Chapels of the Cinquecento and Seicento in the Churches of Rome: Form, Function, Meaning

Chapels of the Cinquecento and Seicento in the Churches of Rome

FORM, FUNCTION, MEANING

Edited by
Chiara Franceschini, Steven F. Ostrow, and Patrizia Tosini

OFFICINA LIBRARIA

LMU LUDWIG-MAXIMILIANS-UNIVERSITÄT MÜNCHEN

SACRIMA

The Normativity
of Sacred Images
in Early Modern Europe

European Research Council
Established by the European Commission

This publication has received funding from the European Research Council (ERC) under the European Union's research and innovation programme Horizon 2020, grant agreement n° 680192/SACRIMA, and from the Adele Hartmann-Programm of the Ludwig Maximilian University of Munich.

Published by
Officina Libraria
Via Carlo Romussi, 4
20125 Milano, Italy

Publisher Marco Jellinek

Editor Wendy Warren Keebler

Designer Tomomot, Venice

Color Separation Premani srl, Pantigliate (Milano)

Printing Galli Thierry stampa, Milano

This book, which is devoted to early modern chapels in Roman churches, has been published under the auspices and with the generous support of the Direzione Centrale per l'Amministrazione del Fondo Edifici di Culto (FEC), a Direction of the Ministry of the Interior of Italy.

The FEC oversees a large part of the artistic, architectural, and cultural patrimony of the city of Rome, conserved in its churches, monasteries, and abbeys, which were placed under its jurisdiction in 1985. The origin of its patrimony—which includes 830 churches of historical and artistic interest in Italy—issues from the Italian State Law 1402, which in 1873 suppressed ecclesiastical control of these sites, thus placing under state jurisdiction some of the most extraordinary complexes on the Italian peninsula.

The mission of the Fondo Edifici di Culto is to assure the protection, appreciation, conservation, and restoration of these monuments. This publication—which is intended not only to offer new scholarly perspectives on some of these artistic treasures, but also to make them better known to a wider public—is an expression of the FEC's mission.

With the sponsorship of the FEC, an extensive photographic campaign was carried out ex novo for this volume, with the goals of bringing to life the integrity of some little-known ecclesiastical spaces, and to invite scholars and visitors to explore their monumental and artistic wealth, as well as their value for the social history of the city of Rome, the cross-roads of early modern cultural experiences.

Table of Contents

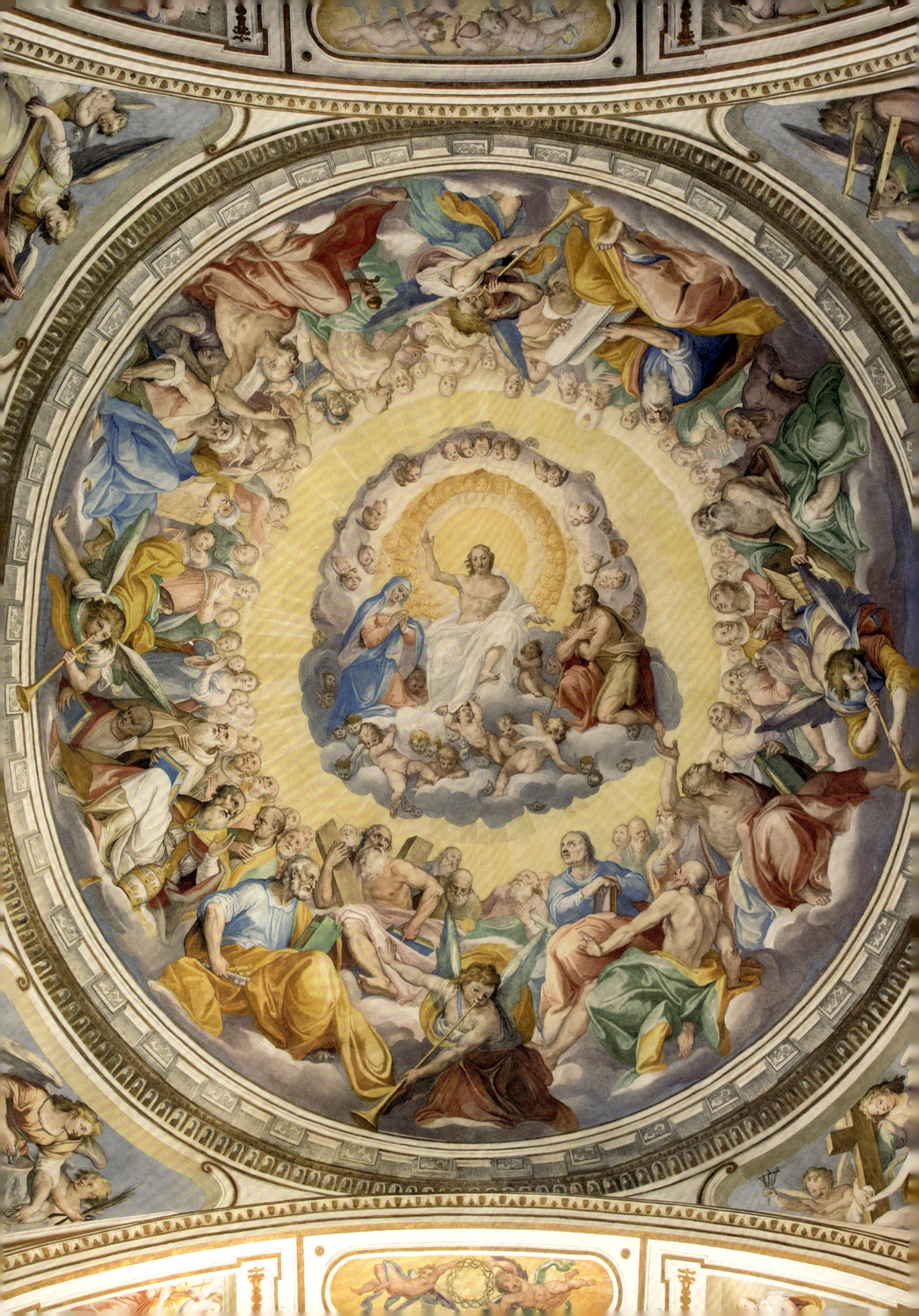

Chapels: An Introduction

Chiara Franceschini, Steven F. Ostrow, and Patrizia Tosini

According to the Accademici della Crusca, in their first *Vocabolario* of 1612, a chapel (*cappella*) is "a place within a church where one situates an altar for celebrating [a Mass]. Lat. *sacellum, aedicula, sacrarium*."[1] This simple definition, as vague and open-ended as it might at first seem, is, in fact, the most appropriate and flexible one to describe a place that in the early modern period assumed and served a variety of forms and functions, as this book demonstrates. The Crusca definition is also useful precisely because it indicates that although every chapel is a sacred space endowed with an altar, it can be a shrine or templelike structure, intimate in its scale or as large as that of an independent church (*sacellum*); it can be a simple architecturally framed altar, either freestanding or placed against a wall (*aedicula*); and it can function as a place for housing liturgical vessels, relics, or tombs (*sacrarium*).[2] The chapel's one constant feature—the altar—and its variety of forms and sizes also figure in Filippo Baldinucci's *Vocabolario* of 1681, in which he defines a chapel as a "place, or room in churches where one situates the altar. Lat. *Sacellum, aedicula, Sacrarium*. And [the term] chapel, one also uses [to describe] a small church, which one also calls [an] oratory."[3]

The root of these definitions can be traced back to Durandus's *Rationale divinorum officiorum* (*Rationale for the Divine Offices*), a late-thirteenth-century liturgical treatise on the symbolism of church architecture, furnishings, and rituals of worship, which—through its thirty-nine published editions between 1473 and 1678 (including in 1568 and 1612)—enjoyed widespread popularity and authority. Durandus, in his discussion of priests, writes that "in many places, priests are called chaplains [*capellani*]; because among the old kings of France, when they went forth to war, they carried with them the cope [*capa*] of Blessed Martin, which they kept in a certain tent; and from [the word] cope [*capa*] the tent was called chapel [*capella*], and the clerics who presided over this place are called chaplains [*capellani*]."[4] This explanation of the origin of "chapel" lives on today, as exemplified in the *Oxford English Dictionary*, where we read that the etymology of the word derives "from the Middle English *chapele*, the Old French *chapele*, and the Latin *cappella*, originally little cloak or cape, diminutive of *cappa* cloak, cape, cope. From the *cappella* or cloak of Saint Martin, preserved by the French kings as a sacred relic, which was borne before them in battle, and used to give sanctity to oaths, the name was applied to the sanctuary in which this was preserved under the care of its *cappellani* or 'chaplains,' and thence generally to a sanctuary containing holy relics, attached to a palace, etc., and so to any private sanctuary or holy place, and finally to any apartment or building for orisons or worship, not being a church."[5]

Durandus's emphasis on the chaplain (*capellanus*), rather than on the physical space over which he presided, also informs the third edition of the

Giovanni Battista Ricci, Frescoes of the vault, ca. 1600–1602. Salviati Chapel, Santi Andrea e Gregorio al Monte Celio, Rome.

Crusca's *Vocabolario* (of 1691), in which the term *cappellania* (chaplaincy) appears, defined as the "benefice that the chaplain (*cappellano*) enjoys."[6] We move, in other words, beyond a space with an altar—the essential furnishing to which others could be and were often added—to a material reward, sometimes in the form of property but most often a financial annuity or income, known as a benefice (*beneficium*), which is given to a priest or cleric (*cappellano*) in exchange for an office (*officium*), which generally required the celebration of Masses in honor of the patron and/or his family and heirs.[7] In the vast majority of cases, a chapel was governed by what is known as *jus patronatus*, the right of patronage established by Roman canon law, which provided a set of rights and obligations of an individual or group—the patron or patrons. It is a legal grant made by the governing body of a church out of gratitude toward a benefactor for the gift of building and endowing the chapel and funding, through a benefice, a chaplain. Thus, *jus patronatus* was intimately tied to both the physical chapel and its chaplain or chaplains.

A chapel's patron—a subject to which the essays in this volume devote considerable attention—in addition to the right of designating a chaplain, bore the responsibility to equip, maintain, and adorn the space that was allocated to him (or her) by the ecclesiastical institution (the church) in which it was located. Equipping or furnishing a chapel, first and foremost, required the provision of an altar and liturgical vessels but most often extended to an altarpiece, and other pictorial or sculptural decorations, including tombs (in the case of burial chapels) and reliquaries. And it was this responsibility that enabled patrons to build and decorate the magnificent chapels that we find in Rome and elsewhere. These patrons, like those for other monuments and works of art, were widely diverse and included individual men and women, both clerical and secular, families, and corporate bodies, such as confraternities or communal organizations. Beyond their obvious function as the site of the celebration of Masses, they also served as vehicles for the expression of individual, familial, communal, civic, and institutional identity and devotion. Each chapel, one could say, speaks, communicating to visitors through its form and visual adornment the message its patron wished to articulate. This practice of creating private chapels seems not to have been active—or was modest at best—during most of the early medieval period, but beginning in the thirteenth century, chapels began to proliferate, especially in the churches of the mendicant Orders, and reached its apogee in the sixteenth and seventeenth centuries. The history of the chapels attached to or within old St. Peter's illustrates this phenomenon well, for it was from the early thirteenth century that private donors began founding, decorating, and endowing numerous chapels, and this practice—which in some cases involved refurbishing or rebuilding an existing chapel—continued well into the sixteenth century, only to come to an end with the demolition of what remained of the Constantinian basilica.[8]

As was the case earlier, but especially during the early modern period, chapels could assume a variety of forms (as alluded to above) and occupy a number of different locales. It could be an independent structure, such as the early-fourteenth-century Arena Chapel in Padua, or, as was more generally the case, a space within or an addition to a larger structure, such as a church, monastery, cemetery, or palace. As a part of a church, a chapel could occupy the high altar area (often the apse); it could be in a space within or attached to the nave, side aisle, apse, or transept; or (as exemplified by the *confessio* chapel discussed here by Steven F. Ostrow) it could be placed underground, below the chancel. Similarly, chapels could vary widely in size, ranging from little more than an adorned altar (as is the case of the example studied here by Guendalina Serafinelli) to a monumental structure as large as many independent churches (such as the Cappella Gregoriana, the subject of Fabio Barry's essay). The one element all chapels have in common, as the definitions cited above make clear, is an altar, which designates them as sacred domains, sites for liturgical celebration (the Mass) and various forms of prayer and devotion. And it is important to stress that the chapels studied here, like all such chapels, although private in the sense of belonging to and having been funded by a particular patron or patrons, were also—at least on certain occasions—open to a larger public as sites for worship, private prayer, and, in some instances, pilgrimage.

Following the Council of Trent, when the majority of the chapels discussed in this volume were created, the form and furnishings of chapels were matters taken up at length by Carlo Borromeo (1538–1584) in his authoritative *Instructiones fabricae et supellectilis ecclesiasticae* (*Instructions on the Building and Furnishings of Churches*) of 1577, the sole post-Tridentine treatise on ecclesiastical architecture. Although primarily concerned with the archdiocese of Milan, of which he was archbishop, Borromeo's text was widely circulated and exerted a considerable influence in Rome, where he had spent his formative years (1560–1565). In the first book of his treatise, he addressed the "main chapel" ("De Cappella Maiori") of a church as occupying the high altar area within the building's "head," which he said should be "properly ornamented with mosaics or some other illustrious pictorial or architectural decoration, corresponding to the characteristics and dignity of the church."[9] Then, after discussing the high altar, choir, and tabernacle of the Sacrament, he turned to "minor chapels and altars" ("De Cappellis et Altaribus Minoribus"), providing detailed instructions about their location, form, size, access, and furnishings. He indicates that suitable spaces for chapels are the transept arms, on either side of the main chapel (apse), at the heads of side aisles, and along both sides of the church, "projecting outwards with respect to the body of the church." He insists on a symmetrical disposition and sufficient distance between chapels "so that the priest celebrating Mass on one altar would not be disturbed by one celebrating at another." If several chapels are to be built projecting outward from the side aisles, they should be equidistant from each other, with "sufficient space between them so that windows for an adequate light can be put into the wall on either side," and in churches with a nave and side aisles, chapels should be placed "directly opposite a bay so that their view is not impeded by columns or piers." Minor chapels should, moreover, "be of the same width, length and height and, as far as possible, similar in all their details"; they should be at least seven cubits (3.05 meters) deep and as wide as 11 cubits (7.145 meters); and they should also be separated from the main body of the church by a gate or railing, and have floors raised above that of the church, with the stairs leading into them made of marble or solid stone.[10] And in accordance with Durandus, all chapels, by definition, are to be equipped with altars.

Borromeo's directives concerning chapels—informed by his desire to reform church buildings, to make them as dignified as possible, and to provide proper settings for the celebration of Masses—were, of course, ideals, primarily directed at those who were building churches with chapels *ex novo*. And although he wished to see his recommendations closely followed, he was also pragmatic about what could be accomplished in reality. Indeed, in his native Milan as well as in Rome, his ideals concerning chapels were rarely, if ever, followed in all their details, as the chapels discussed in this volume make evident. It is notable, too, that he did not address the various functions of chapels—beyond being the site for Masses—such as repositories for tombs, miraculous images, or relics. But the fact that his chapter on "minor chapels" is more than twice as long as any of those that preceded it indicates the significance he attached to them.[11]

Their importance as integral parts of churches (both ancient and modern), as well as their variety in size, location, function, decorative program, and patronage, are vividly demonstrated by the essays in this volume. As noted above, the chapels examined here range in size from a simple *aedicula* (the Boncompagni Corcos Chapel) to a colossal templelike structure (the Cappella Gregoriana). With respect to location, they occupy spaces in early Christian churches (the Rusticucci and Caetani chapels in Santa Susanna and Santa Pudenziana, respectively), a late medieval church (the Salviati Chapel in San Gregorio al Celio), and Renaissance and baroque churches (the Frangipani Chapel in San Marcello al Corso, the Cybo Chapel in Santa Maria del Popolo, the Cappella Gregoriana in St. Peter's, the Boncompagni Corcos Chapel in Santa Maria in Vallicella, the Spada Chapel in San Girolamo della Carità, and the chapel of Saint Francis Xavier in the Gesù). In these churches, they can be found below the chancel (Rusticucci), along the side aisles (Frangipani, Caetani, and Spada), attached to but separate from the side aisle (Salviati), in a transept arm (Saint Francis Xavier), in a sacristy (Boncompagni Corcos), and filling one of the monumental corner spaces of a basilica (Gregoriana). A number of the chapels served as family burial sites (Frangipani, Caetani, Spada, and Cybo), one housed the tomb of a pope (Gregoriana), another contained the tomb of its cardinal patron (Rusticucci), two housed venerated Marian images (Gregoriana and Salviati), and several functioned as reliquary chapels: the Gregoriana for the remains of Saint Gregory Nazianzenus; the Rusticucci for the bodies of Saints Gabinius, Susanna, and Felicita; and the Chapel of Saint Francis Xavier for his right arm and hand. Their decorative programs are no less varied, but one feature common to the majority of the chapels is polychrome marble incrustation, as seen in the Gregoriana, Caetani, Spada, Saint Francis Xavier, and Cybo chapels, or the painted imitation of revetment as found in the Rusticucci and Salviati chapels. And, finally, with respect to the chapels' patrons, they included members of the Capitoline government (Curzio and Mario Frangipani), titular cardinals (Girolamo Rusticucci and Enrico Caetani), a cardinal acting as commendatory abbot (Antonio Maria Salviati), a cardinal who served as Secretary of State (Alderano Cybo), a family of converted Jews (the Boncompagni Corcos), an influential papal cleric (Giovanni Francesco Negroni), a pope (Gregory XIII), and an Oratorian brother and adviser to a pope (Virgilio Spada). Spanning the sixteenth and seventeenth centuries, the nine chapels discussed in this volume are among the most splendid sacred spaces in early modern Rome, and perhaps more significantly, they represent a cross section of chapel types, reflecting and embodying the most important spiritual, ecclesiastical, social, and political concerns of the period.

The chapels discussed here also testify to one of the most striking features of early modern Rome: the continuous cycle of preservation, construction, reconstruction, and decoration, which prompted individual patrons and artists to choose from among a virtual infinite range of architectural and artistic forms, which could never be governed by a strict set of rules and regulations. This small but significant group of chapels also vividly demonstrates how such spaces served as the sites for ongoing artistic experimentation and innovation, as well as for the revival of early Christian and medieval forms—both of which, perhaps paradoxically, could only have been possible in the papal capital. It is our hope that the essays here will provide readers with a sense of the *esquisitezza*, not only of the chapels they examine but of many others as well, and present Rome, as Giovanni Baglione described it, as the true "compendium of the marvels of the whole ... world."[12]

This book of essays began as a two-part session at the 2017 annual meeting of the Renaissance Society of America in Chicago, organized by Steven F. Ostrow and Patrizia Tosini, which was dedicated to the theme "Chapels in Roman Churches between the Cinquecento and Seicento: Form and Meaning." In selecting the papers for this session, the organizers sought contributors who would be able to offer a variety of perspectives on this exceptionally rich subject and introduce those in attendance not only to little-studied and overlooked Renaissance and baroque chapels but also to new readings and interpretations of some of the best-known early modern chapels in the papal capital.

Although this book is an outgrowth of that session, it is not its "proceedings." Of the ten scholars who have contributed to this volume, only six participated in the conference, and in two cases, the subjects of the essays differ from those presented in 2017. And in an effort to expand the parameters of our examination of Roman chapels, the organizers and Chiara Franceschini, one of the original speakers, invited contributions from another speaker at the conference, Guendalina Serafinelli (who had presented a paper in another session but which was central to our enterprise), and from three other scholars (two of them collaborating on a single essay). It is our hope that their contributions, together with those of the original six, will give readers a deeper understanding of the variety, richness, and complexity of sixteenth- and seventeenth-century Roman chapels—as sacred spaces; as sites for liturgical celebration, quiet devotion, and pilgrimage; as burial places and reliquary shrines; and as expressions of individual, familial, and ecclesiastical power and spirituality.

Acknowledgments

At various stages of this book project, the editors have incurred a number of debts, which we would like to acknowledge here. First, we wish to thank the contributors to this volume. We are grateful for their enthusiasm and patience and, most significantly, for bringing their extraordinary expertise to

After Johannes Stradanus and Cornelis Cort, *Allegory of Rome*, in Cornelis de Bie, *Het Gulden Cabinet*, Antwerp 1662. British Museum, London.

their essays. Funding for this volume was generously provided by the Adele Hartmann-Programm of the Ludwig-Maximilians-Universität in Munich, as well as the European Research Council under the European Union's Horizon 2020 research and innovation program (grant agreement no. 680192/ SACRIMA). We also wish to express special thanks to Alison K. Frazier and the Society of Friends of the American Academy in Rome, for their sponsorship of the panels at the RSA 2017 conference that led to this volume; to Maurizio Righini of the Fondo Edifici Culto (Ministero dell'Interno), for his various efforts on behalf of this book; to Mauro Coen, for the photographic campaign that greatly enriched a number of the essays; to the Bibliotheca and Fototeca Hertziana, which generously provided a number of photographs (and we wish to thank particularly Marga Sanchez for her valuable assistance); to a number of friends and colleagues who lent their advice and expertise; and finally, to the publisher and the staff of Officina Libraria, who offered their unequivocal support and encouragement.

Notes

1 — *Vocabolario degli Accademici della Crusca* 1612, 155: "CAPPELLA, luogo nelle Chiese, dove si pongono gli altari per celebrare. Lat. sacellum, aedicula, sacrarium."

2 — Moroni 1853, LX, 132–133, sub vocem "Sacrario." Citing Magri's *Notizia de' vocaboli*, Moroni also defines Sacrario (Sacrarium) as "anticamente era denominato anche il luogo vicino all'Altare, circondato da' cancelli, ove soltanto il sacerdote e altri ministri sagri potevano entrare nel tempo del s. Sacrificio."

3 — Baldinucci 1681, 28: "Cappella f. Luogo, o stanza nelle Chiese dove si pone l'altare. E Cappella dicesi anche una piccola Chiesina, la quale si chiama ancora Oratorio." See also Moroni 1841, VIII, 95, sub vocem "Cappella."

4 — Durando 1612, Lib. II, 8, De Sacerdote, 60v: "In plerisq[ue] locis sacerdotes, capellani vocantur. Nam antiquitus reges Franciae ad bella procedentes, capa[m] B. Martini secum portabant, quae sub quodam tentorio servabatur: quod ab ipsa capa dictum est capella. Et clerici in quorum custodia ipsa capella erat, inde capellani dicebantur."

5 — See the entry "chapel, n." in the Oxford English Dictionary Online (OED) accessible with subscription at https://www.oed.com/. See also the entry for "chapel" in *The Catholic Encyclopedia*, which repeats this etymology: http://www.newadvent.org/cathen/03574b.htm. An overlooked aspect of the origin of the chapel, as both a term and a liturgical space, is its close connection to a vestment--a *cappa* (cape). We are grateful to Kristin Makholm for bringing this to our attention.

6 — *Vocabolario degli Accademici della Crusca* 1691, II, 284.

7 — Franceschini 2002, 345–413, esp. 355–357.

8 — Rice 1997, 19–23.

9 — Borromeo 1577 [1962], I, cap. X, 18. See also the annotated English translation in Voelker 1977 [2008], 124–125, whose translation we follow here and below.

10 — Borromeo 1577 [1962], I, cap. XIV, 24–29; Voelker 1977, 174–182.

11 — As noted by Sénécal 2000, 258. Despite the virtual impossibility of regulating church architecture, a number of churches constructed in Rome in the last decades of the sixteenth century, including notably the Gesù and Santa Maria in Vallicella, conformed to many of Borromeo's "instructions."

12 — Baglione 1642, n.p. (Al Virtuoso Lettore): "E perché Roma è compendio delle maraviglie del tutto, per brevità dell'Opera ho giudicato esser bastevole, che il solamente l'Opere, che in questa Città essi formarono, comprenda anche l'esquisitezza di tutte le altre, che per il Mondo risplendono; che ciò altrove l'Arte disperse, qui la Virtù raccolse."

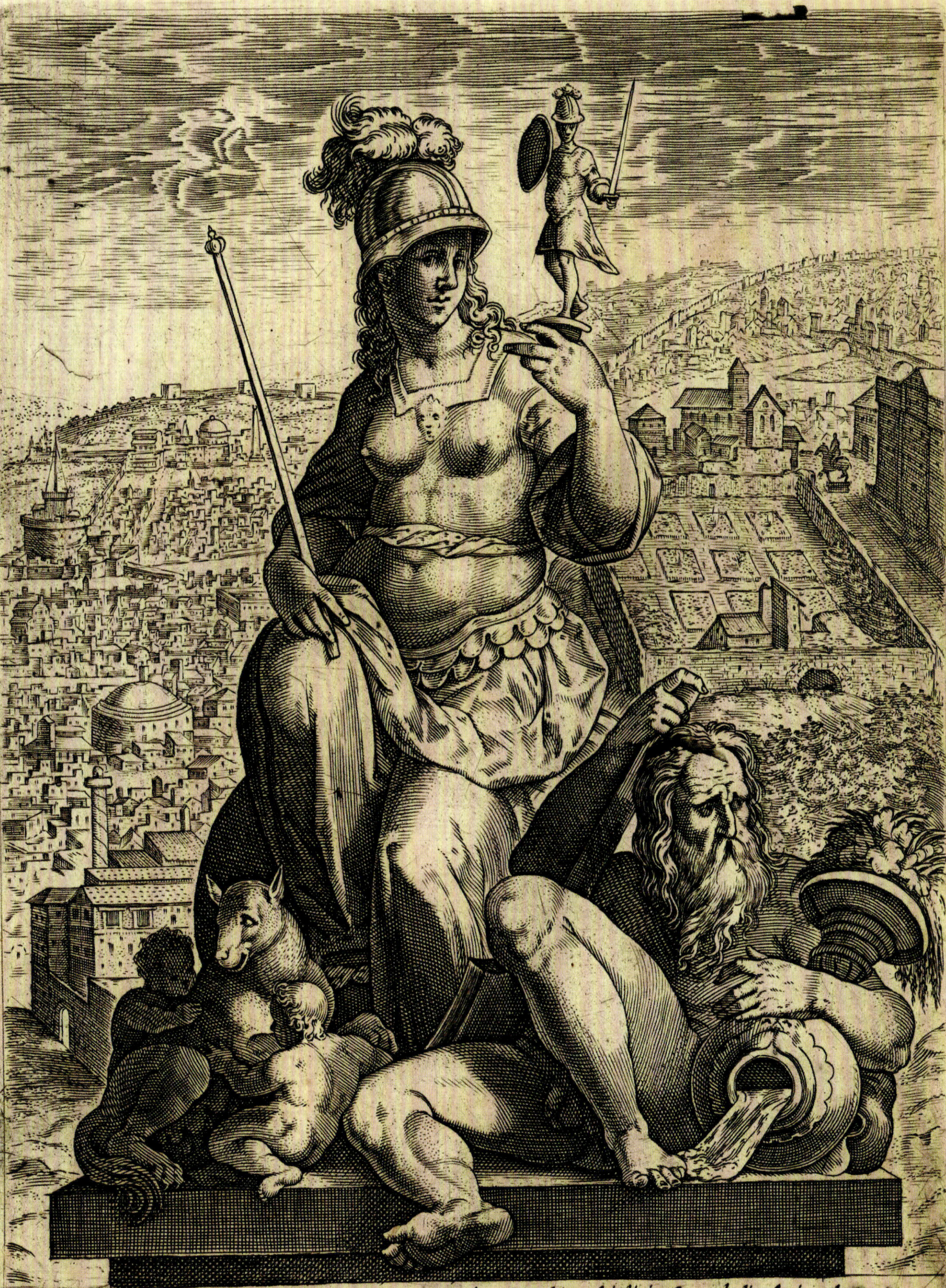

Orbis Roma caput bellorum turbine quondam
Obruta cur fremuit? Martis amica fuit:

Ast ubi multiplicis sese dedit Artis alumnam,
Celsa Triumphatrix se super astra tulit.

Map of the Churches

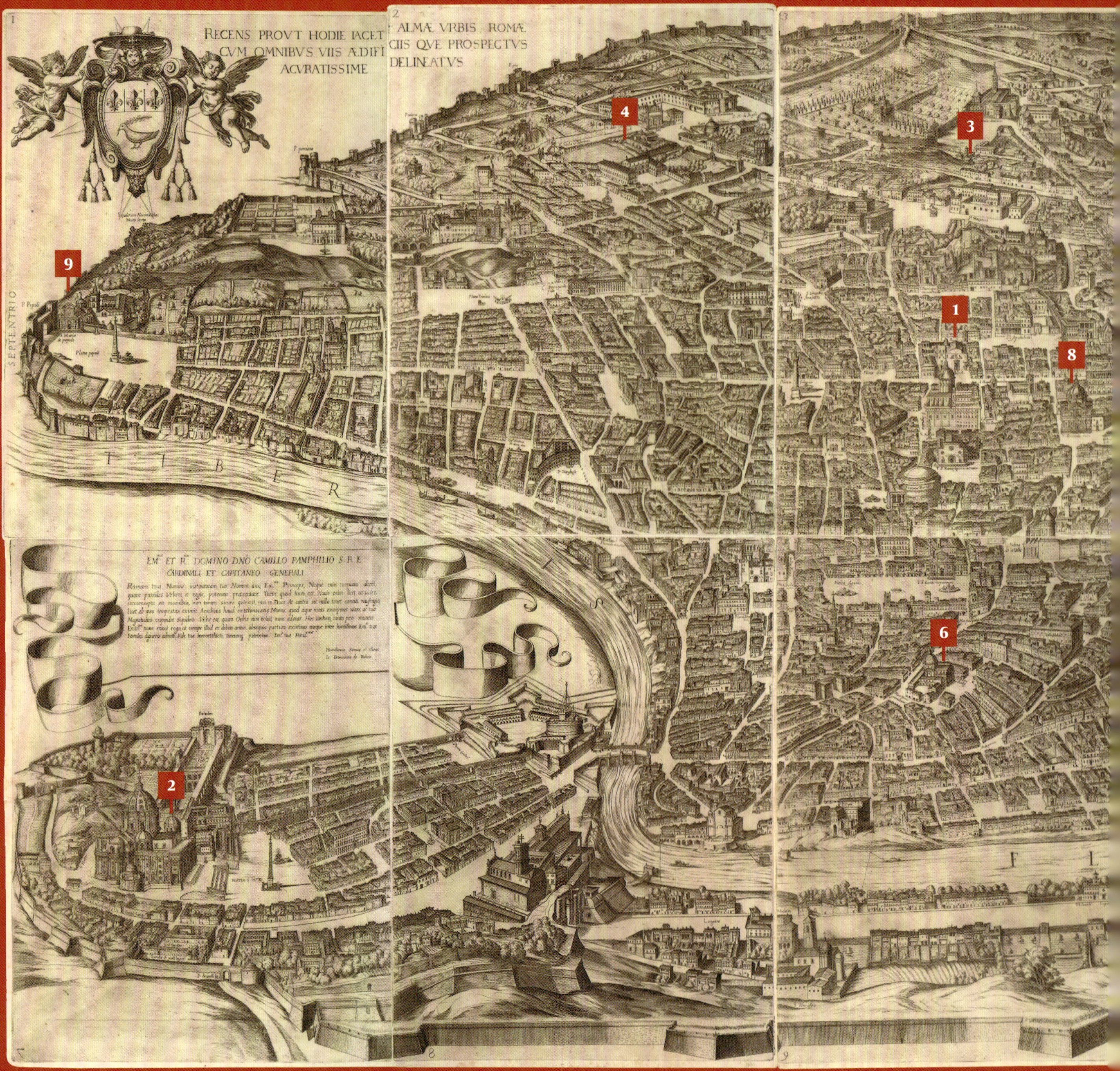

1. San Marcello
2. Saint Peter's
3. Santa Pudenziana
4. Santa Susanna
5. Santi Andrea e Gregorio al Celio
6. Santa Maria in Vallicella
7. San Girolamo della Carità
8. Il Gesù
9. Santa Maria del Popolo

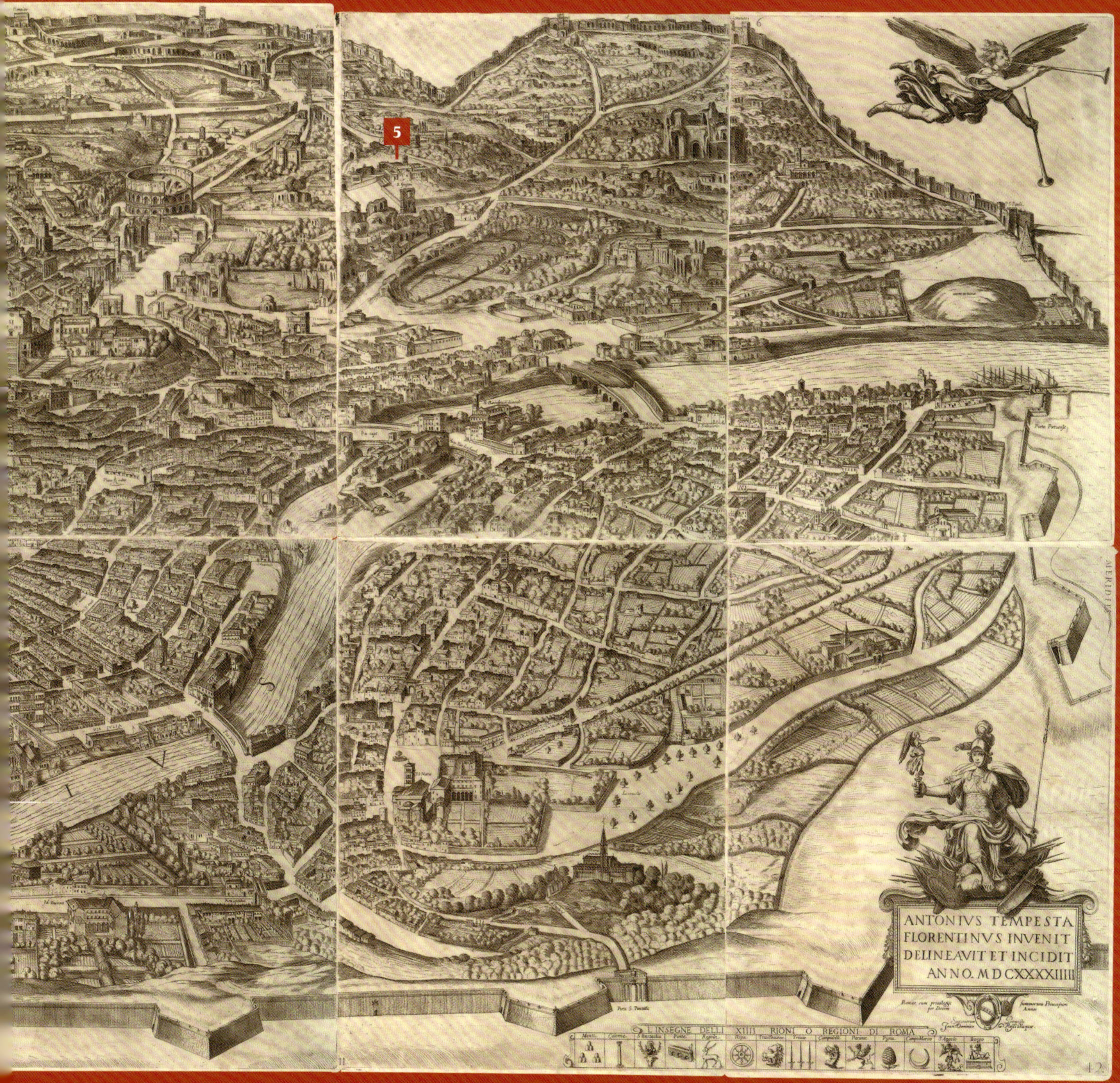

Antonio Tempesta,
Plan of the city of Rome
[1593], reprinted with changes by Giovanni Domenico De Rossi in 1645. New York, The Metropolitan Museum of Art

The Frangipani Chapel in San Marcello

FARNESIAN DEVOTION, ANTIQUARIAN TASTE, AND MUNICIPAL PRIDE

Patrizia Tosini

The church of San Marcello al Corso houses a series of little-known sixteenth-century aristocratic chapels that have been mostly neglected or undervalued in the literature.[1] Among them, perhaps one of the most studied on account of its well-preserved and homogeneous decorations painted by Taddeo and Federico Zuccari, is the one belonging to the Frangipani family, the fourth along the left side of the church (FIG. 1). Despite what has been written about the chapel, however, its patronage and its significance in relation to the role of the Frangipani in the context of the Rome of the Farnese and other powerful Capitoline families have still not been fully investigated. In an effort to fill this scholarly void, this essay examines these very issues; and by considering the Frangipani Chapel in relation to other contemporary chapels in Roman churches, its singularity can be understood as a direct consequence of the specific cultural background of the Frangipani family's Roman lineage.

The pictorial decoration, as is well known, was entrusted to Taddeo Zuccari between 1556 and 1558 and dedicated to the life of Saint Paul.[2] The frescoes represent the *Blinding of Elymas* on the left wall (FIG. 2); the *Healing of the Cripple at Lystra* on the right wall (FIG. 3); on the barrel vault (in rather ruinous condition), the *Resurrection of Eutychus*, *Saint Paul Bitten by a Viper in Malta*, and the *Martyrdom of Saint Paul* (FIG. 4). The altarpiece (FIG. 5), painted in oil on slate, depicts the *Conversion of Saint Paul*, above which appears an inscription with the dedication "D. PAULO APOST. MARIUS FREGEPANIUS DD MDLX," which likely provides the completion date of the chapel.[3]

On each of the side walls are three portrait busts placed within oval niches (FIGS. 6, 7). On the left-hand wall are the portraits of the older members of the family, Antonino (d. 1546),[4] a Capitoline Conservator,[5] and his sons Curzio (d. 1554) and Mario (d. 1569). On the right-hand wall are the busts of Muzio (d. 1588), son of Mario, and his two sons, Lelio (d. 1605) and Roberto (d. 1622). While Alessandro Algardi's authorship of the last three busts is well known,[6] the three splendid older portraits remain anonymous and lack any precise dating. According to Grisebach, the Frangipani Chapel might not have been their original location, a hypothesis that we will discuss later.[7] Below each of the portrait-bust niches are vertical funerary plaques bearing inscriptions written in Roman capitals. As we learn from the inscription below Antonino, his bust was placed according to the wishes of his two sons,[8] while that of Curzio was ordered by his younger brother Mario.[9] The patron who commissioned Mario's bust, however, is not indicated in the inscription.[10]

The Frangipani Family

According to the learned Augustinian friar and historian Onofrio Panvinio, in his introduction to *De gente Fregepania libri quatuor* [1556] (still in manuscript form),[11] the origins of the Frangipani are legendary, dating back to the history of ancient Rome and to the *Gens Anicia*. He writes:

> There was never a family, within memory, of which for many centuries there have been more certain and illustrious testimonies worthy of being remembered, or that has generated a more fecund progeny of great men, than the house named Anicia in ancient times and Fregepania in more recent ones; indeed, the Anicia

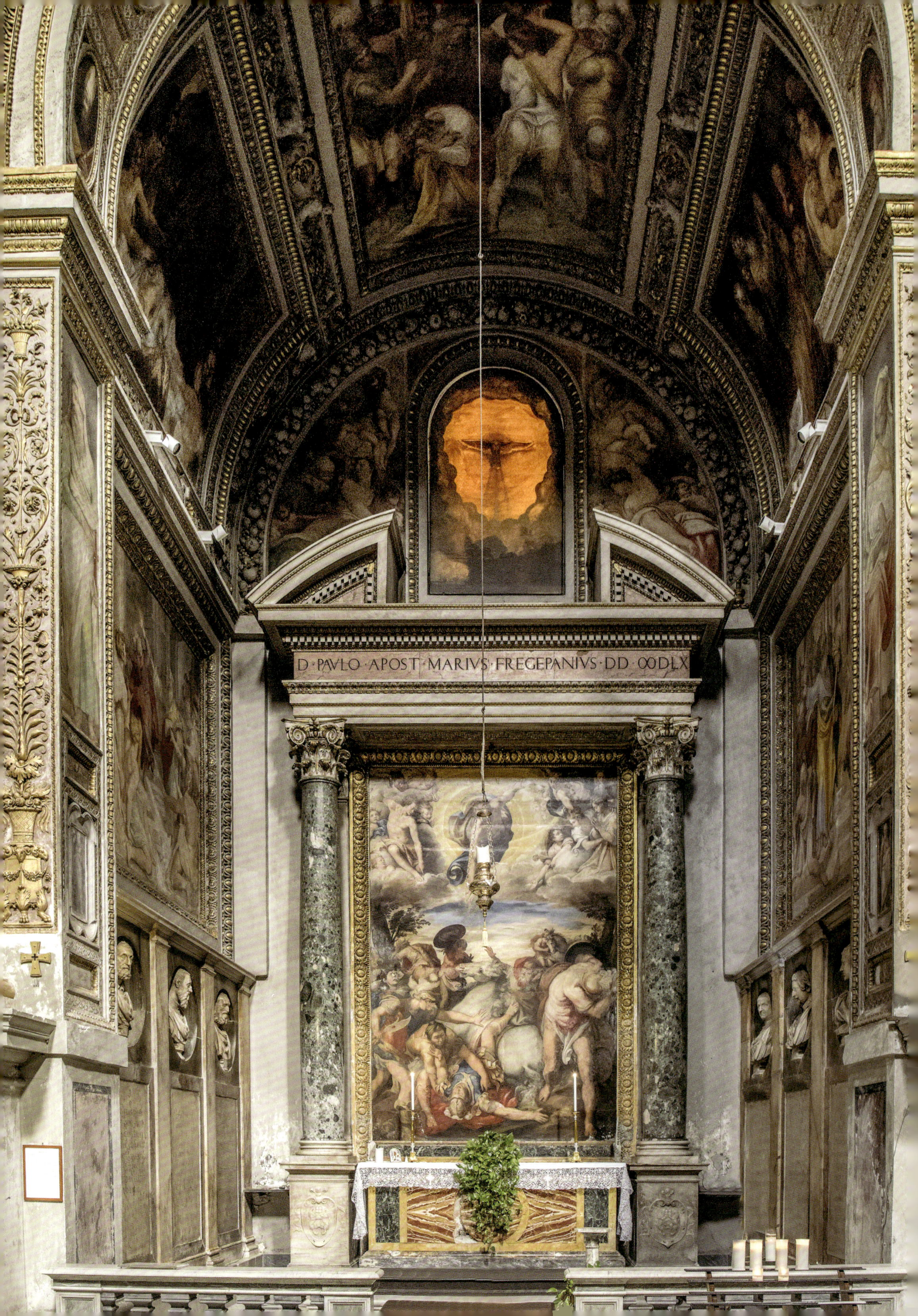
D·PAVLO·APOST·MARIVS·FREGEPANIVS·DD·ↀDLX

lineage has existed since the early Republican age, greatly honored and awarded consular and triumphal status of the highest dignity, and in the successive imperial age [it was] the only one, among the twenty-eight principal families that we shall list, that obtained the consulship ... therefore the house of Frangipani, from that moment, for eight hundred years, excelled among the Roman families.[12]

Panvinio dedicated his work, written in 1556, to Mario Frangipani, as an homage to the *Gens Fregepania*. It was also intended as an expression of gratitude to Curzio, who had died shortly before in 1554 and who, as the *maestro di casa* (house steward) of Cardinal Alessandro Farnese (junior) and a man well versed in art, served as an intermediary between the powerful Farnese and Panvinio in 1552.[13]

Panvinio also reconstructs Curzio's biography, mentioning his familiarity with Pope Paul III Farnese (r. 1534–1549), who kept him at court with great honors, entrusting him with the education of his grandson Ottavio and awarding him with the title of *Urbis Cancellarius* (Chancellor of the Roman People). He informs us that:

Curzio had such an influence and courteous authority over Alessandro [the pope's grandson] that he administered everything on his own with a single command, and at court none of the more serious business was ever dealt with without Curzio being consulted. Indeed, he was above all the other courtiers in his prudence, humanity, and honesty of character.[14]

Panvinio also underlines Curzio's friendship with the antiquarian Mariangelo Accursio from Aquila and with other contemporary intellectuals, including musicians and mathematicians, as well as his interests in moral philosophy and the Etruscan language.[15]

From the papal court, Curzio moved to that of Cardinal Alessandro Farnese, the pope's grandson, where he served (as noted above) as his *maestro di casa*, as well as an intimate and most trusted intermediary in the cardinal's relations with artists and men of letters.[16] And it is in this context of profound erudition—the world of the Farnese court—with its intense focus on antiquity that one must understand the extraordinary event of the discovery in 1546 of the *Fasti Capitolini* in the Roman Forum.[17]

Curzio Frangipani was inextricably tied to the Capitoline Senate and the Campidoglio, on account of his charge as deputy for life (from 1540 to his death in October 1554).[18] In this capacity, he was directly involved in the discovery of the epigraphs of the *Fasti* (FIG. 8), whose excavation was promoted by Cardinal Alessandro Farnese himself, who moved the finds to Villa Farnesina in order to have the inscriptions copied before donating them to the *Popolo Romano*. Degrassi published the Capitoline decree of June 18, 1548, which established that the epigraphs were to be placed on the Capitol—a decree that was underwritten by, among others, Curzio in his capacity as Chancellor of the Roman People.[19] Gentile Delfini and Tommaso de' Cavalieri were charged with reconstructing the *Fasti* in the courtyard of the Palazzo dei Conservatori,[20] with the help of various intellectuals in the court of the "Gran Cardinale" Alessandro, among whom were Panvinio himself, Bartolomeo Marliano, Benedetto Egio, Antonio Agustín, Gabriele Faerno,

FIG. 1. Frangipani Chapel, San Marcello, Rome.

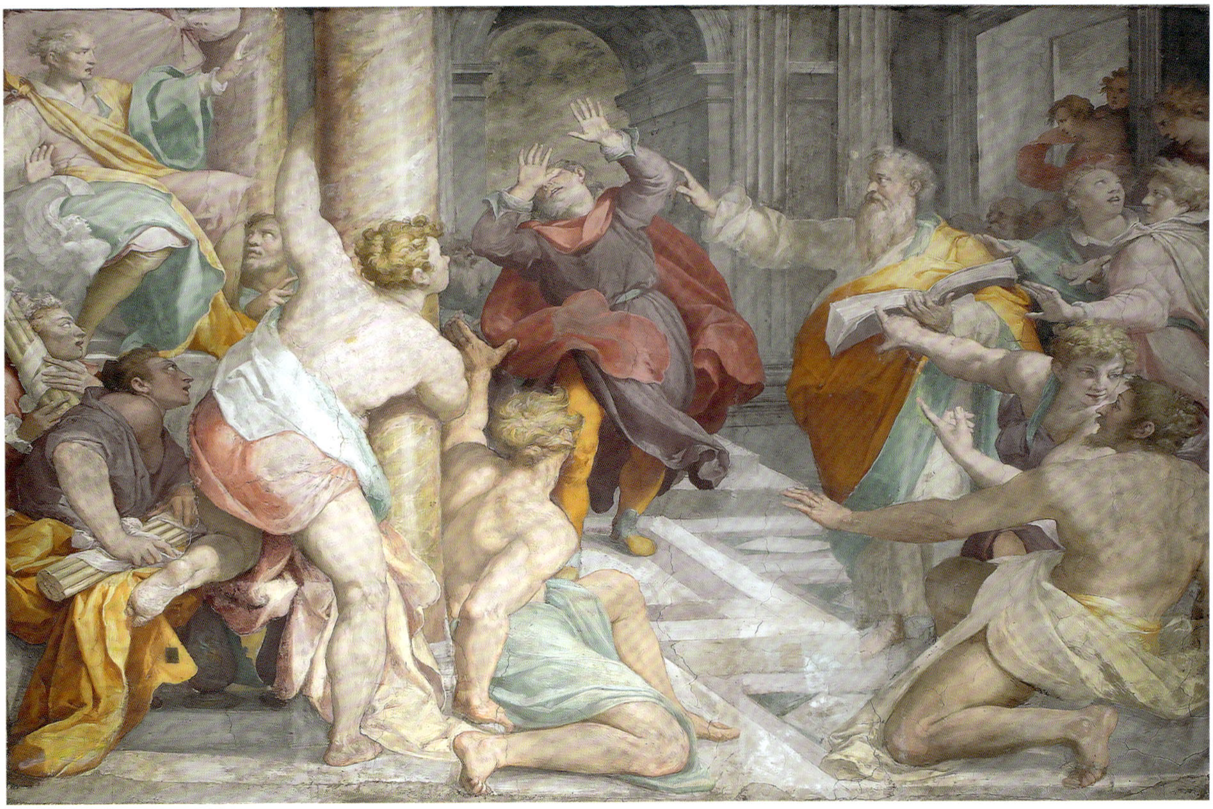

2

and Ottavio Pantagato. The design of their installation—placed on a wall divided by pilasters into three vertical sections—was, according to Panvinio, by Michelangelo, although the attribution has been questioned.[21] In 1558, only two years after writing *De gente Fregepania*, Panvinio published the first annotated transcription of the *Fasti*, meant as another homage to his protector Curzio, in which, through the publication of the lists, he intended to demonstrate his descent from the *Gens Anicia*.[22]

To return to the Frangipani Chapel, it seems evident from the above that it was Curzio, who signed the concession of the chapel by the friars of the church of San Marcello,[23] who was responsible for conceiving the design and program of this sepulchral space, which was intended to be a celebrative monument to himself, in his role as Capitoline Chancellor, as well as a place to immortalize the entire *Gens Fregepania*. Upon Curzio's death in 1554, however, it was his brother Mario who assumed the role of carrying out his brother's wishes with respect to the new chapel.

Mario's uninterrupted engagement with his family's antiquarian tradition was further advanced in December 1556, with his nomination as *Conservatorem Antiquitatum et Statuarum* (Conservator of Antiquities and Statues).[24] His constant interest in ancient finds is also attested by the fact that in 1568, he rented an ancient palace of the Frangipani, near the church of Sant'Anastasia on the slopes of the Palatine, to Giovanni Forti (probably an excavator), with the agreement that Forti would share with his landlord any statue, gold, silver, or other metals that might be found on the site.[25]

FIG. 2. Taddeo Zuccari, *The Blinding of Elymas*, ca. 1564–1566. Frangipani Chapel (left wall), San Marcello, Rome.

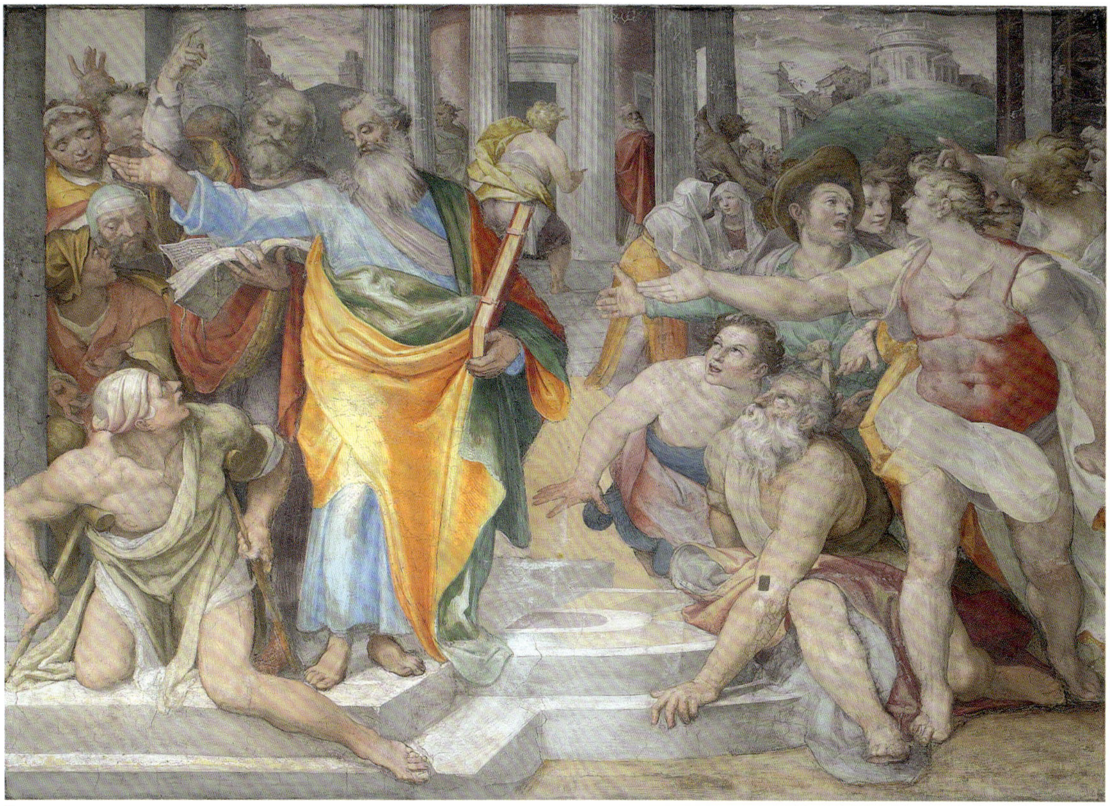

3

The History of the Frangipani Chapel

A consideration of a detailed history of the Frangipani Chapel will allow us to better understand its significance inside the church of San Marcello. That history begins with the father of Curzio and Mario, Antonino, who is described by Panvinio as a man of "modest erudition" but very pious and merciful. At the time of his death, in October 1545, his children, respecting his will, had him provisionally buried in a chapel that had been the property of that branch of the Frangipani family for two centuries, in the church of Santa Maria sopra Minerva.[26] Then, in 1554, although the chapel in the Minerva was still in use, Curzio and Mario decided to build a new chapel to honor their descendants in a different place, one closely associated with the Farnese family.

That different place was the church of San Marcello, which, beginning in the sixteenth century, housed various chapels belonging to individuals and groups who were directly and intimately associated with the circle of Paul III and his grandson, Cardinal Alessandro. These included the chapel of the Confraternita del Santissimo Crocifisso, historically tied to the Farnese through its cardinal protectors, Ranuccio and Alessandro (Farnese), and through Tommaso de' Cavalieri; the chapel of Bishop Ascanio Parisani, treasurer of the pope; and the one assigned to Matteo Grifoni, who was named bishop of Trivento by Paul III and was an intimate of the Gran Cardinale.[27] Thus, in choosing San Marcello as the site for their chapel, Mario and Curzio vividly demonstrated their family's close ties to the Farnese. Moreover, the painters involved in the decoration of these four chapels (from around the middle of

FIG. 3. Taddeo Zuccari, *The Healing of the Cripple at Lystra*, ca. 1564–1566. Frangipani Chapel (right wall), San Marcello, Rome.

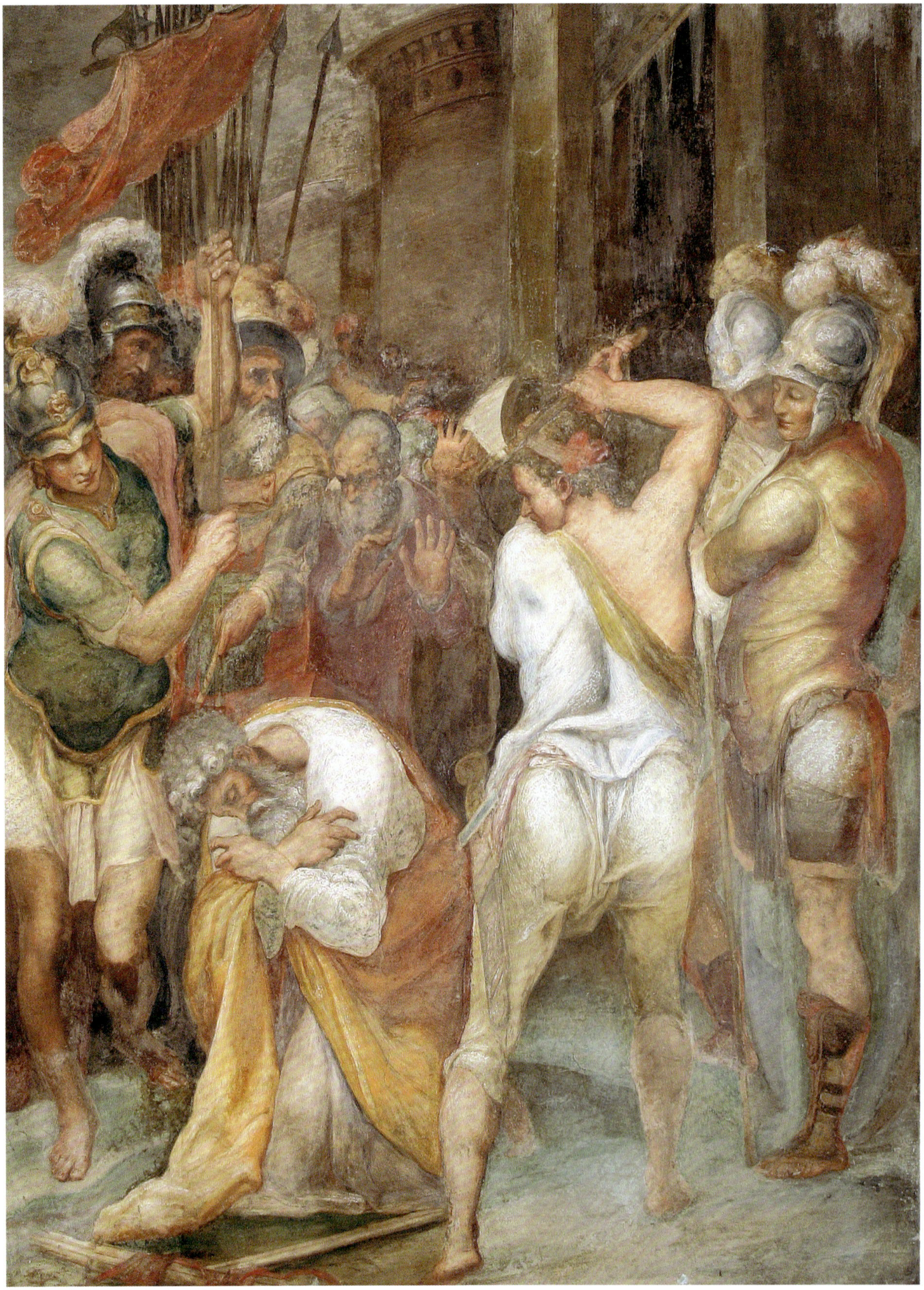

4

the sixteenth century)—Giovanni Paolo del Colle, Perin del Vaga, Daniele da Volterra, Francesco Salviati, and Taddeo and Federico Zuccari—were all principally supported by Farnese patronage, and this artistic "sharing," together with the fact that San Marcello was surrounded by the residences of these family members, further designated the church as a stronghold of the Farnese.

From the inception of Paul III's pontificate, in fact, the Frangipani were among those who felt the attraction of the new Farnesian urban pole, which included the Servite church of San Marcello and the Oratorio del Crocifisso, the latter planned in 1556, the same year the decoration and furnishing of the Frangipani Chapel began.[28] It was probably for the same reason that Antonino and Curzio purchased in 1538–1539 a new building in Piazza San Marco (the future Palazzo Cenci Bolognetti, then Torlonia, demolished in the nineteenth century).[29] And it was in this palace that, in 1556, Ulisse Aldrovandi recorded the presence of an already sizable collection of ancient statutes, acquired most likely by Curzio, given the "modest erudition" attributed to his father, Antonino, by Panvinio.[30]

Of course, the proximity to the Capitoline Hill—the strategic center of the Farnese family in relation to the city and the Capitoline elites—was another impetus to Curzio's decision to acquire a new funerary chapel in San Marcello; there he could celebrate in a distinct fashion that branch of the Frangipani that had shown the greatest devotion to the family of Paul III and had occupied crucial positions in the Capitoline government.

The decision to abandon the chapel of the Minerva as a mortuary space for his descendants should, therefore, be understood as a clear political statement, aimed at signaling a break with other branches of the family and expressing the cultural primacy of the Antonino line, achieved through the deep antiquarian culture embodied by his sons. And we shall see how the decoration of the chapel was meant, on the one hand, to represent the family's profound awareness of its ancient Roman origins and knowledge of the antique and, on the other, to pay homage to Paul III, the pope who had been so important for Antonino's children.

The chronology of the decoration of the chapel is based primarily on the information provided by Vasari (1568) in his *Life* of Taddeo Zuccari and on the *postille* (annotations) added by Federico Zuccari.[31] This information can now be supplemented by newly discovered documents pertaining to the chapel. On April 11, 1554, the prior of the convent of San Marcello offered to Curzio Frangipani a chapel in the church for him and his descendants, in exchange for an endowment of two hundred scudi, to be guaranteed by the purchase of a house by the Frangipani.[32] On June 13, 1556, with Curzio having died in October 1554, the concession of the chapel was formalized with the sale of the house in question by Michele Florio to Mario Frangipani, heir to Curzio and titular of the chapel.[33] Panvinio records that Curzio (who had died in his presence, probably in Palazzo Farnese where Curzio habitually resided, according to the sources)[34] was already buried in the chapel of San Marcello "cura et impensis fratris sui Marii Fregepanii" ("under the care and upkeep of his brother, Mario Frangipani").[35] And the author then provides a valuable bit of information for the chronology of the work in the new chapel, when he, addressing Mario directly in his text, affirms:

> Therefore, you, o Mario, began now to build that chapel in memory of your most beloved brother with such generosity and to adorn it with various marbles, paint-

FIG. 4. Taddeo Zuccari, *The Martyrdom of Saint Paul*, ca. 1556–1560. Frangipani Chapel (vault), San Marcello, Rome.

> ings, and ornaments, such that when it will be finished one must believe that one will not be able to see a work more beautiful in all of Rome.[36]

The passage is proof that at the end of 1556, the chapel, dedicated to the memory of the recently passed Curzio, was already in the process of being built and decorated. The passage "ornare variis marmoribus" ("to adorn [it] with various marbles") suggests furthermore that the splendid marble decoration below the frescoes on the lateral walls had already been planned at that time. This hypothesis accords with the fact that the text of the epigraphs of Antonino and Curzio echoes the words employed by Panvinio in *De gente Fregepania* to celebrate the dead father and son and was therefore probably written by Panvinio himself, as suggested also by the old-style dating "post Christum natum" employed in both epigraphs.[37]

The decision to assign the pictorial decoration of the chapel to Taddeo Zuccari, who at the time was one of the painters most loved by the Farnese family and was a rising star among both the papacy and the Roman nobility, was in all likelihood made by Curzio, notwithstanding the fact that Mario was the one who personally oversaw the work. The choice was certainly an indication of the ambitiousness of the project; however, Taddeo's involvement in many prestigious commissions at the time meant that work on the chapel suffered from several interruptions and delays.

Vasari also gives 1556 as the year the pictorial decoration in the chapel was begun, and he writes that Taddeo "did not do all of it"; although he later resumed painting, he had to stop again to work on the ephemeral *apparati* for Charles V's Roman funeral (March 1559) and once more when he was called to work in Orvieto (June to September 1559).[38] According to Vasari, in the course of Taddeo's work on the chapel, there was also an invitation to Caprarola in 1560, which led him to suspend all other jobs, until he decided "to serve the Farnese and finish the chapel of San Marcello." This occurred in the same period that his brother Federico received one of his first autonomous commissions, to decorate the facade of the Roman palace of Tizio Chermandio da Spoleto, then the *maestro di casa* of Cardinal Alessandro Farnese, which happened around 1559–1560. And when Federico departed for Venice in the summer of 1564, Vasari writes:

> Taddeo continued to paint frescoes all summer in the chapel of San Marcello; for which he finally painted the altarpiece in oils with the Conversion of Saint Paul ... but this work, having remained unfinished on account of his death, was completed by his brother Federico this year and was uncovered with much praise for him.[39]

The pictorial decoration, then, was done in three phases: 1556–1558, ca. 1560, and 1564–1566, presumably starting with the smaller frescoes on the vault, followed by the frescoes on the lateral walls and, finally, the altarpiece.

Strangely enough, critics have failed to consider the most obvious explanation for the choice of the stories of Saint Paul as the subjects of the imagery, namely, the desire, consistent with the extremely close ties between the Frangipani and the Farnese, of celebrating Paul III, Curzio's patron and the one who had enormously facilitated and supported his social elevation.[40] The choice was, after all, perfectly in line with the iconographic politics of the Farnese papacy, in which the figure of the saint, "civis romanus" par excellence, had been

FIG. 5. Taddeo and Federico Zuccari, *The Conversion of Saint Paul*, ca. 1564–1568. Frangipani Chapel (altar), San Marcello, Rome.

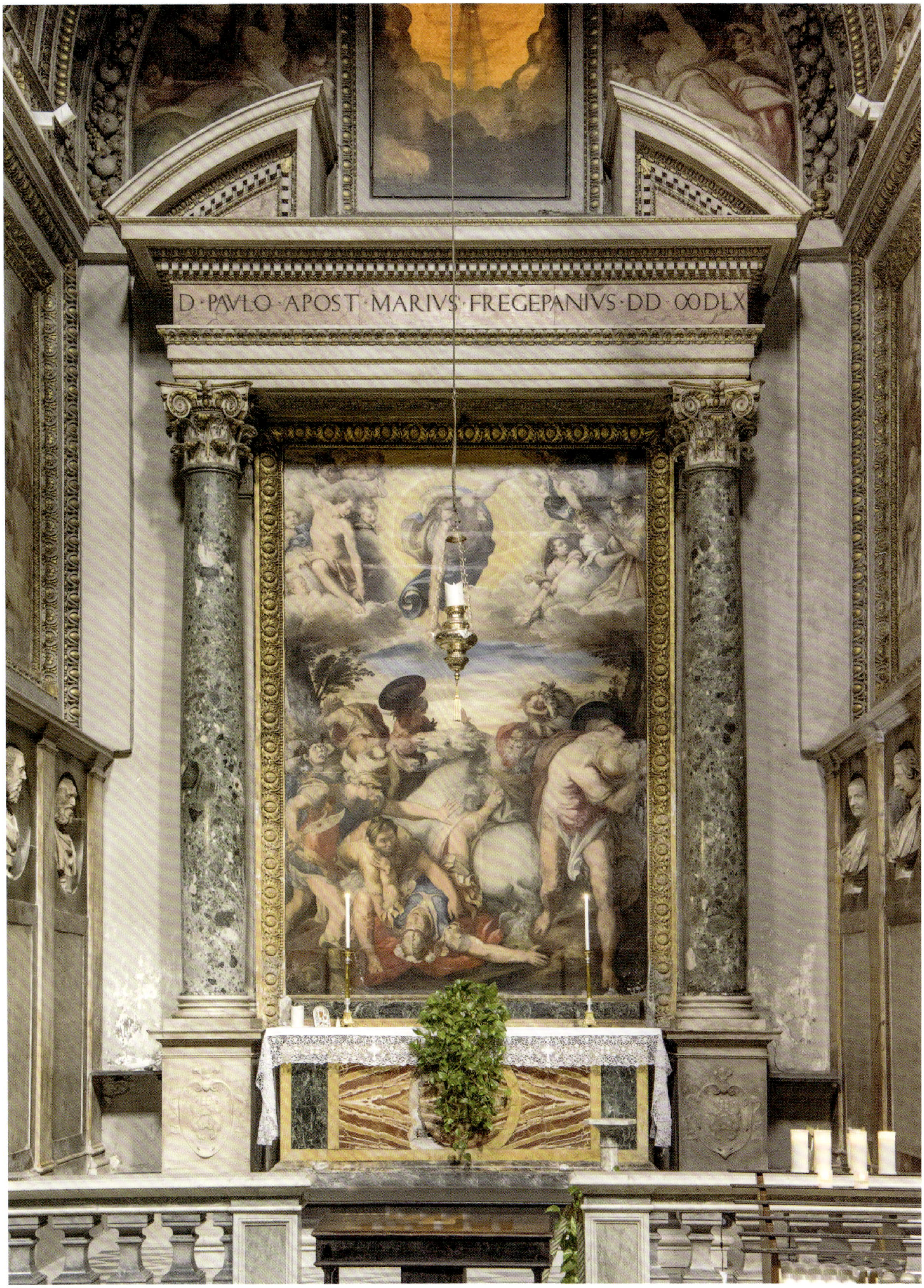

5

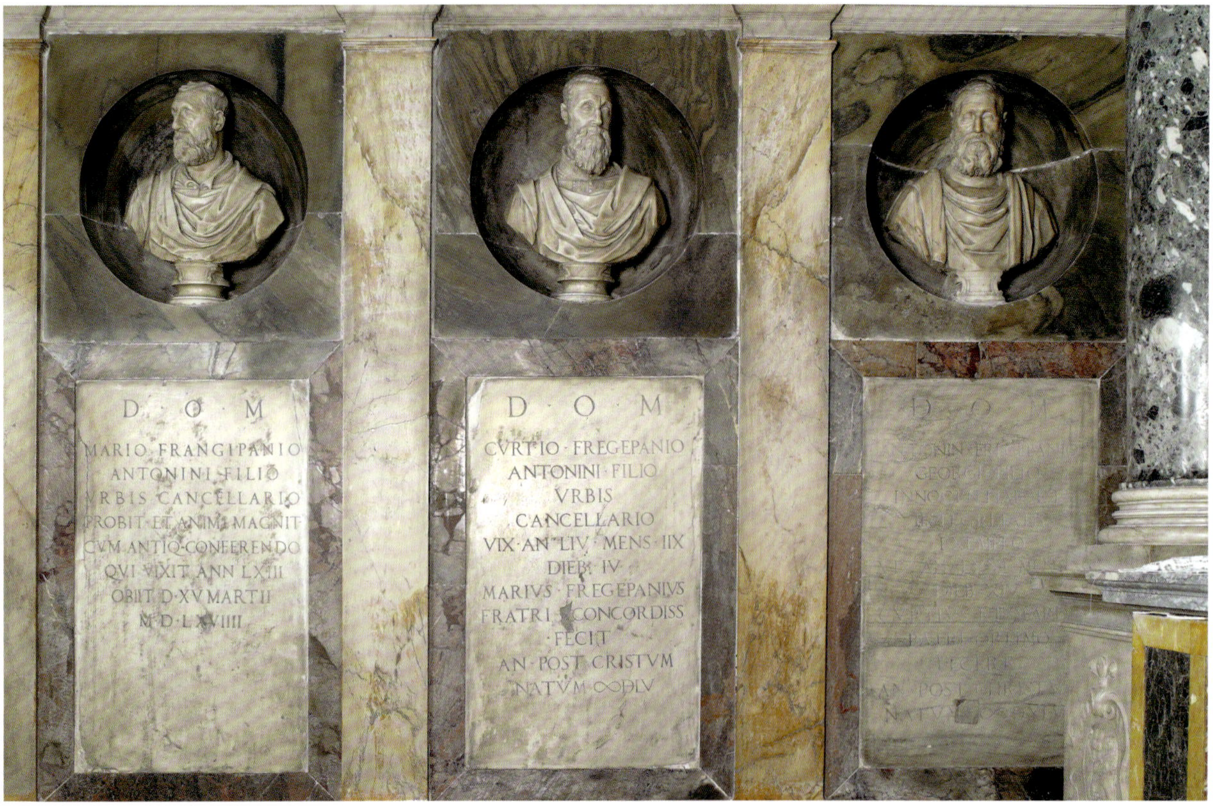
D O M
MARIO FRANGIPANIO
ANTONINI FILIO
VRBIS CANCELLARIO
CVRTIO FREGEPANIO
ANTONINI FILIO
VRBIS
CANCELLARIO
MARIVS FREGEPANIVS
FECIT
AN POST CRISTVM

6

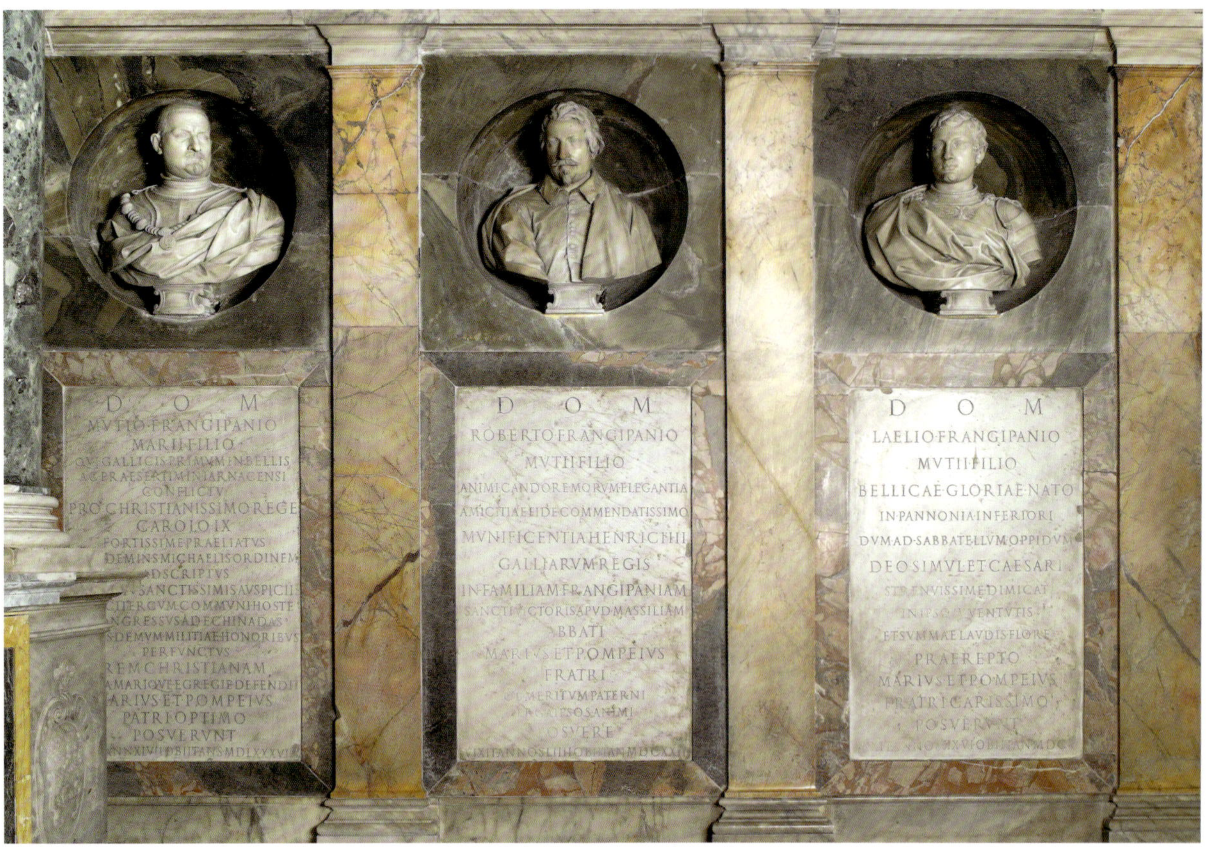
D O M
ROBERTO FRANGIPANIO
MVTII FILIO
GALLIARVM REGIS
MARIVS ET POMPEIVS
FRATRI
LAELIO FRANGIPANIO
MVTII FILIO
BELLICAE GLORIAE NATO
IN PANNONIA INFERIORI
DEO SIMVL ET CAESARI
MARIVS ET POMPEIVS
FRATRI CARISSIMO

7

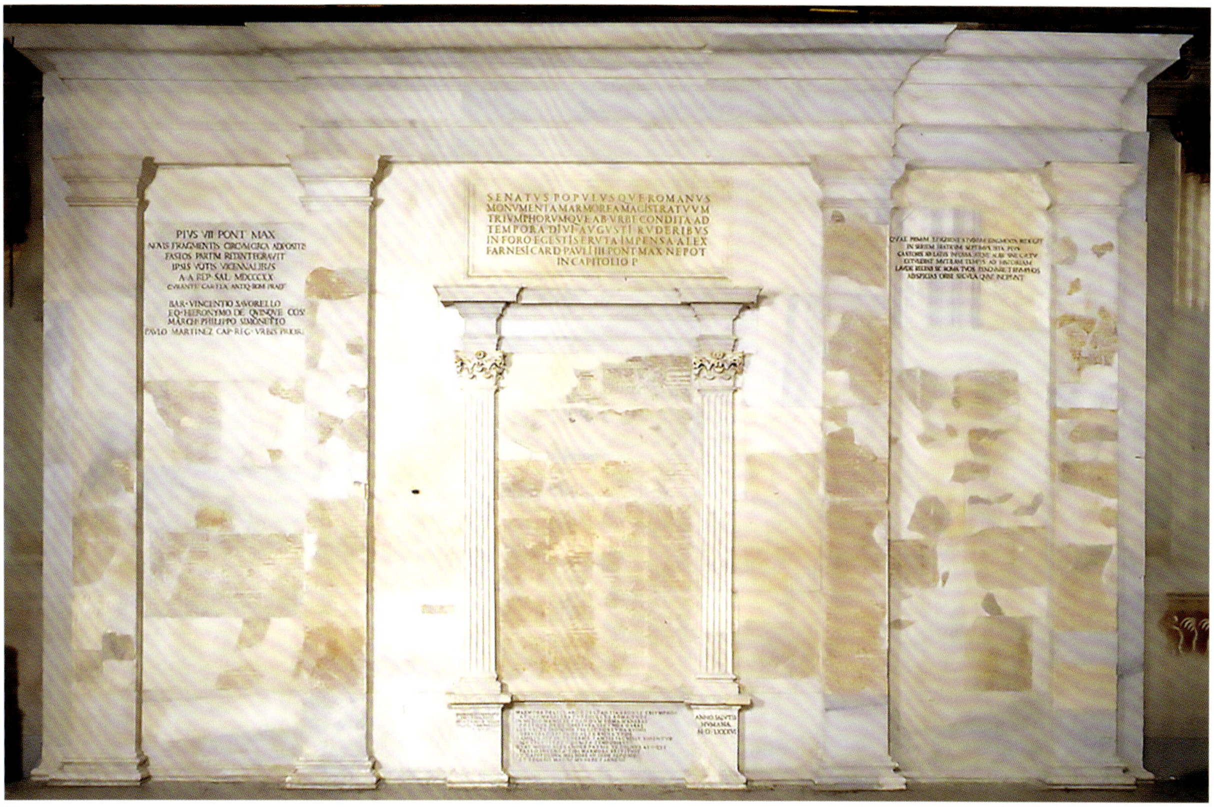

8

celebrated in the main papal pictorial cycles: the Pauline apartment in Castel Sant'Angelo, the Pauline Chapel in the Vatican, and the Chapel of the Pallio in the Palazzo della Cancelleria, the last ordered by the Gran Cardinale himself.

Turning now to the most original element of the chapel—the particular setting of the marble decorations and the busts below the frescoes—it is almost certain, in my opinion, based on the above-cited passage in Panvinio's text, that this was already begun in 1556 and was carried out independently of the slower execution of the paintings.

The decoration of the Frangipani Chapel, with the walls adorned with tall plinths in colored marble animated by the two facing triplets of busts, is almost unique in Rome, although the arrangement of a funerary bust portrait in a semicircular niche with an underlying epigraph had various antecedents, starting in the early sixteenth century. Two noteworthy examples are the tomb of the papal jurist Girolamo Bottigella (1515) and that of the apostolic writer Antonio Castali (1533), both in Santa Maria sopra Minerva, which not coincidentally was the church where the Frangipani were buried.

The extremely high quality of the Frangipani busts (FIGS. 9–12) has been noted almost universally by scholars, starting with Rodolfo Lanciani, who found Mario's bust to be "bellissimo," and including Rudolf Wittkower, who saw them as influential in the formation of the young Gian Lorenzo Bernini's development as a maker of portraits.[41] Unfortunately, the identification of the author(s) remains an enigma. Grisebach attributed the three busts to the hand of a single author, strongly influenced by Venetian portrait art, particularly

FIG. 6. Antonino, Curzio, and Mario Frangipani tombs, ca. 1554–1556. Frangipani Chapel (left wall), San Marcello, Rome.

FIG. 7. Muzio, Lelio, and Roberto Frangipani tombs (busts by Alessandro Algardi), ca. 1634–1638. Frangipani Chapel (right wall), San Marcello, Rome.

FIG. 8. Marble epigraphs of the *Fasti Capitolini*, ca. 1548. Sala della Lupa, Palazzo dei Conservatori, Campidoglio, Rome.

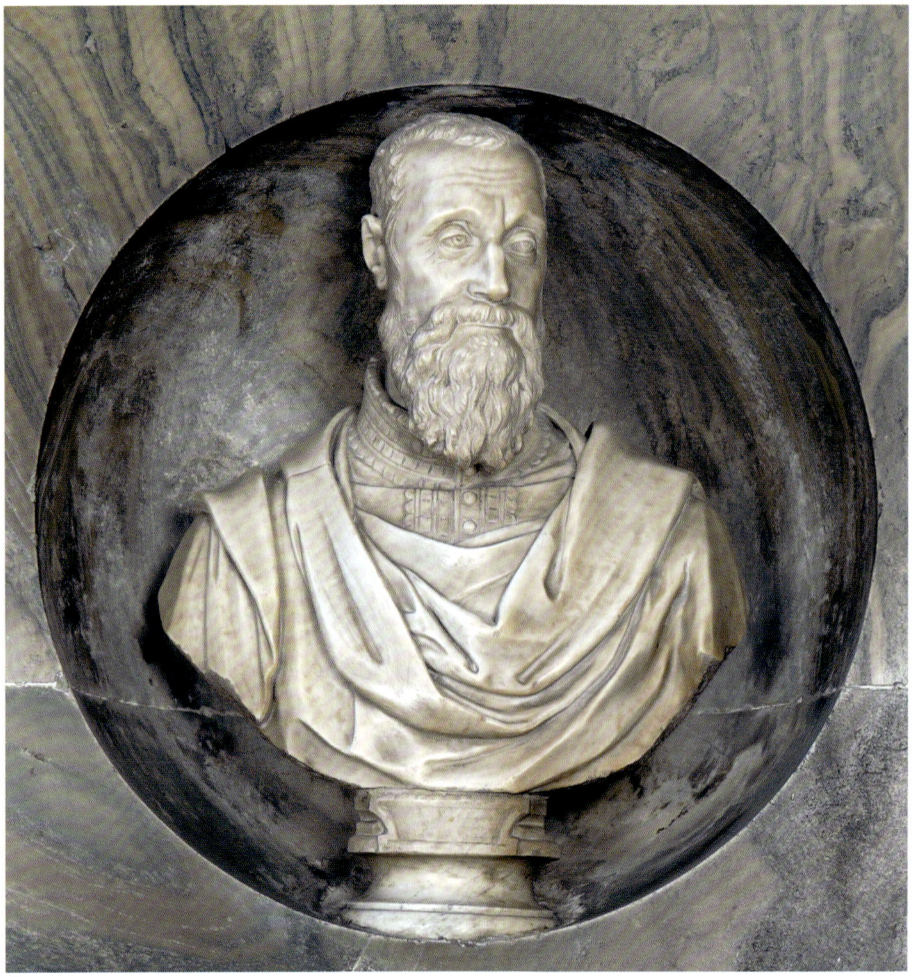

9

the work of Danese Cattaneo, an opinion with which I agree. Convincing, too, are Grisebach's observations about the bust of Antonino (FIG. 13), a work, as he noted, that displays a certain rigidity in the treatment of the beard, the drapery, and the eye sockets, qualities absent in the portraits of the sons, which points to the likelihood of a posthumous execution.[42] Wittkower also saw a strong Venetian influence in the sculptures, which he views as "Romanized versions of a type of Venetian bust."[43] A significant Morellian detail, which may facilitate a possible identification of the bust's author, is the complete absence of any rendering of hair on the protruding arches of the eyebrows, a very rare characteristic in Roman portrait sculpture of the mid-sixteenth century.

A parallel line of investigation worth exploring is the Farnese court—an extremely active site for various patrons allied with the family[44]—which Curzio engaged with intimately and on a daily basis and in which Taddeo Zuccari was involved in the years between 1555 and 1560. It is not easy, however, to identify a likely candidate among the various sculptors working for the Farnese at the time. The style of Guglielmo Della Porta is evidently foreign to the Frangipani busts. Similarly, the few known works by the two sculptors and marble restorers on the Farnese payroll, Giovanni Battista de' Bianchi da Saltrio and Tommaso

FIGS. 9–10. Portrait bust of Curzio Frangipani, ca. 1550–1560. Frangipani Chapel (left wall), San Marcello, Rome.

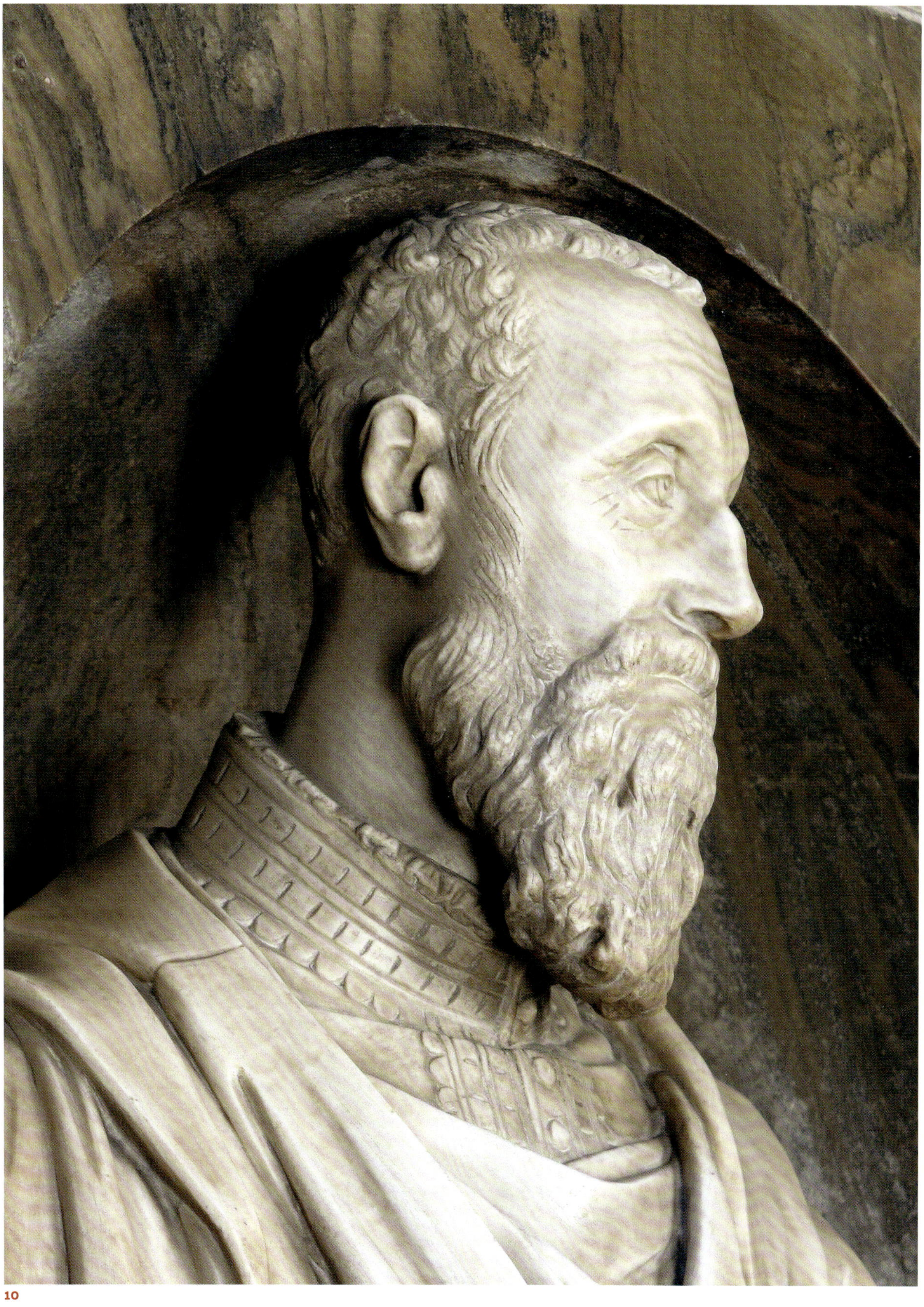

10

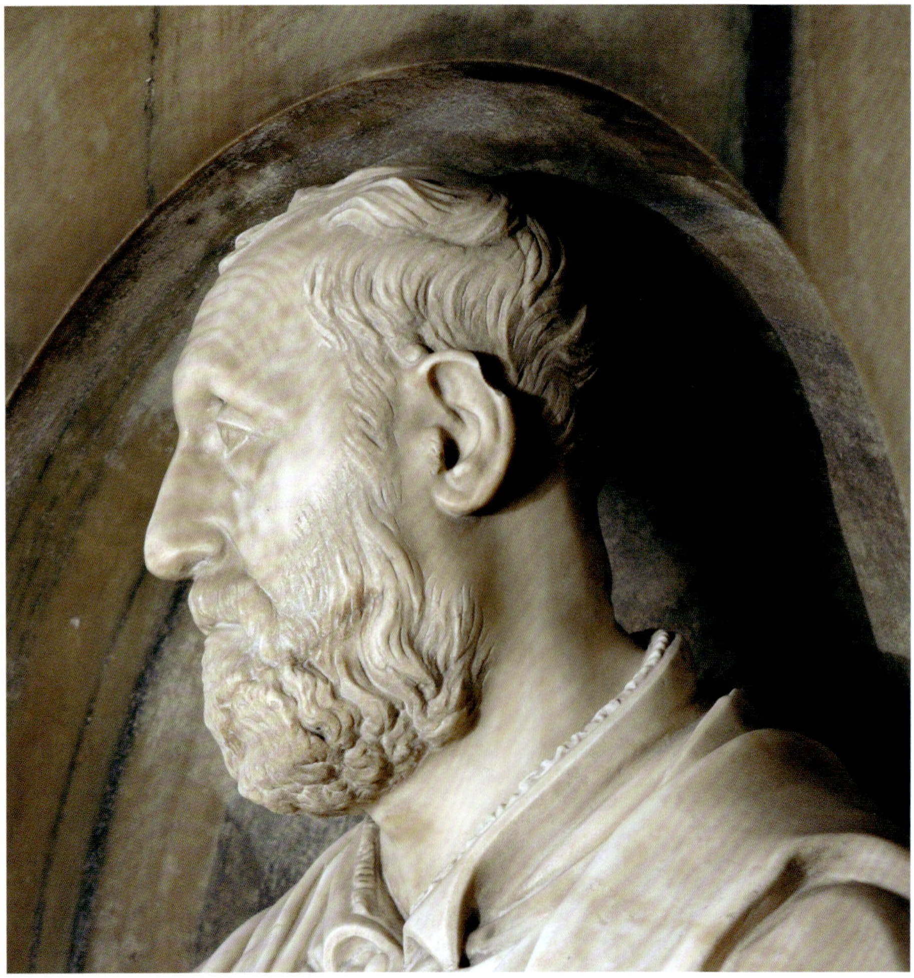

11

Boscoli da Fiesole, bear little resemblance to and pale in comparison with the extraordinary quality of the Frangipani portraits, and both artists joined the Farnese circle at a date later than the hypothetical date of the busts.[45] Thus, the Venetian connection remains the most plausible one until the discovery of new and harder evidence that may help us clarify the issue.

No less appealing and conceivable is Grisebach's hypothesis that the portrait busts of Antonino, Curzio, and Mario were not initially executed for their tombs in the chapel but were only installed in San Marcello at a later time, as suggested by the differences among their pedestals.[46] If this is indeed the case, then we could further hypothesize that the three busts were initially located in the new residence of the Frangipani in Piazza San Marco and were then moved to the chapel when the time came to furnish it.

In the inventory of the palace of San Marco, written a century later in 1654 to accompany the will of the junior Mario Frangipani and in preparation of the *fidecommisso* (legal accounting) of the family properties, there is a description of a room in front of the garden called "of the statues," in which there is mention of some of the marbles described a century earlier by Ulisse Aldrovandi in the loggia of the same building, including a Mercury (with the petasus) and a

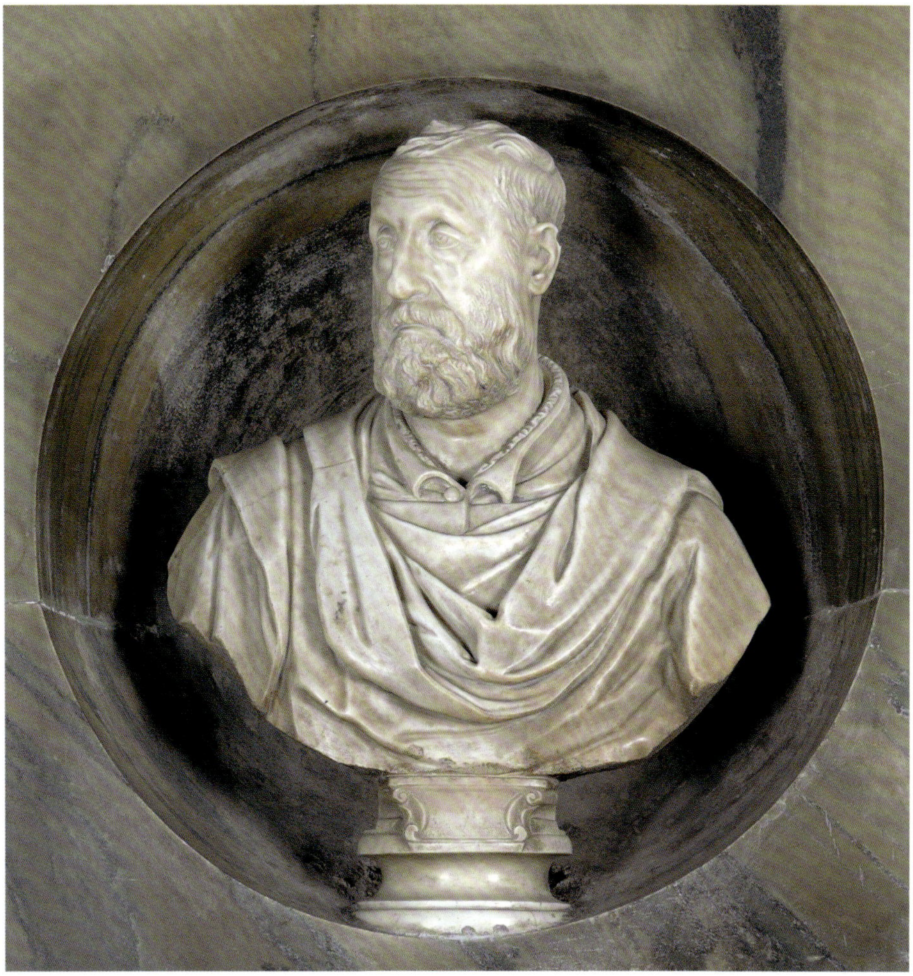

12

rich collection of ancient busts.[47] It is therefore very likely that already toward the mid-sixteenth century, alongside the canonical portraits of the Caesars and the Scipios, the busts *more antiquo* of Antonino and his two sons had been placed in the palace. These could have then been transferred to the chapel in San Marcello, to ennoble the tomb of Curzio and his descendants and as a "sculptural" display of an uninterrupted family tradition of continuity with the antique, the city of Rome, and its earliest protagonists.

Moreover, the particular way in which the busts were installed in the chapel was far from an act of mere "recycling." It was, I would argue, a deliberate and significant effort to arrange the walls as an *all'antica* triptych—a three-panel display—inspired by the setting of the *Fasti Capitolini*, which had played such an important role in Curzio's career as an erudite cultural figure. Not only does the tripartite division of the chapel's walls—articulated by pilasters with Tuscan capitals—echo the framing of the epigraphs of the *Fasti* on the Capitoline Hill, but the epigraphs' *all'antica* lettering and their vertical format closely resemble those used for the lists of Roman notables in the ancient marble tablets. There can be little doubt, then, that the installation of the busts in the chapel was intended as an explicit and intentional reference on the part of

FIGS. 11–12. Portrait bust of Mario Frangipani, ca. 1550–1560. Frangipani Chapel (left wall), San Marcello, Rome.

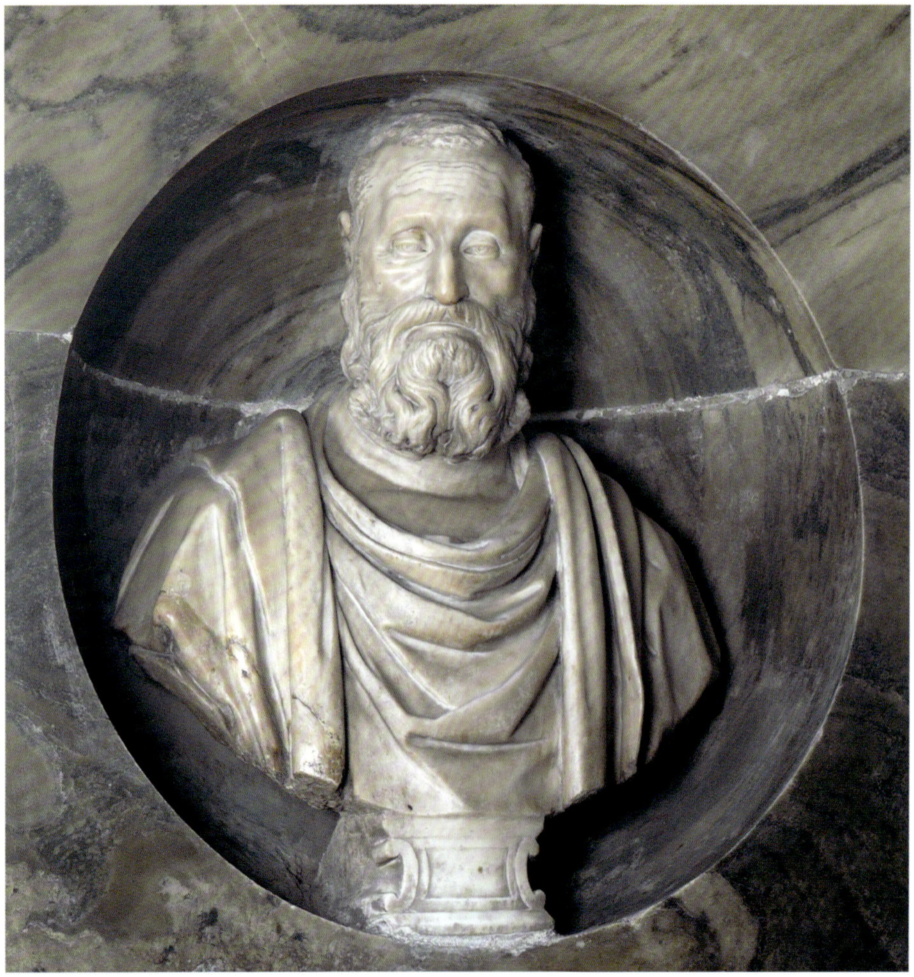

13

FIG. 13. Portrait bust of Antonino Frangipani, ca. 1550–1560. Frangipani Chapel (left wall), San Marcello, Rome.

the Frangipani to this ancient relic, intimately associating the family with the glorious past of ancient Rome.

The unique antiquarian style of the chapel may have been one of the reasons that led the later epigones of the family, the junior Mario and Pompeo Frangipani, to commission the Bolognese sculptor Alessandro Algardi to complete the chapel, sculpting the posthumous busts of Muzio and his sons Lelio and Roberto. This happened toward the mid-1630s, and the busts certainly must have been finished by 1638, the year in which their presence is mentioned by Pompilio Totti.[48] By this time, Algardi was well known for his restoration of some of the Ludovisi's ancient marbles, a type of work he also had done for the Frangipani in the early 1630s, as noted by Bellori.[49] The desire to emulate the form and mastery of the earlier busts and to respect the sense of ancient nobility of the chapel was presumably what guided Algardi's intervention, as can be seen in the shared arcing truncation and the shape of the pedestals of his three posthumous busts (also depicting a father and his two sons), which almost literally replicate the model of those of the bust of Antonino.

In conclusion, the rise of the Frangipani from the time of Paul III encouraged the brothers Curzio and Mario, the foremost representatives of the family and two of the most illustrious figures among the Capitoline elite, to want to retell their most ancient family history through a number of specific cultural projects. Among these, the foundation and decoration of the funerary chapel in San Marcello al Corso, a pendant to the contemporaneous and closely related apologetic history of the Frangipani by Onofrio Panvinio, was certainly the most striking and lavish demonstration to the Roman public.

Appendix

Doc. 1. Archivio di Stato di Roma (ASR), Collegio Notai Capitolini, Notary Bernardino de Comitibus, vol. 621, fols. 408–419, April 11, 1554, "Instrumentum ... concessionis cappellae Sancti Marcelli, et emptionis domum pro dote illius assignata pro d. Mario de Frangipanibus":

> The prior of the convent of San Marcello concedes to Curzio Frangipani Cancellarius Urbis the chapel next to that of the late cardinal of Rimini, with the right to bury himself and his relatives, in exchange for an endowment of two hundred scudi. In case of his death, his place will be taken by his brother Mario and the son of the latter, Muzio, his legitimate heirs. The endowment will be guaranteed through the purchase of the house of Michele Florio de Fabriano on the part of Mario and Muzio, adjoining on one side the properties of Giovan Pietro Caffarelli, on the other the properties of the Chapel of the Visitation and San Martino in San Lorenzo in Damaso, and on the other the public street. The house is consigned to the Provinciale Generale dell'Ordine di San Marcello, Reverendus D. Johannis de Regio.

Doc. 2. ASR, Collegio Notai Capitolini, Notary Bernardino de Comitibus, vol. 622, fols. 45r/v, 51rv, June 13, 1556 (mentioned by Balass 2001, n. 21):

> The deed refers to a previous *instrumento* of April 11, 1554 (document no. 1 above), written down in the presence of the prior of San Marcello and of the late Curzio Frangipani, Cancellarius Urbis. It mentions the endowment of two hundred scudi promised by Curzio in exchange for the concession of the chapel, an endowment that, on account of his death, was not paid in its entirety. Therefore, Mario Frangipani, brother of Curzio, and Muzio, son of Mario, both universal heirs of Curzio, promise to find a property to guarantee the endowment, by purchasing a house in the Rione Arenula from Michele Florio de Fabriano, already identified in the previous deed (see document no. 1). The house, purchased by Mario Frangipani, will be given to the prior of San Marcello and will serve as an endowment for the Frangipani Chapel in the said church.

Doc. 3. ASR, Collegio Notai Capitolini, Notary Bernardino de Comitibus, vol. 623, fols. 284r/v, 295, January 13, 1568:

> Lease on the part of Mario Frangipani to Giovanni Forti of the late Florenzio de Sanctis de Matire [Matera?] of the so-called "palazzo antiquo de Frangipanis" intra moenia Urbis, known as Palazzo Maggiore, near the church of Sant'Anastasia and

the fountain of San Giorgio, for a yearly rent of four scudi. The landlord agrees to share with the tenant half of all the statues, gold, silver, or other metals that will be found in the said place. Every piece of peperino or travertine that will be excavated will belong instead entirely to the tenants, Mario having already leased the place to a stone excavator, Antonio, Roman, and to his partners for the entire month of April with the permission to extract stones.
Present as witness to the act underwritten in the home of Mario Frangipani in the neighborhood of Pigna, are Magistro Mariano di Sandro del Polara, mason from Pisa, and Magistro Antonio of the late Pietro de Mercatello of the State of Urbino … [Antonio de Mercatello was Antonio de Bencivenni, an engraver of wood and trophies].

Doc. 4. Archivio Storico Capitolino, Archivio Notarile Urbano, section V (Fidecommissi) prot. 3, fasc. 63 ("Inventarium bonorum Romae," January 23, 1654, in attachment to the will of Mario Frangipani of January 14, 1654), fols. 267–294:

In the "palazzo grande posto su la piazza di San Marco di Roma … [c. 272r/v] nella 4° stanza respondente al Giardino, dove sono le statue, una statua di Mercurio grande antica con sua base, e piedestallo di marmo, una statua di Venere grande con una conchiglia in mano sopra un piedestallo di marmo, Doi statue di fauni, che s'appoggiano ad un tronco, una più bassa dell'altra con piedistalli di marmo. Una statua d'un satiro nudo con le gnacchere in mano in forma di ballare, l'uno e l'altro, Una statua d'una Diana; nove putti con sue teste, tra quali uno d'alabastro … Giove, Settimio Severo, Iunia Flavilla, Archimede, e dell'altre non si fa il nome; sei teste con suoi pieducci, cioè Anteo, Martio, Aurelio vecchio, e Aurelio Giovane, Scipione maggiore, e Scipion minore, e l'altra non si fa il nome; Doi teste senza peduccio, Doi piedistalli senza statue, un tavolino di noce pietra mischia sotto il camino con suoi piedi di legno."

Notes

I wish to express my gratitude to Stefan Bauer and Andrea Fara for their valuable suggestions about Onofrio Panvinio and the Frangipani family; to Andrea Bacchi, Gregoire Extermann, Fernando Loffredo, Steven F. Ostrow, Massimiliano Rossi, and Susanna Zanuso for conversations about Roman Cinquecento sculpture; to Mauro Mussolin for suggestions about Michelangelo; and to Chiara Franceschini for helpful bibliographic advice. Special thanks to Bianca Maria Tummarello for her revisions to the Latin translations and to Stephanie Leone and Steven F. Ostrow for editing my English translations.

1 — On San Marcello al Corso, see Gigli 1996.

2 — On the pictorial decorations by Taddeo and Federico Zuccari, the main source is Vasari 1568 [1906], VII, 84, 86, 96–97. See also Macioce 1984, 112–118; Strinati 1984, 118–124; Gigli 1996, 123–137; Acidini Luchinat 1998, I, 59–78; Balass 2001; Bailey 2003.

3 — For a credible explanation of the inscription above the altarpiece, see Balass 2001, 178 and n. 17. The same transcription is in J. P. Brutius, *Theatrum Romae Urbis. Ecclesiae Romanae Urbis …*, Biblioteca Apostolica Vaticana (hereafter BAV), Vat. lat. 11881, fol. 247v.

4 — Panvinio (BAV, Barb. lat. 2481: *Onophrii Panvinii Veronensis fratris eremitae Augustiniani de gente Fregepania libri quatuor*, fols. 122r–123r; (hereafter Panvinio [1556]) mentions Antonino Frangipani, son of Lelio Frangipani and Girolama di Angelo Paluzzo degli Albertoni, born around 1477. Orphaned at the age of eighteen months, he grew up in the house of Girolamo Pietro Mattei, under the protection of Cardinal Giambattista Savelli, together with the cardinal's nephews, Troilo and Giacomo. In Antonino's first will, dated June 18, 1540 (Archivio di Stato di Roma [hereafter ASR], *Trenta Notai Capitolini*, Uff. 4, Nicolaus De Straballatis, June 18, 1540, fols. 180v–182r), he elected to be buried in the church of Santa Maria sopra Minerva (where the Frangipani traditionally had their tombs) and named his sons Curzio and Mario as his legitimate heirs. The confraternities of the SS. Salvatore and Santa Maria in Portico were chosen as testamentary executors, receiving twenty-five scudi each. On October 20, 1546, a codicil was added to the first will (Archivio Storico Capitolino [hereafter ASC], *Archivio*

Savorgnan di Brazzà, Maccarani, Archivio proprio, Carte di Paolo Maccarani, b. 137, fasc. 2, testament of Antonino Frangipani on parchment, drawn up by the notary Nicolaus De Straballatis; the copy of the codicil in the Archivio di Stato is now lost). In this second and last will, the testator mentions himself as "infirmus" (ill) and adds as an heir his daughter Ersilia, wife of Giovan Pietro Caffarelli, the latter the author of the famous manuscript on Roman families. At that time, the palace of the Frangipani was at Torre del Melangolo, now the Palazzo Delfini in the Rione Sant'Angelo. In addition to Curzio, Mario, and Ersilia, Antonino had twin sons, Stefano and Lelio, and a daughter, Giulia, all of whom died prematurely (Panvinio [1556], fols. 124r/v). The information on the Frangipani family in Picone 1995 is largely imprecise or incorrect.

5 — Antonino was Conservator of Rome in 1518, 1527, and 1530 (Pucci 1621, 67).

6 — The three busts of Muzio, Lelio, and Roberto were executed posthumously, before 1638, as discussed below. On these busts, see Montagu 1985, II, cat. 147–149, 426–427; Ferrari and Papaldo 1999, 202. Montagu describes "The circular niches in the Frangipani chapel in S. Marcello, reminiscent in their simplicity of a classical columbarium."

7 — Grisebach 1936, 56–58.

8 — The epigraph under Antonino's bust bears the inscription "D. O. M. / ANTONIN(O) FREGEPANIO / GEORGI FILIO / INNOCENTIAE ET / INTEGRITATIS / EXEMPLO / VIX(IT) AN LXXI MENS II / DIEB(US) XIV / CURTIUS ET MARIUS / PATRI OPTIMO / FECERE / AN POST CHRISTUM NATUM / MDXLVI." The identification "Georgi filio" does not match his father's name—Lelio—provided by Panvinio (see note 4 above), unless Lelio also bears the name of Giorgio. It is important to note that the dating "post Christum natum" is an unequivocal sign of antiquarian and classical taste in the inscriptions of Antonino's and Curzio's tombs.

9 — The tablet under Curzio's bust bears the inscription "D. O. M. / CURTIO FREGEPANIO / ANTONINI FILIO / URBIS / CANCELLARIO / VIX(IT) AN(NIS) LIV / MENS(IBUS) IIX / DIEB(US) IV / MARIUS FREGEPANIUS / FRATRI CONCORDISS(IMO) / FECIT / AN POST CRISTUM NATUM / NATUM MDLV." Actually, Panvinio ([1556], fols. 126v–127r]) says that he died at the age of fifty-five from a "quartan" fever (a form of malaria), "quinto calendas novembris anno humanae salutis millesimo quingentesimo quinquagesimo quarto."

10 — The epigraph under Mario's bust reads: " D. O. M. / MARIO FRANGIPANIO / ANTONINI FILIO / URBIS CANCELLARIO / PROBIT ET ANIMI MAGNIT / CUM ANTIQ CONFERENDO / QUI VIXIT ANN LXIII / OBIIT D XV MARTII / MDLXVIIII." In this case, there are some noticeable differences in the inscription, starting with the surname, "Frangipanio," instead of the more correct Latin form "Fregepanio."

11 — Panvinio [1556]. Other copies of the manuscript are in Padua, Biblioteca dell'Università, cod. It. 263, fols. 85–192, and Rome, Biblioteca Angelica, Ms. 77; Bauer (2013, n. 37), however, mentions at least six of them. The information in Panvinio was then repeated in the following histories of the Frangipani family printed at the beginning of the seventeenth century: Zazzera d'Aragonia 1617; Pucci 1621. For an analysis of the *De gente Fregepania*, see Bauer 2013 (with previous bibliography), Bauer 2014, and Bauer 2019.

12 — Panvinio [1556], c. 4r: "Nulla post hominum memoriam familia umquam fuit, cuius per multa saecula certiora et illustriora memoriae tradita monumenta extiterint, vel quae uberiorem clarissimorum hominum copiam tulerit, quam Domus que antiquis Anicia recentioribus vero temporibus Fregepania est appellata, fuit enim Anicia Gens prisca Reipublicae aetate, quod honorificentissimum erat, et supremae dignitatis fastigium consularis et triumphalis, posteriore vero Imperatorum tempore, solae supra duodetrigintas quos omnes max enumerabimus, consulatus est adepta … Fregepaniam autem Domum octingentis ab hinc annis, inter Romanas familias primariam fuisse." ("Non ci fu mai alcuna famiglia, a memoria d'uomo, della quale per molti secoli siano esistite più certe e illustri testimonianze degne di ricordo, o che abbia portato una stirpe più feconda di uomini illustrissimi, quanto il casato che è stato denominato Anicia in tempi antichi e Frangipania in tempi più recenti; ci fu infatti sin dalla prima età repubblicana la stirpe Anicia, che era onoratissima, e [godette] di rango consolare e trionfale della più alta dignità, ma anche nel successivo periodo imperiale, [fu] l'unica, tra le ventotto principali casate che enumereremo, ad ottenere il consolato … dunque la casa Frangipani, da quel momento per ottocento anni, primeggiò tra le famiglie romane.") Author's translation from Latin to Italian.

13 — Balass (2001, 179) also mentions the tie between Onofrio Panvinio and Curzio Frangipani, identifying the Augustinian friar as being responsible for the iconographic program of the paintings in the chapel.

14 — Panvinio [1556], fols. 126v–127r: "Apud Alexandrum [n.d.a. Farnese junior] tanta gratia tantaque auctoritate valuit ut unus ad nutum omnia regeret, nihil prorsus gravioris negocii in aula sua Curtio inconsulto ageretur. Ingenii enim dexteritate, humanitate et prudentia omnes aulicos superabat." ("Curzio, presso Alessandro [Farnese] ebbe una tale influenza e una tale garbata autorevolezza che da solo amministrava ogni cosa con un sol cenno, e a corte proprio nessuno degli affari più seri veniva trattato senza che Curzio venisse consultato. Infatti, superava tutti i cortigiani per prudenza, umanità e rettitudine di indole.") Author's translation from Latin to Italian.

15 — On Mariangelo Accursio, see Campana 1960.

16 — Curzio Frangipani is also mentioned in a letter of Paolo Giovio to Alessandro Farnese in 1546, regarding the frescoes of the Sala dei Cento Giorni at Palazzo della Cancelleria, in which Curzio should have been among the many portraits in the episode of *Paul III Awarding Benefices*: "e vorrebbe messer Curzio nel abito di Testaccio" ("and [Vasari] would like messer Curzio in the clothes of Testaccio"). See also Agosti 2008, 130–131, n. 330. On the "moralistic" character of Curzio, see Spagnolo 2013, 520–522.

17 — The *Fasti Capitolini* are fragments of marble tablets that include lists of the Roman kings and consuls, from the origins of Rome until 13 CE (*Fasti consolari*), and of the victories of Rome (*Fasti trionfali*), with the respective victors, starting from Romulus until Cornelius Balbus in 19 BCE. On their exceptional discovery and display in the Sala della Lupa of the Palazzo dei Conservatori on the Capitoline Hill, together with the bronze Capitoline She-Wolf, during the Cinquecento, see Degrassi 1943, 327–335; Degrassi 1945–1946; Taylor 1950, 84–95; Degrassi 1962;

Bedon 1991; Ferrary 1996, 57–59, 110; Beard 2003, 23–28; Bedon 2008, 75, 135. On the other walls of the room were later placed two celebratory inscriptions, one for the victories of Duke Alessandro Farnese and another in honor of Marcantonio Colonna. See Beard 2003, 26.

18 — Bedon 2008, 59–60. Bedon highlights the wide culture of Curzio, fully ensconced in the inner Farnese circle, where he played the role of *spenditore* of the Farnese house, responsible for the salaries of artists and humanists. Moreover, the entire first phase of the installation of the Capitoline place is due to him, in collaboration with Tommaso de' Cavalieri, who, after Curzio's death, took over this important task (Bedon 2008, 344). On Curzio, see also Pucci 1621, 67–68.

19 — Degrassi 1943, 328; Bedon 2008, 341.

20 — The installation of the *Fasti* in the Sala della Lupa (or Sala dei Fasti antichi) in the Palazzo dei Conservatori, dates to 1586. See Degrassi 1943, 331; Bedon 1991, 76; Bedon 2008, 75.

21 — Bedon (1991, 82, n. 10) believes that the attribution to Michelangelo is based on an erroneous interpretation of the information provided by Panvinio; Mussolin (2009, 85) instead upholds the attribution to Michelangelo, on the basis of the reconstruction published by Marliano (1549).

22 — The first partial transcription of the *Fasti*, without comment, is due to Marliano 1549 (Ferrary 1996, 116), followed by Sigonio (1550; 1556). In 1557, Panvinio published the complete and annotated version (Panvinio 1557), which he then revised in the edition of 1558 (Panvinio 1558); see Beard 2003, 24.

23 — Balass (2001, 179) asserted that the chapel was entrusted to Mario, but the documents clearly demonstrate that before his death, Curzio made the agreement with the friars; see below and Appendix, doc. 1.

24 — Lanciani 1902–1912, III, 1907, 151; Lanciani 1989–2002, III, 1990, 162.

25 — See Appendix, doc. 3.

26 — Panvinio [1556], fols. 124v–125r: "Diem clausit extremum magno apud omnes sui desiderio relicto cadaver in Patrum sacello, quod in templo Sancta Maria super Minervam est honorifico temporario sepulchro conditum est, tribus filiis superstitibus relictis Curtio, Mario et foemina Ersilia que longo tempore ante eius obitum Joanni Pietro Caffarello Nobili Civi Romano nupserat." ("He finished his life, and according to the great wish of all, the body was buried in the tomb of the Fathers, in a temporary honorary sepulcher established in Santa Maria sopra Minerva, having left three surviving children, Curzio, Mario, and Ersilia, who, a long time before his death, got married with the noble Roman citizen Giovan Pietro Caffarelli.")

27 — For the relationships among Grifoni, Parisani, and Farnese, see also Bolzoni 2018, 59–60 (with previous bibliography).

28 — In 1554, Cencio Frangipani and Scipione Orsini initiated the project of an oratory for the Confraternity of the SS. Crocifisso; in 1557, Tommaso de' Cavalieri replaced Orsini. See von Henneberg 1974, 12–14.

29 — I am indebted to Andrea Fara for the information about the Roman houses of the Frangipani. For an in-depth study, see Fara 2018. See also Lanciani 1902–1912, II, 1903, 35–36.

30 — Aldrovandi and Mauro 1556, 262–263; Lanciani 1902–1912, I, 1902, 171–172. See also Christian 2010, 315–317. According to Aldrovandi, a pictorial reproduction of the *Suovetaurilia* reliefs in the Palazzo Venezia (today in the Louvre) were in Curzio's adjacent palace in Piazza San Marco (De Angelis d'Ossat 2011, 34–35). Christian (2010, 316) convincingly suggests that the scene could be part of a painted cycle of Roman history. Since the end of the fifteenth century, other branches of the Frangipani family owned many antiquities, as recorded in Jacopo Frangipani's house in Via dell'Umiltà in the Rione Trevi. See Christian 2010, 315–317.

31 — Vasari 1568 [1906], VII, 84–86, 89, with the *postille* published by Gaetano Milanesi. See also the chronological reconstruction in Acidini Luchinat 1998, I, 59–78.

32 — See Appendix, doc. 1.

33 — See Appendix, doc. 2.

34 — It seems that Curzio died in the house of Cardinal Farnese, in the Palazzo della Cancelleria, if we believe Frangipane 1876, 75, n. 2: "sembra che i più intimi amici del cardinale abitassero il palazzo della Cancelleria Apostolica. Che poi il suo amicissimo Curzio Frangipani in quello compisse la sua vita nel 1554 è manifesto da quanto riferisce un cronista, i cui scritti furono conservati dall'accurato monsignor Galletti. Ivi si dice: 'Morì in S. Giorgio (ossia nel palazzo del Cardinale Raffaele Riario Diacono di S. Giorgio) Curzio Frangipani e fu portato in S. Marcello. Lui giva vestito di rubone con pelli di varo, con un berretto di lama d'oro, e col bastone come Cancelliere di Roma.'" ("It seems that the closest friends of the Cardinal lived in the Palazzo della Cancelleria Apostolica. It is clear that his close friend Curzio Frangipani ended his life there in 1554, according to the report of a chronicler, whose manuscripts were kept by the precise Monsignor Galletti. In them it says: 'Curzio Frangipani died in San Giorgio [that is the palace of Cardinal Raffaele Riario Deacon of San Giorgio] and was carried to San Marcello. He went around dressed in clothing with ermine borders, and a cap in gold leaf, and the baton of Chancellor of Rome.'")

35 — Panvinio ([1556], fols. 126v–127r), affirms that Curzio died at fifty-five years old, after one year of fever, "quinto calendas novembris anno humanae salutis millesimo quingentesimo quinquagesimo quarto [n.d.a.: il 28 ottobre 1554]" ("in the fifth calends of November of the year 1554"), and "cadaver sepultum est in Basilica Sancti Marcelli in via lata, in novo sacello à se ante mortem in eo templo sibi posterisque suis locato, cura et impensis fratris sui Marii Fregepanii viri egregi quem moriens me presente omnium bonorum suorum heredem reliquit. Cum quo ante mortem semper adeo concordissime vixit, ut nulla unquam inter eos patrimonii divisio intercesserit" ("the dead body was buried in the Basilica of San Marcello in via Lata, in a new chapel established in that church before his death, by and for himself and his posterity, through the interest and the expenses of his brother Mario, excellent man, to whom he left, as his heir, dying in my presence, all his goods").

36 — Panvinio [1556], fol. 127r. "Illum autem sacellum modo tu Marii in amantissimi fratris memoria magno sumptu exedificare et ornare variis marmoribus et picturis et emblematibus coepisti, ut quum ad finem perductum fuerit opus nihil pulchrius in Urbe ipsa conspici posse credendum." ("Dunque, tu o Mario, iniziasti ora a costruire quel sacello in memoria del tuo amatissimo fratello con così grande generosità e a ornarlo di vari marmi, pitture e ornamenti, che

quando sarà concluso si dovrà credere di non poter vedere opera più bella in tutta Roma.") Author's translation from Latin to Italian.

37 — For the texts of the epigraphs, see nn. 8–10 above. Panvinio [1556], fol. 123v: "Fuit Antoninus Fregepanius (ut multorum fidedegnorum hominum didici relatione) vir mediocri quidem eruditione sed qui probitate, vitae *innocentia et integritate* pietate quoque, et in pauperos misericordia, omnes sue etatis cives, non tantum adequavit, verum etiam longe post se inferiores reliquit." ("Antonino Frangipani [as I learned by the report of many trustworthy men], man of mediocre erudition but who for honesty, innocence, moral integrity, and devotion and piety towards poor people, not only equaled his contemporaries, but also … by far exceeded them.") Panvinio ([1556], fol. 127r) also highlights the perennial concord between the brothers, Curzio and Mario, mentioned also in the epigraph: "(Marius) cum quo (Curzio, n.d.a.) ante mortem *semper adeo concordissime vixit*, ut nulla unquam inter eos patrimonii divisio intercesserit." ("Mario with whom Curzio, before he died, always lived in complete harmony, so that the division of the patrimony did not come between them.")

38 — On the Zuccaris' stay in Orvieto, see Acidini Luchinat 1998, I, 108–109. Further related documents are published in Tosini 2010, 468.

39 — Vasari 1568 [1906], 97. But in his *postille* to Vasari's *Vite*, Federico himself denies that he finished the painting, instead confirming: "è gloria di Taddeo, perché Federigo quivi fece pocho ho nulla di momento" ("it is a glory of Taddeo, as Federico did little or nothing at that moment").

40 — Macioce (1984, 117–118) generically relates the stories of Saint Paul to the meaning of conversion and conflict with the Protestant heresy; furthermore, she notes that the Frangipani had among their ancestors a certain Benedetto, who, like Saint Paul, abjured the Jewish faith to join Christianity. This latter interpretation is followed by Acidini Luchinat (1998, I, 62). Golda Balass (2001) devotes most of her contribution to an in-depth analysis of the iconography and the style of the frescoes, suggesting that the choice of the Pauline stories, in addition to the Counter-Reformation theme of conversion, could be linked to a saint of the Frangipani, Ottone, whose life shared similarities with that of Saint Paul. She concludes (200, n. 47): "I could not find any documented reason for the Frangipani's choice of a chapel dedicated to St. Paul."

41 — Lanciani 1989–2002, III, 1990, 151; Riccoboni 1942, 136–137; Wittkower 1981, It. ed. 1990, 247. Strinati (1992, 397–398) calls the three sculptures "notevolissime" (very remarkable), attributing them to an anonymous sculptor of the circle of Taddeo Zuccari and comparing them with the anonymous presumed tomb of "Antonio Socher" in the basement of Santa Croce in Gerusalemme. Actually, it is the tomb of Jerôme Souchier, cardinal and General of the Cistercians (d. 1571) in the Gregorian Chapel of the basilica, which has nothing to do with the Frangipani portraits, as it is clearly a later work.

42 — Grisebach 1936, 68. Grisebach compared the composition of the three funeral portraits on each wall to that of the Contarini Chapel in Santa Maria dell'Orto in Venice, but, as rightly underscored by Martin (1998, 134), it is a typology more Roman than Venetian. In fact, it seems to me that the partition of the wall into three sections is the only similarity between the Venetian tombs—characterized by a much more powerful architectural setting—and the layout of the Frangipani Chapel.

43 — Wittkower 1981, It. ed. 1990, 247. The quotation is also cited by Susanna Zanuso in the catalog entry on the bust of Cardinal Agostino Valier by Gian Lorenzo Bernini (Zanuso, in Bernardini and Fagiolo dell'Arco 1999, entry 35, 320–321, illustration at 319). The caption of the photo in the catalog inexplicably attributes the bust of Curzio to Alessandro Vittoria, an attribution not confirmed by Susanna Zanuso (oral communication).

44 — Acidini Luchinat 1998, I, 220, n. 6.

45 — On Giovanni Battista de' Bianchi (or Bianchi), see Riebesell 1991 (with previous bibliography); Robertson 1992, 115, 126, 128, 241, 306, 308–309; Ioele 2013 [2015]; Annibali 2019, forthcoming. On Tommaso Boscoli da Fiesole, see Ghisetti Giavarina 2009 and Loffredo 2011 (who identifies Tommaso Boscoli as two different personalities, one from Fiesole and the other from Montepulciano).

46 — The pedestal of the bust of Antonino is visibly different from the others. Furthermore, the rectangular space for an inscription of the name of the sitter on the bases of Curzio's and Mario's busts is clearly redundant and useless because of the inscriptions beneath, which could confirm that the three sculptures come from another location.

47 — See Appendix, doc. 4. Montagu (1985, I, 259, n. 18) quotes this inventory, pointing out the presence of a bust of "Mutio Frangipane Seniore," which could confirm the existence of a portrait series of family members in the Palazzo Frangipani.

48 — See Totti 1638, 291. Montagu (2009, 187) dates the busts to the 1630s, likely before 1634.

49 — Bellori 1672 [1976], 402: "Spese però Alessandro molti anni in queste occupazioni, restaurando statue antiche, ed alcune che 'l signor Mario Frangipani mandava in Francia, il quale adoperollo ancora per la sua cappella di San Marcello ne' tre ritratti di marmo a man sinistra [sic], di rincontro a tre altri della sua famiglia." ("Alessandro spent many years in these occupations, restoring ancient statues, and some of them that Mario Frangipani sent to France, who made use of him also for his chapel in San Marcello, in the three marble portraits on the left side, in front of three others of his family.") See also Montagu 1985, I, 22, noting that the marbles were sent to Richelieu in France in 1633; and Furlotti 2016, with new material on this subject.

Between *all'Antica* and *Acheiropoieton*

THE CAPPELLA GREGORIANA IN THE EKPHRASES OF LORENZO FRIZOLIO (1582) AND ASCANIO VALENTINO (1583)

Fabio Barry

In 1575, Gregory XIII Boncompagni (1572–1585) appropriated one of the four monumental corner chapels of the unfinished St. Peter's for his personal mausoleum, which would be known from now on as the Cappella Gregoriana (**FIGS. 1–4**). This structure, too, was only half built. Although it had been projected by Michelangelo in the 1550s, its foundations were only dug in 1571, and it was being completed under the supervision of Giacomo Della Porta ("architetto della Fabbrica di San Pietro" from 1573). The vault was closed in 1577, and then every square inch of the chapel was decorated with marble and mosaic between 1578 and 1580, although it was not quite finished until 1584.

This was the first-ever papal mausoleum. To sanctify it, the remains of the Greek Father Saint Gregory Nazianzenus were transferred and reinterred here; it was the Sacrament Chapel of the most important church in the Catholic world, and it was thought that its thaumaturgic altarpiece, the *Madonna del Soccorso*, would work its coredemptive wonders for patron and faithful alike. If all this were not enough, Gregory pulled out all the stops by having an organ installed in the adjoining passage, loud enough to wake the dead.[1]

The decision to inter Gregory Nazianzenus (329–390 CE) here was a milestone in the pope's new policy to unite the Eastern and Western Churches. In 1573, he had established the *congregazione greca*, a committee of cardinals enlisted to oversee relations with the Orthodox. In 1577, as the chapel dome reached completion, Gregory founded the Collegio Greco to train missionaries to proselytize the eastern Christian lands, and the following year, 1578, he also commissioned Della Porta to build a church for it, Sant'Atanasio dei Greci (built 1580–1583), capable of accommodating both the Greek and Latin rites.[2] In the same optimistic spirit of Christian concord, the mosaics in the pendentives of the Cappella Gregoriana displayed two Greek Doctors, Saints Basil and Gregory Nazianzenus, together with two Latin ones, Saints Jerome and Gregory the Great (Basil and Jerome were contemporaries of Nazianzenus, one a friend, the other his spiritual counselor). It was also planned that St. Peter's would eventually contain the relics of luminaries of both the Eastern and Western Churches, all orbiting the grave of Saint Peter and thereby implying the primacy of the Vatican See, with Peter as the rock and foundation of the Universal Church and the Cappella Gregoriana as its cornerstone.[3]

While the Cappella Gregoriana was a chapel in name, it was actually the size of a large church. Gregory went on to lavish two hundred thousand scudi on it (so says one biographer; others say ninety thousand gold pieces), with three hundred and fifty men needed to complete it, and all while the nave still awaited construction, as did the main dome over the crossing.[4] Every inch of the chapel walls was revetted in colored marble, and the dome was totally encrusted with mosaic. It even had the first marbled floor in the basilica. Closed on both its open sides by high iron gates decorated with enamel and brass and occupying the corner of a cavernous stucco-and-travertine basilica rising from a brick floor, with none of the gilding or extravagant marbling the basilica would receive over the next two centuries and no plans yet to execute them, the Cappella Gregoriana was an unearthly oasis of color within the monochrome hulk.[5] There was only one recently built precedent for this marble-and-mosaic scheme in Rome, Raphael's Chigi Chapel (begun in 1513), but it was unfinished and a fraction of the size.

As is well known, the Cappella Gregoriana was built and decorated in a period of intense Christian antiquarianism. Tiberio Alfarano (1525–1596) was

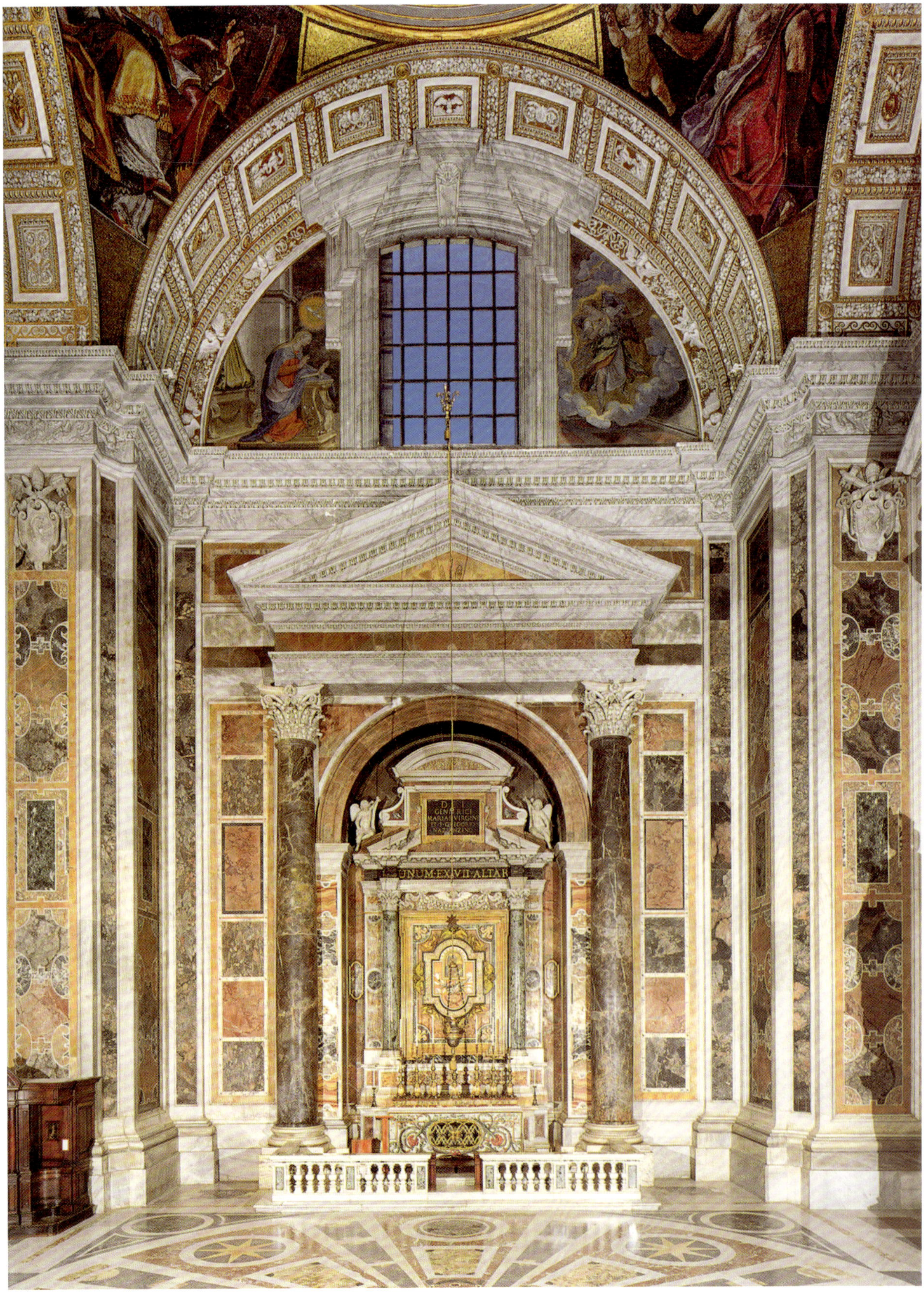

1

writing his guide to the paleo-Christian basilica of St. Peter's that was disappearing before his eyes; Cesare Baronio (1538–1607) was giving the lectures that would become the *Annales*, the authorized Catholic history of the early Church; Pompeo Ugonio (1550?–1614) had accepted an office at St. Peter's and was beginning to catalog Rome's medieval churches; and Christian archaeology traditionally begins with the discovery of catacombs on the Via Salaria in 1578.[6] To clad the Cappella Gregoriana from head to toe with marble and mosaics was self-consciously archaizing, looking back to buildings such as the crumbling Oratory of the Holy Cross (461–468 CE) at the Lateran for material guidance (FIG. 5). Other examples, just as influential, were the Mausoleum of Helena, or Church of Santa Costanza (337–351), whose original revetments and mosaic dome remained relatively intact (until 1620), and the Lateran Baptistery that Gregory XIII had restored in 1575 and whose revetment remained in place until the 1640s.[7] There were still more examples of ancient or paleo-Christian polychrome revetment in Gregory's Rome than survive today.[8] In the Cappella Gregoriana, the two large columns of the altar aedicule were specifically salvaged from the old basilica to the same archaeological end, and its vaults were the first in St. Peter's to receive mosaic.[9]

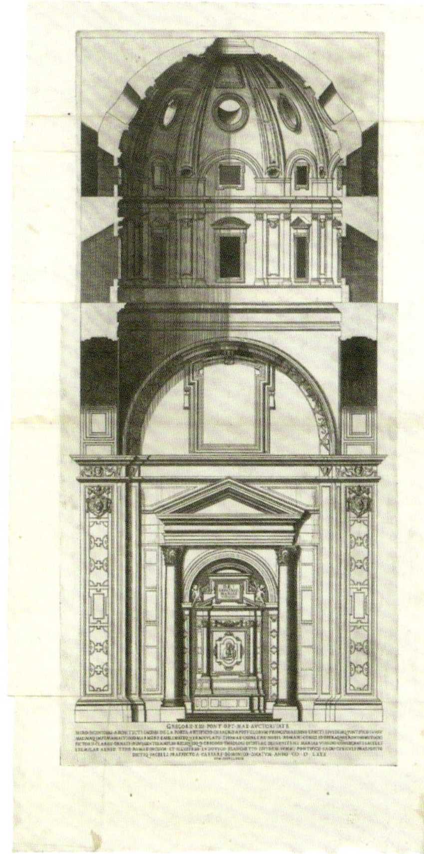

2

As if to acknowledge the fact that this material revival looked back to Christian antiquity, the Cappella Gregoriana also became the subject of renewed ekphrasis. Ekphrases of architecture had reached their acme in Byzantium between the sixth and fourteenth centuries but also featured in Western poetry and epic from Virgil to Romance.[10] The genre now found a new lease life in the compositions on the Cappella Gregoriana written by two *literati*, namely, the verse *Sacellum Gregorianum* (1582) of Lorenzo Frizolio (or Frizzoli, c. 1530–1597) and the prose *Sacelli Gregoriani descriptio* (1583) of Ascanio Valentino (dates unknown). While Valentino's text has drawn the recent attention of Kaspar Zollikofer, Frizolio's poem has escaped any comment since its publication.[11] Moreover, neither has ever been translated from the original Latin (Frizolio is particularly difficult). Likewise, the literary milieu around Gregory XIII that produced both works has gone unrecognized and awaits investigation.[12]

The works of Frizolio and Valentino were both monuments of innovation. There is no underestimating Valentino's achievement. His composition must count as the longest description of a building in prose, let alone Latin, published until this point, and it is difficult to think of any later ones to rival it before the age of strictly academic publication. Frizolio's work became a poetic sensation, eventually appearing in editions of other poets' works, and it was translated into Italian.[13] Both writers had been secretaries to cardinals, Frizolio to Antonio Carafa (1538–1591) and Valentino to Francesco Alciati (1522–1580).[14] Both joined the literary circles that Gregory XIII promoted and protected.[15] Valentino had read philosophy at the Sapienza, where he must have studied Latin composition with the French philologist Marc-Antoine Muret (1526–1585), the acknowledged Cicero of his age who counted Montaigne among his pupils.[16] Frizolio, on the other hand, was so accomplished a poet that his

FIG. 1. Cappella Gregoriana, St. Peter's, Rome (altar wall revetted in 1578–1580 by Giacomo Della Porta).

FIG. 2. Anonymous engraver after Giacomo Della Porta, Cappella Gregoriana (east-west section), St. Peter's, Rome, 1580. Erfurt University, Forschungsbibliothek Gotha.

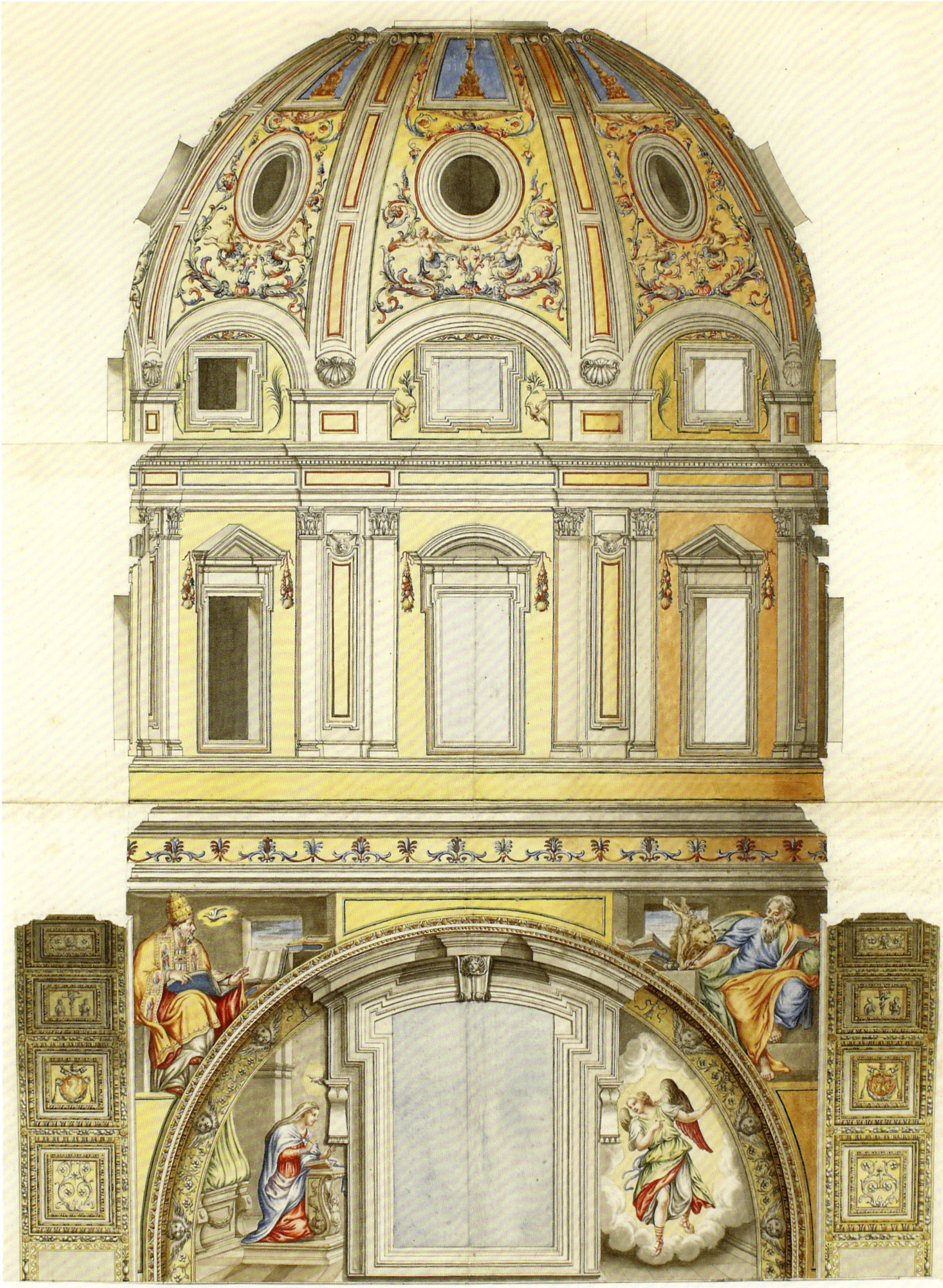

3

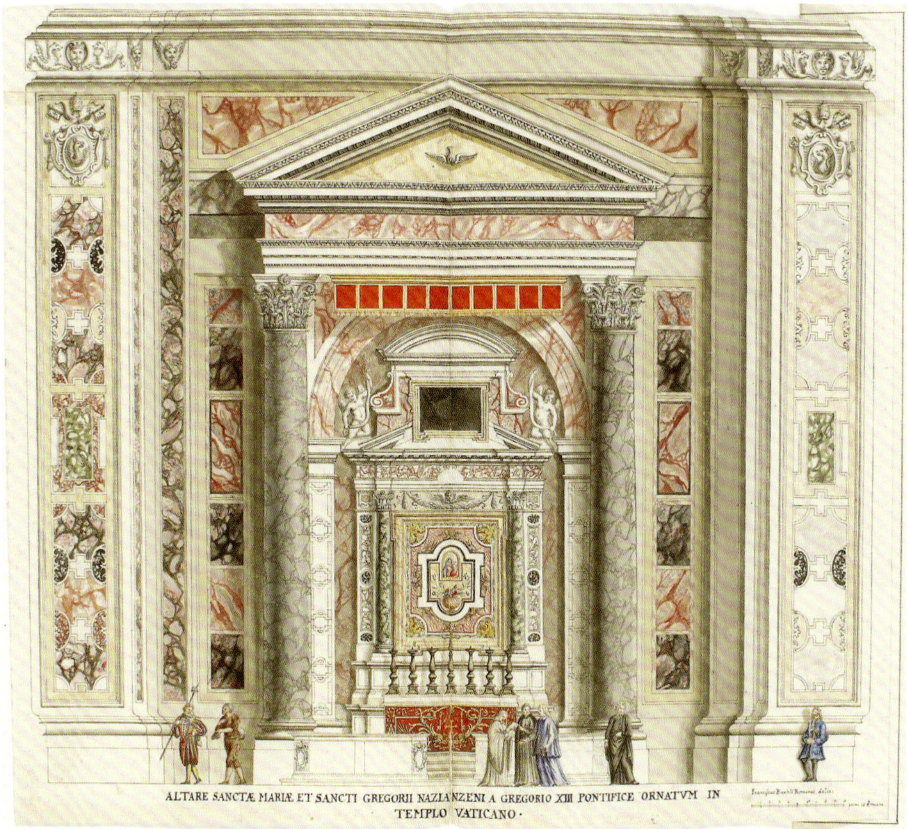

4

work has been mistaken for that of Torquato Tasso, and he may even have influenced Giambattista Marino.[17]

The liminary poems that precede Frizolio's ekphrasis (1583), which were all written by literary associates from the same stable of Gregory XIII, imply that they competed for the honor of composing the poem and that Frizolio's winning submission was formally presented, perhaps recited, to the pope in person ("ante pedes Gregorii"). The motivation was not only the completion of the chapel (1578–1583) but also the translation of Gregory Nazianzenus's body there (June 11, 1580), and the occasion was the synchronized republication of Gregory's *Opera Omnia* in Latin translation (1583). The French Benedictine scholar Jacques de Billy de Prunay (Jacobus Billius) had first compiled an authoritative edition of Gregory's oeuvre in 1569, together with several renowned Byzantine commentaries on him (Elias of Crete, Nicetas of Heraclea, Nonnos of Panopolis, and Michael Psellos), all translated into Latin. Gregory XIII's editors merely reprinted the lot in a deluxe edition but they did add Frizolio's poem as the only modern appendix, an exceptional imprimatur in every sense.[18]

FIG. 3. Francesco Bartoli, Dome and pendentives of the Cappella Gregoriana, sectional elevation, ca. 1712. Wormsley Library, *Pontificalia Insignia Auguralia Sacralia et Sacerdotalia*, vol. I, no. 6a.

FIG. 4. Francesco Bartoli, Altar wall of the Cappella Gregoriana, sectional elevation, ca. 1712. Wormsley Library, *Pontificalia Insignia Auguralia Sacralia et Sacerdotalia*, vol. I, no. 6b.

Mosaics and Grotesques

Frizolio and Valentino had scaled the twin peaks of the classical literary tradition, and, possibly by design, their descriptions rival each other in recreating the building in words. Both authors start from the top and move down, begin-

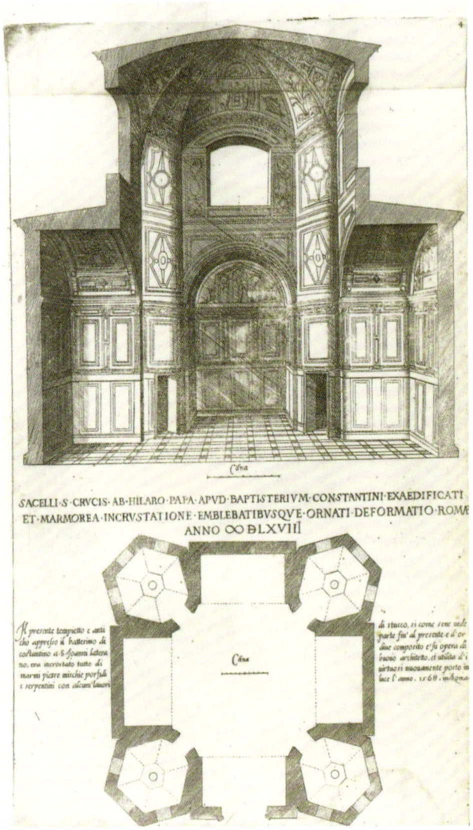

5

FIG. 5. Antonio Labacco (engraved by Antonio Lafréry), Plan and sectional perspective of the Oratory of the Holy Cross (461–468 AD), 1568. A. Labacco, *Libro d'Antonio Labacco appartenente a l'Architettura nel qual si figurano alcune notabili Antiquità di Roma*, Rome 1572, pl. IV.

ning with the dome mosaics that were designed by the painter Girolamo Muziano (c. 1532–1592) but destroyed in the eighteenth century.[19] In Rome, mosaic had ceased to be a living tradition by at least the early fourteenth century, and it has been regularly pointed out that its sixteenth-century revival represented the desire to materialize a continuity with paleo-Christian foundations, not least at old St. Peter's itself. The earliest such archaizing mosaic had been the Chapel of Saint Helen behind the apse of Santa Croce in Gerusalemme, probably executed to the design of Baldassare Peruzzi in 1507–1508, where the quincunx pattern and interlacing borders recall Cosmati floors, while the luminous Christ is a Pantocrator in Renaissance garb (FIG. 6). More recently, in the 1560s, Cardinal Alessandro Farnese had hoped to clad the apse vault of the Gesù with gold mosaic, but nothing came of it.[20]

When Valentino and Frizolio describe the mosaics, even their vocabulary stresses the revival. They use *emblema*, not in the modern sense of an allegorical "emblem" but in its original Greco-Latin meaning of the micro-mosaic (*opus vermiculatum*) centerpieces in ancient floors that had vied with antique easel paintings. Mosaicists were usually termed *pittori di mosaici* or *pictores musivarii*, and contemporaries marveled at how the mosaics were so skillfully executed that they seemed to have been painted with a brush.[21] When Valentino comes to describe the novel technique the mosaicists used to compose the images, he also spells out the desired effect:

> for he [the "contractor," i.e., the chief mosaicist Tarquinio di Cristoforo] shrewdly devised a certain kind of glue which must be used within fifteen days, which he first spread on the walls; he then overlaid the colors in the pattern of the images to be "painted": then a few of the workmen, who were to lay out the works skillfully, assembled varicolored tesserae, which they did not set level but cemented in a certain and fitting order: if they noticed that these had not been assembled artfully with equal spaces, they made sure that they were disassembled within the allotted time, and reset again as art dictates, with the right setting and appropriate spacing so that they joined up properly with those previously set. The result is that the figures are not fused together from tesserae, but the images are created from the fluidity of the dissolved colors: and not only are they expressed in painting, but also shaded exactly like certain solid bodies, so that they even project, with the effect that they seem to stand out from the walls. In this manner, in two years, he entirely completed the work, which, it is certain that, if other practiced artisans had accepted the standard of artistry that was necessary to achieve it in an unfinished work elsewhere at the same scale as the present Vatican one, they would certainly not have accomplished it in many years.[22]

Muziano's dome mosaics were replaced by the present lugubrious and congested composition of angels and putti between 1768 and 1779 (at which time the portholes in the dome were also blocked, hugely diminishing its luminosity).[23] Without Valentino's description and an early-eighteenth-century watercolor by

Francesco Bartoli (FIG. 3), we would be no wiser regarding the dome's original appearance.[24]

Originally, the entire superstructure was covered in gilt-back tesserae, including the drum, not only the dome, vindicating the ekphrasists' rhapsodic descriptions of a dome spilling over with light. Fields of gilt tesserae now survive in only a few early Christian Roman apses, and it is therefore quite possible that these gilded expanses were prompted by the knowledge of Eastern churches and their close relatives in Italy, most notably San Marco in Venice (whose mosaics were recognizably in the *maniera greca*). As early as the 1220s, Pope Honorius III (1216–1227) had turned to Venetian mosaicists to execute the apse of San Paolo fuori le Mura, and despite a brief revival of the craft in Rome toward the end of that century and into the next, Agostino Chigi would still need to turn to Venetian mosaicists when he came to decorate the dome of his own burial chapel at Santa Maria del Popolo, the Chigi Chapel (mosaics signed 1516). Initially, Gregory XIII also looked to Venice for the mosaics of the Gregoriana but to no avail, and it was actually Roman masters who carried out the work from Muziano's cartoons and introduced their own innovations.[25]

The most unusual features in the dome mosaics of the Cappella Gregoriana were the grotesques (FIG. 3). The alternating panels display what look like hippocamps and sirens, their nether regions bifurcating into curling fronds of acanthus. Valentino and Frizolio alert us that they are actually dragons (from the Boncompagni arms) and winged angels.[26] With this newfound knowledge, we can now appreciate that Carlo Maderno must have taken his cue from these now-vanished mosaics when he decided to adorn the window hoods of the nave with identical hybrids (now accompanied by Borghese dragons of Pope Paul V) as he began to stucco its vault in 1614.

Valentino strongly implies that using grotesques was the pragmatic answer to filling the rather awkward remnants left by the ribs, panels, and portholes.[27] This problem, it must be said, was of the architect's making. As Federico Bellini has convincingly argued, the dome of the Cappella Gregoriana did not follow any drawing left by Michelangelo but was a pastiche concocted by Giacomo Della Porta. In fact, the design hybridizes the apse vaults in the transepts with the dome over the crossing, which was still not built but whose intended design was known from the great model that Michelangelo had left on site. In fact, Valentino himself says, "one thing that seizes everyone's admiration is the dome with lunettes (magnificent for its vermiculated mosaic) now restored to Rome by Pope Gregory XIII after a long hiatus, because it surpasses the nearest ancient [examples] as much as the design has been perfected in the intervening years."[28] The problem of fleshing out images between the architectural bones reveals the conflict between opposing desires: on the one hand, to resuscitate paleo-Christian antiquity and, on the other, to sustain the more recent but equally revered legacy of Michelangelo (FIGS. 2–3).

Early Christian and medieval apses had contained branching Christological vines (the best-known examples being the vaults in the narthex of the Lateran Baptistery and the apse of San Clemente), but grotesques per se had been synonymous with ancient vault painting since the discovery of the Domus Aurea in the 1470s. Muziano's design must therefore be seen through the lens of the many Renaissance reinventions of the grotesque, beginning with two of the earliest, Pinturicchio's Basso Della Rovere Chapel (1484–1492)

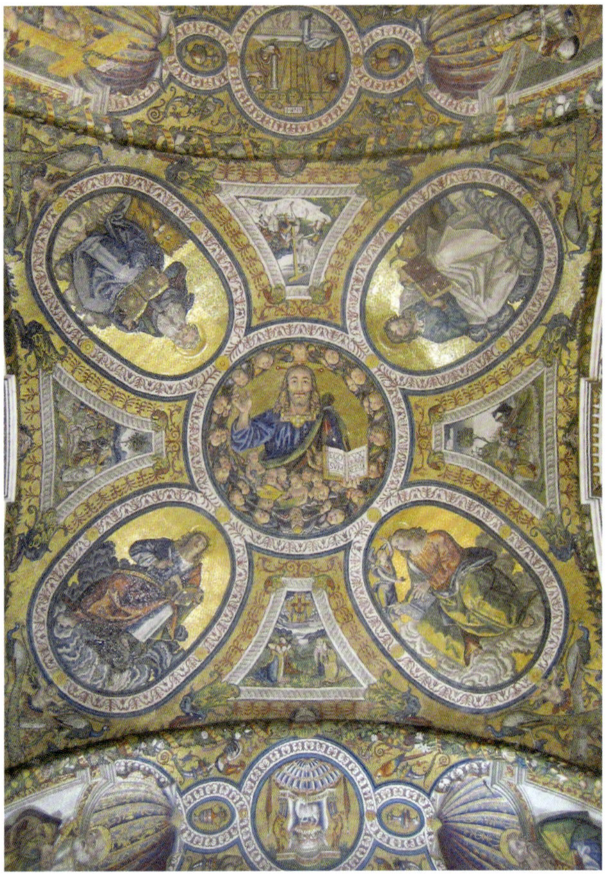

6

and vault of the retrochoir in Santa Maria del Popolo, where grotesques cram the gilded borders of faux mosaic between the panels (FIG. 7). Muziano himself was a past master of grotesque, which he had painted in the rooms of Ippolito d'Este at the Palazzo di Montegiordano in Rome (1560–1566) and at the Villa d'Este in Tivoli (1565–1566).[29]

Nonetheless, the choice of grotesques for such a prominent position in a religious building comes at a moment of mounting tension for their decorative life in religious art. Although Vitruvius had memorably condemned grotesques as unnatural and licentious, to Michelangelo and Vasari they emblematized the unfettered imagination, and Gian Paolo Lomazzo would still commend their inventiveness (1584). Yet, before the Cappella Gregoriana was finished, Cardinal Gabriele Paleotti (1582) would instead excoriate grotesques not only as pagan profanities but also as monsters of the imagination capable of undermining the entire institution of the Church.[30]

Valentino ducks the issue and simply says, "it seemed sufficient to see if, using certain playful things in imitation of the ancients, the gaze would be occupied by the subtlety of the pictures and the varied course of their lineaments."[31] However, the grotesques in the Cappella Gregoriana were also the means of inserting Gregory's heraldic dragon within the vault. They belonged to a larger Gregorian project to rescue this ill-omened beast from any defamatory claims (Protestants, for whom the dragon's equation with the devil was unequivocal, even claimed that Gregory's *stemma* was the badge of the Antichrist).[32] Thus, all of the several writers who tried their pens at rehabilitating the Boncompagni coat of arms as soon as Gregory was elected pointed out that the winged dragon had no tail and therefore no venomous sting. Frizolio was undoubtedly aware of the 256 emblems composed by the Abruzzese priest Principio Fabrizi on the theme, for he characterized the dragon in the chapel dome as a well-meaning defender of the faith:

> Here you should note the guardians of the world, on all sides dragons
> Glowing red, the venom cut from their tails,
> Harmless in their aid and spreading their wings over the people.
> The guardians keep watch with a vigilant eye
> And terrorize the barbarian monsters with their crested heads.[33]

The dome dragons in the Cappella Gregoriana were literally the crowning achievement in the program to save the pope's name. In this particular instance, they also assimilated the apotropaic and psychagogic griffins that accompanied the deceased to *apotheosis in astris* in Greco-Roman art. Indeed,

FIG. 6. Baldassarre Peruzzi (attrib.), Vault mosaics, ca. 1507–1508. Chapel of Saint Helen, Santa Croce in Gerusalemme, Rome.

in 1575, the year in which Gregory set his sights on the Cappella Gregoriana, a "dragon of fire" had appeared in the sky over Rome (FIG. 8).[34]

Architecture and Ekphrasis

The circumstances of Valentino's composition remain unclear, but his work was dedicated to the pope and published, therefore, with his consent. His description is absolutely relentless in detail, and his information plainly came from official sources, from the workmen or administrators, perhaps from Della Porta himself. Della Porta must also have been the source for an engraving of the chapel, unprecedented for its size (680 × 324 mm), which was either traced from the architect's own drawings or derived from a model (FIG. 2). This sectional elevation is exclusively architectural, omitting the mosaics entirely, one of the first genuine "technical drawings" of a building published and quite different from the perspectival cutaways that had begun to appear earlier in the century (FIG. 5). The engraving was perhaps intended to accompany yet another publication project that never came to fruition, and it provides a visual analogue to the technical prose of Valentino rather than the allusive poetry of Frizolio.[35] Valentino also intended to write about every other building Gregory XIII commissioned, an intention that unhappily went unfulfilled.[36] Frizolio's poem, on the other hand, belongs to a wider and growing effort to turn neo-Latin poetry to the ends of architectural ekphrasis, which began to gather steam among the *literati* of the court of Gregory XIII. Frizolio was probably the most intensely original of all of them. Despite the poem's saturation in allusions to Virgil, Ovid, and others, it is neither a collage of stock conventions nor a *cento*, that is a mash-up of sound bites from the gold and silver poets of antiquity.

The opening words of any neo-Latin composition are vital in setting the tone of the remainder and establishing the voice of the author. Frizolio sets the scene with the murmuring populace awaiting the interment of Saint Gregory Nazianzenus in the chapel and with it a new dawn:

> *Extulerat lucem nitido sol aureus ortu,*
> *Et iam tempus erat Petri sub principis aedem*
> *Augustam translata, sacris de more peractis,*
> *Condere Nazanzi monumento antistitis ossa*

> The golden sun had brought forth the light in its gleaming rising,
> And now it was time, having transferred them
> Beneath the venerable shrine of Peter, Prince [of the Apostles],
> Once the holy rites had been duly performed,
> To lay to rest the bones of the bishop of Nazianzus in his monument.

Let us consider the first line. The first two words, *extulerat lucem*, are drawn from Virgil (*Aeneid* 11.183), *nitido ortu* from Ovid (*Met.* 2.112), and *sol aureus* again from Virgil (*Georgics* 1.232; 4.51). Together they signal that we are in epic mode because of the genre they are drawn from, but the specific context of each intertextual reference also resonates with allusions to the contemporary moment. *Extulerat lucem* recalls the dawning day in the *Aeneid* when the truce between the Trojans and the Latins permits them to bury their war dead and, in the present, Gregory's attempts to heal the schism between the Eastern and Western Churches; on this day, Aeneas also superintended construction of the funeral pyres, as Gregory has done with the design of the Cappella Gregoriana. *Nitido ortu* summons Ovid's bedazzling vision of the Palace of the Sun (*Metamorphoses* 2.1–30), the paragon of an architecture of light in classical poetry; together with *sol aureus*, it also evokes the arrival of the golden sun that expels the cold winter and may therefore allude to the warming rapprochement between East and West. The phrase *sol aureus* on its own also summons the chapel's gilded vault not only in light but also in shape, as Virgil continues that "the golden sun [that] commands his ecliptic, split into fixed segments, through twelve heavenly constellations" (*Georgics* 1.231–232: *Idcirco certis dimensum partibus orbem / per duodena regit mundi Sol aureus astra*). These phrases all recur in the same metric positions as the originals, no easy thing to do, and altogether bring ancient and modern into a reverberant simultaneity—all this in just six words.

The "monument" in which Gregory's bones will be interred is not only the chapel but also Frizolio's poem about it and on him, a poem that was itself deposited in the *monumentum* of Gregory's *Opera Omnia*, composed not just of orations but also of poems, for Gregory was as much a pioneering Christian poet as he was a theologian.[37] Frizolio's own poem is the "monument more lasting than bronze" (Horace, *Carmina* 3.30: *monumentum aere perennius*), the text immemorial of which Horace had written, a monument loftier than the pyramids, which neither time nor the elements can destroy. Virgil had also compared the monumental poem with the monumental building as repositories of memory (*monumentum* means "remembrance"), when he promised to erect a temple at Mantua to honor Augustus (*Georgics* 3.12–18), perhaps in synchrony with a real temple that the emperor was building to culminate his triumph (29 BCE).[38] This concept of the poem as a building in words reached back at least as far as Pindar, who, in the *Sixth Olympian Ode* (468 BCE), had compared his poetic undertaking to a wondrous megaron (6.1–4) belonging to a treasure house of hymns (6.5–18) and elsewhere (*Nemean* 4; 473 BCE?) compared another ode to a stele whiter than Parian marble. The same parallelism of text and building, construct and construction, infused Byzantine ekphrases of buildings where not only did the written word comment on the artifact, but the spoken one resounded through the space that was its subject, and together they reassembled the building in words. Paul the Silentiary's ekphrasis of Hagia Sophia was intoned at a church's consecration, and others were inscribed on church walls, so that the building spoke for itself, and its words returned to life each time a visitor recited them.[39] Ekphrases were, therefore, anything but textual adjuncts after the constructional fact and enjoyed a more reflexive relationship.

Roy Eriksen has more particularly argued that a "topomorphical analysis" of early modern literary texts reveals poetic tectonics—the desire to shape form, instill order, maintain symmetry, and generally "edify"—that parallel those of architectural theory. Many poets, he argues, saw their works as edifices enacted through the careful placement of words, while "extrasyntactic" structures manifest themselves in rhetorical tropes such as chiasmus, antithesis, parallelism, and repetition.[40] If this is true, it depends on close analysis of textual gestalt or hard attention to the rhythms of verse for effect.

Valentino and Frizolio sought more immediate imagery to answer the question of how one made a building present in words (*hypotyposis*). In theory, this was the inverse of the idea that a building could translate into visual form a *concetto* expressed in words. Ekphrasis offered three basic strategies: *enargeia*, *periegesis*, and *periphrasis*. When Valentino begins his text by announcing that he will "describe the Gregorian Chapel, from the work itself, exactly as it stands, so that those present who could not gaze upon it should have the thing everywhere before their eyes," he sets the agenda for all three.[41] *Enargeia* ("vividness"), the goal of making the architecture readily present to the absent reader trying to imagine the spectacle from the words on the page, is Frizolio's Bible. He had personally participated in the procession that accompanied the translation of the Greek Father's body, and he begins his description with the moment of interment, dwelling on the concourse of devoted populace, whose communal awe only increased as the rays of the dawn sun flooded the dome, like a resurrection.[42] *Enargeia* could be partly achieved through *periegesis* ("leading around"), a retracing in words of the path of the eyes or the feet around the building, to bring image and text into unison as well as to avoid a descriptive pause in the narrative. Frizolio encourages the conceit by casting his own ekphrasis as a dialogue between an ignorant, though enthusiastic, interlocutor (the poet himself) and a learned correspondent back in his hometown of Rimini, to whom he describes every sight of his searching eyes. The instructions and injunctions that punctuate the text—"Behold!" or "Turn your eyes to this!"—reinforce the conceit that the reader is present, that the poet is not only bringing the building to the reader but is also bringing the observer to the building. Even were Frizolio's poem never recited in the chapel, it is as though it had been. An equally important tool was *periphrasis* ("talking around"), not in the pejorative sense of beating around the bush but rather with the aim of possessing the object as fully as possible in words (*ekphrasis* literally means a "telling in full"). Analogously, the richness of the text might parallel the richness of the artifact in a *copia* of description, with a language as wrought as the artifact, altogether resulting in what we might call "archi-texture."

A liminary poem by Aurelio Orsi (one of the prefatory poems introducing Frizolio's own composition) recognizes the poet's ambition when he says that "one art calls forth another":

> Here marvel at the shrine of the bishop of Nazianzos on par with Heaven;
>   There at the noble work of a mighty poet.
> How variously it glitters, a picture in interwoven jewels!
>   How sweet the song sounds to the learned ear!
> Together the stones do not gleam by a single skill, nor is there a single glory in the song.
>   How both smile with the ornaments dispersed within them!
> One art calls forth another. In one moment Victory favors the chapel,
>   In another you, Lorenzo; to whom will the laurel go?[43]

Architecture and Marbles

Both Frizolio and Valentino extolled the nobility of the architecture, the latter exclaiming that it was "admirable for its symmetry, singular in its design, in structure comparable with those of the ancients."[44] Accordingly, the first thing Valentino had to get right was his vocabulary, scouring Vitruvius and Pliny for recondite terminology, though only with partial success. He correctly translated *zophorus*, for example, as "frieze," but surprisingly mistranslated *epistylium* as "capital," when it actually means "architrave."[45] Where Vitruvius and Pliny were found wanting, Valentino stepped in with neologisms such as *lunulatum hemisphaerium* (a *cupola lunettata*, "a dome with lunettes") to describe structures that had either never existed in antiquity or, if they did (for example, the vault of the Piazza d'Oro at Hadrian's Villa, Tivoli, after 117 CE), postdated the first-century BCE/CE authors on whom he relied. As few people would have been conversant with all these technical terms, Valentino appended a glossary to his pamphlet, with Italian explanations of them. He included the names of all the various marbles as well, getting a few of them wildly wrong, although understandably, as the provenances of many were not nailed down until the twentieth century, and several still await identification.[46]

The always well-informed Valentino also lays great store by the technical skills that made the walls shine:

> On all sides the raised walls gleam with manifold and mottled marble, which has been sawn into slabs; then lightly chiseled so that the slabs are not deformed by any cavity but have uniform surfaces; then smoothed with solid globulettes of pumice until they are so polished that if one lays a hand to them one feels no roughness or projection at all. The segments are joined together with glue, and in such a way that the parts unite among themselves, so that it seems as though a single nature has been fused from dissimilar things.[47]

Valentino stresses the organic unity achieved ("joined ... in such a way ... that it seems as though a single nature has been fused from dissimilar things"), which stood in notable contrast to the ad hoc spolia assemblies of the later Middle Ages and which fulfilled the higher aesthetic criterion of "ex uno lapide," the long-cherished idea that a statue or building might appear as though carved from one block of stone. A particular problem at the Cappella Gregoriana, and all the chapels that followed it, was that not only were ancient marbles favored for their intrinsic beauty and ready associations with hallowed antiquity, but there was also as yet precious little modern quarrying of colored marbles in Italy. As all the ancient marbles were spoliated from the ruins, they came in fragments of differing shape and size and had to be pieced together with meandering cuts that disguised the joins in the veining. They were also sliced as thinly as possible to maximize the output from a single chunk. Valentino reveals a particular trick the chapel masons used when he describes that "twin panels of marble, large enough that they are liable to crack because of their size, have indeed been glued together very delicately, and color added to the appearance of the marble, so the joins are concealed in such a way that they are thought to be natural."[48]

Indeed, it was the marble cladding of the chapel that really caught the attention of both Valentino and Frizolio, and they left no stone unturned. The second half of the sixteenth century had seen a resurgence in the use of colored marbles as a medium for architecture, beginning with Vasari's abortive scheme (c. 1550) for the Cappella Del Monte in San Pietro in Montorio, Rome.[49] In the 1560s, interest in the medium accelerated. Jacopo Barozzi da Vignola designed rich fireplaces and tabletops for the Palazzo Farnese, and Pius V (1566–1572) commissioned tomb monuments in Rome, Naples, and Piedmont. Chief among these was the grand tomb of Paul IV (1566) that Pirro Ligorio

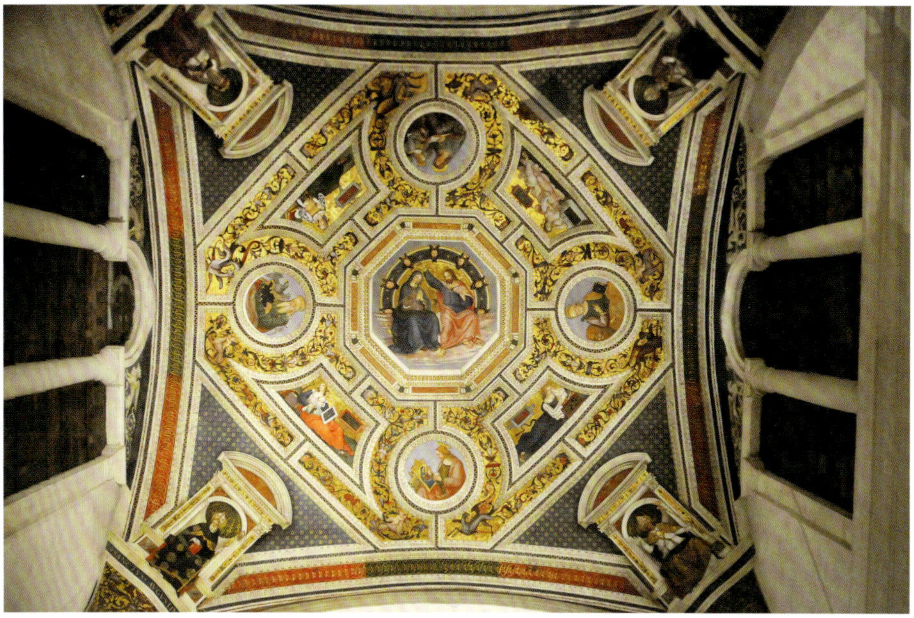

7

(ca. 1512/1513–1583) designed for the Carafa Chapel in Santa Maria sopra Minerva, which, in turn, inspired the equally impressive sepulcher that Pius V built himself (but never used) in the vast new church of Santa Croce (1567–1571) at Bosco Marengo, Piedmont.[50] The rekindled desire for colored marbles, the majority of which had to be pilfered from ruins in Rome, resulted in a demand so great that Gregory XIII eventually issued a series of proclamations prohibiting their excavation for architectural use.[51] Meanwhile, a colored-marble revival was also under way in Florence. In 1576, Giovanni Antonio Dosio (1533–1611) returned from Rome to Florence and initiated a long sequence of colored-marble chapels and altars throughout the city with his Gaddi Chapel in Santa Maria Novella (1575–1576) and the Niccolini Chapel in Santa Croce (begun 1579).[52]

As artful and accomplished as all these projects were, none of them could match the scale and prestige, not to mention showcase location, of the Cappella Gregoriana. While the Cappella dei Principi at San Lorenzo, Florence, was comparable in scale and ambition and had been planned by Vasari in 1561–1568, it was not begun until 1605 and not encrusted in marbles and hardstones until 1613–1624, and the result is a mottled and saturated cacophony.[53] The Florentine friar and natural scientist Agostino del Riccio was compelled to admit at the outset of his *Delle Lodi delle Pietre* (1597) that of all the chapels and churches now being adorned with varicolored stones, the Cappella Gregoriana was "the most beautiful and honored that has been made until our time."[54] It can hardly be coincidence that Ferdinando I de' Medici decided to resume the project for the grand chapel at San Lorenzo and founded the Galleria dei Lavori (now called the Opificio delle Pietre Dure) in 1588 to aid in its realization. Indeed, the fact that Giacomo Della Porta visited Florence in 1598 and provided a model for the chapel in 1601 may owe as much to his accomplishment in revetting the Cappella Gregoriana as to his expertise in completing the dome of St. Peter's (1588–1590).

Where Valentino dryly concentrates on nomenclature and technique, Frizolio waxes lyrical. His longest passage on the marble panoply, which was

FIG. 7. Bernardino di Betto, called Pinturicchio, Vault of the choir, ca. 1503–1506. Santa Maria del Popolo, Rome.

the most shocking aspect of the chapel when it was built besides the great mosaic dome, is one of the most original in the whole poem. He does not rely on an extended paraphrase of Ovid's Palace of the Sun (*Met.* 2.1-4) or fall back on the hackneyed trope that the chapel exceeds the Temple of Solomon (1 Kings 6).[55] Nor does he draw on Statius or any of the late antique poets (e.g., Sidonius Apollinaris) whose verse was rich in marble imagery. He instead writes a dense description whose allusions are all of the poet's own invention:

> [T]hink you that the sawn marbles,
> That dazzle by their varied color,
> Can be understood by our descriptions alone?
> Here in brilliance they vie with driven snow;
> The green ones surpass emeralds by far;
> These dunny ones in their polished glow
> Resemble topaz and flaming bronze.
> And do not these others surpass black ebony, or jet?
> Still others are distinguished by their innate blots or sprinkled droplets,
> And these things are joined together by wondrous art,
> And dull the lights of the stars with their new weavings.
> The floor radiates with the light of them, and the wall resplends,
> Just as the various fields laugh with expanses of every sort of color
> On Timolus in Cilicia, or in the valleys of Sicilian Enna;
> Just as marigolds, violets, white privet,
> Narcissus flowers, or blue cornflowers shine budding like gems in their garden beds;
> Just as woven hangings glitter, when the varicolored weft weaves in and out stitched with Arabian patterns.
> As you look at these things, also marvel at the flowers that burn in the lofty coffers, and do not ask for more.[56]

The passage is laced with allusion. Frizolio's mention of flaming, bronze-colored stones ("Pyropian") is a cue to Ovid's Palace of the Sun; when he talks of "dun-colored" stones, he adopts an adjective also used of piebald horses and thence summons the image of dappling, even the idea that they are creations of divine painting. Mount Timolus in Lydia was famed for its saffron crops and gold deposits; Enna had not only a famous temple of Ceres (and corn is golden, too), but from its flower-scattered meadows Proserpina was abducted by Pluto. As Frizolio's gaze shifts from the walls to the vault, the subject remains floral, and the path of the eyes traces a continuum of thought. His comparison of flower beds to the chapel's paneled walls may recall villa parterres, but if so, he is modernizing the floral imagery that filled much paleo-Christian ekphrasis (e.g., Prudentius). The closing words, "do not ask for more," recall the *Distichs of Cato* (third or fourth century CE) that one should not inquire about the nature of the gods, implying that however visible the spectacle and however many words are spent describing it, its workings remained a divine engineered mystery.[57]

Frizolio makes it clear that he was well read in the works of Gregory Nazianzenus himself. As he specifically mentions Gregory's funeral oration (374 CE) for his father—also called Gregory—he can hardly have been unaware of the mini-ekphrasis that this contains, describing the church that the senior Gregory had built at Nazianzos in Cappadocia (after 328/329 CE):

For it is surrounded by eight regular equilaterals, and surges aloft in the elegance of stories of columns and porticos, and in fact it is adorned with pictures of such a kind that they concede nothing to nature itself. The vault illuminates from above, and it dazzles the eyes with abundant sources of light on every side, so that it is truly the dwelling place of light. It is surrounded by excrescent equiangular ambulatories of the most splendid material, with a wide area in the midst, while its doors and vestibules shine forth with their comeliness and offer from a distance their welcome to those who are drawing near. I have not yet mentioned the external ornament, the beauty and size of the squared and dovetailed stonework, whether it be of marble in the bases and capitals, which divide the angles, or from our own quarries, which are in no wise inferior to those abroad; nor of the belts of many shapes and colors, projecting or inlaid from the foundation to the summit, which robs the spectator by limiting his view.[58]

Although Frizolio modeled neither his language nor his description on this passage, it is important that Gregory Nazianzenus was describing a centrally planned church with a dome, therefore comparable to the Cappella Gregoriana, and that he expatiates on its facture and radiance. The church at Nazianzos would have looked something like San Vitale, Ravenna, but the description would have evoked a much richer image of the Byzantine church much as we see it, half building and half Eden, in an illumination of Saint Gregory himself at work on his *Liturgical Homilies* (FIG. 9). Frizolio must also have known the extensive commentary on this oration (by Elias of Crete, ca. 1120/1130), also conveniently translated into Latin in the *Opera Omnia*, which carefully explained every phrase and which shortened the distance between the medieval Greek world and Counter-Reformation Rome. It is equally significant that just as the Cappella Gregoriana was being completed, Giacomo Della Porta, as noted above, was also building a church for the Greek College in Rome, Sant'Atanasio dei Greci (1580–1583), which was not only to vaunt a high dome (never built) over a centralizing plan but even to feature an archaizing triconch.[59]

All this said, Valentino risks, by comparison to Frizolio, appearing simply a dutiful and studiously antiquarian prose writer. Yet one passage in his work is perhaps more original still than any in Frizolio's poem. Valentino zooms in on a small panel in the altar frame around the icon of the Virgin:

Looking into the amethyst, the thought of some river enters the mind; which, discharged from the heights of the mountains, flows in a fine line, twisting and turning through the harsh lands, then bursts in more abundantly, just as clashing waves do, swells and billows, and dashing against the crags it catches up the surge in its assault, and washes against towns, whose *idols* [εἴδωλα] fall before the eyes.

He continues:

On the stylobates on every side three slabs of the most beautiful alabaster of all have been set in place: in one of these [slabs] one may look with the utmost pleasure upon the semblance (perceived by the mind) of water, in another [slab] that of earth; and as though water originating in the mountain ridges is snatched downhill, then bent into a second course when opposed by the rocky obstacles, the gullies covered

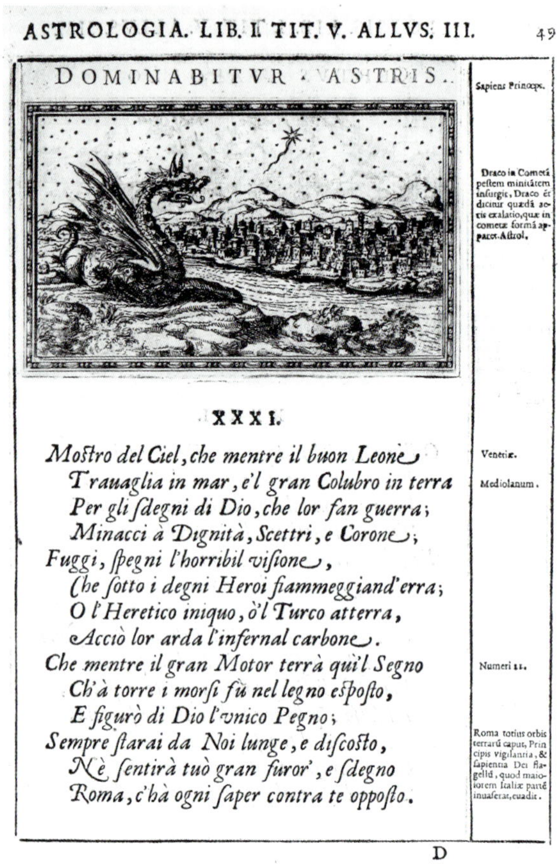

ASTROLOGIA. LIB. I. TIT. V. ALLVS. III. 49

DOMINABITVR · ASTRIS.

Sapiens Princeps.

Draco in Cometá pestem minitãtem insurgit, Draco ẽt dicitur quædã aeris exalatio, quæ in cometæ formã apparet. Astrol.

XXXI.

Mostro del Ciel, che mentre il buon Leone
Trauaglia in mar, e'l gran Colubro in terra
Per gli sdegni di Dio, che lor fan guerra;
Minacci à Dignità, Scettri, e Corone;
Fuggi, spegni l'horribil visione,
Che sotto i degni Heroi fiammeggiand'erra;
O l'Heretico iniquo, ò'l Turco atterra,
Acciò lor arda l'infernal carbone.
Che mentre il gran Motor terrà qui'l Segno
Ch'à torre i morsi fù nel legno esposto,
E figurò di Dio l'vnico Pegno;
Sempre starai da Noi lunge, e discosto,
Nè sentirà tuò gran furor', e sdegno
Roma, c'hà ogni saper contra te opposto.

Venetiæ. Mediolanum. Numeri 21. Roma totius orbis terrarũ caput, Principis vigilantia, & sapientia Dei flagellũ, quod maiorem Italiæ partẽ inuaserat, euadit.

D

8

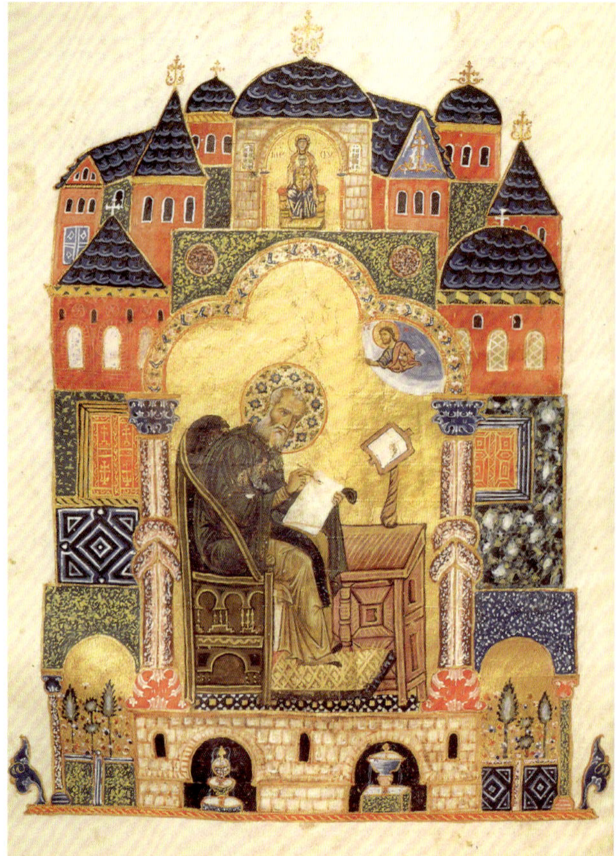

9

over by the billowing; in the way they irrigate the plowed soil; the way they flow together in one place, dispersed by the mass of rocks, and spread over the whole earth: in another [slab,] mountains, just as they are divided among themselves in equal intervals, cascade into hills underlying each other, some of them greater in height, while others appear more pinched because of the windings of their peaks.[60]

One will not find this mode of description in any contemporary text, not even Frizolio's, and it recalls the rhapsodies of Byzantine ekphrases, notably Prokopios (ca. 554–560), who saw blooming meadows in every panel of Hagia Sophia, or Paul the Silentiary (563), who envisioned "flower-banked streams, wheat fields and sheltering woods, playful flocks of sheep and gnarled olive trees, spreading vines." Valentino could not have known Paul the Silentiary, whose work only became known in western Europe in 1606 and did not see print until 1670, but Latin translations of Prokopios had been printed in 1537 and 1538 and an Italian one in 1547, and copies of all three are still in the Vatican library.[61] Knowledge of Byzantine ekphrasis of marbles was probably limited to Prokopios, for had Valentino or Frizolio been acquainted with Nikolaos Mesarites's description (1198–1203) of the Apostoleion, where Gregory of Nazianzus's body had been transferred (950) before it made its way to Rome (1204), they would have known and surely alluded to the fact that the saint "who breathed fire from his mouth and consumed every heresy with fire" had been buried in a sarcophagus "of

FIG. 8. Emblem of a comet with a dragon's tail, 1588. Principio Fabrizi, *Delle allusioni, imprese, et emblemi . . . sopra la vita, opere, et attioni di Gregorio XIII*, Rome 1588, 49.

FIG. 9. *Gregory of Nazianzus*, in Gregory of Nazianzus, *Liturgical Homilies*, 1136–1155. Monastery of Saint Catherine, Sinai, cod. 339, fol. 4v.

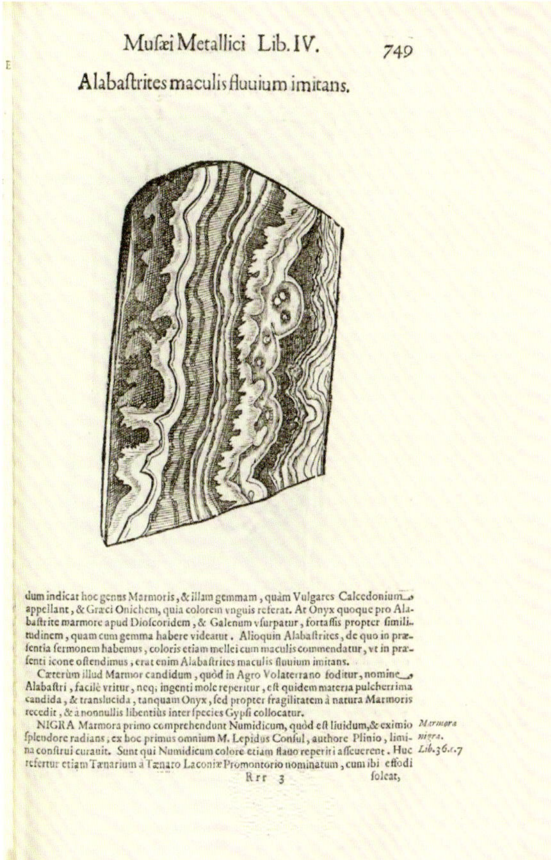

Muſæi Metallici Lib. IV. 749

Alabaſtrites maculis fluuium imitans.

dum indicat hoc genus Marmoris, & illam gemmam, quàm Vulgares Calcedonium appellant, & Græci Onichem, quia colorem vnguis referat. At Onyx quoque pro Alabaſtrite marmore apud Dioſcoridem, & Galenum vſurpatur, fortaſſis propter ſimilitudinem, quam cum gemma habere videatur. Alioquin Alabaſtrites, de quo in præſentia ſermonem habemus, coloris etiam mellei cum maculis commendatur, vt in præſenti icone oſtendimus; erat enim Alabaſtrites maculis fluuium imitans.

Cæterùm illud Marmor candidum, quòd in Agro Volaterrano foditur, nomine Alabaſtri, facilè vritur, neq; ingenti mole reperitur, eſt quidem materia pulcherrima candida, & translucida, tanquam Onyx, ſed propter fragilitatem à natura Marmoris recedit, & à nonnullis libentiùs inter ſpecies Gypſi collocatur.

NIGRA Marmora primo comprehendunt Numidicum, quòd eſt liuidum, & eximio ſplendore radians, ex hoc primus omnium M. Lepidus Conſul, authore Plinio, limina conſtrui curauit. Sunt qui Numidicum colore etiam flauo reperiri aſſeuerent. Huc refertur etiam Tænarium à Tænaro Laconiæ Promontorio nominatum, cum ibi effodi *Marmora nigra. Lib. 36. c. 7*

Rrr 3 ſoleat,

10

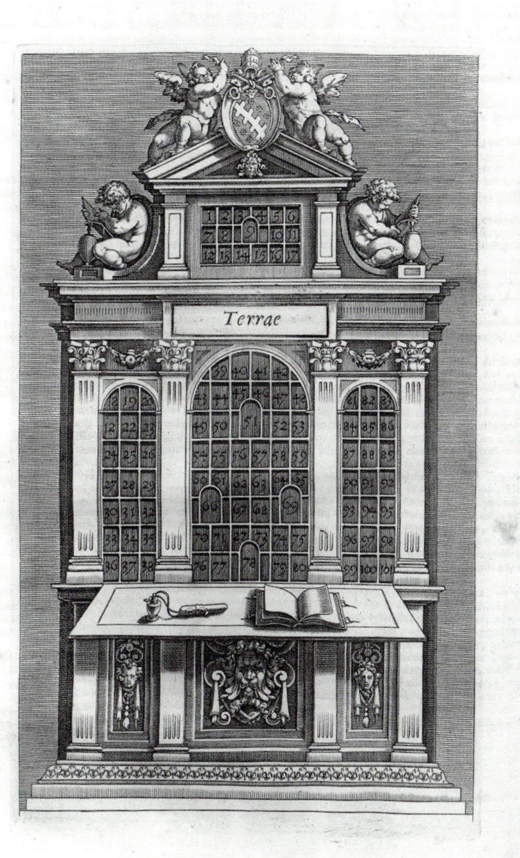

11

ruddy color, because he who lies in it was ruddy with spiritual beauty, glowing ever in mind and heart with the fire of the spirit."[62]

Nonetheless, it is certainly striking that the only Greek word Valentino uses in his description is εἴδωλον (*eidōlon*), the word invariably used to mean false idols throughout the Septuagint and the New Testament.[63] The subtext, which requires some prompting now, lies in the distinction between these idols, which are carved and therefore require the hand of man, and the pareidolic images naturally figured in the living rock, the artworks of nature, and therefore sanctioned by the Almighty. As Valentino says separately, "He restored sight to those born blind, so they could see various colors, and so that they should recognize [God] the Artist from the things that they saw."[64] As with Hagia Sophia, we are encouraged to think of the walls of the Cappella Gregoriana as petrous acheiropoieta that complement the paintings in stone (mosaics) above them.

But this scrutiny of the stone, of its every vein, as if under a microscope, also points to the contemporary and renascent science of geology. A stone in the collection of the Bolognese naturalist Ulisse Aldrovandi (1522–1605) recalls Valentino's river stone (**FIG. 10**), and, like the other stones in the collection, its patterns were considered to be "painted" by *Natura Pictrix*, at the behest of the Almighty himself.[65] Aldrovandi's *Musaeum Metallicum* was not published until 1648, and a more immediate example was the Vatican geology collection (*Metallotheca*) that had been founded for Gregory XIII by Michele Mercati

FIG. 10. *Alabaster That Imitates a River with Its Veining (Alabastrites maculis fluvium imitans)*, in Ulisse Aldrovandi, *Musaeum Metallicum*, Bononiae 1648, cap. LVII (*De Marmore*), 749.

FIG. 11. Frontispiece to *Armarium I (De lapidibus)*, in Michele Mercati, *Metallotheca*, Rome 1717.

(1541–1593), the papal physician and director of the Vatican botanical garden.[66] Frizolio wrote commendatory poems for Mercati's catalog, the *Metallotheca* (ca. 1574–1589), and would subsequently do the same for Mercati's volume on the obelisks of Rome.[67] In Mercati's gallery of nature, minerals were sorted in cupboards or cabinets, and the latter look very much like altars themselves (FIG. 11).

However, Valentino's lively description of marbles in the Cappella Gregoriana was just as likely influenced by another scholar in the Boncompagni stable, Alfonso Chacón (1530–1599). This Spanish Dominican had come to Rome in 1567, in the reign of Pius V, to become a confessor at St. Peter's. He now embarked upon a staggeringly ambitious program of writings, both religious and antiquarian, most of which remained unpublished. The best known are his *Lives and Deeds of the Popes and Cardinals* and the first fully illustrated book on Trajan's Column (1576). In the preface to the latter, Chacón announced he was preparing two "huge books," one a catalog of all the books in the world (!), the other a work "on gems, stones, marbles, rocks, juices, metals, and anything else to do with mines and quarries." Neither publication materialized, but one third of his manuscript on stones survives in the archive of Sant'Isidoro, the Roman convent of the Irish Franciscans.[68] This describes the classical marbles mentioned by Pliny and repeated by Valentino, but, more important, it dwells at great length, more than the *De Re Metallica* (1556) of Georgius Agricola or any other text since *On Stones* by Theophrastos (315/314 BCE), on their earthly generation.[69]

For all its proto-modern taxonomy, Mercati's *Metallotheca* still followed the Aristotelian division of minerals into "things that can be mined" (*ta metalleuomena*) and "things that can be quarried" (*ta orukta*), between the ductile and the carvable or, roughly speaking, metals and stones.[70] There was no periodic table, and scientists were still under the spell of the Four Elements. Modern geological classifications—sedimentary, igneous, metamorphic—lay far in the future, and stones still seemed to owe their color and veining to a varying cocktail of air, earth, moisture, and colored ores. It was the mottled and veined marbles, the so-called *marmi mischi*, that best seemed to confirm antique doctrine that all marbles were congelations of terrestrial exhalations, replenishing themselves in the core of an earth constantly channeled by generative streams and procreated by nature under the influence of a God-given "lapidifying virtue."

Valentino itemizes the marbles of the Cappella Gregoriana as being here more earthy, there more aqueous, or he describes their veining as mountain peaks poking through cloud or clotted masses traversed by snowy rivulets. It is a language that sometimes evokes modern satellite photography but at heart one that regards the stone as being only in a temporary stasis before it will disassemble and return to its elemental origins. As I have argued elsewhere, this elemental vision of marbles culminates in the metamorphic architecture of Gian Lorenzo Bernini, in buildings such as the Cornaro Chapel, where the walls are apparently in a phase transition from one element to another, effecting a transformation from earth, through air, to ether.[71]

It is now impossible to appreciate the "shock of the new" that greeted the Cappella Gregoriana when it finally became accessible to an elite primed by the thick description and allusive verse of Valentino and Frizolio, as well as a general public stirred by the sheer spectacle of its materiality. However, it was destined by its own success to dissolve from view after generations of popes decided to multiply its marvelous materials throughout the basilica. The cupola of the Cappella Gregoriana was soon eclipsed by the massive dome of St. Peter's (1588–1593), brilliant with its own acres of mosaics (1598–1600, 1603–1612). A few years later, it surrendered its splendid isolation when Della Porta built its near facsimile, the Cappella Clementina (marbled 1601–1602), as a pendent in the opposite aisle; and thereafter every other chapel in the basilica was dressed with marble cladding, as was the nave, while a marble floor spread over the crossing, nave, and aisles. When Gregory XIII had gated his mausoleum, he can only have intended his successors to close off chapels to similar ends, but when the iron screens of the Cappella Gregoriana were removed in the seventeenth century, it became as much a pilgrims' thoroughfare as every other part of the basilica.

Beyond St. Peter's, it was inevitable that the chapel should also set the standard for the papal mausoleums that Sixtus V and Paul V would build at Santa Maria Maggiore (1585–1590; 1605–1615), and as the decades passed, the rich marble panoply would be mimicked in the chapels and oratories of the nobility and confraternities, and, after a century or more had passed, eventually whole churches. As this became the norm, the Cappella Gregoriana became still more invisible. Yet when the chapel was being built, it was visionary, an ideal church in the midst of what was little more than a building site. Michelangelo's basilica had been travertine and stucco, and its floor was brick. In 1580, the still-unfinished basilica with its crossing open to the air was hardly distinguishable from the ruined imperial bath complexes that loomed on the Roman skyline. However incomplete, it offered the promise of a resurgent and glorious world Church. Within it, the Cappella Gregoriana seemed to augur heaven itself, as visitor after visitor recalled. There was, as yet, nothing to compare with the unprecedented (since antiquity) merging of colossal architecture, petrified painting, and animated marbles that enshrined a Father of the Church and his namesake, Pope Gregory XIII.

Notes

1 — The most comprehensive study of the chapel is Zollikofer 2016, with previous bibliography. The construction history was established by Bellini 2002; Bellini 2011, 1, 195–203. For the artisans, see Lamouche 2018 (my thanks to the author for providing me with his paper before publication). The chapel was mainly decorated in 1579–1580, but the metal gates were only installed in 1583, and work on the pavement and revetment continued until 1584. The most recent publication on the chapel by Möller (2018, 46–94) synthesizes preexisting literature. Möller does publish a new drawing (Albertina, Az Rom 754r; Möller 2018, Abb. 20), which she ascribes to Giacomo Della Porta; however, it is plainly a survey drawing done post-construction and therefore by a visiting architect. For the *Madonna del Soccorso* (a fifteenth-century replica of a twelfth-century icon), see Zander 2016; Zander 2020, forthcoming, with bibliography.

2 — Bedon 1983; Tancredi 1998; Tancredi 2000; Fiore 2018.

3 — The chapel in front (which would become the Cappella Clementina) was also meant to host the images of Ambrose and Augustine, John Chrysostom, and Athanasius; Gregory the Great was interred here. This iconographical scheme was later resurrected on the *Cathedra Petri*. See Rice 1997.

4 — Turner 1583, 64: "The work is still unfinished, but, so you may admire the splendor, the part that is finished, cost ninety thousand gold pieces. At first fifty workmen began the work, not much later three hundred and fifty pushed it on." ("Imperfectus est opus adhuc, sed, ut mireris splendorem, quae est confecta pars, nonaginta millibus aureorum confecta est. Quinquaginta operae inchoarunt prius opus, urserunt paulo post trecentae quinquaginta.")

5 — Valentino 1583, 8–9: "On the south and west sides iron gratings shut off the chapel, the entrance into which is through three openings: the iron is wrought into bars above these openings, but beneath and to each side it is fashioned in a net pattern, each one two cubits in length: next the *meniana* (which is generally called a balustrade) of cast brass, and lofty candelabra enclose it, interspersed with olive branches covered with spreading leaves. On all sides the painted colors both make ornament and this lends convenience besides, lest the iron become spoiled with age and covered with rust." ("Sacellum a Meridie, & occidente cancelli ferrei praecludunt, ad quod tribus ostiis aditus patet:

ferrum in regulas formatum supra eadem ostia, atque infra a lateribus reticulatim nectitur, quaque versus longum cubitos duos: tum meniana (quae passim Balaustia vocantur) ex aurichalco ductili, & excelsa candelabra circumscribunt, olivae ramo interiecto, patulisque foliis diffuso. Undique colores inducti, & ornatum faciunt, & hoc praeterea commodi afferunt, ne vetustate ferrum, obducta rubigine, vitietur.") *Maenianum* (Italian: *mignano*) classically refers to a projecting balcony.

6 — Alfarano 16th cent. [1914]; Baronio 1588–1607; Ugonio 1588. For the 1578 discovery of the catacombs, truth and myth, see Oryshkevich 2003.

7 — Chapel of the Holy Cross: Kelly 1987, 267–268 (cat. no. 44); Johnson 1995; Romano 1996; Mackie 1997. Santa Costanza: Stern 1958, 208–212; Amadio 1986, 23–26 (cat. nos. 3–4), 38–39 (nos. 12–13), 40–41 (no. 14), 50–51 (no. 21), 89–90 (no. 65). Lateran Baptistery: Giovenale 1929, 122–123, 128–139; Kelly 1987, 265–266 (cat. no. 43); Romano 1991, 34; the wall revetment of the central space (removed under Urban VIII) is recorded in BAV, Barb. lat. 4333, fol. 69v, and Barb. lat. 4424, fol. 31r.

8 — E.g., the Curia Senatus (Sant'Adriano), Hall of the Praefectus Urbis (later Santi Cosma e Damiano), Basilica of Junius Bassus (Sant'Andrea in Catabarbara or Sant'Andrea ad Praesepe), Portico of St. Peter's, Santa Lucia in Selci, Santa Maria Maggiore, Santa Sabina, Santo Stefano Rotondo and, of course, the Pantheon. Curia: Bartoli 1963, 58–60; Mancini 1966–1967. Hall of the Praefectus Urbis: Lanciani 1882, 37–40; Luschi 1998, 447–449. Basilica of Junius Bassus: Lanciani 1902–1912, 4, 66. Portico of St. Peter's, "spartimenti di pietre mischie ... come si vede nella Ritonda e nel portico di S. Pietro": Vasari 1568 [1906], VI, 554–555. Santa Lucia in Selci, "marmora et lapides porphireticos diversorum colorum septaque in statuis pictorum more reducta, ut apparet in porticu Sancti Petri et Sanctae Mariae Transtyberinae et in ecclesia Sancti Andreae miro artificio incrustata ... et in ecclesia Sanctae Luciae in Silice, in quibus ecclesiis picturae animalium aviumque ac si musivo et pictura essent depictae": Albertini 1510, 37. Santa Maria Maggiore, "aedes fuit lastricata ... in aula interius ubi supra portas desunt tabule lapidee": Panvinio, cited in Biasiotti 1915, 23. Santa Sabina: Rickert 1998. Santo Stefano Rotondo, "marmoreis columnis et crustatis varij coloris marmore parietibus musivoque opere:" Flavio Biondo, in D'Onofrio 1989, 151; Stern 1958, 208–212.

9 — Valentino 1583, 12: "The twin columns of the holy altar, which is built on the right wall of the chapel, were supplied from the demolition of the antique church, and which for that reason they intentionally did not take them away." ("Sacrae arae, quae ad Sacelli dexteram exstructa est, binae Columnae ex antiqui templi demolitione adiectae sunt, quas eo consilio non amoverunt.") In 1584, the four granite columns of the monumental aedicules were substituted in *africano*. For the imitation of paleo-Christian revetment in the Cappella Gregoriana and Cappella Sistina in Santa Maria Maggiore, see Ostrow 1990.

10 — See, for example, James and Webb 1991, esp. 6, 11; Webb 1999a; Webb 1999b; Newlands 2013.

11 — Frizolio 1582; Valentino 1583. Zollikofer (2016, 268–276) published a transcription of Valentino (without translation) but mentions Frizolio's ekphrasis only in passing (21–23).

12 — Barry and Gwynne forthcoming.

13 — Guicciardi 1589. Extremely rare, this copy is in the Biblioteca Estense Universitaria, Modena, E 080 H 021 (inv. A 4383).

14 — Valentino was secretary to Cardinal Alciati by 1574 (Lucidi 1796, 269). Frizolio is recorded as *Secretarius* of the *Congregatio Cardinalium Concilii Tridentini Interpretum* (the commission of cardinals that interpreted and ensured application of the disciplinary decrees of the Council of Trent) in 1584–1590 (Tromp 1959, 528–529).

15 — Maffei 1742, 2, 459–460: "Fu però propria del solo Gregorio di aver ristabilito nell'Italia i buoni studi e le scienze più sublimi. Poiché sebbene non avesse egli atteso molto alle belle lettere, alle Poesie, alle Matematiche, ed alle applicazioni Teologiche, contuttociò favorì gl'uomini più eruditi, ed i più bell'ingegni de'suoi tempi, cosa tanto più lodevole in un Principe, quanto più di rado da questi vedesi praticare. Quindi tra i molti promossi alle cariche più ragguardevoli, e ad altri beneficati con Vescovadi, o con altri ecclesiastici Benefizi, stipendiava col suo proprio denaro i seguenti: Vincenzo Laureo da Tropea, Cesare Baronio da Sora, Ignazio Dante Perugino Domenicano, Antonio Agellio Napolitano, Fulvio Orsino, Antonio Boccapaduli, Silvio Antoniano, e Ascanio Valentino Romani, i due Amaltei Udertini Giambattista, ed Attilio, Alessandro Petronio da Civita Castellana suo medico. Paolo Manuzio Veneziano, Carlo Sigonio Modenese, Flaminio de' Nobili da Lucca, Fabio Benvoglienti Sanese, Jacopo Mazzone da Cesena, Girolamo Mercuriale da Forlì, Pietro Magno d'Arpino, Uberto Foglietta Genovese, Lorenzo Frizolio da Rimini, Lorenzo Gambara Bresciano, Antonio Querengo da Padova, Giovanni Carga Furlano, Jacopo Billio, Emondo Eugerio, Giliberto Genebrardo, Marcantonio Mureto, Pietro Morino Francesi, Francesco Toledo, Martino Azpilqueta detto il Navarro, Francesco Torres, Pietro Maldonato, Pietro Giaccone Spagnuoli; Girolamo Osorio, ed Achille Stazio Portoghesi; Pietro Canisio, Cristoforo Clavio, Giorgio Edero Tedeschi; Gulielmo Alano, Edueno Lodovico, Niccolò Sandero Inglesi; Alessandro Seronio, Emondo Hajo, Giovanni Lesleo Scozzesi; Gulielmo Lindano, Jacopo Pamelio, e Gherardo Vossio Fiaminghi: a' quali tutti andava anche somministrando aiuti straordinari nelle necessità di ciascheduno, e per stimare il loro merito servivasi delle bilancie, particolarmente de' Cardinali Sirleto, Antonio Carafa, e del Contarello." On Frizolio, see Brigidi 1885, 347–357, with older bibliography. Frizolio's oeuvre is most extensively cataloged in Leuker 2013, 697–724. Unpublished letters of 1772 from Giovanni Cristofano Amaduzzi to Girolamo Ferri, conserved in the Rubiconia Accademia dei Filopatridi at Savignano sul Rubicone, contain information that was to have been included in an unfinished biography. Ferri's replies (nos. 66–68, 75, and 77) are published in Donati 2005, 137–263. A more penetrating study of Frizolio will appear in Barry and Gwynne forthcoming.

16 — August 16, 1570, "che maestro Ascanio Valentino figlio di maestro Damiano legga filosofia straordinaria senza salario": Archivio Segreto Vaticano (ASV), arm. XI, vol. 93, fol. 54, in Pometti 1901, 89. Muret, from Limoges, had taught in Bordeaux and (from 1554) in Venice, Padua, Ferrara, and (1563) Rome. In 1576, he took holy orders, and in 1578, Gregory XIII doubled his salary to stop him from taking up a post at Cracow offered by the king of Poland (Dejob 1881; Summers 2006; Girot 2012).

17 — Riikonen 1982. On the false attribution of the ode *Ad Nubes* to Tasso, see Poma 1993. Leuker (2009, 244, n. 6) argues that verses from Frizolio's panegyric to the poet Aurelio Orsi were

the model for Giambattista Marino's homage to the same poet in his *La Galeria* (1619).

18 — Gregorius Nazianzenus ed. 1569; anon. 1583. The *editio princeps* of Gregory Nazianzenus's poems with a Latin translation had been printed in 1504, and Gregory XIII owned a copy (Falcone 1998, 68–69). For the transmission and sources, see Palla 1989–1998; Palla 2002; Palla et al. 2010.

19 — On the role of Girolamo Muziano in the Cappella Gregoriana, see Tosini 2008, 220–232.

20 — Robertson 1992, 196.

21 — Borghini 1584, 577: "tutti i musaici, che vi sono con tanta bella maniera composti insieme, e con tant'arte, che parono dipinti col pennello, e con i colori." For *emblema*, see, e.g., Lucilius in Cic. *Or.* 44; Varr. *Rust.* 3.2.4.

22 — Valentino 1583, 16–17: "is enim glutinis genus quoddam scite commentus est in dies quindecim usum servandum, quo parietes primum illevit; tum ad imaginum pingendarum exemplar colores induxit: inde opera aliquot hominum, qui affabre struerent, versicolores laterculos coegit, quos non exegit ad perpendiculum, sed ordine quodam apposite coagmentavit: hos si comparibus coniunctionibus minus ex arte coactos depraehendisset; dissolvi intra certos illos dies, atque ad praescriptum artis rursus disponi curabat, recta quadam collocatione, aptaque consequentium rerum cum primis coniunctione. Quo fit, ut non ex tessellis conflatae figurae, sed humore solutis coloribus effictae imagines: neque pictura solum expressae, sed tamquam solida quaedam corpora ea etiam eminentia sint adumbratae, ut parietibus exstare videantur. Ita annis ferme duobus opus absoluit, quod caeteros artifices si ad eam artis, quam callent, normam perficiendam suscepissent, constat ex inchoati alibi operis commensione ad praesentem Vaticanam relata, ne multis quidem annis effecturos."

23 — Nicola La Piccola and Salvatore Monosilio (Di Federico 1983, 62–63).

24 — Francesco Bartoli (1675–1733), c. 1712. *Pontificalia Insignia Auguralia Sacralia et Sacerdotalia*, vol. I, n. 6a, Wormsley Library; pen, brown ink, traces of graphite, watercolor and bodycolor on paper, on three sheets glued together, overall size 786 × 601 mm. A separate sheet (vol. I, n. 6b, 528 × 597 mm) depicts the altar wall of the chapel in the same technique and to the same scale. John Talman presumably commissioned the drawing on one of his visits to Rome between April 1710 and February 1717 (Sicca 1996, 114–115, with bibliography). Bartoli presumably used the anonymous engraving (fig. 2) as his template.

25 — Paul 2015. The master mosaicist was Tarquinio di Cristoforo (called Tarquinio Perugino), assisted by Evangelista Saldino and Giorgio Vasaro (Lamouche 2018, 56). On the chapel mosaics, see Tosini 2008, 412–418; Turriziani 2011, 208–215; Tosini 2012, 283–284. The richness of the decor is remarked upon in Ciappi 1591, 5–6.

26 — Frizolio 1582, 44–52; Valentino 1583, 19–20.

27 — Valentino 1583, 18–19: "Tum spectra quaedam adsurgunt consulto propter loci excelsitatem, angustiamque figurata: quod illa oculorum acies perstringeretur, ne suis symmetriis integrae figurae suspicerentur; hac vero certum non esset, praestaret ne similes inter sese, aut omnino dissimiles pingere: quod satietatem similitudo attulisset; dissimilitudo in eam spatii contractionem cadere non posset, cum varii corporum flexus ex iliis ad verticem essent adiiciendi, ducendique certi cum venustate membrorum fines."

28 — Valentino 1583, 15: "Quod omnes in admirationem rapit unum est lunulatum hemisphaerium, emblemate vermiculato magnificum, a GREGORIO XIII. P. O. M. nunc longo intervallo Romae restitutum, quod tanto praestat proximis antiquis, quanto est interiecto tempore ichnographia perfectior effecta."

29 — Tosini 2008, 109–155.

30 — Gabriele Paleotti, *Discorso intorno alle imagine sacre et profane* (1582), and Gian Paolo Lomazzo, *Trattato dell'arte della pittura, scoltura et architettura* (1584), in Barocchi 1960–1962, 2, 2639–2665, 2692–2697. See also Dacos 1969.

31 — Valentino 1583, 19: "Satis igitur visum probari, si ludicris quibusdam, antiquorum imitatione, oculi tenerentur picturarum subtilitate, varioque lineamentorum tractu."

32 — On the Boncompagni dragon, see Ruffini 2005; Ruffini 2009.

33 — Frizolio 1582, 63–67: "Tutelam hic orbis non una ex parte dracones / desecto caudae videas rutilare veneno, / auxilio innocuas et pandere gentibus alas. / Excubat in vigili custodia lumine, monstris / Barbaricis oritur cristato e vertice terror." Fabrizi 1588; De Lillo 2012. Although Fabrizi's work was not printed until 1588, it circulated in manuscript long before.

34 — Pisanelli 1575.

35 — Rome, Istituto Nazionale per la Grafica, inv. S0072406, overall size 680 × 324 mm, engraved from two separate plates. (Bellini 2002, fig. 4; Bellini 2011, 195–197, fig. 162; Tosini 2012, 283; Raspe 2014). Although the engraving bears the date 1580, the aedicule frieze is pulvinated, unlike the finished object, indicating that it predates the cladding (1578–1580). See also Raspe 2000 for a discussion of the foundation medal for the chapel that unusually shows it in sectional perspective, emphasizing its centralized volume. The medal also proves (if any proof were needed) that a design model was available.

36 — Valentino 1583, 3: "In the meantime let me wish that you approve the plan … my contriving to describe thoroughly (unless you refuse) the other monuments that you build from day to day, that you make worthy of your grace and approval." ("Velim interea, ut consilium probes… imo parantem me describere (nisi abnueris) caetera monumenta, quae in dies edis, dignum reddas gratia, & approbatione tua.")

37 — On Gregory Nazianzenus as a poet, see, among many, Gilbert 1994, 122–142.

38 — Wilkinson 1970; Balot 1998; Harrison 2005; Meban 2008.

39 — Macrides and Magdalino 1988; Papalexandrou 2001; Connor 1999; Whitby 2006.

40 — Eriksen 2001.

41 — Valentino 1583, 3: "Gregorianum Sacellum, ex ipso opere, ut exstat, descripsi, ut qui praesentes intueri non poterunt, rem ubique ante oculos habeant."

42 — On the procession, see Pittiglio 2012.

43 — Valentino 1583, 7: "Hinc caelo aequatam Nazanzi antistitis aedem / Mirare: hinc magni nobile vatis opus. / Quam varie micat intextis pictura lapillis! / Quam placidum docta carmen in aure sonat! / Non una nitet arte lapis, non carminis una / Gloria. Ut aspersum ridet utrinque decus! / Provocat ars artem. Victoria nunc favet aedi, / Nunc tibi Laurenti; laurea cuius erit?" *Pictura* (line 3) means both "picture" and "painting," so Orsi may have had mosaics specifically in mind.

44 — Valentino 1583, 36: "Symmetria admirabile, dispositione singulare, structura cum antiquis comparandum."

45 — Valentino 1583, 28: "Epistylia. Capitelli nelle Colonne." The *zophorus* (frieze) fills the interval between the *epistylium* (architrave) and the *coronis* (cornice): Vitr. 3.5.10; 4.1.2. For *epistylium*, e.g., Vitr. 3.1ff.; 4.3; 5.1; Plin. *HN* 35.49.172; Paul. ex Fest. 58, p. 72 ("trabs, quae super columnas ponitur"). Valentino was perhaps misled by 1 Kings 7.6 (on Solomon's Temple) "in facie maioris porticus et columnas et epistylia super columnas."

46 — "Augustenae Columnae. Colonne Cipolline hoggi si chiamano" (27). Pliny (*HN* 36.9.55-56) mentions "Augustean [marble, in which the markings] curl over like waves so as to form curls" ("Augusteum undatim crispum in vertices"), but this is possibly Metagabbro granite (*granito verde della sedia*), not Carystian marble, from Euboea in Greece, whose green and white veining readily evoked waves. On the same page (27), Valentino compounds matters by defining "Cariystium [*sic*] marmor. Marmo bianco di Carrara." He also comments, "Leucophaeus color. Color giallo simile al Zafferano" (29). "Rubens punicum. Marmo africano rosso" (30). It is unclear what Valentino means by red *africano*. For *leucophaeus* (λευκόφαιος), "ash-" or "dun-colored," see Plin. 32, 10, 38, § 114: Vitr. 8, 3 *med.*

47 — Valentino 1583, 10: "Parietes undique ducti collucent multiplici maculoso marmore, quod sectum in crustas, tum scalptum leviter nullo curvamine inflectitur, sed aequabili est superficie, solidisque globusculis e pumice levigatum usque adeo expolitum est, ut admota manu nihil asperitatis habeat, nihil offensionis: glutine compacta segmenta, ac partes ita coeunt inter se, ut una dissimilibus ex rebus natura conflata videatur." On joining and staining marbles, see Barry 2017, with references.

48 — Valentino 1583, 36: "binae tabulae marmoreae satis insignes, quae propter amplitudinem rimas quidem agunt, verum tenuissime iuncto glutine, additoque ad marmoris speciem colore ita latent, ut adnatae venae iudicentur."

49 — Morrogh 1985; Satkowski 1993, 15-16; Conforti 1993, 129-142.

50 — Naples: Caldwell 2011. Carafa Chapel: Cerasoli 1894; Pressouyre 1984, 181; Palmerio and Villetti 1989, 159-161; Ieni 1985; Ieni 2002. For Santa Croce, Bosco Marengo, see Ieni 1985; Ieni 2002; Extermann 2016. The overall architect was Nanni di Baccio Bigio, but the tomb has been convincingly attributed to Giacomo Vignola: Frommel 2012, 38-40.

51 — Gregory issued *bandi* in 1572, 1576, and 1578 (Lanciani 1902-1912, 4, 51, 54-56). "Tavole di porfido o simili atre sorte di marmo grande o piccola tanto colonna come altra sorte di mischi di chiese di roma da fare fornimenti di tavole o di pavimenti et pili" and "serpentini porfidi graniti orientali che sieno stati ornamenti di chiese" and "sorte di marmo che sia lavorato da famosi aparamenti ed ornamento dell'architettura" (Tuena 1989a).

52 — Acidini Luchinat 1991; Martellacci 1995; Bosman 2005; delli Santi 2000.

53 — Baldini, Giusti, and Martelli 1979; Przyborowski 1982; Cresti 1988; Guarraccino 2009; Morrogh 2017; Barry 2019.

54 — Gnoli and Sironi 1996, 164 (f. 79r): "Chi potrebbe a pieno dir come le pietre di varie sorti abbelliscono i tempii e le bellissime cappelle, come si vede oggidì fatto in Roma, una dalla' santa memoria di papa Gregorio Terzodecimo, la più bella e più onorata che sia stata fatta a di nostri?" Del Riccio's manuscript dates from 1597.

55 — Compare the more conventional description by the Scottish priest and professor of rhetoric Robert Turner (1583, 64): "And what can I say about the chapel? The upper part is distinguished by pictures in vermiculated mosaic and beautiful designs in small tesserae; the middle part, on the other hand, all over, and right down to the pavement, of Greek and African marble, which resembles bronze or flame; easily they say (though they hold their tongues) this chapel equals the Temple of Jerusalem, and even—if such a small thing may be compared with such a large one, something so august with something so august—exceeds it." ("De sacello quid dico? Aeditior pars emblemate vermiculato, & tesserulis pulchre compositis distincta, media autem pars longe lateque ad pavimentum usque Graeci atque Aphricani marmoris, quod imitetur Pyropum aut flammam, facile dicunt, dum tacent, Ierosolomitanum templum aequari hic, atque adeo [si tantulum cum tanto, tam angustum cum tam augusto conferatur] superari. imperfectus est opus adhuc, sed, ut mireris splendorem, quae est confecta pars, nonaginta millibus aureorum confecta est. quinquaginta operae inchoarunt prius opus, urserunt paulo post trecentae quinquaginta.")

56 — Frizolio 1582, 417434: "diverso splendent quae secta colore, / Nostris posse putes comprendi marmora dictis? / Haec puris certant nivibus candore: smaragdos / Haec virides superant longe, flammasque pyropi, / Chrysolithos gilva haec referent laevata nitore. / Non nigrum haec vincunt hebenum? Non succina nigra? / At maculis alia innatis, guttisve notantur / Aspersis, mira inter se iunguntur et arte, / Signorumque novis perstringunt lumina textis. / Quorum luce solum radiat, pariesque renidet, / Ut Cilicis Timoli, Siculae aut convallibus Ennae / Omnigenum arva plagis rident distincta colorum. / Ut calthae areolis, violaeve, albive ligustri, / Narcissi, Cyanive nitent gemmantibus horti. / Ut vario signante vias subtegmine, lucent / Textilia arabijs illusa tapeta figuris. / Haec tu, quique altis flores laquearibus ardent,/Aspiciens mirari ultro, nec quare moneri." Compare Guicciardi 1589, 49-50: "E gl'altri marmor di vario colore / Che tagliati risplendono cotanto / Pensi che noi col poetico ardore / Possiamo à pien sphiegarli'n verun canto? / Questi à nevi par sono di candore, / Vincono i bei Smeraldi con gran vanto, / E del Piropo le fiamme illustranti; / Il splendor vago, le luci micanti. / De i Chrisoliti, e'l Giggiolin candor questi? / Non vincon l'Hebeno attro e ascuro que / Nò i negri Elettri? ma'n se alto colore / Tengono e innate macchie, e segni insesti, / E congionti trà se son con stupore, / Con modo eccelso; e gl'occhi di celesti / Segni perstringon con inusitate / Tessitur rar, e non mai essercitate. / Per la luce de quali alto splendore / La terra spande e il muro parimente, / Come del Cilico Timol del cultore / O d'Enna di Sicilia, e suol clemente / Nelle convalli pel vario colore / Ridono i vaghi fior distintamente / L'herbette molli, i gigli ameni e grati, / E di tanti stupor gl'adorni prati. / Ligustri over, Narcisi over distinti, / Over horti turchini, e pullulanti, / Come risplendon tapeti dipinti / D'Arabiche figur'aurati manti, / Le vie mostrando i fil del stame avinti / Sotto e tessuti, con gl'occhi guardanti / Questi mirando, e i tetti bei pe'i fiori, / Non più nò addimandar, scaccia i stupori." *Chrysolithos* (= χρυσόλιθος) presumably refers to yellow topaz (Plin. *HN* 37.42.126; Prop. 2.16, 44; Ov. *Metam.* 2.109; Prud. *Psych.* 854; Isid. *Orig.* 16.15.2). "Black ambers" must signify jet. *Gemmare* means both "to bud" and "to sparkle like a gem," as *gemma* means both "bud" and "gem."

57 — Ov. *Metam.* 2.1-2: "Regia Solis erat sublimibus alta columnis / clara

micante auro flammasque imitante pyropo." For *gilvus* ("dun-colored"): Servius *ad Georg.* 3.81 (piebald horses). Cf. *Catonis Disticha* 2.2.1 "ne quare ducere." Mount Timolus in Lydia was famed for its saffron (Verg. *Georg.* 1.56), and the River Pactolus was rich in gold dust (Ov. *Metam.* 11.136–141; Strabo 13.1.23, 13.4.5). Proserpina's abduction from the "valleys of Sicilian Enna": Ov. Metam. 5.385 ff. Pliny characterized nature as an artist, *Natura Pictrix*, because she painted the seasons with flowers, speckled the shells of crustaceans, dappled the hides of wildlife: *HN* 7.3, 9.52, 21.1.

58 — Frizolio 1582, 162–164: "The cities of Asia have heard him proclaim his tempered outpourings on the sad funeral of his dear father bereft of life." ("Audivere urbes Asiae carique parentis / Defuncti vita … / Edentem in tristi moderatos funere fletus.") Oratio 18 (*funebris in patrem*), §39, "Nam et octo aequilateris rectis in se occurrit, et columnarum ac porticum elegantia per laquearia in altum assurgit, et quidem eiusmodi picturis ornata, ut nec naturae ipsi concedant. Quid quod coelo desuper collustratur, uberrimisque lucis fontibus spectantium oculis irradiat, ut vere lucis domicilium! Adhaec orbicularibus et aequiangulis splendissimae materiae cursibus, atque ingentem in medio locum ambientibus cingitur, ac portarum et vestibulorum venustate praelucet, atque accedentes eminus excipit. Nondum de externo ornatu loquor, de quadrati lapidis, atque in crinem concinnati pulchritudine et magnitudine, tam qui marmoreus est, nempe in basibus et capitibus, quibus anguli intercipiuntur, quam qui patriis, nulla tamen in re externo cedens. Nondum de variis et multiplicibus zonis, a fundamentis ad cacumen usque protensis et intextis, quod spectatorem damno afficit, visum circunscribens." For the Greek original (which differs slightly), see *PG* 35, 1037–1038: "ὀκτὼ μὲν ἰσοπλεύροις εὐθείαις εἰς ἑαυτὸν ἀπαντῶντα, κιόνων δὲ καὶ στοῶν κάλλεσι διωρόφων εἰς ὕψος αἰρόμενον, καὶ τοῖς ὑπὲρ αὐτῶν πλάσμασιν οὐ λειπομένοις τῆς φύσεως· οὐρανῷ δὲ ἄνωθεν καταστράπτοντα, πηγαῖς δὲ φωτὸς πλουσίαις τὰς ὄψεις περιαυγάζοντα, ὥσπερ ἀληθῶς φωτὸς οἰκητήριον· δρόμοις τε ἀμφιθέτοις ὕλης τῆς λαμπροτάτης ἰσογωνίοις κυκλούμενον, καὶ πολὺν τὸν ἐν μέσῳ τόπον περιλαμβάνουσι· πυλῶν δὲ καὶ προπυλαίων προλάμποντα χάρισι, καὶ πόρρωθεν τοὺς προσιόντας δεξιούμενον. Καὶ οὔπω λέγω τὸν ἔξωθεν κόσμον, λίθου τετραπέδου, καὶ εἰς τρίχα συνηρμοσμένου κάλλος καὶ μέγεθος, ὅσος τε καὶ μαρμάρεος ἐν ἕδραις καὶ κεφαλίσιν, αἳ τὰς γωνίας διειλήφασι, καὶ ὅσος ἐπιχώριος μηδὲν τοῦ ξένου λειπόμενος· ζώνας τε πολυειδεῖς καὶ ποικίλας προβεβλημένας τε καὶ ἐνυφασμένας, ἀπὸ κρηπῖδος εἰς κορυφὴν, ἣ ζημιοῖ τὸν θεατὴν, τὴν ὄψιν ὁρίζουσα."

59 — Bedon 1983; Tancredi 1998; Tancredi 2000; Fiore 2018.

60 — Valentino 1583, 31–32: "Amethysti inspectione mentem subit cogitatio fluivi cuiusdam; qui e montium finibus emissus vario flexu per aspera tenuis profluit, tum irrumpens uberius, quasi undis concursantibus, tumescit in fluctus, atque impetu illisus ad scopulos exsilientem excipit, alluitque oppida, quorum εἴδωλα oculis subiiciuntur.… Undequaque in stylobatis ex alabastrite omnium pulcherrimo adpositae crustae ternae: in quarum altera aquae, altera terrae speciem, animo conceptam, summa iocunditate licet intueri: Atque e montium quasi iugis manantem aquam in proclive rapi, tum rupium obiectu aversam inflecti secundo cursu, rivos fluctibus operiri; modo subactam humum irrigare; modo in locum unum confluere, lapidum mole disiungi, atque terra tota diffundi: Altera crusta montes, veluti aequabili inter sese spatio discreti, procumbunt in colles sibi subiectos, quorum nonnulli proceritate ampliores sunt, angustiores alii ob cacuminum flexiones apparent."

61 — For the manuscripts and editions of Paul the Silentiary, see De Stefani 2011, xiv–xxi. See Prokopios's ekphrases of Hagia Sophia in the editions of van Craneveldt and Svallemberg 1537, 3–8; Haldrein 1538, 11–18; Egio 1547, 2–4.

62 — Nikolaos Mesarites 38.4; Downey 1957, 890, 915: "Γρηγόριος ὁ τῆς θεολογίας ἐπώνυμος, τὸ πῦρ πνεῦσαν στόμα καὶ πᾶσαν αἵρεσιν καταφλέξαν, ἐν τετραγώνῳ ἑτερομήκει περιγραφόμενος λάρνακι πυρρακιζούσῃ τὴν χρόαν, ὅτι καὶ ὁ κείμενος ἐν αὐτῇ πυρράκης ἦν μετὰ κάλλους πνευματικοῦ, τῷ πυρὶ μὲν τῷ τοῦ πνεύματος τὸν νοῦν καὶ τὴν καρδίαν ἐς εἰ διαθερμαινόμενος, τῷ δὲ κάλλει τῶν λόγων τὴν γλῶτταν κατακοσμούμενος." It is unclear when the manuscript entered the collection of Cardinal Federico Borromeo and thence the Biblioteca Ambrosiana in Milan, but it was not rediscovered until 1898 and was published in Heisenberg 1908.

63 — Suggit 1985; Griffith 2002.

64 — Valentino 1583, 301–302: "Caecigenoque dedit solem, variosque colores / Cernere, et artificem visis ex noscere rebus."

65 — For Aldrovandi's museum, see Torricelli, Tugnoli Pattaro, and Scappini 1993, 99–109, with catalog of marbles at 114–117; Vai and Cavazza 2006. For Aldrovandi's library, see Folli 1993. For the stone, see Bernia, Ambrosini, and Aldrovandi 1648, cap. LVII (*De Marmore*), 749: "Alabastrites maculis fluvium imitans."

66 — Accordi 1980; Cooper 1995.

67 — "Laurentii Frizoli de Michael Mercato," in Mercati 1717, lvii–lviii. Mercati's fleeting section on marbles (*Armarium X. Marmora*) begins at p. 351.

68 — Alfonso Chacón, *De Marmorum Liber Tertius*, Sant'Isidoro degli Irlandesi, Rome, Archive (Ms. 2/49, fols. 80r–93r, 94r–99v, 100r–110r). The other projected books in the tome are missing. Chacón 1576, 1 (dedication to Philip II, 5 Idus Octobris 1576): "Proinde loeta fronte suscipe hoc munusculum clementissime Princeps, interim dum tuis auspiciis libros duos ingentes paro: alterum, de gemmis, lapidibus, marmoribus, saxis, succis, metallis, rebusque cunctis metalliferis: quae maxime reges decent, quorum interest, thesauros in publicos usus conservare, qui gemmis praecipue, & metallis constant: alterum, bilbliothecam universalem librorum omnium, tam eorum qui typis excussi." Chacón 1601 was revised and updated by Luke Wadding (1588–1657), the prior of Sant'Isidoro degli Irlandesi, in 1630, which may explain how this manuscript entered the college's archive. The manuscript is hitherto unknown and was brought to my attention by Irina Oryshkevich.

69 — Caley and Richards 1956; Eichholz 1965; Halleux 1974; Agricola 1556.

70 — Arist. *Mete.* 1.339a 11–339b 2, 1.340b 19–28, 2.359b 29–360a 13, 3.378a 14–378b 6, 4.378b 10–25, 4.379b 10–26, 4.388a 10–15.

71 — Barry 2016.

Caetani's Blood

MAGNIFICENCE, LINEAGE, AND MARTYRDOM IN THE FAMILY CHAPEL OF SANTA PUDENZIANA

Enrico Parlato

"Cardinal Enrico Caetani titular of this [Santa Pudenziana] renovated it entirely sparing no expense, building in it such a noble and magnificent chapel, considered among the most beautiful in Rome, imperial more than cardinalesque."[1] These words of unconditional praise by the Servite Pietro Martire Felini for Cardinal Enrico Caetani (1550–1599) were written in 1600, when the decoration was still not entirely finished. Indeed, the rarity and cost of the materials and the use of sophisticated artistic techniques produced an uncommonly opulent appearance, placing the Caetani Chapel of Santa Pudenziana—as noted early on (ca. 1597) by Agostino del Riccio (1541–1598)—within a select group of outstanding late-sixteenth-century Roman chapels: the Gregorian in St. Peter's, the Sistine in Santa Maria Maggiore, and the Aldobrandini in Santa Maria sopra Minerva.[2] As is typical in sacred art, the openly flaunted opulence of the materials combines the anagogic mystique of the reliquary with the more mundane exaltation of the magnificence of the patrons. These two aspects are at the root of the history of the decoration of the chapel.

When it was commissioned in 1588, the Caetani were already the titulars of a very ancient shrine, the altar of Saint Boniface on the counterfacade of old St. Peter's, located in a position of great prestige in a central site of Christianity, close to the tomb of Boniface VIII, forefather and glory of the lineage. Not long before, in 1574, Onorato Caetani had commissioned an altarpiece from Girolamo Siciolante for this chapel.[3] One wonders, then, what led the family, and in particular its high prelates, Cardinal Enrico and the patriarch Camillo (1552–1602), to commission a major work like the chapel in Santa Pudenziana, "sparing no expense," as Felini wrote.

The chapel (**FIG. 1**) is located on the south side of the basilica, with its main axis perpendicular to that of the church.[4] Its plan is rectangular. On the short sides are, respectively, the niche with the main altar and, opposite, a symmetrical space that serves as a vestibule. The main chamber of the chapel is vaulted, and the atrium and the niche have barrel vaults, evoking the triumphal arches of the classical tradition.

The chapel stands on the area previously occupied by the oratory of Saint Pastor, described by Onofrio Panvinio and, immediately before its demolition, by Pompeo Ugonio. According to their concordant testimony, there was a well in the area where, according to tradition, the blood of martyrs was kept, as well as a pulpit from the time of Gregory VII. Ugonio also cites the presence "at the foot of the altar ... of two small iron *cratelle* that have underneath, on the stone, certain small circular signs, which, it is said, were made by the holy host in falling from the hands of a Priest who was celebrating at the said altar."[5] Following the renovation, the well disappeared, while the *cratelle*—the two small hexagonal iron balustrades fixed to the floor protecting the blood spots on the stone—were moved along with the stone sections to the foot of the main altar, on the left side.

The iconography of the chapel centers on the *Adoration of the Magi* (**FIG. 2**), the monumental marble altarpiece sculpted by Pietro Paolo Olivieri (1551–1599),[6] and is integrated by related themes, articulated according to the spatial subdivision of the chapel: the niche, the main chamber, and the atrium. The different materials and techniques—mosaic, stucco, marble encrustation, low-relief and high-relief sculpture—also serve to distinguish the themes. For example,

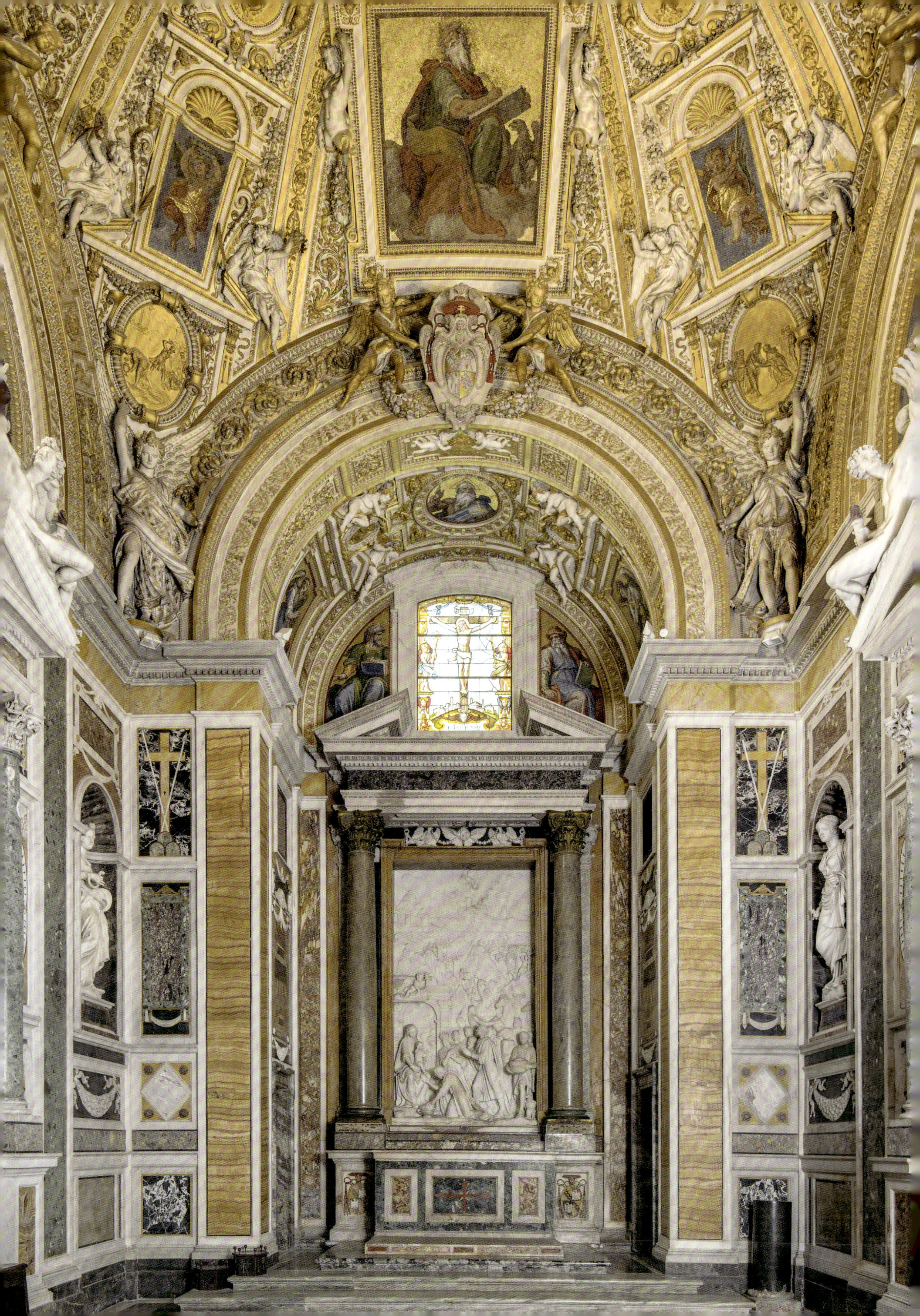

there is a rather evident internal narrative continuity within the stucco low-reliefs or the mosaics; at the same time, there is no lack of cross-references and connections among the various sections and media.

Besides the *Adoration of the Magi* and the commemoration of the departed—the latter two present in effigy, flanked by the Virtues, and by heraldic elements in stucco, sculpted, or depicted with marble *tarsiae*—as we have seen, various visual themes combine in the chapel. The spreading of the Word is the theme in the mosaics of the vault and the niche (FIGS. 3–4); in the center of the vault, we see the Holy Spirit surrounded by the Evangelists; on the walls are the four Sybils, mirrored by the two Prophets at the back of the niche. In the vault of the latter, the image of adoring angels in front of God the Father can be associated with the Passion of Christ, insistently evoked by the Crucifixion in the stained-glass window and by the marble inlays depicting the *arma Christi*.[7] In an almost cyclical pattern, the Passion is again triumphantly evoked in the vault, where angels in stucco or in mosaic hold the martyrs' palms and crowns. In the center of the vault, the traditional representation of the diffusion of the Holy Spirit starts from the mosaic oval—where the dove is surrounded by pairs of angels holding flaming candelabra, as well as by heraldic Caetani eagles, all modeled in stucco—and ends with four *clypei* (tondi) with the three Theological Virtues, to which (for reasons of symmetry) Justice was added, all made in gilded stucco.

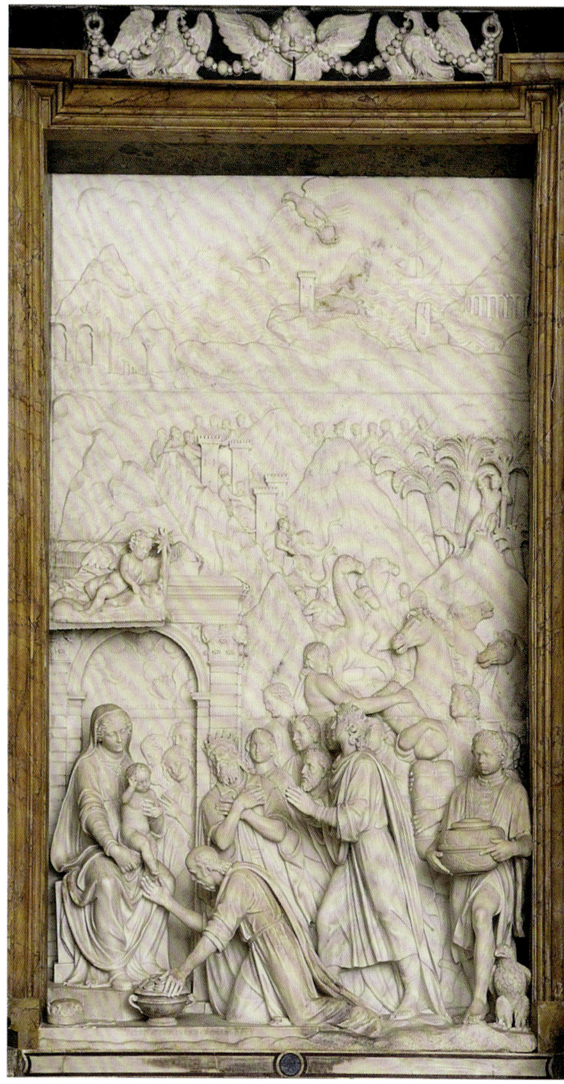

2

The theme of the cult of the bodies and blood of the martyrs practiced by the pious sisters Pudentiana and Praxedis has its visual center in the mosaic lunette in the counterfacade (FIG. 5); it is evoked again in one of the gilded stucco *clypei* positioned against the corbels of the vault and extends to the marble *tarsiae*—two extraordinary *pinakes* on the lateral walls of the niche (FIG. 6)—and is also found in certain details of the marble decoration, such as the sponge in the talons of the Caetani eagle (FIG. 5), an image that combines the family heraldry with the *passio* of the titular saint of the basilica. According to the testimony of Bruzio (1668), the two lateral windows originally bore stained-glass depictions of Saint Pudentiana and Saint Praxedis.[8] Finally, the story of Saint Peter's apostolate in Rome—central to the story of the basilica—is mainly entrusted to the stucco low-reliefs. In the four ovals in the corbels of the vault, four episodes are represented, which refer to the presence of Saint Peter in the house of Pudente, Pudentiana's father, to the latter's conversion, and to the consecration of the church or of the Oratory of Saint Pastor, even if the only clearly recognizable subject is the relief with *Saint Pudentiana Collecting the Blood of the Martyrs*, while the *Baptism* most likely refers to that of Pudente. It is again Bruzio who defines the ovals as

FIG. 1. Caetani Chapel, Santa Pudenziana, Rome.

FIG. 2. Pietro Paolo Olivieri, *Adoration of the Magi*, 1599. Caetani Chapel (altar), Santa Pudenziana, Rome.

the "stories of Saint Peter and Saint Pudente ... when Saint Peter is received in the home of the said Holy Senator, when he baptizes him."[9]

For its position, size, and material, the *Adorations of the Magi* (FIG. 2) on the main altar is the visually outstanding element in this arrangement. Gelasio Caetani in his *Domus Caietana*—a fundamental documentary study on the history of the family—identifies in the vast landscape in the background the presence of "heraldic and historical allusions" to the lineage and sees the maritime landscape as a reference to the family fiefs.[10] The eagle with spread wings and the laurel wreath in its talons is certainly a symbol of victory and, in combination with the maritime landscape and with the marching army, could refer to a military episode, perhaps the Battle of Lepanto, in which the Caetani family participated, more than to the trip of the Magi.[11] In terms of iconography, the *Adoration of the Magi* is not a particularly frequent subject in sixteenth-century Rome. As suggested by Gina Möller, the choice could be explained as an homage to Arnolfo di Cambio's *Nativity* in the crypt of the nearby Sistine Chapel in Santa Maria Maggiore, commissioned by Sixtus V (1585–1590). The idea that the Caetani may have chosen the subject to honor the pope to whom they owed the good fortune of the family is entirely convincing.[12]

History of the Chapel: 1587–1668

I will begin by offering a brief overview of the architectural and decorative history of the chapel. It all started when Enrico Caetani was named cardinal on December 18, 1585, and received, on the following January 15, the presbyterial title of Santa Pudenziana.[13] The church is positioned on the slopes of the Viminale, in the valley that separates it from the Esquiline Hill. It has an extremely ancient history, closely connected to the birth of Christianity and Saint Peter's apostolate in Rome. According to tradition, when Saint Peter arrived in Rome, he remained there for seven years, a guest of Senator Pudente and his two daughters. The story was told by Panvinio, Ugonio, and Baronio and amplified by the building of a chapel dedicated to Saint Peter in the church around 1590, in which a fragment of the saint's altar was said to be kept.[14] According to the hagiography, Saints Pudentiana and Praxedis, during the persecution of Christians, collected the bodies and blood of martyrs, storing them in wells, whose remains are cited in late-sixteenth-century guides. The increasing development of Christian historiography and, in particular, the monumental work by Cesare Baronio, the *Annales Ecclesiastici*, conferred on this tradition a significant relevance in regard to the ongoing European religious conflict.[15]

Another and equally important factor in the renovation of the church was its location: Santa Pudenziana and the annexed convent of the Foglianti bordered the villa that Cardinal Felice Peretti had built between Santa Maria Maggiore and the Baths of Diocletian.[16] It was also close to the Liberian Basilica, where Peretti, now Pope Sixtus V, had ordered the Sistine Chapel to be built, and, more generally, was located in an area of the city that had been the object of special attention from the new pope. Among the various urban development projects, a major one was the construction of the Felice Aqueduct, which brought water to the higher parts of the area, including the Viminale and Esquiline Hills; to this we might add the work done in the area

FIG. 3. Mosaics by Paolo Rossetti (after cartoons by Cristoforo Roncalli) and stuccos by Ambrogio Bonvicino and Stefano Fuccari, 1591–1597. Caetani Chapel (vault), Santa Pudenziana, Rome.

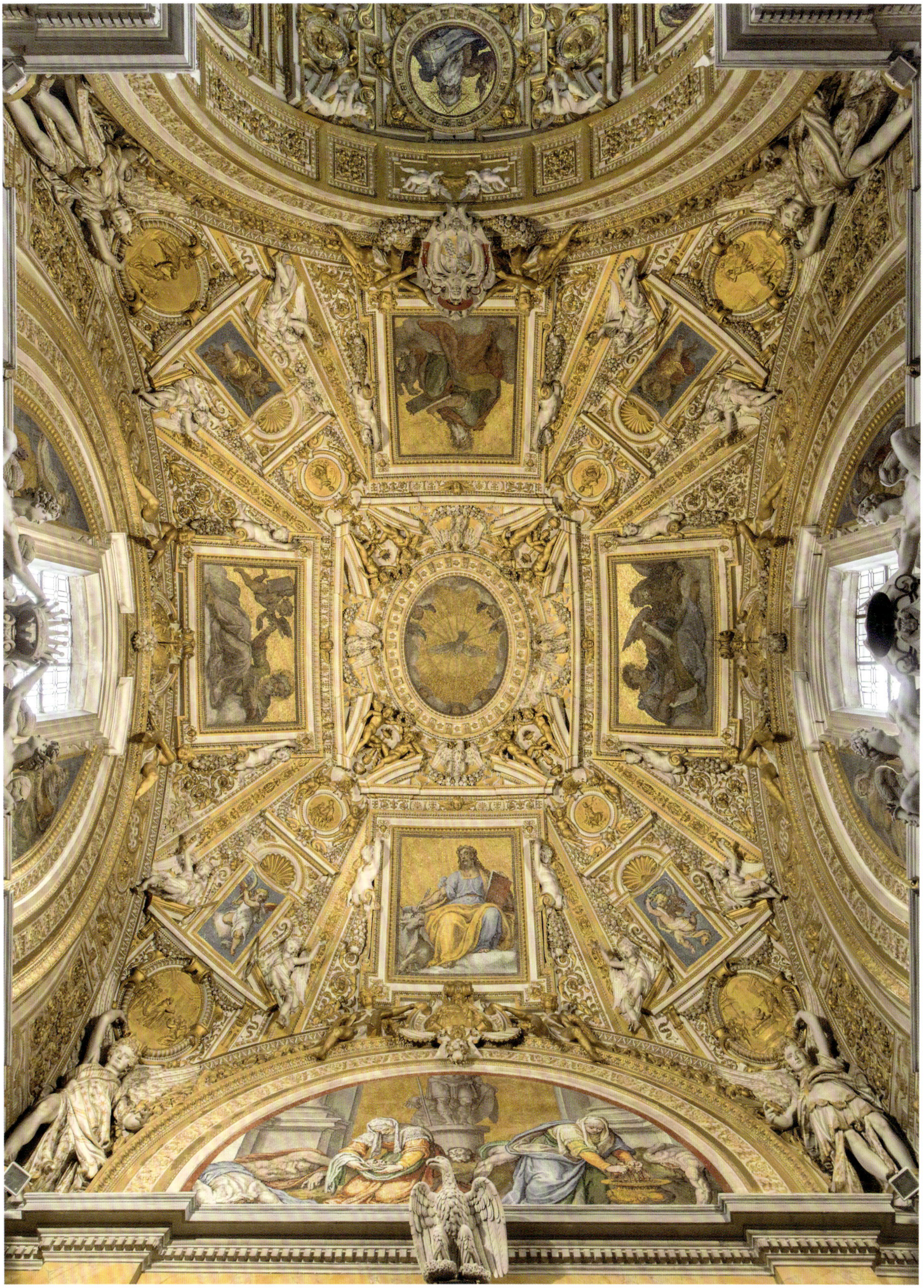

3

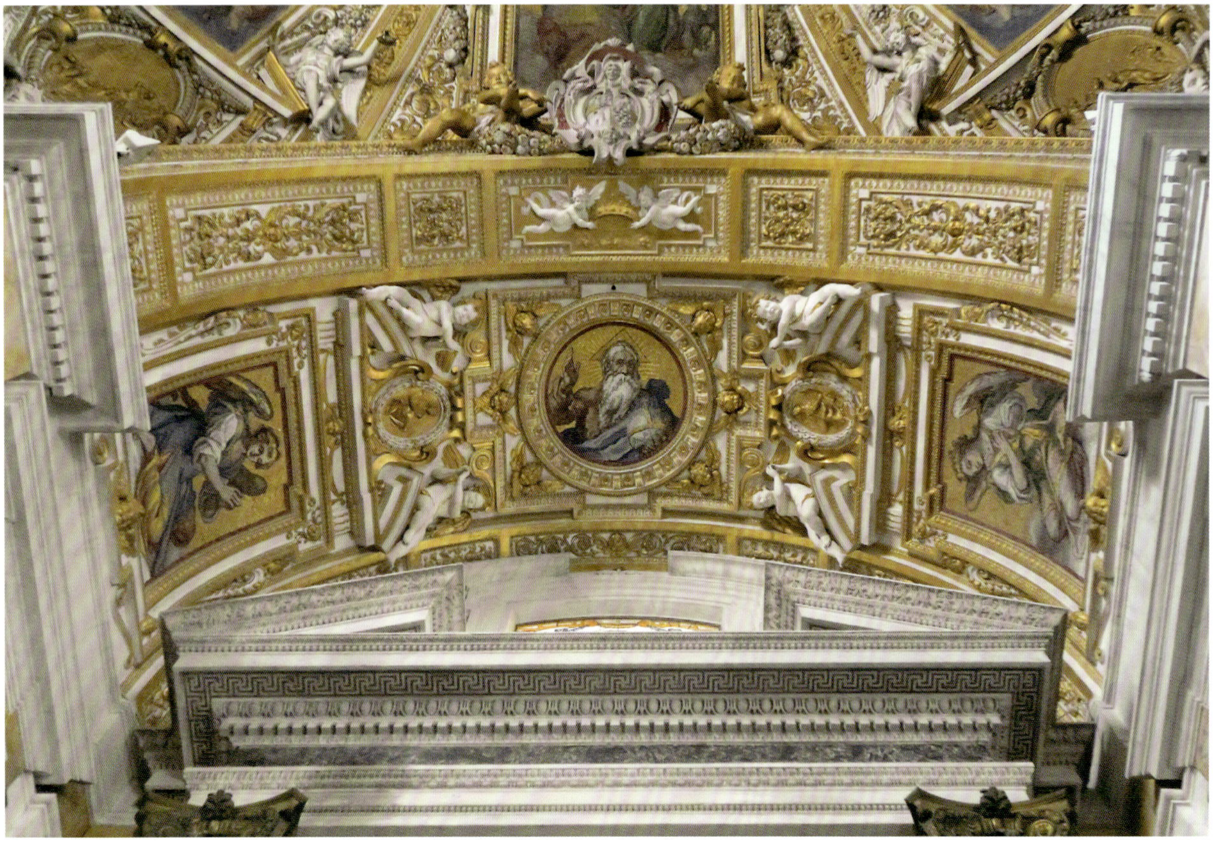

4

FIG. 4. Paolo Rossetti after cartoons by Cristoforo Roncalli, Mosaics of the vault, 1591–1597. Caetani Chapel (altar niche), Santa Pudenziana, Rome.

between Santa Maria Maggiore and Villa Peretti, with the raising of the level of the street facing the entrance of Santa Pudenziana.[17] Assigning to a cardinal with notable financial means a titular church in this area was a gesture that implicitly involved certain obligations, a message that was promptly understood by Enrico Caetani.

In 1587, work on the church started, directed by architect Francesco Capriani da Volterra (1535–1594) and with the participation of the painter Niccolò Circignani (ca. 1530–1598). The old and precarious structure was consolidated, the church was renovated according to the principles of the Tridentine Council, the vault was built ex novo and decorated anew, and the famous fifth-century mosaic in the apse was restored.[18] The church's present aspect is largely the result of this intervention. The area of the oratory of Saint Pastor was taken over by the Caetani Chapel, whose construction began in 1587 and must have been mostly finished by 1591, when the first payments for the decoration of the vault were made (FIG. 3). The new architecture was designed by Capriani and, after his death, was finished with small modifications by Carlo Maderno, who "inherited" the project.[19] The internal decoration began with the stuccos in the vault entrusted to Stefano Fuccari from Trento[20] and to one "Ambrogio from Milan," no doubt Ambrogio Bonvicino (1552–1622), while the mosaics were installed by Paolo Rossetti, based on Cristoforo Roncalli's cartoons.[21] These interventions took place in the years 1591 to 1597. Starting from 1594, work on the walls also began; payments are documented for the marble incrustations that

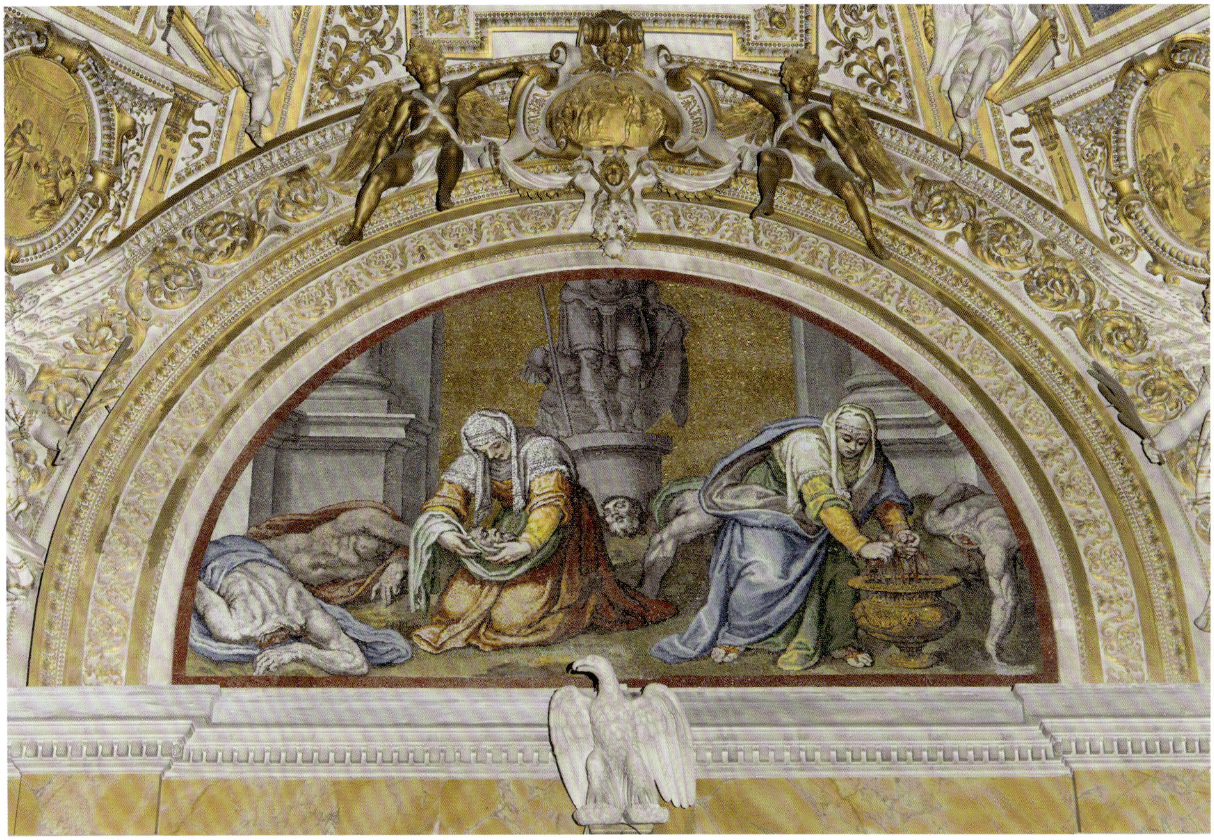

5

line them, for the marble columns, and for the bronze capitals and bases of the altar. The artists involved were the sculptors Giovan Battista Della Porta and Giovanni Antonio Paracca the Younger, known as Valsoldino, and the founder Bastiano Torrigiani.[22] Finally, the busts of the two patrons, Enrico Caetani and his brother Camillo, were placed in the niches in the center of the lateral walls, and the monumental marble altarpiece, the *Adoration of the Magi*, sculpted by Pietro Paolo Olivieri, was also installed (FIG. 2). This phase of the work was finished no later than 1603.

More than sixty years later, in 1668, Duke Francesco Caetani (1594–1683) decided that the chapel was to become the pantheon of the entire family. Up to now, no documentary evidence of this work has been found, but we have the testimony from the early eighteenth century of Francesco Posterla, who writes: "In the year 1668, Duke Francesco Caetani lined it with fine inlaid marbles and opened under it the Cemetery for the Departed of this Family."[23] In other words, a crypt was built underneath the chapel, or perhaps only expanded, where the remains of the members of the family could be entombed. At the same time, in the chapel, a new pavement in *opus sectile* was installed, with a monumental heraldic eagle, possibly the work of Giovanni Somazzi;[24] the bust of Duke Filippo (1565–1614; attributed to Paolo Naldini) with the symbol of the chivalric order of Saint James prominently displayed, replaced that of the patriarch Camillo.[25] Finally, the niches symmetrically arranged beside the two funerary monuments (by Francesco da Volterra and designed to remain emp-

FIG. 5. Paolo Rossetti after cartoons by Cristoforo Roncalli, *Saints Praxedis and Pudentiana Gathering the Martyrs' Bodies and Blood*, 1591–1597. Caetani Chapel, Santa Pudenziana, Rome.

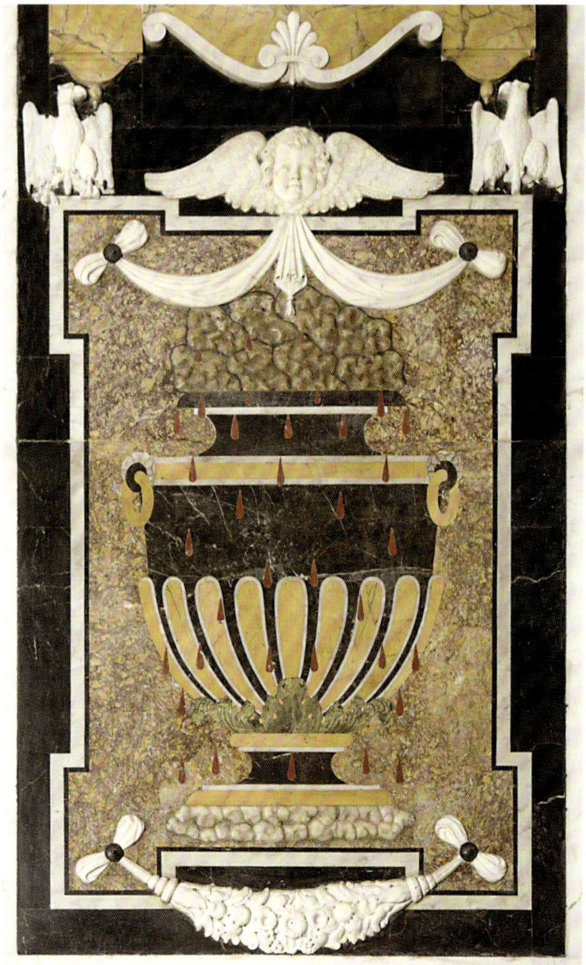

6

ty) were adorned with four marble statues representing the Cardinal Virtues. *Justice* and *Prudence* were inserted in the left wall, alongside the tomb of Cardinal Enrico, respectively assigned to Ambrogio Parisi and Adam Claude Bréfort (Adamo Lorenese); on the right-hand wall, next to the bust of Duke Filippo, *Temperance* was placed on the left and *Fortitude* on the right, respectively attributed to Carlo Malavista and Vincenzo Mari.[26] Bruzio's description of the Caetani Chapel offers some additional information on this alteration. His text can be dated to 1668, since it names Rinaldo d'Este (nominated on March 12 of that year) as titular cardinal, but in describing the chapel, he makes no mention of the alterations ordered by Francesco Caetani, which date to the same year, nor does he refer to Filippo Caetani's funerary monument, the statues of the Virtues, or the marble floor. The testimony also allows us to date the marble inlay work on the walls to the first phase of the decoration. "The tomb [on the opposite side]," writes Bruzio, describing the tomb in front of that of Enrico Caetani, "bears no inscription even though, after Cardinal Henrico, three cardinals of this very noble family have died."[27] This information suggests that the sepulcher of the patriarch Camillo might have been dismantled before the intervention of Francesco Caetani, perhaps to make room for one of the various cardinals of the family who at some time had the title to the basilica.

To conclude, in the first phase of the works, ending in 1603, the chapel had been conceived as a monument to the two prelates, Cardinal Enrico and the patriarch Camillo, and a sepulcher for the prelates of the family. As already mentioned, from the death of Enrico Caetani (1599) up to 1642, Santa Pudenziana was almost constantly entitled to one of the cardinals of the family, although Felini (as quoted at the beginning of this essay) stated that the chapel was "imperial more than cardinalesque."[28] Only in 1668, when the Caetani Vatican shrine was already demolished, through the renovation ordered by Duke Francesco, did the Caetani Chapel become the mausoleum of the entire *Gens Caietana*.

The Caetani Family in the Late Sixteenth Century

The relationship between the Caetani family and Sixtus V was decisive for the history of this architectural and decorative enterprise. However, we get a better understanding of the situation when we consider the history of the Caetani as a whole, starting from the 1560s.[29] The decision to engage in the building of an expensive chapel in a moment of dramatic financial straits for the family cannot be explained in terms of an obsession with social status. Indeed, the irrationality of the enterprise is only apparent.[30] It was rather a question of complet-

FIG. 6. Giovan Battista Della Porta and workshop, Urn with a sponge dripping blood, ca. 1594–1600. Caetani Chapel (altar niche), Santa Pudenziana, Rome.

ing a difficult journey, begun with a change in the family policy that the Caetani had cautiously started more than twenty years before. During the "government" of Bonifacio Caetani (1514–1574) and Cardinal Nicola (1526–1585), the Caetani, rulers of Sermoneta, decided to try to overcome their traditional antagonism with the Colonna, distancing themselves from the French party in favor of the Habsburg one. An important step in this process was the marriage between Onorato Caetani and Agnesina Colonna (sister of Marcantonio), which was celebrated in 1560 but whose contract had been signed in 1558. The union, besides attenuating the territorial controversies between the two families, cemented the alliance between the two brothers-in-law. Starting from 1570, Onorato joined Marcantonio in the anti-Turkish expeditions of the Spanish-Pontifical fleet and played an important role in the Battle of Lepanto (October 7, 1571), as commander of a ship that distinguished itself in the battle. The resonance of the event, the triumph offered to Marcantonio (but also to Onorato himself),[31] was a turning point for the family. Furthermore, in the conclave of May 1572, in which Pope Gregory XIII (1572–1585) was elected, Nicola Caetani played a decisive role in orienting the vote toward the candidate favored by Spain. With this step, the Caetani definitely severed their traditional ties with the French crown. In the following years, however, the tensions between the Caetani and the new pope grew, finally leading Cardinal Nicola to abandon Rome and retire to his fiefs. The almost contemporary death of Nicola and Pope Gregory, followed by the election of Sixtus V (April 1585), changed the fortunes of the Caetani once again. A few months after his election, the new pope, who had been a friend to Cardinal Nicola, nominated his nephew Enrico as cardinal, and in October 1586, he turned the fief of Sermoneta into a dukedom. This had always been the ambition of the Caetani, since it meant joining the highest rank of Roman aristocracy, alongside the Colonna and the Orsini.[32] The family continued to rise rapidly. In February 1587, Philip II bestowed on the newly appointed Duke Onorato the Order of the Golden Fleece, which only Marcantonio Colonna, among the aristocrats of Rome, had received until then.[33] In the meantime, Cardinal Enrico Caetani had been nominated legate in Bologna (August 1586), after which, with the help of the entire family (including his acquired relative Cardinal Farnese), in September 1587, he purchased for the considerable sum of fifty thousand ducats the position of camerlengo (this, however, was to prove an unsatisfactory investment). The solid relations with the pope are also evidenced by the family heraldry, with the insertion of the lion rampant of the Peretti at the center of the arms of the Caetani. This variant appears in Rome in a coat of arms of Cardinal Enrico, now in the courtyard of Santa Pudenziana (FIG. 7), and in Bologna in the cistern outside the current town hall, a palace that was once the seat of the legate, where, in the Sala Urbana, we find the same version of his coat of arms.[34]

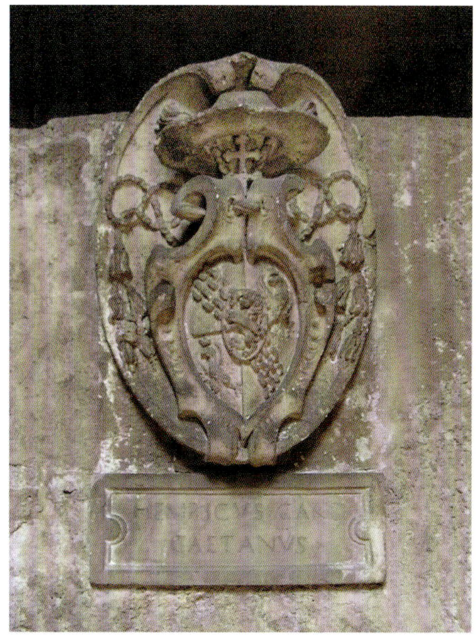

7

FIG. 7. Coat of arms of Cardinal Enrico Caetani, south courtyard (formerly on the facade). Santa Pudenziana, Rome.

During the most critical moment in the religious wars in France and the dynastic crisis (culminating in the assassination of Henry III in August 1589), in September 1589, Sixtus V entrusted to Cardinal Enrico the role of legate at the French court. This prestigious mission, however, resulted in a failure, on both a political and a financial level—a very critical situation for the family that was definitively overcome only after the death of Pope Sixtus V (August 27, 1590) and the return of the cardinal to Rome.

Enrico Caetani and his retinue arrived in Paris in January 1590. In March, the delegation remained trapped inside the city during a siege laid by the king of Navarre, and it was only in early September that they managed to return to Rome. Traditionally, being legate involved considerable expenses, which quite often were not entirely covered by the funds provided by the pope. In this case, the situation was made worse by the conspicuous military expenditures required to help repel the siege. On a political level, in an extremely intricate situation, Enrico Caetani interpreted the instructions of the pope in too rigid a fashion, also due to his connections with the Spanish crown, failing to take into account the different orientations within the French Catholic faction, and was unable to exercise an effective diplomatic action. This lack of flexibility was probably also a result of the influence of the Jesuit Roberto Bellarmino, theological adviser to the legate, who firmly opposed any conciliatory policy.[35] The final result was a break with Pope Sixtus V, who recalled the cardinal. The conflict extended to the Jesuits who defended the legate (and Bellarmino) against the pope's ambivalent policy, which seemed increasingly oriented toward acknowledging Navarre as the new king of France. We know about this also from a letter from Giovanni Niccolini, the Medici ambassador in Rome, to Grand Duke Ferdinando, dated June 9, 1590, which reports a conversation between Pope Sixtus and François de Luxembourg, who had arrived in Rome to defend the position of the French Catholic aristocrats who had sided with Henry of Bourbon.[36] According to Niccolini, Luxembourg complained that the pope allowed the Jesuits to "publicly preach in Rome and in the church of the Gesù, as they had done on Sunday, and praise the acts committed by the legate in Paris against the heretics; where they arrived at saying that Gaetano, besides the actions done in service of the Catholic faith, had spent all he could and risked his life against the heretics in imitation of the martyrs, which turned the noses of everyone."[37]

While the bitter conflict was resolved only with the death of Sixtus V, the connection of the Caetani with the Jesuits and, in particular, the rhetoric of the cardinal's "martyrdom" left a trace in the decoration of the Caetani Chapel. The narration in images of this subject was a result of the Jesuits' patronage, as is also the case for the martyrology painted by Niccolò Circignani around 1582 in the church of Santo Stefano Rotondo, but also likely influenced by the history of the martyrs (*Trattato de gli instrumenti del martirio*), published in 1591 by the Oratorian Antonio Gallonio.[38]

The above survey offers a better understanding of the context in which the decision to build the chapel was made. However, besides the motives and goals of the patrons, one should also keep in mind the institutional role of the family and the important positions of the two cardinals, Nicola first and then Enrico, and of other figures, notably the secretary Giovan Francesco Peranda (ca. 1529–1602/1612), a man who, behind the curtains, played an important supporting role in the activities of the two prelates.[39] Peranda's letters (published and unpublished) clearly evidence his role as adviser, in particular during Cardinal Enrico's missions to Bologna and Paris as papal legate, a period during which Peranda worked to ensure that Enrico's absence from the Roman court did not damage the family. Of course, the use of letters as historical sources requires caution on account of the semipublic character of correspondence during that period; furthermore, it is evident that any correspondence, the more so when published by its author, as in this case, is meant to extol the virtues of the author and as such must be carefully weighed.

Peranda began working as secretary and member of the Curia in 1561, serving Francesco Gonzaga (1538–1566) when the latter became cardinal; the young cardinal died in January 1566, during the conclave, and in May of that year, Peranda became a trusted collaborator of Cardinal Nicola Caetani, whose family he continued to serve throughout his life.[40] Peranda's previous relations with the Gonzaga and Mantua are reflected in his relations with artists and his role as adviser in this specific area.[41]

Peranda possibly also played such a role in the decorating of the Caetani Chapel, although up to now, no definitive evidence of this has been found.[42] As noted by Gelasio Caetani, around 1575, Peranda supervised the pictorial decoration of Palazzo di Cisterna, as shown by his correspondence with the French architect and engraver Etienne Dupérac.[43] According to the *Domus Caietana*, Peranda was involved in the system of recommendations that was a necessary step in the recruiting of any artist. His role is evident, for example, in a letter to him from the sculptor Silla Longhi, dated August 11, 1577, discovered by Laura Gori, in which Longhi asks Peranda to help him obtain from Cardinal Luigi d'Este the commission for the tomb of Ippolito, by speaking in his favor to Nicola Caetani and having the latter recommend him to Cardinal Luigi.[44]

A few years later, around 1578, the secretary also played a part in the planning of the funerary monument for Nicola Caetani in Loreto, mediating the relations with various artists and selecting the final project; this emerges clearly from a well-known letter sent by Peranda to the architect Francesco Capriani da Volterra.[45] Here, after paying his respects to "Your Madonna Diana" (Diana Scultori [1547–1612], Francesco's wife and a member of a famous family of Mantuan engravers), he turns to business. "From Loreto," Peranda continues, "came another drawing by N. [Boccalini] for the tomb of Signor Cardinale, the said drawing being in my possession, of which I shall not give you my opinion, because when we are together you will judge it yourself and with better competence: it is very similar to the first, and where it differs it does not bear invention deserving praise and in truth the poverty of the author and the sterility of his genius is well known, and is not helped in any way by technique or scrupulousness."[46] The issue was the funerary monument that Nicola Caetani had ordered for the sanctuary of Loreto. The two projects mentioned are those presented by the architect of the Santa Casa, Giovanni Boccalini (ca. 1520–1580). As one can see, the artist was very severely judged: lacking in invention, arid in ornament, and incapable of following the rules of architecture.[47] This condemnation is followed in the letter by a request for precise information on an architectural plan for the project. The intent of the letter seems clearly to entrust the project to Capriani instead, as indeed was the case in the end.

Another trait of Peranda was his interest in classical antiquity, which in a letter to Camillo Caetani he justifies in terms that are fully in line with Counter-Reformation culture: "I beg you be so kind as to take pity on this infirmity of mine, if the study of ancient things is indeed an infirmity, when it is applied to the Christian goal and reinforces it. Our very Holy See has surpassed through humility the temporal power of all the world, and it is therefore useful to obtain information on these things, which in other times were worldly great."[48]

The idea that the study of antiquity could be "applied to the Christian goal" seems to me to be echoed in the decoration of the Caetani Chapel, at once Christian and antiquarian, as, for example, in the case of the marble inlays, which had a very long tradition in Rome. In practice, the antiquarian and Christian perspectives often overlap and are difficult to distinguish. Peranda's identity as an erudite antiquarian is further complicated by his role as collector and merchant, as client and purveyor. This complexity, discussed by Laura Gori, emerges also in his relation with the Caetani, to whom he sold his own collection (1591) and for whom he served as intermediary in the purchasing of precious marbles and also in a business he set up with Giovan Battista Della Porta, author of the marble encrustation in the chapel of Santa Pudenziana, for the purpose of extracting ancient marbles and statues and selling them on the market.[49] On the other hand, this diversification was not entirely unusual, as suggested by the case of Diomede Leoni, for example, who in the previous two decades had also engaged in similarly diversified activities.[50]

Stuccos and Mosaics

Let us return to the chapel and its decoration. One of its outstanding characteristics is the way in which the stones, the shiny surfaces of the marble statues and colored marbles, and the tesserae of the mosaics all contribute to produce an overall effect of precious luminosity, in which even the opaque stucco is enlivened and turned into a reflecting surface by the gilded leaves that adorn it. It is an artistic whole, which, only for practical purposes, will be discussed according to media and chronology.

The stucco vault, as we have seen, was first made by Fuccari and Boncivino. Already at a first glance, one discerns an evident relation with the decoration of the Orsini Chapel in Trinità dei Monti, begun around 1575 but finished about twenty-five years later. This relation has, in fact, already been noted and is easily explained by the identity of the clients: Onorato, Enrico, and Camillo Caetani were the grandsons of the commissioner of the chapel, Cecilia Orsini.[51] When we examine the Caetani Chapel in more detail, it becomes evident how its stucco decorations—a technique that enjoyed an extraordinary success and diffusion—are influenced by the post-Raphaelesque and Farnesian tradition, a fact that can in turn be explained by the relations between the Caetani and the Farnese.[52]

On the other hand, unlike in the Orsini Chapel, the vault and walls of the Caetani Chapel are adorned by mosaics. Besides aesthetic reasons, the decision to revive this ancient technique was certainly also the result of the availability of the materials (vitreous paste tesserae) and specialized artisans, due to the work being done in the Gregorian Chapel in St. Peter's and the establishing of the Vatican Studio del Mosaico during the Boncompagni papacy.[53] There is no doubt, however, that in Santa Pudenziana, the use of mosaic was also motivated by the presence of the great fifth-century mosaic in the apse, which had mostly survived the renovation of the church, although Enrico certainly intervened to order additions to it, most notably the heraldic ornament on the left post of the throne.[54] It seems evident, in other words, that the mosaic on the vault and on parts of the walls of the chapel is the result of the antiquarian taste that permeates the entire environment. What Steven F. Ostrow wrote about the marble revetment in the Sistine Chapel in the Basilica Liberiana, that it endowed the space with the character of a reliquary, applies as well to the Caetani Chapel, in which the ornamentation also serves to exalt its role as a liturgical space.[55]

After the stuccos were finished, the great mosaics were entrusted to Paolo Rossetti,[56] who, as mentioned earlier, based them on the drawings by Cristoforo Roncalli. The cartoons mentioned in the ledger seem to have been lost. When I published the payments in the ledger, I overlooked an important article by David McTavish,[57] in which the author discusses a drawing now in Rennes picturing *Saint Mark* (FIG. 8), reiterating its attribution to Federico Zuccari. McTavish's argument is based on an old inscription and goes counter to authoritative modern scholars who tend toward an attribution to Correggio.[58] The reason for this radical change in attribution lies in the iconographic relationship between the drawing and the mosaic of the same subject in the vault of the Caetani Chapel (FIG. 9). The correspondence between the Rennes drawing and the mosaic noted by McTavish is certainly striking. Furthermore, the presence of the grid in the drawing indicates that it was meant to be copied and expanded, consistent with traditional mosaic practice. There are a few differences between the drawing and the mosaic: in the *rotulo* in the right hand of the Evangelist, in the posture of the lion, and, above all, in the relationship between the visage of Saint Mark and the lion, his symbolic animal—in the drawing, the two look at each other, creating an intense psychological rapport, whereas in the mosaic, they both have their faces turned toward the viewer. These variances, perhaps introduced by Rossetti, suggest the possibility of intermediate stages between the drawing and the mosaic. They are also proof that the drawing was not derived from the mosaic. Starting from these elements and taking into consideration the Perinesque echoes of the invention and, above all, the testimony of Baglione, who attributed the cartoons for the mosaics to Federico Zuccari, McTavish also attributed the *Saint Mark* in Rennes to Zuccari or, alternatively, to Rossetti. On the other hand, the fact that the payments for the cartoons of the mosaics in the Caetani Chapel were made to Cristoforo Roncalli raises a major question about this hypothesis, making it more likely that the author of the Rennes drawing was Roncalli, as hypothesized by Laura Gori.[59] The critically problematic history of the drawing (whose attribution to Federico Zuccari, an artist with a well-defined style, has been questioned by John Gere) certainly invites caution, something that, in any case, McTavish himself seemed well aware of.[60]

Nevertheless, Roncalli's style seems clear from the close study of the mosaics.[61] The use of putty, a material characterized by a longer setting time than mortar, offered more control over the inclination of the tesserae and therefore over the way they reflect the light. In the head of *Saint Luke* (FIGS. 10–11), one notices a profoundly pictorial interpretation of mosaic technique and an "impressionist" use of color, evident, for example, in the yellow overtones around the head of the Evangelist, which suggests the vibrant drawing and colors of Roncalli, inspired by the acid and spirited colors of the pictorial tradition of Siena.

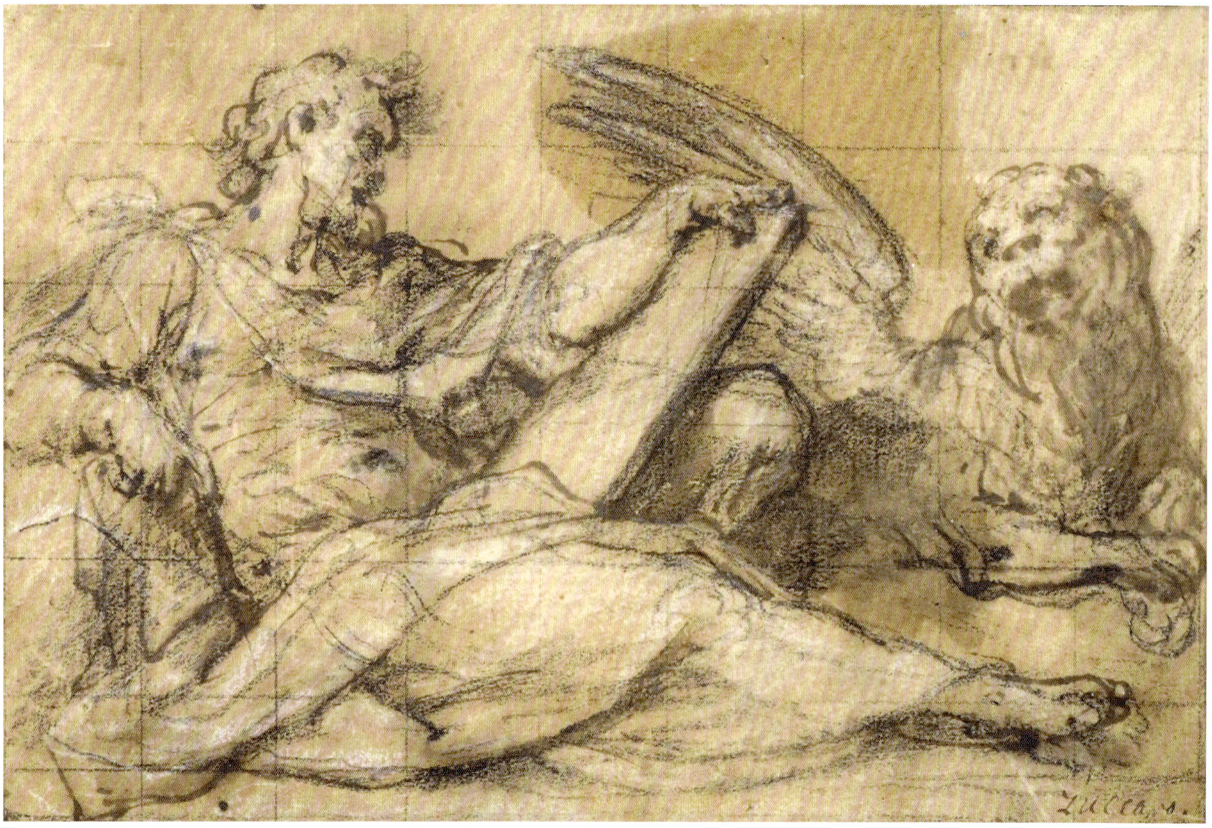

8

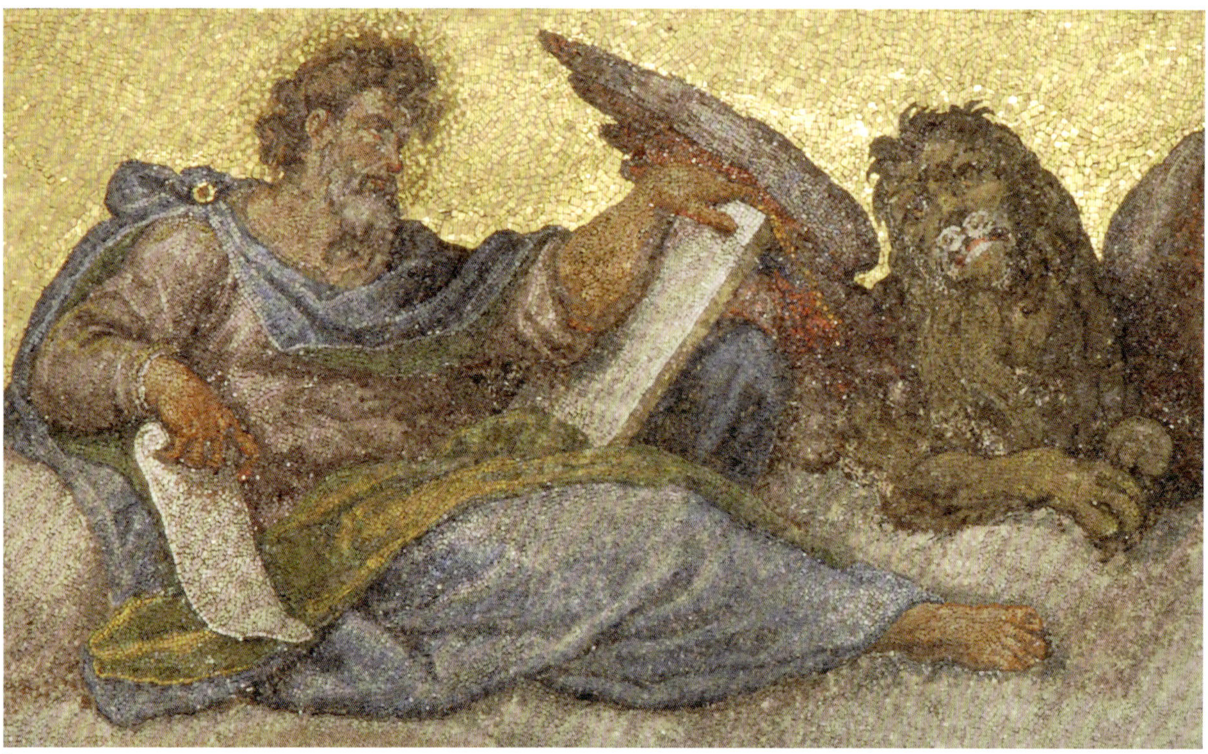

9

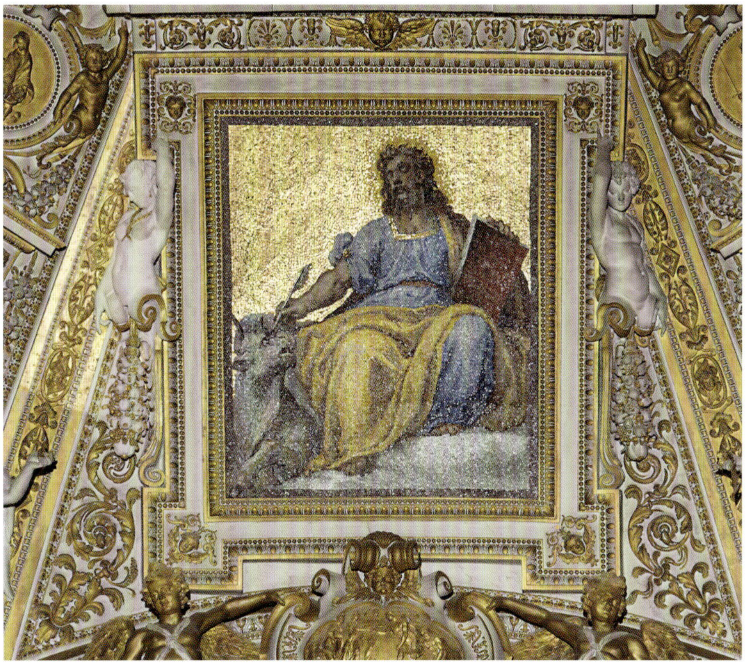

10

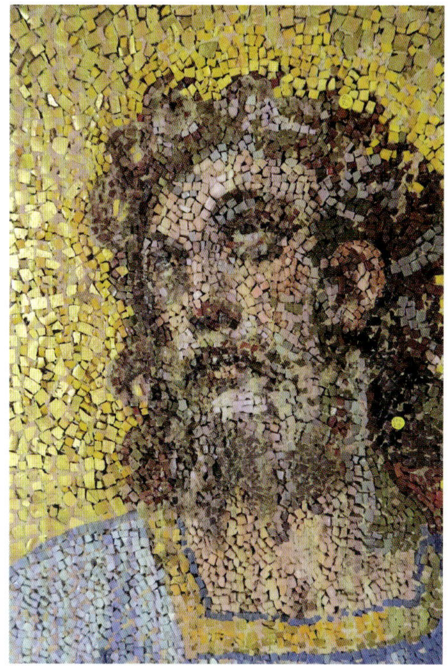

11

The Colors of the Marbles

Marble inlaid decorations were extensively used in the chapel and are one of its distinctive traits. I will consider here only the first phase of the decoration (ending in 1603), which was certainly the most significant one. This phase was entrusted, as already noted, to Giovan Battista Della Porta and his workshop, possibly in collaboration with Silla Longhi.[62] We have already noted the immediate precedents for these decorative choices, namely, three important papal chapels: the Gregorian in St. Peter's, the Sistine in Santa Maria Maggiore, and the Aldobrandini in the Minerva. This list has been expanded by studies of the last few decades, which have brought to light other antecedents, less illustrious, perhaps, but certainly significant.[63] In my opinion, there are yet more references that can be tangentially added to this main group. We can start with the Mignanelli Chapel in Santa Maria della Pace and the funerary monument to the Venetian Cardinal Francesco Pisani in San Marco. In the Mignanelli Chapel, completed in 1576–1577, the ornamental marble cladding (FIG. 12) adopts a very simple and almost austere geometrical pattern, which seems foreign to the Roman tradition. Recently, Andrea Donati has suggested a relationship to the Cavalcanti Chapel in Santo Spirito in Florence, designed around 1560 by Antonio Dosio.[64] The funerary monument to Pisani by the Lombard stonemason Giovanni Marchesi da Saltrio (FIG. 13) was finished by 1571.[65] In the context of a (micro) architecture with evident Michelangelesque overtones, the opulence of the rare colored marbles is disciplined by the geometrical minimalism of the design. In regard to these echoes, one should note that the altarpiece in the Mignanelli Chapel was commissioned to the painter Marcello Venusti, a faithful follower of Michelangelo; in the case of the Pisani monument, instead, not only do we have evidence that Giovanni Marchesi da Saltrio was involved in the building of the monument for Julius II in San Pietro

FIG. 8. Cristoforo Roncalli, *Saint Mark*, end of the sixteenth century. Musée des Beaux Arts, Rennes.

FIG. 9. Paolo Rossetti after cartoon by Cristoforo Roncalli, *Saint Mark*, mosaic of the vault, 1591–1597. Caetani Chapel, Santa Pudenziana, Rome.

FIG. 10. Paolo Rossetti after cartoon by Cristoforo Roncalli, *Saint Luke*, mosaic of the vault, 1591–1597. Caetani Chapel, Santa Pudenziana, Rome.

FIG. 11. Paolo Rossetti after cartoon by Cristoforo Roncalli, *Saint Luke* (detail), mosaic of the vault, 1591–1597. Caetani Chapel, Santa Pudenziana, Rome.

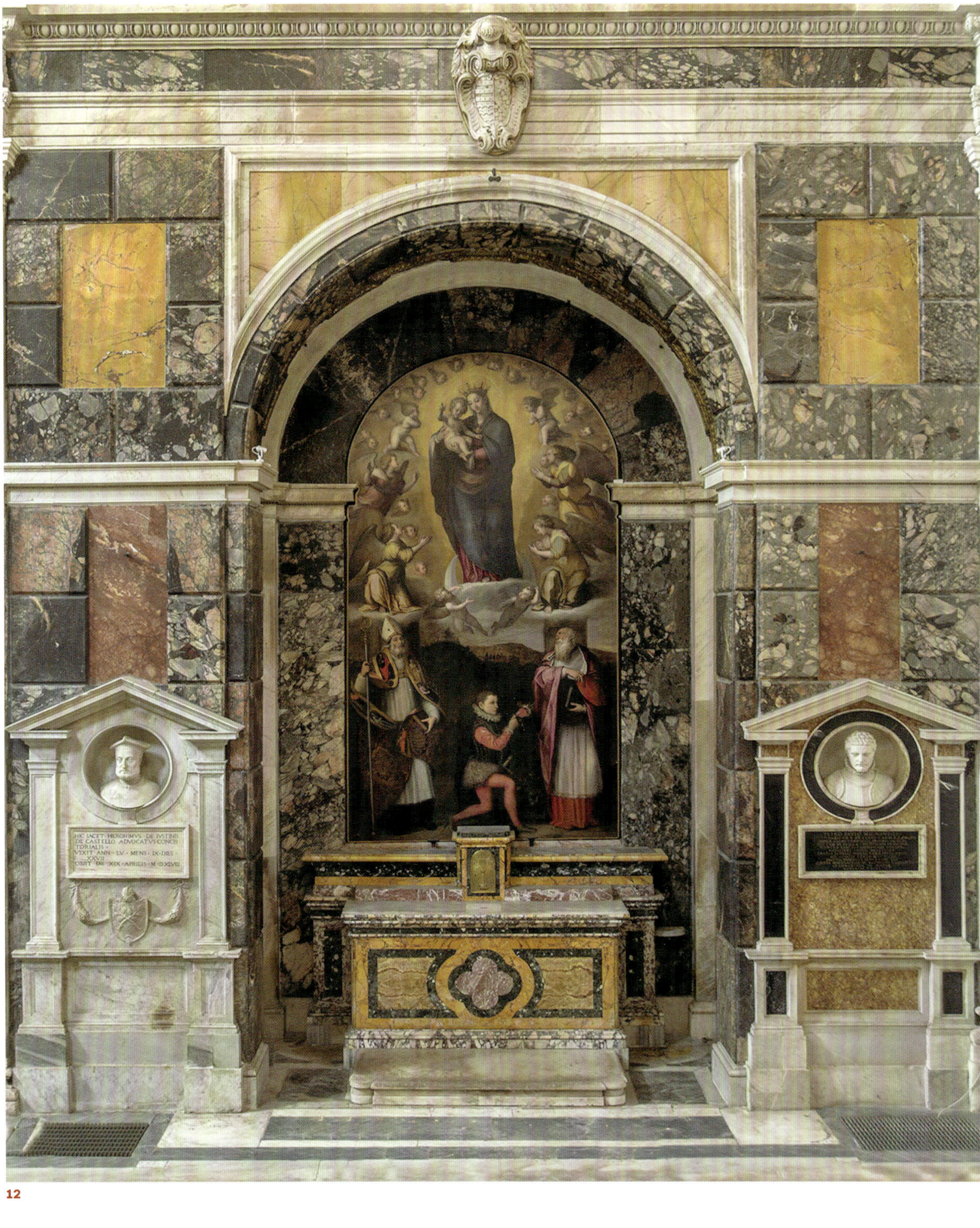

12

in Vincoli, but we also know that Diomede Leoni, too, worked on the Pisani monument. Leoni was also tied to the Michelangelo circle, besides being on the payroll of Cardinal Pisani, and was known to be involved in the commerce of antiquities and ancient marbles. He might also have had connections with the Mignanelli family, since he was from Siena like them, although at the moment, we lack the hard evidence to support this hypothesis.

The opulence of the Caetani Chapel, which was unanimously acknowledged from the start, is to a significant extent the result of the marble inlays, which were mostly the work of Giovan Battista Della Porta.[66] The traditional motifs are subject to a sophisticated *variatio*, also chromatic, made more effective by the insertion of precious and rare materials. Even before it became the subject of modern studies on marble incrustation, this characteristic had been already noted by the erudite Giovanni Antonio Bruzio, who writes: "From the cornice going down, the walls are covered with fine Oriental marbles, most of them extremely rare." In another passage, Bruzio remembers, almost enthusiastically, the two columns on the side of the altar, "of Oriental *pidocchioso*, possibly the only ones in Rome." He goes on to list the different types of marble adorning the walls of the chapel: *alabastro cotognino* (Egyptian alabaster), Chios marble ("vulgarly known as *portasanta*"), and *diasprata* breccia.[67]

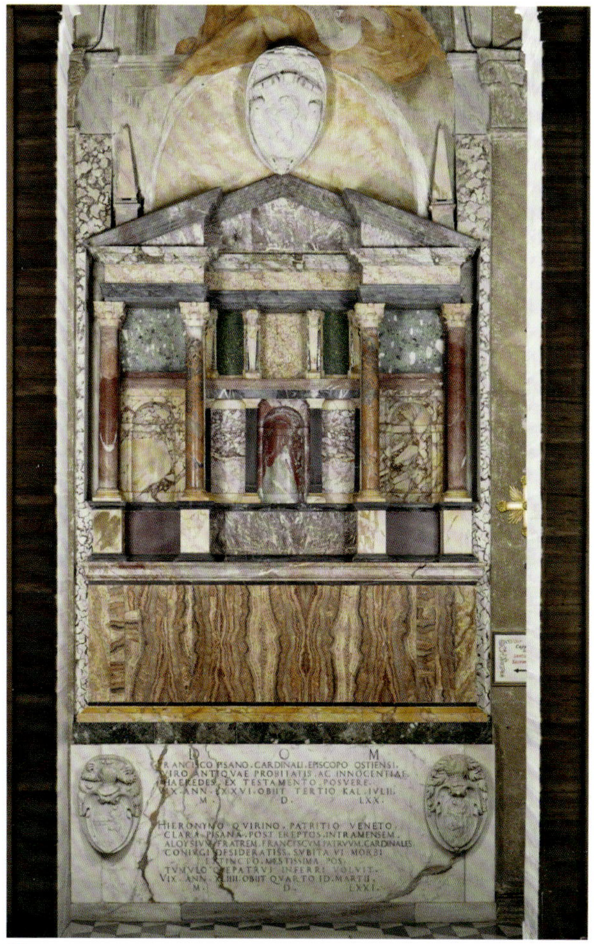

13

Bruzio then comments on a series of sophisticated details: the pair of pod-design vases in the small apse (**FIG. 6**) on the *broccatello trompe-l'oeil* slabs with the low-relief of the blood-dripping sponge, the blood made with pieces of *rosso antico* marble, and the heraldic eagles, also in low-relief. He also notes marginal details such as the "base of red stone inlaid with white marble" in the plinth of the columns of the altar.[68] And the presence in the chapel of a breccia so rare that it came to be known as *breccia dei Caetani* is cited in nineteenth-century studies and has been further explored by Raniero Gnoli.[69]

The rarity of the materials raises the question of Peranda's ambivalent role as a collector and purveyor of marbles, which emerges also from the accounts of the Caetani, studied by Laura Gori,[70] and returns us to the aesthetic decisions made by Giovan Battista Della Porta. The Caetani Chapel was an important step in the evolution of the marble inlay tradition in Rome and served as a model, at least in the years immediately after it was built. The novelty was the deliberate use of models taken from late antiquity, sometimes integrated with trompe l'oeil details possibly inspired by painting, such as the low-relief drapes, which seem to merge material reality with art. In this category fall also the alabaster shields with mother-of-pearl, lapislazuli and *rosso antico* marble inlays (**FIG. 14**), the panels in black Africano marble with, at the top, a motif that

FIG. 12. Mignanelli Chapel, ca. 1570–1580. Santa Maria della Pace, Rome.

FIG. 13. Giovanni Marchesi da Saltrio, Funerary monument of Francesco Pisani, 1571. San Marco (right aisle), Rome.

transfigures in a striking fashion the shell-shaped niches and, below, the eel-shaped design, which subtly evokes the rippling frieze of the Caetani heraldry.

The marble inlay is applied in a fashion that one may call mimetic and naturalistic, and it is precisely this aspect that helps integrate it with the iconography of the chapel. The most evident examples are the pod-design vases, eloquent emblems of Saint Pudentiana and of the tradition of martyrdom evoked in the chapel (FIG. 6). To these we can add the *arma Christi* (FIG. 15), significantly positioned on the short sides of the chapel, where they are visually connected with the altar. Here the backdrop in black Africano marble with white veining evokes the nocturnal, stormy, tragic sense of the Crucifixion, anticipating the seventeenth-century "figurative" use of marble, exemplified, for example, by the lapis-lazuli sky framing the *Salus Populi Romani* in the Borghese Chapel in Santa Maria Maggiore.[71] The stories of the Passion and of the sacrifice of the martyrs are almost condensed here, following a procedure analogous to that of *emblemata*. The dialogue between the classical tradition and the Christian imagination, the "study of ancient things ... applied to the Christian goal," in the words of Peranda, is here marvelously expressed. The theme evokes the birth of Christianity, to which the basilica of Santa Pudenziana is a material testimony, and also the biography of Enrico Caetani, defender of the Catholic faith and "martyr" in France.

The discussion of the marbles must necessarily also take into account their ceremonial and liturgical significance. This is evident, for example, in the use of porphyry or in the mimetic relationship between blood and *pavonazzetto* marble, with its violet stains. Fabio Barry's essay in this volume offers interesting suggestions in this direction.[72] The interpretation of the Gregorian Chapel in two apologetic texts published in 1582 and 1583 provides some insights into the meaning of the use of marble encrustation in the Caetani Chapel. For Lorenzo Frizolio, the description of the marbles in the Vatican chapel interweaves with theological aspects, while Ascanio Valentino compares the chapel ordered by the Boncompagni pope with Hagia Sophia in Constantinople, suggesting an anagogic interpretation of the marble decorations.[73] We should be wary, however, of reading too much into the marbles beyond the traditional conceptual association between rare and precious materials and the sacred.

The Sculptures

The high-relief sculptures and sculptures in the round are prominent in the chapel's decoration. In the first phase of the project, the busts of Enrico and Camillo Caetani commemorate the founders, and the monumental marble altarpiece plays a central role.[74]

The latter (FIG. 2), as we have noted, is the visual focus of the chapel and its most outstanding element. It combines high- and low-relief elements, plastic but also pictorial aspects. This monumental work, consisting of three large blocks horizontally arranged on top of one another, has been rightly considered a milestone in the Roman history of the genre, which had significant development in the seventeenth century, as attested by works such as the famous *Meeting of Leo the Great and Attila* by Algardi in St. Peter's and the *Ecstasy of St. Francis* in Bernini's Raimondi Chapel in San Pietro in Montorio.[75] As for the immediate antecedents of the altarpiece of the Caetani Chapel, these include the

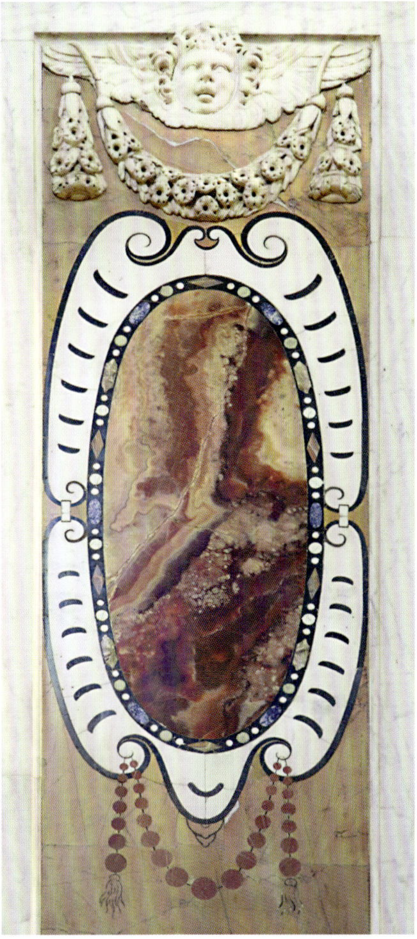

14

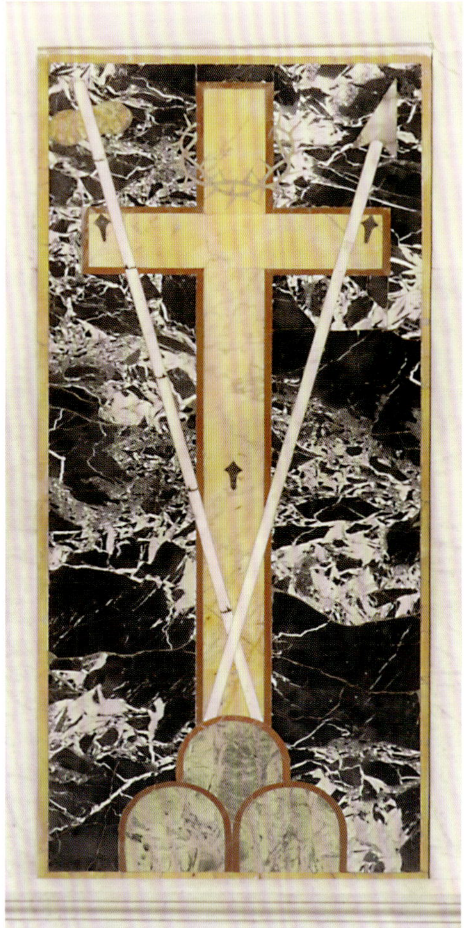

15

historical relief on the monument to Gregory XI in Santa Maria Nova, sculpted by Olivieri (completed in 1589), and the great reliefs on the papal tombs in the Sistine Chapel in Santa Maria Maggiore, where Olivieri worked in those same years.

We noted the connection between the *Adoration of the Magi* in Santa Pudenziana and that made by Arnolfo di Cambio in the Liberian basilica, as suggested by Möller. The similarity can also be seen as an expression of "servitude" from Enrico Caetani to Pope Sixtus V. There is an even more evident connection in the case of the *Madonna and Child*, attributed to Olivieri, that was added to Arnolfo's sculpted group in the late sixteenth century, a work that is clearly echoed in the altarpiece of the Caetani Chapel. However, the hypothesis of an homage to the pope is problematized by the dating of the altarpiece, which was commissioned to Olivieri after the break between the Sixtus V and Cardinal Enrico Caetani (the first payment being dated 1596).[76] One can speculate that the subject of the altarpiece, which depends on the dedication of the chapel, could not evidently be changed at this stage, despite the relations between the two parties.

In regard to the reliefs in the Sistine Chapel and on the monument to Gregory XI in Santa Maria Nova, it should be noted that none of them is an al-

FIG. 14. Giovan Battista Della Porta and workshop, Decorative escutcheon, ca. 1594–1600. Caetani Chapel, Santa Pudenziana, Rome.

FIG. 15. Giovan Battista Della Porta and workshop, *Arma Christi*, ca. 1594–1600. Caetani Chapel, Santa Pudenziana, Rome.

tarpiece, and the latter is not only smaller than the one in Santa Pudenziana, but it also conspicuously lacks the bold plasticity of the Caetani relief. If we look to Naples, however, we find that marble altarpieces had a much longer tradition there, as noted by Vasari in his biography of Girolamo Santacroce. The historian writes that in Naples, "it is very much the custom to make chapels and altarpieces of marble," and examples dating to the sixteenth century are indeed common in Naples and in Campania in general.[77] The possibility that the Caetani, historically tied to the Kingdom and Vice Kingdom of Naples, might have decided to model their altarpiece on a genre common in the southern city can be explained in terms of the artistic exchanges between the Roman and Neapolitan "schools," as well as the traveling habits of the clients, who, in following the Neapolitan taste, may have also been influenced by nonaesthetic criteria. After all, as is well known, the theme of the *Adoration* of Santa Pudenziana is not simply the Epiphany. As mentioned above, Gelasio Caetani saw the depiction of the sea with the indented coastline and the two ships in the background as an allusion to Caetani estates and possibly to their victorious military deeds, a triumphal element echoed in the relief by the spread eagle with the laurel wreath in its talons, dominating the entire scene from above.[78]

At the end of this long journey through the chapel of the lords of Sermoneta, a number of questions remain inevitably open, which would require further investigation. Nevertheless, it is clear how the political and family history and the combination of factors outlined above left their mark on the extremely sophisticated decorations in the chapel, in which aesthetic criteria combine with ideological and political ones, celebrating the Caetani family and promoting their future memory.

Notes

I warmly thank Chiara Franceschini, Steven F. Ostrow, and Patrizia Tosini for inviting me to join the panel at Chicago RSA (2017) and then to write this contribution, which is an expanded version of the paper presented in Chicago, improved by the comments and the discussion I have benefited from during the panel and by the editors' careful reading. Many thanks to Maria Beltramini and Giulio Archinà for the Mignanelli's Chapel photograph.

1 — Felini 1600, I, 95: "Henrico Cardinal Caetano Titolare di questa [Santa Pudenziana] la rinovò del tutto non sparagnando à spesa alcuna, facendovi una cappella tanto nobile & magnifica, tenuta delle più belle di Roma, la quale ha più dell'Imperiale che del Cardinalicio." On Felini (1565–1613), see Ceresa 1996. The magnificent aspect of the Caetani Chapel at Santa Pudenziana was already noted by Ugonio 1588, 163r. Baglione (1642, 76): "ricchissima cappella" (lavish chapel). Martinelli (1653, 289): "spectabilem ornatissimamque capellam" (worthy and very ornate chapel).

2 — Del Riccio 1597 [1996], 179, 186 (quoted from Gori 2012, 263): "chi andrà a Roma vedrà tutte le sorti pietre nelle gran fabbriche, che si maraviglierà, e particularmente nella gran cappella che fece fare la Santa memoria di Papa Gregorio XIII, così come in quella che fece fare Papa Sisto V in Santa Maria Maggiore e molt'altre cappelle che son fatte nelle chiese di Roma, come alla Potenziana ed in altri tempii della città che oggi dì si fanno . . . ma chi si vuol saziare e vedere bei alabastri insieme con una infinità di pietre rare e belle, vadi alla città di Roma per tutti i palazzi e casamenti, ma in particulare in San Pietro, nella Gregoriana ed in Santa Maria Maggiore ed alla Potenziana e nelli altri tempii di Roma" ("whoever will visit Rome will see all sorts of stones in the majestic edifices being built, that he will be astonished, and in particular in the huge chapel that was built in the sacred memory of Pope Gregory XIII, as well as the one which Sixtus V had built at Santa Maria Maggiore, and many other chapels which are now under construction . . . but whoever wants to satisfy his appetite and see beautiful alabasters together with plenty of rare stones shall go to Rome into every palace and building, but in particular in St. Peter's in the Gregoriana and in Santa Maria Maggiore and in Santa Pudenziana, and in the other temples of Rome"). Since del Riccio's *Istoria delle pietre* was written in 1597, the author could have seen or received information on the Caetani Chapel when its decoration was not yet completed. On late-sixteenth-century Roman chapel marble decorations, see Ostrow 1990;

Sénécal 1995; Möller 2018; and Fabio Barry's chapter in this volume.

3 — The altarpiece is now located in San Tommaso in Formis (Rome). See Toesca 1965, 87; Hunter 1983a, 44–45, figs. 30, 31, nn. 112–114; Hunter 1983b, 366–374, 533; Pugliatti 1983, 105, fig. 30, n. 36; Hunter 1996, 188–191, cat. no. 35, fig. 91; Rice 1997, 22, 233, nn. 12, 32.

4 — In addition to the previous notes, on the Caetani Chapel, see Biblioteca Apostolica Vaticana (BAV), G. A. Bruzio, Vat. lat. 11886, fols. 171r–73r (new printed numbering), quoted from Hülsen 1927 [2000], 452; Felini 1600, I, 95 (and subsequent editions); Celio 1638 [1967], 81–83, nn. 243, 244; Baglione 1642, 76, 114, 170; Martinelli 1644, 80; Ugurgieri Azzolini 1649, II, 368; Titi 1674–1763 [1987], 42; Posterla 1707, 656–657; Pascoli 1730–1736 [1992], 850, n. 11; Caetani 1933, II, 325–327; Riccoboni 1942, 100; Montini 1960, 32–36, 78–81; Vanmaele 1965, 70–73, 124–134; Gnoli 1971, 216–217; Hibbard 2001, 147; Cozzi Beccarini 1976; Barroero 1984, 140; Borghini 1989, 5, 145, 161, 164, 183, 194; Gnoli 1989, 15; Napoleone 1989, 104, n. 44; Tuena 1989b, 92, n. 51; Marcucci 1991, 180–186; Di Castro 1994, 22, figs. 51–53; Ferrari 1996; Del Riccio 1597 [1996], pl. XLVIII–XLIX; Ferrari and Papaldo 1999, 382–386; Marcucci 1999, 501–502, 506, 517–518; Aurigemma 2004, 198–199, figs. 16–23; Gori 2007; McTavish 2008; Trivellone 2007, 318–319 and notes; De Lotto 2009, 178–179; Parlato 2009, 148–155; Angelelli 2010, 306, 309–311, 315; Gori 2011, 102–103; Gori 2012; Ioele 2012, 157–158; Gori 2016; Braconi 2016, 36–38; Ioele 2016, 58–61, 227–231, cat. no. 20, figs. 48–52; Antonucci 2018.

5 — Panvinio 1570, 341–342; Ugonio 1588, 165v: "ai piedi dell'altare … di due cratelle di ferro che hanno sotto, in su la pietra segnati certi circoletti, i quali segni è fama che siano fatti cadendo l'hostia sacra di mano ad un Sacerdote che al detto altare celebrava."

6 — The signature, located under the kneeling Magus, reads: "PETRI PAVLI OLIVERII ROMANI OPVS."

7 — The stained-glass window above the altar bears the date 1951, but it replaces an older one. G. A. Bruzio (ca. 1668, BAV, Vat. lat. 11886, fol. 173r) describes this section of the chapel as follows: "Sopra il frontespizio una finestra nel cui vetro è dipinto Christo crucifisso col motto di Isaia: *Cuius livore sanati sumus.*" ("Above the pediment there is a window, on whose glass is painted the crucified Christ with Isaias's motto: 'and with his stripes we are healed'" [Isaias 53:5].)

8 — Ibid.: "Sopra i Depositi vi sono le due finestre …: i vetri di esse sono dipinti in uno S. Prassede, nell'altro S. Pudenziana." ("Two windows are located above the tombs …: their stained-glass images representing in one Saint Praxedis, and the other Saint Pudentiana.")

9 — Ibid.: "Storie di San Pietro e di San Pudente … quando San Pietro è ricevuto in casa del detto Santo Senatore, quando lo battezza."

10 — Gelasio Caetani (1933, 326) proposes the identification of the two islands in the background as Ponza and Ventotene.

11 — The eagle with the laurel wreath is unrelated to the iconography of the Adoration of the Magi, being instead an obvious reference to triumph and to the Caetani coat of arms.

12 — Möller 2013, 45.

13 — On Enrico Caetani, see Eubel, van Gulik, and Ritzler 1923, 50; Caetani 1933, II, esp. 189–245; De Caro 1973; Gardi 1985, with bibliography.On the renewal of Santa Pudenziana under the cardinal's tenure, see also Tafuri 1976; Braconi 2015.

14 — *Acta sanctarum Pudentianae et Praxedis*, in *Acta Sanctorum* …, Maii, IV, Antwerp 1685, 299–301; quoted from Scorza Barcellona 2000, 220–221; Ugonio 1588, 160. On St. Peter's Chapel, in particular the sculptures by Giovan Battista Della Porta, see Ioele 2016, 63–65, 231–233, cat. no. 21, figs. 58–59, 61, 63, with bibliography.

15 — The first volume of the *Annales* was published in Rome in 1588, under the pontificate of Sixtus V; the subsequent volumes came to light from 1590 to 1607.

16 — In May 1586, Sixtus V bestowed to this branch of the Cistercian Order the convent of Santa Pudenziana, where the monks resided until the time of the French Revolution.

17 — Ugonio 1588, 162r.

18 — Both the architect and the painter were born near Volterra, and both enjoyed the long-lasting patronage of the Caetani. Baglione (1642, 42) states that at Santa Pudenziana, Niccolò Circignani frescoed the dome and the facade (lost): "In Santa Pudentiana è di suo la facciata di fuori; e di dentro le pitture della cupola in fresco." Later, Circignani worked in Valvisciolo Abbey, a Caetani fief. On the painter, among others, see Cordaro 1981; Aurigemma 2004, 198–200; Galassi 2007; Loisel 2014; Loisel 2015. On Capriani and his relations with the Caetani family, see Tafuri 1976; Marcucci 1991, 23–25, 127–135, 160–169, 180–186; Marcucci 1999.

19 — For the chapel architecture, see Cozzi Beccarini 1976; Marcucci 1991, 180–186. For Maderno's contribution, see Hibbard 2001, 147.

20 — On Fuccari (or Fuccheri, or Furcheri), documented in Rome from 1585 to 1615, see Lombardi 1993; Pupillo 1998.

21 — On the drawings by Roncalli (and not by Federico Zuccari, as believed for a long time), see the independent findings by Gori 2007, 87–88; Parlato 2009, 154–155, n. 63.

22 — On Giovan Battista Della Porta, see Ioele 2016, 61, 227–231, cat. no. 20. On Valsoldino (c. 1558–1646), see Di Giammaria 2012; Di Giammaria 2014; Grandolfo 2014. On Bastiano Torrigiani (documented 1577–1596), see Petraroia 1993; Lamouche 2012; Ostrow 2015.

23 — Posterla 1707, 657: "L'anno 1668, il Duca Francesco Gaetano lastricolla vagamente con marmi fini intersiati, e vi aprì sotto d'essa il Cemeterio per i Defonti di questa Famiglia." For the works commissioned by Francesco Caetani, the date 1668 is also written on an epigraph on the floor; see Angelelli 2010, 315, n. 148.

24 — On the basis of the comparison with the pavement of the Spada Chapel (Santa Maria in Vallicella, Rome) (Ferrari 1996, 79).

25 — Ferrari (1996, 78) proposes this attribution; he also remarks that the chivalric insignia reiterates the family's Spanish affiliation.

26 — Titi (1674–1763 [1987], 42) was the first to mention the authorship of Adamo Lorenese, Vincenzo Mari, and Carlo Malavista. On this question, see the important contributions in Ferrari 1996; Ferrari and Papaldo 1999, 382–386.

27 — Bruzio, BAV, Vat. lat. 11886, fol. 173r: "Il Deposito incontro non ha iscrizione alcuna ancora che dopo il Card. Henrico sono morti tre cardinali di questa nobilissima famiglia."

28 — The Caetani titular cardinals of Santa Pudenziana were Bonifacio (1607–1617), Antonio (1621–1623), and Luigi (1626–1642). They were all buried in this chapel. See Eubel et al. 1935, 10, no. 7, nn. 9–10; 16, nn. 3–4,;17, n. 1; 19, no. 5, n. 1; 49, n. 4; Vanmaele 1965, 76. Felini 1600, I, 95: "ha più dell'Imperiale che del Cardinalicio."

29 — On the historical context, see Caetani 1933, II, esp. 136–163; De Caro 1973; Gardi 1985; Gori 2014.

30 — Visceglia (2001, 201) has pointed out the nonexclusively economic dynamics of an aristocratic coterie.

31 — In a letter addressed on November 11 to Enrico and Camillo Caetani, Giovan Francesco Peranda lists the furnishings for Marcantonio Colonna's triumph, a ceremony attended also by Onorato. Later, Peranda describes the celebrations for Onorato held in Rome in January 1573. A comedy was performed, followed by a banquet, a tournament, and a ball. Peranda 1601, 29–31, 41–42; Caetani 1933, II, 160. For Onorato Caetani's correspondence see also Carinci 1870 [1893].

32 — Among other evidence, the Caetani's new political affiliation emerges from a letter from Cardinal Enrico (but possibly written by Peranda) to Philip II of Spain, immediately after Enrico had been nominated cardinal. Enrico Caetani not only thanks the Spanish ambassador who supported his nomination but also states his compliance, offering to the king his "humilissima servitù, supplicandolo ad accettarla benignamente; et credami che se ben in obedirla non arrivarò né al valor né alle forze del Cardinal mio Zio [Nicola Caetani], non mi trovarà però manco ardente di lui in eseguir i suoi ordini" ("most humble servitude, begging his benevolent reception. Even though in my obedience I will not attain the merit and the strength of the cardinal my uncle [Nicola Caetani], however you will find me as much fervent in executing his highness's orders.") Peranda 1601, 380.

33 — The importance of this advancement emerges in a letter published in Peranda 1601, 249–251.

34 — Originally, the stone coat of arms in Santa Pudenziana was located on the facade. Bruzio reports that three stone escutcheons were located there: those of Sixtus V, of Cardinal Caetani, and of the city of Rome. Bruzio, BAV, Vat. lat. 11886, f. 167r. For the coats of arms in Bologna, see Gardi 1985, figs. 7–8. The water well is located in the second courtyard of the city hall.

35 — For the French legation, see Caetani 1933, II, 189–245; De Caro 1973.

36 — Peranda (1601, 165) labels Luxembourg "Ambasciator de i Prencipi del sangue" ("ambassador of the royal princes").

37 — Canestrini and Desjardin 1875, 5, 133: "Sua Beatitudine comportasse, che in Roma e nella chiesa del Jesu, li preti riformati [i Gesuiti] predicassero publicamente, come fecero domenica, e esaltassino i fatti egregii del legato in Parigi per la difesa delli [but read "dalli"] eretici; dove hanno per sin detto, che Gaetano, oltre all'azioni sue fatte in servizio della fede cattolica, egli spendeva ed aveva speso quello che egli poteva, e esponeva la vita contro gli eretici a imitazione de' martiri, cosa veramente che ha dato nel naso ad ognuno." The ambassador's complaint continues: "soggiungendoli Luxembourg, che la Santità Sua doveva aver l'occhio e non comportare che questi preti cominciassero a parlare di questa maniera; perché piglierebbono tanto ardire che direbbono poi male anco della Santità Sua; e che interverrebbono como quelli della Sorbona, la quale cominciò a poco a poco a voler riprendere quest' e quell'altra cosa, e perché non li fu dato sulle mani dai re, si è ridotta in tanta arroganza, che dice male del re e d'ognuno" ("adding Luxembourg that His Holiness should be careful and not permit these priests to speak in such way: otherwise they will begin to reproach even His Holiness; and they will interfere as those of the Sorbonne, who little by little have begun to dissent on this and that issue, and since they have not had their hands beaten by the king, they have become so arrogant as to speak badly of the king and everyone else"). According to Niccolini's reports, Camillo Caetani on June 22 was confined in his palace, and two preachers who had supported the papal legate were jailed. Canestrini and Desjardin 1875, 5, 139.

38 — The Roman church of Santo Stefano Rotondo was attached to the Jesuit German-Hungarian novitiate. Circignani is also the author of a lost pictorial cycle representing the English martyrs frescoed in 1584 in the church of San Tommaso di Canterbury, immediately reproduced in a series of engravings (Cavalieri 1584). It reminds one of the treatise on martyrdom by the Oratorian Antonio Gallonio, with illustrations by Antonio Tempesta (Gallonio 1591b), and Gallonio (1591a, 72–82), which reconstructs Pudentiana's and Praxedis's *passio*. On this subject, see also Zuccari 2012.

39 — On Peranda, see Caetani 1933, II, esp. 102–109, 285–286; Marcucci 1999, 523–524; Gori 2011; Testa 2015. The first edition of Peranda's correspondence was published in Venice in 1601, when the author was still alive. Thereafter, the correspondence was republished nineteen times until 1647, a literary success that attests to the author's fame. See Peranda 1601; Caetani 1933, II, 109, n. b. The original letters are preserved in Rome at the Archivio Caetani. The Caetani patronage has been studied by Fiorani, Hunter, and Pugliatti 1983; Aurigemma 2004; Fiorani 2007; Amendola 2010; Ioele 2012, 157–161; Ioele 2016.

40 — Caetani 1933, II, 102–109. In the catalog of the Archivio Caetani (AC), there is mention of a letter sent to Peranda on June 30, 1566, in which the latter is described as "segretario del cardinale di Sermoneta" ("secretary of the cardinal from Sermoneta") (AC, *Fondo generale*, 74968). The close relationship between Peranda and Cardinal Nicola is also attested by the prelate's portrait painted by Bartolomeo Cesi (Galleria Spada, Rome). Laura Gori (2011, 104, n. 86) has persuasively identified Peranda in the figure in black standing behind Nicola Caetani.

41 — Laura Marcucci has stressed the significance of Peranda's Gonzaga connection for the Caetani's taste. Also, Francesco Capriani had previously worked for Cesare Gonzaga at Guastalla, where he met Diana Scultori. See Marcucci 1991, 27–68, 341–343; Marcucci 1999, 523–524; Gori 2011, 97–98.

42 — Gori 2011.

43 — Caetani 1933, II, 116–117; Gori 2011, 98–99 and notes; Gori 2012, 266, n. 29; AC, *Fondo generale*, 142098. Also relevant is the connection with Giulio Clovio, also mentioned by Gori 2011, 99.

44 — Gori 2011, 99, n. 36.

45 — Peranda 1601, 105–106. The printed text is undated, but it could have been written around June 1578, based on a letter that Capriani sent to the secretary. AC, *Racc. generale*, 89377, quoted from Tafuri 1976, and partially published in Marcucci 1991, 133, n. 8; Marcucci 1999, 502, n. 5.

46 — "Da Loreto venne un altro disegno del N. [Giovanni Boccalini] per la sepoltura del Signor Cardinale, il qual disegno è appresso di me, non entro a dirvene il mio giudicio, perché quando saremo insieme lo giudicarete voi et con miglior fondamento: ha gran similitudine col primo, et dove è diverso da quella non porta inventione che meriti laude et nel vero si conosce la povertà dell'auttore et la sterilità del suo ingegno, al qual non dà nessun aiuto né l'artificio ne l'osservanza." Peranda 1601, 105; Caetani 1933, II, 172.

47 — Peranda 1601, 105. On Nicola Caetani's monument at Loreto, see Caetani 1933, II, 171–173; Tafuri 1976; Marcucci 1991, 132–135; Gori 2011, 100, fig. 4; Ioele 2012, 157; Coltrinari 2016a, 308–309; Coltrinari 2016b; Ioele 2016, 200–2005, cat. no. 7.
48 — Peranda 1601, 119 (undated): "Io la supplico si degni di compatir questa mia infermità, se però è infermità lo studio delle cose antiche, il qual applicato al fine Christiano edifica esso ancora. La nostra sede Santissima ha superato con la humiltà l'Imperio di tutto il mondo, et perciò è utile l'havere notitia di quelle cose, che altre volte furono mondanamente grandi."
49 — Picozzi 2007; Gori 2011, 100, n. 51.
50 — On Diomede Leoni, see Parlato 2014, 340, n. 79; Sickel 2014, 236, n. 37, with bibliography.
51 — Gori 2012, 267–268; Gori 2016, 97–98; Ioele 2012, 159, n. 75.
52 — Bonifacio Caetani and his brother Nicola were first cousins of Paul III.
53 — Barral Altet and Bertelli 1988, 229–232. For the *Studio vaticano del mosaico*, see Cornini 2012.
54 — For the ancient restorations of the apse mosaic, see Parlato 2009, 146; Braconi 2015, 79–97; Braconi 2016.
55 — Ostrow 1996, 1.
56 — Antonella Pampalone has kindly informed me about her discovery of Rossetti's contract. She will publish it in a forthcoming book in honor of Bishop Edoardo Cerrato.
57 — Parlato 2009, 154, n. 63; McTavish 2008.
58 — Rennes, Musée des Beaux Arts, inv. 794.I.2892, 122 × 183 mm. McTavish 2008, esp. 5, nn. 2–3, with bibliography. The attribution to Correggio was proposed by Gere 1977.
59 — Gori 2012, 272–73, n. 90.
60 — At the end of his article, McTavish (2008, 9) reaffirms the probable attribution to Federico Zuccari, even though he does not exclude a role by Paolo Rossetti, but adds, "it would be wise to remain flexible on a precise attribution of the drawing."
61 — In winter 2016–2017, during the restoration of a section of the chapel's mosaics by the team of Istituto Superiore per la Conservazione e il Restauro, I had the opportunity to see them from the scaffolding. I would like to thank colleague and friend Dora Catalano and staff for their generous help and for sharing their information.
62 — Ioele 2016, 227–231, cat. no. 20.
63 — Gonzáles-Palacios 1988, esp. 45–47; Tuena 1988; Tuena 1989b; Di Castro 1994; Gori 2012, 268; Gori 2016.
64 — I warmly thank Andrea Donati for this information, which he will be publish in his forthcoming catalogue raisonné of Marcello Venusti. Among the chapels with marble incrustations that predate the Caetani, it should be also included the Fonseca Chapel (1584) in S. Giacomo degli Spagnoli in Rome.
65 — Parlato 2014, 338–339, nn. 72–75.
66 — For Della Porta's marble inlays, see Ioele 2016, 44, 47, n. 25, 84–87, 144–149.
67 — Bruzio, BAV, Vat. lat. 11886, 172r–173r.: "Dalla cornice in giù ha le mura ricoperte di marmi fini orientali la maggior parte rarissimi ... di pidocchioso orientale, forse uniche a Roma ... volgarmente chiamato il portasanta."
68 — Ibid.
69 — Gnoli 1971, 216; Borghini 1989; Del Bufalo 2000; Extermann and Varela Braga 2016.
70 — AC, *Fondo economico*, 1701 (account book for the years 1593–1595). Gori 2007, 91, 116–120.
71 — Ostrow 1996, 158–166, esp. 158 and n. 189.
72 — This subject was also discussed by Barry at RSA (Chicago, 2017).
73 — Frizolio 1582, esp. 22; Valentino 1583; Valentino 1584, cited in Barry's essay in this volume. The latter mentions a manuscript by Chacón in which the Dominican discusses the nature of different marbles. Also relevant is Michele Mercati's (1541–1593) *Metallotheca* (1717) and, in particular, the tenth chapter dedicated to the marbles' nature, without attributing to them a specific significance.
74 — Besides the marble altarpiece by Olivieri, the sculptures pertaining to the late Cinquecento decoration are assigned as follows: Valsoldino is the author of the two pairs of angels topping the pediments of the tombs and the frieze with eagles and cherubs within Enrico Caetani's aedicule, whereas Guglielmo Mido is responsible for those on the opposite wall, within Filippo Caetani's monument. See Ferrari and Papaldo 1999, 384–385; De Lotto 2009, 178–179; Ioele 2016, 144–149.
75 — Montagu 1985, I 138–149, esp. 146. On Olivieri's altarpiece, see also Montagu 1985, I, 135–136, 138; Pierguidi 2017, 34–37. In his monograph on the history of the marble altarpiece, Pierguidi (2017, 116–133) discusses Algardi's work in St. Peter's and Bernini's in San Pietro in Montorio.
76 — Caetani 1933, II, 326; Pressouyre 1984, 214, n. 26.
77 — Vasari 1550–1568 [1966–1997], IV, 417: "Molto si costuma fare le cappelle e le tavole di marmo." I would like to thank Fernando Loffredo for drawing my attention to this passage from Vasari's *Lives*.
78 — Baglione (1642, 114) states that when Olivieri died, the marble altarpiece was finished by Camillo Mariani, information that does not conflict with the presence of both Olivieri and Mariani at the Lateran or with the latter's collaboration with Valsoldino. However, as is made clear by Teresa De Lotto (2009), it was only on July 6, 1599 (Olivieri's death), that the altarpiece was completed. After that date, Pasquale Pasqualini—Mariani's apprentice—was charged with the finishing and polishing of the monumental marble relief. According to Caetani (1933, II, 263, n. a), the polishing was paid for in August 1599 to "Giovanpietro lustratore." De Lotto (2009, 24, 54, 58–59, 62, 83, 178–179) also notes that the Gualdo family, Mariani's protectors in Vicenza, had a long familiarity with the Caetani, and very likely they were instrumental for the connection between Mariani and Olivieri. See also Parlato 2009, 149–150, n. 42; Ioele 2015, 52, n. 21.

"A Gem Set in Most Resplendent Gold"

GIROLAMO RUSTICUCCI'S CONFESSIO CHAPEL IN SANTA SUSANNA

Steven F. Ostrow

Beneath the raised chancel of the church of Santa Susanna is an oval *confessio* that was built and decorated during the last decade of the sixteenth century (**FIGS. 1, 4**). Unprecedented in its plan and complexity of decoration, this subterranean place of prayer, in one of Rome's oldest churches, has received remarkably little scholarly attention, despite the fact that it was considered by early viewers to be a "venerable place," "beautiful and dignified . . . a gem set in most resplendent gold."[1] To fill this scholarly gap, this essay traces the history of the *confessio* with respect to its origins and place within Santa Susanna. It considers its patron and the architects and painters involved in its creation and adornment; analyzes its plan, altar, and pictorial program; and addresses its function as a martyrium, funerary chapel, and site for veneration and liturgical celebration. From this multifaceted exploration of the *confessio*, my goal is to enrich our understanding of this little-explored and little-understood monument and to situate it within the context of post-Tridentine Rome.

The Early History of Santa Susanna

In order to understand the sixteenth-century *confessio*, knowledge of the church's history—however briefly sketched—is essential. The origins of the church of Santa Susanna can be traced to the end of the third century, when a Christian house of worship was first established on the site. According to early sources, the church was constructed "ad duas domos" (at the site of two houses), in reference to the homes of Gabinius, a nephew of Emperor Diocletian and the father of Susanna, and Gaius, Gabinius's brother.[2] The three family members were Christians: Gabinius a presbyter, Gaius a pope, and Susanna a devout virgin, all of whom, according to tradition, were martyred by Diocletian—Susanna in 295 and the other two in 296—and subsequently elevated to sainthood.[3] By the fifth century, the church was designated a *titulus*, and during the reign of Pope Leo III (795–816), who had served the church as its titular priest, it was largely rebuilt.[4] In addition to richly outfitting the church with an apse mosaic, marble pavements and columns, and other liturgical gifts, Leo III is also credited with having created a semiannular crypt below the high altar to house the bodies of Saints Gabinius and Susanna, who were martyred on the site. To these precious remains Leo also added the body of the second-century Roman martyr Saint Felicita, which he translated from the cemetery of Maximus on the via Salaria.[5] Following Leo III's interventions at Santa Susanna, no major work was carried out until the last quarter of the fifteenth century, when Sixtus IV oversaw extensive work on the building, both inside and outside, including the addition of a new facade.[6] This was, to a great extent, the church inherited by Cardinal Girolamo Rusticucci when Pius V named him its titular cardinal in 1570.

The Patron: Girolamo Rusticucci

The church of Santa Susanna that we see today is largely the result of Girolamo Rusticucci's extensive interventions in its structure and decoration, most of which have been well studied.[7] Exactly when he began his renovation is uncertain, but Pompeo Ugonio, in his *Historia delle Stationi di Roma* of 1588, noted that "in our times, he [Rusticucci] has put it [the church] commodiously in order," suggesting that considerable work was already carried out by that time.[8]

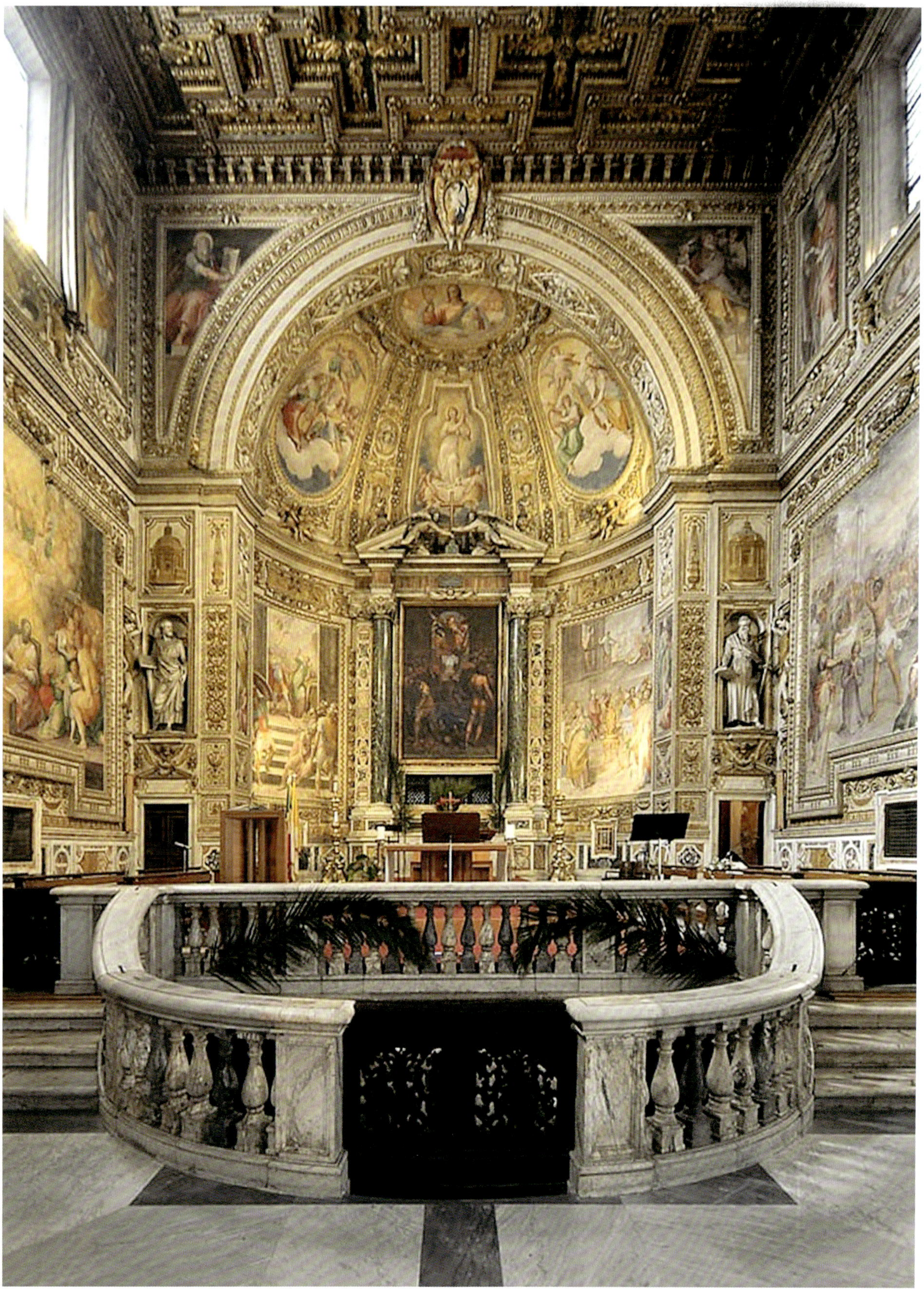

1

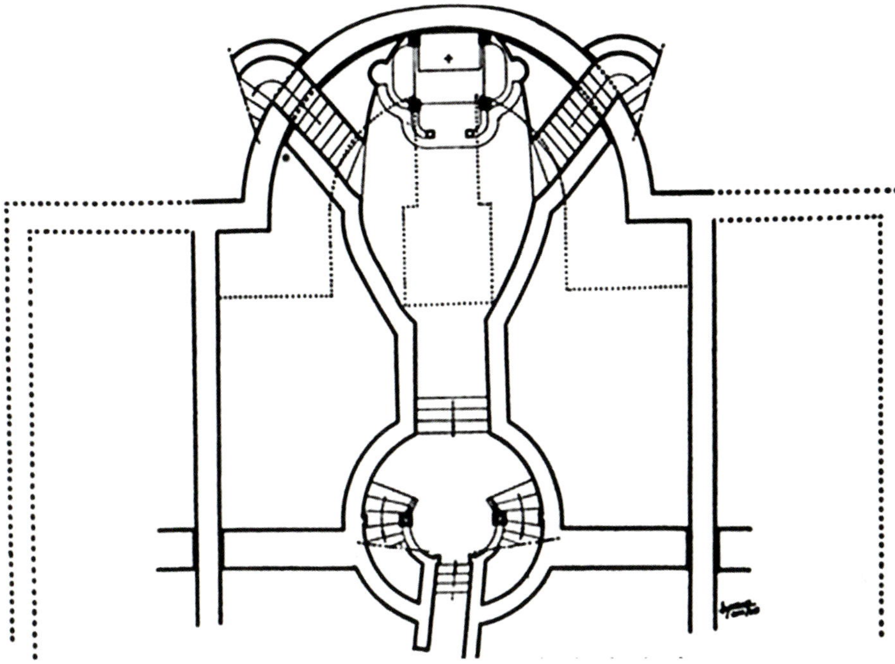

2

Well documented, however, are the architectural restoration, new wooden ceiling, and pictorial decoration of the chancel, carried out from 1593 to 1597 by Domenico Fontana and Carlo Maderno and the painters Cesare Nebbia, Baldassarre Croce, Paris Nogari, and Tommaso Laureti (FIG. 1); Maderno's new facade erected between 1597 and 1603; the new Maderno-designed wooden ceiling in the nave, completed in 1598; and the frescoes on the nave walls and counterfacade by Croce, executed between 1598 and 1601.[9] The *confessio*, the central element of his elaborate renovation project, is the exception with respect to documentation; but before turning to it, a consideration of its patron is in order, as he remains, to a great extent, little known.

Born in Cartoceto—near Fano, in the Marches—in 1537, the son of Ludovico, a jurisconsult and nobleman, and Diamante Leonardi, Girolamo received a classical education before moving to Rome in 1557.[10] There he entered the court of Cardinal Michele Ghislieri, the future Pius V, serving as his *secretarius intimus*, a position he continued to hold after Ghislieri's election in 1566. Four years later, Pius elevated Rusticucci to the purple and named him titular cardinal of Santa Susanna and bishop of Senigallia. Throughout his pontificate (1566–1572), Pius relied heavily on the Marchegian cardinal, placing him in charge, during the absences of the papal nephew, Cardinal Michele Bonelli, of managing many of the Church's affairs, naming him legate to Spain and France to promote the league against the Turks, and appointing him cardinal protector of the Cistercian Order. Although Pius's successor, Gregory XIII (1572–1585), named him governor of Bolsena in 1581, Rusticucci enjoyed little of that pope's favor. However, upon the election of Felice Peretti as Sixtus V in 1585, his fortunes changed. The two men shared Marchegian origins, both had been elevated to the cardinalate in 1570, and both owed much of their success to Pius V. And Sixtus demonstrated his favor toward Rusticucci in three significant ways:

FIG. 1. Chancel with Confessio Chapel balustrade, Santa Susanna, Rome.

FIG. 2. Modern plan of Confessio Chapel, Santa Susanna, Rome.

naming him his secretary of state in 1585, appointing him to the all-important role of *Cardinal Vicario* of Rome in 1587 (which he retained until his death in 1603), and, in 1590, elevating him to the position of camerlengo of the College of Cardinals.[11] During the papacy of Clement VIII (1592–1605), Rusticucci continued to enjoy papal favor, being named bishop of Albano (1598), then of Sabina (1600), and finally of Porto (1603). Clement also appointed him titular cardinal of Santa Maria in Trastevere in 1597 but granted Rusticucci the unusual privilege of retaining that role at Santa Susanna for the remainder of his life.

According to diplomatic correspondence of the time, Rusticucci was of "modest intelligence, but sagacious, slow in manner, but diligent, a man of good sentiments, but very slow expression, [who] has more prudence than doctrine."[12] Cardinal Giulio Antonio Santori, who was also raised to the cardinalate in 1570, described him as neither particularly cultured nor learned.[13] Over the course of his career, however, Rusticucci acquired a reputation as a pious reformer, who was devoted to the education of the clergy and to carrying out the principles of the Council of Trent. As bishop of Senigallia, from 1570 to 1577, he dutifully made pastoral visits to the churches and monasteries of his see, scrupulously inspecting their fabrics, altars, and altarpieces to ensure their integrity and decorum. In his role as Cardinal Vicar of Rome, according to Alfonso Chacón (Ciacconius), his earliest biographer, he demonstrated "most honorable oversight, religious devotion, supervision, justice, and shrewdness."[14] One manifestation of this was his edict on sacred art of 1593, issued on behalf of Clement VIII, which directed all clergymen and artists to maintain sacred decorum in the artworks made for chapels and churches. In addition to prohibiting lascivious images, in adherence to the Council of Trent's decree on sacred art, the edict required artists "before commencing work on any new fresco or panel picture intended for a church or chapel to submit [to Church authorities] a cartoon or preparatory drawing demonstrating the proper display of church history and decorous figures."[15] Rusticucci's rigorous oversight of religious imagery, which he first demonstrated under Pius V when he advocated the removal of Michelangelo's *Last Judgment* fresco, was also entirely in keeping with Clement's crusade against indecent art, as demonstrated by the decrees he issued following his pastoral visits, in which he personally inspected (in the company of his Cardinal Vicar and others) the churches of Rome.[16]

What emerges from the sources is an image of Rusticucci as an austere, even zealous, churchman, who was determined to make certain that religious imagery conformed to orthodoxy and principles of decorum. For his undertakings at Santa Susanna, he demonstrated a preference for the reform painters that Sixtus V had employed—Nebbia, Laureti, Nogari, and Croce—and similarly followed the Peretti pope in his architectural taste as well, employing Fontana and his nephew Maderno.[17] Like Sixtus, too, he could be indifferent to both ancient and medieval works, as evidenced by his selling off of architectural fragments from the Pantheon and destruction of Leo III's mosaic in the apse of Santa Susanna.[18] And with respect to Croce's frescoes on the nave walls and counterfacade of Santa Susanna, we know that he strictly applied his own edict of 1593, requiring the painter to submit his cartoons to his "ministro," the cleric Giovanni Angelo Frumenti (ca. 1541–1621), who was also entrusted with approving the painter's finished frescoes.[19] The same oversight certainly applied to the decoration of the *confessio*.

The *Confessio*: Its Date, Architects, and Plan

As already noted, the documentation for much of Rusticucci's renovation of Santa Susanna spans the years 1593 to 1603, but some work appears to have been begun by the late 1580s. Hibbard assumed, no doubt correctly, that the earlier work was directed by Domenico Fontana, who at the time was working on the Palazzo Rusticucci in the Borgo and was considered the cardinal's architect.[20] Unfortunately, no documents for the *confessio* have come to light, but circumstantial evidence suggests that its architecture, at least, must have been completed by late 1593 or early the next year. Two pieces of that evidence are contracts for work in the chancel. The earlier of the two, dated April 16, 1593, obliged the stonemasons to execute "all of the work … in the choir of the church," including "all of the stairs" that lead up to the elevated chancel, as well as "all of the balustrades," to the satisfaction of "architects Cavalier Fontana or ms. Carlo Maderno, his nephew." The other contract, dated December 7, 1593, required the woodworker, Alessandro Castaldo, to execute the wooden "ceiling of the Cappella mag[g]iore … according to the design … of ms. Carlo Maderno Architect" and to complete it by mid-March 1594.[21] As the *confessio* lies beneath the raised chancel, it must have been built prior to the chancel's elevation, the construction of the stairs, and the execution of the ceiling above. Moreover, that the two curving flights of stairs that lead down to the *confessio* are circumscribed by marble balustrades that are of a piece with the one that runs across the front of the chancel, it is highly likely that they were made at the same time (FIG. 1).

With respect to the architect responsible for the *confessio*, the majority of scholars who have had anything to say about it have attributed it solely to Maderno. But there is good reason to believe that Domenico Fontana played a key role in its conception and, in all likelihood, its construction as well.[22] He was, after all, Rusticucci's architect; he is named coarchitect in the contract of April 1593 for the chancel's construction; and, most significantly, he was the most experienced designer of crypts in Rome at the time, having created two just a few years earlier on behalf of Sixtus V. One, in the church of Santa Sabina, dating to 1586–1588, is perhaps the first *confessio* to be created in post-Tridentine Rome. Described by Pompeo Ugonio as "the *confessione* or *grotta* below the high altar," it was built to replace a preexisting crypt and to house an altar dedicated to Saint Dominic. Like the *confessio* in Santa Susanna, as we will see, it was also described as a subterranean chapel and was situated at the threshold of a raised chancel and accessed by a wide, eleven-step staircase, circumscribed by a balustrade very similar to the one in Santa Susanna.[23] The other and more widely known of Fontana's crypts was built in 1587 at the center of Sixtus's burial chapel in Santa Maria Maggiore. It was created to enshrine the small early-thirteenth-century Cappella del Presepio—a simulacrum of the grotto in Bethlehem—containing relics of Christ's birth, which Fontana translated from its previous location in the side aisle of the basilica into a subterranean space at the chapel's center. As at Santa Susanna, the *confessio* is open, with a U-shaped balustrade circumscribing the opening at floor level and two curving staircases descending to the lower chamber.[24]

Maderno, of course, went on to design the most famous *confessio* of all, the one in St. Peter's, which was built and decorated between 1615 and 1617 on behalf of Paul V. It was conceived earlier, however, in 1606, as we learn from an

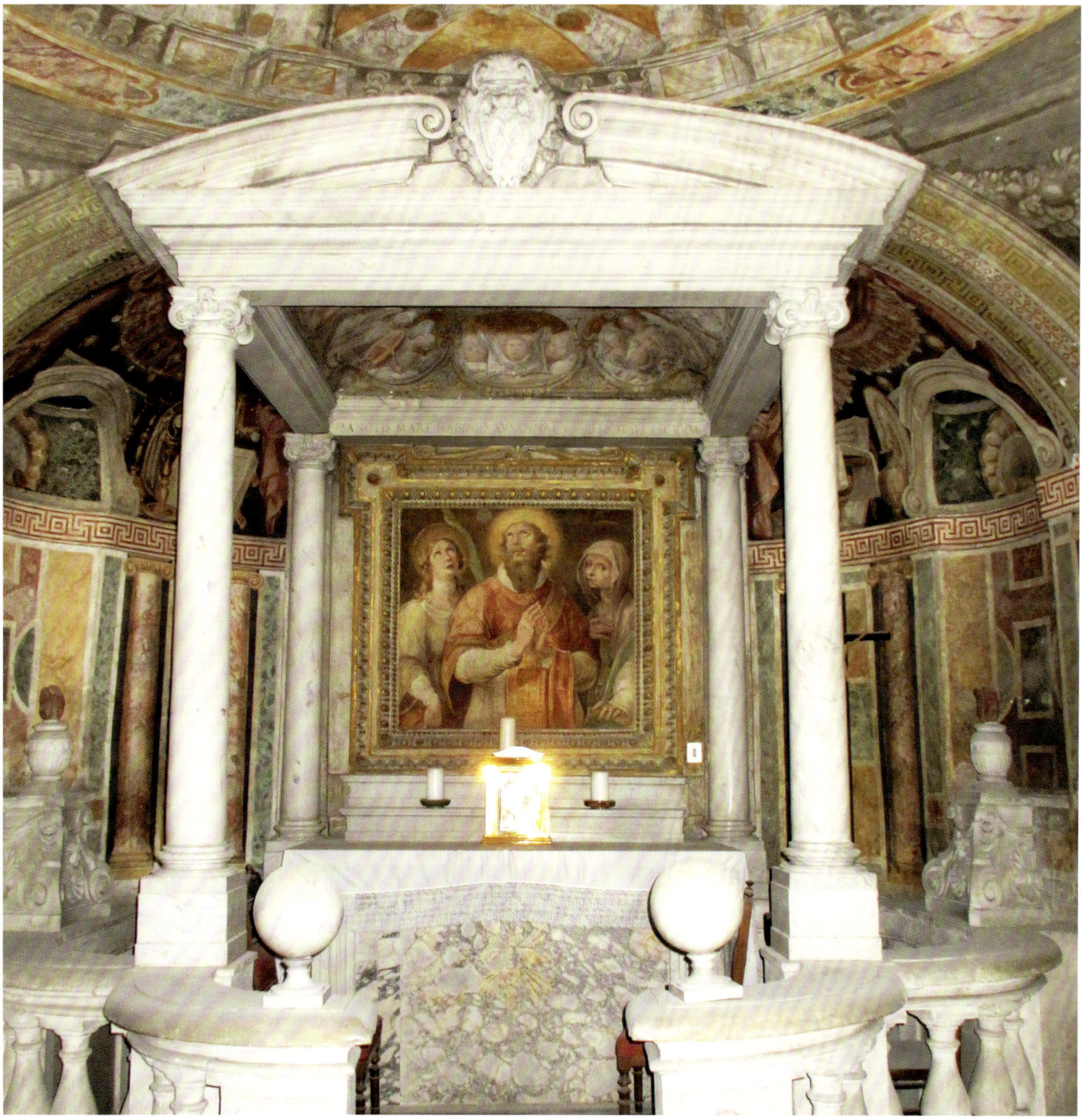

3

FIG. 3. Carlo Maderno,
Ciborium, ca. 1593–1594.
Confessio Chapel,
Santa Susanna, Rome.

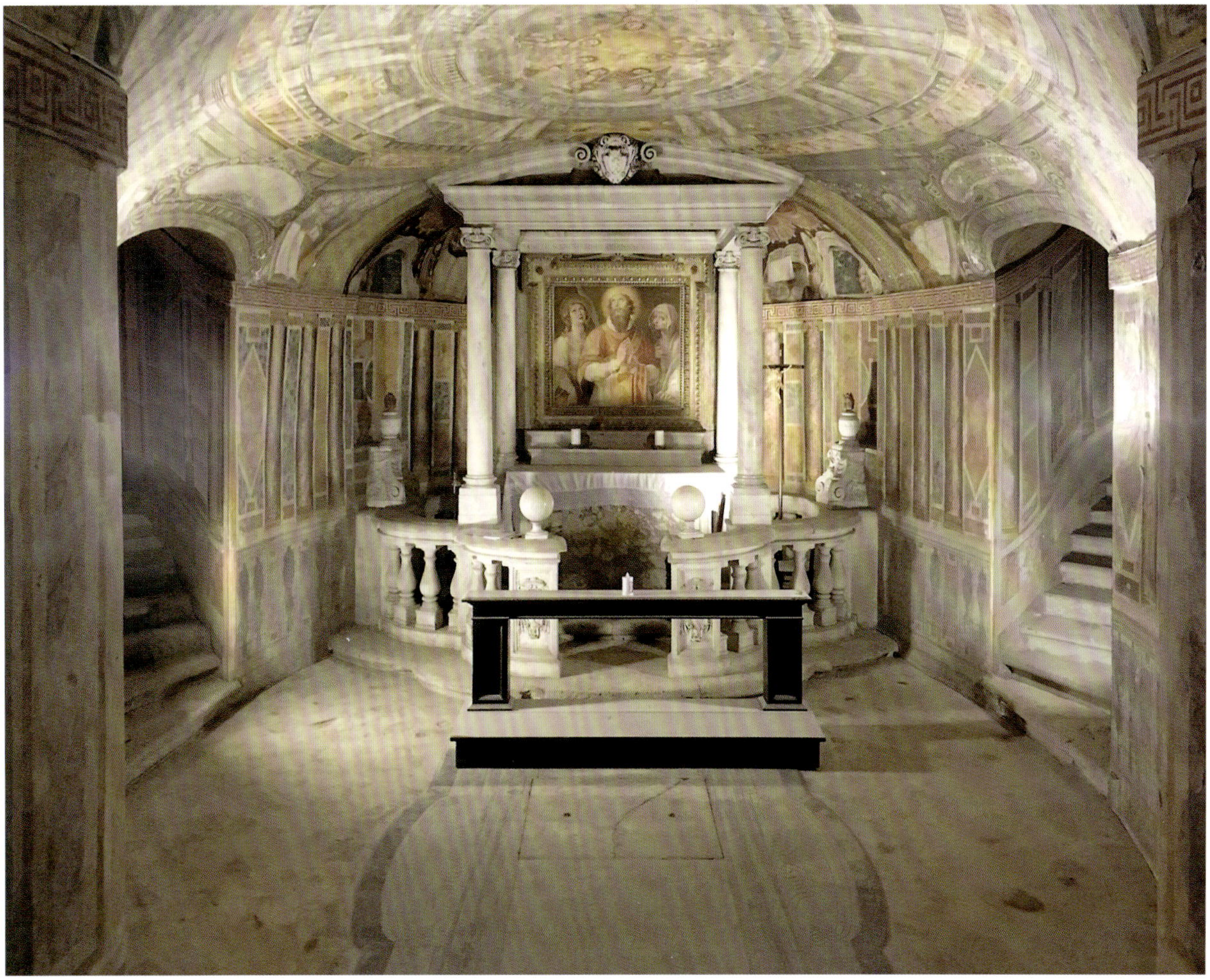

4

avviso that describes its design as consisting of a subterranean space, circumscribed at floor level by a "balustrade around" the opening and "with flights of steps so as to be able to descend below to go and celebrate Mass at the altar and bodies of the ... Holy Apostles."[25] Nothing immediately came of this plan, but as an *avviso* of 1611 informs us, the idea was taken up again, with the pope having "resolved to open under the high altar of Saint Peter's a pair of staircases, so that from the same church one can go to say and to hear Mass at the altar of the Apostles ... in a manner like that of the chapel beneath the ... altar ... of the Presepio in Santa Maria Maggiore."[26] Maderno, in other words, based his design for the *confessio* in St. Peter's on Fontana's in Santa Maria Maggiore, and it is virtually inconceivable that Rusticucci would not have turned to the older architect to conceptualize the new *confessio* in Santa Susanna.[27]

Maderno did, however, play an important role in the design, in my view, providing the idea for its novel plan (FIG. 2). That plan consists of a circular vestibule, approximately five meters in diameter, into which the descending staircases lead, which is followed by an approximately three-meter-long vaulted corridor (separated from the vestibule by an iron gate), which in turn leads to the main space, a gently vaulted longitudinal oval, measuring approximately

FIG. 4. Confessio Chapel, ca. 1593–1595. Santa Susanna, Rome.

five meters wide, nine meters in length, and four meters high. Branching off from this space, just past its midpoint at both left and right, are arched openings, which lead to narrow vaulted corridors that ascend diagonally and then dogleg back and up to doors that open at both sides of the chancel (**FIGS. 1–2, 4**).

In contrast to the crypts in Santa Sabina and Santa Maria Maggiore, which are essentially rectangular in plan, the *confessio* in Santa Susanna consists of multiple spaces, the primary one being an oval.[28] The oval plan, which would flourish in the seventeenth century but was already being experimented with in the sixteenth, was no doubt inspired by a series of oval churches, both designed and actually built: Sebastiano Serlio's designs (published in his treatises), Jacopo Vignola's Sant'Anna dei Palafranieri (ca. 1565–1583), Ottaviano Mascherino's project for Santo Spirito dei Napoletani (ca. 1584–1585), and especially Francesco da Volterra's San Giacomo in Augusta (begun ca. 1590).[29] This last example is particularly noteworthy, as Maderno appears to have been involved in the design process of the church, alongside da Volterra, almost from its inception, and upon his death, he oversaw its completion.[30] The idea of an oval plan was thus fresh on Maderno's mind.

Perhaps more significant than attributing the oval plan to Fontana or Maderno, or identifying its sources, is the relationship between the plan and the function of the space. Like the churches that may have inspired it, the *confessio* is the site of liturgical celebration—a chapel—outfitted with an altar (to which we will return below). This was a point repeatedly made by early writers such as Ottavio Panciroli, who, in his *I tesori nascosti nell'alma città di Roma* of 1600, described it as the "cappella di sotto" and in the 1625 edition of his book referred to it as "the *confessione*, below [the high altar], which occupies a grand space, and with beautiful marble stairs opens to a place to visit the bodies of the ... Saints, well accommodated in an altar."[31]

Panciroli's later description (in 1625) alerts us to its second function, a martyrium—the tomb of a martyr or the repository of the relics of martyrs—in keeping with the majority of crypts built in Rome since the fifth century.[32] Rusticucci's *confessio*, in fact, replaced the preexisting one built by Leo III and, like its predecessor, enshrined the bodies of Saints Susanna, Gabinius, and Felicita. Prior to the construction of the new crypt, Pompeo Ugonio recorded the presence of these relics: "below [the high altar is] the *confessione* or Martyrium, where the bodies of the saints rest." And this assertion of bodily presence was repeated by a number of early writers with respect to Rusticucci's new *confessio* and proclaimed by the cardinal himself in an inscription on the rear lintel of the altar canopy: "SANCTIS MART[IRIBUS] GABINIO SVSANNAE ET FELICITATI SACRUM" (**FIG. 3**).[33]

Although it is a mistake to assume that symbolic meanings should always be read into architectural forms, here, I would argue, the oval plan of Rusticucci's *confessio* chapel was a deliberate choice in relation to its function as a martyrium.[34] As Sinding-Larsen has shown, the majority of Renaissance buildings erected to serve as martyria, *memoriae*, or sepulchral monuments were centralized structures—in keeping with a long tradition in both the Western and Eastern Churches—and like their earlier models, they were designed according to circular, square, octagonal, or Greek-cross plans.[35] The new *confessio* in Santa Susanna, which was built to house the bodies of three martyrs and, according to tradition, on the very site where two of them, Susanna and Gabinius, were martyred, follows this architectural tradition, albeit in a new, more dynamic variant of the circle: the oval.[36] And the oval plan was not without related symbolic associations, as it had long been connected to amphitheaters; and in the funeral orations for Cardinal Antonio Maria Salviati, held in San Giacomo in Augusta (of which he was the patron), its oval plan was likened to "ancient temples" by one orator, Paolino Arnolfini, and by the other, Pompeo Ugonio, to both the Mausoleum of Augustus and an amphitheater, thus, as Hibbard remarked, "specifically calling to mind the oval plan of the Colosseum," the site of Christian martyrdom.[37]

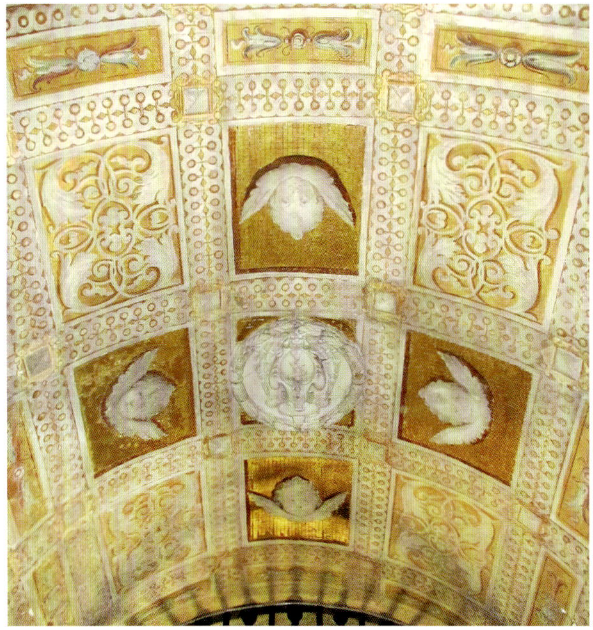

5

If the oval plan can be symbolically related to the function of the *confessio* as a martyrium, it can also be associated with its role as a funerary chapel, as it was here that Rusticucci chose to be buried, below the pavement at the center of the oval space, which he marked with a simple incised tomb slab that he placed in 1595, eight years before his death (FIG. 4). In opting for *depositio ad sanctos* (burial in proximity to the saints), the cardinal followed a long-standing tradition, going back to the early Christian period. And although Saint Augustine argued that "all Christians should, at their end, enjoy the proximity of the saints," given the control the Church exerted over relics, it was a privilege only the elite, as the cardinal was, could obtain.[38] His burial in proximity to the relics was a potent expression of his belief in their *potentia* (power) and *praesentia* (presence) as vehicles for salvation. But it was also an expression of his personal devotion to Susanna, Gabinius, and Felicita, which he articulated in the inscription on his tomb slab: "Girolamo Rusticucci, Cardinal Priest and Titular Cardinal of this Church, Vicar of the Pope, out of devotion, while still alive, placed this monument himself [in honor of] the Holy Martyrs, at the age of fifty-nine, in 1595."[39]

As a funerary chapel, martyrium, and site for liturgical celebration, Rusticucci's *confessio* is unique among the crypts built in Rome during the post-Tridentine period. With its saintly bodies, it was a place for veneration and pilgrimage, especially on feast days. Masses were celebrated there, too, perhaps for the public but without doubt for the Cistercian nuns and the members, both *consorelle* and *confratelli*, of the Confraternita di San Bernardo, to whose community the church had been given by Sixtus V in 1587.[40] The latter consisted of laywomen and both ecclesiastics and laymen, respectively. The former (the nuns) were cloistered in the monastery adjacent to Santa Susanna but met in prayer in the large nuns' choir directly behind the church's chancel, which was constructed by Rusticucci. These various worshippers may explain the highly unusual inclusion of the two additional routes of access to the *confessio*, the narrow, vaulted corridors that lead from the chancel to the subterranean space; they could have provided privileged access for the clergy and members of the confraternity from the chancel and a discreet means of entry for the nuns, who were not permitted contact with the outside world. The

FIG. 5. Vault of the corridor to Confessio Chapel, Santa Susanna, Rome.

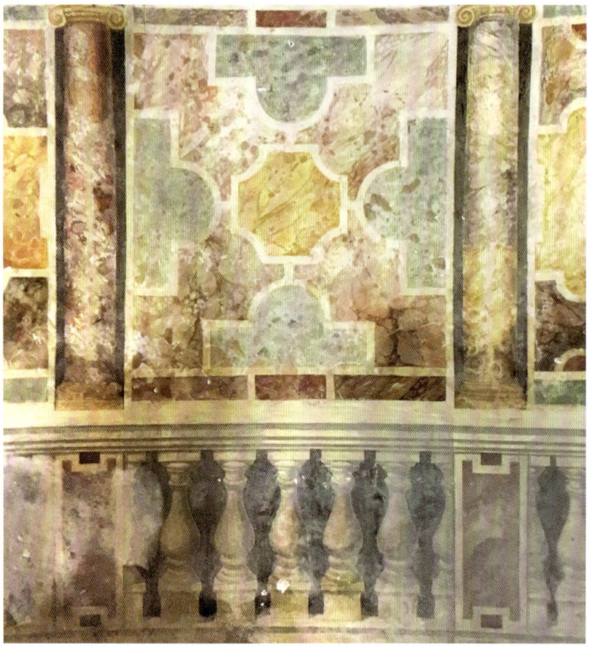

6

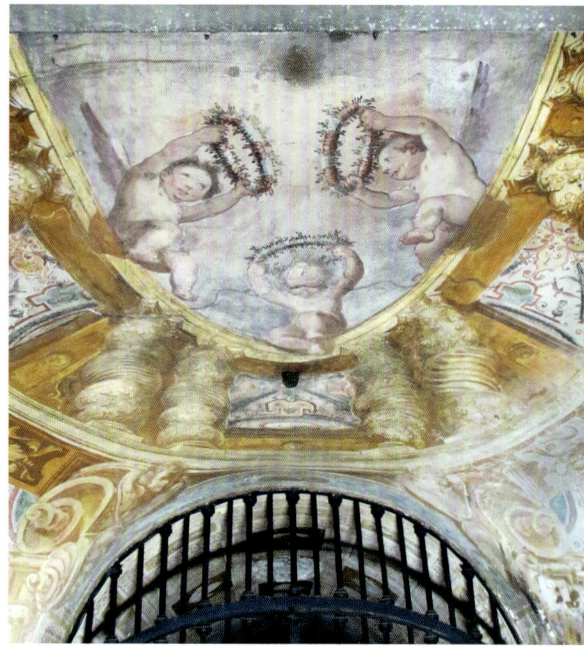

7

corridors' paths were likely determined, as Apollonj Ghetti first suggested, by a desire to utilize parts of the preexisting semiannular crypt, but their function was clearly to offer an alternative access to the shrine.[41]

The Altar and Its Ciborium

Tradition tells us that following the martyrdom of Susanna and before his own demise, Pope Gaius, her uncle, celebrated Masses in her honor at an altar that he erected on the site of her death. And according to the erudite cleric and scholar Carlo Bartolomeo Piazza, it was this very altar, containing the remains of Susanna, Gabinius, and (later) Felicita, that Rusticucci placed in his *confessio*.[42] Although we lack definitive proof of this claim, the altar, located at the far end of the oval chapel, is a patchwork of old and new marbles, some of which, specifically the *breccia di pavonazzetto* front, may derive from the altar at which Gaius was said to have celebrated (FIG. 3). If indeed this is the case, it would indicate Rusticucci's interest in preserving the venerable altar and underscoring the continuity between his *confessio* and the site's early Christian origins.

The same holds true, I believe, for Maderno's elegant marble ciborium (FIG. 3), which rises above the altar on four Ionic columns, supporting a slightly domical canopy. Fronting the canopy is a simple broken pediment, echoing in shape the curve of the vault above it and bearing Rusticucci's coat of arms at its center. Although an independent structure, it is attached to the rear wall, and its forward columns rest on plinths that emerge from the lobed balustrade, or altar rail, which projects out into the space of the chapel. Marble spheres, resting on the balustrade, flank the opening at its center above the cardinal's *stemmi*, while marble candelabra, with *marmo rosso* flames, rest atop the rear sides of the balustrade.[43] Typologically, Maderno's ciborium derives from, and recreates in a modern and miniaturized form,

FIG. 6. Fictive marble revetment (detail), Confessio Chapel, Santa Susanna, Rome.

FIG. 7. Baldassarre Croce, *Angels Bearing Floral Crowns*, ca. 1593–1595. Confessio Chapel (vault of entrance vestibule), Santa Susanna, Rome.

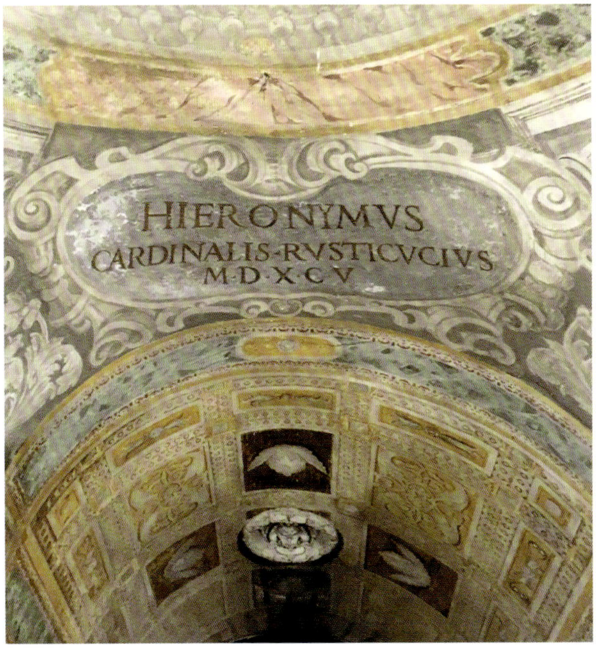

8

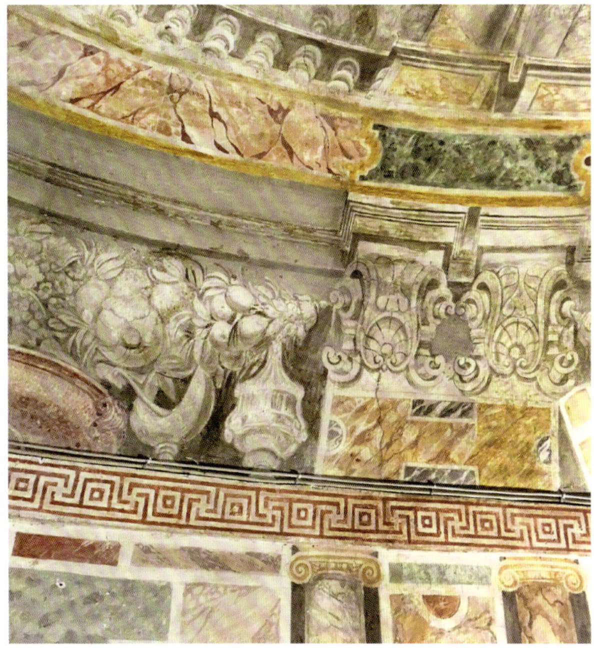

9

medieval altar canopies, such as the mid-twelfth-century ciborium in Santa Maria di Castello in Tarquinia and that in Santa Maria Maggiore in Tuscania, which dates to the eleventh century. It also shares a simplicity and likeness of form to many medieval altar tables.[44] This was an intentional evocation of earlier Christian forms, I suspect. And so, too, was the very decision to erect a medievalizing canopy over the altar, for it replicated the arrangement of the preexisting high altar of the church, which Ugonio described as having a "marble ciborium [above], and below the *confessione* or Martyrium, where the holy bodies rest."[45] The altar and ciborium not only provide the space with a visual focus—with the air of the Christian antique—but also give purpose to the chapel as a site for veneration and prayer.

The Fresco Decorations

In the 1625 edition of his *Tesori nascosti*, Ottavio Panciroli described Rusticucci's *confessio* as having "decorations throughout," and Piazza similarly reported that it was "nobly adorned by Cardinal Rusticucci with marbles and beautiful paintings."[46] In fact, frescoes cover every wall surface and vault of the vestibule, connecting corridor, oval chapel, and front and rear entryways, endowing the crypt with an extraordinary richness (FIG. 4). The walls of the descending stairs, from both the nave and the chancel, are adorned with fictive marble revetment, imitating inlays of *marmo rosso*, *giallo antico*, and *verde antico*. In the circular vestibule and rear corridors, the panels alternate with fictive red marble columns, capped by gold Ionic capitals, beneath a continuous meander-pattern frieze. The walls of the corridor connecting the vestibule to the chapel are similarly adorned, but here, below the cladding and columns, is a painted balustrade, the balusters of which match those of the altar rail and of the balustrades that run along the descending staircases from the nave. The

FIG. 8. Dedicatory inscription, 1595. Confessio Chapel, Santa Susanna, Rome.

FIG. 9. Baldassarre Croce, *Frieze of Liturgical Objects*, ca. 1593–1595. Confessio Chapel, Santa Susanna, Rome.

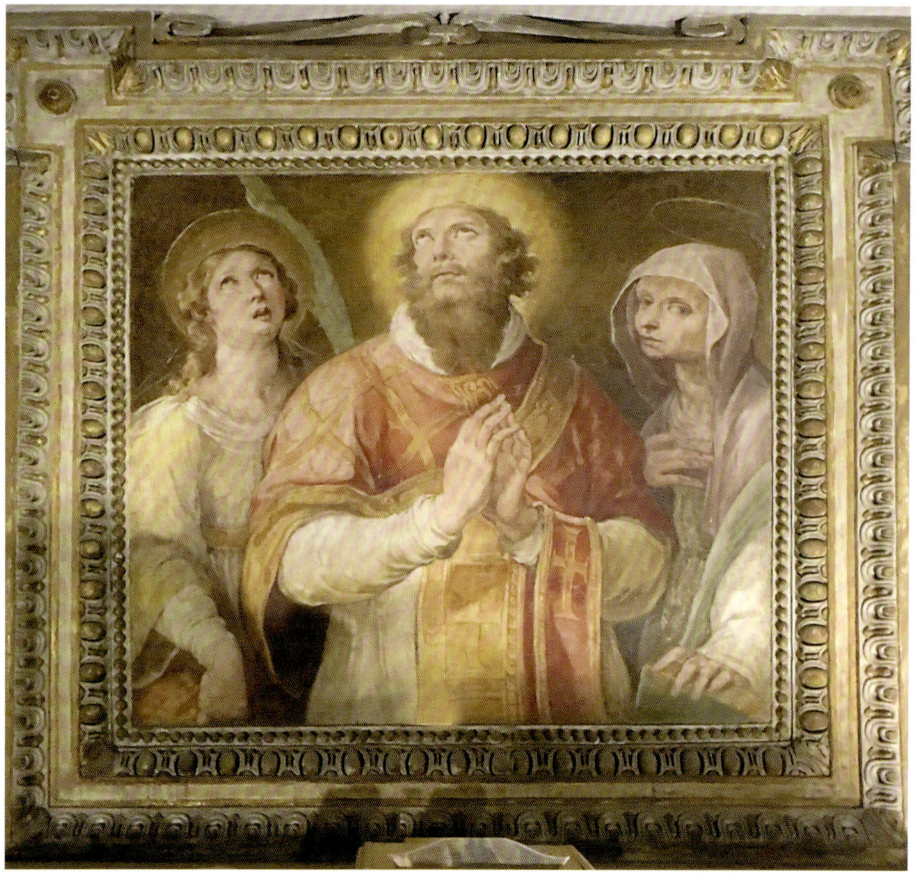

10

vault of this corridor is covered with feigned stucco coffers, decorated with white floral patterns alternating with seraphim on fictive gold mosaic grounds and, at the very center, a marble *stemma* of Rusticucci (FIG. 5). And the walls of the chapel match those of the corridor, with a fictive balustrade rising to the height of the altar rail, fictive marble cladding alternating with columns, and a meander-pattern frieze above (FIGS. 4, 6). Although the walls of the *confessio* lack any architectonic elements, as Lotz and Hubala first observed, the faux marble cladding, colonnade, and balustrade serve to articulate the spaces and to unify them visually.[47]

More significantly, the fictive marble revetment—like the real marble cladding in the Cappella Gregoriana in St. Peter's,[48] Sixtus V's chapel in Santa Maria Maggiore, and the Caetani Chapel in Santa Pudenziana,[49] to name just a few among many examples created in Rome in the late sixteenth century—recreates, in a modern idiom, the marble revetment that adorned Rome's early Christian churches, such as the sixth-century encrustation in Santi Cosma e Damiano and the fifth-century cladding in the Oratorio della Santa Croce (see fig. 5 in Fabio Barry's essay in this volume).[50] It was, as I have argued elsewhere, an intentional evocation of the past, another aspect of the post-Tridentine early Christian revival, paralleling the medievalizing ciborium and the fictive mosaics in the entrance corridor. And as Hubala discussed in his now classic article of 1965, the *confessio* itself—in Santa Susanna as well as those built in

FIG. 10. Baldassarre Croce, *Saints Gabinius, Susanna, and Felicita*, ca. 1593–1595. Confessio Chapel (altar), Santa Susanna, Rome.

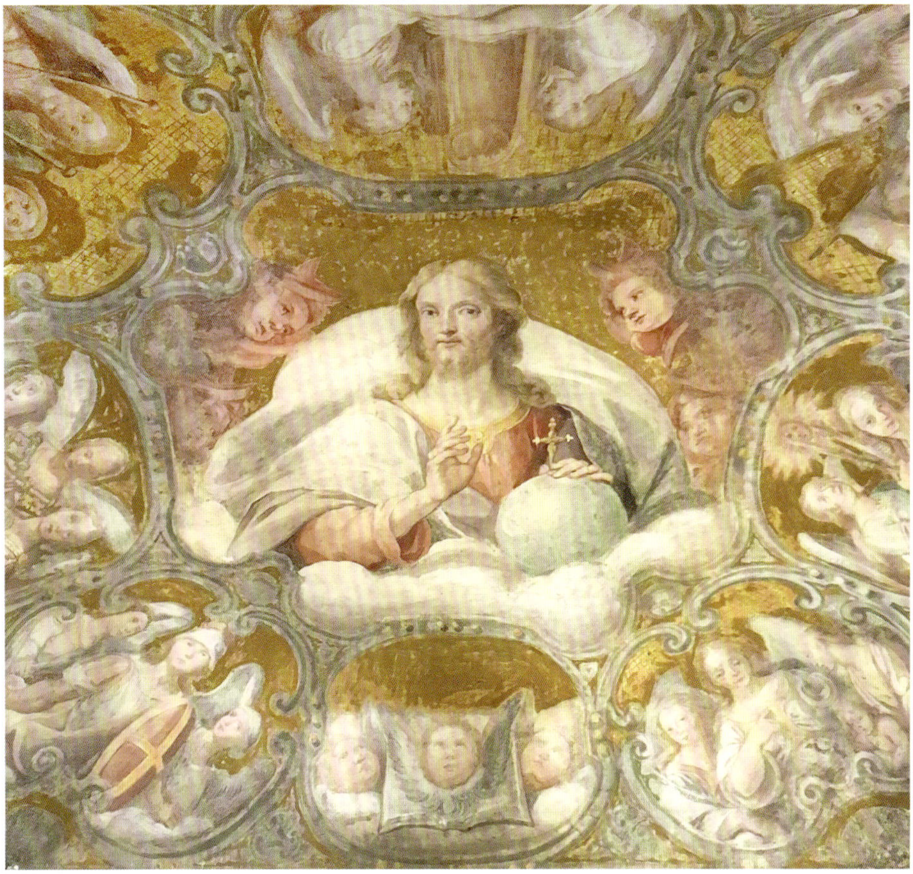

11

other churches at the time—was deeply expressive of the period's cult of early martyrs and of the broader revival of early Christian forms.[51]

The remaining frescoes in the *confessio* expand upon the language of fictive architecture seen on the walls and introduce figural and other forms of representation into the program. They begin in the vestibule at the base of the curving stairs, a space that serves as a narthex or forecourt, through which one passes before entering the liturgical space of the chapel. Here, on the vault, above a fictive colonnade of paired Solomonic columns, depicted *dal di sotto in sù*, are an open sky and three angels bearing floral crowns, heavenly gifts for the three sainted martyrs commemorated at the altar (FIG. 7).[52] Around the circumference of the *confessio* chapel, above the arched openings from the entrance and lateral corridors, are three frescoed inscriptions within fictive cartouches. The first, above the right lateral arched opening, reads: "CORPORA SANCTORUM IN PACE SEPULTA SUNT," in reference to the saintly bodies of Susanna, Gabinius, and Felicita that repose in the altar. The second, "HIERONYMVS CARDINALIS RVSTICVCIVS MDXCV," above the entrance corridor arch, celebrates the patron of the *confessio*, provides the likely completion date of the project, and marks the thirteen-hundredth anniversary of Susanna's martyrdom in 295 (FIG. 8). The third, largely abraded, records the restoration of the frescoes in 1955. The inscriptions form part of a frescoed frieze that runs around the space of the chapel, above the fictive revetment, in which books and an array of litur-

FIG. 11. Baldassarre Croce, *Christ with Angelic Hierarchies*, ca. 1593–1595. Confessio Chapel (underside of altar ciborium), Santa Susanna, Rome.

gical objects—incense boats and censers, candlesticks, monstrances, patens, water pitchers, and pyxes, all foreshortened from below and arranged beneath garlands of fruit (painted in grisaille) and tessellated canopies—serve to emphasize the liturgical and sacramental function of the chapel (**FIG. 9**).

The chapel's altarpiece (**FIG. 10**), also executed in fresco, presents three-quarter-length figures of the three sainted martyrs whose relics are contained in the altar below: Gabinius at the center, flanked by Susanna and Felicita at left and right, respectively, whose bodily presence, as noted earlier, is also recorded in the inscription on the rear lintel of the ciborium above the painting.[53] Felicita engages the viewer with her eyes, rests her left hand on a book, and raises her right hand to her breast; Susanna, in turn, holds a martyr's palm; and Gabinius, wearing a chasuble, joins his hands in a gesture of prayer. All three are nimbed, the lateral female saints with traditional circular disclike halos, Gabinius with a golden aura surrounding his head.

Susanna and Gabinius direct their gazes to the underside of the ciborium canopy, which, like many medieval ciboria, is adorned with a fresco (**FIG. 11**).[54] The square field is divided into nine sections or medallions, each within a delicate frame. At the center is a half-figure of Christ as Salvator Mundi, who rests his left hand on a *globus cruciger* and makes a gesture of blessing with his right hand. In the surrounding eight sections, disposed symmetrically, are angels, set against fictive gold mosaic grounds. But these are not generic angels, as the few scholars who have mentioned the fresco have said;[55] rather, together with the angelic beings that flank Christ in the central medallion, they represent—albeit in an unprecedented way—the nine angelic hierarchies, closely conforming to the way they are described by the late-fifth-century writer known as Pseudo-Dionysius the Areopagite in the *Celestial Hierarchy*.[56] Although not all of the angelic ranks in the fresco can be identified with certainty, the majority appear much as the author described them in terms of their physical manifestation and attributes and may be tentatively named as follows: Seraphim appear to the left and right of Christ as fiery, multiwinged heads; Cherubim inhabit the medallion directly below, the central one of which takes the form of a winged head on an opened book; Thrones, above Christ, take the form of two angels flanking a throne; Dominations, at the upper left, are winged creatures holding scepters; Principalities, in the upper right, hold banners; Authorities, at center left, are winged half-length beings bearing keys; opposite are two half-length Archangels, one of whom holds a forceps-like tool bearing a radiant sun; and at the lower left and right corners are Powers (the central one helmeted and holding a shield) and Angels, respectively.

As for why the subject of the angelic hierarchies was selected for the fresco above the altar, it is noteworthy that the *Celestial Hierarchy* enjoyed renewed and ardent support among Catholic theologians during the post-Tridentine period in response to attacks against Pseudo-Dionysius by Protestant reformers and as part of a broader flowering of devotion to angels. And Bernard of Clairvaux—perhaps the most celebrated member of the Cistercian order, to which the nuns of Santa Susanna belonged and of which Rusticucci was cardinal protector—wrote frequently about angels, embracing the Dionysian hierarchies, with a slight shift in their order, and equating each with a corresponding spiritual path. In fact, although the ciborium fresco adheres for the most part to the Dionysian text, the depiction of an Archangel with a radiant sun and a Power with a shield and helmet seems to follow Bernard's association of the former with light and the latter with the role of guarding.[57] And there can be little doubt that the Cistercian nuns would have been familiar with Bernard's writings (at least on a general level), and so would the *confratelli* of the Confraternita di San Bernardo, which was founded to promote devotion to him. Domes featuring the nine angelic choirs, largely based on the *Celestial Hierarchy*, also proliferated in Rome in the late sixteenth century, albeit in their traditional configuration in nine concentric rings. Nowhere do they appear more conspicuously, however, than in Sixtus V's funerary chapel in Santa Maria Maggiore, a work well known to Rusticucci and his team of architects and painters. There, as in the ciborium fresco in the *confessio*, the angelic hierarchies manifest the beatific vision, "the direct, intuitive, intellectual vision of God ... [by which] the blessed are brought to fruition in ... a union with God."[58] It is the gift, as Saint Thomas Aquinas wrote, bestowed by God at man's end; and, as Saint Augustine had earlier described it, it is "the vision of the holy angels, who are also called our angels, because we, being rescued out of the power of darkness, and receiving the earnest of the Spirit, are translated into the kingdom of Christ."[59] The angels are participants with Christ in the economy of salvation and the process of sanctification, bringing true bliss, happiness, and solace to the soul.[60] The fresco of the angelic hierarchies is thus a fitting image for Rusticucci's martyrium and funerary chapel, as it represents the gift of salvation to the saints whose bodies are enshrined in the altar below and to the patron, who would in 1603 be interred just a few feet away.

The last and largest fresco, adorning the vault of the main chapel, is, like the fresco on the vault of the vestibule, a trompe l'oeil, combining fictive architecture and figures (**FIGS. 4, 12**). Above a thin band of faux marble inlays and the frieze of books and liturgical objects that ring the oval space, we see a balustrade from which rise pairs of marble columns, which, in turn, support a second balustrade crowned above the columns with gold candelabra. Beyond, the vault opens to a view of heaven, a cloud-filled sky in which, surrounding a central dove within an aureole of golden light, are seven angels who sit, kneel, or stand upon the clouds. Like the fresco on the underside of the ciborium's dome, this one, too, has confounded scholars regarding its subject. Those who have ventured an identification have called it a "glory of angels," "a view of Heaven with angels," "a glory of cherubs," or "Heaven, with the Dove of the Holy Spirit, ringed by putti."[61] A far more plausible reading of the fresco is as the representation of the Seven Gifts of the Holy Spirit, a subject that finds its origin in Isaias (11:2), in which the "spirit of the Lord" is described in terms of seven spiritual gifts—wisdom, understanding, counsel, knowledge, fortitude, piety, and fear of the Lord—which will come to rest upon the "flower" that will rise up out of the root of Jesse.

Part of a prophecy of the coming of Christ as the Messiah, the Seven Gifts became the subject of extensive exegetical study and commentary by theologians from the second century onward, beginning with Irenaeus, Origen, Victorinus of Pettau, Augustine, and Gregory the Great, among others.[62] Scholastic theologians, however, devoted even more attention to the gifts, some of the most important being Rupert of Deutz (*De operibus Spiritus Sancti*), Bonaventure (*Collationes de septem donis Spiritus Sancti*), Bernard (Sermon XIV, "De septem donis Spiritus Sancti contra septem vitia"), and, most notably,

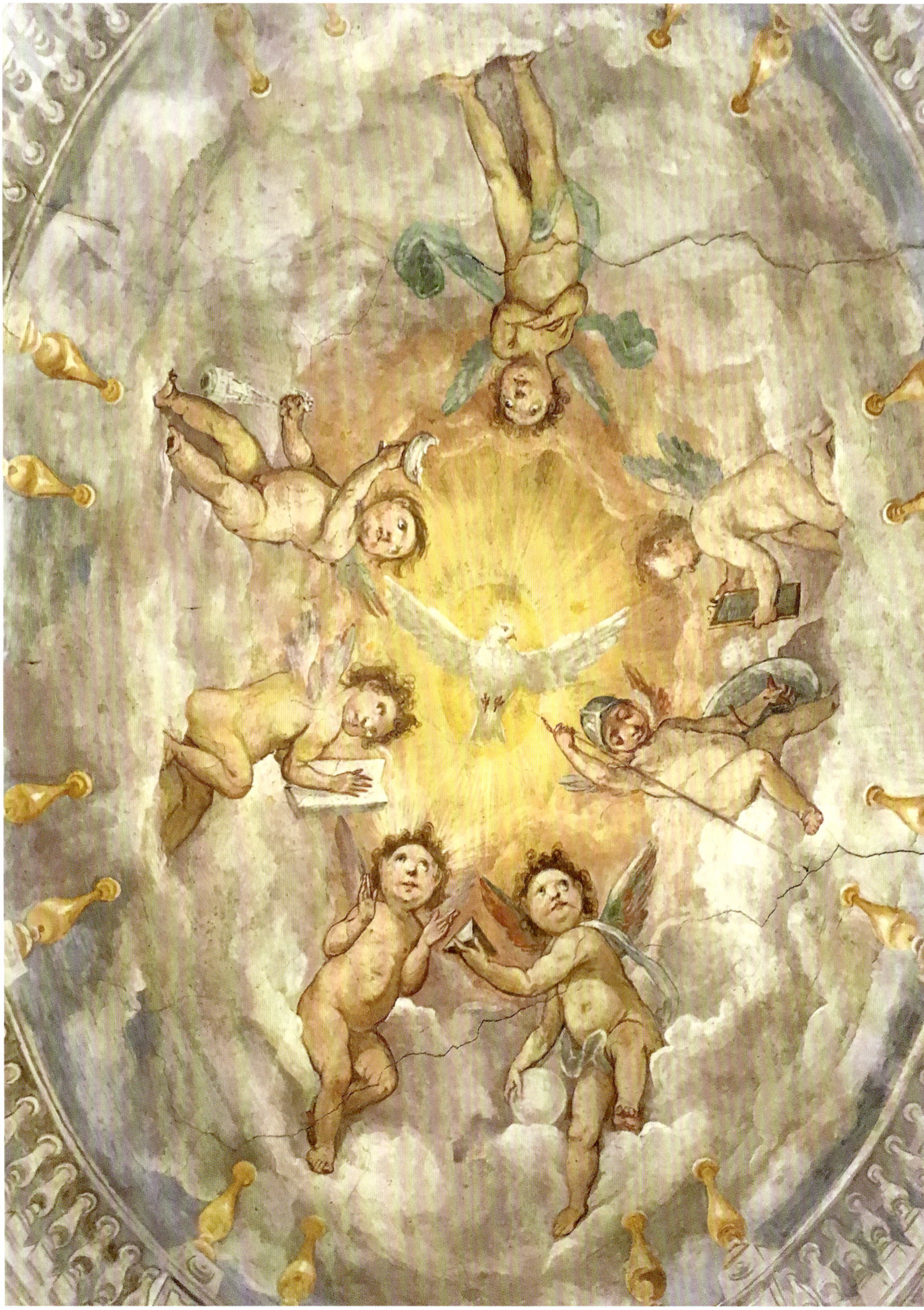

12

Thomas Aquinas (in the *Summa Theologiae*).[63] According to Church teaching, the Seven Gifts promised in Isaias manifested themselves at the baptism of Christ and to the Apostles at Pentecost, and through the gifts, the Holy Spirit—what Victorinus of Pettau called the *Spiritus septiformis*—directs the supernatural life of the soul. The gifts, Bernard tells us, work against sins and vices, and according to the Angelic Doctor—as Aquinas is aptly called—without the gifts, salvation is impossible. He also asserts that "just as the moral virtues are connected with one another in prudence, so the Gifts of the Holy Spirit are connected with one another in charity, in such wise that one who has charity has all the Gifts of the Holy Spirit."[64] And Bonaventure interprets the gifts as embodying the mystery of grace, which nourishes the soul and, in the end, brings people in union with God.

The idea to depict the Seven Gifts on the vault of the chapel may, in part, have been inspired by the fact that they were singled out in the *Catechismo del Concilio di Trento* of 1568, written on behalf of and dedicated to Rusticucci's great mentor, Pius V, as "the most noble and most propitious effects of the Holy Spirit" and—in keeping with Bonaventure—closely connected to the idea of grace.[65] And just a few years before the fresco was begun, in a volume of sermons published in 1590 by Cornelio Musso (1511–1574), the bishop of Bitonto, the Holy Spirit and the Seven Gifts figure prominently. Among all that he has to say on the subject, perhaps the most significant and relevant are his assertions that "he who has these gifts of the Holy Spirit, has all of the virtues," and "He who has the Spirit of God is always joyful, always content, delights in travails, laughs in the face of insults ... [and] triumphs over death."[66] It should also be noted that Bernard's sermon on the Seven Gifts was a *monastic* one, given to the monks at Clairvaux, and thus would also have been appropriate for the nuns of Santa Susanna and the *confratelli* of San Bernardo who would have prayed in the *confessio* chapel, either aloud or silently, and perhaps would even have read or listened to excerpts from Bernard's works. In many respects, too, the fresco of the Seven Gifts complements that of the angelic hierarchies, as both subjects relate to the idea of one's personal relationship to God. The angelic choirs act as vehicles for transmitting knowledge of God to humankind and as collaborators with him in the economy of salvation, while the Seven Gifts are one of the primary vehicles for approaching Christ and, through Christ, the Father, without whom salvation is unattainable.

As embodiments of grace, salvation, and charity, then, the Seven Gifts of the Holy Spirit was a subject well suited to the *confessio*'s multiple functions. But how does an artist depict such an abstract subject? Beginning around the twelfth century, seven doves were used to represent the Seven Gifts—an iconography that persisted until the fifteenth century.[67] A very different iconographic conception of the Seven Gifts appears at the top of Andrea di Bonaiuto's fresco of ca. 1368, *The Triumph of St. Thomas Aquinas*, in the Spanish Chapel in Santa Maria Novella, Florence, where they appear as seven hovering angels bearing various attributes.[68] Closer in date to the *confessio*'s fresco is Giorgio Vasari's *Descent of the Holy Spirit* in Santa Croce, Florence, which he completed in 1568 according to a program conceived by Vincenzo Borghini. In the upper zone of the altarpiece, above a traditional scene of the Pentecost, the Seven Gifts appear as seven angels, arranged around the dove of the Holy Spirit, each of which is distinguished by color, costume, and attribute. The "inventione" was,

FIG. 12. Baldassarre Croce, *The Seven Gifts of the Holy Spirit*, ca. 1593–1595. Confessio Chapel (vault), Santa Susanna, Rome.

as Borghini himself declared in the written program, completely "nuova," and although he intended the iconography to be easily understood, the fact is that it remains a complicated visual puzzle.[69]

Returning to the fresco in the *confessio*, what we encounter is somewhat similar to Borghini's iconography, but in contrast to Vasari's painting, there is no scene of the Pentecost, only seven nude, winged angels amid an oval ring of clouds around a central dove. But like Andrea di Bonaiuto's and Vasari's angels, each one here was clearly intended to symbolize one of the Seven Gifts. Unfortunately, neither their poses and gestures (standing, sitting, kneeling, crossing arms, etc.) nor their attributes (a pyramid and orb; a spear, helmet, and shield; a tablet or mirror; a book; and a censer) allow us to identify each as a specific gift. If the painter was inspired by Vasari's altarpiece, which he could have known from Cornelis Cort's reproductive engraving of 1574, he must have been advised to alter it, simplifying its obscure iconography.

Although the vault fresco conceptually relates to the other imagery in the *confessio*, it is, as far as I am able to determine, unique in being the only image in which all seven of the Gifts of the Holy Spirit appear together and physically independent of any other subject.[70] It is, in other words, as unprecedented as the fresco on the underside of the ciborium. As no written program for the pictorial cycle in the *confessio* has been discovered, we can only conjecture about who its inventor might have been. Rusticucci, as the patron, must have played a key role in both selecting and arranging the subjects. So, too, one would suspect, did his "ministro," Giovanni Angelo Frumenti, who was responsible for approving virtually all of the work carried out in Santa Susanna on behalf of the cardinal. Just as he controlled the ideation of the program for the chancel and nave paintings, Frumenti likely contributed significantly to conceiving (and approving) the imagery in the *confessio*.[71]

The Painter

Unlike the paintings in the chancel and the nave, no documents provide us with the name of the artist responsible for the frescoes in the *confessio*. There is general consensus, however, that Baldassarre Croce, who executed the frescoes on the walls of the nave and the counterfacade and contributed to the pictorial decoration of the chancel, is responsible for the subterranean altarpiece and the fresco on the underside of the ciborium.[72] As for the vault frescoes in the vestibule and the chapel, Alessandro Zuccari rejected an attribution to Croce, while Rossella Vodret and Elisabeth Priedl have suggested that Croce was the author of these frescoes as well.[73] There is, I believe, no reason to doubt this attribution, as the figures throughout the *confessio* have a close stylistic affinity with those in Croce's documented works in the chancel and the nave, as well as with a number of his other paintings and drawings.[74]

Especially noteworthy is the appearance in the vestibule of the rising colonnade of Solomonic columns (FIG. 7), which anticipate the twisted columns that flank Croce's Susanna scenes along the nave, which were begun in 1598. These columns are often credited to Matteo Zaccolini, the *quadratura* specialist, who arrived in Rome in 1599 and found employment as Croce's assistant. The attribution derives from Giovanni Baglione's *vita* of Zaccolini, in which he claims that he was responsible for "all of the ornamental decorations, and the grand colonnades of spiral columns" in the nave.[75] But as is clearly demonstrated by Croce's design in Chatsworth for a portion of the nave in which spiral columns are shown flanking the narrative scene, he was more than capable of such an invention. The idea for Solomonic columns in the nave must, therefore, have been based on what he had already painted in the *confessio* and intended to visually connect the imagery in the crypt to that of the church above.[76]

The *quadratura* illusionism of the vault fresco in the main chapel space is similar to that of the vault fresco in the vestibule. Here, however, the fictive architecture is more complex and, rather than Solomonic columns, the colonnade is made up of columns with straight shafts, painted to resemble *breccia di pavonazzetto* (the same marble as the altar frontal), and crowned with gold composite capitals. It is a bold invention, which unifies the space with the vestibule, and in many respects looks forward to the *quadratura* frescoes carried out by the Alberti brothers (and others) in San Silvestro al Quirinale and the Cappella Aldobrandini in Santa Maria sopra Minerva. At the same time, it looks back to and must certainly have been derived from Giovanni Guerra's fictive cupola in San Girolamo degli Schiavoni, painted in 1589–1591, where Solomonic columns rise up from a balustrade to form a drum pierced with *oculi*, which opens up to a celestial vision of the Trinity with Saint John the Baptist and the Virgin.[77] But in contrast to the successful illusionism of Guerra's fictive dome, by virtue of its distance from the viewer below, Croce's vault falls short; within the relatively shallow space of the chapel, the viewer is simply too close to the vault for the perspective to do its magic (FIG. 4).

Conclusion

The *confessio* in Santa Susanna is a remarkable example of the early Christian revival in post-Tridentine Rome, a recreation *alla moderna* of a subterranean *memoria*, in which the fictive marble revetment, faux mosaics, and altar ciborium emulate models from the Christian antique.[78] While it is true, as Alessandro Zuccari has argued, that Rusticucci lacked the archaeological rigor and respect for Christian antiquities demonstrated by Cesare Baronio and some other cardinals of the period in restoring their titular churches, he nevertheless appears to have endeavored to retain at least part of the Leonine semiannular crypt and, possibly, portions of the original altar and to commemorate the early Christian martyr-saints Susanna, Gabinius, and Felicita in as splendid a way as possible.[79]

Although indebted to Sixtus V's crypts in Santa Maria Maggiore and Santa Sabina, Rusticucci's *confessio* stands apart from its predecessors for the complexity of both its architectural design and its pictorial program. It also anticipates, and no doubt influenced, the new crypt of Santa Cecilia of 1600 by Cardinal Paolo Camillo Sfondrato in the saint's eponymous church, as well as the crypt chapel of Santa Prisca in her titular church, created on behalf of Cardinal Benedetto Giustiniani at the same time.[80] But in contrast to the shrine in Santa Cecilia, which announces its contents with a cult statue of the saint before the high altar, in Santa Susanna, the *confessio* is a hidden treasure, a "tesoro nascosto," to borrow from the title of Panciroli's devotional guidebook, which can only be discovered by descending to it. And unlike the crypt chapel of Santa Prisca, which is adorned with narrative paintings, the frescoes in Rusticucci's *confessio* are iconic, abstract, and theological in nature. The saints' holy deaths are narrated above, in the chancel, in Tommaso Laureti's altarpiece and the frescoes by Croce and Nogari. In the sacred domain of Rusticucci's *confessio*—which, with its self-contained spatial effect, gently vaulted ceiling, and minimal light, powerfully evokes the space of the catacombs—there was no need to narrate the saints' martyrdoms. Here, instead, in the devotional heart of Santa Susanna, the faithful visitor comes face-to-face with their likenesses in the altarpiece and with their sacred remains in the altar, experiencing what the English Catholic writer Gregory Martin wrote in 1581 about the tombs of saints he encountered in Rome:

> if any where a man stand nigh to these tombes, he perceaveth his sense, by and by ravished with this sayd force, for the sight of the coffin entring into the hart, pierceth it, stirreth it up, and moveth it in such a manner, as if he that lyeth there dead, did pray with us, and were visibly present to be seen.[81]

Notes

I wish to express my heartfelt thanks to Paul Barolsky, Fabio Barry, James Clifton, Chiara Franceschini, Pamela Jones, Lucia Morganti, Irina Oryshkevich, Livio Pestilli, Elisabeth Priedl, Conrad Rudolph, and Patrizia Tosini for their generous encouragement, help, and guidance.

1 — Respectively, Totti 1638, 272 ("questo sotterraneo, e venerando luogo"), and Panciroli 1600, 790, who asks rhetorically: "Ma che dirò ... della Capella di sotto? Qual cosa più bella, e degna: qual gemma legata in oro più risplende?" In calling the *confessio* unprecedented in its plan and richness of decoration, my reference is to other crypts created in Cinquecento Rome (on which, see below). The Cappella del Succorpo in the Duomo of Naples, dating to 1497–1506, which also serves as a subterranean funerary and reliquary chapel, is, in fact, richer in its decoration but not as innovative in its plan.

2 — These include the fifth-century *Martyrologium Hieronymianum* and the *Passio Sanctae Susannae*, both cited in Krautheimer, Corbett, and Frankl 1937–1980 [1970], 255. See also Ugonio 1588, 191; Kirsch 1918, 70–71; Apollonj Ghetti 1965, 10–13; Diefenbach 2007, 343–345. Gaius is often spelled Caius.

3 — On the legends and traditions surrounding their lives and martyrdoms, see Baronio 1586, 91 (Gabinius: February 19), 176 (Gaius: April 22), 360 (Susanna: August 11); Gallonio 1591a, 145–154; Baronio 1617, II, 675–680; Panciroli 1625, 334–340; Baronio 1656, 695–699; Ribadeneyra 1604, 80–82 (Susanna, Feste di Agosto), 219 (Gaius: Feste di Aprile).

4 — Duchesne 1892, II, 3–4; Baronio 1588–1607 [1600], IX, 476–477; Apollonj Ghetti 1965, 28–32, 42–43; Krautheimer, Corbett, and Frankl 1937–1980 [1970], 256. For an excellent summary of the early history of the church, with references both to the early sources and the archaeological evidence, see Priedl 2004, 27–49.

5 — On the semiannular crypt, see Apollonj Ghetti 1965, 52–54; Krautheimer, Corbett, and Frankl 1937–1980 [1970], 272; Apollonj Ghetti 1984, 207; de Blaauw 1995, 567; Priedl 2004, 37–42; Emerick 2005, 61–62. Only Guidobaldi and Sabbi (2016, 551) reject the argument that the crypt of Leo III was semiannular. On the martyrdom of Santa Felicita, see Baronio 1586, 528 (November 23); Baronio 1617, II, 191–192; Baronio 1656, part I, 446. On Leo's translation of the body of Santa Felicita, see Bosio 1650, 449–453; Piazza 1675, 90. According to Bosio and other early writers, Leo's translation of Felicita's body to the church of Santa Susanna was determined by the fact that Susanna was herself originally buried in the same cemetery on the via Salaria. On the veracity of the translation of the body of Santa Felicita and of the actual bodies of the saints housed in the crypt, see Priedl 2004, 43–53.

6 — The work is generally dated 1475–1477. Sixtus's facade is illustrated in the woodcut in Santi 1588, 59v (republished in Francino 1595, 113). On Sixtus IV's work on the church, see Urban 1961–1962, 272–273.

7 — On the architectural interventions, see especially Apollonj Ghetti 1965, 56–63, 74; Hibbard 1971, 39–40, 111–114. On the pictorial decorations, see Apollonj Ghetti 1965, 63–73; Buchowiecki 1974, 1005–1008, 1011–1013; Abromson 1981, 135–141, 355–356; Macioce 1990, 144–145; Affanni, Cogotti, and Vodret 1993, 21, 28–46; Steinemann 1996, esp. 2–9, 77–79; Zuccari 2004; Priedl

2004, esp. 138–167; Jones 2008, 13–74, esp. 21–38; Priedl 2014.

8 — Ugonio 1588, 193v: "Girolamo Cardinale Rusticucci Titolare à nostri tempi l'ha commodamente rassettata." This passage is cited by Hibbard 1971, 111.

9 — The nave also features four stucco statues of prophets, generally attributed to Giovanni Antonio Paracca il Valsoldo. See di Giammaria 2012, 228–229.

10 — The following biographical sketch of Rusticucci is drawn primarily from Chacón 1630, II, cols. 1717–1719; Farlati 1753, 606; Cardella 1793, 148–150; Castellani 1900; Davis 1962; Prete 2001–2002; Bellavia 2003, esp. 25–30; Jones 2008, 20–21; Brunelli 2017.

11 — Although named to this last position in January 1590, he was not confirmed in this post until February 1592.

12 — Von Pastor 1951, XVII, 167, n. 4: "di ingegno posato, ma sagace, di moto tardo, ma diligente, di buoni sentimenti, ma di tardissima espressione ... ha più prudenza che dottrina."

13 — See Davis 1962, 334–335.

14 — Chacón 1630, II, col. 1718.

15 — The edict, dated December 22, 1593, was first published by Beggiao 1978, 106. See also Zuccari 1984, 16–17; Hecht 1997, 35–36.

16 — On his criticism of the *Last Judgment*, see De Maio 1978, 40; on Clement VIII's pastoral visits and his decrees concerning art, see Beggiao 1978; Mansour 2013.

17 — Between 1589 and 1591, Sixtus V's sister, Camilla, entrusted the building and decoration of the Chapel of Saint Lawrence in Santa Susanna to Fontana, Nebbia, and another Sistine painter, Giovanni Battista Pozzo. See Guerrieri Borsoi 1993b. Rusticucci had earlier (ca. 1584–1591) shown his preference for Fontana and Maderno, when he entrusted them with the enlargement and remodeling of his palace in the Borgo, purchased ca. 1570. See Hibbard 1971, 109–110. On Rusticucci's earlier artistic patronage, see Davis 1962; Prete 2001–2002, 158–163; Bellavia 2003, 30–35.

18 — Davis 1962, 335; Bellavia 2003, 28–29. Ironically, Rusticucci was serving as cardinal protector of the Pantheon. The destruction of Leo III's apse mosaic in 1595 was lamented by contemporary writers, as Chacón (1630, col. 1718) records.

19 — See Ostrow 2016, 518–519, with additional bibliography.

20 — Hibbard 1971, 109, 111.

21 — Archivio di Stato di Roma (hereafter ASR), Notai Auditor Camerae, b. 4024, G. B. Maynus notarius, fols. 1038–1039v; b. 4027, G. B. Maynus notarius, fols. 482r–v and 487r–v; b. 6236, D. Ricci notarius, fols. 343–344, respectively; cited and partially transcribed in Hibbard 1971, 112.

22 — Lotz 1955, 93; Hubala 1965, 161; Krautheimer, Corbett, and Frankl 1937–1980 [1970], 259; Hibbard 1971, 39–40, 112; Buchowiecki 1974, 1013. As far as I am aware, only Priedl (2004, 111, 115) and Kämpf (2015, 122) have suggested that Fontana also played a role in its design. Although Fontana initially left Rome for Naples in June 1592, he did not settle in the southern city until mid-1594, and documents attest to his being in and out of Rome until 1596. See Hibbard 1971, 37; Verde 2009, 82.

23 — Roma, Biblioteca Casanatense, Pompeo Ugonio, ms. 878: "la confessione, o sia grotta sotto l'altare maggiore" (transcribed—with the incorrect *segnatura* and without fol. number—in Berthier 1910, 323, n. 1); and Ugonio 1588, 11, respectively. Its plan is recorded in Francesco Borromini's drawing in the Albertina (IT.AZ.250). It was dismantled ca. 1918 during the renovation of the church. For more on this *confessio*, see Berthier 1910, 87–92; Muñoz 1919, 35; Muñoz 1938, 16, 37, 48–53 (with photographs prior to its removal); Darsy 1961, 38; Krautheimer, Corbett, and Frankl 1937–1980 [1976], 73, 78; Levy 1999–2000, 406.

24 — See Ostrow 1996, 25, 30–35; Ostrow 2009, 22–23.

25 — "vi farà una baluastrata intorno con scalini per poter scendere a basso et andar a celebrar messa all'altare e corpi de detti Santi Apostoli." First published in Orbaan 1919, 44; republished in Hibbard 1971, 185.

26 — Paul V "resolve di far aprire sotto l'altare maggiore di San Pietro un paio di scalette, accioché dalla medesima chiesa si possa andar a dire et udir messa nell'altar delli Apostoli ... in quella guisa, che stanno le cappelle sotto l'altar maggiore di San Giovannj Laterano et del Presepio in Santa Maria Maggiore." First published in Orbaan 1919, 98; republished in Hibbard 1971, 186. The other reference in the *avviso* is to the *confessio* in the Lateran, restructured by Clement VIII, on which see Freiberg 1995, 38, 282–283. On the relationship between the *confessio* in Santa Susanna and that in St. Peter's, see Hibbard 1971, 72; Bellini 1999, 50–51. See also Apollonj Ghetti 1965, 82, where he inexplicably attributes the conception of the *confessio* in St. Peter's to Giacomo Della Porta.

27 — Fontana would also go on to renovate and enlarge the crypts in the Duomo of Salerno (enshrining the relics of Saint Matthew) and in the Duomo of Amalfi (housing relics of Saint Andrew), in both of which the architectural vocabulary is close to that in the *confessio* of Santa Susanna. See Restaino and Zampino 2012.

28 — I use the word *oval* instead of *ellipse*, as the latter term denotes an oval form with precise mathematical measurements, which this space does not have.

29 — Lotz (1955, 93) cites the influence of Vignola and Francesco da Volterra. Vignola also produced oval designs for the church of the Gesù. Although the design process for San Giacomo began in 1590, its founding was in 1592.

30 — When, exactly, Maderno began to work with da Volterra on the church has been debated. Lotz (1955, 61–64) argued for his definitive role beginning in 1590; Pecchiai and Montini (1958, 23) argue for 1592; Hibbard (1971, 118) claims 1594.

31 — Panciroli 1600, 790; Panciroli 1625, 340. See also Totti 1638, 272, who repeats Panciroli's description of 1625, as do several later guidebooks to Rome.

32 — On the origins and meanings of the *confessio*, see Leclercq 1914, cols. 2503–2508.

33 — Ugonio 1588, 192v (see below, n. 45); Ugonio (192v) also transcribes an inscription in the earlier crypt, lost during its renovation, which recorded the presence of the bodies of Susanna and Gabinius: "Olim Presbyteri Gabini filia felix / Hic Susanna iacet in pace patri sociata." Among other early writers to record the presence of the three bodies in Rusticucci's crypt are Felini (1610, 193–194) and Bosio (1650, 453), who also transcribes the early inscription.

34 — See Krautheimer (1942, 9) on the danger of always reading meaning into architectural plans.

35 — Sinding-Larsen 1965, 219–220, 230; see also Lotz 1955; Lotz 1977, 66–73.

36 — Vincenzo Scamozzi (in his *L'idea dell'architettura universale*, 1615) wrote: "appresso la rotondità perfetta, le forme ovali sono più vicine a quella." Quoted in Lotz 1955, 16. Scamozzi

was here rephrasing what Serlio had written about ovals in his *Quinto libro d'architettura* (1547).

37 — On its association with amphitheaters, see Lotz 1955, 16–17, with additional bibliography. Arnolfini (1603, 8) and Ugonio (1603, 22), respectively; both are cited in Hibbard 1971, 119.

38 — I quote the passage as cited in Brown 1981, 35. For more on the tradition of *depositio ad sanctos*, see Brown 1981, esp. 27, 32–35.

39 — The full inscription reads: "HIERONYMVS RVSTICVCIVS / S.R.E. PRESB. CARD / TITVLI HVIVS ECCLESIAE / VICARIVS PAPAE / MONVMENTVM AD SS. MARTRES / DEVOTIONIS CAVSA / VIVENS SIBI POSVIT / ANNO AETATIS SVAE LIX / SAL. HVM. M.D.XCV / OBIIT XIV IVNII M.DCIII." As the inscription makes evident, the tomb slab was placed in 1595, eight years prior to his death in 1603.

40 — For a cogent synthesis of the relationship between Santa Susanna, the Cistercian nuns, and the Confraternita di San Bernardo, see Jones 2008, 45–49. In his *Trattato di tutte l'opera pie di alma città di Roma* of 1601 (207), dedicated to Girolamo Rusticucci, Camillo Fanucci, after describing the cardinal's transformation of the Cappella Maggiore (or chancel), writes that he rebuilt "un altra Cappella [in reference to the *confessio*] ... veramente Regia e degna di tal Signore," which "visitano i fratelli della Confraternita."

41 — Apollonj Ghetti 1965, 53, 82; and Apollonj Ghetti 1984, 207.

42 — Piazza 1675, 77: "Nell'oratorio sotterraneo magnificamente ristorato, & abbellito in S. Susanna vi è l'Altare, ove questo s. Pontefice [Gaius] celebrò più volte Messa in onore della Santa sua Nipote Susanna." See also Panciroli 1600, 788; Panciroli 1625, 339; Piazza 1690, 334; Piazza 1702, 220; Piazza 1703, 363.

43 — The candelabra are very close cousins of the pair that top Maderno's Santa Susanna facade, while the Ionic capitals anticipate those he designed for the Cappella Salviati in San Gregorio Magno. See Hibbard 1971, figs. 11C, 13.

44 — On medieval altar tables and canopies, see Braun 1924, I, 135–174, pls. 11–22; II, 189–242, pls. 151–169. Braun (II, 237, pl. 173) cites and illustrates Maderno's Santa Susanna ciborium in his larger discussion. Livio Pestilli (written communication, June 11, 2018) has suggested that the lobed altar rail was an intentional evocation, in its shape, of early baptismal pools, an allusion to the fact that the day of martyrdom is considered the *dies natalis*, a (re-)birth in Christ, like baptism itself.

45 — Ugonio 1588, 192v: "Vi è in capo l'altar maggiore con il ciborio di marmo, & sotto la confessione ò Martirio, dove i corpi santi riposano."

46 — Panciroli 1625, 341: "ornamenti per tutta la cappella di questo sotteranneo." Piazza 1702, 220: "ornate nobilmente d'intorno di marmi, e di vaghe pitture dal Cardinal Rusticucci." Piazza (1690, 334) describes it as "sontuosamente ornata." The pictorial program has largely been ignored but has been described, in whole or in part, by Hubala 1965, 161; Apollonj Ghetti 1965, 82–83; Buchowiecki 1974, 1013; and Affanni, Cogotti, and Vodret 1993, 46. Priedl (2004, 118–122) offers the most complete consideration of the frescoes but misidentifies the iconography of two of the most important parts of the pictorial program. The frescoes were rather poorly restored in the late eighteenth century and again in 1955. Despite much overpainting, the original program was not altered. I am grateful to Lucia Morganti, who is currently engaged in restoring much of Santa Susanna, for discussing the earlier interventions and confirming the integrity of the original fresco program.

47 — Lotz 1955, 92; Hubala 1965, 161.

48 — See the essay by Fabio Barry in this volume.

49 — See the essay by Enrico Parlato in this volume.

50 — On the revival of early Christian revetment at this time, see Ostrow 1990; Ostrow 2000, esp. 247–249. The cladding in Santi Cosma e Damiano is recorded in a drawing by Pirro Ligorio (BAV, Vat. lat. 3439); that in the Oratorio della Santa Croce is recorded in a drawing attributed to Giuliano da Sangallo (BAV, Barb. lat. 4424) and in an engraving by Antonio Lafréry.

51 — Hubala 1965; see also Ostrow 2009.

52 — In the spandrel-like spaces below the fictive colonnade, as well as on the vaults of the entrance corridors that lead to the vestibule are oval and octagonal medallions, painted in tones of brown and gold to simulate bronze, depicting additional angels bearing crowns.

53 — The altarpiece is briefly discussed by (in addition to those cited above, n. 46) Abromson 1981, 138; Steinemann 1996, 78, cat. no. 18; Zuccari 2004, 53, n. 9.

54 — The underside of the canopy of the eleventh-century ciborium in Tuscania, referred to above as a possible model for Maderno's, is painted with images of the Evangelists, which were added sometime later. This emulation is also seen in the ciborium erected (between 1597 and 1603) by Cesare Baronio in San Cesareo de Appia, where the underside of the canopy is adorned with a ring of cherubim and, at their center, the dove of the Holy Spirit.

55 — Apollonj Ghetti 1965, 83: "Christ surrounded by angels." Buchowiecki 1974, 1013: "Half-figure of the blessing Christ." Abromson 1981, 138: "a figure of the Savior." Affanni, Cogotti, and Vodret 1993, 46: "*Christ in the act of blessing* the globe and cross, surrounded by angels bearing symbols of Christ." Steinemann 1996, 77: "The Blessing Christ within a glory of angels." Priedl 2004, 123: "Christ."

56 — On the Dionysian *Celestial Hierarchy*—its meanings, polemical status in the post-Tridentine period, and depiction in art—see Ostrow 1996, 105–109; Gill 2014.

57 — See Saint Bernard of Clairvaux's *On Consideration*, V.5.12, quoted in Chase 2002, 107.

58 — Redle 1967, 186.

59 — Aquinas, *Summa Theologiae*, as cited in Redle 1967, 187. Augustine, *De civitate Dei*, in Augustine ed. 1948, II, 656.

60 — Chase 2002, 71.

61 — Apollonj Ghetti 1965, 83; Buchowiecki 1974, 1013; Affanni, Cogotti, and Vodret 1993, 46; Priedl 2004, 123, respectively.

62 — My discussion of the Seven Gifts of the Holy Spirit is drawn primarily from Edward D. O'Connor's commentary in Aquinas ed. 2006, 80–115; Stroud 2012; Mulhern 2003.

63 — Rupert of Deutz ed. 1854, CLXVII; Bonaventure ed. 2008; Bernard ed. 1887, 553–554; and Aquinas ed. 2006, Question 68, 1–8, respectively.

64 — Aquinas ed. 2006, 13, 19, 27, Question 68, Ia 2ae. 68, 2, 4, and 5.

65 — *Catechismo* 1568, 103–104.
66 — Musso 1590, 582 and 226, respectively. Musso's sermons were preached for Lent in 1542 before Paul III but not published prior to this edition.
67 — They appear in this form, for example, in the Tree of Jesse window of Saint Denis of ca. 1144 (see Rudolph 2011, 402–404) and again in a manuscript in the Walters Art Museum, Baltimore, *Duke Albrecht's Table of Christian Faith* (Walters ms. W. 171, fol. 53r), dated to 1400–1404, in an illuminated initial.
68 — Bargellini (1954, 24), Diek (1997, 86–87), and Berger (2017, 30) identify these hovering figures as the Seven Gifts. In contrast, Meiss (1951, 100), Romano (1976, 188), and Polzer (1995, 264) identify them as the seven virtues. I am grateful to Babette Bohn for alerting me to this fresco.
69 — See Hall 1979, 136–140, where she also transcribes Borghini's program for the painting. The gifts and their characterization are (from left to right): Wisdom, with the rays of the sun on his chest and behind his head; Counsel, holding a scepter and wearing a floral crown; Piety, holding a censer and wearing a crown of grain and lilies; Fear of the Lord, kneeling, holding a cross, and crowned with olive; Knowledge, holding a book and wearing a gemmed crown; Fortitude, wearing armor and holding a shield and palm branches; and Understanding, wearing a winged crown studded with stars. However obscure Borghini's invention was, it was soon repeated by Santi di Tito, with modest changes, in his *God the Father with the Seven Gifts of the Holy Spirit* of 1582 in the Santuario di Santa Maria del Soccorso in Prato, which was clearly based on Vasari's painting. See Spalding 1982, 361–364; Bastogi 2002, 23–49. In contrast to Vasari's angels, Santi di Tito's are nude. The painter would also incorporate the Seven Gifts in his *Annunciation* of ca. 1602/1603 in Santa Maria Novella. Another Tuscan altarpiece to include the same iconography is the *Pentecost* of ca. 1590, attributed to the school of Giovanni Bizzelli, in San Pietro a Grignano.
70 — At almost the same time this fresco was completed (ca. 1595), a set of seven prints representing the Seven Gifts, by Adriaen Collaert, after Johannes Stradanus, was published, with each gift represented by an Old Testament narrative scene. Around 1580, Collaert also produced a suite of seven prints after Maarten de Vos, in which each of the Seven Gifts is represented by an allegorical female figure. I am grateful to James Clifton for alerting me to this second series. It should also be noted that the Seven Gifts in the fresco do not correspond in their iconography to the way they are described in Cesare Ripa's *Iconologia* of 1593.
71 — Zuccari (2004, 39) asserts that Frumenti "esercitò un ruolo di rilievo nella fase di elaborazione delle iconografie dell'intera decorazione. Quasi certamente fu lo stesso Frumenti a controllare l'ideazione e l'esecuzione dei dipinti che decorano l'area del presbiterio."
72 — Possanzini 1985; Steinemann 1996, 77–78; Zuccari 2004, 53, n. 9.
73 — Zuccari 2004, 53, n. 9; Affanni, Cogotti, and Vodret 1993, 46; Priedl 2004, 118–119.
74 — The angels on both vaults are very closely related to those in Croce's study for a *Pentecost*, which sold at auction at Sotheby's London in 2013 (its present whereabouts are unknown to me).
75 — Baglione 1642, 316 (also in his *vita* of Baldassarre Croce, 298). This attribution, repeated in subsequent guidebooks to Rome, has been widely accepted; see, for example, Bell 1985, 233–236; Macioce 1990, 144; Affanni, Cogotti, and Vodret 1993, 29; Zuccari 2004, 38–39.
76 — Priedl (2001, 116), argued this point with respect to the nave columns but not in relation to the frescoes in the *confessio*. The Chatsworth drawing is reproduced as her fig. 5. Croce's frescoes in the Sala Regia in the Palazzo dei Priori, Viterbo, painted between 1588 and 1591, also demonstrate his abilities as a painter of fictive architecture.
77 — On Guerra's fictive dome fresco, see Mangia Renda 1993. I arrived at this comparison independently of Priedl (2004, 121), who makes the same claim for Guerra's fresco being a source for Croce's.
78 — In calling it *alla moderna*, I follow Cesare Baronio, who in a letter dated February 22, 1597, described the recently renovated *confessio* in S. Paolo fuori le Mura—with its open form and staircase down to the shrine—as being "rinovato … alla moderna," a designation diametrically opposed to the closed and more traditional crypts he created in Santi Nereo ed Achilleo and San Cesareo de Appia and the one he planned for the Chiesa Nuova, all of which, in his mind, were properly "all'antica." See Ostrow 2009, 21–24, esp. 24, nn. 32–33.
79 — Zuccari 1985, 501–503; Zuccari 2004, 38.
80 — On the crypt of Santa Cecilia and its debt to Rusticucci's *confessio*, see Kämpf 2015, esp. 120, 124. On Giustiniani's renovation and decoration of the crypt of Santa Prisca, see Krautheimer, Corbett, and Frankl 1937–1980 [1971], 263–279; Zuccari 1984, 93; Zuccari 2001; Gallavotti Cavallero 2010, 59–65.
81 — Martin 1581 [1969], 27.

A Splendid Shrine for an Ugly Image

VISUAL INTERACTIONS IN THE SALVIATI CHAPEL AT SAN GREGORIO AL CELIO

Chiara Franceschini

"There you saw a noble chapel, part of the house of Gregory, where the image of the heavenly Virgin is shown, which is said to have spoken to that most holy Pontiff. The old age and long span of time (*vetustas*) have removed any beauty (*venustas*) from this image; this [chapel] now, thanks to the generous munificence of Salviati, for the mottled columns, the gilded vault, and the elegant work of painting, shines so brightly that the ornament of the place responds admirably to the dignity of the religion."[1]

Lacking beauty

In his funerary oration for Cardinal Antonio Maria Salviati, held in the church of San Giacomo in Augusta on January 22, 1603, ten months following the cardinal's death, Pompeo Ugonio thus described the cardinal's chapel (*sacrarium*) within the church of San Gregorio al Celio (FIG. 1).[2] The passage is remarkable, as it offers a comprehensive interpretation of the conception and decoration of the "noble chapel" as a modern project, which, both in its entirety and in its details, was oriented around the reinstallation of a Marian image valued for its antiquity and associations but considered lacking in "any beauty" due to the passage of time.

As in other cases in this volume, important studies exist as well on certain aspects of the Salviati Chapel; however, they primarily have focused on its architecture.[3] Although Ugonio clearly had done so, modern scholars have rarely considered the various decorative elements of the chapel in relation to one another within their spatial context. Furthermore, the chapel in San Gregorio al Celio has never been considered in relation to the other contemporary works promoted by the cardinal, which help to clarify its genesis and meaning. This essay therefore examines the history and decoration of the Salviati Chapel—as the repository of the image of the Virgin—in its entirety and in relation to two other chapels created by the same patron in the church of San Giacomo. In considering this dialogue among the chapels, I analyze the rationale behind the project at San Gregorio and its purpose to valorize antique images and the role played by Pope Gregory the Great in promoting the cult of the Virgin. I also discuss the artistic experimentation that took place in Rome at the turn of the seventeenth century. As I will argue, the Salviati Chapel reveals a new awareness, simultaneously conservative and expository, that should be considered in light of previous and contemporary projects aimed to enhance miraculous images, as promoted by Salviati himself and other Roman patrons. And through a consideration of its peculiarities and novel elements, the chapel—designed and decorated *ex novo* by the cardinal's artists—can be understood as the site at which an unprecedented dialogue between antiquity and modernity played out. This dialogue was aimed not only at the recovery of devotional and proto-archaeological elements of the Christian past but also at an original and modern creation that resulted from an experimental form of visual analysis and a new discourse of stylistic judgment.

Two issues need to be kept in mind with respect to an understanding of Salviati's chapel at San Gregorio. First of all, it has changed considerably since its unveiling. Giovanni Battista Ricci's frescoes are damaged, at least as far as the two lateral walls are concerned. The right wall was completely repainted in

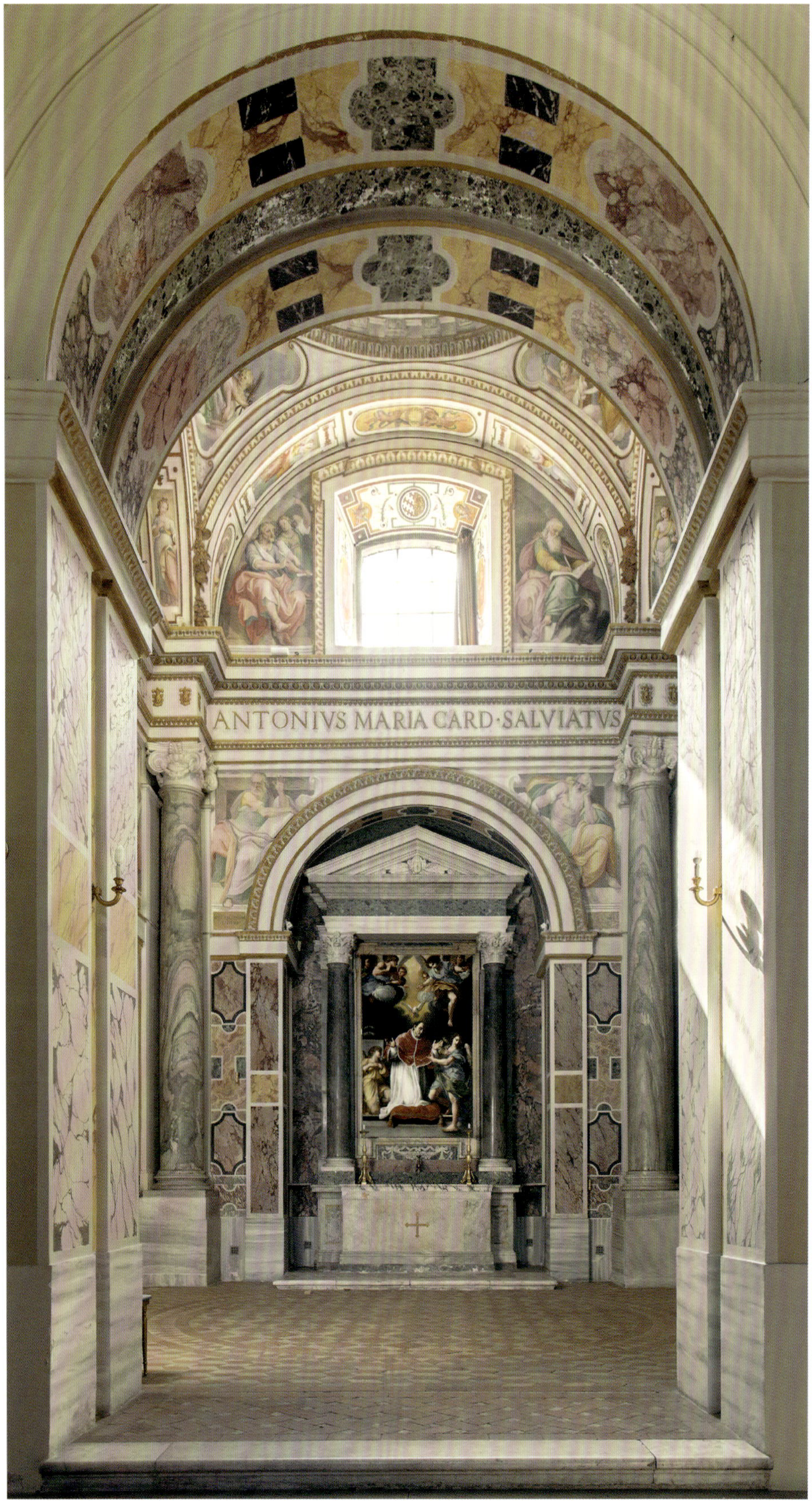

1

FIG. 1. Salviati Chapel, Santi Andrea e Gregorio al Monte Celio, Rome.

1839 by the Danish painter Christen Købke, and the modern restoration appears to be only partial (FIG. 3).[4] The wall to the left of the altar is largely obscured, due to the 1757 relocation there of what was once the high altar of San Gregorio, commissioned in 1469 by the abbot Gregorio Amatisco Romano and dismantled in 1733 (FIG. 2).[5] The biggest change, however, concerns the replacement of the altarpiece by Annibale Carracci with a copy executed in 1800 when French troops removed the original from the church and sent it to Paris (FIG. 4). This action led to an irrevocable loss because the painting, intercepted in Genoa by Vincenzo Camuccini and purchased in London in 1801 by Lord Radstock, ended up in the Bridgewater House collection that was destroyed in 1941.[6] The second issue concerns the type of chapel it is: unlike many of the cases dealt with in other essays in this volume, Salviati's commission is not a sepulchral chapel.

Salviati's Chapels, Salviati's Madonnas

As early as April 1593, Antonio Maria Salviati (1537–1602) had chosen the apse of the church of San Giacomo in Augusta—the church that he himself had built—as his future burial site rather than the family chapel at Santa Maria sopra Minerva.[7] A bronze commemorative plaque to the right of the high altar of San Giacomo bears an inscription of the works promoted by the cardinal (provisioned for in his will of 1593 and installed by his nephew in 1604).[8] His coat of arms and the commemorative plaque are integrated into the two apse frescoes by Vespasiano Strada (ca. 1582–1622), depicting, respectively, *The Fall of Manna* and the more rarely depicted scene of *Melchizedek Delivering the Blessed Bread to Abraham* (Genesis 14:18 and Hebrews 7:3; FIGS. 5–6). Together the scenes have a Eucharistic meaning (the first perhaps also a supersessionist connotation by presenting Melchizedek as a non-Jewish priest). Regardless, the two scenes also allude to the cardinal's much-praised charitable works; in particular, the delivery of the bread (placed in direct visual relationship with the funerary inscription below) seems to refer to the recurrent donations of white bread to the poor ordered by the cardinal in the last years of his life.[9] Here, as well as in the chapel of San Gregorio, it is worth noting the preeminence of signs of personal representation, particularly the crests and inscriptions of a cardinal, whose fame, however, was linked not so much with pomp and monumental self-representation but rather with his great financial and material commitment to charity. Even so, his name and his coat of arms—which in the apse fresco of San Giacomo even takes the place of a basket to collect the manna held by a woman in the foreground (FIG. 5)—are omnipresent, as prominent "media" of the cardinal's person and body.[10]

While the exact chronology of the chapel of San Gregorio al Celio is not entirely known, it is possible to hypothesize that its conception dates back to the end of the same year of 1593. Antonio Maria Salviati returned to Rome in June 1578, after having been the apostolic nuncio to France for seven years (1572–1578), and was raised to the cardinalate on December 12, 1583, by Gregory XIII. Over the last twenty years of his life, Salviati distinguished himself through his generosity. He rebuilt the hospital of San Giacomo (1587), of which he had been appointed guardian-prelate; built the church of San Giacomo in Augusta (first stone laid on May 20, 1592); founded the hospital of San Rocco delle Partorienti; and established the Collegio Salviati for the orphans of Santa Maria in Aquiro

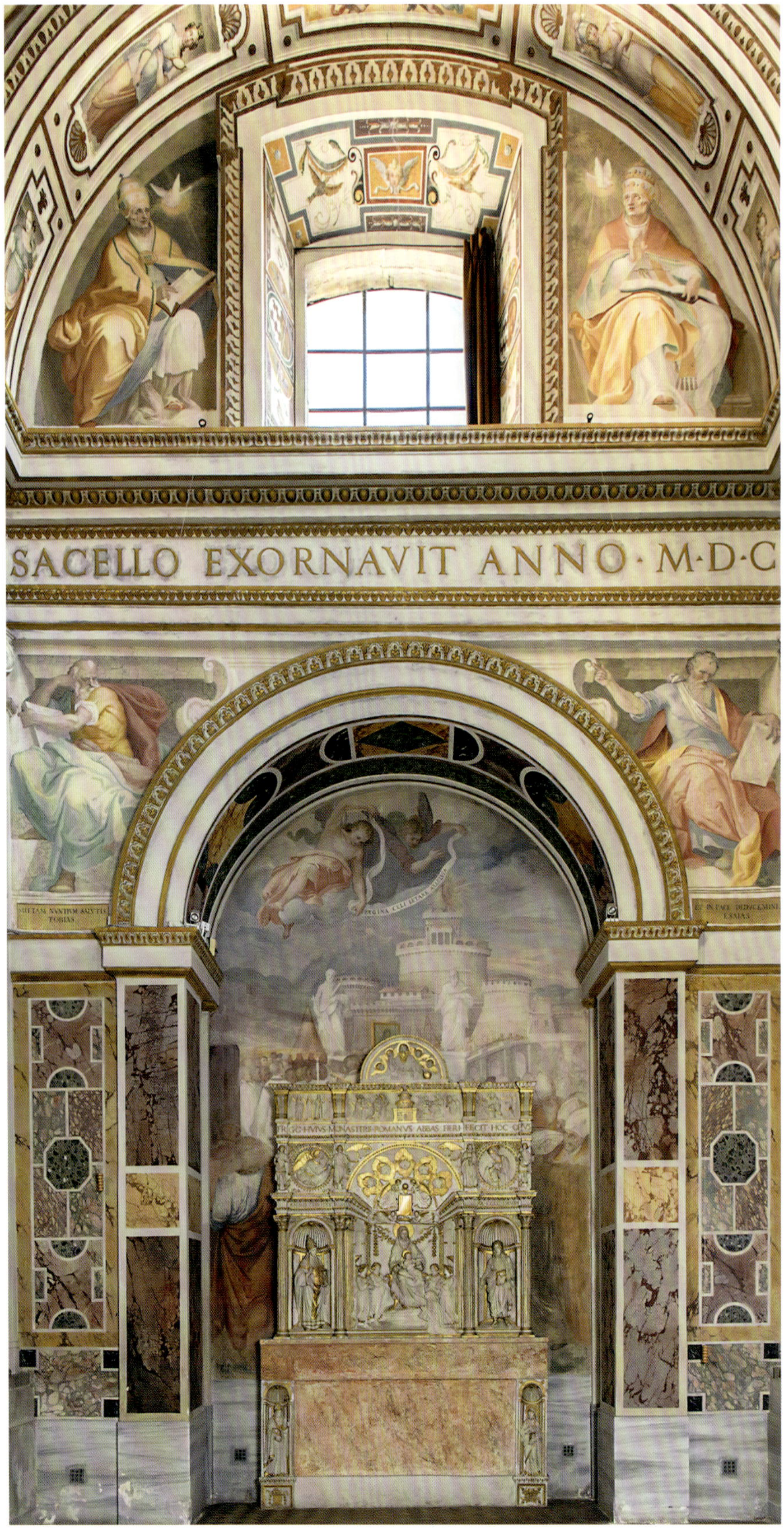

2

FIG. 2. Salviati Chapel (left wall), Santi Andrea e Gregorio al Monte Celio, Rome.

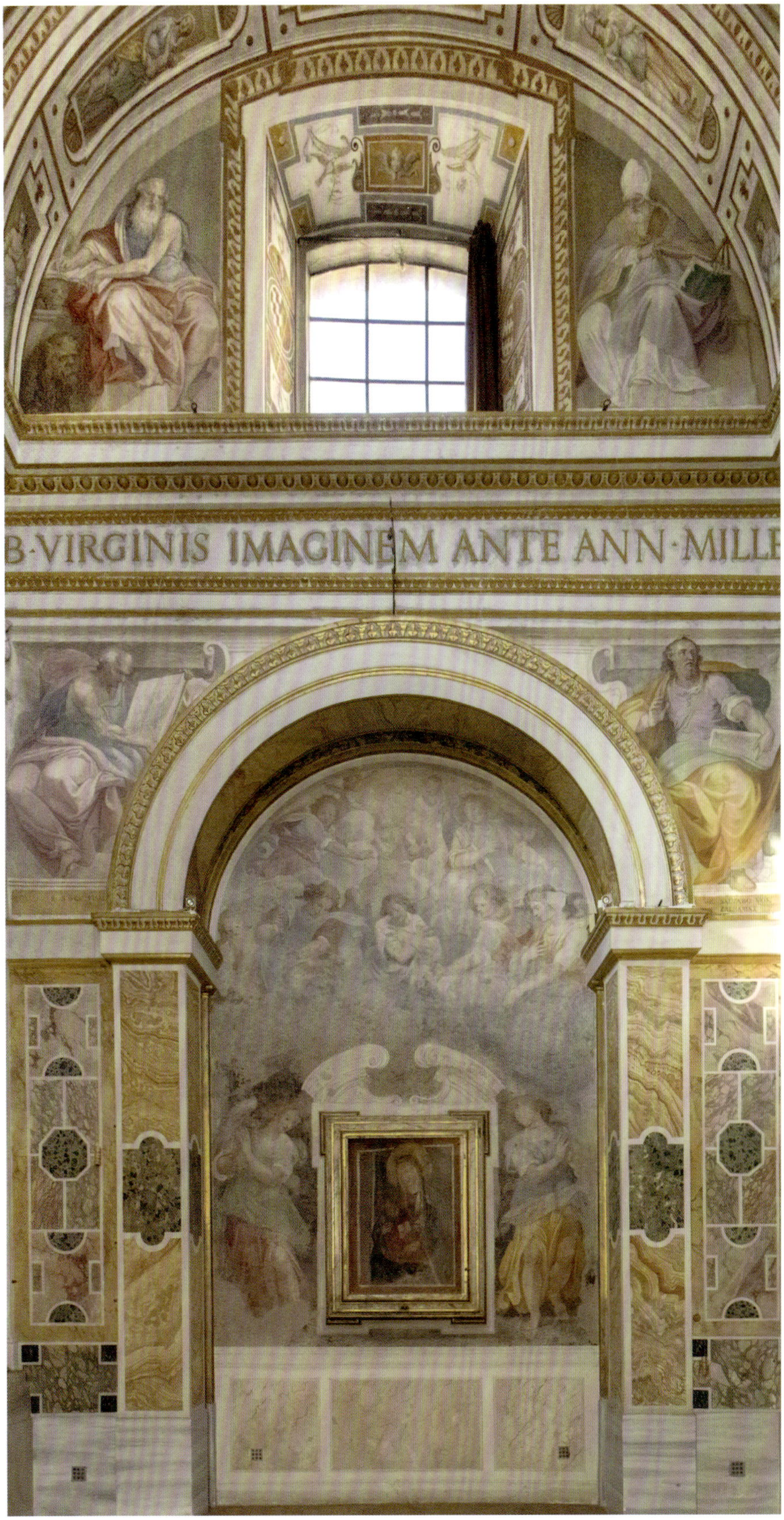

3

FIG. 3. Salviati Chapel (right wall), Santi Andrea e Gregorio al Monte Celio, Rome.

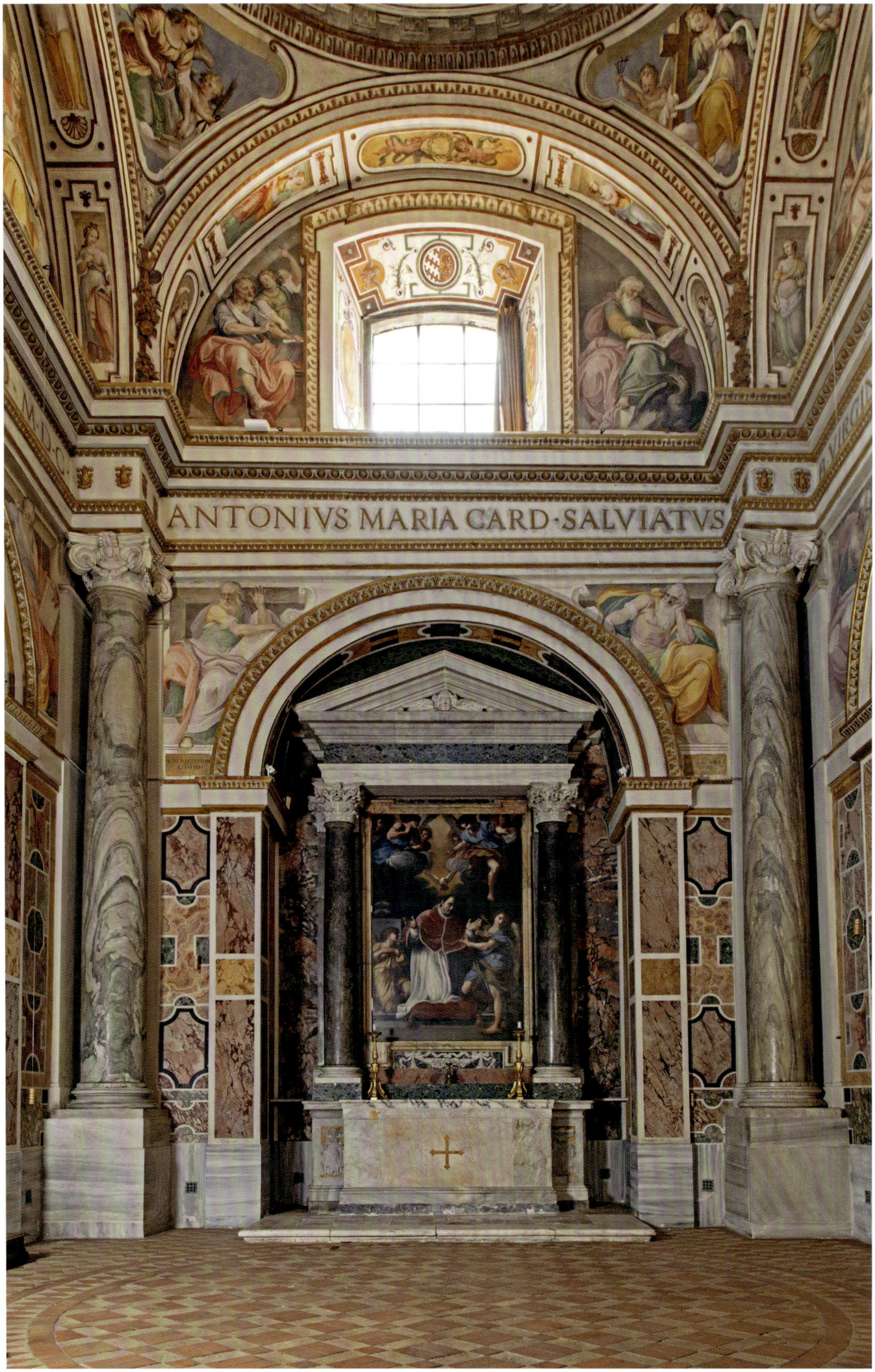

4

and restored its eponymous church. The cardinal also undertook the reorganization of the monastery of San Gregorio, which was united in 1573 with the congregation of the Camaldolese by Gregory XIII, where he had become commendatory abbot. Jacob Hess already noted the contribution of Antonio Maria Salviati to the reconstruction of this church, which had fallen into disuse during the sixteenth century, as "the most important," although greater credit was subsequently attributed to his successors, Cesare Baronio and Cardinal Scipione Borghese.[11] On September 13, 1593, Clement VIII, who had also been involved in promoting the publication of the works of Saint Gregory the Great, issued a brief that lashed out against those who wanted to prevent Salviati from taking possession of this title.[12] The projects at San Gregorio therefore must have begun after this date. To facilitate access to the church, the cardinal opened the square in front of it by paving an adjacent vineyard; this work was completed before June 7, 1600, when Ottavio Panciroli, in his *Tesori nascosti*, praised the recently opened "beautiful and large square."[13] Salviati then widened the staircase, in the middle of which, according to the *Annales Camaldulenses*, he included an image, painted on a false door, of the Septizonium recently demolished by Sixtus V.[14] Nothing else is known about this pictorial reproduction, although its inclusion points to the archaeological interests of the cardinal. In a comparable spirit of recovery, but focused on a late medieval pictorial relic of the Virgin originally located in the area of the cemetery of the church (FIG. 7),[15] Salviati turned to the construction of the chapel, which constituted the first step in the enhancement of the "memorie gregoriane" (the memory of Gregory the Great) at San Gregorio, which would subsequently continue under Baronio. A second brief of Clement VIII attests that on December 14, 1593, the pope granted indulgences to those who participated in the litanies to be held on Saturdays before the Marian image.[16] It is likely that the Marian image had not yet been moved by this date, which can therefore be considered a *terminus ante quem non* for the conception of the chapel.

Built on the same ancient burial grounds of the church,[17] the Salviati Chapel at San Gregorio is a square building independent of the body of the sanctuary. A plan by Robert de Cotte shows the original structure prior to the 1744 renovations to the church (FIG. 9), in which we can see that the externally constructed chapel is in line with the three church apses but exceeds them in size. Its interior is preceded by a rectangular atrium (modified and extended after 1744) connected by a door to the left side aisle of the church but also has an independent external entrance. Today, the viewer still enters the chapel from the vestibule (FIG. 1), his gaze guided into the space by an imposing inscription painted in fictive bronze letters running along the four sides of the upper cornice: "The year 1600 Cardinal Antonio Maria Salviati adorned with a chapel (*sacellum*) the image of the Virgin Mary that, 1000 years before, had spoken to the Blessed Gregory in his parents' house."[18] The inscription is carefully distributed on the four sides of the chapel to highlight the name of Cardinal Salviati and explain the desired function and meaning of the space. The cardinal's name appears prominently directly above the effigy of the pope (FIG. 4), instead of the expected name of Gregory (which is relegated to the entrance wall, behind the entering viewer), while the reference to the image corresponds with the Marian aedicule (FIG. 3). Beyond providing the year 1600 as the completion date, this inscription also leaves no doubt

FIG. 4. Salviati Chapel (altar wall with copy of Annibale Carracci's lost altarpiece), Santi Andrea e Gregorio al Monte Celio, Rome.

that the chapel's devotional focus was the Marian image reinstalled there. The church of San Gregorio (often indicated with the toponym "ad clivum Scauri") was, in fact, built on the site where the monastery dedicated to the apostle Andrew had been located, which, at least starting from the end of the sixth century, was believed to have been founded by Saint Gregory the Great in his own paternal home.[19] In the absence of sources prior to the sixteenth century that describe the image (and in particular, prior to 1573, when the Camaldolese moved to San Gregorio), the very fact that the image was found in this area was sufficient to prove its association with the saint.[20] Among the various Roman Madonnas known to have spoken to Saint Gregory, only this one could aspire to the role of domestic devotional image.[21]

While it was common practice for a cardinal to choose a place distinct from that of his family for his burial site, to design an entire chapel without an explicit sepulchral purpose but only to honor an image of dubious origin was a more unusual occurrence. Several Marian images already had been recovered and reinstalled as altarpieces, including the *Madonna della Colonna* in St. Peter's, the *Madonna del Latte* in the church of San Giovanni Decollato, and the image of Mary on the altar of the Grifoni Chapel in San Marcello, where Giovanni Battista Ricci himself had worked. However, at the time of the Salviati project, no large-scale chapel was built exclusively for this purpose.[22] The most important models for Salviati were undoubtedly the Gregorian Chapel in St. Peter's, on whose altar Gregory XIII had reinstalled the beautiful *Madonna del Soccorso* with a solemn ceremony on February 12, 1578, and the Altemps Chapel commissioned by Marco Sittico Altemps (1589) in Santa Maria in Trastevere, which housed the precious ancient encaustic image of the *Madonna della Clemenza*.[23] However, both chapels were conceived as monumental burial sites, for Gregory XIII (and Saint Gregory Nazianzenus) and the Altemps family, respectively. The Cappella della *Madonna della Strada* in the church of the Gesù is another precedent, but it is not a private chapel and functions mostly as a repository of relics, which do not play an important role in the Salviati Chapel. Instead, here everything revolves around the image of the Virgin—which was restaged almost as a contact relic of Saint Gregory and served as the chapel's generating element—reflecting the patron's particular interest in this type of Marian image recovery.

The ideas at work in the Salviati Chapel at San Gregorio al Celio are in fact closely related to some other contemporary projects. On the one hand are those promoted by Salviati himself, as already mentioned, at San Giacomo in Augusta and, on the other, the Cerasi Chapel in Santa Maria del Popolo, where the same artists (with the notable exception of Caravaggio) were employed, namely, Carlo Maderno, Annibale Carracci, and Ricci.[24] It has been suggested that the Cerasi Chapel was completed shortly after the Salviati Chapel; in fact, some elements of the decorative apparatus are similar (not only the use of fictive polychrome marble revetment but also the simple, two-toned floor design).[25]

As at San Giacomo, Salviati first entrusted the project of the chapel at San Gregorio to Francesco Capriani, called il Volterra, who died on February 15, 1594, before finishing the commission.[26] No documents survive detailing to what extent the design of the San Gregorio chapel was completed by the date of Volterra's death, at which time the project (along with the church of San Giacomo)

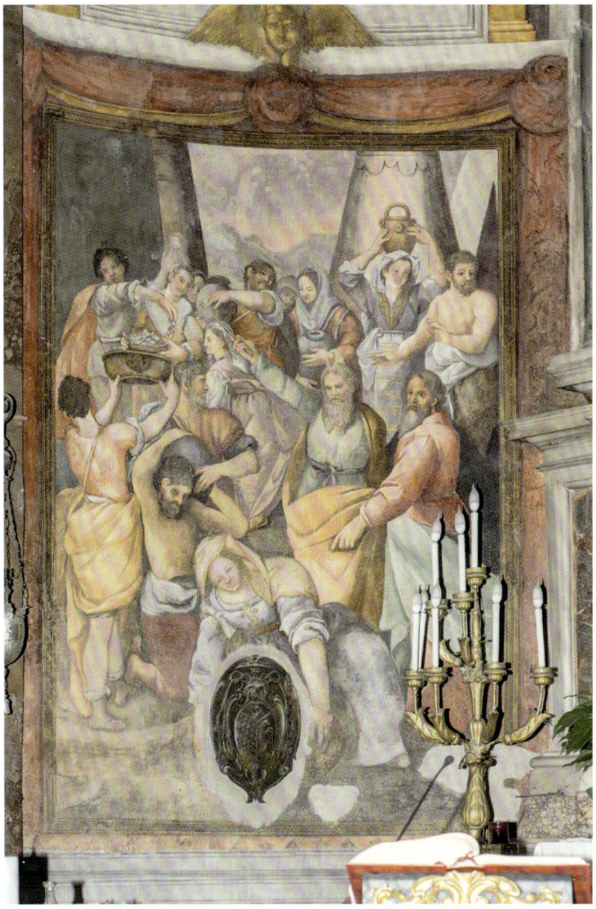

5

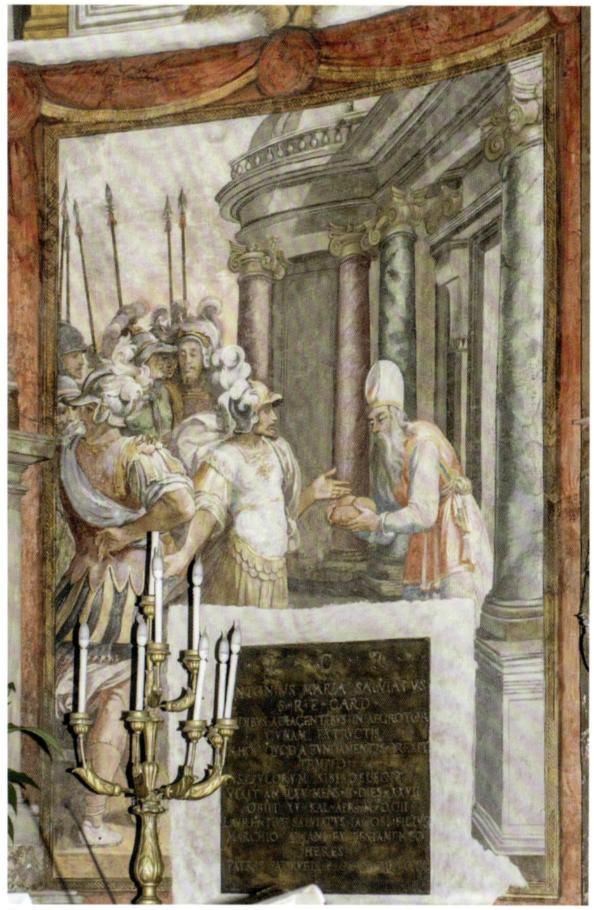

6

FIG. 5. Vespasiano Strada, *The Fall of Manna* with Salviati coats of arms, ca. 1600. San Giacomo in Augusta (apse, left side), Rome.

FIG. 6. Vespasiano Strada, *Melchizedek Delivering the Blessed Bread to Abraham* with Salviati epitaph (1604), ca. 1600. San Giacomo in Augusta (apse, right side), Rome.

passed into the hands of Carlo Maderno. According to Howard Hibbard, the chapel as we see it today is entirely the fruit of Maderno's intervention.[27] However, the considerations put forward by Margherita Eichberg, together with the widespread claims in various Roman sources (from Baglione onward) that associate the beginning of the work with Francesco Capriani, seem sufficient (in the absence of supporting documents) to maintain the double attribution. It seems reasonable to attribute the design of the chapel and its fundamental elements to Francesco Capriani and the subsequent completion of some decorative elements (including, perhaps, the choice of capitals) to Maderno.[28] At San Giacomo, the cardinal used the same artists. He entrusted the project to Volterra as well as the pictorial decoration of one of the chapels (that of Saint John) and the lost altarpiece depicting the *Last Supper* to Giovanni Battista Ricci of Novara.[29]

The projects for San Giacomo and those at San Gregorio must therefore be read in parallel. The most important element uniting the projects is the fact that the cardinal promoted the transport and reinstallation of yet another devotional image, known as the *Madonna dei Miracoli*, inside the church of San Giacomo. This fifteenth-century frescoed image was known for having performed a miracle in 1525 in its original location, on the inner side of one of the towers of the Aurelian walls near the Tiber.[30] Following the reputed miracle,

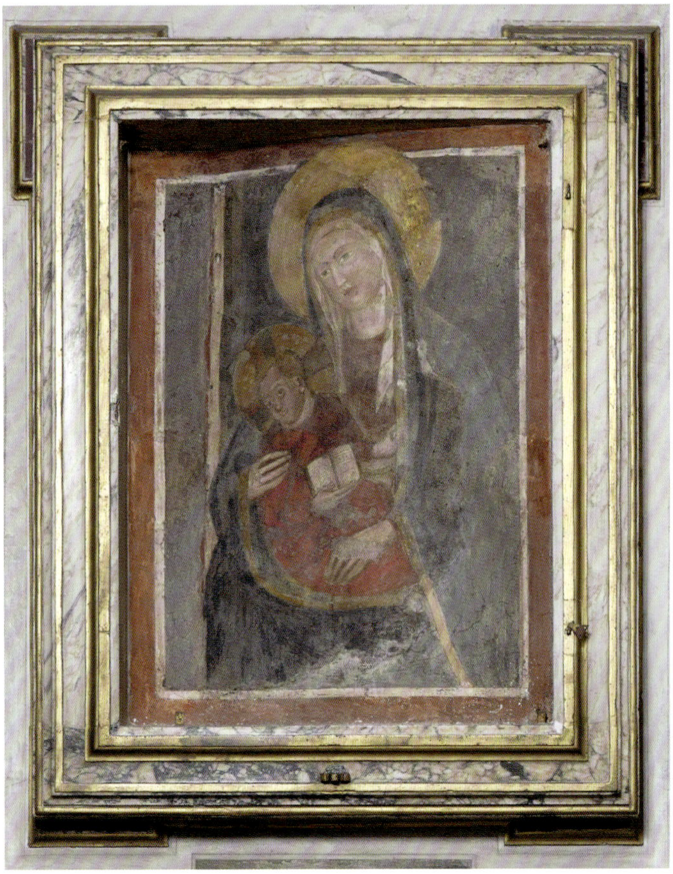

7

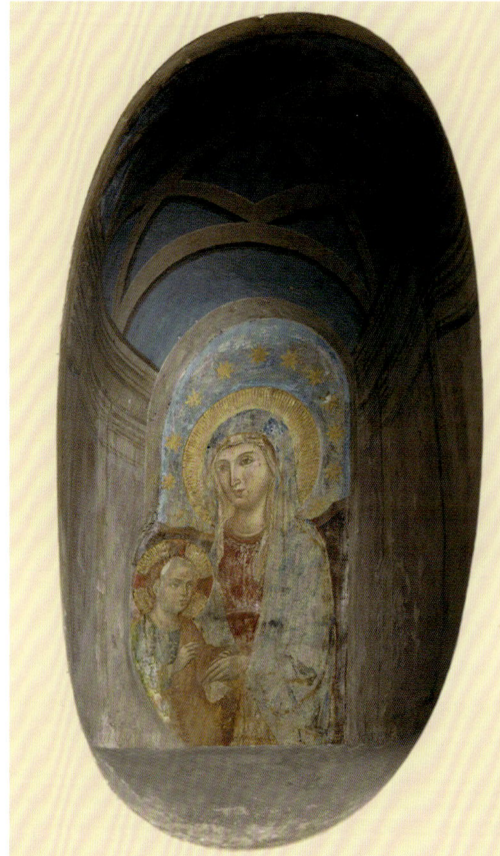

8

FIG. 7. *Virgin and Child* (first half of the fourteenth century), reframed and retouched, ca. 1600. Salviati Chapel (right wall), Santi Andrea e Gregorio al Monte Celio, Rome.

FIG. 8. *Virgin and Child*, early fourteenth century. Vestibule of the Salviati Chapel (visible through an oval hole on the right of the entrance to the chapel), Santi Andrea e Gregorio al Monte Celio, Rome.

the image was first exhibited in a small chapel erected around the exposed image by the Archconfraternity of San Giacomo near the Tiber, a chapel that appears in Bufalini's map of Rome in 1551 and again in Tempesta's in 1593 (see the map on pp. 16–17). In 1598, on the initiative of Cardinal Salviati, the image was finally transported into the church of San Giacomo.[31] The arrangement commissioned by the cardinal for the Madonna in San Giacomo has been partially lost, since the image is now inserted in a large sculptural altarpiece with *San Francesco di Paola* executed by Pierre Legros between 1714 and 1716 (when the church was under the control of the Minims).[32] However, notwithstanding the later additions, the image is still located in the second chapel on the right (FIG. 11). The original altar, still in the chapel and bearing the Salviati insignia, is remembered and described in a notarial deed dated February 13, 1601, a *donatio* that reports all the bequests and investments provided by the cardinal for the hospital:

> he also built from the foundations and completed at great expense the new temple or church of San Giacomo, added to the same Archihospital, completed with a sacred double tower, or bell tower, sacristies, choirs from one side to the other, chapels and altars arranged around an ellipse or a circle, and all of its other parts, and recently [he] adorned the apse, or tribune, and the main altar with paintings, columns, colored marbles, and a tabernacle inlaid with varied stones, and at the

> same time [the space was] richly honored by a new statue in marble (*statua nova marmorea*) of Saint James above the altar of one of the aforementioned chapels dedicated to this saint, and by an ancient and devout image (*vetere devotaque imagine*) of the Most Holy Virgin Mother, called Santa Maria dei Miracoli, transferred from a less honorable place (*e loco minus decenti*) near the Tiber to another of the aforementioned chapels on an honorific altar.[33]

The two chapels of San Giacomo and the Madonna dei Miracoli—the one with the "new statue" executed by Ippolito Buzzi (or Buzio) (FIG. 10) and the other with an "ancient and devout image" recovered from a less decent place (FIG. 11)—are the two main chapels of this innovative elliptical building. They face each other along the latitudinal axis of the church, and their layout and decorative elements as imagined by Volterra for Salviati have been preserved (particularly in the Chapel of San Giacomo). Originally, the image of the Virgin was surrounded by "some angels and putti" painted by Paris Nogari, presumably as a frame not unlike those of Ricci at San Gregorio.[34] Concomitantly, as in a shell game, the cardinal had a substitutive copy of the Marian image painted in the small chapel of the Madonna dei Miracoli beside the Tiber. This copy is today in the church of Santa Maria dei Miracoli in Piazza del Popolo, a building that was constructed by Alexander VII in 1661 because the old freestanding Chapel of the Miracoli was subjected to excessive humidity and flooding. We do not know to whom Salviati entrusted the task of painting the replacement copy of the Marian image, executed on canvas rather than fresco, but further research will likely clarify this point.[35]

The three projects at San Giacomo, San Gregorio, and the Chapel of the Madonna dei Miracoli, focusing on the recovery, reinstallation, and substitution of Marian images, respectively demonstrate the systematic approach of the cardinal's simultaneous archaeological, devotional, and curatorial vision. Surviving information does not allow us to establish which project came first, although it is clear that the 1600 jubilee precipitated completion. The earliest known documents regarding the chapel at San Gregorio are prior to 1598, which is the transfer date of the *Madonna dei Miracoli*. However, considering that the chapel of the Madonna dei Miracoli beside the Tiber was already under the aegis of the hospital, the first Salviatian idea for the *Madonna dei Miracoli* could date back a few years earlier (since the work at San Giacomo in Augusta began on May 20, 1592).

Vetustas and *Venustas* at San Gregorio

The first documents relating to the chapel in San Gregorio date to February and March of 1595. These are payments to the *scarpellino* Stefano Longo for two columns of *cipollino* marble coming from the church of the Santi Apostoli and another column, of the same material, from the Ospedale del Salvatore;[36] on July 8 of the same year, four columns of the same type were purchased and transported to San Gregorio.[37] A subsequent payment found by Hibbard concerns "a statement of the work performed by the *scarpellino* Bartolomeo, or Meo Bassi, dated 25 September 1600"; this report records the invoice for the making of pedestals, bases and capitals of columns, work on the columns themselves, on the architrave, and also on the stone frame "around the Madonna."[38] All these

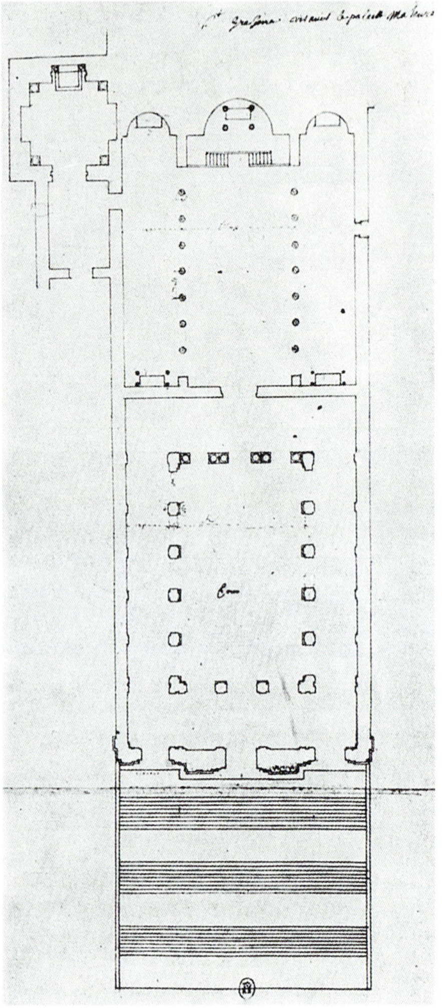

9

additions were valued at 4,322.77 scudi. The entry seems to confirm that the installation of the image of the Madonna in the chapel must have taken place by September 1600.

The *maculosae columnae* (mottled columns) mentioned by Ugonio as the first element of the decoration, that is, the four freestanding shafts of *cipollino* marble placed in the corners of the quadrangular space to support the ribbed vault (FIGS. 1, 9, 12), are the dominant elements of the chapel's architecture. In addition to the reference to the San Zeno Chapel in Santa Prassede, built under Paschal I (817–824), where, however, the columns actually do not serve a supporting function, the design also corresponds to the sepulcher of the Cerceni on the Via Appia, a monument that was often reprised and copied by Renaissance architects.[39] It is also very relevant to note a comparison offered by Eichberg with the chapel of the Madonna in the church of San Benedetto in Piscinula, which exhibits elements from the same Cerceni mausoleum. Due to the similar shape of the aedicule housing the image of the Madonna, this chapel seems to constitute an influence on Salviati's commission. Inspired by these ancient models, the four corner columns in the San Gregorio chapel not only serve a decorative role but also have a manifestly structural function: together with the trabeation, including the inscription, they highlight the "architectural frame" built to house the image (FIGS. 4, 12).[40] The four large windows that open into the upper subarches contribute to the height and illuminate the space.

The words *camera inaurata* (gilded vault) in Ugonio's description of the chapel surely refer to the ornament and pictorial decoration of the dome, elliptical like the plan of San Giacomo, and of the walls, articulated by three niches of differing depths, shallower along the lateral walls and deeper on the altar wall (FIG. 9). The projecting moldings, arches, and other structural and decorative elements of the vault (including the now darkened stuccos), as well as the mostly white stone frame of the Marian image, are highlighted with gilding. In the dome fresco (FIG. 12), a blessing Christ flanked by Saints Mary and John the Baptist appears in a heavenly *gloria* with cherubs before a circle of apostles, saints, and martyrs. Among them, the eponymous Saints Andrew and Gregory (who is dressed in blue and red like the Virgin Mary and looks up at her), as well as Peter, John the Evangelist, Noah, Moses, and Abraham and David, in between whom we see Isaac, appear prominently, along with other more distant patriarchs (including the naked Eve and Adam) and some female saints. Bright yellow tones dominate the composition, perhaps another distant call to the traditional medium of mosaic (as in the Chapel of San Zeno). Even the fictive marble inlay simulated in stucco continues the yellow tone (although these stuccos, as well as the gilding, have been retouched). Projecting their trumpets downward from the base of the luminous composition, four figures of angels (which recall those of the Last Judgment) connect the figures of the dome to the rest of the space painted by Ricci. In their entirety, the frescoes are exuberant and rich in iconographic and decorative detail.[41] Eight figures of Prophets

FIG. 9. Robert de Cotte, Plan of the church of San Gregorio al Celio, ca. 1713.

FIG. 10. Ippolito Buzzi, *Saint James*, ca. 1600–1602. Chapel of San Giacomo, San Giacomo in Augusta, Rome.

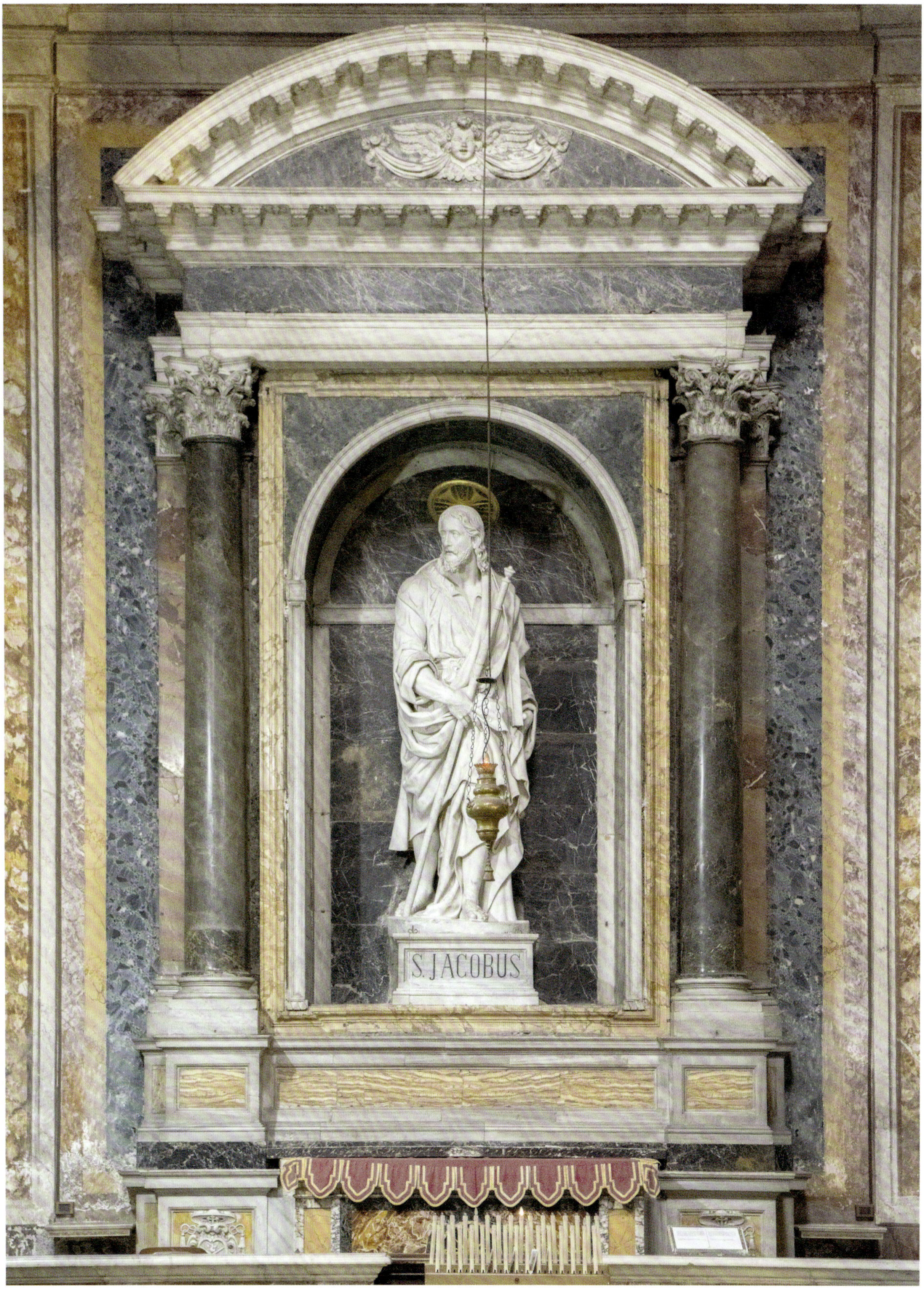

10

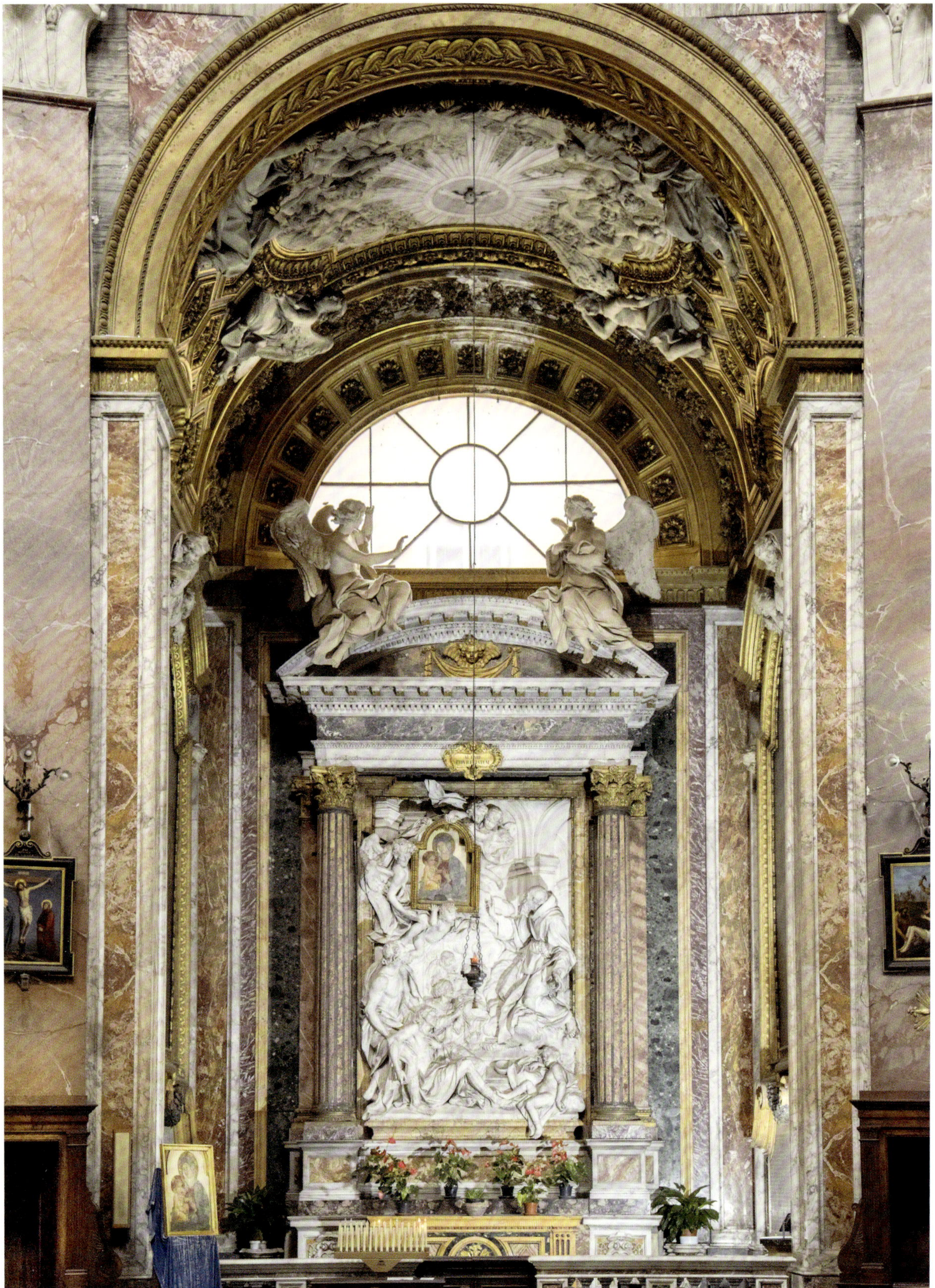

11

appear above the arches of the low register (and below the inscription), from left to right, starting from the altar wall: Ezekiel, Hosea (FIG. 4); perhaps Habakkuk and Zechariah (FIG. 3); Daniel and Jonah; Tobias and Isaiah (FIG. 2). Above are the Evangelists in the lunettes flanking the large windows in the upper register of the main wall (Matthew and John, FIG. 4) and on the entrance wall (Luke and Mark), and finally, four figures of Fathers of the Church are on the lateral walls. Here (FIG. 2) Gregory seems to be repeated twice in the lunettes of the upper left register of the left wall, while Saints Jerome and presumably Augustine appear in the register on the right (FIG. 3). The four pendentives at the corners of the dome simulate triangular openings onto a blue sky through which angels and cherubs fly with the instruments of the Passion. Other graceful pairs of winged putti float on a golden yellow background in the squares at the center of the upper subarches, and others bear the *arma Christi*. Each pair of cherubs is flanked by four personifications of Virtues (sixteen in total), while in the window openings we see cherubic heads or the cardinal's coat of arms surrounded by birds and other finely painted elements alluding to early Christian decorations. Finally, the Salviati double-merled crest is repeated obsessively, painted on the fictive entablature encircling the base of the dome (FIG. 12).

While the early Christian references and the allusion to mosaic yellow can be associated with the archaeological interests of the cardinal and of Ricci himself, the allegorical details (especially the sixteen personifications of Virtues) signal a further interest of Cardinal Salviati, who was the dedicatee of the first-ever edition (not illustrated) of Cesare Ripa's *Iconologia*.[42] The imagery in the dome and the second register of the chapel, starting from above the arches, insists on a combination of prophetic, Christological, Marian, and salvific themes (accentuated by the centrality of John the Baptist, next to Mary, and the visibility of the nude Adam and Eve just above the figure of the blessing Christ, FIG. 12).[43] These upper frescoes therefore have a complementary and ascendant function with respect to the uniquely Marian and Gregorian themes unfolding below across the three main walls.

Beyond stylistic associations, the attribution of these frescoes to Giovanni Battista Ricci is based on the testimony of Baglione, who briefly mentions the glory of the dome and describes in detail only the fresco on the left wall, a fresco, whose subject refers to a further and better-known effigy of Mary connected with Gregory: "When Saint Gregory had the holy image carried in procession through Rome" (FIG. 2).[44] This composition was prepared presumably by Ricci in a drawing now preserved in the British Museum (FIG. 13).[45] It derives from an invention of Federico Zuccari for the now-lost altarpiece of the Ghiselli Chapel in the church of Santa Maria del Baraccano in Bologna (1580).[46] From an iconographic perspective, Ricci's fresco—only partially visible today—constitutes his greatest contribution to the Marian-Gregorian meaning of the chapel. The scene focuses on the public procession of Gregory the Great with the thaumaturgic image of the Virgin before the immense Castel Sant'Angelo. As far as we can reconstruct from what remains of the fresco and from the preparatory drawing, which admittedly differs in some details, the Marian image (FIG. 14) seems closer to the icon of Santa Maria Maggiore than to the image in the chapel and is represented at the center of the composition, with the pontiff kneeling in the foreground at prayer.[47] Thus, the uni-

FIG. 11. Altar of the *Madonna dei Miracoli* (fifteenth century), ca. 1600–1602 and 1714–1716. Chapel of the Madonna dei Miracoli, San Giacomo in Augusta, Rome.

versal *Salus Populi Romani* (as it would later be called) faces and mirrors the domestic image from the house of Gregory on the opposite wall. An angelic apparition dominates from a distance, and, closer to the spectator, two angels in flight bear a scroll celebrating Mary ("Regina celi letari [*sic*] alleluia"). The message of the fresco unequivocally points to Gregory's renewed emphasis on the value of Marian images, and its composition mirrors the scene enacted in the space of the chapel through the dynamic visual relationship between the chapel's two principal images (Carracci's altarpiece and the ancient Madonna), to which I now turn.

What distinguishes the Salviati Chapel from all of the previous and subsequent reinstallations of Marian images (such as the two Maderno tabernacles in San Giovanni dei Fiorentini, 1612–1613, and Santa Maria della Pace, 1614, and the Pauline Chapel in Santa Maria Maggiore),[48] is that the aedicule on the high altar was intended to frame not the old Madonna but rather a modern painting. It is tempting to identify the modern composition by Annibale Carracci with the *pictura perelegans* ("very fine painting") mentioned by Ugonio.[49]

The surviving structure of the shrine that housed Carracci's painting resembles that of the Madonna in the chapel of San Benedetto in Piscinula and also the frame for the *Madonna della Clemenza* in the Altemps Chapel. A simply formed frame with two columns, perhaps ancient and sometimes identified with a rare marble called *marmo rodio*, with Corinthian capitals supports an entablature composed of a slab of *verde antico* and a simple, triangular pediment (FIG. 4).[50] As the chapel is dedicated to the recreation of a moment in the life of Saint Gregory, it is not surprising to find his image, albeit in the dress of a sixteenth-century pope, in the altarpiece.[51] However, given the emphasis placed on the Marian image by the imposing inscription in fictive bronze letters and the evident reference to ideas implemented in previous Marian chapels, it becomes necessary to question why the Madonna was placed on the side wall in a position apparently secondary to the modern painting. The particular shape of the image not only helps us to comprehend this decision but also allows us to fully understand the genesis of the composition by Annibale Carracci, today lost but fortunately documented by a rich series of drawings already studied by Donald Posner followed by successive scholars.

The Marian image, immured obliquely in the right wall of the chapel, is all that remains of a fresco apparently dating from the fourteenth century (FIG. 7).[52] Its irregular shape is characteristic of the original rounded surface to which the painting was once attached, perhaps a column or otherwise curved surface. Despite the prestige accorded to the Marian effigy, the creators of this chapel must have considered that its shape did not make an entirely suitable main altarpiece. The effect of its irregular format potentially affected its location more than the fresco's poor quality; thus, it was decided to place the image on the right side wall and in this manner, given its curvature, literally oriented toward the main altar (FIG. 15). Contemporaneously, Antonio Maria Salviati, who must have had some contact with the Carracci since at least 1598 (having been the dedicatee of an engraved replica of the *Pietà di Caprarola*),[53] commissioned the altarpiece from Annibale, which was probably executed between 1600 and the second half of 1602. This altar was consecrated together with others in the church on October 30, 1603, by Bishop Sidone Leonardo Abel (following Salviati's death more than a year earlier).[54] Even so,

FIG. 12. Giovanni Battista Ricci, Frescoes of the upper walls and the vault, ca. 1600–1602. Salviati Chapel, Santi Andrea e Gregorio al Monte Celio, Rome.

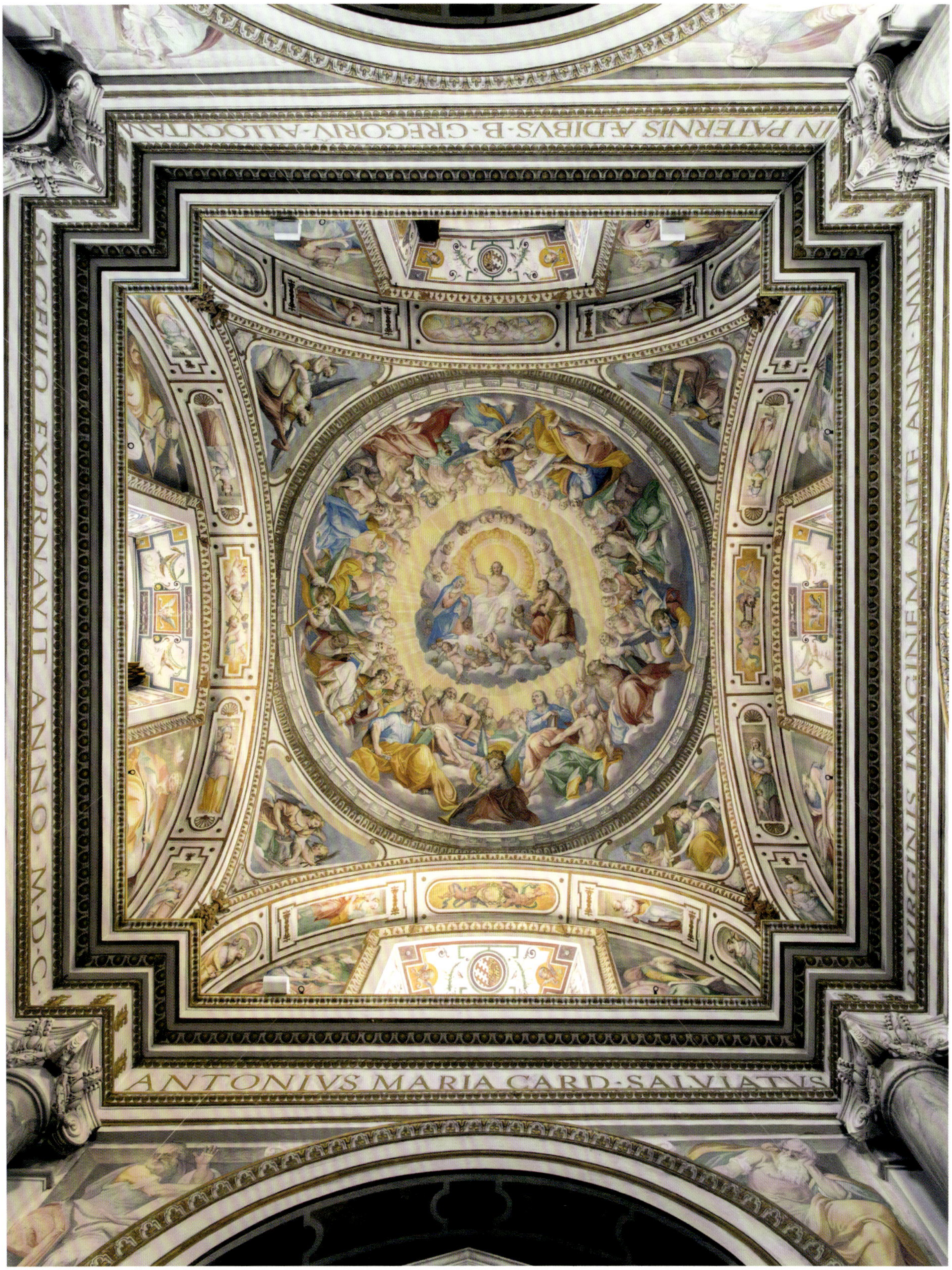
IN PATERNIS ÆDIBVS·B·GREGORIV·ALLOCVTAM
B·VIRGINIS IMAGINEM ANTE ANN·MILLE
ANTONIVS MARIA CARD·SALVIATVS
SACELLO EXORNAVIT ANNO·M·D·C

12

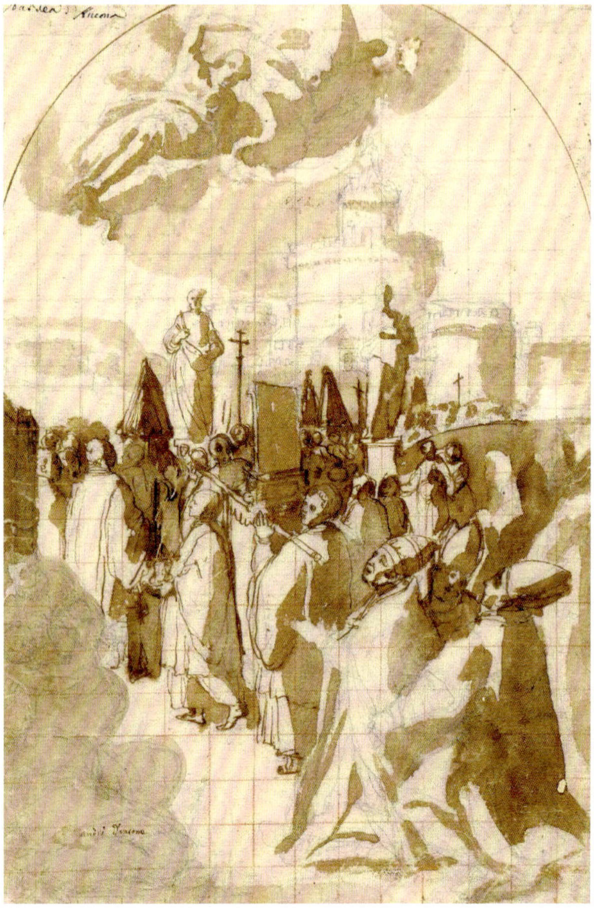

13

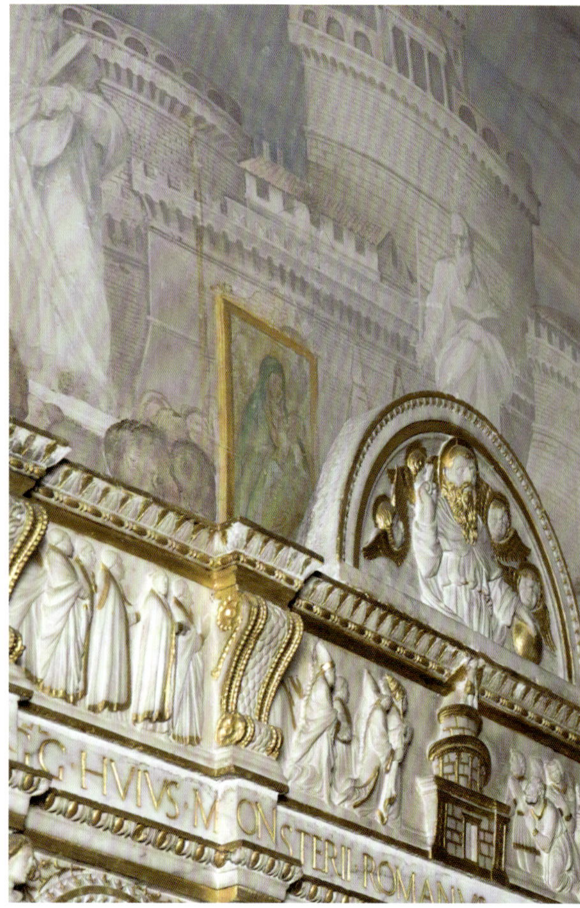

14

FIG. 13. Giovanni Battista Ricci, *Saint Gregory's Procession with the Icon of the Virgin Mary and the Vision at Castel Sant'Angelo*, ca. 1600–1602. British Museum, London.

FIG. 14. Giovanni Battista Ricci, *St. Gregory's Procession with the Icon of the Virgin Mary and the Vision at Castel Sant'Angelo* (detail of the icon), ca. 1600–1602. Salviati Chapel, Santi Andrea e Gregorio al Monte Celio, Rome.

FIG. 15. Lateral view of the right wall as seen from the main altar. Salviati Chapel, Santi Andrea e Gregorio al Monte Celio, Rome.

a testimony by Mancini reassures us that the painting was ordered by the cardinal himself and had been finished, or nearly so, while the cardinal was still alive.[55] Although the copy remaining in situ lacks in quality, it still gives us a sense of the relationship between the two images (FIG. 16). Saint Gregory turns slightly toward the Virgin, who in response looks toward the kneeling saint. In this moment, the humble saint not only prays to the Virgin (as the scene is often simply described) but also actively receives divine grace, and even potentially listens to the voice of the Madonna through her image.[56]

Annibale thus found himself having to solve the following complex and unprecedented problem: how to create an altar painting with a frontal orientation yet simultaneously engage in dialogue with a devotional focus on a lateral wall. Some studies have already reflected on this dialogue between adjacent images in space and on the theme of side walls in chapel spaces.[57] This preoccupation likely aroused interest in contemporary artists, especially if we consider the work of Caravaggio in his lateral paintings for chapels at San Luigi dei Francesi and Santa Maria del Popolo. In any case, here the orientation is reversed: it is the altarpiece that must show a certain level of deference toward the right wall (i.e., to the left of the figures represented).

The original composition by Annibale is preserved only in a photograph, which Heinrich Bodmer obtained before 1937 from the Earl of Mayo in London

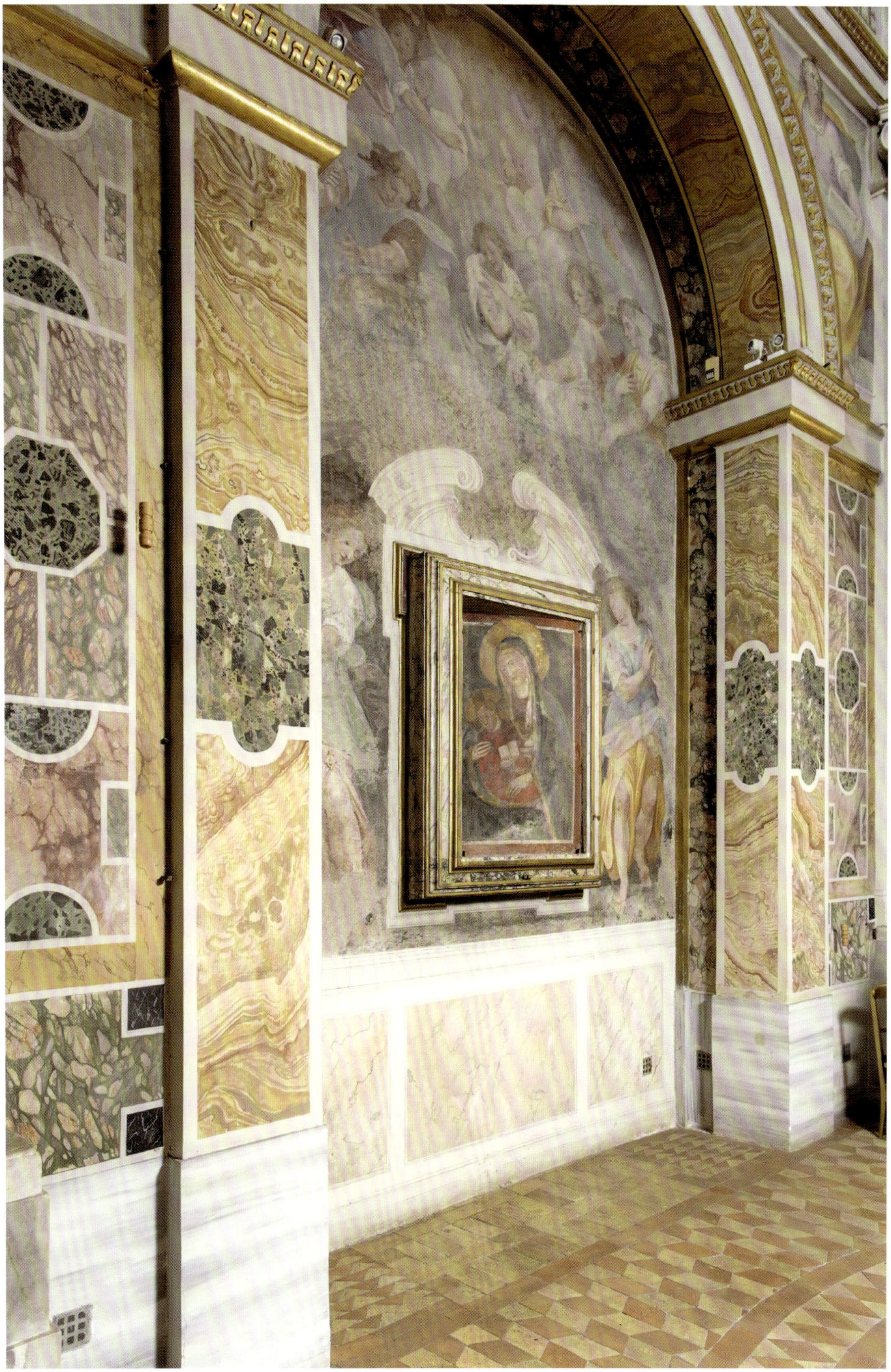

15

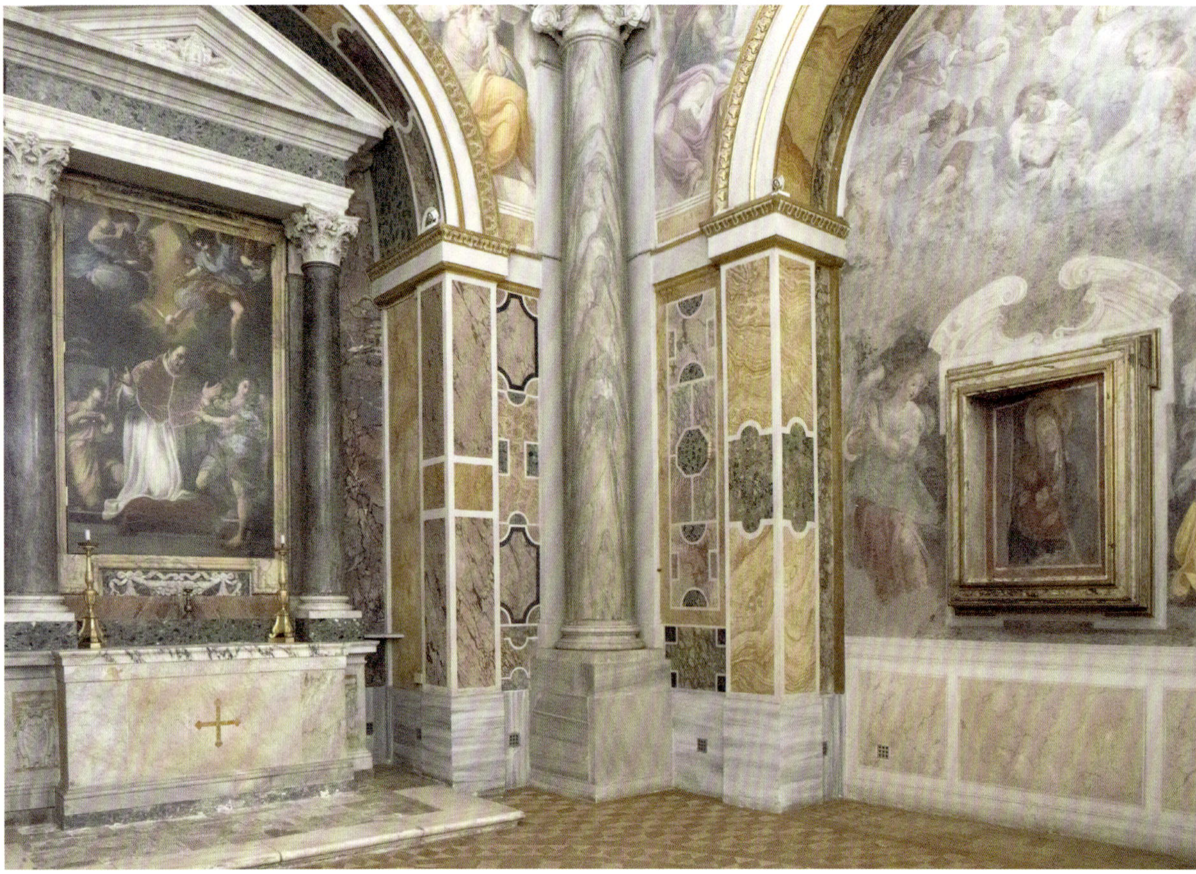

16

and later donated to the Kunsthistorisches Institut (**FIG. 17**). Comparing the copy with the original composition by Annibale (**FIGS. 4, 16, 17**), one notices how the former alters important details of the original painting, including the position of Gregory and the exact shape and inclination of the cushion on which he kneels. In the analysis that follows, I will therefore refer to the pre-1937 photograph of the original. Since 1971, the complex composition of Annibale's painting has been reconstructed thanks to a series of at least six surviving drawings.[58] It has already been noted several times that Annibale sought to achieve a "fusion between painting and surrounding space"[59] and a certain degree of illusionistic effect, perhaps in competition with Caravaggio.[60] The first known *bozzetto* by Annibale for the San Gregorio altarpiece is identified as the drawing now in Chatsworth (**FIG. 18**), which is often described as much freer and more "illusionistic" than the final painting.[61] According to Posner, who was interested in developing the idea of the "reform" of Italian painting, Annibale progressively eliminated every "ease and warmth" from the composition, which resulted in an "unpleasantly rigid and cold" painting. This influential reading of the surviving drawings depends on Posner's more general assumption that the "late style" of Annibale consisted of "hyper-idealism," according to which illusionistic elements had to be abandoned in favor of monumentalizing "expressive gestures" and "pious attitudes."[62] Recent studies have now modified this point of view, emphasizing instead the interests of the late

FIG. 16. Salviati Chapel (dialogue between right wall and main altarpiece), Santi Andrea e Gregorio al Monte Celio, Rome.

Annibale in Correggio's naturalism and Venetian painting.[63] In relation to the chapel's lost altarpiece, it is worth pursuing this analysis, since Posner's interpretation is in contrast to all of the period descriptions of the painting.

From Baglione (1642) to Bellori (1672), up to the engraver Jakob Frey (1733, FIG. 19), who offers us one of the best reproductions of the work (which was engraved several times previously),[64] all observers noticed not only the extremely vivid colors of the composition[65] but also the actual "dialogue" between Gregory and the Virgin Mary—that is, the interaction between the two images across the space of the chapel from the central altarpiece to the right wall.[66] Bellori describes how "color enlivens the efficacy of the Holy Pontiff,"[67] while Frey praises how Annibale "had expressed in colors" (*coloribus expresserat*) the figure of Gregory the Great, "who, kneeling toward the image of the Virgin Mary that was depicted on the opposite wall, deserved that she talked to him during his life."[68]

These impressions are definitively confirmed by a lesser-known source: documentation relating to the crowning of the Marian image by the Chapter of Saint Peter. In 1658, the image at San Gregorio al Celio received a golden crown (stolen for the first time before 1786) in recognition of its status as a miraculous image. As is well known, this systematic crowning campaign of the Madonnas by the Chapter began in 1631, becoming a perpetual honor in 1636 thanks to a rich legacy bequeathed to the Chapter by Count Alessandro Sforza.[69] The bestowal of the crown represented an official recognition of the prestige of Marian images (at first those predominantly located in Rome and then elsewhere) that could aspire to obtain this status. For each Madonna, a small dossier is kept in the archive of the Chapter, and it is worth reading the complete justification for the crown granted to the Madonna at San Gregorio:

> The most prestigious and excellent glory of this most respectable place is the image of Mary painted on the wall (*dipinta in muro*), which once was in Saint Gregory's parents' house, and is now venerated in the most beautiful Salviati Chapel. This chapel was fabricated in 1600 by the illustrious piety of cardinal Antonio Maria of that name, who praiseworthily deployed his munificence for the decoration (*condecorazione*) of this most precious image. This is the image in front of which the devout St Gregory, from his earlier years, frequently directed to God his fervent prayers. And this is the image that delighted to talk repeatedly (*compiacquesi di parlar più volte*) to this beloved son of God, as we are assured by a continual tradition and by the inscription on the frame on the chapel. What more? The painting on panel (*il quadro in tavola*) painted by the famous Annibale Carracci represents the Holy Pontiff humbly kneeling and praying, and with his face turned toward this image.[70]

"With his face turned toward this image" offers us the most direct and effective description of how the interaction between the two images was understood in 1658. Moreover, as already noted by Ugonio, we are shown once again the reciprocal hierarchy between the two images. The beautiful painting by the "famous" Annibale Carracci confers decisive value on the ancient and prestigious Marian image, not only in artistic terms (as a restitution of that beauty deprived by time) but also from a normative point of view. That is to say, the miracle of the Virgin speaking to Gregory occurred *because* the painting by the famous Carracci (together with the inscription painted on the

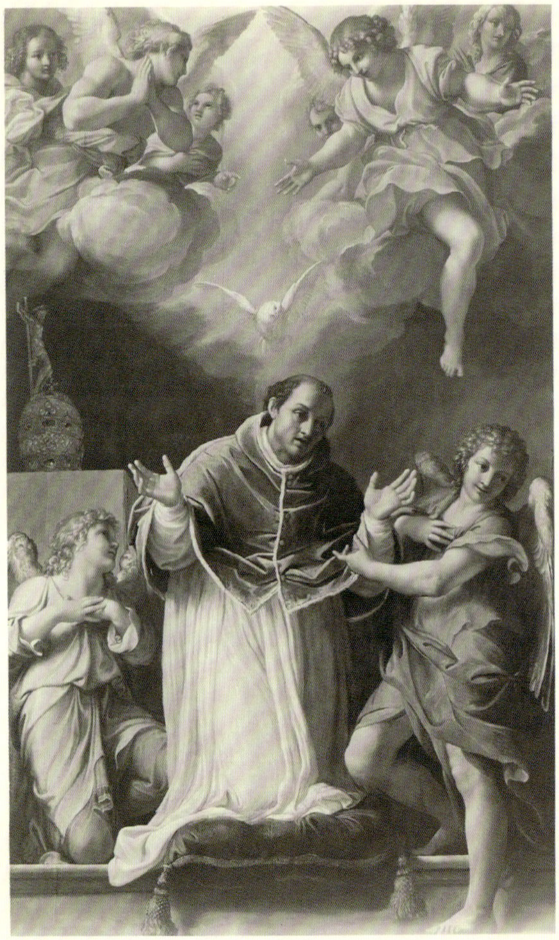

17

FIG. 17. Annibale Carracci, *Saint Gregory Altarpiece* (from the Salviati Chapel), formerly Ellesmere collection, Bridgewater House, Westminster, London. Kunsthistorisches Institut in Florenz, Photo Library, inv. 115117, pre-1937.

frame), here and now (in 1658), proves it.[71] If the underestimation of Annibale's completed altarpiece stems from preconceived prejudice toward the artist's supposed late style, then it is worthwhile to go back one last time to the surviving preparatory studies. By reconsidering this series, not so much in relation to the internal development of the painter's style but rather in relation to the space of the chapel in terms of a search for a progressive laterality, Annibale's solution reveals a deceptively effective design.

The "strong three-dimensional implications" of the first sketch (FIG. 18) are due to the inclusion in the represented space of the entrance arch within the chapel and to the gesture of the angel on the right, which projects beyond the arch and points toward the image of the Virgin.[72] It should also be noted that the background of this sketch is not completely resolved. An open landscape appears on the right, while on the left we see an altar with a tiara and a crucifix. The relationship between inside and outside is not entirely clear at this point in the artist's process. Regarding the gestures of the angel on the left, the one hand beckons the attention of the pope, while the other points toward the background of the painting in the direction of one or two souls in flight, probably freed from Purgatory. This element—which refers to another and better-known legend linked to Gregory the Great and is still present in a second stage of Annibale's process (documented by a study copy at the Louvre)[73]—was subsequently eliminated from the composition, most likely because it was not relevant to the particular historic episode staged in this chapel (specifically, the image of the Virgin that spoke to Gregory in his parents' house).[74] Further, from a compositional point of view, the double movement suggested by the opposing gestures of the angel unnecessarily complicates the composition.[75]

The development toward the final composition is documented by a sheet containing a series of at least four pen studies now in Windsor (FIG. 20). These sketches not only explore the spectrum of appropriate gestures for a figure in the act of receiving a divine message (a series of solutions comparable to those possible for an Annunciate Virgin) but also introduce other small but fundamental changes, in particular with respect to the position of the angel on the right, which evolves into the second key figure in the composition (as evidenced by a further drawing dedicated solely to this figure in a sheet at the Metropolitan Museum).[76] The first study seems to be the central one, with the saint clasping his hands to his chest and the angel on the right. Unlike both the first sketch and the intermediate stage documented by the copy in the Louvre, the angel here is no longer placed behind the pontiff (Chatsworth) or at the same level (Louvre) but descends one step in the direction of the image

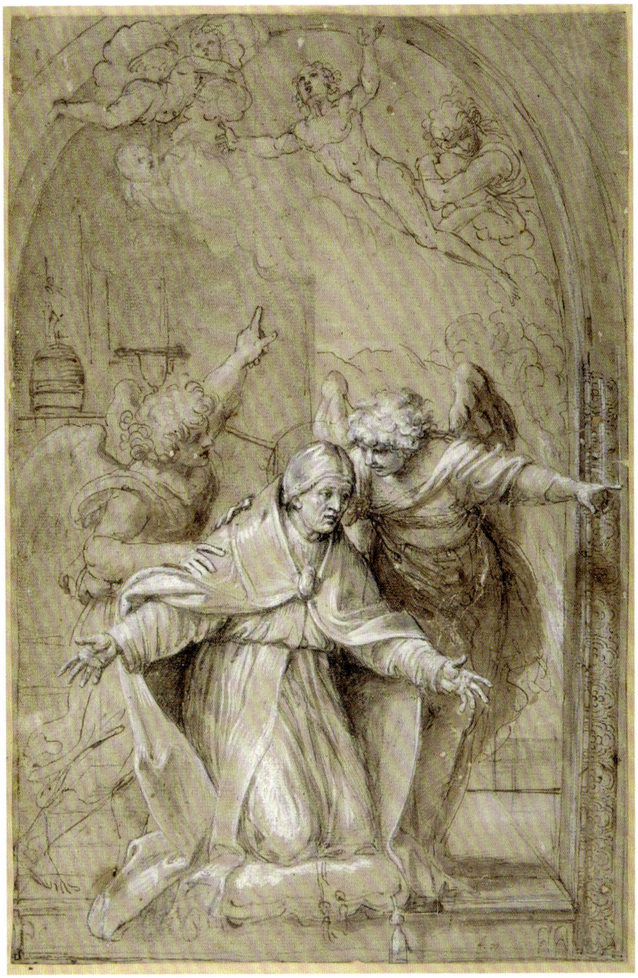

18

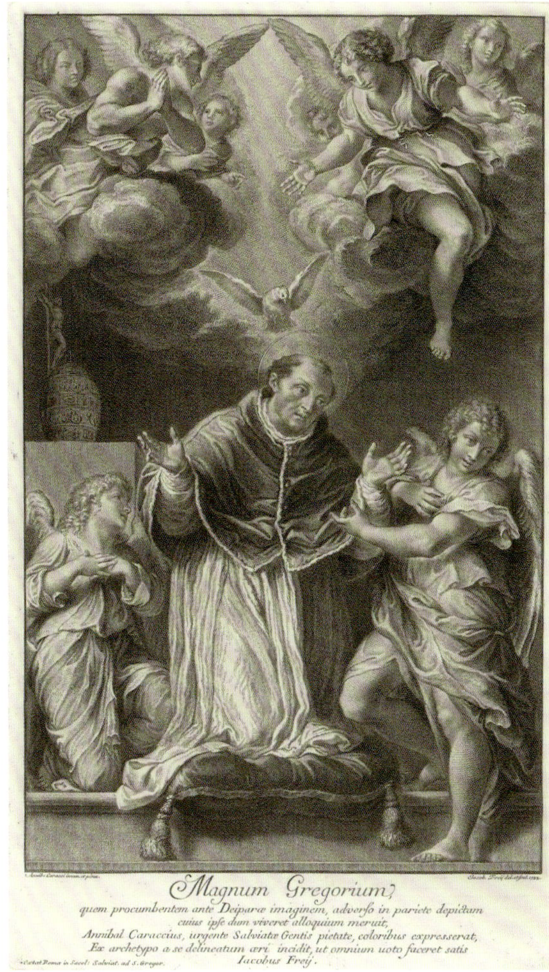

19

of the Virgin and toward the viewer. The position of this angel in the space is moreover isolated in a second sketch in the right background (although it is unclear if this drawing was executed before or after the central scene). And here the angel on the left barely appears, being only hinted at in a secondary position behind Gregory. The unsuitable flying angels that accompanied the souls from Purgatory into the sky have now been replaced by a *gloria* of flying angels culminating in the figure of the dove that slightly inclines to the right. These two first studies are followed by the two remaining designs represented on the left side of the sheet. In the lower left corner, the artist works through another variant of the pontiff's listening gesture. The last in-depth analysis appears in the squared vignette, placed against the left margin of the sheet; in my opinion, this miniature study of the relationship between the two figures represents an attempt to render an angled view of the altarpiece, that is, from the point of view of the image of the Madonna on the right wall (compare the detail of this vignette with the photograph taken from an acute angle of the painting's copy; **FIGS. 20, 21**).

While in the first *bozzetto* the three figures and the corresponding line of the cushion are all parallel and horizontal to the picture plane, the ultimate

FIG. 18. Annibale Carracci, First composition for the Saint Gregory altarpiece (pen and brown ink and wash, heightened with white), ca. 1600–1602. Collection of the Duke of Devonshire, Chatsworth House, inv. 435.

FIG. 19. Jakob Frey after Annibale Carracci, *Saint Gregory Altarpiece* (etching), 1733. British Museum, London.

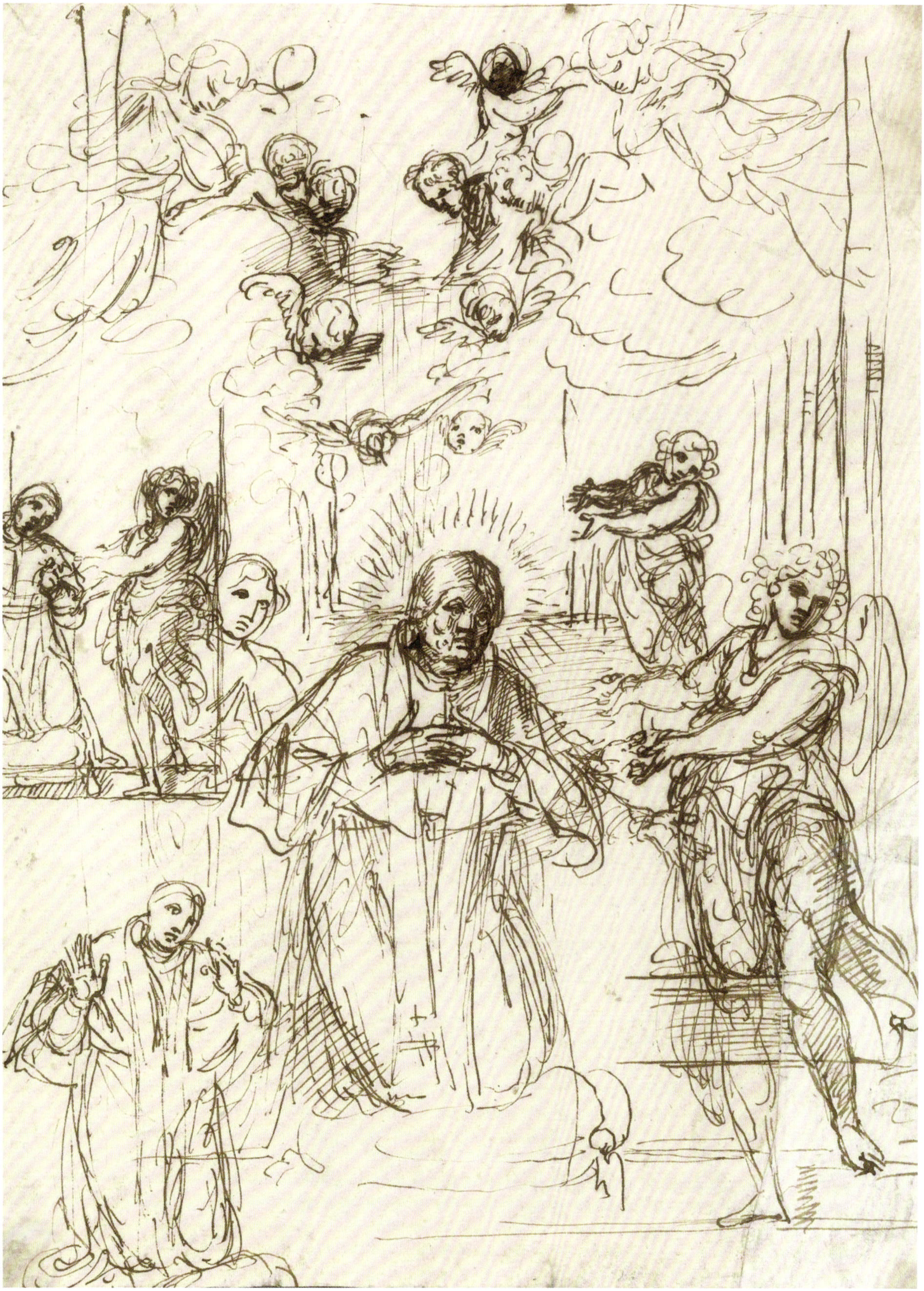

20

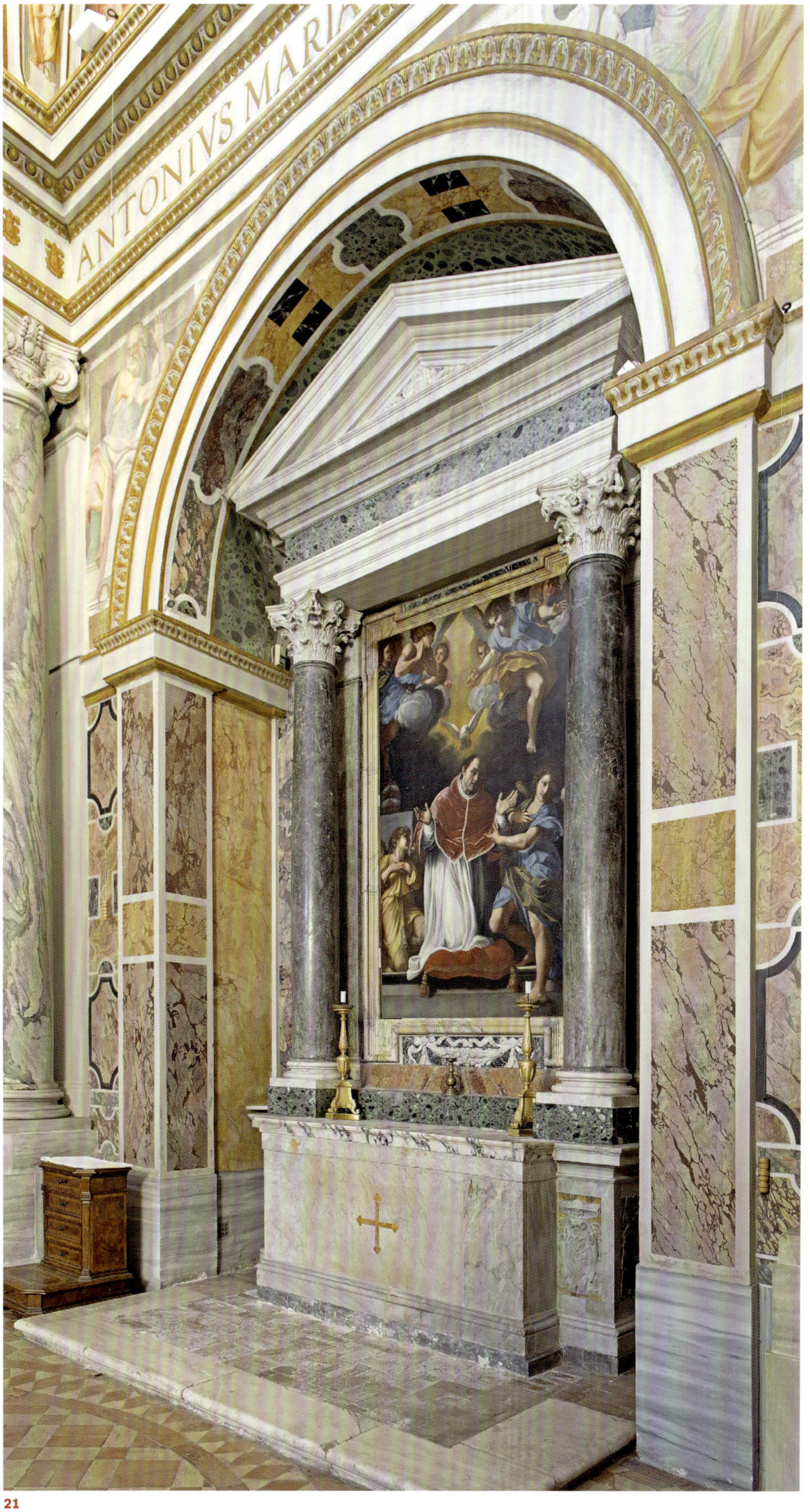

21

FIG. 20. Annibale Carracci, *Studies for Saint Gregory Altarpiece* (pen and brown ink on cream paper). Royal Collection Trust, Windsor Castle, Collection of H.M. the Queen, inv. 2335.

FIG. 21. Lateral view of the main altar with the copy of the altarpiece (after Annibale Carracci) as seen from the right wall. Salviati Chapel, Santi Andrea e Gregorio al Monte Celio.

solution executed by Annibale sets the three figures on a diagonal line, from the knee of the angel on the left to the foot of the main angel on the right which now firmly rests on the ground near the viewer (FIG. 18, 17). A further modification, with respect to the Windsor folio, is the repositioning of the primary angel, which serves to connect the figure of the pontiff and the image of the Madonna through the space of the chapel even more effectively: the angelic leg now firmly resting on the ground echoes the function of the corner column (almost a reference to the typical column included in Annunciation scenes). At the same time, the final version (documented by the pre-1937 photograph) orients the cushion diagonally, at an opposing angle to the figures represented. The cushion therefore heightens the spontaneous twist of Gregory toward the image of the Virgin, a movement accentuated by the prominence of the saint's right knee leaning more clearly on the cushion and confirmed by the position of the dove above his head, which, like the saint, has "eyes turned" in the direction of the speaking image. In addition, while Gregory was represented in both the Chatsworth and Windsor drawings with the red velvet and satin cap typically worn by the Pope (*camauro*), in the final painting the absence of the cap presents to the viewer the still black hair of a young Gregory, as the future pope should have been at the time of the episode in the house of his parents.

These adjustments, minimal yet decisive, are not to be attributed only to a stylistic evolution of Annibale between his first sketch and the final composition but instead represent a study of the function of the painting in the chapel interior and its dialogue with the old and private image of the Virgin on the right wall: the interaction between the two images was intended to recreate the real private space in which the young Gregory allegedly prayed and listened to the voice of the Marian image. The brilliant colors praised by all observers had to compete with the fictive polychrome marbles and frame of the Madonna and probably sought to accentuate the "effectiveness" of the recreation, as emphasized by Bellori.[77]

Conclusion

In 1586, Giovanni Battista Armenini, speaking of "sacred images," posed a sharp contrast between those that contained "certain figures made in the Greek manner, very awkward, disagreeable, and completely darkened with soot," and "beautiful images" painted by Renaissance artists, such as "Titian, Correggio, and Giulio Romano." These modern paintings, according to Armenini, were to be considered much more effective—capable of bringing tears to viewers' "eyes out of emotion"—because the eye can perceive the "divinity [in such images] almost like the very ones who are in heaven."[78]

Around 1600, the experiment designed and implemented in the Salviati chapels by Volterra, Maderno, Giovanni Battista Ricci, Annibale Carracci, and a series of stonemasons and marble workers (Stefano Longo, Bartolomeo Bassi) aimed to overcome this sharp contrast between the clumsy "Greek" figures and the "beautiful images" of the Renaissance. The "divinity" emerges here from the combination and integration of artifacts of different epochs. In the new and luminous space of the Salviati Chapel in San Gregorio, gilded and brightly decorated, the old and private Marian image received new life from the added brilliant frescoes of the walls and the vault (showing respectively two other images of Mary related to Gregory: the public *Salus Populi Romani* and the interceding Virgin Mary in the vault, to whom the Saint Gregory in the vault, dressed in the same colour, raises his gaze) and from the most elegant contemporary painting ("pictura perelegans"), which in the 1763 edition of Filippo Titi's guide was called "one of Rome's most famous paintings."[79] This reputation no doubt stemmed from the fact that the altarpiece was conceived not as an independent work but in relation to the chapel's space and more precisely in a way that enhanced, aesthetically, iconographically, and symbolically, an image otherwise lacking "any beauty" (Ugonio). At San Giacomo, Salviati sought a similar reconciliation between the "new" statue of the saint commissioned from Ippolito Buzzi and the "ancient" image of the *Madonna dei Miracoli* in the two central chapels across the new architectural interior (**FIGS. 10, 11**).

This juxtaposition of antiquity (*vetustas*) and modern beauty (*venustas*), thematized both in the cardinal's *donatio* and in Ugonio's passage, emerges as the most innovative element of the chapels commissioned by Cardinal Salviati, wherein contemporary works (in painting and sculpture) were cleverly conceived and positioned in relation to prestigious ancient images, whose importance was enhanced by their reinstallation in new spaces.

In both San Gregorio al Celio and San Giacomo in Augusta, the emphasis is not so much on the Virgin's role as abstract intercessor[80] but rather on the value and effectiveness of Mary's material images. The desire to conserve (in the modern sense) and arrange new spaces suitable for each image's presentation was the impetus for the creation and decoration of the Salviati chapels.[81] Experimentation in the case of the chapel in San Gregorio was made all the more daring by the defects of the image itself and by the decision to exploit these very defects in order to recreate in the space of the chapel the historical role and miraculous activity of the image itself (an image and an event not mentioned in documents before the sixteenth century).[82] The architecture and the decoration of the chapel, culminating in the altarpiece by Carracci, fundamentally contribute to the historic recreation, the effectiveness of which is attested by all of the sources prior to 1800. While this unusual solution may have inspired other artists engaged in similar commissions,[83] the reciprocal visual hierarchy between the old Madonna and the elegant modern painting in the Salviati Chapel was sanctioned officially by the image's coronation in 1658. When the Madonna received her golden crown from the Vatican Chapter, the altarpiece painted by the "celebrated Annibale Carracci" was called out specifically in the documentation in order to confer prestige and recognition on the Marian image.

In San Giacomo in Augusta, and even more so in the "cautiously experimental" chapel of San Gregorio al Celio,[84] the authorship and beauty of the chapels' architecture and ornamentation served to restore splendor to the two prestigious yet ruined Madonnas, in what emerges as a specific theory of conservation and enhancement of ancient images. In these carefully articulated interiors, the Madonnas were thus restored from a devotional as well as an aesthetic point of view, in spaces designed to exploit their full potential and reveal them in their divine materiality.

Appendix

Doc. 1. Copy of the will of Cardinal Salviati, written on April 9, 1593, and opened in 1602 on the death of the cardinal, Archivio di Stato di Roma (ASR), Ospedale di San Giacomo, b. 228, n 2 (register bound in parchment), fols. 24–66:

> /24/ Testamentum bonae mem(oriae) Eminentissimi Cardinalis Antonii Mariae Salviati rogatum die 9 aprilis 1593 et apertum die 16 Aprilis 1602. . . . /28v/ Corpus vero suum sepelliri voluit sine aliqua pompa in Ecclesia S. Jacobi Incurabilium quae modo edificatur et in Cappella Maiori sub lapide eneo et cum epitaffio congruenti. Item reliquit pro Anima sua celebrari Missas S. Gregorii, et in singulo anno Anniversarium in eadem ecclesia in qua erit sepultus. Item reliquit. . . .

Doc. 2. *Donatio* of Cardinal Salviati to the Ospedale di San Giacomo, ASR, Archivio dell'Ospedale di San Giacomo degli Incurabili, 44, *Protocollum instrumentorum Venerabilis Archiconfraternitatis Sancti Jacobi Incurabilium in Augusta de Urbe. Petrus Martinus Truccha est Notarius*, fols. 49–63v (the passage translated in the text appears at the end in italics):

> /49/ [on the margin] Presens donatio fuit insinuate per acta d. Octavii Capogalli notarii r. coll. sub die 15 martii 1602
>
> Donatio facta per illustrissimum et reverendissimum d. Antonium Mariam Cardinalem Salviatum ad favorem V. Archiospedalis, Confraternitatis et Ecclesiae Sancti Jacobi Incurabilium et Collegii Salviati.
>
> In Dei nomine amen. Anno a nativitate eiusdem D. N. Jesu Christi millesimo sexcentesimo primo inditione decima quarta die vero decimatertia februarii pontificatus s.mi in Christo patris et D. N. D. Clementis Divina providentia papae octavi anno decimo.
>
> Cum fuerit et sit quod illustrissimus et reverendissimus D. Antonius Maria Tituli S. Mariae Transtiberim presbiter cardinalis Salviatus, et ac presens venerabilium Archiospedalis S. Jacobi Incurabilium, et Archiconfraternitatis Domusque Orfanorum et Orphanarum sub titulo Visitationis B. Mariae in Aquiro, et SS. Quatuor Coronatorum de Urbe Protector pro Pia sui animi propensione, quam semper habuit ad procurandum et propagandum optimum statum dictorum Archiospedalis et Archiconfraternitatis Domusque Orphanorum et Orphanarum omni tempore maxima cura invigilaverit et intenderit ac protegendum et amplificandum dicta loca, ipsorumque incrementum sua continue promoverit beneficentia et propterea ex una parte ad gloriam Dei Optimi Maximi, honorem S. Jacobi Apostoli, et Christifidelium salutare commodum propriis ipsius illustrissimi d. Cardinalis sumptibus Hospitale maius a Sancti Rocchi via inceptum, et ad alteram viam Flaminiam, quam Cursum appellant, recta linea protensum suis partibus inferioribus et superioribus ad infirmerum infirmarumque usum distincte fabre factum ac et domum et habitationem pro officialibus, sacerdotibus et ministris Ecclesiae, Confraternitatis, et Archiospedalis S. Jacobi prefati inter Hospitale Vetus ac domus maius Hospitale Novum consistentem a funda/49r/mentis edificaverit *nec non templum seu Ecclesiam Novam S. Jacobi eiidem Archiospedali adiunctam, duplici turri sacra, seu campanili, sachristiis, chorisque ab uno, et altero cornu, cappellis, et altaribus per orbem seu circum circa dispositis, ceterisque suis partibus absolutam, et nuper maxime ad apsida seu tribunam, et altare maius picturis, columnis,*

marmoribus versicoloribus, tabernaculoque mixtis lapidibus contexto adornatam, simul et statua nova marmorea S. Jacobi ad altare, in una prefatarum Capellarum suo peculiari dicatum nomini, ac vetere devotaque Sanctissime Deiparae semper Virginis Imagine, Sancta Maria Miraculorum nuncupata, e loco prope Tiberim minus decenti ad alteram dictarum capellarum in altare honorificum translata, munifice insignitam pariter a fundamentis extruxerit, ac perfecerit.

This *Donatio* starts with a separate register, from 1601, compiled by Vincentio Castronio "computista." On fol. 2:

item mandat illustrissimus Bonae memoriae quod singulis annis de mense septembris post dominicam quartam ipsius mensis die prima non impedita sequeri fiat officium de Spiritu Sancto pro salute eiusdem.... Item quod in eodem die dicti mensis septembris quotannis donec vixerit detur a confraternitate per manus camerarii infra deputandi seu eodem deficiente alterius vel aliourm manus unum inseprum rubrum tritici boni in tot panes albos ex eo conficiendos pro elemosina in salutem ipsius cardinalis distribuendum pauperibus eodie ad ecclesiam accedentibus qui hortantur fundere preces pro eiusdem cardinalis salute. Post vero mortem loco dicti oficii Spirius Sancti mandat quod fiat anniversarium solemni funere annis singulis in perpetuum et rogat eosdem custodes qui velint interesse. Et vult quod distributio panum que fieri... post obitum etiam fiat in die anniversarii et sic in perpetuum.

Doc. 3. Biblioteca Apostolica Vaticana (BAV), Archivio del Capitolo di San Pietro, Madonne Coronate (1648–1667), 2, fol. 166r–v, Madonna nella chiesa di S. Gregorio sul Monte Celio, 1657–1658:

La gloria più pregevole ed eccellente di questo rispettabilissimo luogo è l'imagin di Maria dipinta in muro, che un tempo era nella paterna abitazione di S. Gregorio, e ora si venera nella bellissima Cappella Salviati, fabbricata l'anno 1600 dall'insigne pietà del cardinale Antonmaria di tal nome, il quale sì lodevolmente impiegò la sua munificenza alla condecorazione di questa preziosissima immagine. Imperocchè dessa è quella, innanzi alla quale il divotissimo S. Gregorio, sin dai teneri anni, frequentemente mandava a Dio le sue fervide preghiere, dessa è che a questo suo amatissimo figliuolo compiacquesi di parlar più volte, come ne vediamo assicurati dalla constante tradizione, e dalle parole a gran caratteri impresse nel fregio del cornicione della detta cappella: "Antonius [Maria] cardinalis Salviatus B. V. imaginem ante annos mille in paternis aedibus B. Gregorium allocutam sacello exornavit anno MDC." Che più? *Il quadro in tavola dipinto dal celebre Annibale Caracci rappresenta il Santo Pontefice umilmente genuflesso ed orante, e colla faccia rivolta a questa imagine.* Anzi l'altare stesso fu con ecclesiastico rito a Dio consacrato in memoria appunto della Beatissima Vergine, e di S. Gregorio Papa: ecco quel che vi si legge: "Sacris ritibus Deo consecratum in memoriam Dei genitricis V. Mariae et S. Gregorii papae die 30 octobris 1603." /166v/ Clemente VIII con suo Breve de' 14 Dicembre 1593 concede amplissime Indulgenze a quei che visitano questa sacra imagine, e intervengono alle litanie solite a cantarsi in onor di Maria, ossequio religioso, che ogni sabbato dopo la compieta rendonle in chiesa i divotissimi Monaci Camaldolesi, ai quali mancava la consolazione di vedere questa sì veneranda effigie coronata.

Notes

The research leading to this essay has received funding from the European Research Council (ERC) under the European Union's Horizon 2020 research and innovation programme (grant agreement n° 680192/SACRIMA: The Normativity of Sacred Images in Early Modern Europe). I wish to thank Erin Giffin, who has kindly translated an advanced draft of this text from Italian into English, as well as Olivier Bonfait, Cloe Cavero, David Ekserdjian, Sefy Hendler, Steven F. Ostrow, Enrico Parlato, Ulrich Pfisterer, and Patrizia Tosini for having discussed with me this work at different stages, offering helpful suggestions and sound advice. Special thanks go to Mauro Coen, for the new photos of the chapels at San Gregorio and San Giacomo; and to Miriam Kreischer and Christina Vetter, who helped with image and copyright acquisition.

1 — "Vidistis ibidem sacrarium nobile, partem Gregorianae domus, ubi caelestis Virginis imago monstratur, quae Pontificiem illum sanctissimum affata traditur, cui omnem venustatem vetustas longae aetatis abstulerat; id nunc munifica Salviati impensa, maculosis columnis, camera inaurata, picture pereleganti ita collucet, ut dignitati religionis egregie ornatus loci respondeat." Ugonio 1603, 23.

2 — On Salviati's funerals see Schraven 2014, 236–237. The date of the cardinal's death, April 16, 1602, is noted in a copy of his will; see Appendix, doc. 2 (fol. 25). The complete title and dedication of the church on Celio is Santi Andrea e Gregorio al Monte Celio, but San Gregorio Magno, or San Gregorio al Celio, are the most commonly used denominations.

3 — Hibbard 1971, 121; Eichberg 1994; see also Pedrocchi 1993, 60–67, mostly based on Hibbard and on Gibelli 1888.

4 — After a first sample cleaning in 1983, the nineteenth-century frescoes were completely removed. A photo of the previous situation with Christen Købke's frescoes is available in the Photographic Collection of the Bibliotheca Hertziana.

5 — Gibelli 1888, 10, n. 3. Traditionally associated with Andrea Bregno, this altar is attributed today to the so-called Maestro di Pio II (Caglioti 1997, 235). Its move into the chapel is probably due to the association of the stories of Saint Gregory in the reliefs with the frescoes in the chapel (see below).

6 — Posner 1971, II, 57, no. 130.

7 — This choice is expressed already in 1593 in his will (see Appendix, doc. 2). The Salviati family possessed the *iuspatronatus* of a chapel entitled to Saint James in Santa Maria sopra Minerva (subsequently passed to other patrons). Thus, the idea that the chapel at San Gregorio might originally have had a funerary function (Eichberg 1994, 49) does not seem plausible.

8 — Appendix, doc. 2. The inscription runs as follows: "I.C.R. ANTONIUS MARIA SALVIATUS / S.R.E. CARD(INALIS) / AEDIBUS ADIACENTIBUS IN AEGROTOR(UM) / CURAM EXTRUCTIS / IN HOC QUOD A FUNDAMENTIS EREXIT / TEMPLO / SEPVLCRVM SIBI DELEGIT / VIXIT AN. LXV MENS. II. DIES XXVII / OBIIT XV. KAL. APR. MDCII / LAURENTIUS SALVIATUS IACOBI FILIUS / MARCHIO IULIANI EX TESTAMENTO / HERES / PATRIS PATRUELI P.C. AN. MDCIV." See also Pecchiai and Montini 1958, figs. 10–11.

9 — See Appendix, docs. 1 and 2.

10 — "Medien des Körpers," according to Belting 2001, 130–133.

11 — Hess 1943, 56.

12 — Hurtubise 1985, 311.

13 — Panciroli 1600, 395; Ugonio 1603, 22–23: "Vidistis in Caelio, ad Magni Gregorii aedem huius quondam fidei commendatam, patefactam aream, gradus ad ascensum templi dilatatos, ubi antea ob locorum angustias, confluente ad festos dies turba populorum, molestissime premebatur."

14 — Mittarelli and Costadoni 1764, 194: "scalas similter ampliavit, et cum antiquum Septizonium, quod prope ecclesiam sancti Gregorii extabat, jussu Sixti V. fuisset eversum, in medio scalarum ecclesiae ex una parte fingens ianuam, ad memoriam Septizonii conservandam depingi ipsum voluit expresse, et prout integrum iacebat, apposita inscriptione: *Antonius Maria cardinalis Salviatus aream confluenti populo aperuit.*" Mittarelli and Costadoni (1764, 195) refer to Michele Losanna's manuscript *Descriptio monasterii Sancti Gregorii*, from around 1640, which is also used by Gibelli 1888, 18–19, n. 6. This text is currently untraceable.

15 — BAV, Vat. lat., 11911, Francesco del Sodo, "Conpendio delle chiese di Roma con le loro fondatione, consegratione e titoli de' Cardinali delle parochie," 1575, fols. 133–135: "Questa è una chiesa nel Monte Celio in luogo antico detto Clivo Scauro qual chiesa era la casa paterna di detto San Gregorio. La casata sua non si sa sicura, ma la commune oppenione è che lui fussi di casa Frangipane el quale l'anno secondo del suo pontificato che fu l'anno secondo del suo pontificato 592 la dedicò e consagrò a Sant'Andrea apostolo e vi fece li quattro sottoscritti altari consagrati di sua mano e previlegiati per li defunti: l'altar grande fu il primo e vi pose alquante reliquie come le mani di Sant'Andrea a molte altre reliquie in un vaso e la dotò d'assai indulgentie; il secondo fu quel a mano manca di detto ad honore di San Tomaso ...; l'altro è a mano diritta qual ad honore di San Pantaleo et ivi vi pose il suo santo corpore et altre reliquie; l'altro in nel entrare in chiesa a mano diritta ad honore della gloriosa Vergine e qui vi pose del latte e i capelli della Madonna et altre reliquie qual altare hanno di molte indulgenze come per le bolle in sagrestia si vedeno *et drento al cimiterio v'è una Imagine della Regina del Cielo quale dicono che parlò con San Gregorio.* Quel luogo che cala abasso nel detto cimiterio dove è il Pozzo di San Gregorio lì dicono che vi faceva penitenzia. Là fuora [vi era] la tavola dove il glorioso Santo dava da mangiare a dodeci poveri ogni giorno... Questa Chiesa è assai devota con gran concorso di devotione alli Christiani, e per l'Ottava de' morti ve si dicono assaissime messe per li defunti e non tanto in la detta Ottava, quanto in tutto l'anno nella qual Ottava v'è indulgentia plenaria." See Eichberg 1994, 51, n. 6; Gibelli 1888, 19 ("dipinta nel muro di un antico luogo non sempre visibile") and 20, n. 2. Gibelli mentions a copy, which would have been left in the place where the original image was on the basis of Michele Losanna's manuscript quoted above (n. 14): "Haec sacra imago B.V. Mariae est remota, sed in loco, in quo erat, asservata." Unfortunately, I have not yet been able to retrace either this painted copy or Losanna's manuscript. According to Romano (2017, 433, n. 7), the image in the chapel is "staccata e di ignota provenienza ... la sua *facies* attuale è compatibile con una datazione alla prima metà del Trecento" (entry by Daniela Sgherri). Just before entering the chapel, it is possible to see, through a hole in the right wall of the vestibule to the chapel, another image of the Virgin (FIG. 8). However, this image appears to be different in iconography and certainly cannot be considered a copy, as it seems to be from the early fourteenth century (not commented on

in Romano 2017). The matter deserves further investigation.

16 — Bombelli 1792, 2, 83.

17 — See Eichberg 1994, 50.

18 — "ANTONIUS MARIA CARD[INALIS] SALVIATUS / B[EATAE] VIRGINIS IMAGINEM ANTE ANN[OS] MILLE / IN PATERNIS AEDIBUS B[EATUM] GREGORIU[M] ALLOCUTAM / SACELLO EXORNAVIT ANNO 1600." The indication of the interlapsed one thousand years, marking a sort of Gregorian jubilaeum, aspires to be quite precise if we consider that the date of the foundation of the monastery (as specified by the *Conpendio* quoted above in n. 15) was thought to be in the year 592.

19 — See n. 15 above. The earliest documentation on this foundation dates to the end of the sixth century; references to the institution of a monastic community in the Celimontan properties of Gregory the Great's family are present in the *Dialogi* and in the *Registrum Epistolarum*; subsequent sources (*Liber Pontificalis* and *Vita Gregorii* by Giovanni Diacono, 873–876) "registrano la notizia della fondazione del monastero all'interno di un complesso immobiliare di proprietà del pontefice sul colle Celio nei pressi del Clivo di Scauro." Bartola 2003, vi–viii.

20 — The absence of documents is noted in the application submitted to the Chapter of St. Peter's in 1657–1658 for the coronation of this image: "Non essendo i Monaci Camaldolesi entrati al possesso della Chiesa o Monastero di S. Gregorio di Roma prima dell'anno 1573 non possono avere notizie più antiche dell'anno suddetto circa la mentovata chiesa, e le imagini sacre in essa contenute, giacchè loro non fu lasciato archivio fornito di scritture, che potessero somministrare simili notizie." BAV, Archivio del Capitolo di San Pietro, Madonne Coronate, 1648–1667, 2, fol. 168 and fols. 175v–176; see below and Appendix, doc. 3.

21 — The legend of a Marian image having spoken to Saint Gregory was attached to at least four other works in Rome, including in St. Peter's (Muffel 1452 [1999], 50); Santa Maria del Buon Aiuto (Mariano da Firenze 1518 [1931], 161); Santa Maria Imperatrice (among others Palladio 1554, 54); and Santi Cosma e Damiano (Panciroli 1600, 282–283). See Weißenberger 2007, esp. 62, with her very useful appendix of texts.

22 — Later examples include the *Madonna delle Grazie* in San Salvatore in Lauro and the Rivaldi Chapel in Santa Maria della Pace. Subsequently, the same Ricci also painted the *frontale*, or framing altarpiece, around the Madonna of SS. Trinità dei Pellegrini. For a typology of Roman reframing projects from the 1570s to the Pauline Chapel (1613), see Ostrow 1996, 151–168. A useful chronology of *translationes* of Roman Madonnas from the year 431 to 1593 (*Madonna della Clemenza*) is offered by Weißenberger 2007, *Anhang*, 50.

23 — For the Gregorian Chapel and the *Madonna del Soccorso*, see the essay by Fabio Barry in this volume; Zander 2016; Zander 2020, forthcoming.

24 — According to Bernardini and Mignosi Tantillo (2001, 49–75), Ricci was asked to work in the Cerasi project by Maderno, after the completion of a great part of the Salviati Chapel.

25 — Bernardini and Mignosi Tantillo 2001, 49–75.

26 — For San Giacomo, it is possible to attribute to Capriani (to whom is attributed a project preserved in the Albertina; Pecchiai and Montini 1958, 26) not only the original oval plan of the church but also the building of the edifice to the height of the cornice (Pecchiai and Montini 1958, 25).

27 — Hibbard 1971, 121; Hibbard 2001, 77, n. 10.

28 — Eichberg 1994.

29 — Wiedmann 2004. The altarpiece was replaced in the first half of the nineteenth century by a *Death of Saint John of God* by Giovanni Silvagni (1844), which in turn was substituted by the currently visible *SS. Trinità* by Francesco Grandi. Pecchiai and Montini 1958, 32.

30 — Fulvio 1527, book 5, cap. 15: "Imago deiparae Virginis quae nuperrime in quadam fumosa proseuca in proximis moenibus iuxta Tiberim coli frequentiarique coepta est proximo anno iubilei MDXXV." See Weißenberger 2007, *Katalog*, 83–84; Montini 1953, 17, 31 (quoting "ampie notizie manoscritte del padre V. Sauré presso l'Archivio dei Padri di Bétharram" on the two Madonne dei Miracoli).

31 — Panciroli 1600, 534–535: "li Guardiani dell'hospitale de gl'Incurabili dall'elemosine raccolta fabricarono qui l'anno 1525 che fu del Giubileo, a di 20. di Giugno, questa chiesa a canto le mura della vicina porta detta del Popolo, e da quel luogo qua riportarono l'imagine, et è stata gran tempo sotto la prottettione, e cura delli Padri Francescani Conventuali riformati. . . . Poi l'anno 1598 per essere il luogo molto rimoto, et havendo il Cardinale Salviati adornato l'hospitale de S. Giacomo de gl'Incurabili con si bella, e vaga fabrica, . . . volse con quest'Imagine ancora arrichirla." See Weißenberger 2007, *Anhang* 30; Bombelli 1792, 1, 85. Romano 2017, 434, n. 25: "è probabile che la cronologia si attesti al primo Quattrocento, accanto al gruppo affine a Taddeo di Bartolo."

32 — Pecchiai and Montini 1958, 54.

33 — See Appendix, doc. 2. This *donatio* is incorrectly considered to be a will by Hibbard 1971, 121.

34 — Baglione 1642, 89: "colorì in s. Giacomo de gl'Incurabili alcuni angioli, e puttini intorno alla Madonna."

35 — Bombelli (1792, 1, 85) specifies this difference of media. In BAV, Archivio del Capitolo di San Pietro, Madonne Coronate, 2, fol. 208 (1659), the substitutive copy on canvas is described as "di eccellentissimo lavoro."

36 — Hibbard 1971, 121; Eichberg 1994, 44, 52, n. 20 (ASV, Fondo Borghese Salviati, b. 4374).

37 — Hibbard 1971, 121.

38 — Hibbard 2001, 139. Meo Bassi worked at least since 1593 for the cardinal, and he is recorded in BAV, Archivio Salviati, 315, "Libro di spese datte dal Card. Giovann [ma Antonio Maria] Salviati per il Palazzo alla Lungara, 1583 [*sic*; actually 1593] a 1599," fols. 15r, 72v, 73r, 91v, 98v, 99r. The "fascicolo sciolto" mentioned by Hibbard (relevant fols. 10v, 13), presumably containing the reference to the frame of the Madonna, corresponds today to BAV, Archivio Salviati, 316: "Nota delli lavori di scalpello fatti nel Palazzo dell'ill.mo cardinale Salviati [1600]." Due to the significant state of deterioration of the small file, consultation is not allowed.

39 — Eichberg 1994, 44–45.

40 — Eichberg 1994, 47: "telaio architettonico."

41 — Previous studies on these frescoes, however, have been rather dismissive of this program. See, for example, Abromson 1976, 177–180.

42 — Ripa 1593, 2r–v.

43 — On images of the Patriarchs as a salvific theme in private chapels, see Franceschini 2017, 287–298.

44 — Baglione 1642, 149: "per il medesimo cardinale dipinse a S. Gregorio al Celio la cappella al Santo dedicata; e nella cupoletta havvi una gloria con li Santi del Cielo; e da basso incontro all'immagine di Maria, v'è quando S. Gregorio fece portare la santa immagine in processione per

Roma, fatte a fresco." The attribution and description are repeated by several subsequent Roman guides, such as Martinelli (1581 [1969], 72); Nicola Pio (Enggass and Enggass 1977, 88); and others (e.g., Giacomo Gregorio Terribilini).

45 — Gere and Pouncey 1983, n. 246, and online entry at: britishmuseum.org (n. 1979,1006.87). For a later chapel fresco design by Ricci (at San Francesco a Ripa), see Tosini 2003.

46 — The work by Zuccari displeased the patron and was subsequently replaced; the painting now in the chapel is a procession of Saint Gregory the Great by Cesare Aretusi (1552–1614). See Acidini and Capretti 2009, 174–183, with previous bibliography.

47 — Eichberg (1994, 54, n. 49) states that the represented icon is not of the type of the *Salus Populi Romani* but of the type of the image in the chapel; after close inspection, this seems not to be the case.

48 — Ostrow 1996, 151–158.

49 — However, *pictura* can also refer to the entire work of painting, including the frescoes by Ricci.

50 — Corsi 1825, 56–57.

51 — The anachronistic representation of Gregory, who is shown already as a pope (while the episode occurred supposedly when he was still living in his parents' house) and more specifically as a sixteenth-century pope (here in white tunic and *mozzetta* and without a beard as in Raphael's *Disputa*), was repeated in both sculpture (Nicolas Cordier) and painting (Antonio Viviani) in the Oratory of Santa Barbara with Saint Gregory's *triclinium*, following Baronio's instructions. Hendler 2007, 177–178.

52 — See n. 15 above.

53 — A silver plate for this engraving, dated 1598, is preserved in Naples, Museo di Capodimonte. The plate replicates in reverse an etching made by Agostino on the model of Annibale's etching from 1597, known as the *Pietà di Caprarola*. The plate bears the inscriptions in reverse, "A.C.I.F.," and on the right "Ant. Mar. Card. Salv. 1598." See DeGrazia 1984, 190, n. 209; Bernardini and Mignosi Tantillo 2001, 75, n. 43. As suggested by Posner (1971, II, 82–83), it is therefore likely that the executor of the plate was Agostino Carracci and not Annibale.

54 — "M. DC. III. DIE XXX. MENSIS OCTOBRIS EGO LEONARDUS ABEL EPISCOPUS SIDONIENSIS ET IN URBE SUFFRAGANEVS DEPVTATVS CONSECRAVI ALTARE HOC IN HONOREM BEATAE VIRGINIS MARIAE ET SANCTI GREGORII PAPAE; ET RELIQVIAS SACRI SPIRIDIONIS CONFESSORIS SANCTAE MARIAE EGYPTIACAE. . . . " See Gibelli 1888, 21–22.

55 — Mancini ca. 1620 [1956–1957], I, 218: "tra tanto Anniballe attende a finire la gallaria et in questo tempo, con suo disegno e ritocco, fu il quadro di S. Gregorio per il cardinale Salviati, e il Deposto di Croce in S. Francesco di Ripa con alcune altre cose particolari." See Ginzburg Carignani 2000, 97–110. According to Mittarelli and Costadoni (1764, 194), Salviati obtained the *altare privilegiato* through a *breve* by Clemente VIII of April 5, 1601; see also Pedrocchi 1993, 64. In this case, the Saint Gregory altarpiece would follow, and not precede, the *Assumption of the Virgin* in the Cerasi Chapel, which is usually dated "by March" (Strinati 2001) or June 1601 (by the time of the Farnese Gallery *scoprimento*, on June 2, 1601). The Cerasi Chapel was then consacrated only on November 11, 1606, when Cerasi was already dead (May 5, 1601).

56 — A similar arrangement was repeated in the Pauline Chapel in Santa Maria Maggiore, where Paul V directs his prayers from his tomb to the Marian icon on the altar; however, the difference is that here the icon is on the main altar, and the figure of the pope acts from the lateral wall.

57 — Steinberg 1959; for Venice, Matile 1997.

58 — Posner 1971, 1, 126–128.

59 — Pedrocchi 1993, 64.

60 — Ginzburg Carignani (2000, 97–110) interestingly suggests a comparison between the cushion in this painting and Matthew's tottering stool in the second version of Caravaggio's Saint Matthew altarpiece.

61 — Posner (1971, 128), followed by several others (e.g., Bernardini and Mignosi Tantillo 2001, 75: "i suoi studi preparatori, di un illusionismo molto più accentuato").

62 — Where, according to Posner (1971, 1, 128), "little remains of the illusionistic ideas with which Annibale started some years before." In the same way, Posner compares and contrasts the Capodimonte *Pietà* and the *Pietà* at the Louvre. For the influence of Posner on subsequent judgment, see Ginzburg 2011, 160.

63 — Ginzburg Carignani 2000.

64 — Borea (1986) lists and reproduces three other engravings, for a total of four (while only three are known of the *Assunta* in the Cerasi Chapel; Jean Collin engraved both the San Gregorio altarpiece and the *Assunta*).

65 — Also noted by Ottley and Tomkins 1818, no. 30, who saw the painting in London and described the "crudeness or over brilliancy of its colours," considering it "too gay in its colouring" (Posner 1971, 2, 57, no. 130). However, Gibelli (1888, 21, n. 1) reports the notice (from the untraceable *Memorie del monastero*) that in 1731 the work was restored at the orders of Duca Salviati: "dal coloraro Pietro Michelini, il quale facendo uso di uno suo segreto lavò il quadro e l'accomodò così bene, che sembrava dipinto da poco tempo."

66 — Baglione 1642, 107: "Per il Cardinale Antonio Maria Salviati fece in S. Gregorio nella cappella a questo Santo dedicata sopra l'altare un s. Gregorio Papa, ginocchione in atto di orare ad una imagine della Beatissima Vergine, con angioli, e puttini a olio dipinto, e diligentissimamente condotto."

67 — Bellori 1672 [1976], 93–94: "Nella Chiesa di San Gregorio su 'l monte Celio, entro la cappella edificata dal cardinale Antonio Maria Salviati, ammirasi il quadro del Santo ginocchione con le braccia aperte, pregando per l'anime del Purgatorio. Vive il colore nell'efficacia del Santo Pontefice in abito col camice e con la mozzetta su le spalle. Sta in mezzo a due angeli, che accompagnano le sue preghiere; l'uno con le mani al petto, l'altro accenna il Santo alla Vergine dipinta in una divota immagine per fianco nella medesima cappella, che si tiene parlasse a San Gregorio; e sopra il Santo si vede lo Spirito Santo in forma di colomba, che infonde la luce con altri angeli in adorazione."

68 — "Magnum Gregorium / quem procumbentem ante Deiparae imaginem, adverso in pariete / depictam / cuius ipse dum viveret alloquium meruit, / Annibal Caraccius, urgente Salviatae Gentis pietate, coloribus expresserat, / Ex archetypo a se delineatum aerae incidit, ut omnium voto facere satis / Jacobus Frey" is the inscription that appears a the bottom of the engraved reproduction by Frey (FIG. 19).

69 — For more general information on the history of the *madonne coronate* and the role of Fra Girolamo Paulucci de' Calboli da Forlì (d. 1620), see Bombelli 1792; Ilarino da Milano 1950; Ottavio da Alatri 1933; Bonci 2004, 60, 20–29. See also Ostrow 1996, 130, 318, n. 60; Garnett and Rosser 2013, 26, 283–285.

70 — See Appendix, doc. 3, and Bombelli 1782, 2, 79, and following pages. The crowns were already stolen before 1786 when the following note was written: "Noi sottoscritti per la pura verità attestiamo, qualmente abbiamo sempre inteso a dire, e pubblicamente, che la corona d'oro posta alla Madonna della Capella Salviati in S. Gregorio, fu rubbata, ed attestiamo avere ciò inteso a dire da vecchi dimoranti nel Monastero di S. Gregorio, i quali riferivano il sudetto furto, come certo, e indubitato, e nelli anni più addietro a tempo loro pubblico, e notorio. Io fra Fedele Brancoli Calmaldolese; io Andrea Puggelli vecchio ortolano di detto monasterio" (note subsequently included in the same file quoted in Appendix, doc. 3, that is, BAV, Archivio del Capitolo di San Pietro, Madonne Coronate [1648–1667], 2, at fols. 178–179).

71 — The idea that the inscription and, above all, the painting by Annibale *document* the miracle is expressed elsewhere in the same file, for example, in this passage: "Da alcuni documenti però non tanto recenti, che tuttavia sussistono, si può sufficientemente raccogliere essere stata la predetta imagine avuta sempre in grande venerazione, non solo per i miracoli, ma ancora per essersi riconosciuta per quella, che parlò già a san Gregorio il grande fondatore del monastero. Nel fregio del cornicione dell'accennata cappella Salviati.... La tavola medesima dell'altare di S. Gregorio nella stessa cappella Salviati esprime cosa coerente alle descritte parole [i.e., the inscription], giacchè rappresenta S. Gregorio in ginocchio con la faccia rivolta alla menzionata imagine posta in altro altare in fianco in atto di adorarla." BAV, Archivio del Capitolo di San Pietro, Madonne Coronate, 1648–1667, 2, fol. 170v, which is the continuation of the text quoted above, n. 20.

72 — Posner (1971, 1, 126–127, 173, n. 22) suggests that at this stage, the idea "was to paint the picture in fresco, which would have been the only logical way to execute this design." It is difficult to assess this hypothesis in relation to the overall project of the chapel.

73 — Posner 1971, 1, 127, and 2, fig. 130c.

74 — The chapel might have been finished after 1600 and even after the death of Salviati by his successor, Cardinal Cesare Baronio, who was certainly in charge of the 1603 consecration of this and other altars in the church (see Posner 1971, 172, n. 24; Eichberg 1994, 50); however, for what concerns this change of iconography, there is no need to posit an intervention by Baronio, as it is not possible to establish any certain connection between Baronio and the San Gregorio altarpiece, even if Baronio was certainly in charge of all the subsequent Gregorian interventions at San Gregorio al Celio. Posner (1971, 1, 172, and 2, 57, n. 130) dated the executed altarpiece to ca. 1601 or 1601–1602; see n. 55 above. For a discussion of this drawing in relation to the painting (wrongly entitled *Saint Gregory Praying for the Souls in Purgatory*), see also Loisel Legrand 1999.

75 — Posner (1971, 1, 127) notes the "rather odd presentation of a slightly bewildered saint being pulled in opposing, but equally legitimate directions."

76 — The Metropolitan Museum of Art, inv. 62.120.1, recto.

77 — Posner (1971, 2, n. 130, 57) mentions the possibility (on the basis of Mancini, quoted in n. 55 above) of a degree of intervention of the workshop in the execution of the painting. However, this hypothesis does not seem to be necessary, and it is rarely taken up in the subsequent literature. Among the original liturgical furnishings was probably also a small altar below the image of Mary "in commesso di marmi preziosi." See Pedrocchi 1993, 64: "risulta dai documenti che fin dall'inizio del '600, sotto l'icona della Madonna, c'era un piccolo altare, solo da pochi anni rimosso, costituito da una mensa in commesso di marmi preziosi, citato sia nell'Inventario dei Beni della Chiesa del 1727 che in quello del 1825."

78 — Armenini 1586, 188–189: "certe figure fatte alla Greca, goffissime, dispiacevoli e tutte affumicate...."

79 — Titi 1763, 75: "nel quadro dell'altare è dipinto a olio s. Gregorio orante alla B. Vergine, con angioli, e puttini, con gran maniera condotto da Annibale Carracci, ed è una delle insigni tavole di Roma."

80 — As suggested by Eichberg 1994, 50: "tradurre formalmente ... il cammino ascensionale del popolo di Dio attraverso le preghiere alla Vergine."

81 — These commissions follow Cardinal Salviati's diplomatic mission in France (1572–1578), during which time he would have been intimately aware of the Saint Bartholomew's Day massacre, gaining firsthand knowledge of iconoclastic fervor. Earlier, as bishop of Saint-Papoul (since 1561), Salviati went to Trent on November 28, 1561 (Hurtubise 1985, 1, 10). Here, from January 18 to the beginning of December 1562, he took part in the Council, speaking in favor of a strict interpretation of the residence duty. He left before the discussion of the decrees on Purgatory and the veneration of saints and images.

82 — See above and n. 20.

83 — It has been widely recognized that at the moment of planning his major altarpiece for the *Madonna della Vallicella*, Peter Paul Rubens knew the San Gregorio al Celio chapel. In fact, Rubens's first and refused proposal—the Grenoble version—offers, among other things, a sophisticated combination of laterality (the figure of Saint Gregory) and frontality (the image of the Virgin), while in the final version, the figures of the saints are more "normally" situated at the sides of the Marian image. See Buttler 2011 and *La regola e la fama* 1995, 158.

84 — The quotation about the architecture of this chapel is from Tafuri 1976.

Carving Out Identity

THE BONCOMPAGNI FAMILY, ALESSANDRO ALGARDI, AND THE CHAPEL IN THE SACRISTY OF SANTA MARIA IN VALLICELLA

Guendalina Serafinelli

On April 23, 1636, a fire broke out in the wood storage of Giovanni Zaccarello, tenant of Duke Salviati's vineyard, and expanded to the neighboring house of the Bolognese artist Alessandro Algardi (1598–1654), located in Rome in Via della Lungara.[1] The unfortunate sculptor, who was at first accused by Zaccarello of having set the fire, was the one who suffered considerable damage.[2] From the legal examinations recorded in the *Tribunale Criminale del Governatore* and the deposition of Algardi's assistant Francesco Maria Ricci, who was in the house of the sculptor when the fire broke out, we learn that if not for several people who came to the artist's aid, his house would have burned to the ground.[3] Aside from providing an account of what happened to Algardi, the legal records are of pivotal importance because they shed light on the sculptor's projects at the time. In fact, thanks to the deposition of Ricci, we learn that when the fire broke out, another assistant of Algardi's was present in the house, working "intorno a San Filippo Neri," a work correctly identified as the sculpture of *Saint Philip Neri and the Angel*, a three-meter-tall marble group destined for the chapel in the sacristy of the church of Santa Maria in Vallicella (FIG. 1).[4]

Arguably, the artist received the commission only sometime before and was not even at the preliminary stage of his carving process, having his assistant working "alla gagliarda," that is, taking off the rough parts of the marble block and cutting out the principal features of the sculptural ensemble.[5] The statue was commissioned by the layman and converted Jew Pietro Boncompagni (1592–1664), but the payment of two hundred scudi and another for the two columns flanking the marble group were made, respectively, by Pietro's uncles, the convert Agostino Boncompagni (d. 1640) and his brother Ippolito (d. 1652).[6] The three characters came from the Jewish family of the Corcos, a branch of famous rabbis and wealthy bankers from the Roman Ghetto, several members of which embraced Christianity under the auspices of Philip Neri, being baptized, as will be explained in more detail, with the Bolognese and noble family name Boncompagni.

The commissioning of the statue was investigated by Minna Heimbürger Ravalli in 1973 and by Jennifer Montagu in a seminal article published in 1977 and again in her monograph on Algardi in 1985.[7] Aside from his Jewish origins, little was known about Pietro Boncompagni at the time. This lack of information about his artistic patronage and his relationship with artists made it difficult, as both scholars observed, to postulate why Pietro chose Algardi.[8]

By placing the circumstances of this commission in the broader context of the Corcos family's transition from Judaism to Catholicism, I will examine this episode of patronage in connection with the vicissitudes that led the family to embrace Christianity and its subsequent efforts to refashion its identities. In investigating the relationship of Pietro to Agostino and Ippolito, I will delve further into the lives of the latter two and suggest, on the basis of new documentary evidence, that because of Agostino's role within the Oratory and Ippolito's friendship with Bolognese artists, the two played a key role in envisioning the commission. I will thus explore the embellishment of their chapel as a collective enterprise, conceived with the intention both to emphasize the Boncompagni family's devotion and special bond to Saint Philip Neri as advocate of their conversion and to publicly consolidate their new social and religious identity.

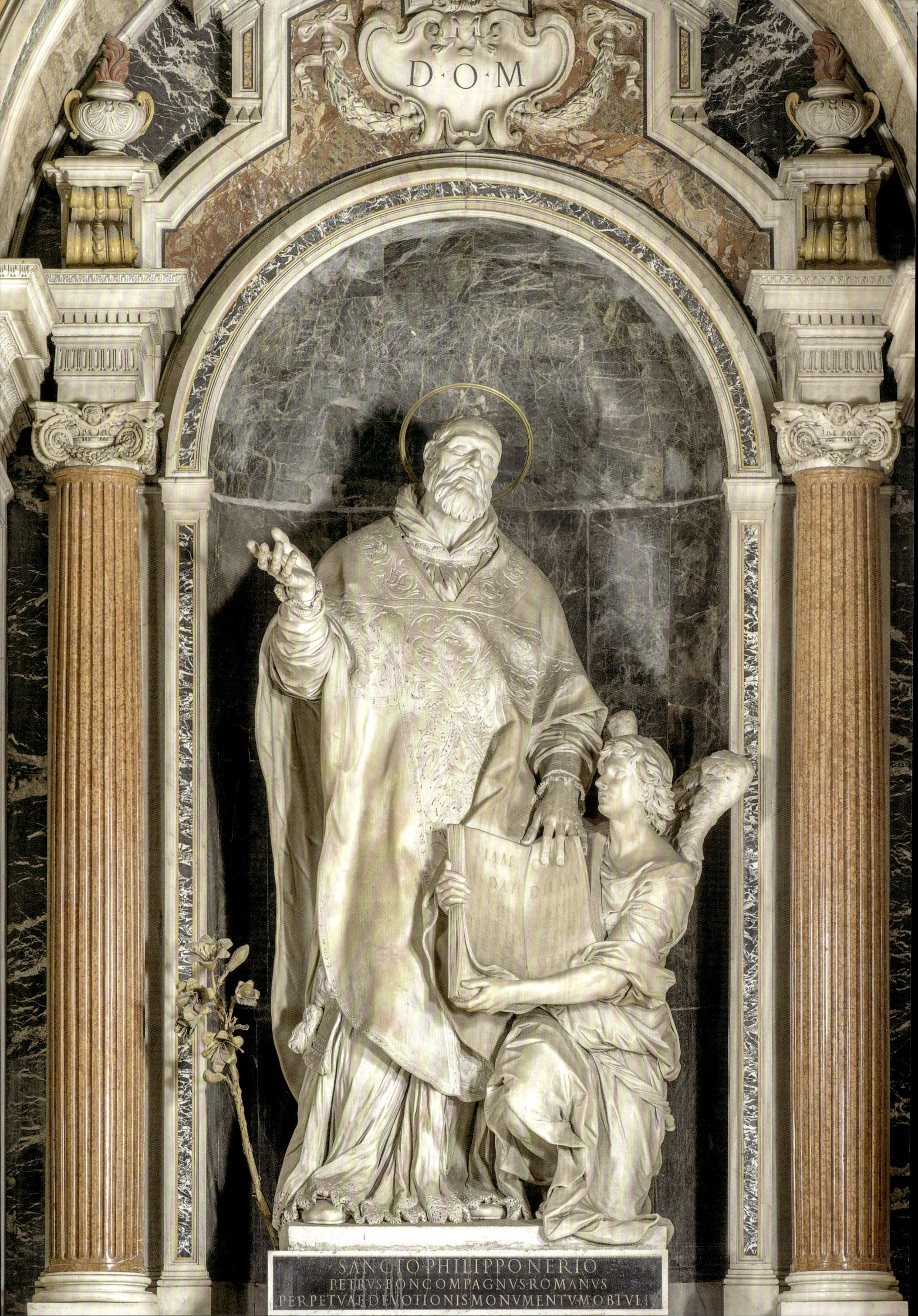
D·O·M
SANCTO·PHILIPPO·NERIO
PETRVS·BONCOMPAGNVS·ROMANVS
PERPETVAE·DEVOTIONIS·MONVMENTVM·OBTVLIT

Before addressing these issues, it should be clarified that although the project—consisting of an altar within the sacristy—is not in the strictest sense of the term a chapel, it nevertheless conveys the same meanings as a chapel opening onto a nave of a church. Accordingly, the Boncompagni altar—a microcosm annexed to the Vallicella church,[9] endowed by wealthy patrons as a demonstration of piety and social standing—is always referred to in coeval documents as "cappella" or "cappella di sagrestia."[10] The fully adorned altar for the celebration of the Mass, the prominent display of the Boncompagni coat of arms, and the inscription of the donor at the base of Algardi's statue emphasize, in fact, the dual nature of this space as one for devotion and one for self-representation.

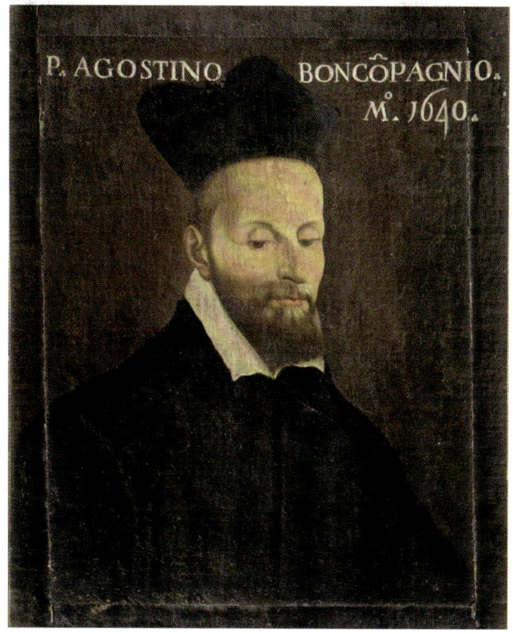

2

Becoming Boncompagni

The story of the conversion of the Corcos (Boncompagni) took place during the last two decades of the sixteenth century, beginning with two preeminent members of the family: Lazzaro and his father, Salomone, who were baptized, respectively, in 1581 and 1582 in St. Peter's Basilica with the names Gregorio and Ugo Boncompagni in honor of the then-ruling Pope Gregory XIII Boncompagni (1572–1585).[11] Both father and son embodied the establishment of the Roman Ghetto; thus, their confessional change was hailed as the most successful outcome of Gregory XIII's policy of conversion.[12] In this respect, not only did the pope offer them the extraordinary privilege of adopting his family name, Boncompagni, and his coat of arms, but by means of a *motu proprio* issued in 1582, he also elevated the converts to the Roman nobility, creating them Counts Palatine and granting them several public offices.[13]

The previously mentioned Ippolito and Agostino, who contributed to the making of the chapel in the Vallicella sacristy, were nephews to Ugo. On August 1592, together with their other two brothers (Alessandro and Clemente), they were snatched away from their widowed mother, Gemma Luzzatti, and entrusted by Ugo to the pastoral care of Philip Neri and the Oratorians.[14]

As will be explained below in greater detail, shortly before Pope Clement VIII Aldobrandini (1592–1605) promulgated two papal bulls on Jews (1593, *Caeca et Obdurata* and *Cum Hebraeorum Malitia*), the four brothers had been led to conversion through a miracle worked by Philip Neri and were baptized by the pope in the baptistery of San Giovanni in Fonte on October 28, 1592. The four brothers, who were born Ruben, Salomone, Leone-Juda, and Abramo Corcos, converted to Christianity with the names Ippolito, Agostino, Alessandro, and Clemente, and because of the *motu proprio* of 1582, they were granted the same privilege as their predecessors of adopting the Boncompagni family name and coat of arms.[15]

Detailed accounts of the miraculous episode of the conversion of the Corcos are reported in the multiple depositions of 1595, 1600, and 1610 by Ippolito and Agostino Boncompagni at the canonization process of Philip Neri (beatified in 1615 and proclaimed saint in 1622).[16] These depositions had been delivered during the years in which the four brothers were accomplishing their integra-

FIG. 1. Alessandro Algardi, *Saint Philip Neri and the Angel*, 1636–1638. Sacristy of Santa Maria in Vallicella, Rome.

FIG. 2. Anonymous, *Portrait of Father Agostino Boncompagni*, seventeenth century. Archivio della Congregazione dell'Oratorio, Rome.

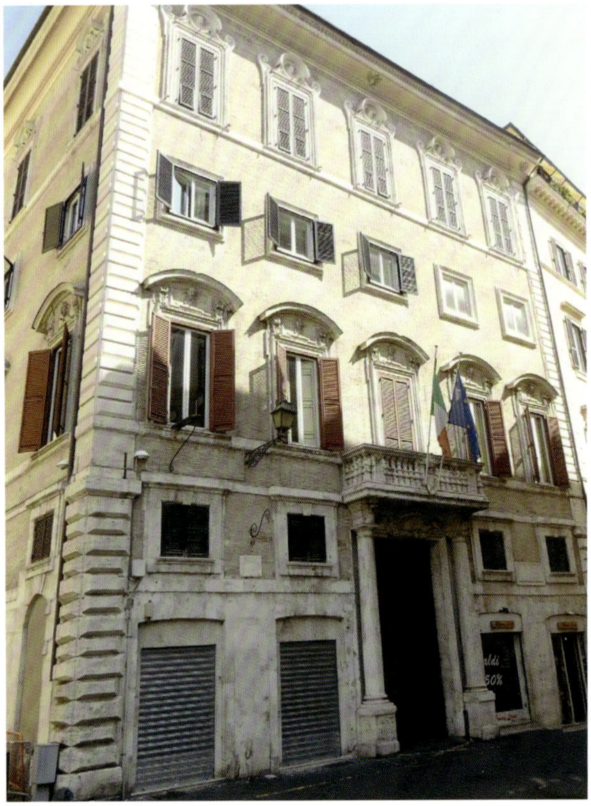

3

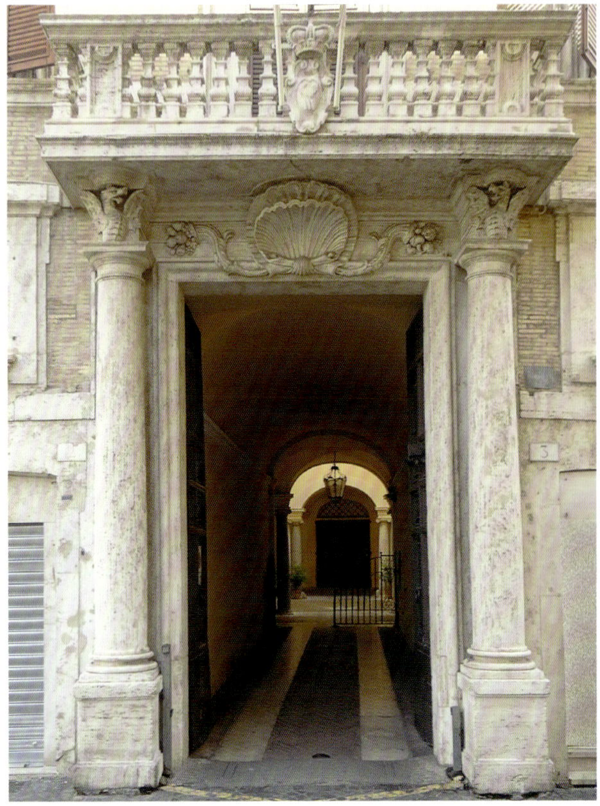

4

FIG. 3. Giovanni Antonio De Rossi, Facade of Boncompagni Corcos Palace at Monte Giordano, Rome.

FIG. 4. Giovanni Antonio De Rossi, Portal of Boncompagni Corcos Palace at Monte Giordano, Rome.

tion into Catholic society and the conversion of their relatives was taking place, including that of Pietro, Algardi's future patron. A new interpretation of the deposition by Agostino, who in 1602 became an Oratorian father (FIG. 2),[17] provides significant insights into his and Ippolito's bond to Pietro, which after several years would take tangible form in their joint chapel commission. In 1600, Agostino reported that, despite the fact that his mother, Gemma, was entrusted in 1594 to the care of the Marquess Giulia Orsini Rangoni, she refused conversion and was sent back to the Ghetto.[18] Philip Neri prophesied that the time was not yet ripe for her conversion and that she would have to commit to become Christian "un'altra volta," that is to say, in the future.[19] Gemma, living in the Ghetto, had two married daughters (among other children), both of whom were parents themselves. One was Maddalena (Pietro's mother), who in around 1595 became a widow of her Jewish husband, Servideo. Agostino narrates that when Maddalena and her other sister concurrently lost their husbands, "we, as uncles of the said children, undertook their tutelage. And, so, in this role we were able to remove the said children from the Ghetto."[20] In other words, because Agostino and his brothers were related to these "putti"—among whom was Pietro—they took them out of the Ghetto and became their tutors until around 1599, the year when Maddalena, Gemma, and other members of the family embraced conversion, as Philip Neri had miraculously predicted.[21] We are uncertain exactly when the conversion of Pietro took place, but in light of Agostino's deposition, there are reasons to surmise that their uncles had been responsible for his religious education, which likely occurred within the Oratorian context.

The Choice of Algardi

When Pietro commissioned the sculpture of *Saint Philip Neri and the Angel* around 1636, he was also taking his first step in an even more ambitious project that would eventually lead him to establish an overt connection of his personal story to the Oratorians and their mother church. Thanks to the studies of Bevilacqua, Gigli, and Uttaro, we know that when Pietro married Sulplizia della Vetera in 1643, he concurrently bought from the Pandolfini family a monumental palace facing Piazza Monte Giordano right behind the Vallicella church (FIG. 3).[22] Pietro's choice for the location of his dwelling was "explicitly evocative of the family's affairs, a site—between the *via papale* and the seat of the Oratiorians—that embodied both papal protection and the spiritual guidance of the saint."[23] From the mid-1640s until his death, Pietro spent all of his economic resources on the enhancement of his palace, entrusted to the architect Giovanni Antonio De Rossi, in which he ostentatiously displayed his coat of arms—not only on top of the two columns flanking the main entrance of his palace (FIG. 4) but also over the body of the building as a declaration of his new social standing. This obsession, through which the converted Jew Pietro publicly proclaimed himself a "true" Boncompagni, is also reflected in the private sphere, if we consider the many furnishings ("suppellettili") richly decorated with the Boncompagni emblem, which are described in the inventory of his goods (1664).[24]

Based on this inventory, in which only a limited number of works of art are recorded, we might assume that Pietro did not have a significant inclination toward artistic patronage and collecting.[25] Admittedly, before commissioning the statue from Algardi, Pietro was not involved in any relevant activity of patronage. Single exceptions of limited significance can be found in a hitherto unpublished document of 1628, which testifies to a payment of thirty scudi by Pietro to Francesco Porri for the making of two "silver candlesticks" (July 7) and, most important, another of seventy scudi to his uncle Agostino "per paramenti della Chiesa Nova" (August 12), that is, for unspecified decorations or vestments destined for the church of the Vallicella.[26] Not only does the latter payment prove Pietro's first timid attempt to step in as a patron within the context of the Vallicella, but it also proves that his initiative was channeled through his uncle Agostino, who, as an Oratorian, clearly had a say in such matters.[27] We might assume that Pietro relied again on Agostino when on October 21, 1635, the Oratorians discussed in Congregation Pietro's offer to commission at his own expense a marble statue of Saint Philip Neri.[28]

Why Algardi was selected to carry out the commission has been a recurring question in the studies devoted to the chapel in the Vallicella sacristy.[29] Although, as Montagu observed, "the sculptor was becoming recognized by the more observant connoisseurs as a promising young artist," he had yet to produce, as she also noted, "marble works of any significance."[30] Indeed, following the Bolognese local tradition, Algardi received no training in the carving of stone; rather, he learned his profession working mainly in terracotta and stucco. Accordingly, when in 1625 he moved to Rome with a recommendation to Cardinal Ludovico Ludovisi—nephew to the former Pope Gregory XV—he was largely employed as a restorer of antique sculptures, ultimately suffering the prejudice "put about by some, that he was not good at anything but modeling."[31]

In his *Life* of Algardi, Giovan Pietro Bellori wrote that after having "languished for so long, ... numerous noble and esteemed commissions came his way. First he was chosen by Signor Pietro Buoncompagni for the statue of Saint Philip Neri."[32] The Boncompagni commission was entrusted to the sculptor in a period that marked a watershed between his past career and the future. In the summer of 1634, Algardi received the commission from Cardinal Roberto Ubaldini for the *Tomb of Leo XI* in St. Peter's Basilica (completed in 1644), and a few months later, the Oratorian Virgilio Spada contracted him for the marble group of the *Beheading of Saint Paul*, installed on the main altar of the church of San Paolo Maggiore in Bologna in 1647.[33] With her usual acumen, Montagu perceived that the bond between Pietro and the Oratory could have led to a connection with Spada, who, as a patron of Algardi, might have introduced the sculptor to Boncompagni.[34] This hypothesis is also strengthened by the fact that, according to Spada's indications, in 1640, Algardi's bronze *Bust of Pope Gregory XV* was installed above the entrance of the Vallicella sacristy directly opposite the marble group commissioned by Boncompagni.[35]

Considering that Pietro was not involved in any relevant activities of artistic patronage before the mid-1630s, it is possible to surmise that the ones who pulled the strings of the chapel project had been his older uncles Agostino and Ippolito. Indeed, the fact that both of Pietro's uncles had financially contributed to the making of the chapel suggests that they took an active role in envisioning this artistic project—one destined to permanently communicate their family's devotion to Saint Philip Neri and to publicly declare the authenticity of their conversion.

Arguably, Pietro's connection with Spada was mediated through his uncle Agostino. From the testament of Agostino, opened on March 10, 1640, we learn that he bequeathed to the Oratory the remarkable amount of fifteen hundred scudi for the purchase of some textiles to adorn the pilasters of the Chiesa Nuova on the occasion of the feast day of Saint Philip Neri.[36] In his will, Agostino also bequeathed to his heirs —his brothers Ippolito and Clemente—some relics of Saint Philip Neri and donated to Spada "la pelliccia del Glorioso S. Filippo Neri," the fur coat the saint wore to mortify himself.[37] While Agostino's endowment of the saint's relics to his brothers bears the symbolical memory of their joint conversion, his precious donation to Spada testifies to a strong personal bond between the two. Such evidence might suggest that had Spada spoken in favor of Algardi, his privileged interlocutor might have been Agostino.

Of no less importance was the role of Ippolito, who, as anticipated, financed the two columns flanking Algardi's sculpture. New archival evidence proves that, unlike Pietro, Ippolito was fully immersed in the artistic patronage system of his time.[38] A well-off ecclesiastic who lived on his private income,[39] Ippolito, contrary to what Carlo Cesare Malvasia reports, was not an Oratorian father.[40] At the beginning of the 1620s, Ippolito played the prestigious role of privy chaplain to the Bolognese Pope Gregory XV—the pope who proclaimed Philip Neri a saint—living in the Apostolic Palace as a member of the pontifical household.[41] Ippolito was known to Malvasia for having been a close friend to Guido Reni and one of his privileged correspondents.[42] In his palace, located in the Parione area not far from the Vallicella, Ippolito built up, together with his brother Clemente—to whom in 1652 he bequeathed all his goods[43]—a collection of around 250 paintings, which featured a considerable number of works by

FIG. 5. Durante Alberti, *The Annunciation*, 1588. Santa Maria ai Monti, Rome.

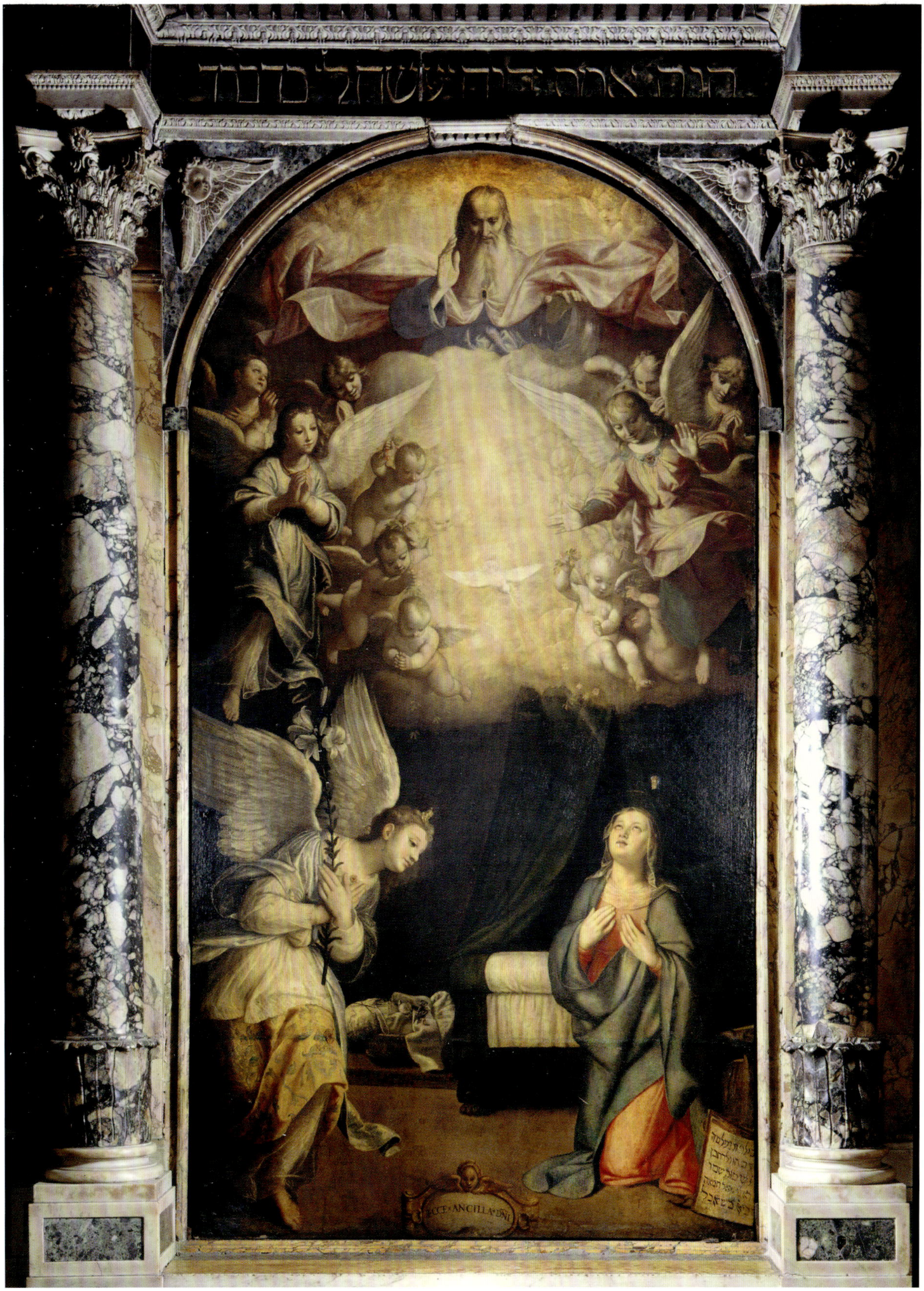

5

Emilian artists (Domenichino, Guercino, Giovan Giacomo Sementi, and Giovanni Lanfranco) and, most important, fifteen works by Reni.[44] The presence in this collection of many paintings by Emilians can now be explained as the logical consequence of Ippolito's personal acquaintance with some of the most important Bolognese masters of his time, among whom were the already mentioned Reni, Guido Signorini (Reni's cousin and heir), and Domenichino.[45] It is striking to observe that because of his friendship with Domenichino, Boncompagni was appointed his procurator and entrusted with the management of his finances and investments in Rome, even after the artist's departure for Naples.[46]

Seen in this new light, it is inevitable to wonder whether the choice of Algardi for the Boncompagni chapel might have originated from concurrent factors: Virgilio Spada's advocacy as well as Ippolito's connection with the Ludovisi family and Domenichino. If Algardi had been introduced to Ippolito by Cardinal Ludovisi, to whom the sculptor was recommended when he moved to Rome, then it had to have occurred before 1632, the year Ludovisi died; alternatively, had it been Domenichino, with whom Algardi notoriously had collaborated in Rome and "formed a close friendship,"[47] then it might have happened before or even after the painter moved to Naples.[48] Clearly, this is a hypothesis; however, Ippolito's connection with the Bolognese community in Rome, notably with Domenichino, can hardly be overestimated.

What leads us to believe that Ippolito played a role in the choice of Algardi[49] and in conceiving the sacristy chapel project is the fact that he had been one of the first members of his family to be involved in artistic patronage and collecting and to employ art as a means of self-representation and construction of social legitimacy. His immersion in the art world and familiarity with artists, most of whom were Bolognese, would have been regarded by Agostino and Pietro as an asset for their joint commission. One of the most striking features of the collection of paintings that Ippolito shared with his brother Clemente is that the majority of the works by Emilians, listed in the inventory of Boncompagni's goods of 1657, appear prominently displayed in the area of the palace that traditionally constituted the space for self-representation: the gallery.[50]

Of no less importance is the fact that the first two paintings to be displayed at the entrance of the gallery were a portrait of Pope Gregory XIII Boncompagni, the catalyst of the new Boncompagni social identity and noble status, and one of Saint Philip Neri, the saint responsible for their new religious identity.[51] For reasons of brevity, it is not possible to delve further into this matter here, other than to emphasize that the decision to group the works by Emilians and the two portraits in the gallery reflects Ippolito's (and probably his brother's) wish to express his family's geographical ties (although fictitious) to the city of Bologna and to be seen as a "true" Boncompagni and a "true" Christian devoted to Saint Philip Neri.

This strategic use of images is conceptually analogous to the main features of the commissioning of the Boncompagni Chapel at the Vallicella, notably the choice of a Bolognese sculptor, the presence of the Boncompagni coat of arms, and the declared devotion to Saint Philip Neri. This pattern strengthens Montagu's hypothesis that with the family name and coat of arms of the Bolognese Boncompagni family, Pietro (and now also Ippolito and Agostino) took over "a loyalty to the city and its artists which might influence him towards a Bolognese sculptor."[52]

Psalm 118.32: The Question of the Inscription

Despite the chronological proximity of the religious conversions of the Boncompagni family members, the gradual process of establishing a new religious identity varied considerably among the members of each generation. For instance, after his conversion, the old Ugo (former Salomone) chiefly engaged in proselytizing, completing his chapel in the church of the Madonna ai Monti with a pictorial cycle, which stands as a remarkable example in Rome of a decoration that incorporates Hebrew inscriptions into the visual narrative (FIG. 5).[53] With this figurative program, Ugo not only legitimized himself as a member of the Boncompagni family through the multiple displays of his coat of arms, but he also called attention to his activities as a convert who contributed in proselytizing to the catechumens of the Confraternity of Saint Joseph of the Catechumens, to which the church of the Madonna ai Monti had been assigned by Pope Gregory XIII.[54]

As a consequence of their integration into Catholic society at an early stage of their lives, the Boncompagni members of the second and third generations—notably Agostino, Ippolito, and Pietro—made a break with their past, being more concerned with consolidating their status as genuine Christians and authentic Boncompagni. In this respect, their joint public commission at the Vallicella is exemplary, as its message of devotion is addressed not to the catechumens but to the Oratorians and, more generally, to the larger Catholic community. Like Ugo's chapel, the Vallicella chapel features elements of considerable novelty.

In an article devoted to the sculptural altarpiece, Damian Dombrowski argued that the tradition of creating individual statues of saints for altars dramatically declined in the papal city after the Sack of Rome and during the following decades.[55] The closeness between statues on altars and pagan idols, their proximity to "truth" (as claimed by sixteenth-century art theorists), and, later, Gabriele Paleotti's admonitions against them resulted in a general reluctance regarding the sculptural altarpiece.[56] The reappearance of this tradition in post-Tridentine Rome "was made possible by situating the statue in a decorative frame that goes beyond the space of the niche and serves to integrate the sister arts," according to a manner that anticipates the *bel composto*.[57] One of the most remarkable examples of such a revival in Roman chapels is provided by the statue of *Saint Silvia* on the altar of the homonymous Oratory of San Gregorio al Celio, commissioned from Nicolas Cordier by Cardinal Cesare Baronio (1603–1604).[58] Together with the statue of *Saint Silvia* and that by Bernini in the church of Santa Bibiana (1624–1626), Algardi's work at the Vallicella stands as one of the earliest examples of the three-dimensional statue-on-altar's revival, conceived as part of a larger scheme.[59] Indeed, the marble group of *Saint Philip Neri and the Angel* ideally dialogues with Pietro da Cortona's preexisting fresco of the *Arma Christi* on the sacristy vault (1633) and, most important, with the previously mentioned *Bust of Pope Gregory XV*—the pope responsible for the canonization of the saint—on the wall opposite the altar.[60]

That Pietro commissioned a monumental statue instead of a painting reflects his (and most probably his uncles') intentions to emphasize not only his status, given the remarkable cost of the project, but also the physical and living presence of the saint—a presence and vividness underscored by Paolo Sebastiano Medici in his *Catalogo dei Neofiti Illustri* (an account of distinguished

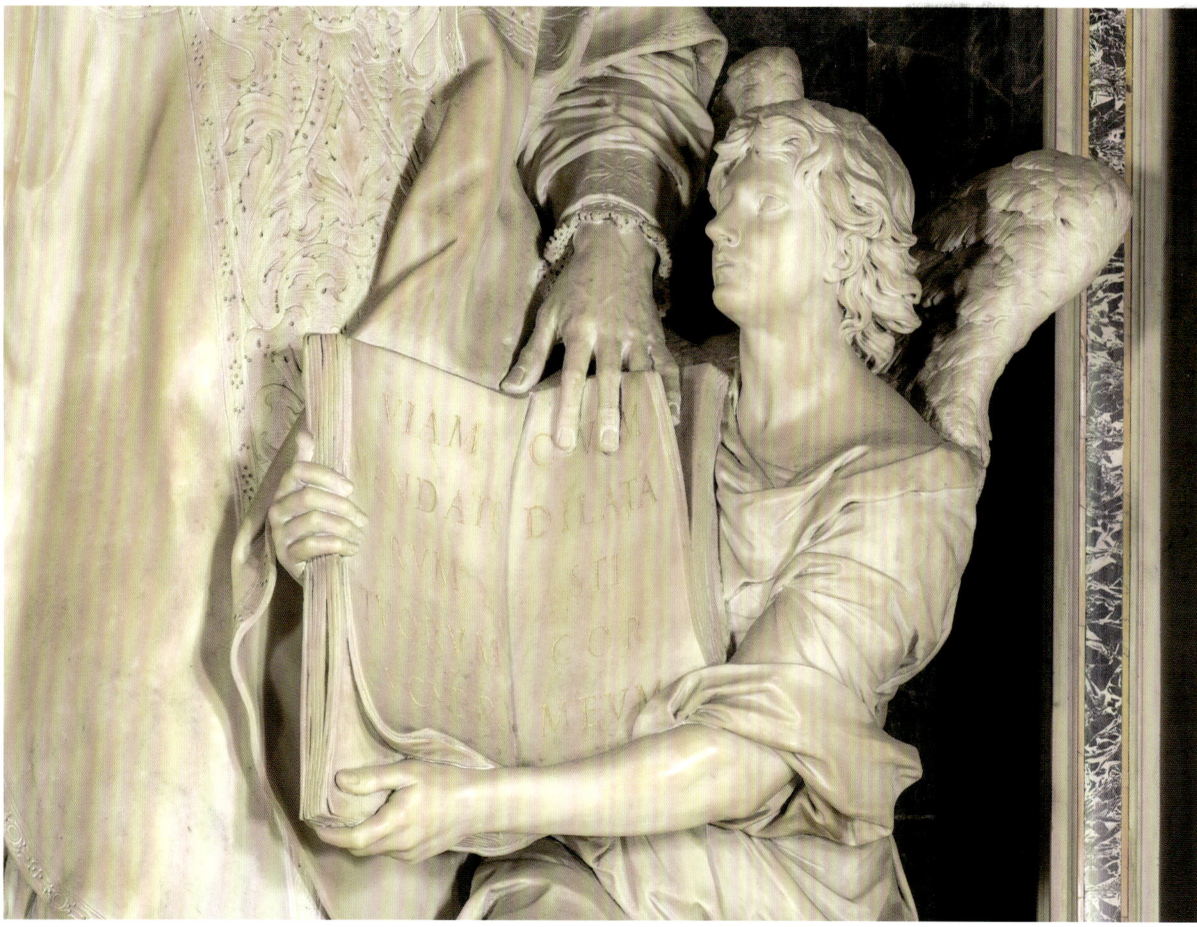

6

FIG. 6. Alessandro Algardi, *Saint Philip Neri and the Angel* (detail of the book with the inscription), 1636–1638. Sacristy of Santa Maria in Vallicella, Rome.

converted Jews), where he describes the work as representing Saint Philip Neri "al vivo" ("alive").[61] Prior to Medici, Bellori had already stressed the lifelike nature of the marble group's figures, "which live and breathe in the *affetto* of the elderly saint and the exceedingly sweet grace of the angel."[62]

In describing the statue, Bellori wrote that Algardi sculpted "the aged saint in priestly robes, wearing a chasuble," adding that "he opens one hand and rests the other on the book of his rule."[63] Yet what we see here are not the Constitutions of the Oratorian Order. The angel of utmost beauty, who is kneeling beside the saint, carries a monumental book that features the verse of Psalm 118:32: "Viam mandatorum tuorum cucurri cum dilatasti cor meum" ("I have run the way of thy commandments, when thou didst enlarge my heart") (FIG. 6).[64] The intimate correlation between the inscription and the hand gestures of Saint Philip Neri offers the impression that the saint himself, with his face gazing upward, is pronouncing the words traditionally attributed to King David. Accordingly, through a subtle semantic transposition, the original meaning of the verse of the Old Testament gains a new sense, becoming a powerful metaphor for the miraculous enlargement of Neri's heart prompted by his love of God.

Primary sources on Philip Neri provide accurate accounts of his mystic palpitations, commencing with Antonio Gallonio, who, in his *Life* of the

Oratorian, reports that in 1544, he "felt himself filled with such a violent inrush of the divine Spirit that his heart began to pounce within his breast."[65] Thanks to the testimony of Pietro Consolini, we know that this miraculous phenomenon, which resulted in the displacement of two of Neri's ribs, occurred in the Catacombs of San Sebastiano, during the Pentecost, while the future saint was praying to the Holy Spirit.[66] This episode, which marks the beginning of miracle-working palpitations that would affect him for the rest of his life, prompted the so-called iconography of the Pentecost of Philip Neri, where the saint, either alone or sustained by an angel, is represented enraptured in ecstasy, often in the catacombs, wearing the black robe of his order.[67]

Scholars agree on the fact that the verse of Psalm 118:32 is central to Algardi's composition. While Montagu, who examined the hand gestures of the saint in connection to the inscription, argued that in this text "lies the meaning of the statue,"[68] Preimesberger stressed that the complementarity (in both form and content) between words and images suggests that the incorporation of the inscription into the visual narrative, which resulted in an unprecedented iconography of the saint, was envisaged from the outset of the project.[69] Central to the understanding of this iconography is the question as to where the association of Neri's palpitations with Psalm 118:32 originates. While it is correct to affirm that Psalm 118:32 appears in the Offertory antiphon of the Mass celebrated for the feast day of the saint,[70] the text of the *Missa Propria S. Philippi* (which features the verse of the psalm) had been approved only on February 11, 1690, several decades after the commissioning of Algardi's statue.[71] According to the Decrees of the Sacred Congregation of Rites, no text of the individual (Proper) Mass for Saint Philip Neri had been validated prior to 1690, and a generic formula for all the saints—the *Missa de Communi Confessorum*—was thus adopted before that time.[72] Thus, it may be argued that the association of the biblical passage with the mystic palpitations of the saint—which decades later was destined to have a significant place in the saint's proper liturgy—made its first appearance in the marble group commissioned by the Boncompagni for their chapel.[73] As for who was responsible for the semantic transposition featured in the marble inscription, it is inevitable to think that it was a member of the Boncompagni family who undoubtedly was acquainted with both the life of the saint and the sacred Scriptures. I would argue, in view of his biography, that the most probable candidate for this erudite choice was the Oratorian Agostino Boncompagni, who was an expert in the Holy Scriptures,[74] was conversant with the Old Testament,[75] and was in charge of delivering sermons at the Vallicella.[76]

Because in the text of the psalm, as Montagu argued, lies the meaning of Algardi's statue, we might ask which message the Boncompagni meant to convey by stressing the centrality of the verse within their chapel and by proposing a likely unprecedented association of its contents with the mystic experience of the saint. Aside from its primary message (Saint Philip Neri's enlargement of heart), it is legitimate to wonder whether this unique formula suggests a further dimension of significance, notably one associated with the most memorable event in the story of the Boncompagni family: their conversion, from which stemmed their new religious and social identity. To answer this question, and before delving into the interpretation of the inscription, it is essential to consider the vestment worn by the saint and its possible symbolic meaning.

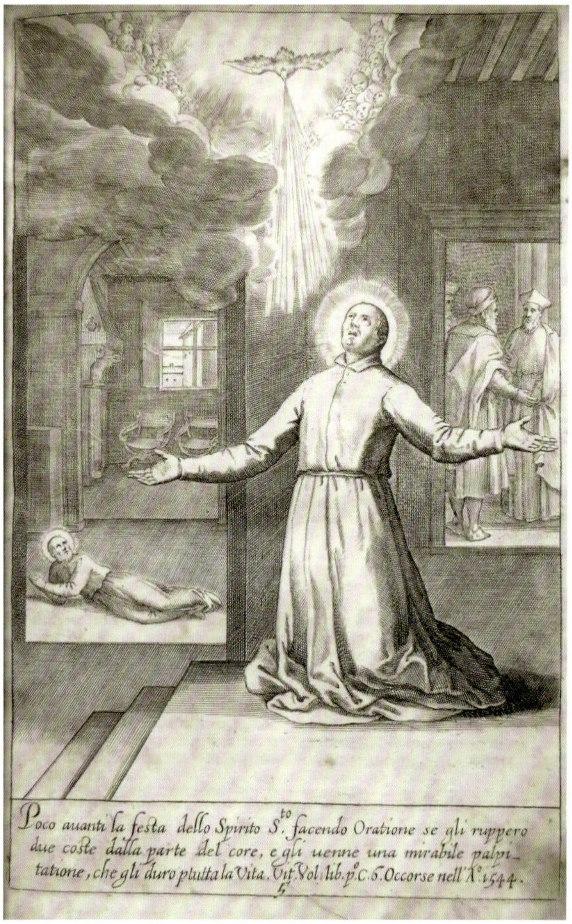

7

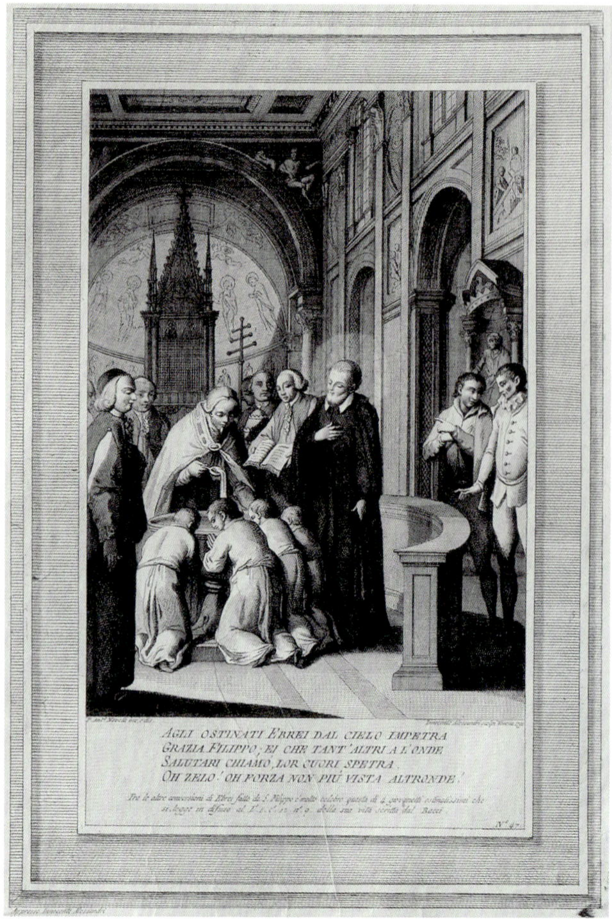

8

FIG. 7. Luca Ciamberlano, *The Pentecost of Saint Philip Neri* (from a drawing by Guido Reni, 1610), in Pietro Giacomo Bacci, *Vita di San Filippo Neri fiorentino fondatore della Congregazione dell'Oratorio*, Rome, 1625. Archivio della Congregazione dell'Oratorio, Rome.

FIG. 8. Innocente Alessandri, *The Baptism of the Corcos Brothers* (from a drawing by Pietro Antonio Novelli), 1786–1793. Private collection, Rome.

Unlike early scenes of the Pentecost of Philip Neri, in which he often wears the Oratorian's robe (FIG. 7),[77] the saint sculpted by Algardi wears a chasuble, a liturgical vestment for the celebration of the Mass, which underscores his priestly office. It is worth noting that the Boncompagni family's spiritual rebirth is associated with the ritual of the Mass celebrated by Philip Neri, and the conversion of Agostino, Ippolito, and their other two brothers (which was the catalyst for the full conversion of their relatives, including that of Pietro) is related to the miracle performed by Philip Neri when he celebrated the Mass for their conversion. When introduced to the Oratorian, the former Corcos, including Ippolito and Agostino, were firmly reluctant to convert.[78] As Gallonio wrote, they were "obstinate like devils," for they "wanted to live and die in their ancestral ancient religion."[79]

Father Philip, who was "burning with the desire to work for their salvation" (this notion evokes the mystic palpitations of his heart), exhorted them to pray to God, predicting that the next day, they would abandon Judaism.[80] "We will compel God," said Neri, who, as Ponnelle and Bordet explained, had such a way of praying with all his soul that God granted his wishes.[81] Accordingly, the next day, despite being "determined to stick to their religion,"[82] the brothers had committed to become Christians while Neri was celebrating the Mass. His prediction had been fulfilled: the most important Jews in Rome, the members

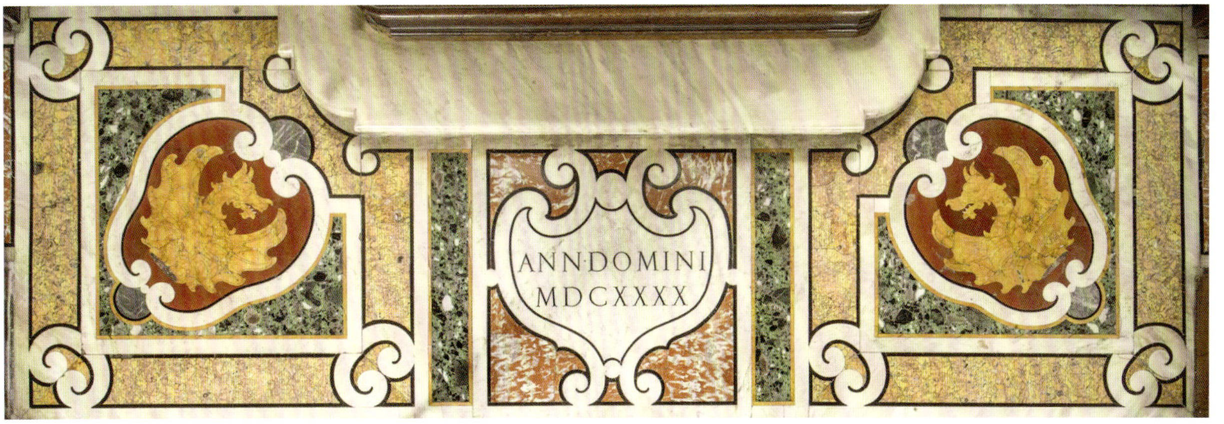

9

of one of the richest Jewish families of Italy, abandoned Judaism by means of a miracle. Because of its resounding appeal,[83] this miracle, which is reported in the biographies of the saint and was first illustrated by Luca Ciamberlano in his series of engravings of scenes from the life of Neri (1609–1614),[84] was included among the proofs of his sanctity presented in his canonization process; indeed, in referring to the miracle of the Mass, at the opening of Neri's canonization process of 1595, Ippolito Boncompagni declared: "I have always deemed that our conversion was due to the prayers of Father Philip."[85]

Considering the fame of this miracle and its profound impact on the destiny of the Corcos family, it seems likely that the chasuble worn by the saint on the altar of the Boncompagni Chapel should be understood symbolically—as referring to the miracle of the Mass and as an evocation of the Boncompagni's own conversion.[86] If this interpretation is correct, we may go back to the verse of Psalm 118:32—whose primary explanation in Algardi's sculpture is the Holy Spirit enlarging the saint's heart with divine love—and wonder whether it might be understood, in a broader sense, as a metaphor chosen by the Boncompagni to also evoke the conversion of their family advocated by Philip Neri.

In his *Commentary* on the verses of Psalm 118:30–32 ("I have chosen the way of truth: thy judgments I have not forgotten. I have stuck to thy testimonies.... I have run the way of thy commandments, when thou didst enlarge my heart"), Saint Augustine wrote: "*I could not run hadst Thou not widened my heart.* The sense of the words, *I have chosen the way of truth and Thy judgements I have not forgotten* ... is clearly explained in this verse."[87] It is interesting to observe that the notion of spiritual enlightenment (the enlargement of heart) that prompts one to follow the "way of truth" (the way of God's commandments)—implied in the inscription of Algardi's marble group—is a leitmotif of firsthand sources related to Boncompagni's conversion of 1592. For example, in his deposition of 1595 in the canonization process of Philip Neri, Agostino Boncompagni, the one who possibly conceived the unprecedented theme of Algardi's sculpture, recited the verse of a *giaculatoria* that he had been taught by Neri: "My Lord, I'd want to love you, but I cannot find the way."[88] Meaningfully, Father Consolini, who personally witnessed the miracle of the Mass, testified in 1595 to the very words addressed by Philip Neri to the four Jews: "Pray God

FIG. 9. Polychrome marble decoration of the floor of the sacristy with the Boncompagni coat of arms, 1640. Sacristy of Santa Maria in Vallicella, Rome.

that He would show you the truth."[89] In his account of the conversion of the Boncompagni, Gallonio reported the same words as Consolini, adding that while Philip Neri was celebrating the Mass, the brothers had been unexpectedly driven to Christianity by a spiritual force.[90] Among Gallonio's sources was the deposition of Ippolito Boncompagni, who, in testifying to his conversion, declared that as a result of Neri's prayers, he had felt as if driven by a spirit to become Christian.[91] Gallonio's and Ippolito's words epitomize the intimate sense of the verse of Psalm 118:32; the supernatural force they mentioned is the grace of the Holy Spirit bestowed upon the Boncompagni to follow the way of truth, the grace of the enlargement of their hearts obtained through the intercession of Philip Neri's prayers.

This interpretation of the inscription on Algardi's sculpture resonates well with one of the rarest representations of the Boncompagni conversion, *The Baptism of the Corcos Brothers*, featured in a series of drawings on the life of the saint conceived by Pietro Antonio Novelli in 1786–1793 and etched by Innocente Alessandri (FIG. 8).[92] Erroneously located in the Basilica of San Giovanni in Laterano, the baptism of the four Jews, administered by Pope Clement VIII, takes place in the presence of their godfathers and Philip Neri, who, meaningfully, holds his hand to his heart while lovingly gazing at them. The engraving bears an inscription that reads: "Philip [Neri] prays to bestow Grace upon the obstinate Jews; he, whom many other [infidels] summoned to the waters of salvation, softens the stoniness of their hearts; Oh Zeal! Oh power not seen elsewhere." The content of this inscription seems to paraphrase that featured in Algardi's sculpture: being himself recipient of the grace of a widened heart, Philip Neri invokes to bestow grace upon the former Corcos; through his advocacy, the hardness of their hearts is softened, and then they are summoned to salvation.[93]

In his *Ritratto di Roma moderna* of 1638, Pompilio Totti described the statue as already installed in the sacristy; thus the first monumental marble group executed by Algardi was probably completed.[94] From the choice of a Bolognese master to the inclusion of the verse of the psalm, the sculpture of Saint Philip Neri, with its unprecedented iconography, most probably reflected the great depth and refinement of thought of Agostino and Ippolito Boncompagni. The chapel was inaugurated only in 1640; in the meantime, Pietro Boncompagni stepped in and set the stage for an unplanned self-representation destined to alter the perception of the sacristy chapel.

Pietro Boncompagni's Self-Representation

In 1639, Pietro Boncompagni obtained from the Congregation of the Oratory the authorization to add the polychrome marble Boncompagni coat of arms to the floor of the sacristy right before the altar (FIG. 9) and an inscription on the base of Algardi's sculpture which states that Pietro offered the monument to the saint for his devotion: "SANCTO PHILIPPO NERIO / PETRUS BONCOMPAGNUS ROMANUS / PERPETUAE DEVOTIONIS MONUMENTUM OBTULIT."[95] Unlike the verse of Psalm 118:32, these inclusions were not envisaged at the outset of the project; while the coat of arms on the floor evokes the memory and the status of the Boncompagni family, the dedicatory inscription identifies Pietro as the one and only munificent donor of the work. The inscription produces an alteration in the understanding of the chapel project, which originated from the collective efforts of Pietro,

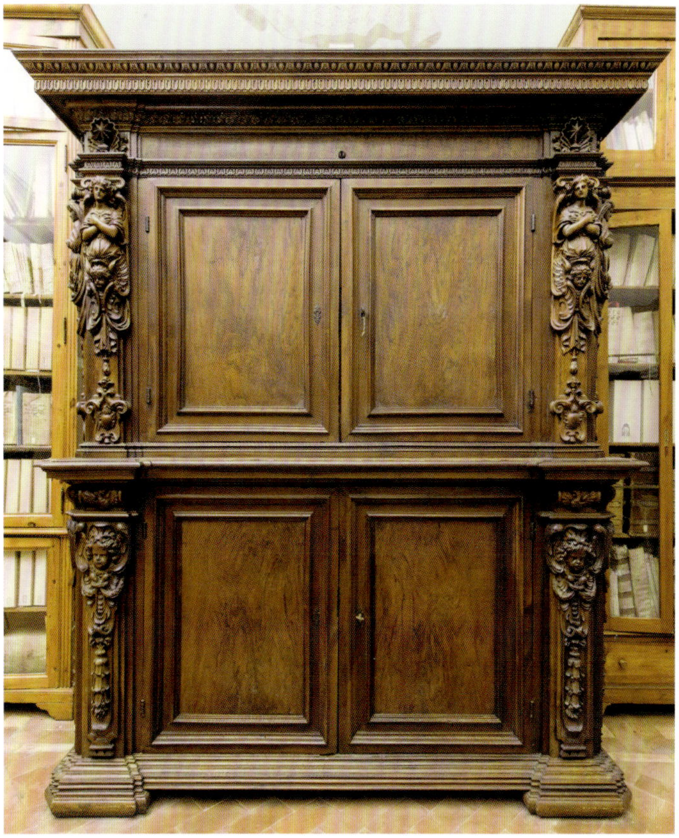

10

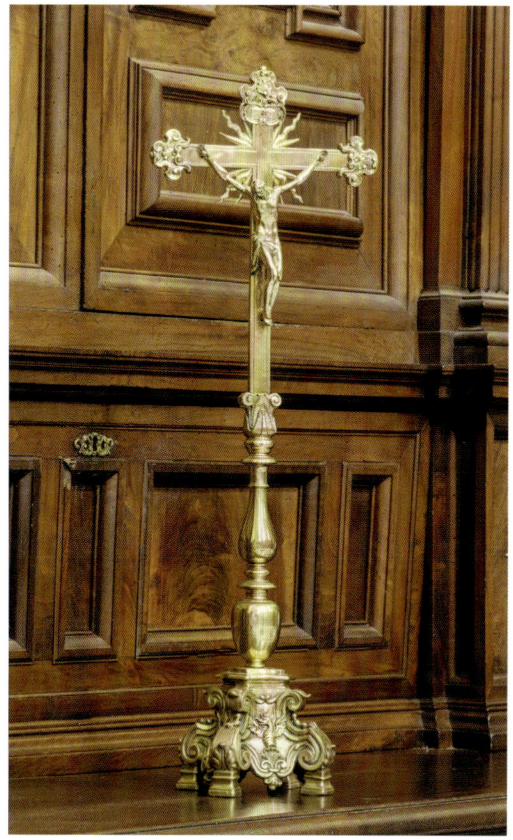

11

Agostino, and Ippolito, as we read in the accounts of the General Congregation's meetings of 1635–1636;[96] furthermore, it reflects a departure from the original intentions, agreed on in the Congregation of 1635, to erect a monument only for the sake of charity, without any display of arms or inscriptions that could be read as family aggrandizement.[97] At the end of the project, only the clerics Ippolito and Agostino, renowned for their modesty, kept faith with their vows; as a result, Pietro came to prominence, and by virtue of his late inclusions, he raised a monument in honor of himself rather than the saint.[98]

By consecrating their lives to Christ, the clerics Agostino and Ippolito, unlike their nephew, had already consolidated their full integration into Catholic society, and their participation in the chapel project was the ultimate, outward, "silent" proclamation of a genuine religious conversion that transpired over a lifetime. Conversely, at the beginning of the 1640s, the layman Pietro had not yet acquired the palace behind the church of the Vallicella; the sacristy chapel therefore constituted the ideal and only means for his self-representation and demonstration of full acceptance of Christian faith.

On May 16, 1640, Pietro's donation of the chapel was ratified.[99] The notarial act encompasses a list of furniture—including the wooden cupboard attributed to Algardi (**FIG. 10**)—and liturgical objects that Pietro donated for the celebration of the Mass on the sacristy altar.[100] Meaningfully, among these objects were the four brass candlesticks and a cross for the altar (still in place), featuring the heraldic dragons of the Boncompagni arms, repeated on each side of their bas-

FIG. 10. Alessandro Algardi (attr.), Cupboard, seventeenth century. Archivio della Congregazione dell'Oratorio, Rome.

FIG. 11. Cross with the Boncompagni coat of arms, seventeenth century. Sacristy of Santa Maria in Vallicella, Rome.

es (FIG. 11), and four vases with their handles chiseled in the shape of heraldic dragons.[101] Fully adorned with the Boncompagni emblems, these refined objects, destined to be placed on the altar before the statue of the saint,[102] abundantly amplified the message of identity and noble status already expressed in the inscription on the base of the sculpture and in the coat of arms on the floor.

Several decades before (1582), Cardinal Paleotti had thundered against the execrable practice of donors showing off their coats of arms in churches[103] and most notably on liturgical objects,[104] making it very clear that "such arms do not serve God in the least and are nothing but instruments allowing us to make ourselves known to others," in other words, a means to honor ourselves.[105] The question at stake is, did Pietro want to propel himself to the forefront of artistic patronage just for personal honor and to convey his noble status? In part, he did, but for those who were acquainted with the conversion history of the Boncompagni, a detail would not have been left unnoticed. In the inscription on the base of the sculpture, Pietro proclaimed himself not as "Bolognese"—as one would naively expect, given the profusion of his coat of arms—but rather as "Romanus," a status, that of Roman citizenship, that he and his family obtained through their conversion.[106] The declaration of being Roman is thus an indicator of conversion, a signal of a fully achieved integration into society that further establishes the complex nature of this chapel as a sacred space to both celebrate the glory of Saint Philip Neri and publicly cement Pietro's (and his family's) Christian identity.

Notes

I presented a shorter version of this essay at the 2014 Annual Meeting of the RSA, in a panel I organized (Art and Politics in the Chapels of Early Modern Rome), and wrote this essay during my postdoctoral fellowship at the Bibliotheca Hertziana Max-Planck Institut für Kunstgeschichte, Rome, where I conducted a research project on the artistic patronage of the Boncompagni family. I want to thank directors Tanja Michalsky, Tristan Weddigen, and the director Emerita Sybille Ebert-Schifferer. My gratitude goes to the editors of this book, Chiara Franceschini, Steven F. Ostrow, and Patrizia Tosini, and to Alexandra Hoare and Richard Spear for their invaluable help. I dedicate this essay to the memory of Pierfrancesco Pangallo.

1 — Masetti Zannini 1973. The artist moved to the house across the Tiber in 1635. Montagu 1985, I, 30, 240, n. 66.

2 — Archivio di Stato di Roma (ASR), *Tribunale Criminale del Governatore di Roma*, Processi Criminali, vol. 314, f. 538r, in Masetti Zannini 1973, 239.

3 — Masetti Zannini 1973, 235, 240.

4 — Masetti Zannini 1973, 235–237; Montagu 1977, 79; Montagu 1985, II, 381.

5 — Montagu 1985, II, 381.

6 — The project was proposed in the General Congregation of October 21, 1635: "Il Padre propose, che il signor Pietro Boncompagno si era essibito di fare à sue spese una statua di marmo con l'effigie del Santo Padre per collocarla in faccia della Sagrestia, et che similmente il Padre Agostino si era essibito di dare 200 scudi, et il signor Hipolito due colonne pure per questo effetto ... il tutto questi Signori fratelli fanno senza pretensione, ne di mettere l'arme, ne inscrittioni, ne obligo alcuno di qual si vogli sorte, ma solo per carità." Rome, Archivio della Congregazione dell'Oratorio (ACOR), *Libro Quinto dei Decreti*, C.I.6, f. 267 (my transcription), in Heimbürger Ravalli 1973, 71–72; Montagu 1977, 78.

7 — Heimbürger Ravalli 1973, 71–74, cat. 15; Montagu 1977; Montagu 1985, I, 64–66, II, 380–381, cat. 75. For the *modelletto* in clay possibly presented by Pietro Boncompagni to the Congregation (Rome, Museo Nazionale del Palazzo di Venezia, inv. 13467, acquired in 1999), see Montagu 1990; Montagu 1992; Giometti 2011, 40–41, cat. 14. For the altar, projected by Paolo Marucelli and rearranged by Taddeo Landi with the support of Francesco Borromini, see Pollak 1928–1931, I, 1928, 431–436; Connors 1980, 203–205; Incisa della Rocchetta and Connors 1981, *ad indicem* "sacrestia."

8 — Heimbürger Ravalli 1973, 72; Montagu 1977, 79. It should also be noted that very little information was available about Agostino and Ippolito Boncompagni.

9 — As declared by Virgilio Spada, Algardi's statue was intended to be engaged in a symbolic dialogue with the urban fabric of Rome. See n. 35 below.

10 — For instance, see the account of the Congregation meeting of January 27, 1640, ACOR, *Libro Sesto dei Decreti*, C.I.7, f. 106. See also the donation act of the chapel of May 16, 1640: ASR, Notai Auditor Camerae, A. Gallus, vol. 3489, fols. 192r–v, 221r, 193r–v, 220r; the testament of Pietro Boncompagni opened on September 21, 1664 (ASR, Notai Auditor Camerae, G. Simoncellus, vol. 32, fols. 733–ff.). For these documents, see Montagu 1977,

esp. 80; Montagu 1985, II, 380–381. For the transcription of Boncompagni's testament, see Uttaro and Gigli 2003, 133–138.

11 — On both conversions, see Ciappi 1596, 69; Bartolocci 1675–1693, III, 1683, 759, 822–823; Medici 1701, 53–59; Incisa della Rocchetta and Vian 1957–1963, I, 1957, 44–45, n. 170; Bevilacqua 2003, 149–152.

12 — Their apostasy occurred in a period marked by an increasingly intense policy of conversion, culminating with the emanation of Gregory XIII's bull on Jews, the infamous *Antiqua Iudaeorum Improbitas* (1581), anticipated a few years before by the bull *Vice Ejus Nos* (1577), through which the pope founded at Rome the College of Neophytes—an institution for the education of converts—and established forced preaching as a weekly practice at which Jewish attendance was compulsory. On Gregory XIII's policy toward the Jews, see van Boxel 2016, with bibliography.

13 — For the *motu proprio*, see Bartolocci 1675–1693, III, 1683, 822–823.

14 — Incisa della Rocchetta and Vian 1957–1963, I, 1957, 93–94, n. 305; Bianco 2009; Serafinelli 2011, 182; Serafinelli 2020, forthcoming.

15 — Serafinelli 2020, forthcoming.

16 — For this deposition see Incisa della Rocchetta and Vian 1957–1963, I, 1957, 91–94, 96–99; II, 1958, 268–270; III, 1960, 229–231; IV, 1963, 47. See also Caffiero 2016, 174–180.

17 — Incisa della Rocchetta 1961, 6; Bianco 2009, 168.

18 — Incisa della Rocchetta and Vian 1957–1963, II, 1958, 268–270.

19 — Incisa della Rocchetta and Vian 1957–1963, II, 1958, 268.

20 — "Noi, come avunculi di detti pupilli, cominciammo a pretendere la loro tutela. Et così, sotto questa pretensione, ottenemmo di poter levare dal Ghetto li detti putti." Incisa della Rocchetta and Vian 1957–1963, II, 1958, 269.

21 — Incisa della Rocchetta and Vian 1957–1963, II, 1958, 268–270; Serafinelli 2020, forthcoming.

22 — Bevilacqua 2003, 154; Uttaro and Gigli 2003, 28.

23 — "Una scelta esplicitamente evocativa della propria vicenda famigliare, dove—tra la via papale e l'insediamento filippino—si riassumono la protezione pontificia e la guida spirituale del santo." Bevilacqua 2003, 154.

24 — For the transcription of this inventory (cited in Montagu 1977, 78–79), see Uttaro and Gigli 2003, 139–144.

25 — Uttaro and Gigli 2003, 139–144. Bevilacqua 2003, 156–157.

26 — Archivio Storico Unicredit Banca di Roma (ASUCBR), Banco di Santo Spirito, *Libro Mastro*, 1628, II.I. 31, f. 699.

27 — In the manuscript biography of Agostino Boncompagni, we read that the Oratorian also contributed extensively to the adornament of the Vallicella. See Rome, Biblioteca Vallicelliana (BVR), ms. O.59, ch. XV, f. 264r.

28 — See n. 6 above. On that occasion, for the making of the niche, the Congregation offered "alcune pietre mischie … le quali pietre sono in casa." It is unclear whether Agostino gave two hundred scudi as a contribution for the making of either the sculpture or the niche of the altar. In the Congregation of November 14, 1636, in fact, it is suggested that more than one contributor was involved in the commission of the statue: "la statua, che fanno fare li signori Buoncompagni per mettere nella Sagrestia." ACOR, *Libro Sesto dei Decreti*, C.I.7, f. 13, transcribed in Montagu 1977, 78.

29 — Heimbürger Ravalli 1973, 72.

30 — Montagu 1977, 79.

31 — Bellori 1672 [2005], 297. Bellori reported that Cardinal Ludovisi, who among other things commissioned from the sculptor the restoration of antique statues (e.g., the *Torchbearer* and the *Putto with a Mask*) as well as "a seated putto in marble" of the artist's own invention, "entrusted him to Domenichino, with whom he formed a close friendship because they had both come from the same school of Ludovico [Carracci], and because of their natural love of their native land." Bellori 1672 [2005], 296. As will be explained in greater detail below, there are reasons to surmise that the bond of Pietro's uncle, Ippolito, both to the Ludovisi family and to Domenichino had an impact on the final choice of Algardi for the Vallicella commission.

32 — Bellori 1672 [2005], 296–297.

33 — For both commissions, see Montagu 1985, II, 369–372, cat. 68; 434–436, cat. 161.

34 — Montagu 1977, 79; Montagu 1985, I, 64.

35 — Montagu 1985, II, 427, cat. 150. In his *Dialogo* on the construction of the Roman Oratory, Spada wrote: "Lascio di parlare della sacrestia, quale fu fatta, senza che io ne avessi pensiero alcuno, nei primi anni, ch'entrai in Congregazione"; with reference to Algardi's sculpture on the altar of the sacristy, he added: "col tempo, dovrà incontrare la porta di fianco della chiesa (che si dovrà fare una strada, d'aprirsi da Parione alla piazza della facciata) di dove si vedrà detta statua, in lunghezza maggiore, che non è oggi tutta la chiesa." Incisa della Rocchetta 1967, 193–195.

36 — "Li pilastri controtagliati per compimento dell'apparato della Chiesa Nova, con ordine, che li damaschi, che si leveranno dalli pilastri si mettono per parare le navi di detta Chiesa nella prossima festa di S. Filippo Neri." Archivio Storico Capitolino (ASC), *Archivio Urbano*, sez. 42, vol. 67, A. Gallus, 1636–1644, unpaginated.

37 — ASC, *Archivio Urbano*, sez. 42, vol. 67, A. Gallus, 1636–1644, unpaginated. On the fur worn by Philip Neri, see Incisa della Rocchetta and Vian 1957–1963, III, 1960, 68.

38 — For the new archival documentation, see Serafinelli 2020, forthcoming.

39 — At the canonization process of Philip Neri, Ippolito declared in 1610: "vivo delle entrate mie del patrimonio." See Incisa della Rocchetta and Vian 1957–1963, IV, 1963, 47.

40 — Malvasia 1678 [1841], II, 55; Serafinelli 2020, forthcoming.

41 — Serafinelli 2020, forthcoming. In Agostino's biography, we are told that when he fell sick, "consigliato da medici à mutar aria, il S. Hippolito suo fratello, ch'era in quel tempo cameriero di honore e cappellano secreto di Gregorio XV, ottenne licenza da Padri di condurlo per alquanti giorni alle sue stanze di S. Pietro per quivi ristorarlo." BVR, ms. O.59, ch. XV, f. 262v.

42 — Malvasia 1678 [1841], II, 55; Malvasia 1980, 131.

43 — Serafinelli 2020, forthcoming.

44 — For this collection, the inventory of the goods of Clemente Boncompagni (1657), and that of his heir Filippo Boncompagni (1676), see Serafinelli 2011.

45 — Serafinelli 2020, forthcoming.

46 — Ippolito administered Domenichino's finances even during the painter's sojourn in Naples (1631–1641), looking after his economic interests following the artist's death (1641). Serafinelli 2020, forthcoming.

47 — Bellori 1672 [2015], 296. Thanks to the support of his coreligionist painter, the sculptor received the commission for two stucco statues in the Bandini Chapel in the church of San Silvestro

al Quirinale (ca. 1628–1629, Montagu 1985, I, 16–22; II, 358, cat. 58). Richard Spear hypothesized that thanks to Domenichino, Algardi was also involved in the works for the Chapel of the Strada Cupa in Santa Maria in Trastevere, where the sculptor might have modeled one of the eight large stucco telamones adjacent to Zampieri's fresco. Spear 1969a; Spear 1969b, 19, fig. 30; Montagu 1985, II, 453, cat. 195.

48 — Despite a quarrel over Giovanni Battista Ruggieri (one of Domenichino's collaborator and Algardi's friend), in his *Life* of Giuliano Finelli, Giovanni Battista Passeri wrote that when Domenichino was in Naples, working in the Cappella del Tesoro in the cathedral, the painter "negoziava per l'Algardi il lavoro di tredici statue di metallo per detta Cappella." Domenichino's efforts to involve Algardi resulted in nothing; however, Passeri's account testifies to the long-standing friendship between the two, despite their physical distance. Passeri 1934, 250–251; Montagu 1985, I, 21–22.

49 — In his *Life* of Reni, Malvasia referred to Algardi as "un nuovo Guido in marmo." Malvasia 1678 [1841], II, 26.

50 — Serafinelli 2011, 194–196.

51 — Serafinelli 2011, 194.

52 — Montagu 1977, 79. As evidenced by the inventories of their goods, the taste for Bolognese artists is more typical of Ippolito and his brother Clemente (Serafinelli 2011; Serafinelli 2020, forthcoming) than of Pietro, who in the second half of the seventeenth century commissioned the decoration of the rooms of his palace from Carlo Cesi, a painter from Antrodoco (Rieti; see Uttaro and Gigli 2003, 40 ff.).

53 — After his conversion, Ugo was appointed by his step-uncle, the converted Andrea de Monte (d. 1587), his heir and executor of his will. In this capacity, Ugo commissioned from Durante Alberti the completion of the decoration of the chapel in the church of the Madonna ai Monti, which became the burial place of the first generation of the Boncompagni. On the chapel, see Guerrieri Borsoi 1993a, 235–237. On Andrea de Monte, see Parente 1990, 663–667.

54 — Erected in 1580 by will of Pope Gregory XIII, the church was assigned by the pope himself to the Confraternity of Saint Joseph of the Catechumens; this was an institution founded in 1543 by Pope Paul III Farnese with the purpose of welcoming and hosting Jews, Muslims, and others to promote their conversion to Catholicism, whether forced or voluntary. Piazza 1679, 361–363. On the Casa dei Catecumeni, see Caffiero 2004, 21–26.

55 — Dombrowski 2014, 119.

56 — Dombrowski 2014, 120–122.

57 — Dombrowski 2014, 120.

58 — Dombrowski 2014, 127–130. The project for the overall decoration of the Oratory envisaged by Baronio—Church historian and member of the Congregation of the Oratory—was unrealized owing to his death (1607). The frescoes by Guido Reni, with which Cordier's statue is engaged in dialogue, were executed only when Cardinal Scipione Borghese became abbot. See Smith O'Neil 1985, 156.

59 — Dombrowski 2014, 129–132.

60 — Preimesberger 1993, 153–157. On Pietro da Cortona and the Oratorians, see Lo Bianco 1995.

61 — Medici 1701, 58.

62 — Bellori 1672 [2005], 297.

63 — Bellori 1672 [2005], 297.

64 — Montagu 1977, 82–83.

65 — Gallonio 1601, 16. On the saint's mystic palpitations, see also Incisa della Rocchetta and Vian 1957–1963, IV, 1963, 299, ad indicem.

66 — Brix 1995 and, most recently, Barchiesi 2017, 231.

67 — On this specific iconography, see Pampalone 2000.

68 — "The saint is both offering himself to God and accepting the grace which God will bestow upon him by the enlargement of his heart." Montagu 1985, I, 66.

69 — Preimesberger 1993, 157–159. Earlier representations of Philip Neri (from Antonio Tempesta to Guido Reni) illustrate him either kneeling or standing with outstretched arms or enraptured in the vision of the Virgin and Child. The literature on the iconography of the saint is rich. Due to the limitation of space, see Pampalone 2017.

70 — Montagu 1977, 82; Preimesberger 1993, 157 (where it is suggested that the psalm can be associated with the Mass for Philip Neri's canonization in 1622). I was not able to verify this information, because no documentation was provided. For instance, in the Canonization Bull of Saint Philip Neri (1622), it is possible to find references to his mystic palpitations ("Mirabilem patitur palpitationem cordis et fracturam costarum"); however, no association with Psalm 118:32 is present. See *Bullarium* 1868, esp. 14, n. 24.

71 — Vatican City, Archivio Storico della Congregazione per le Cause dei Santi (ACCS), Decreta Sac. Rit. Congr. Ann. 1689–1690, *Missa Propria S. Philippi*, fols. 85r–86v. The Proper Mass for the saint was approved on 1690 and thus included in the Roman Missal, in the section *Missae propriae Sanctorum* for the Universal Church. I thank Sandro Corradini and Alberto Bianco for their help in the course of my research. As clarified by Corradini (oral communication), for economic purposes, it was customary in the past to attach to earlier editions of Roman Missals sheets with updated texts (which, of course, don't follow the pagination of the text). For instance, a Roman Missal of 1660 curiously might contain the text of the proper Mass for Saint Philip Neri that was not approved until 1690; this is evident, for example, in the copy of a Roman Missal of 1661 in the Staatliche Bibliothek of Regensburg (*Missale* 1661, 477–479); see http://reader.digitale-sammlungen.de/de/fs1/object/display/bsb11057588_00549.html.

72 — ACCS, Decreta Sac. Rit. Congr. Augus. 1610 usque ad an. 1621, *Urbis-Beati Philippi Nerii*, fols. 120r–121r.

73 — It might be interesting to observe that in his deposition to the canonization process of Philip Neri (1595), Gallonio associated the father's mystic palpitations of the heart to the text of Psalm 83:3: "cor meum et caro mea exultaverunt in Deum vivum"; see Incisa della Rocchetta and Vian 1957–1963, I, 1957, 185.

74 — Agostino had been educated "nella letione della scrittura sacra, e nell'intelligenza di luoghi più difficoltosi di quella." BVR, ms. O59, ch. XV, f. 261r.

75 — "Insieme con la grazia della fede egli [Agostino] fu tra quelli che meglio assimilarono lo spirito genuinamente filippino, fatto di semplicità, mitezza e grande generosità. Uomo di studio e insieme assiduo consigliere d'anime, profuse l'ingente sua sostanza nel beneficare i poveri e la Congregazione." Cistellini 1989, II, 1546. On Agostino's intellectual activities and his study of the Hebrew Bible, see Cistellini 1989, III, 1761, n. 287.

76 — BVR, ms. O59, ch. XV, f. 262r.

77 — For instance, see Antonio Tempesta-Pietro Coel's engraving of 1600 and that by Matthäus Greuter of 1606, republished in Pampalone 2017, 40–41, figs. 34–35.

78 — Gallonio 1601, 215.

79 — Gallonio 1601, 215.

80 — Gallonio 1601, 215.
81 — "Ha una maniera di pregare alla quale bisogna per forza che Iddio si arrenda, ed è quella di pregare con tutta l'anima.... Chiama questo metodo 'sforzar Idio.' Vedendo che la conversione dei quattro piccoli Ebrei raccolti alla Vallicella va per le lunghe, 'domattina,' annunzia, 'sforzaremo Idio et alla mia messa diranno di sì.'" Ponnelle and Bordet 1986, 504.
82 — "Stando eglino pure ostinatissimi nella perfidia loro, e pertinaci, volendosi rimaner Giudei, come erano. Cosa stupenda nella medesima hora che il servo di Dio Filippo diceva la Santa Messa, in quella medesima appunto si sentirono i giovinetti all'improviso [*sic*] come sforzati à dire che si volevano far Christiani." Gallonio 1601, 215–216.
83 — See the *Avviso di Roma* (Vatican City, Biblioteca Apostolica Vaticana, Urb. lat., 1060, pt. II, fols. 552v/646v), cited in Incisa della Rocchetta and Vian 1957–1963, I, 1957, 93.
84 — For the iconographical analysis of this engraving, see Serafinelli 2020, forthcoming. Only after the canonization of Philip Neri were the engravings by Ciamberlano adopted to complement the second edition of the saint's biography by Pietro Giacomo Bacci (1625). Pampalone 2017, 74–95.
85 — Incisa della Rocchetta and Vian 1957–1963, I, 94.
86 — Clearly, the chasuble is not an unrelated element to the iconography of the saint, who significantly wears the Mass vestment in the image of canonization by Matthäus Greuter (however, he is represented with open arms in a devotional attitude toward the Virgin Mary and the Child). See O. Melasecchi in *La regola e la fama* 1995, 450–451, cat. 2. A vague source of inspiration for Algardi's statue might have been Greuter's engraving of 1606. For this engraving, which is in ACOR, 1 XLVII,3, see Barchiesi 2017, 202–206.
87 — Augustine 1853, 353.
88 — "Gesù mio te vorria amare ma non trovo la via." Incisa della Rocchetta and Vian 1957–1963, I, 1957, 98.
89 — Incisa della Rocchetta and Vian 1957–1963, I, 1957, 44.
90 — See n. 82.
91 — "Finalmente, mi risolsi de sì. Il che disse con forza, perché mi pareva che uno spirito mi dicesse: *'di' de sì.'*" Incisa della Rocchetta and Vian 1957–1963, I, 1957, 93.
92 — The series is reproduced in *La regola e la fama* 1995, 248–254.
93 — On a more general level and with no specific reference to the conversion of the Boncompagni, echoes of this notion reverberate in Ignazio Orsolini's *Riflessioni Spirituali e Morali sopra la Vita di S. Filippo Neri*, notably in his *Discorso XXIII*, largely devoted to the interpretation of Psalm 118:32. Orsolini addressed to Neri the following invocation: "May you, most Glorious Saint Father Philip ..., who have with ease run the way of the Divine Commandments, God having prodigiously enlarged your heart, also beseech for your devotees this wondrous enlargement, so that we too may run the way of the celestial Commandments, as fervent imitators of your sanctity, saying unto the Lord as did the Prophet King [David]: *Lead me into the path of Thy Commandments; for this same I have desired.*" Orsolini 1701, 380.
94 — Totti 1638, 228; Heimbürger Ravalli 1973, 72.
95 — ACOR, *Libro Sesto dei Decreti*, vol. C.I.7, f. 100v, in Heimbürger Ravalli 1973, 72; Montagu 1977, 79–80. Because of his liberality, Pietro, after a long negotiation, also obtained from the Congregation (January 27, 1640) the right to set his burial place in the space of the church, closest to the chapel and tomb of Saint Philip Neri, that is, "il sito sotto l'archetto del pilastro della cupola incontro alla cappella del Santo." ACOR, *Libro Sesto dei Decreti*, vol. C.I.7, f. 106v; see Montagu 1977, 80. On December 26, 1642, he also obtained "parte della sepultura commune dell'altare della Presentatione, con che esso ne faccia un'altra in un altro luogo della Chiesa." ACOR, *Libro Sesto dei Decreti*, vol. C.I.7, f. 175v. The making of the sacristy chapel assured Pietro and his family of the eternal guidance and protection of the saint even in the afterlife.
96 — See nn. 6 and 28 above.
97 — See n. 6 above.
98 — See also Montagu 1990, 171.
99 — ASR, Notai Auditor Camerae, A. Gallus, vol. 3489, fols. 192r–v,221r; 193r–v, 220r, in Incisa della Rocchetta 1967, 195–196, nn. 47–48; Montagu 1977, 80.
100 – On this cupboard, featuring heads of angels, inflamed hearts, and the Boncompagni emblems, currently preserved in the archive of the Roman Oratory, see Incisa della Rocchetta 1966; Incisa della Rocchetta 1967, 196, n. 48; Montagu 1985, II, 460, cat. A.209.
101 – "Un piede da Croce quadrangolo lavorato cisellato con un drago per faccia con suo vaso e balaustro tondo liscio tornito col suo fiore in cima con la sua Croce con quattro testate cisellate, e suo Crocifisso di ottone fino di getto; Quattro candelieri col piede di triangolo con un drago per facciata con suo balaustro liscio e tondo ...; Quattro vasi di fiori con due draghi in luogo de manichi cisellati gettati di rame et indorati." ASR, Notai Auditor Camerae, A. Gallus, vol. 3489, f. 193v.
102 – ASR, Notai Auditor Camerae, A. Gallus, vol. 3489, f. 193v.
103 – "There may be an error in the mode of using one's coat of arms, which happens when a man employs them with much ostentation and excessive affectation, seeking to multiply them everywhere, although there is no evident reason for doing so.... It is also possible to err greatly in the matter of place by affixing these coats of arms in churches, or having them added to things that are sacred and dedicated to the divine cult." Paleotti 1582 [2012], 297; see also 298–301.
104 – "But what ought to be pondered even more is that these wordly arms are carved with great artifice not just on the walls but also on altarpieces, chasubles, copes, candlesticks, lighting fixtures, crosses ...." Paleotti 1582 [2012], 299.
105 – Paleotti 1582 [2012], 300.
106 – With their conversion, the Boncompagni had been ascribed to Roman nobility and gained Roman citizenship. See n. 13 above.

The Angelic Balustrade of the Spada Chapel in San Girolamo della Carità

Louise Rice

The balustrade is a feature of chapel architecture that seldom gets much attention. It is, in a sense, designed to be overlooked, for with its low profile it invites the eye to penetrate the chapel's interior even as it acts as a barrier, blocking the way in. Those alert to the fine points of ecclesiastical decor might admire the rare marbles out of which it is made, or cast an appreciative glance at the ornamental turn of its balusters; or they might pause to inspect the coats of arms or other sculptured features that sometimes adorn it. But the function of the balustrade is usually taken for granted, and little consideration is given to the paradoxical roles it plays in both delimiting and expanding the chapel's space. It seems appropriate to preface the case study at the heart of this essay, therefore, with a few general remarks on the origins and evolution of balustrades in church interiors, the multiple uses to which they are put, and, above all, the capacity they have to shift the shape and extend the reach of the chapels they guard.

Chapel Balustrades: Form and Function

The definition and origins of the chapel balustrade are not entirely easy to pin down. From the earliest days of the Church, it was customary (although apparently never obligatory) to protect altars behind an enclosure of some kind.[1] Tall wooden or metal gates or stone parapets or *transenne* (solid or pierced screens of varying height) were commonly used. In the fifteenth century, as private family chapels proliferated, low railings of wood or stone started to appear. At first, these were supported on colonettes. At the Tempio Malatestiano in Rimini, for example, two side chapels are enclosed with colonette rails, while the rest feature ornamental *transenne* of the same height. Colonette rails soon gave way to true balustrades, that is, railings supported on candelabrum-shaped or vase-shaped balusters. The true balustrade, it should be noted, is not an antique form; no examples of it survive in the archaeological record of ancient Greece and Rome.[2] It is a Renaissance adaptation, which seems to have first appeared in the 1460s in painted and intarsia representations of architecture.[3] Built examples began showing up soon afterward and by the 1480s had found their way into the vocabulary of chapel design. The balustrade at the entrance to the Basso Della Rovere Chapel in Santa Maria del Popolo (third on the right), datable to around 1484, is one early example.[4] Another is the balustrade enclosing the Carafa Chapel in Santa Maria sopra Minerva (1488-1493).[5]

Although it was to become a standard feature of chapel design, eventually winning out over most other forms of enclosure, the balustrade did not immediately catch on. Metal grilles remained in common use right through the end of the sixteenth century and even beyond.[6] As late as 1577, Carlo Borromeo made it plain that he considered tall iron gates (*cancelli*) the best kind of barrier to place at the entrances of chapels.[7] In his view, a balustrade was a suitable alternative only when adequate metal for gates was unavailable:

> Where finding the amount of iron needed for the chapel railings is difficult, then little columns of marble or other solid stone, where such materials are available, can be used. Called "balustrio" or balustrade, it is surmounted by a cornice, and is much lower than a metal railing and will enclose and decorate the front part of chapels.[8]

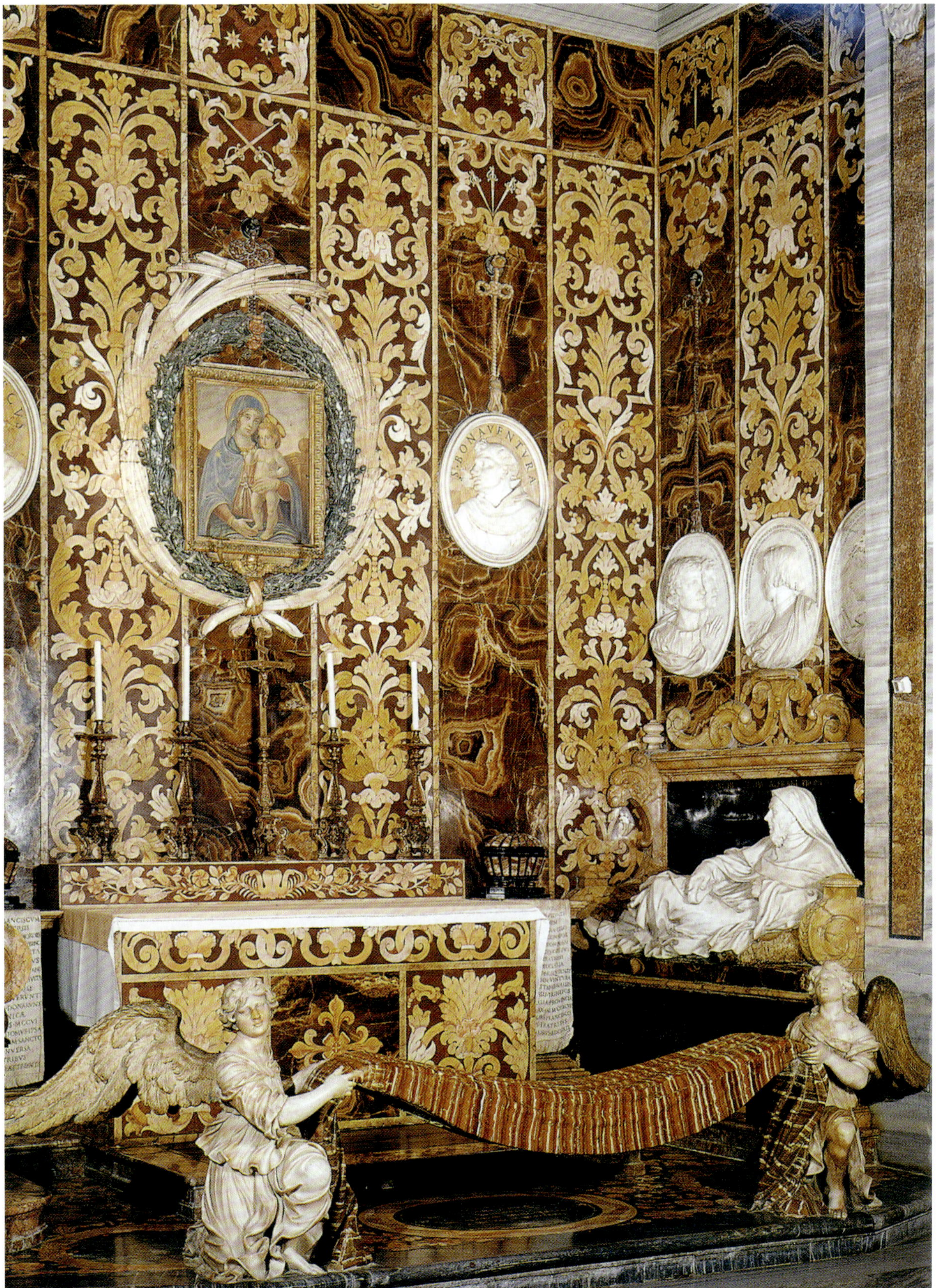

1

Borromeo's awkward wording reminds us that the very term "balustrade" was still something of a neologism at the time he was writing. It is no wonder if he viewed the thing itself as a fashionable novelty to be used only when metal fencing was not to be had.

All the same, it is surprising that Borromeo, the great reformer and writer on Church architecture and furnishings, failed to mention the significant advantages that balustrades have over other forms of chapel enclosure. He seemed to regard metal grilles and stone rails as functionally equivalent. For him, the main purpose of both was to protect the altar by keeping out unauthorized persons and stray animals. He did acknowledge, at least implicitly, one other important function, that of separating the officiating clergy from the laity:

> Where the chapels of the side altars are large enough to hold a certain number of faithful during Mass, even if they already have iron railings at the entrance, they must also be furnished with wooden gates inside, near the altar, which will enclose the altar and keep the crowds at a distance from the celebrating priest, leaving the space necessary for the assistant cleric.[9]

The passage concerns those relatively exceptional chapels spacious enough to accommodate all or part of the congregation inside the chapel confines. But the majority of family chapels in Italian churches are too small to admit more than the priest and his assistants, and Borromeo clearly understood that in these spatially more restricted chapels, there was no need for altar rails, because the gate or balustrade at the chapel's entrance served essentially the same function. In other words, the enclosure, whatever its form, was there not only to protect against trespassers but also to establish a ritual boundary between the sanctuary within and the congregational area without.

In preferring tall iron grilles to balustrades, Borromeo may have been thinking of the greater security they afford. But when Mass is in progress—and particularly during the distribution of the Eucharist, when priest and communicant necessarily interact—it is the balustrade that proves the more convenient of the two. The priest cannot dispense the consecrated wafer through a grille without violating liturgical decorum. Even where there is space enough for his hand to pass through the bars, there is no convenient way of positioning a cloth or paten underneath to catch stray crumbs. In small chapels fenced with iron, therefore, either the priest must exit the chapel in order to distribute the Eucharist outside its confines, or he must summon anyone wishing to receive the sacrament to the little opening, or *porticella*, at the center of the grille. Inevitably, in either case, the accommodation complicates and slows down the progress of the ritual. In contrast, a chapel balustrade, being low and open, is ideally designed to do double duty as a Communion rail. Kneeling outside with their knees on the lip of the chapel's raised floor, the faithful can receive the host by mouth directly over the balustrade, while the priest remains inside the sanctuary. Borromeo makes no mention of this practice, nor does he appear to recognize its advantageousness. He recommends, instead, the use of a Communion bench (*scabellum oblongum*), a movable piece of wooden furniture a little less than three feet high, which when covered with a linen cloth and placed between the priest and the communicant during the administration of the Eucharist acts as a kind of Communion table.[10] Such a bench would serve a

FIG. 1. Spada Chapel, San Girolamo della Carità, Rome.

useful purpose when placed in front of a high altar or any altar lacking a suitable altar rail or when set up at the open *porticella* or outside a chapel enclosed with a metal fence. But in chapels with balustrades, there is no need for it, for its function is taken over by the balustrade itself. It is probably no coincidence that the growing popularity of balustrades in chapel architecture coincided with the period of Catholic Reform. At a time when the Church was actively promoting the idea of frequent Communion and instructing the faithful on the seemliness of kneeling to receive the Eucharist, the chapel balustrade created a permanent architectural environment for taking the sacrament. One might almost think of it as an invitation in stone to join in the ritual of the Mass.

In a typical side chapel, then, the balustrade has several distinct functions. It is a protective barrier, preserving the privacy of the *jus patronatus* and guarding against trespass of all kinds; it is an altar rail, separating the sanctuary from the congregational space; it is a Communion table, providing a fixed site for the distribution of the Eucharist; and, finally, it is a kind of permanent *prie-dieu*, where the faithful may kneel in private veneration even when no ceremony is in progress. Its different functions kick in at different moments. When the chapel is not in use, the balustrade establishes its perimeter. Positioned just inside the edge of the elevated floor, it defines where the *architectural* space of the chapel begins and ends. But during the Mass, its role subtly shifts. At that point, rather than enclosing the chapel, it throws it open, temporarily expanding its boundaries. For with the clergy on one side and the congregants on the other co-participating in a sacramental act that stretches across it, the balustrade becomes the hub of a *ritual* space that extends beyond the chapel's architectural space, spilling out into the public area of the nave, side aisle, or transept. The balustrade is thus a powerful space shifter, narrowing or broadening the chapel's reach according to the circumstances of its use.[11]

By the end of the sixteenth century, the balustrade had become by far the most common form of chapel enclosure. Its unobtrusive height made it more accommodative as a barrier and more flexible as a definer of space. It could be used in tandem with a raised floor to generate a chapel around any altar, even one installed in a common area of the church, such as a side aisle or transept. In purpose-built chapels with defined architectural precincts, the balustrade usually spanned the arched opening and was therefore aligned with the wall of the church, but it could also be deployed to make surreptitious "land grabs," projecting out into common areas to steal additional square footage for the chapel. In such cases, the motive for pushing the boundaries usually had less to do with enlarging the chapel than with stamping its presence more assertively onto the surrounding churchscape.[12] A chapel that juts out into the public space of the church will naturally catch the eye and make a more imposing statement than its neighbors with their balustrades modestly in line with the church wall. In this regard, chapels could act very much like their owners' palaces, which jostled and shoved for maximum visibility, occasionally pushing out into the street or piazza to gain a better vantage point.[13] Of course, church authorities had something to say about private chapels appropriating public space, and the privilege of having a projecting balustrade normally had to be negotiated and paid for.[14]

But the balustrade could also be made to retreat inside the architectural boundaries of the chapel when there were practical reasons for requiring it to

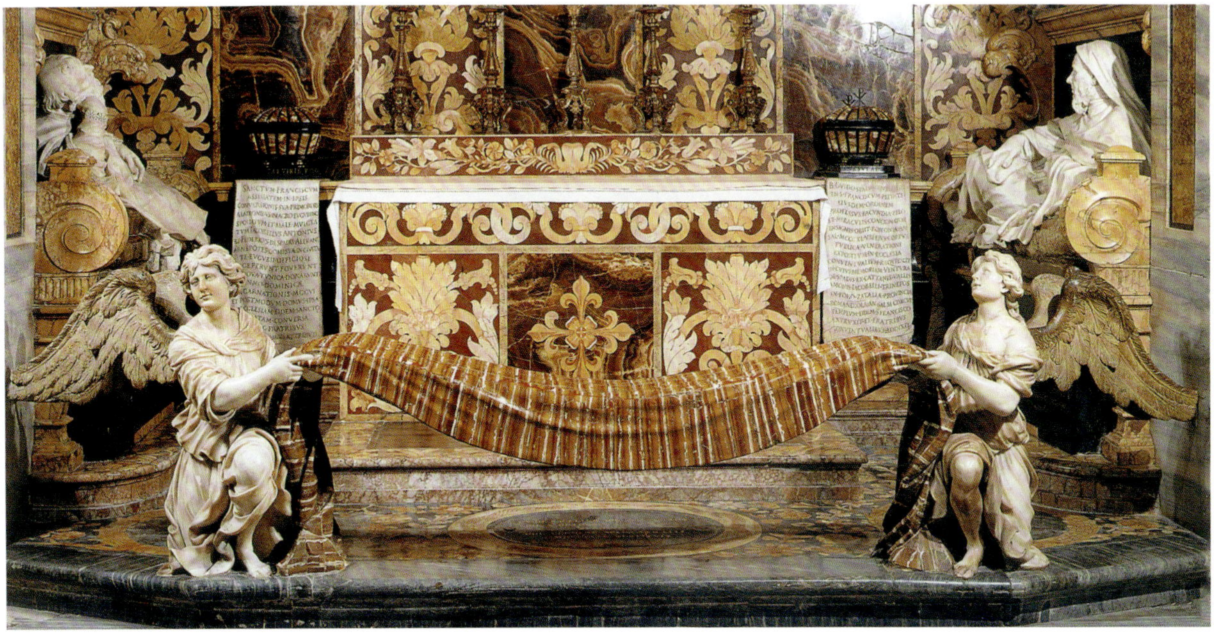

2

do so. The balustrades of the nave chapels in Sant'Andrea della Valle were not originally set up at the arched entrances into the chapels, where one would normally expect them to be (and where they are today), but were pulled back around the altar platforms. The explanation lies in the fact that Sant'Andrea has no side aisles. Instead, its nave chapels are interconnecting, and it was to ensure public access to the passageways between them that the chapels were left open to the nave. The solution must have been very disagreeable to the owners of those chapels, who cannot have appreciated having a public right-of-way cutting across their private space, and not surprisingly, it was rectified in a later remodeling of the church.[15]

The case of the nave chapels in Sant'Andrea della Valle reminds us that balustrades were added, removed, repositioned, or modified probably more often than any other feature of chapel design. We need to keep this in mind whenever we consider the numerous permutations of chapel enclosures in Roman churches. The Aldobrandini Chapel in Santa Maria sopra Minerva or the Chapel of the Shepherds in Santa Maria della Consolazione, for example, have tall metal grilles *and* marble balustrades, the one planted just inside the other. Since there would seem to be no obvious utility or logic to this doubling of elements, only one of them is likely to be original. Early printed views and plans can help us sort out puzzles of this kind, but these, too, can be misleading.[16] A survey of the many varieties and combinations of chapel barriers, with attention to whether the feature is original or not, would make a valuable contribution to our understanding of chapel design and would doubtless bring to light many fascinating instances of adaptation and accommodation.

This brief overview of the typology and uses of chapel balustrades introduces the case study that follows. The figurative balustrade of the Spada Chapel in San Girolamo della Carità is in many ways atypical. It experiments with both form and function, stretching the meaning of the rail in new and imaginative

FIG. 2. Antonio Giorgetti, Angelic balustrade, 1657–1659. Spada Chapel, San Girolamo della Carità, Rome.

ways. This is one balustrade that refuses to be overlooked but claims center stage in a Eucharistic drama witnessed by angels. And yet, by its very exceptionalness, the Spada rail helps focus our attention on a neglected feature of chapel design. For all its difference, it has much to teach us about chapel balustrades in general and about the crucial role they play in defining space and determining ritual boundaries.

The Balustrade of the Spada Chapel in San Girolamo della Carità

Just up the street from Palazzo Spada is the little confraternal church of San Girolamo della Carità in which the Spada have their family chapel. Prominently positioned to the right of the main entrance and to the left of the side entrance into the church, the chapel was acquired by Orazio Spada in 1595 but underwent a radical makeover between 1654 and 1659, when it was transformed into one of the richest and most eccentric marble chapels in Rome (FIGS. 1–2). The design is not the work of a professional architect but is rather the brainchild of Orazio's nephew, the Oratorian priest and expert consultant on architectural matters Padre Virgilio Spada, who directed the renovation from beginning to end.[17] The construction history of the Spada Chapel is for the most part well documented and has been much discussed in the literature.[18] This essay will focus exclusively on the balustrade, therefore, and will not address other aspects of the chapel's design, except to point out what is widely recognized, namely, that the decoration of the chapel imitates the kind of ephemeral *apparato* that one might see in churches or chapels on high feast days or other special celebrations.[19] We are meant to imagine that the *festaiuoli* have just finished their work and departed, leaving the walls hung with lengths of brown and gold figured damask, the image of the Virgin and Child encircled with fresh green laurel and palm fronds, and the floor strewn with flowers that release a sweet scent as they are trod underfoot. A painting of the interior of the Chiesa Nuova—the nearby church of the Oratorians—decked out in all its finery for the canonization of Philip Neri in 1622, with alternating lengths of red and yellow damask hanging from the cornice and flowers scattered in abundance across the floor, illustrates precisely the kind of effect that Virgilio Spada had in mind.[20]

Quite a bit is known about Virgilio's ideas for the rest of the chapel because he recorded them in letters and descriptions that have come down to us. But about the angelic balustrade, arguably the most unusual and arresting feature of the chapel, his thoughts have not been preserved. All we know for sure is that in its present form, it was something of an afterthought. Initially, he planned a more conventional architectural balustrade, with a centrally positioned wooden gate.[21] By the end of 1656, however, he had come up with the idea for the figurative balustrade that we see today. Executed between 1657 and 1659 by the young Antonio Giorgetti, it consists of two angels made of marble who kneel and stretch between them a length of boldly striped fabric pieced together of Sicilian jasper mounted on a substructure of iron-reinforced mortar (FIG. 2).[22] There is no central gate into the chapel. Instead, the wings of the angel on the right are made of wood and hinged to his torso in such a way that they can be swung to the side to allow access into the sanctuary (FIG. 3). This clever (if somewhat sadistic) device, meant to surprise and delight, is entirely of Virgilio Spada's own invention; a sketch in his clumsy amateurish hand records the genesis of the idea (FIG. 4).[23]

From the start, even before he conceived of a figurative balustrade, Spada determined to use the element to make a small land grab. In the earliest floor plans, the railing projects out on angled arms into the public space of the nave.[24] Although the maneuver gains little in terms of square footage, it dramatically increases the visibility of the balustrade and thus draws attention to the chapel. This mattered to Virgilio, who was clearly concerned that the chapel should catch the eye and stand out from the others around it. When the Archconfraternity offered him the opportunity to exchange the space acquired by his uncle for either of the transept chapels immediately to the left or right of the high altar, he turned it down, explaining in a letter to his nephew that "even if it seems that being near the door makes this site less noble than a chapel next to the high altar, nevertheless our chapel will be seen by everyone who enters the church, whereas that other one seems to me to be hidden from view, such that only someone who goes looking for it on purpose will find it."[25] The projection of the balustrade into the nave may have encouraged, in turn, the idea of introducing a sculptural element, since the angels, by virtue of being set in front of (rather than in line with) the arched opening into the chapel, can be seen more or less in the round, their angled wings replacing the angled sections of balustrade originally planned. The angel on the left makes especially good use of his protruding vantage point, for turning outward and to the left as he does, he takes in the length of the nave with his glance.

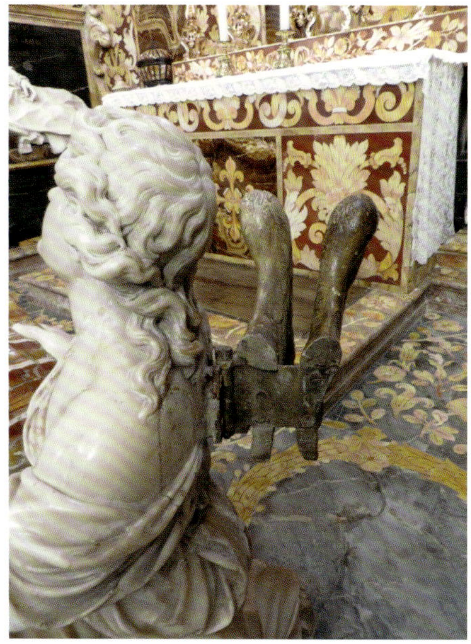

3

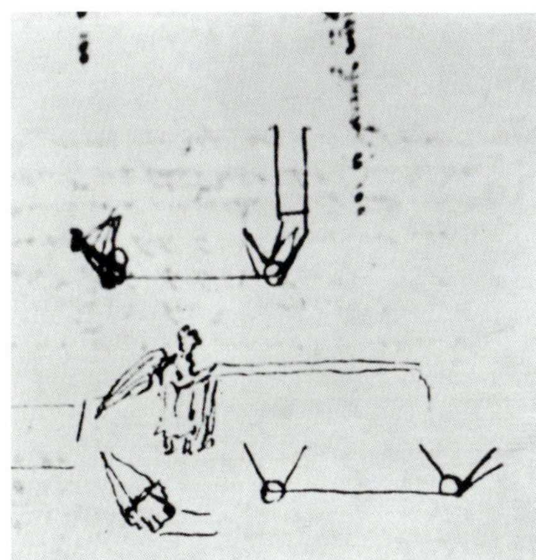

4

The angelic balustrade of the Spada Chapel is very much an anomaly; it has no obvious precursors in any church in Rome, nor does it have any immediate imitators.[26] That said, no Seicento viewer would have had any difficulty recognizing what it represents. Passeri put it succinctly: "In place of the usual balustrade enclosing the altar [are] two angels, one on each side, who kneel and stretch out a cloth, as it is customary to do, for the sake of propriety and decorum, for those receiving that most holy food of the Eucharist."[27] The angels, in other words, are holding a Communion cloth, also known as a Communion veil or houseling cloth, a long strip of fabric held by two assistants during the distribution of the host, for the double purpose of catching stray crumbs of consecrated wafer that might accidentally fall and keeping the communicant's hands from accidentally touching the sacrament. The practice of holding the Communion cloth suspended between two acolytes originated in the Middle Ages, before altar rails or balustrades had become essential features of chapel design (FIG. 5).[28] Often extraordinarily long, they are mentioned in church and palace inventories[29] and are described in accounts of festive liturgies, such as the Easter Sunday Mass attended by Queen Elizabeth I in 1593, during which the monarch, kneeling, received the sacrament over "a most princely linen cloth … borne at the four ends by the noble Earl of Hereford, the Earl of Essex, the Earl

FIG. 3. Antonio Giorgetti, Angelic balustrade (detail showing the angel wings swung to the side), 1657–1659. Spada Chapel, San Girolamo della Carità, Rome.

FIG. 4. Virgilio Spada, Sketch for the balustrade of the Spada Chapel, 1656. Archivio di Stato di Roma, Archivio Spada Veralli, vol. 495, fasc. 15.

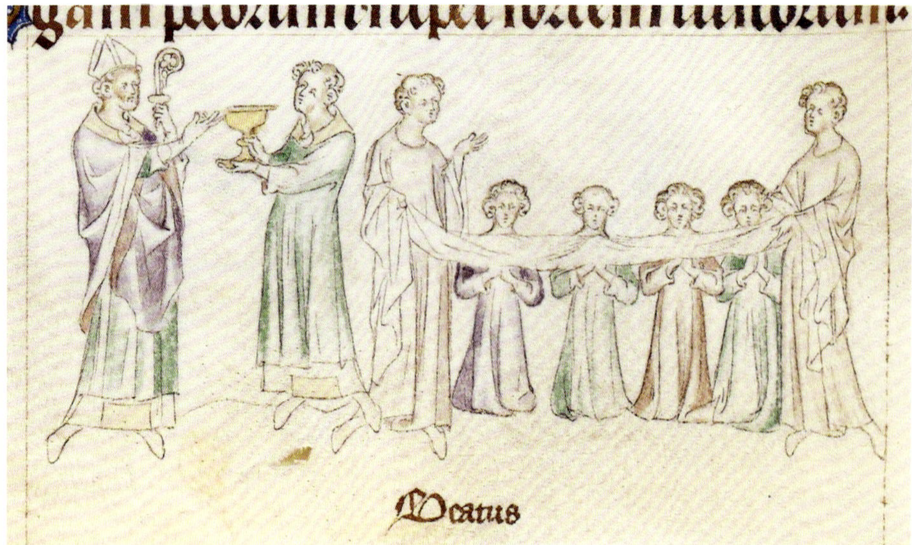

5

of Worcester, and the Earl of Oxford."[30] With the introduction of Communion benches, altar rails, and chapel balustrades, the veil no longer needed to be held up by hand and was more often laid over these surfaces like a tablecloth (FIGS. 6–7).[31] At the same time, the paten, or Communion plate, overtook the Communion cloth as a more convenient all-purpose crumb catcher. Evidence has proved hard to come by with regard to how frequently and under what circumstances the houseling cloth held by acolytes continued to be used in seventeenth-century Rome. The practice was never completely abandoned—it continued to be called for in the *Caeremoniale episcoporum* of 1600—but it was probably less and less on view as the balustrade became an increasingly standard feature of both high altars and side chapels, essentially eliminating the need for it.[32]

Handheld Communion cloths do show up with some frequency in paintings and prints, on the other hand, and nearly always in one of two contexts. The first is the Communion of a saint, whether his or her last Communion (viaticum) or any other miraculous episode in which he or she receives the Eucharist. It should be noted that even in scenes of this kind, it is more usual for the priest to be shown holding a paten under the host, obviating the need for a Communion cloth. When a cloth is depicted, more often than not it is the communicant who holds it. But the old-fashioned houseling veil stretched between two attendants does appear in a handful of instances, and when it does, the attendants are usually angels, accompanying the saint in his or her final hour or otherwise attesting to the miraculous nature of the event.[33] The motif of the angel-held houseling cloth enters the iconographic lexicon sometime around 1600; we find it, for example, in the *Last Communion of Saint Mary Magdalen* from the workshop of Alessandro Allori (FIG. 8)[34] and in Francisco Pacheco's 1611 *Last Communion of Saint Raymond Nonnatus* (FIG. 9).[35] Seemingly gaining in popularity as the century progressed, it appears in late-seventeenth- and eighteenth-century representations of the miraculous Communions of Saint Teresa of Ávila and Saint Maria Maddalena de' Pazzi;[36] while in images of the

FIG. 5. *Saint Donatus restoring the broken chalice*, The Queen Mary Psalter, ca. 1310–1320. London, British Library, ms. Royal 2 B VII, f. 259v (detail).

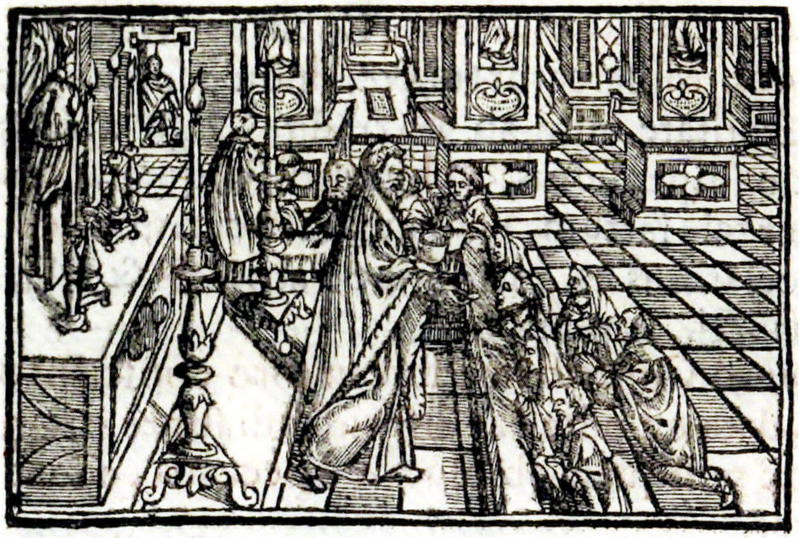

6

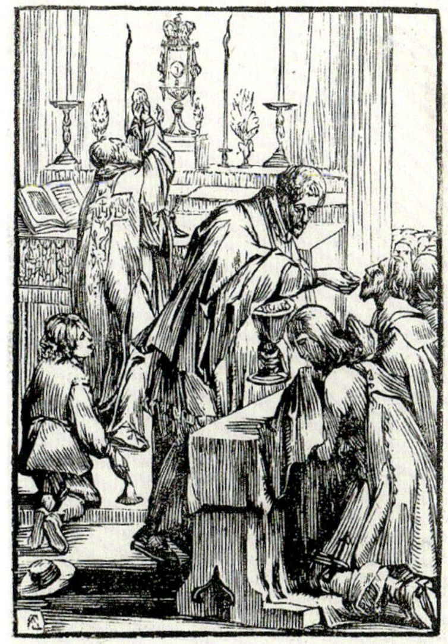

7

viaticum of Saint Mary of Egypt, it shows up with such regularity that it might almost be called a standard part of her iconography (FIGS. 10–11).[37]

The other pictorial context in which the houseling cloth held by angels makes an occasional appearance is the scene of the Virgin receiving the sacrament from Saint John the Evangelist. This subject was unknown in art before the late sixteenth century and was very much a product of the Counter-Reformation. Émile Mâle traced it to the writings of the Spanish Carmelite Jerónimo Gracián (1545–1614), spiritual adviser to Saint Teresa of Ávila, and the Portuguese Jesuit João Rebelo (1541–1602), both of whom described how, in the last years of her life, the Virgin took the sacrament daily from Saint John; and he convincingly connected the sudden emergence of the theme with the Church's promotion of frequent Communion at around the same time.[38] As in depictions of saints' Communions, here, too, there is considerable variation in the method used to distribute the Eucharist. Sometimes John is shown holding a paten, sometimes the Virgin holds up her own Communion cloth, and sometimes the two of them make doubly sure that no crumb hits the floor by combining their actions, as in altarpieces by Giovanni Battista Speranza (by 1640; Santa Lucia in Selci, Rome) and Giacinto Gimignani (1668; church of the Jesuits, Marseilles).[39] But in one early illustration of the Virgin's Communion—an engraving by Anton Wierix III from the first quarter of the seventeenth century (FIG. 12)—two kneeling angels stretch a houseling cloth between the Virgin and Saint John; and several later artists, including Salvi Castellucci and Giovanni Battista Galestruzzi, picked up on the motif and incorporated it into their own versions of the subject.[40] In contrast to the viatica of saints, which usually occur outside of a church setting and often outdoors, the Communion of the Virgin is always pictured as if taking place in front of an altar, and thus the angels supporting the Communion veil as she takes the Eucharist seem especially akin to their sculptured cousins in the Spada Chapel. In an engraving by Schelte Adamsz. Bolswert after a design by Erasmus Quellin II (FIG. 13), the parallels are even more compelling, for the flowers scattered across the chapel floor exactly

FIG. 6. *Distribution of the Eucharist*, in *Rituale Romanum Pauli V Pont. Max. iussu editum*, Rome, 1652, 46.

FIG. 7. Anthonis Sallaert and Jan Christoffel Jeghers, *Distribution of the Eucharist*, in Jodocus Andries, *Necessaria ad salutem scientia partim necessitate medii, partim necessitate praecepti, per iconas quinquaginta duas repraesentata*, Antwerp, 1654, 110. British Museum, London.

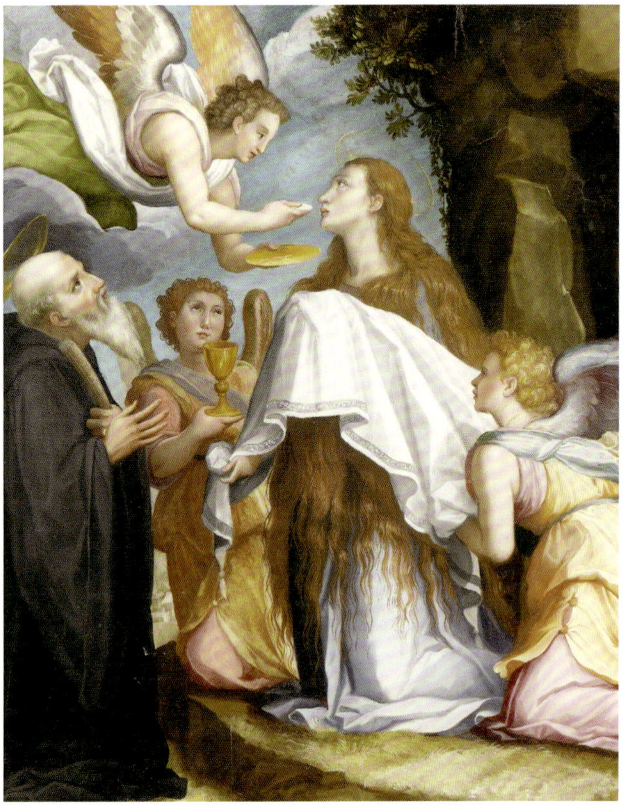

8

resemble the flowers of inlaid marble that decorate the floor of the Spada Chapel. We might recall, in this regard, that the Spada Chapel is dedicated to the Virgin Mary, and that the blossoms across its pavement are described in at least one related document as "rose e gigli," the two flowers most closely associated with her.[41]

These examples prove that the Communion veil held by angels was, if not a commonplace, at least a recognized motif in depictions of miraculous Communions. Spada's innovation was to give sculptural form to a pictorial conceit. Where he got the idea for the angelic balustrade we will probably never know for sure, but there is one painting in particular—a painting he almost certainly would have known—that may have first planted the seed in his imagination. I refer to the altarpiece representing the *Last Communion of Saint Jerome*, executed around 1625 by the Bolognese painter Lucio Massari for the Ariosti Chapel in San Paolo Maggiore in Bologna (FIG. 14). Massari's composition owes much to Agostino Carracci's more famous version of the subject formerly in the Certosa of Bologna, as Malvasia rightly noted.[42] The main difference lies in the greater emphasis that Massari puts on the mystical nature of the Eucharist. As the host is passed from priest to saintly communicant, it lines up precisely with the image of Christ crucified on the altar above it, the action contemplated with tender understanding by two kneeling angels who stretch a houseling cloth directly below it. We can be virtually assured that Virgilio was acquainted with Massari's painting, for the church of San Paolo Maggiore was a Spada foundation. The Spada, who self-identified as a Bolognese family, had acquired the *jus patronatus* in 1634, using money left by Virgilio's father, Paolo Spada. In the following years, under Virgilio's careful supervision, the family undertook and paid for the construction of the ornate brick-and-stone facade, topped with the Spada coat of arms and embellished all over with Spada swords and fleurs-de-lis. The family also took over the rights to the high altar. Here, again under the direction of Virgilio Spada, they commissioned Alessandro Algardi to create a marble group representing the *Martyrdom of Saint Paul*, set within a sumptuous architectural *teatro* designed by Gian Lorenzo Bernini (1634–1648).[43] Virgilio resided in Rome and directed the work at San Paolo mostly from a distance. But we know that he visited Bologna on at least one occasion, and he would surely have looked at Massari's painting while he was there.[44] It could, of course, be purely coincidental that an altarpiece in the Spada church in Bologna and the balustrade of the Spada Chapel in Rome happen to feature the same motif of paired angels holding a houseling cloth, but I think it at least as likely that a recollection of some sort informed Spada's invention.

FIG. 8. Workshop of Alessandro Allori, *Last Communion of Saint Mary Magdalen*, ca. 1600. Present whereabouts unknown.

It makes sense, too, that Spada would have paid close attention to Massari's picture, for it shares its subject—the last Communion of Saint Jerome—with the

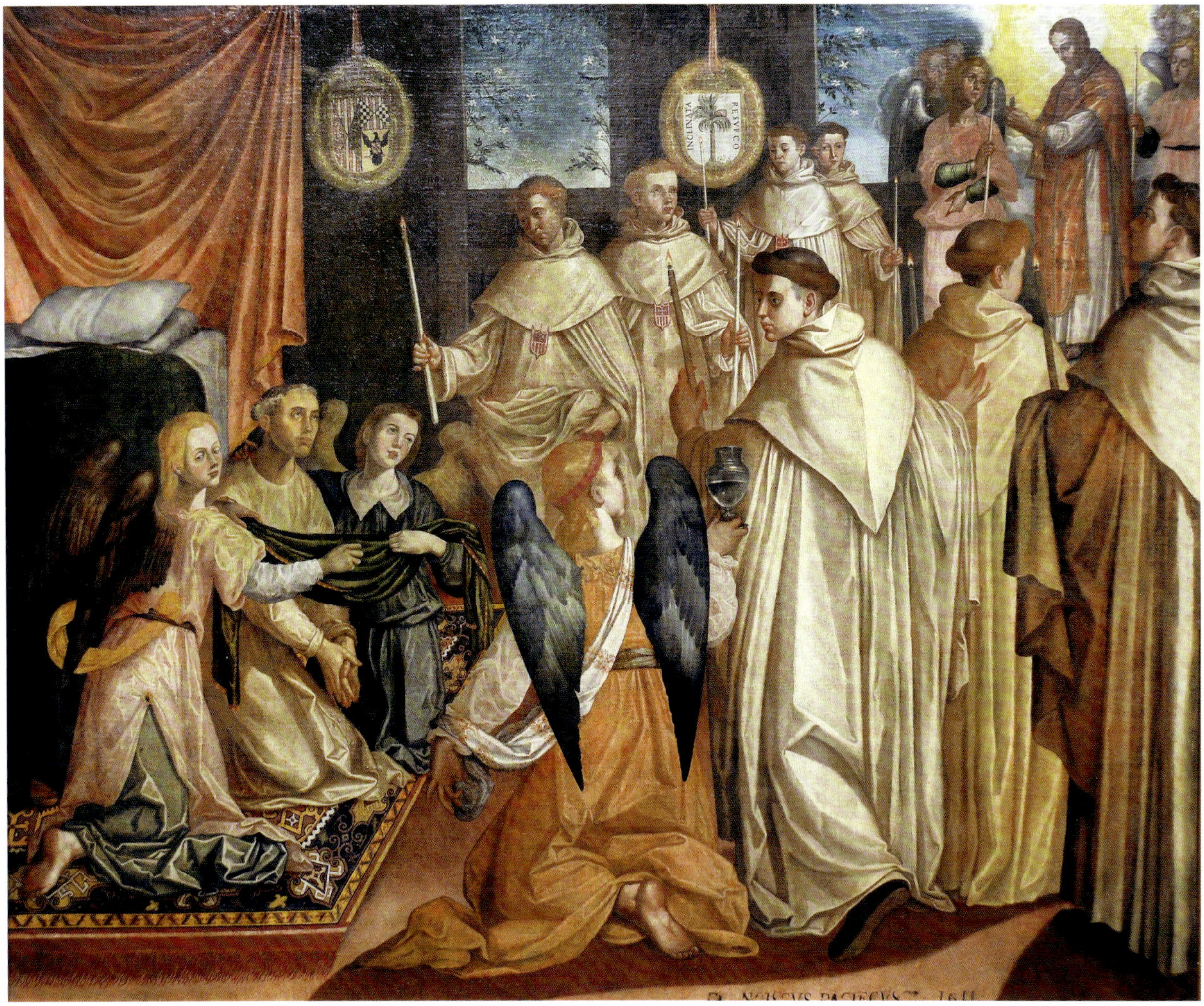

9

high altarpiece of San Girolamo della Carità, painted in 1614 by Domenichino.[45] Like Massari, Domenichino based his composition on the altarpiece by his teacher Agostino Carracci. Indeed, as Spada was probably aware, the painter had been accused by his rivals of partially plagiarizing Agostino's invention, passing it off to a Roman audience as if it were entirely his own.[46] Under the circumstances, it would be only natural for a connoisseur like Virgilio Spada, with strong Roman and Bolognese connections, to indulge in an art-critical exercise in *paragone* by closely examining and comparing all three paintings. Given that Massari's altarpiece hung in the Spada church in Bologna and Domenichino's in a church with Spada connections in Rome, the association between them would have been all the more obvious.

At the very least, whether or not they directly inspired Spada's invention, Massari's angels help us to visualize the balustrade's liturgical function and affective form. Just as they fix their eyes on the ritual in progress, one of them gazing at the consecrated wafer in the priest's right hand and the other at the ciborium in his left, so the angel on the right of the Spada balustrade contemplates the act of Communion taking place above him. The upward

FIG. 9. Francisco Pacheco, *Last Communion of Saint Raymond Nonnatus*, 1611. Bowes Museum, Barnard Castle, County Durham.

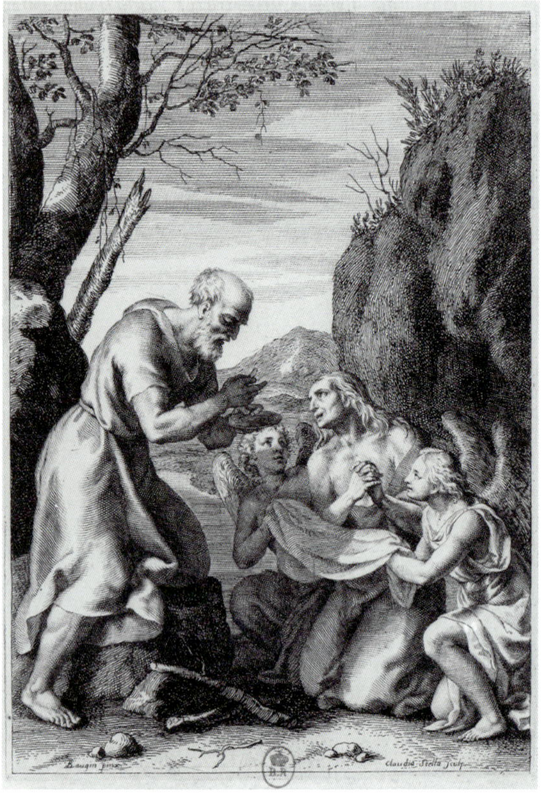

10

FIG. 10. Claudine Bouzonnet-Stella (after a lost altarpiece by Lubin Baugin in Notre-Dame), *Last Communion of Saint Mary of Egypt*, ca. 1653. Paris, Bibliothèque nationale de France.

turn and tilt of his head is almost identical to that of his painted counterpart (FIGS. 15–16). There is no other possible explanation for the direction of his gaze; he, too, must be looking at the host. His twin, meanwhile, faces outward, inviting the faithful to approach and bear witness. In the same way that the walls and floor of the Spada Chapel are decorated as if for a festive celebration, the marble angels perpetually act out the holiest moment in the Mass, when the communicant kneels and partakes of the Eucharistic bread.

It may be helpful to know something of the history and sacred character of the church in which the Spada Chapel is located in order to understand the unusual emphasis on the act of Communion implied by the design of the angelic balustrade. In 1524, San Girolamo was assigned to the Archconfraternity of the Carità, or Charity, one of the earliest and most powerful of the lay confraternities established during the period of Catholic Reform.[47] Dedicated to good works, the group took as its symbol the Eucharistic host, in recognition of the theological notion that the Eucharist is "the sacrament of Charity."[48] Consequently, the host—a circle inscribing a cross—is repeated everywhere throughout the church.[49] It replaces the usual fleurons in the Corinthian capitals both outside and inside the building. It appears in the pediment over the side entrance and again above the door into the confraternal rooms, where it is superimposed like a shield over the resurrected body of Christ. The same motif—the host over the body of Christ—is featured in the central panel of the elaborate wooden ceiling over the nave (1587–1597), while in the somewhat later transept ceiling (ca. 1654), carved and painted hosts emerge like flowers out of curling rinceaux. Nowhere is the host more emphatically on display than over the high altar, where it is the focal point of Domenichino's *Last Communion of Saint Jerome*. For Domenichino's altarpiece not only celebrates the saint to whom the church is dedicated, it also depicts a solemn Eucharistic act and thus cleverly links the titular saint and the Archconfraternity's symbol within an iconography of mutual relevance. Domenichino was careful to accentuate the sacramental theme, brightly illuminating the host and setting it against a tondo of darkness so that it stands out even from a distance. Thus, the Spada Chapel is situated in a church positively steeped in Eucharistic imagery, both inside and out; and although the chapel is a private foundation (that is to say, it was acquired from the Archconfraternity but was otherwise independent of it), the state of perpetual readiness for the Mass suggested by the design of its balustrade is very much in keeping with the Eucharistic emphasis of the church as a whole.

As an Oratorian priest, moreover, Virgilio Spada would have been acutely aware of the fact that San Girolamo della Carità had been home for more than thirty years to Philip Neri, the founder of his Congregation and a passionate devotee of the Eucharist. Employed by the Archconfraternity to say Mass at its altars, Neri lived in rooms above the church from 1551 to 1583.[50] It was there

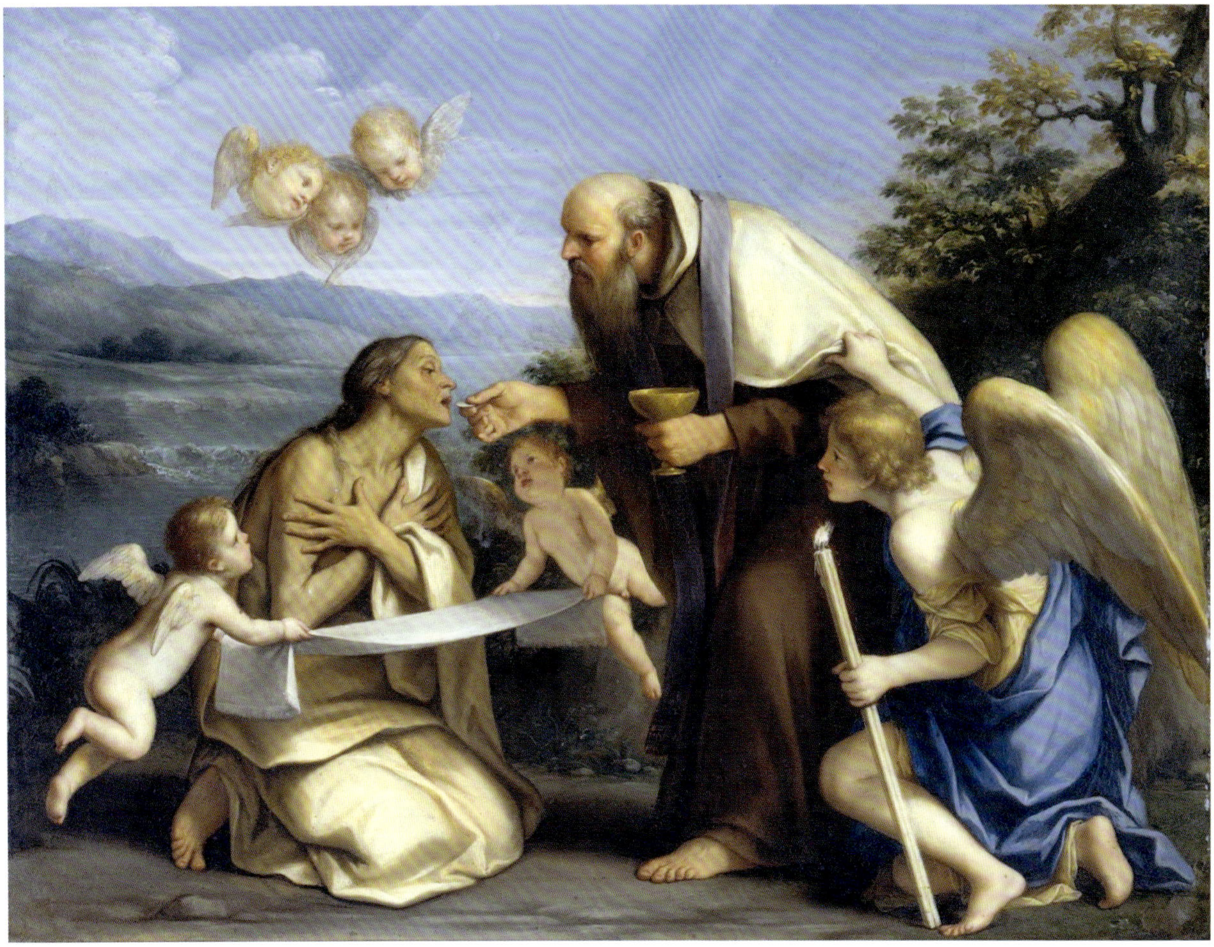

11

that he gathered around him a group of like-minded churchmen that eventually coalesced into the Congregation of the Oratory. Among them was Orazio Spada, Virgilio's uncle and the original founder of the Spada Chapel.[51] Neri's more than usual reverence for the Eucharist was noted by all his early biographers, who described how he took Communion daily, could not sleep until he had tasted his Lord's body, greedily claimed for himself the largest piece of the host so that he could savor its sweetness longer, suffered violent tremors and levitations while consecrating the wafer, experienced visions and fell into ecstatic swoons while adoring it.[52] His mystical connection to the Eucharist and his desire to share that sacrament with his congregants are the reasons he is traditionally depicted wearing the chasuble of an officiating priest, an iconography already well established in the years leading up to his beatification in 1615 and canonization in 1622. In more practical terms, Neri was a vociferous proponent of frequent Communion, urging his priestly followers to say Mass every day, a practice that "was by no means common in those days," and "anxious also that laymen, as well as priests, should frequent this Sacrament."[53] San Girolamo della Carità must have been a center of intense Eucharistic activity during the decades when Neri was in residence there. Virgilio would not have been insensible to the sacred history of the church and its connection to the

FIG. 11. Marcantonio Franceschini, *Last Communion of Saint Mary of Egypt*, 1680. The Metropolitan Museum of Art, New York.

founder of his order, and it is conceivable that he intended the balustrade, with its angelic attendants, to recall the kind of ecstatic adoration of the Eucharist that Neri himself so fervently promoted.

Given the history of the church, it is intriguing to note that Antonio Giorgetti, the sculptor of the balustrade, modeled the angel on the right on the angel in Alessandro Algardi's marble sculpture of Saint Philip Neri that stands over the altar in the sacristy of the Chiesa Nuova, the mother church of the Oratorians, situated barely five hundred meters away from San Girolamo (see fig. 1 in Guendalina Serafinelli's essay in this volume).[54] The borrowing is yet another suggestive link between the Spada balustrade and the spirit of Nerian devotion that permeates the church.

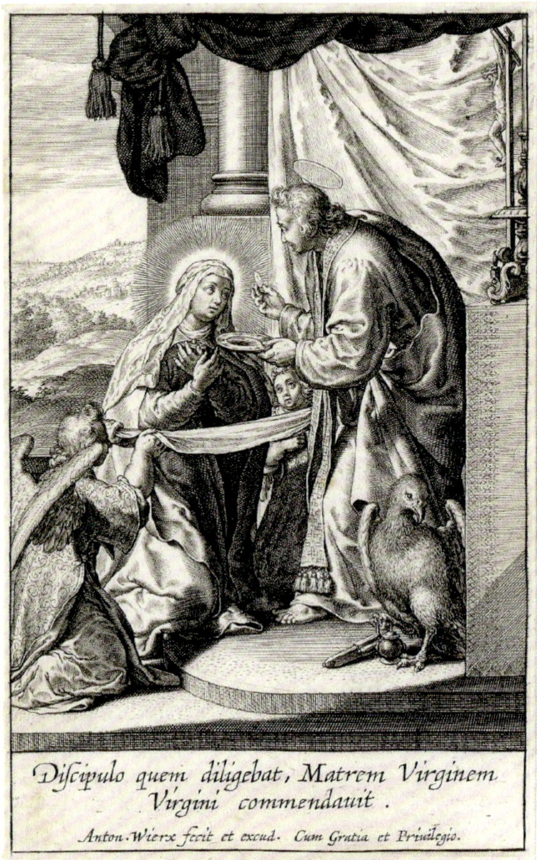

12

The Failure of the Spada Balustrade

Despite its obvious novelty and charm, the Spada balustrade met with a muted response. The fact that it had no immediate progeny and was never imitated in any Roman church suggests that it was regarded as an eccentric and perhaps even a frivolous experiment that did not quite work out. How to explain this? What was it about the conceit or the design that failed to please? No contemporary critiques have survived, as far as I am aware, but even without them, it is easy to spot the logical flaws in Virgilio's invention and to guess the kinds of things that may have been said about it, relating to three main areas of concern: (1) the garishly striped Communion cloth, (2) the angels' unsynchronized gazes, and (3) the indecorousness of the very idea of angel attendants at the Communion of non-saints. A few words follow about each of these in turn.

The cloth. The colorful jasper out of which the cloth is made harmonizes with the polychrome decoration of the chapel walls and precisely matches the material used in the reliquary caskets to the right and left of the altar. Nevertheless, it complicates our understanding of the balustrade. Communion cloths are usually made of white linen. There are exceptions. The cloth held by the angels in Pacheco's *Last Communion of Saint Raymond Nonnatus* (1611) is green with embroidered edges (**FIG. 9**), Saint Teresa of Ávila clutches a deep blue cloth fringed in gold in a depiction of her Communion by Juan Martín Cabezalero (ca. 1670),[55] and Andrea Commodi represents a Communion bench covered with a fitted green cloth with gold trim in his *Saint Ignatius Attending Mass at Manresa* (ca. 1602).[56] All the same, colored Communion cloths are not the norm, to say nothing of outlandishly striped ones in orange, red, and white. So why did Spada instruct the artist to craft so vibrant a fabric, when it was bound to detract from the very illusion he was trying to create? After all, "linens" made of white marble appear elsewhere in the chapel—fringed strips of the stuff hang from each of the reliquary caskets—and the houseling cloth could have been cut from this same material. The only explanation I can offer—

FIG. 12. Anton Wierix III, *The Virgin Receiving Communion from Saint John the Evangelist*, before 1624. British Museum, London.

FIG. 13. Erasmus Quellin II and Schelte Adamsz. Bolswert, *The Virgin Receiving Communion from Saint John the Evangelist*, before 1660. Rijksmuseum, Amsterdam.

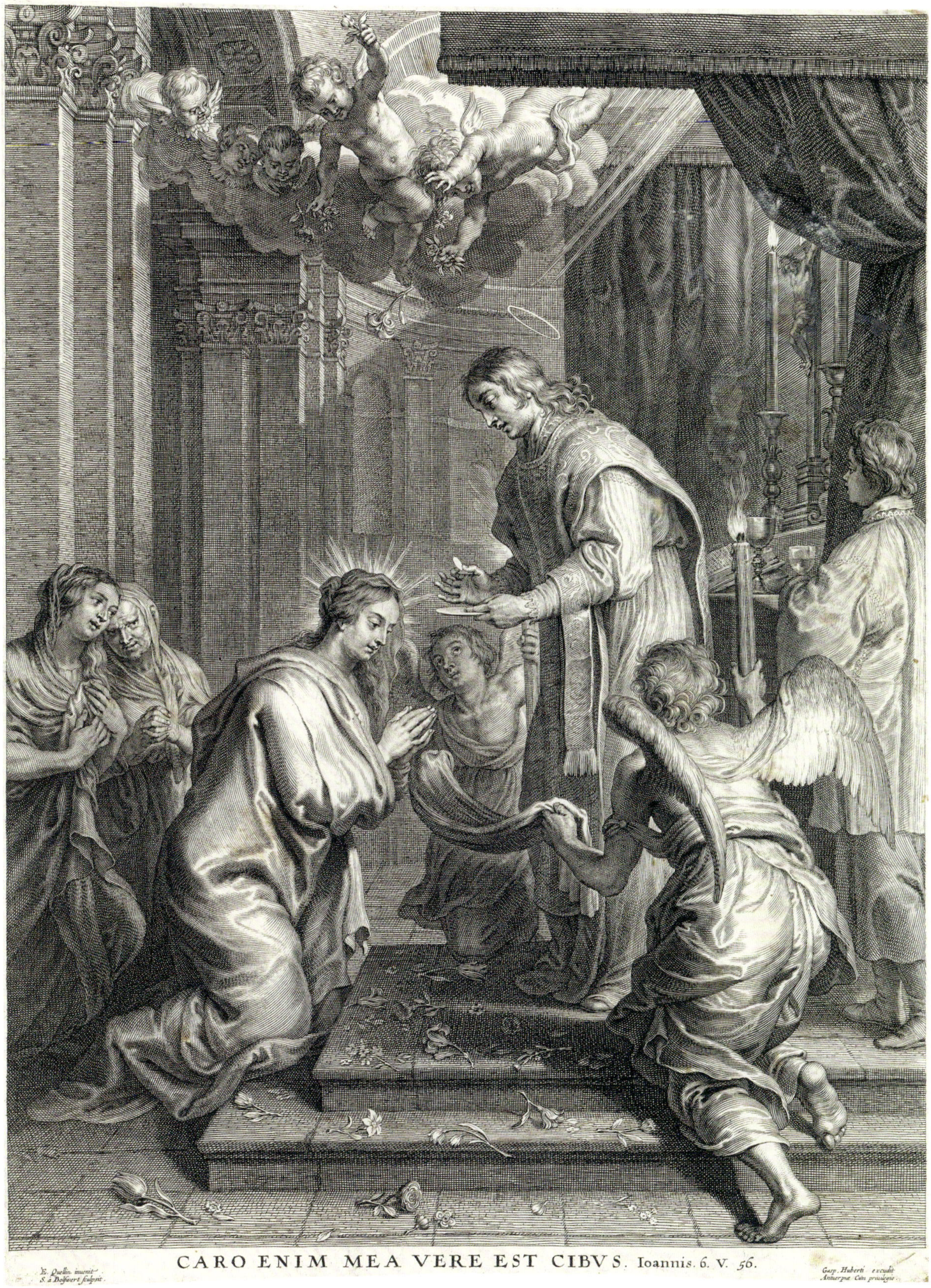
E. Quellin. invenit
S. à Bolswert sculpsit.
CARO ENIM MEA VERE EST CIBVS. Ioannis. 6. V. 56.
Gasp. Huberti excudit
Antverpiæ Cum privilegio.

13

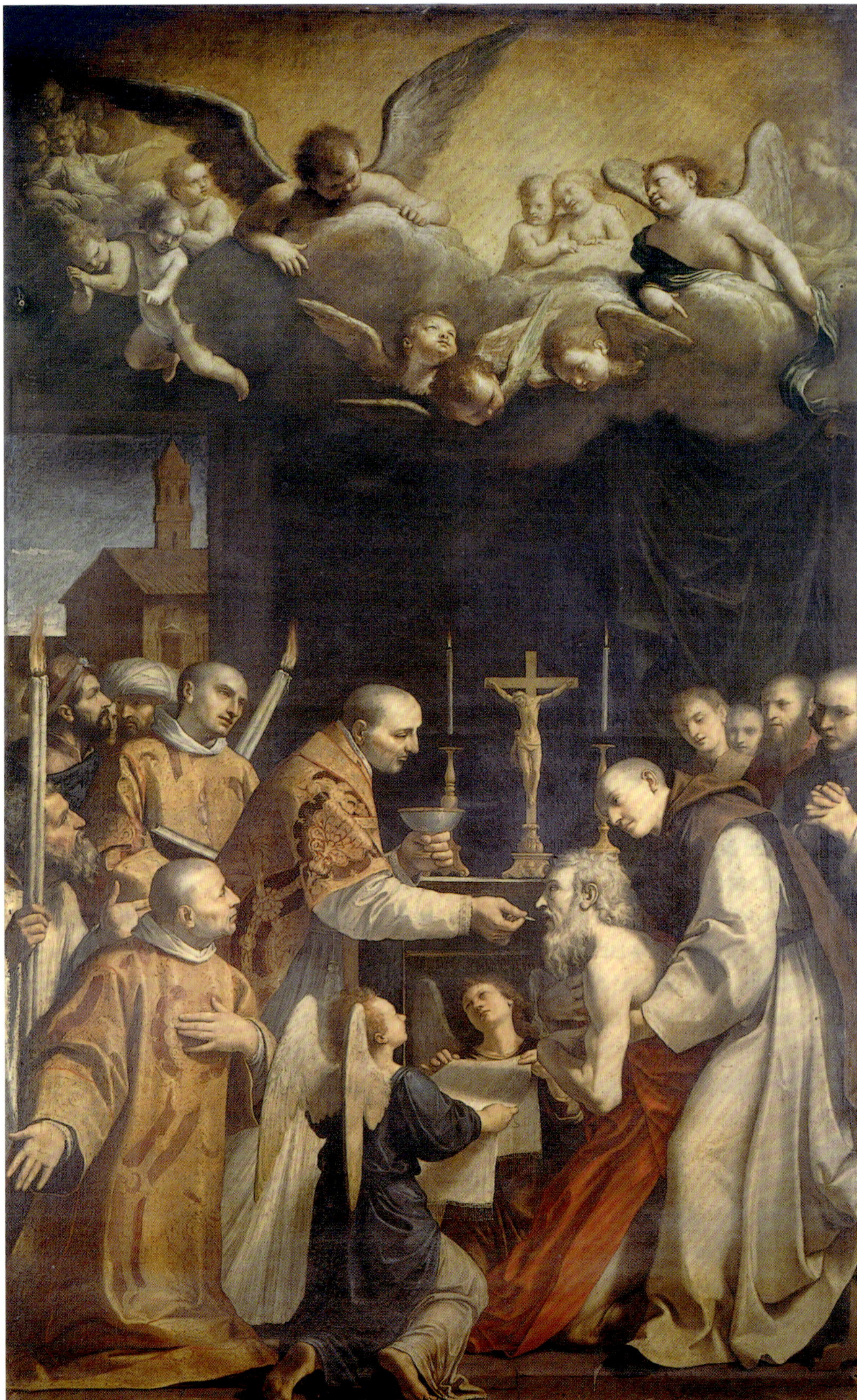

14

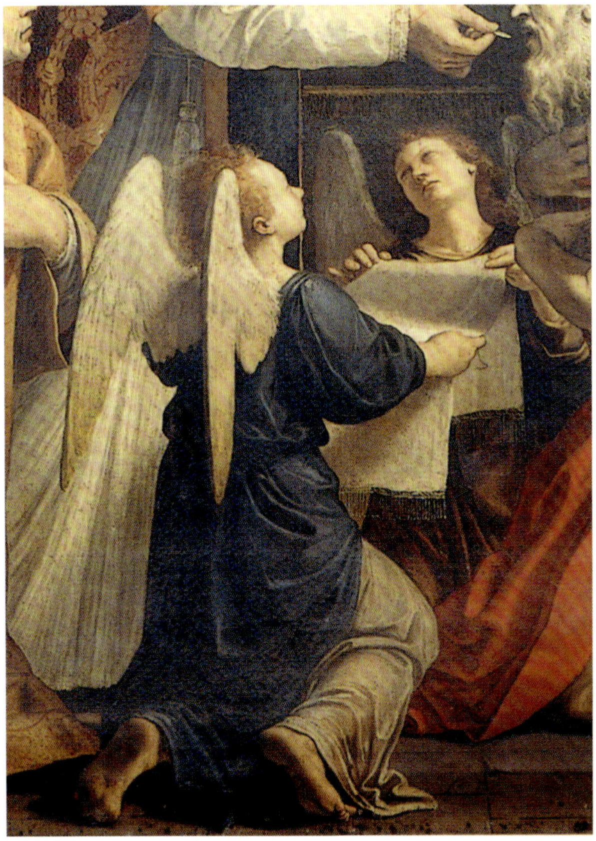

15

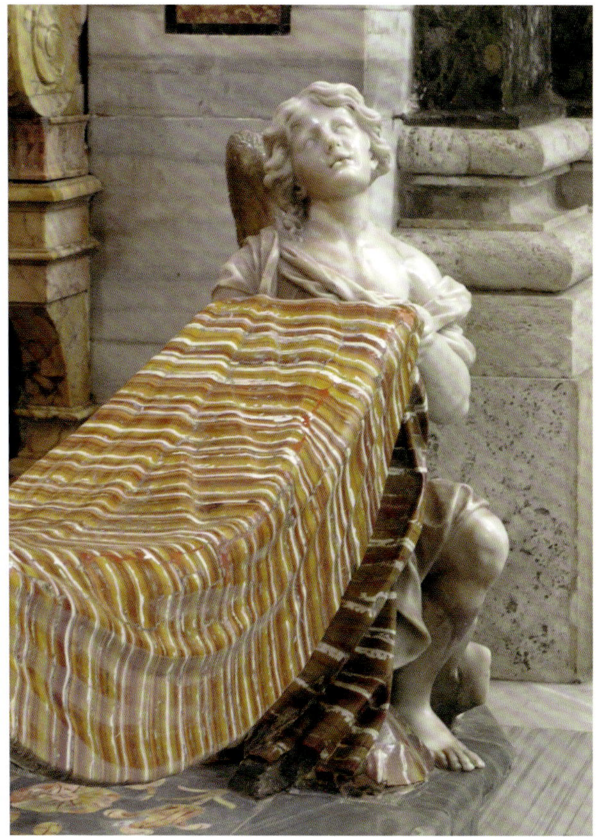

16

and it is, admittedly, a clumsy one—is that Spada intended or expected that the fictive fabric of the balustrade would be covered with a real Communion cloth during the Mass. If so, whenever the chapel was in ritual use, the angels would appear to be holding a length of white linen, whereas as soon as the Mass was over, the jasper cloth would reemerge, its flamboyant pattern so different from the liturgical white that no one would be likely to confuse the two. The very gaudiness of the sculptured fabric may have been decided on as a way of coping with the fundamental dilemma posed by the angelic balustrade, namely, how to ensure that it makes visual and conceptual sense not only when Communion is in progress but also when it is not; or, to put it another way, how to make the length of fabric look like a Communion veil in one context and like something else altogether—something more like the festive stone "hangings" that decorate the chapel's walls—in the other.

The angels. Another peculiarity of the balustrade is the unsynchronized manner in which Giorgetti's angels direct their attention. While the one on the right looks upward, his eyes notionally fixed on the host as it passes from priest to communicant, the other on the left looks away. His glance is directed toward the door that leads upstairs to the rooms once inhabited by Philip Neri; he seems to address the person descending from that holy place or, at any rate, someone approaching from the left.[57] And yet, as long as the direction of his companion's gaze implies that Communion is in progress, his own turning away seems incongruous, for at that ritually charged moment, both

FIG. 14. Lucio Massari, *Last Communion of Saint Jerome*, ca. 1625. Ariosti Chapel, San Paolo Maggiore, Bologna.

FIG. 15. Lucio Massari, *Last Communion of Saint Jerome* (detail), ca. 1625. Ariosti Chapel, San Paolo Maggiore, Bologna.

FIG. 16. Antonio Giorgetti, Angelic balustrade (detail), 1657–1659. Spada Chapel, San Girolamo della Carità, Rome.

angels should be adoring the miraculous bread, as they do in every pictorial representation of Communion mentioned above. There seems to be a curious kind of temporal disconnect between the two figures: the pose and attitude of the right-hand angel make sense only at the moment of Communion, whereas the outward address of the left-hand angel seems proper and appropriate only at any other point in time. Is the incongruence of their gazes due to carelessness on the part of the sculptor? Or is this another calculated measure to ensure that the balustrade remains conceptually viable whether Mass is in progress or not?[58]

The questionable decorum of Spada's invention. In paintings and prints, as we have seen, the motif of the angel-held houseling cloth is almost always associated with the Communion of saints or of the Virgin Mary; it also shows up, although more rarely, in images of Christ.[59] The notional man or woman kneeling in front of the Spada balustrade, on the other hand, has no claim to exceptional sanctity. Why, then, should he or she be attended by angels? One could, of course, argue that the transubstantiated host is by itself a sufficiently miraculous object to merit their divine presence, regardless of the worldliness of those who partake of it. After all, angels have always been intimately associated with the Eucharist—the *panis angelorum*—which is why they often flank sacrament tabernacles and monstrances. All the same, when the motif of the angel-held houseling cloth is extracted from the hagiographic or Marian context of a painted altarpiece, turned into a life-size three-dimensional tableau, and inserted into a space inhabited by the living, the result is unsettling. It is possible that Spada conceived of the angelic balustrade as a kind of visual alternative to an altarpiece. For his chapel lacks the large narrative painting that is the central visual feature of most private family chapels of the period. The small image of the Virgin and Child on the altar wall, piously retained from his uncle's day, communicates the Marian dedication but is hardly an eye-catcher. Instead, it is the balustrade, with its altarpiece-inspired subject matter, that gives the chapel its figural focal point. But an altarpiece and a chapel balustrade are hardly interchangeable, and a motif perfectly at home in a painting, where its poetic nature is taken for granted, becomes disturbingly literal and potentially indecorous when translated into stone and brought down to earth.

Ultimately, all of these infelicities stem from the essential illogic of a statuary group that requires the presence of living actors to bring it to completion. Baroque sculptors loved to imply the possibility of communication between marble and living beings, persuading their viewers with the mimetic power of their art. But in the Spada Chapel, the game was taken too far. A composition that depends for its meaning on the participation of a priest and a communicant becomes meaningless and confused when they are not there and ends up trivializing the mystical event it is meant to celebrate.

These are the telltale signs that the Spada balustrade was conceived by an enthusiastic but heedless amateur. The idea for the angelic railing has been attributed to Gian Lorenzo Bernini by at least one distinguished scholar, and on the face of it, Giorgetti's substitution of an architectural element with figurative sculpture is undeniably Berninesque.[60] Spada knew Bernini well, sometimes consulted him, more often sparred with him, and on occasion employed him (at San Paolo Maggiore in Bologna, for example, where Bernini provided the architectural design of the high altar), so it is certainly possible that the

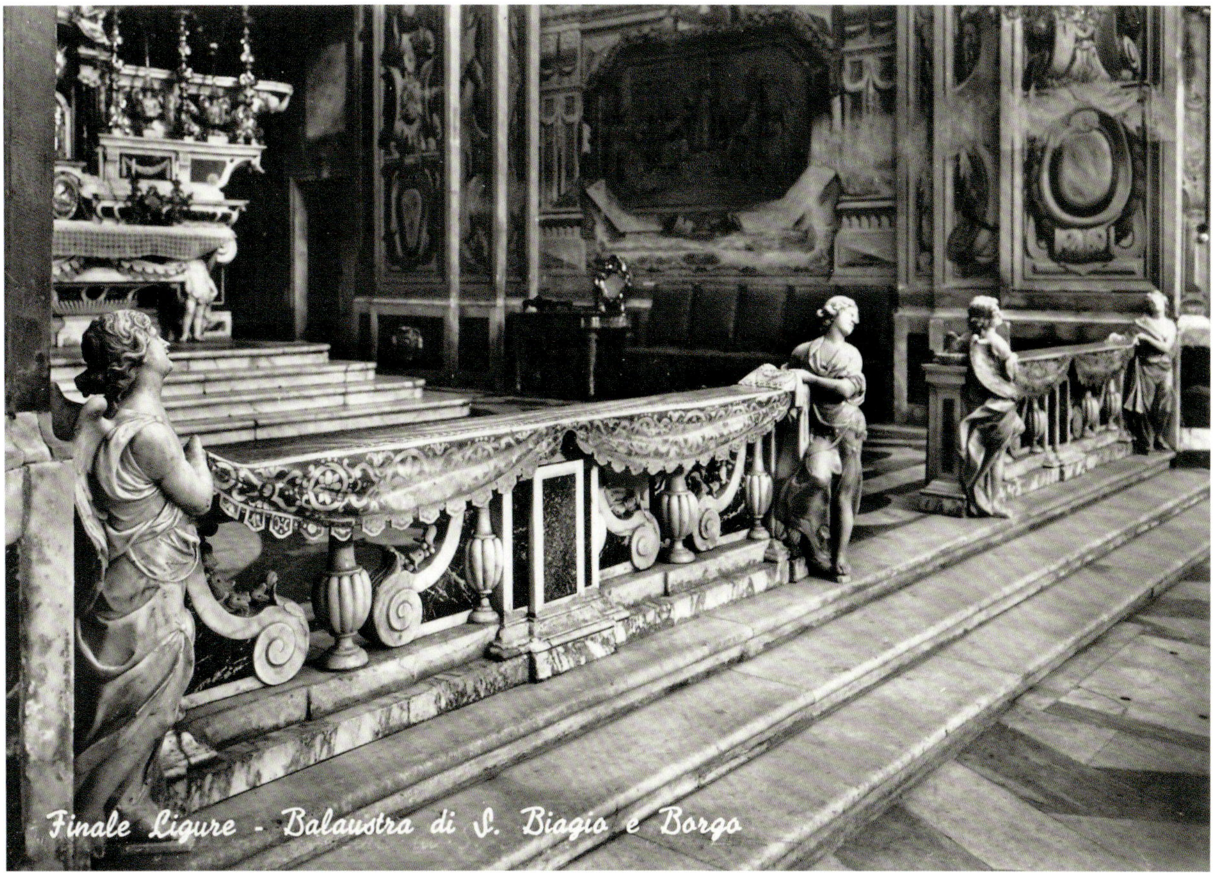

17

two men conversed about the refitting of the Spada Chapel.[61] Nevertheless, it seems to me unlikely that Bernini had a hand in the design of the balustrade. Bernini's inventions are always scrupulously logical. His sculptures may reach out to address the viewer, but they never require the viewer's presence to complete their configuration or render them meaningful; and although they tend to be highly theatrical, they are rarely gimmicky.

In the apse of the basilican church of San Biagio in Finalborgo in Liguria, marble angels spread a white Communion cloth over a balustrade of polychrome marble (FIG. 17).[62] Attributed to Domenico Bocciardo, a lesser-known member of a prolific Finalese dynasty of painters and sculptors, the ensemble was completed in 1799 in a style entirely derived from an earlier age. In this work, clearly inspired by the Spada balustrade, all of the shortcomings of the original are pleasingly resolved. The Communion cloth is made of white marble, tooled in imitation of the finest worked linen or lace. The angels stand rather than kneel and spread the cloth over an actual balustrade rather than support it themselves, all of which suggests a more casual kind of attendance. The two central angels look out but not off to the side; their attention is fixed on the approach to the high altar. And finally, the larger scale of the Ligurian balustrade—and the inclusion of four rather than two angels—eliminates any residual association with saints' Communions; this is a balustrade meant for a congregation and not for an individual. The "corrections" that Bocciardi

FIG. 17. Domenico Bocciardo, Angelic balustrade at the high altar, 1799. San Biagio, Finalborgo, Liguria.

has introduced give us insight into the kind of criticisms that may have been leveled at the Spada balustrade. More to the point, they demonstrate how a conceit that fits awkwardly in the smaller, more intimate setting of a private family chapel can be charmingly effective and problem-free in the wider, more public space of the apse.

Despite its conceptual flaws, its lively and ingenious design has meant that the Spada rail has always enjoyed a certain fame. In the end, though, the most significant thing about it may be not its exceptionalness but its conventionality. It differs in form but not in function from the hundreds of other balustrades that fill the churches of Rome, and by drawing attention to itself, it encourages us to think more deeply about this crucial and paradoxical feature of chapel design which stands as a protean boundary between private and public, between celebrant and congregation, and between architectural and ritual space.

Notes

1 — Braun 1924, II, 649–670, pls. 145, 364–371; Jungmann 1951, II, 374–376.

2 — Heydenreich 1977; Davies and Hemsoll 1983; Catitti 2013–2014. On the derivation of the word "baluster" from the Italian for the bud of the pomegranate flower, see Llewellyn 1977, 292–300.

3 — Davies and Hemsoll 1983, 5. The uppermost floor of the loggia on the turret facade of the Ducal Palace in Urbino, completed around 1470, is apparently one of the earliest structures to feature a true balustrade in stone. Davies and Hemsoll 1983, 6; Catitti 2013–2014, 23, figs. 7, 25.

4 — It is worth noting that the balustrade of the Basso Della Rovere Chapel closely imitates the painted decoration of the chapel by Pinturicchio, which features illusionistic benches supported on identical balusters. Other chapels in Santa Maria del Popolo—for example, the Della Rovere Chapel (fourth on the right) and the Cybo-Soderini Chapel (fourth on the left)—are enclosed with low parapets, which, although different in form, are identical to the Basso Della Rovere balustrade in height and function.

5 — Here, too, the marble balustrade echoes a painted balustrade in one of the frescoes by Filippino Lippi that decorate the chapel's walls.

6 — One finds ornate iron grilles, for example, at the entrances to the Aldobrandini Chapel in Santa Maria sopra Minerva, the Lante-Della Rovere Chapel in San Nicola da Tolentino, and several chapels in Santa Maria della Consolazione.

7 — Voelker 1977 [2008], I, 46–47: "On the front part at the entrance to every chapel, including the main chapel, iron railings will be set on the topmost step. They will be three cubits [approximately four feet] high, or even higher where it is advisable that they be safer and more secure. Where possible, all railings must be decorated at the top and bottom and in the middle with ornamental motifs, such as small pillars or small vase-shaped swellings, well made, to obtain a nice aesthetic effect. . . . The rather artful ironwork in the lower part, about a cubit high, should be compact enough so that dogs cannot enter. There will be a double gate at the center of the railing. It will also be of iron and in the same style, and will close on both sides with bolt and lock." Borromeo 1577 [1962], 31–32.

8 — Voelker 1977 [2008], I, 47. Borromeo 1577 [1962], 32: "Ubi vero vis et copia ferri, quo ad cappellarum instruendarum usum clathra conflentur, haberi minus potest, si ibi lapides solidi marmorave apparari queant, e marmore aliove solido lapide columellae opere quod vocant *balustrio*, addita coronice, fieri poterunt, aliquanto clathris ferreis humiliores, quibus cappellarum pars anterior saepta ornetur atque instruatur."

9 — Voelker 1977 [2008], I, 47; Borromeo 1577 [1962], 32.

10 — Voelker 1977 [2008], II, Dicta 80.1–2.

11 — A striking example of a side chapel whose ritual and devotional space extends well beyond its narrow architectural confines can be seen today in the church of Sant'Andrea delle Fratte. Religious activity in that church is centered around the cult of the *Madonna del Miracolo*, whose nineteenth-century image over the altar in the third chapel on the left is greatly revered, and such is the popularity of her cult that the pews that nearly fill the nave are now oriented semipermanently toward the side chapel rather than toward the high altar.

12 — Borromeo (1577 [1962], 27) strongly disapproved of the practice: "ne quicquam de ecclesiae parte, aut navi, cancellis occupetur." Chapels with protruding balustrades were always somewhat exceptional, but one does come across them in Roman churches; see, for example, the Gavotti Chapel in San Nicola da Tolentino, the Benedetti Chapel in San Luigi dei Francesi, and the Spada and Antamoro Chapels in San Girolamo della Carità.

13 — On palaces that push and shove, see Connors 1989, esp. 209–232.

14 — In 1739, the family who held the *jus patronatus* of the altar in the left transept of Sant'Eustachio requested permission to build a balustrade around it, hoping in this way to extend their private reach into what was a public area of the church, but they met with resistance from the Chapter, which argued that "se si ponesse la balaustrata nell'altare a mano manca, bisognerebbe altresì porlo all'altro a man dritta e la

chiesa restarebbe patentemente più angusta" (the documents are cited and discussed in Franceschini 2002, 379). The passage is revealing for a couple of reasons. It not only illustrates the role played by those in charge of the church in overseeing potential land grabs using balustrades, but it also reveals their predilection for maintaining strict symmetry throughout.

15 — The original position of the balustrades in the Ginnetti and Strozzi Chapels (first and second on the right) is recorded in De Rossi 1713, pls. 6–7, 38–39. Even without De Rossi's engravings, the fact that the chapels' floors, instead of being raised a step, are flush with the floor of the nave alerts us that something unusual is going on here. Balustrades are normally erected just inside the lip of a chapel's elevated floor, leaving enough space on the outside to serve as a kneeler. But in Sant'Andrea, the repositioned balustrades are raised up on narrow strips of masonry, which provide the usual space for kneeling on the outside but end abruptly on the inside. Another clue that the present balustrades are not original is the fact that the Strozzi balustrade exactly matches the balustrade of the chapel opposite, suggesting that they were products of a churchwide remodeling.

16 — In seventeenth-century views of the interior of the nave of Santa Maria della Pace, made after Cortona's intervention (1656–1659), balustrades matching the one he designed for the newly renovated Chigi Chapel are shown in front of the other three nave chapels. Falda and later engravers indicate all four balustrades standing on elevated floors that jut out from the interiors of the chapels into the nave. But in fact, the sixteenth-century Cesi Chapel to the left of the Chigi Chapel seems never to have had an elevated floor, and the balustrade it was given in the seventeenth century rested directly on the floor of the nave, with a wooden kneeler running around the outside of it (see the watercolor by Filippo Anivitti recently sold at auction; https://www.mutualart.com/Artwork/Die-Cappella-Cesi-in-Santa-Maria-della-P/FF7577991AEF4BBB). Falda's prints and others that show the Cesi Chapel with Cortona's balustrade set on a raised floor are recording an ideal arrangement rather than a reality.

17 — On Virgilio Spada, see Aringhi 1788; Heimbürger Ravalli 1977, 24–30; Sickel 2011; Righini 2012, 6–24. In his forthcoming monograph on Francesco Borrromini, Joseph Connors has a substantial chapter on Virgilio Spada, including a thorough and insightful account of Spada's involvement in the chapel in San Girolamo, and I thank him for allowing me to preview it.

18 — See, in particular, Neppi 1975, 292; Heimbürger Ravalli 1977, 82–113, 315–316; Ferrari and Papaldo 1999, 155–157; Fagiolo 2006, 62–63; Lenzo 2008, 383–428.

19 — Heimbürger Ravalli (1977, 111) very much exaggerates the secular quality of the decoration. Picking up on a phrase of Virgilio's that describes the chapel as a "stanza addobata" (a decorated chamber) and "cubiculum" (a private room), she claims that "Le sole cose che facciano pensare ad una cappella sono la mensa e gli angeli in ginocchio." In fact, nothing in the chapel is out of a place in a religious setting; even the statues of Bernardino and Giovanni Spada stretched out on day beds against the side walls are modeled on tombs in earlier chapels such as the Aldobrandini Chapel in Santa Maria sopra Minerva.

20 — Pinacoteca Vaticana, inv. 42343. The painting, usually attributed to Andrea Sacchi, is discussed in detail and illustrated in *La regola e la fama* 1995, 322, 448–450.

21 — Spada's ideas about the balustrade seem to have changed several times over the course of construction. At first, he may have intended to keep the original balustrade, which had been in place since the 1630s (Heimbürger Ravalli 1977, 105). In January 1656, however, he sent to Siena for six double balusters made of alabaster from the quarry at Montalcino (Neppi 1975, 282; Heimbürger Ravalli 1977, 105, n. 98; Lenzo 2008, 399). These, it seems, were never installed, and in an undated letter to his nephew, he described a different sort of enclosure: a low *transenna* of veined marble pierced with oval openings, with a central faux-marble wooden gate (Heimbürger Ravalli 1977, 113, n. 116; Lenzo 2008, 399).

22 — Montagu 1970, 279–280; Ferrari and Papaldo 1999, 156–157; Dickerson and Sigel 2016, 190–203. Most scholars assume that the angels are made of marble; Dario Del Bufalo (2002, 193, 195) additionally specifies that they are made of Carrara marble ("marmo bianco statuario di Luni"). Dickerson and Sigel (2016, 197), on the other hand, state that the material is alabaster. The stone is discolored in places and has been rubbed to an appearance of waxy softness, making identification difficult.

23 — The sketch is drawn on a sheet of paper, on the verso of which is a memo referring to a payment of September 14, 1656, making it likely that Spada came up with the idea for the angels around that time. Heimbürger Ravalli 1977, 106; Lenzo 2008, 399, n. 58.

24 — See the plans by Francesco Righi (Biblioteca Apostolica Vaticana [BAV], Vat. lat. 11258, f. 72; illustrated in Heimbürger Ravalli 1977, fig. 82) and Francesco Borromini (Vienna, Albertina, Az. Rom 474; illustrated in Lenzo 2008, 428, fig. 14).

25 — Archivio di Stato di Roma (ASR), Spada Archive, vol. 406, no. 19, transcribed in Heimbürger Ravalli 1977, 87–88, n. 40.

26 — There are earlier chapels that have balustrades or *transenne* decorated with putti—the Della Rovere Chapel in Santa Maria del Popolo, for example, or the Del Monte and Ricci Chapels in the transept of San Pietro in Montorio—but none of them is comparable to the Spada Chapel in replacing the architectural element with a purely figurative design. As for its influence, Fagiolo (2006, 62, n. 11) mentions two later imitations. One is the marble balustrade in the sanctuary of the Madonna del Buon Consiglio in Genazzano. Carved in the guise of a rumpled fringed cloth supported by six cloud-borne putti who strain under the weight of it, it is traditionally but erroneously attributed to Bernini (it appears to be eighteenth-century) and is said to have come from the little church of Santa Maria in Posterula in Rome, which was destroyed around 1888. The other is the high altar balustrade of the church of San Biagio in Finalborgo in Liguria (ca. 1799), about which I will say a few words toward the end of this essay.

27 — Passeri 1934, 363: "in cambio della solita balaustrata, che richiude l'Altare, vi fece due Angioli uno per parte, li quali, inginocchiati, tengono steso un mantile, come è solito per convenienza, e decoro, che si stende a quelli che riceveno il cibo sagratissimo dell'Eucaristia." See also Montagu 1970, 279. Alternative interpretations—for example, that the angels are exhibiting the shroud of Christ (Blunt 1982, 59; Fagiolo 2006, 62–63, n. 11) or that they are holding up the tunic that a Spada

ancestor is said to have given to Saint Francis (Fagiolo dell'Arco and Fagiolo 1967, 261)—are not supported by any of the early sources and frankly make little sense.

28 — Bond 1916, 140–142; Duffy 2005, 110, 128; Fortescue, O'Connell, and Reid 2009, 149. The word *houseling* (*housling*, *houselling*) is derived from the obsolete English noun *housel*, meaning Eucharist.

29 — Bond 1916, 141–142.

30 — Boden 2005, 63.

31 — Jungmann 1951, II, 375: "Since the thirteenth century it was customary here and there to spread a cloth (held by two acolytes) for those communicants kneeling at the altar. Later on, in the sixteenth century, this cloth began to be laid over a table or a bench which was placed before the communicants between the nave and the *presbyterium*. This was found very convenient for an orderly coming and going. Various synods now laid down prescriptions along these lines. However, in place of table or bench, solid rails of wood or stone gradually came into use ...—our Communion rail, which since the seventeenth century has almost everywhere [become the norm]." Bond 1916, 140; Voelker 1977 [2008], II, Dicta 79, 1–2.

32 — The *Rituale Romanum*, the basic manual for the administration of the sacraments first issued in 1614, does not mention the handheld houseling cloth; on the contrary, the woodcut that accompanies the passage on the distribution of the Eucharist (in the illustrated edition of 1652, 46) shows congregants gathered at a Communion bench or balustrade covered with a Communion cloth. On the other hand, the *Caeremoniale episcoporum Clementis VIII*, first published in 1600, does call for the use of a Communion cloth held by acolytes during the episcopal Mass on Easter Sunday: "eodemque tempore vocantur duo cappellani, seu Acoliti cottis induti cum albo mantili, quod genuflexi sustinent [ante communicandos], inde ambabus manibus per quatuor angulos quousque perfecta fuerit communio." (*Caeremoniale episcoporum* 1600, 262–263; the woodcut illustration of the ceremony is reproduced in Cropper 2005, 80, fig. 49). Today the use of the handheld houseling cloth is being revived in certain traditionalist enclaves of the Catholic Church; for example, at SS. Trinità dei Pellegrini, where the Priestly Fraternity of Saint Peter, a conservative society of churchmen dedicated to preserving the Mass as it existed before the reforms of the Second Vatican Council, has held services since 2008.

33 — Although the houseling cloth, when represented in connection with a saint, is usually supported by angels, there are exceptions. In Giacomo Giorgetti's *Last Communion of Saint Lucy* (ca. 1650; San Martino, Esanatoglia [Macerata]), it is the saint's youthful companions who hold it up, while in scenes of the last Communions of sainted monastics, the task is often performed by the saint's fellow religious, as in depictions of the viaticum of Saint Benedict by Daniel Hallé (1664; Saint-Ouen, Rouen) and Giovanni Battista Rossi (eighteenth century; Montecassino Abbey, presumably destroyed).

34 — Sotheby's, London, December 6, 2012, lot 312; Bonhams, London, Knightsbridge, October 29, 2014, lot 7.

35 — Bowes Museum, County Durham, inv. 1007. Signed and dated, the work is one of nine large canvases produced by Pacheco and Alonso Vázquez for the Mercedarian convent in Seville.

36 — See, for example, Niccolò Bambini's *Miraculous Mass of Saint Teresa of Ávila* (late seventeenth century; in the Ruzzini Chapel in Santa Maria degli Scalzi, Venice) or Felice Cignani's *Miraculous Mass of Saint Maria Maddalena de' Pazzi* (late seventeenth century; in the church of the Conversion of Saint Paul, Imola).

37 — In addition to the examples illustrated here, see Sebastiano Ricci's depiction of the subject, ca. 1695 (National Gallery of Art, inv. 2003.85.1), and the charming *pietra dura* reliquary containing a piece of the saint's remains in the treasury of San Lorenzo in Florence, where the scene of her Communion, carved in colored stones, appears to be based on Baugin's lost altarpiece in Notre-Dame. (On Baugin's altarpiece, probably painted in the 1650s and known through several engraved reproductions, see Notter and Daguerre de Hureaux 2002, 178, 190–193).

38 — Mâle 1951, 81–82.

39 — Sometimes attributed to Camassei, the altarpiece in Santa Lucia in Selci is illustrated in Cropper 2005, 87, fig. 57. For Gimignani's painting, see Gloton 1998.

40 — On Castellucci's altarpiece, painted ca. 1658–1660 for the Chapel of the Holy Sacrament in the cathedral of Cortona, see Fornasari 1996, 41–42, cat. VI, where it is suggested that the artist may have modeled his interpretation on a lost altarpiece of the same subject by Giovan Francesco Romanelli, commissioned by Anna Colonna for the church of Regina Coeli between 1654 and 1658. Galestruzzi produced his version of the subject a year or two later, between 1661 and 1663; part of a series of scenes from the life of the Virgin by French and Italian artists painted in Rome but destined for the chapel of the "Congrégation des Messieurs" in the Jesuit college in Aix, it was recently discovered in the Hôpital de Saint-Jacques in Aix (see Mâle 1951, 82; Gloton-Rinville 1990). It is surely significant that both Castellucci and Galestruzzi were exploring the motif of the angel-held Communion cloth right around the time that the Spada balustrade was installed. It is, of course, possible that the painters derived the idea from the balustrade. On the other hand, if Romanelli's lost altarpiece included the same motif (and we do not know that it did), then it may have been the primary inspiration not only for the two paintings but for the balustrade as well.

41 — Lenzo 2008, 420, doc. 7.

42 — Malvasia 1678 [1841], I, 392: "Il S. Girolamo comunicato per viatico nella cappella Areosti in S. Paolo, e nel quale fu forza similmente seguisse il gran pensiero di Agostino alla Certosa, avendo questa proprietà le cose de' Carracci, che più proprie, nè espressive possano rappresentarsi." Agostino's painting is now in the Pinacoteca Nazionale in Bologna.

43 — Heimbürger Ravalli 1977, 37–59; Montagu 1985, II, 369–376; Righini 2012, 78–101; Delbeke 2014.

44 — Virgilio was in Bologna in 1636 (Heimbürger Ravalli 1977, 42, n. 19), by which time he was already thinking about the family chapel in San Girolamo della Carità (Heimbürger Ravalli 1977, 82, n. 20).

45 — Spear 1982, I, 57–58, 175–178; II, pl. 141; Cropper 2005. The painting over the high altar in San Girolamo della Carità today is a copy; the original is preserved in the Pinacoteca Vaticana.

46 — The episode is described and analyzed in detail in Cropper 2005.

47 — On the Archconfraternity of the Carità, approved by Pope Leo X, see Piazza 1679, 391-395; Marchetti 2004 (with additional bibliography, 253); Cropper 2005, 73-74.

48 — Thomas Aquinas, *Summae Theologiae*, part III, question 73, article 3.

49 — The symbol also appears on the title pages of the Archconfraternity's publications (see, e.g., *Gli Statuti della Compagnia della Charità di Roma*, Rome, 1536; *Constitutiones Archiconfraternitatis Charitatis de Urbe*, Rome, 1603) and can be seen on numerous buildings in the vicinity of the church, marking the organization's extensive holdings in real estate.

50 — Bacci 1902, I, 78-113 and passim; Gallonio 2005, 28-29 and passim; Cropper 2005, 74-76.

51 — Aringhi 1788, 19; Lenzo 2008, 386.

52 — Bacci 1902, I, 142-150, 169, 337-338, 347-348; Gallonio 2005, 31-32, 131-132, 169. Neri's "devotion to the Blessed Sacrament of the Altar was more tender than can be expressed" (Bacci 1902, I, 142). "In administering this Sacrament to others, he felt such fevour that his whole body bounded, to the great marvel of those who saw him... When he took the pyx into his hand,... his face gleamed as if it were on fire, whilst after the Communion he was deadly pale." He trembled so violently when handling the host that those present, "fearing lest some particles should fall (though no such accident ever did occur to the Saint), reverently took hold of his arm, and held it steady until he had given Communion" (Bacci 1902, I, 149). Gallonio (2005, 31-32) adds that he "was so taken by delight in the divine Sacrament that he would retain the sweet flesh of Christ and His most precious Blood in his mouth, not swallowing it at once but letting it pass slowly, drop by drop, into his stomach. His devotion in celebrating the Mass, and in distributing the Body of Christ to others was no less than in his partaking of it." Alone in his private chapel, "he would often not consume the sacred Eucharist, nor drink the Precious Blood, before he had passed two hours, more or less, in contemplation of the Blessed Sacrament, with deep feelings of devotion and much shedding of tears" (Gallonio 2005, 169). Appropriately, he died on the feast of Corpus Christi (Gallonio 2005, 203).

53 — Bacci 1902, I, 43: "He was one of the first... who revived in Rome the practice of frequent confession and Communion." See also Bacci 1902, I, 118-119, 144-145, 199-200, 258.

54 — The similarity of the two angels was first noted by Montagu (1970, 280). On Algardi's statue, see Montagu 1985, I, 64-66, pl. III; II, 380-384, figs. 47, 49.

55 — Madrid, Museo Lázaro Galdiano, inv. 05694 (formerly attributed to Claudio Coello).

56 — Rome, Casa Professa, chapel of Cardinal Odoardo Farnese.

57 — Above the door in the church that leads to the saint's room is an inscription that reads: "Visit and venerate the place up above where Philip Neri initiated the Congregation of the Sacred Oratory through the pious exercises that were long held here by the fathers. These exercises have now moved elsewhere on account of the new building; but let not this little corner be forgotten, out of which a wellspring of piety poured forth into the world." ("Suspice ac venerare locum supra positum in quo s. Philippus Nerius Sac. Oratorii congregationem inchoavit per pias exercitationes quae diu hic habitae a patribus ob novam aedificationem alio translatae sunt non debet ignorari angulus ex quo manavit in orbem fons pietatis.")

58 — In an early bozzetto (Berlin, Bode Museum), the pose of the right-hand angel is almost the mirror image of his twin's. He, too, looks outward and, in his case, slightly to the right. Given that the chapel is nestled between the main and side entrances into the church, the initial intention may have been to have both angels outward-looking, the better to catch the attention of anyone arriving through either of the doors. This might, indeed, have been a happier solution, since it would not have required an ongoing act of Communion to make sense of the angel's gaze. The bozzetto is illustrated in Ferrari and Papaldo 1999, 157, or visit the museum's online collections database.

59 — Fagiolo (2006, 62, n. 11) points to a fresco in the sanctuary of Santa Maria della Fontenuova in Monsummano Terme (Tuscany), painted by Giovanni da San Giovanni in 1630-1633, in which Christ is portrayed in the role of priest presenting the chalice and wafer over a Communion veil stretched between two airborne angels and inscribed with the words "I am the living bread which came down from heaven" (John 6:51).

60 — Fagiolo 2006, 62-63. The action of the angels holding an object between them (the veil) reminds him of the angels holding the tempietto-shaped tabernacle in an early drawing for the Sacrament altar in St. Peter's, while the veil itself he likens to the rumpled fabrics of colored stone in the tomb of Alexander VII and the altar of Blessed Ludovica Albertoni. Interestingly, all of these works postdate the Spada balustrade (although the idea for the fabric-flung tomb of Alexander goes back to ca. 1657 and is therefore contemporaneous with it). Lenzo (2008, 399) compares the cloth to the great swatch of drapery that Bernini was installing in the Sala Ducale of the Vatican Palace in 1656-1657, around the time that Giorgetti was beginning work on the balustrade.

61 — Their relationship was a troubled one. Spada's involvement in the decision to take down Bernini's bell tower at St. Peter's and his later criticism of Bernini's design for the piazza earned him the artist's deep resentment. It did not help matters that Spada consistently championed Bernini's great rival, Francesco Borromini. On the relationship between Spada and Bernini, see McPhee 2002, 85-86 and passim; Mormando 2011, 150-152, 207-208; Sickel 2011.

62 — See n. 26 above.

The Arm Relic as Index of the Body

THE CHAPEL OF FRANCIS XAVIER IN THE GESÙ

Alison C. Fleming and Stephanie C. Leone

Held by the hand of the hovering gilt-bronze angel, the crystal-covered medallion reliquary of Saint Francis Xavier (1506–1552), containing the precious relic of his right arm and hand, floats above the altar, in the right transept chapel of the Gesù, the mother church of the Society of Jesus (FIGS. 1–3). As Evonne Levy has shown, the patron Monsignor Giovanni Francesco Negroni declared that Xavier's arm relic was vital not only to the altar but to the whole chapel: "it must always show, describe, and enrich, not only the altar, but also the whole chapel."[1] Under Negroni's patronage, the Chapel of Francis Xavier was mostly realized from March 1672 to February 1679, and the reliquary was installed by 1684.[2] Negroni's devotion to the relic led to a conflict with the Jesuits over its possession and display. This story, with its illumination of a shift in reliquary display in baroque chapels, has been told.[3] Along with the patronage, the scholarship on the chapel has focused on the architectural design and Carlo Maratti's altarpiece (FIG. 5).[4] Despite this scholarly attention, no comprehensive study of this space's multimedia components exists, and the function of the relic as propagating the whole chapel has not been fully considered.

Artists and artisans of many specializations worked in a variety of materials and techniques to create this sacred space. The sculptor Girolamo Lucenti designed the gilt-bronze angel with reliquary (FIG. 2). Pietro da Cortona and Luca Berrettini were responsible for the design and execution of the architecture and stonework (FIGS. 3–4). Carlo Maratti painted the oil-on-canvas altarpiece of the *Death of St. Francis Xavier* (FIG. 5) and probably designed the stucco sculpture of Francis Xavier lifted by angels in the altar's pediment. In the arch of the upper wall and on the vault, Giovanni Andrea Carlone frescoed five narrative scenes of the saint's life (FIG. 6). Surprisingly, only one prior publication fully identifies the subject matter of every scene, even though, as we will argue, the frescoes play an essential role in the chapel.[5] Furthermore, unnamed artisans made the precious metalwork objects furnishing the chapel.[6] The chapel's function and meaning can only be understood through the analysis of these individual components in relationship to one another and the whole.

Treating the chapel as an integrated spatial environment, this study argues that its reliquary function generates the visual rhetoric of sanctity for Francis Xavier within the coordinated space of the chapel.[7] Specifically, the arm relic catalyzes defining episodes of Xavier's hagiography, culminating in his body's incorruptibility, which was evidence of his fervent devotion to Jesus Christ.[8] Though depicting only a few episodes from Xavier's life, the frescoes represent his missionary work in Asia, where he fought heresy by preaching, baptizing, and saving the faithful through miraculous intervention. This iconography symbolizes Xavier's imitation of Jesus Christ and the resulting power of his incorrupt corpse. Further, the precious metalwork objects specify Christ's centrality in Xavier's life, and the purposeful use of polychrome stone extends the evocation of his incorruptible body to the architectural framework. The elements of the chapel, therefore, work together to celebrate the strength of Xavier's arm. This precious relic—as index of (stand-in for) the saint's whole body—guides the viewer through the space, unifying the pictorial, architectural, and decorative design.[9] By analyzing and reassembling the disparate elements, this essay offers a new interpretation of the Chapel of Saint Francis Xavier: the "whole chapel" visualizes the rhetoric of Xavier's sanctity.[10]

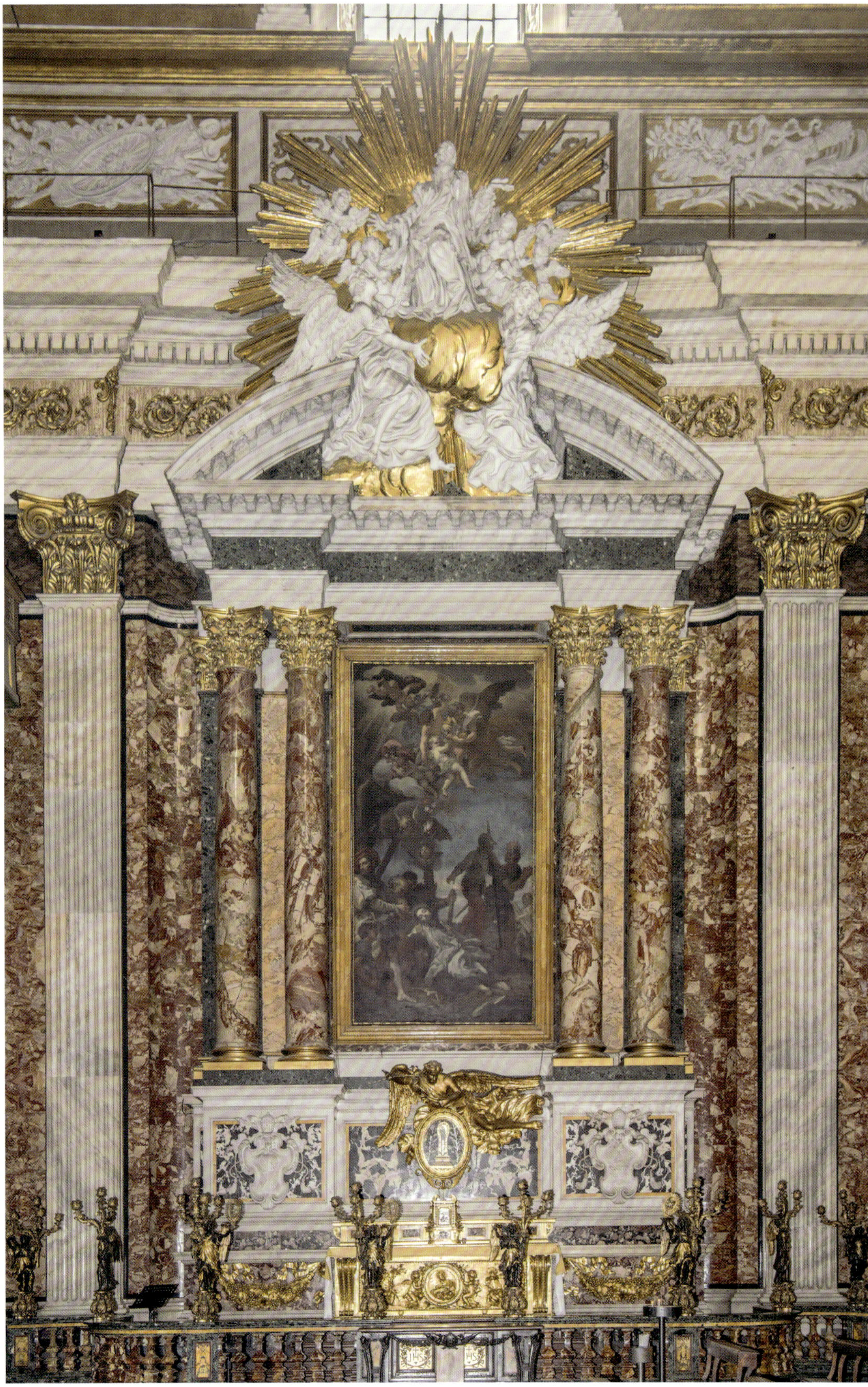

1

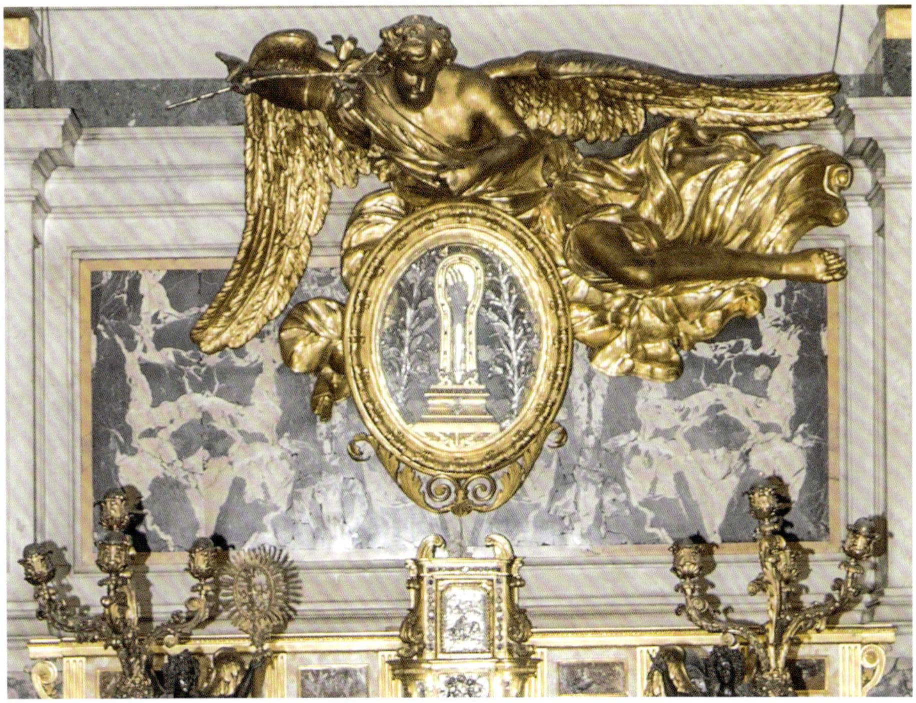

2

The Incorrupt Body of Francis Xavier

In many hagiographies, death is a defining moment, and in the case of Francis Xavier, the afterlife of the body accrues crucial significance. Central to his cult is his body's incorruptibility, which was first recognized when his intact body was disinterred three months after burial, and this grew in significance in the years leading to his canonization as his body worked miracles and proved his holiness. Indeed, incorruptibility is the defining feature of his hagiography and of his chapel in Rome.[11]

In March 1554, fifteen months after Xavier's death, his body was returned (from Malacca) to Goa, where it was found to be extraordinarily fresh and well preserved.[12] After news of Xavier's canonization reached Goa in 1624, it was moved into the Church of the Bom Jesus (constructed 1594–1605).[13] In 1636–1637, his body was placed in a new silver casket with removable reliefs covering crystal panels, through which the body could be viewed during its annual exposition on Xavier's feast day.[14] The Jesuits in Goa had always carefully controlled the faithful's access to the body, limiting exposure to protect the relic and heighten its value. This new feature of crystal windows offered an optimal solution, both restricting and providing access as appropriate.[15] As we shall see, the control and exposure of the body are issues in the Roman counterpart of this reliquary.

Xavier's earliest biographers, notably Orazio Torsellino and João de Lucena, stress that the miraculous preservation of the body was an indication of, and reward for, Xavier's imitation of Christ.[16] Subsequent hagiographies repeat the idea that God preserved the body and allowed it to work miracles, encouraging the display and veneration of the incorrupt corpse to facilitate these miracles.[17] The Chapel of Francis Xavier in Rome unites the principal features of the saint's hagiography: the relic of his incorruptible body, the episodes as-

FIG. 1. Chapel of Saint Francis Xavier, ca. 1672–1684. Il Gesù, Rome.

FIG. 2. Girolamo Lucenti, Arm reliquary of Saint Francis Xavier, 1679–1684. Chapel of Saint Francis Xavier, Il Gesù, Rome.

sociated with his ministry in Asia, represented in the frescoes, and the death of the saint off the coast of China, depicted in the altarpiece. Xavier's arm—both its physical presence and its role as an index of the saint—guides the viewer through the space and furthers an understanding of his significance as a missionary and founding member of the Society of Jesus.

Francis Xavier's Arm Relic and Reliquary

The most crucial component of the Chapel of Francis Xavier is the precious body-part relic (FIG. 2). Body-part relics—and the "speaking" reliquaries that encase them—embody the actions, gestures, and expressions of the human form. Associated with "the most communicative parts of the human body," they have been studied as a particular type.[18] While head reliquaries date to the ninth century, the earliest surviving arm reliquary is mid-twelfth-century.[19] Arm relics are capable of continuing the living acts of blessing, baptizing, and healing, as they "testify to the importance of sacred and imitable gesture."[20]

In the case of Francis Xavier's arm, we will see that the narrative frescoes repeat and reinforce these actions. The scenes depict the saint using his arm to preach to followers, bless the faithful, baptize the newly converted, stop the attacking infidels, and retrieve his miraculous crucifix. It is the role of the audience to recognize and identify the relic's significance, and here the paintings facilitate this process; this is executed by reading the paintings and associating them with the relic on the altar.[21] We must also consider the notion that the part represents the whole, a concept with origins in the fifth-century writings of Paulinus of Nola, who explained that a saint's power is present in every part, no matter how small or where it ends up.[22] Xavier's arm is not just his arm but the index of his whole body. In other words, "The relic is fragmentary, but its spiritual power is as strong as if it were whole."[23]

Francis Xavier's arm relic is the source of power in the chapel. In 1614, at Pope Paul V's request, Superior General Claudio Acquaviva ordered the Jesuits in Goa to send him a relic of the saint, specifically his right arm.[24] Even before the Society of Jesus was officially approved in 1540, Ignatius sent Xavier to India to initiate missionary work at the request of King João III of Portugal. In just more than a decade, Xavier traveled extensively, preaching and baptizing, ministering to Christians, and seeking to convert others. His right arm also was instrumental in his acts of healing the sick, restoring sight, and resuscitating the deceased. One purpose of the operation was to determine, once and for all, the incorruptibility of the corpse, but the body part chosen for the relic is significant because the arm recalls these and other works of ministry and miracles.[25] While many in Goa were less than enthusiastic about the task, given the quantity of relics already in Rome, later Jesuits regarded the request as extraordinarily meaningful.[26] In 1694, Antonio Vieira, noting the need for Xavier's arm relic to complement Ignatius's relics, in the left chapel of the Gesù, interpreted the significance: The saint's holiness would extend from "the east in Goa, head of the church in Asia, and the other in the West in Rome, head of the church and of the entire world."[27] Also of consequence is the long-held belief that the translation of relics was only possible with the "permission" of the saint.[28] The Jesuits had attempted to remove other parts of Xavier's body but were unsuccessful, whereas the saint's "permission" allowed them to succeed in amputat-

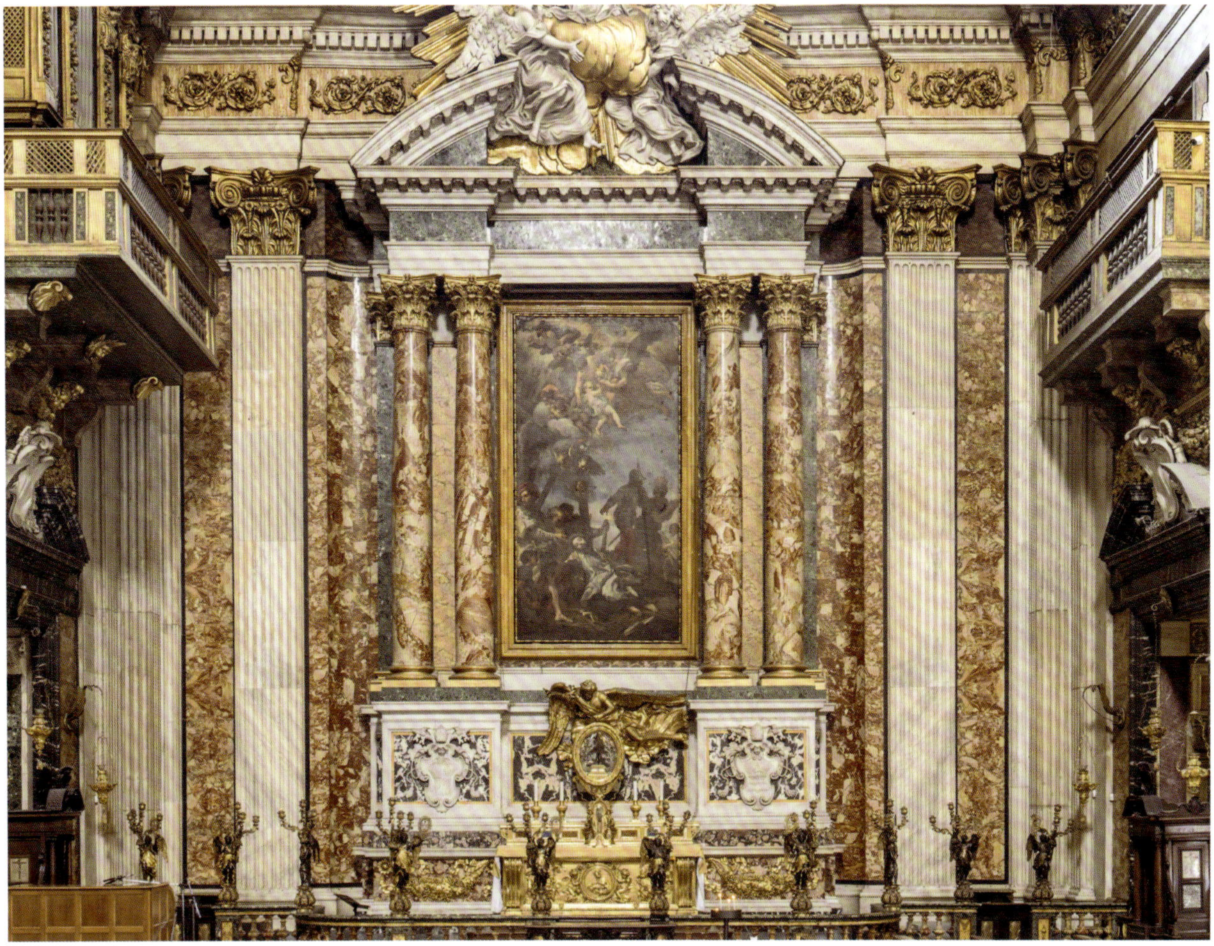

3

ing the arm.[29] This belief reinforces the power of the arm as a synecdoche of his missionary work and an index of the whole saint.

Understanding the relic's crucial role in the chapel, Monsignor Negroni commissioned a reliquary to visualize its primacy. In earlier centuries, relics were kept in reliquary cupboards or chests, away from public view, or concealed in reliquaries. They were brought out on feast days or other special occasions, to be carried in processions or displayed for short, fixed periods.[30] Only in the late Middle Ages are crystal or glass panels inserted into reliquaries to make the encased relics more visible.[31]

In the seventeenth century, Gian Lorenzo Bernini heightened the visibility of reliquary display by placing relics at the center of permanent and cohesive architectural designs, using rich materials with associative meanings. For instance, the *Cathedra Petri* encases the giant relic of Saint Peter's chair in a setting of alabaster, bronze, and gilded stucco, which spectacularly concretizes the miraculous appearance of the chair and promotes papal primacy.[32] Bernini's innovative designs of large-scale reliquary display inspired the installation of the relic in the Chapel of Francis Xavier.[33]

FIG. 3. Altar wall, ca. 1672–1678. Chapel of Saint Francis Xavier, Il Gesù, Rome.

In late 1678, the display of Xavier's arm relic became a matter of discussion between the Jesuits and Negroni. Letters suggest that the relic had been

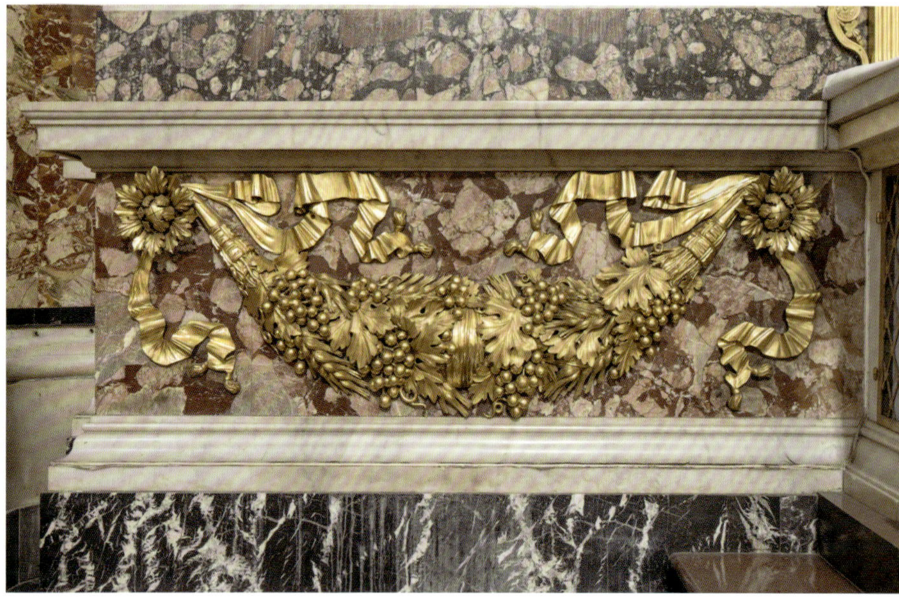

4

located below the altar, and Superior General Gian Paolo Oliva asked that it be moved above the altar. Negroni, who sought total control of the chapel, complied with Oliva's request and placed the relic in "a majestic box, protected by the air."[34] But the Jesuits were unsatisfied with the apparently wooden reliquary, whose ornamentation did not signify the relic's sanctity. At some point between the chapel consecration on February 13, 1679, and 1684, Negroni commissioned a reliquary from Girolamo Lucenti that met expectations for the material splendor of reliquaries. Moreover, in the permanent installation, "Lucenti's angel enacts the appearance of the most historically charged limb of the preacher and baptiser of the Indians' earthly activities, his arm."[35]

Based on Negroni's description of the reliquary (1702), it seems the one on display today is only partially original:

> the design of a medallion, of gilt bronze, the work of Lucenti, and this held by an angel in flight, also of gilt bronze, and the cavity of the medallion encloses the Holy Arm, between two large crystals, that cannot be opened, as is customary, the holy relic having suffered not a little, in the time of the saint's freedom, that he enjoyed, and therefore the Holy Arm remains restricted, with the accompaniment of the precious things, as it now appears.[36]

Negroni's words confirm that the gilt bronze angel and medallion are original but do not mention the inner encasement and decoration. They also confirm that the reliquary was sealed, as was customary to protect its authenticity, and was accompanied by its "accompagnamento pretioso," or jewels inside the medallion. A later inventory made before the despoliation by Napoleon's troops, in 1798–1799, lists the jewels "that are inside the oval [medallion]," left by the devoted. One gift was the large jewel of gold, enamel, diamonds, pearls, and other gems, representing Saint Michael and the Devil, donated by Cardinal Giovanni Alberto, prince of Poland, who died in 1621.[37] The date indicates that

FIG. 4. Socle with bronze relief of grapes and wheat, ca. 1672–1678. Chapel of Saint Francis Xavier, Il Gesù, Rome.

long before Negroni commissioned the new reliquary, the arm relic was the recipient of acts of devotion that took expensive, material form.

The inventory also describes the original silver-gilt container of the arm inscribed with Negroni's name: "This sealed and authentic case is embedded in the inside part in a silver gilt case, which is divided into two pieces, one that is all rays, covered by some gems, the other is the pedestal, where on the bas-relief is sculpted the brazier with flame that burns."[38] This description nearly matches an engraving published by Levy (FIG. 7), except that the engraving adds adoring angels flanking the silver-gilt case.[39] At Jennifer Montagu's suggestion, Levy proposed that the engraving might represent the cover of the medallion reliquary. However, the correlation between the inventory and the engraving seems to indicate that the image represents the original container of the arm relic inside the medallion. If that is correct, the engraving shows how the relic was perpetually visible while doubly protected and adorned by the inner partial encasement of the arm and the outer bronze medallion whose crystal faces allowed visual access.

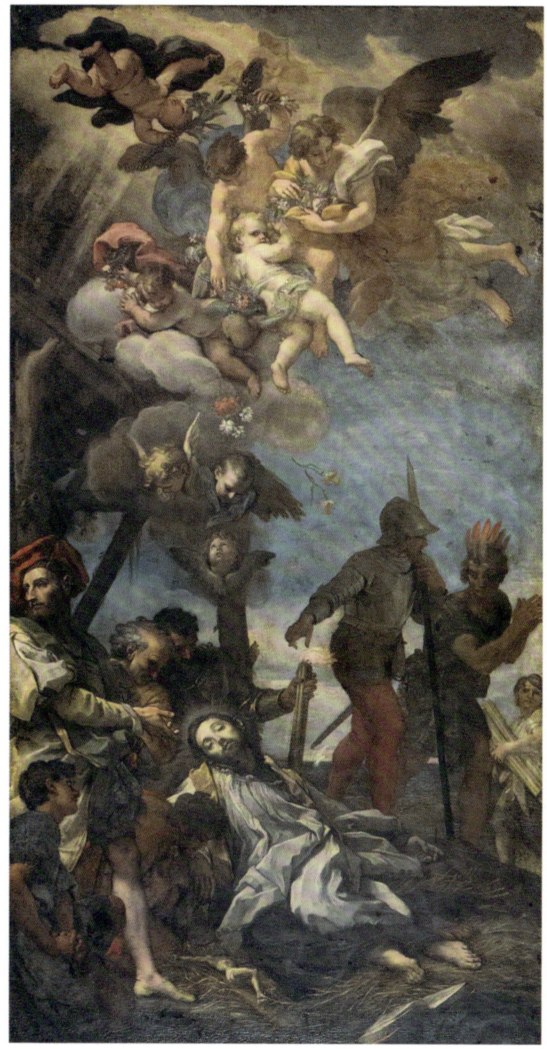

5

The making of the reliquary coincides with a major achievement in Monsignor Negroni's ecclesiastical career. In 1681, Innocent XI elected him treasurer general of the Camera Apostolica. The rich and visible treatment of the relic, indeed of the whole chapel, accords with Negroni's prominent status and his patronage ambitions. Contemporary to this commission was his acquisition (1682) of the Palazzo di Santa Lucia alle Botteghe Oscure (today Palazzo Caetani) from Girolamo Mattei.[40] Prelates of Negroni's status, which rose again in 1686 when he became cardinal, were expected to spend lavishly on devotional acts. Furthermore, the use of precious materials continues the long tradition of associating physical splendor and wealth with holy persons. Silver and other precious metals signaled the sacred because they were considered pure like saints, and the smelting process was analogous to purification by fire. Heat and flame were used in the process of making the arm reliquary, and they had particular meaning to Xavier because the symbol of the flaming heart, depicted on the original inner reliquary, represents his great love of God.[41] Pure metals were considered incorruptible; thus, the silver encasing Xavier's arm relic was as incorruptible as his body, protecting but revealing the charged limb of the saint.[42]

In 1680, General Oliva forbade further access to Xavier's corpse in Goa.[43] His decision was in response to reports that Xavier's remains, though incorrupt, were suffering from desiccation.[44] However, it also allowed the body part that had been removed to Rome to assume greater visibility and, thus, greater authority. That the decision about the body in Goa coincides with the perpet-

FIG. 5. Carlo Maratti, *Death of Saint Francis Xavier*, 1679. Chapel of Saint Francis Xavier, Il Gesù, Rome.

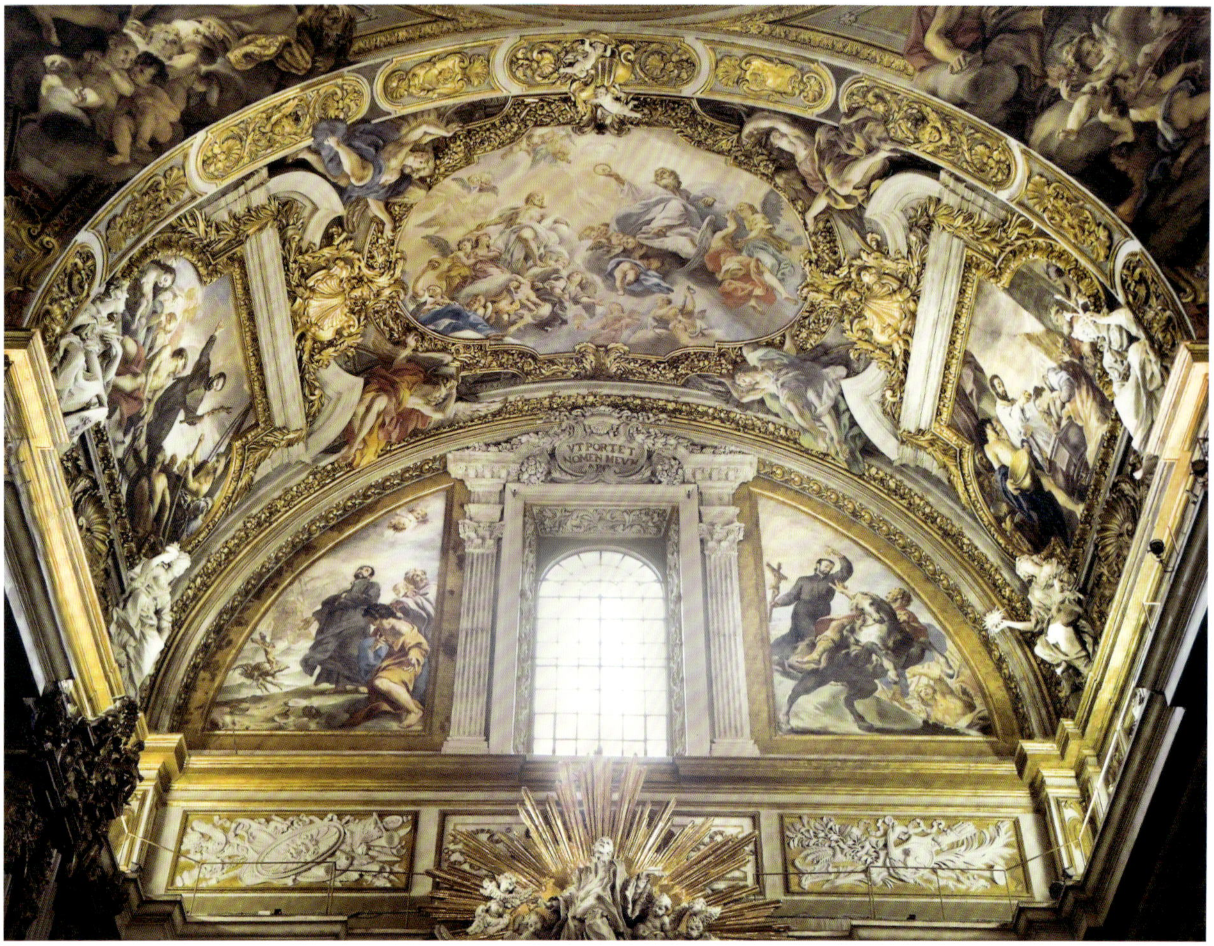

6

FIG. 6. Giovanni Andrea Carlone, *Life and Miracles of Francis Xavier*, ca. 1672–1674. Chapel of Saint Francis Xavier (vault and upper wall), Il Gesù, Rome.

ual exposure of the arm in Rome, therefore, may not be coincidental. Other components of the chapel—especially the body's representation in the altarpiece and the red-hued jasper stone of the architecture, considered in the next section—work with the relic to make present Xavier's miraculous body. The arm in Rome invokes the body in Goa, and together they remind the faithful of Xavier's spiritual relevance to both Europe and Asia.

From Reliquary to Reliquary Chapel

The Chapel of Francis Xavier functions as a reliquary chapel, a place to encase and display a relic, to construct the visual rhetoric of sanctity, and to promote reverence of the holy person. The relic in its container is the essential element, but the entire chapel with furnishings extends the reliquary function to the surrounding space.[45] Drawing upon the extensive scholarship of holy shrines and reliquaries, this argument places the chapel in an enduring tradition of cohesively assembled chapels concentrated on a powerful relic that began in the medieval period and continued in the early modern period.[46]

In promoting the cult of a revered saint through reliquary display, the Jesuits were following the practices of other orders such as the Franciscans. At

Il Santo in Padua, the Franciscans assembled the venerated relics of Saint Anthony in a powerful, rhetorical display promoting his thaumaturgic abilities (ca. 1470–1570).[47] In the left transept chapel, the saint's body rests in a sarcophagus that is "elevated on columns so that, as the early sources tell us, the sick and lame could be placed underneath it."[48] The installation focuses attention on the body relic and facilitates its posthumous healings. Like Anthony's body relic in Padua, Xavier's body in Goa rapidly became a cult site and the location of miracles. The Jesuits' decision to separate his right arm with hand and transfer this relic to Rome was an effort to share in his sanctity and led to the placement of the reliquary in a visible, permanent, and elevated position.[49]

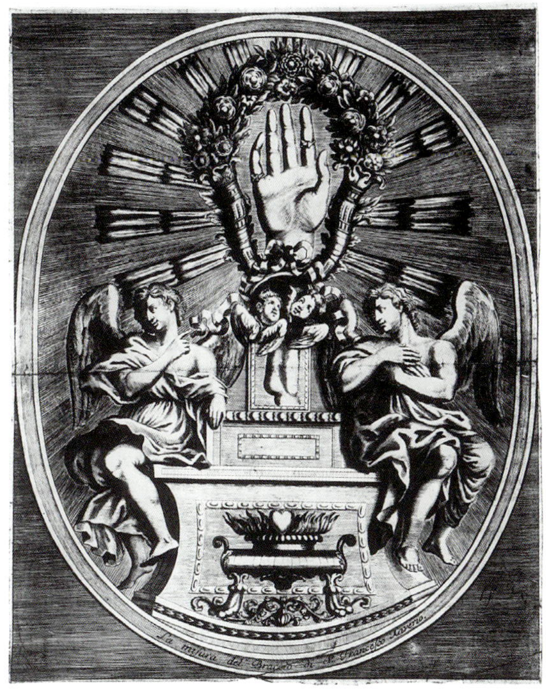

7

During the Catholic Reformation of the late sixteenth and seventeenth centuries, the fervent devotion to saints resulted in new dedications of buildings or segregated spaces within them to encase relics, much as smaller containers do. The Sistine Chapel in Santa Maria Maggiore, Rome (1585–1590), was designed as a cohesive, multimedia sacred space, in which the tombs and relics are coordinated with the painted and sculptural decoration to promote the cult of relics of Christ's crib, effectively constructing "Bethlehem in Rome."[50] Almost contemporary with the Chapel of Francis Xavier, Guarino Guarini's Chapel of the Holy Shroud in Turin was described in 1674 as a giant "reliquary case."[51] The specific use of materials, including polished black marble and bronze, and the space's geometric ornamentation surrounding the "sacred effigy of Christ" reinforce the function of the reliquary chapel and the political aspect of this royal chapel of the Savoy duchy.[52] Like these examples, the Chapel of Francis Xavier privileges the display of the reliquary, while depending on the coordination of all components "in creating or constructing the saint and his or her spiritual meaning for (and by) the viewer."[53]

The Architectural Design and Materials

Executed between 1672 and 1676, the architectural design and materials contribute to constructing the spiritual meaning of Francis Xavier's reliquary in the chapel. Despite Filippo Titi's attribution of the Negroni Chapel, in 1674, to Pietro da Cortona, the early sources leave the architect uncertain; however, Levy has convincingly argued that the architectural design represents the intelligent modification of a Cortona design by his stonecutter cousin Luca Berrettini, and Leone has developed the joint attribution by arguing for Berrettini's greater role in the invention through the selection, use, and meaning of the precious stone.[54] The architecture's organizing principle is the verticality of the altar aedicule (FIG. 3). Its plinth is broken into two projecting pedestals, on which are placed the double Corinthian columns that support the broken curved pediment. The curved wall and the colossal pilasters that support the main entablature visually frame and reinforce this central aedicule.

FIG. 7. Anonymous, Original cointainer of the relic of the arm of Saint Francis Xavier (engraving), seventeenth century. Archivum Romanum Societatis Iesu, Rome.

The architecture's vertical axis coordinates the components of the chapel into a unified entity and structures the chapel's meaning. The formal and iconographic linkage moves from the altar frontal up to the vault: from the *imago clipeata* ("materialized vision") of the deceased Francis Xavier, to the arm reliquary, then to the pictorial altarpiece of the saint's death, the stucco sculpture of the saint, and, finally, to the fresco of the Trinity in heaven (**FIGS. 1, 8**).[55]

Together, these stacked representations narrate the death and apotheosis of Francis Xavier, which prove his love of Christ as his spiritual motivation and the source of his sanctity. The saint's expiration is the main event. Maratti's altarpiece follows contemporary accounts of his death caused by fever while fervently contemplating the crucifix (**FIG. 5**). Xavier was awaiting the opportunity to spread his missionary work to China, on Sanchien Island, where conditions were difficult. The saint had eaten little, became ill, and developed a fever. For nearly two weeks, he passed in and out of consciousness. Despite this physical suffering, he maintained patience and cheerfulness and prayed. The account of his death by his Chinese Christian interpreter Antonio, which became the source of his early biographies, emphasizes his frequent invocations of Jesus's name, his prayers to the Trinity, and the constant fixation of his eyes upon the Crucifix.[56] These biographical details are represented in the altarpiece which dramatically depicts the limp body of the saint, in a pose that imitates and turns toward Christ's body on the Crucifix, to the saint's left near his knees. The saint's peaceful countenance and expired body contrast with the active drapery that implies his great spiritual fervor associated with his death. Above the saint and the surrounding onlookers—one of whom with feathered headdress and hands in prayer appears to convert upon the saint's death—are flower-bearing angels that signal God's immediate, welcoming response.[57]

The materialization of Xavier's body extends his death and its aftermath beyond the altarpiece. Below it, the saint is (partially) incarnate in the arm relic and, on the altar frontal, appears as the *imago clipeata*, which Bernini popularized in baroque art.[58] Above the altarpiece, his soul materializes in sculptural form as it rises through the pediment to the Trinity, to whom Francis Xavier was devoted, which is frescoed in the center of the vault. This glorious reception into heaven is the saint's reward for his devotion to Christ and the Trinity. The coordinated components of this vertical axis place on center stage the saint's death and apotheosis and together substitute for his miraculous incorruptible body.[59]

Through Luca Berrettini's expert work in stone, the central meaning of Xavier's incorruptible body and its powerful connection to Christ extend beyond the central axis into the structure and substance of the chapel. The symbolic use of stone follows a long tradition that began in antiquity and early Christianity, continued in medieval sacred spaces, and was reignited in early modern chapel design. The Christian custom of associating holiness and precious stones is epitomized in Revelation 21:18–21, where the heavenly Jerusalem has walls of jasper, sapphire, emerald, amethyst, and other stones. Thus, the rich materials used in medieval reliquaries and shrines signify and authenticate the sanctity of the holy person and the relic. Medieval writings compared saints to precious stones, and body part reliquaries like Xavier's arm reliquary fuse them.[60] In early modern Rome, the Cappella Gregoriana in St. Peter's (1572–1584) revived the medieval tradition of ornamenting holy spaces with marble revet-

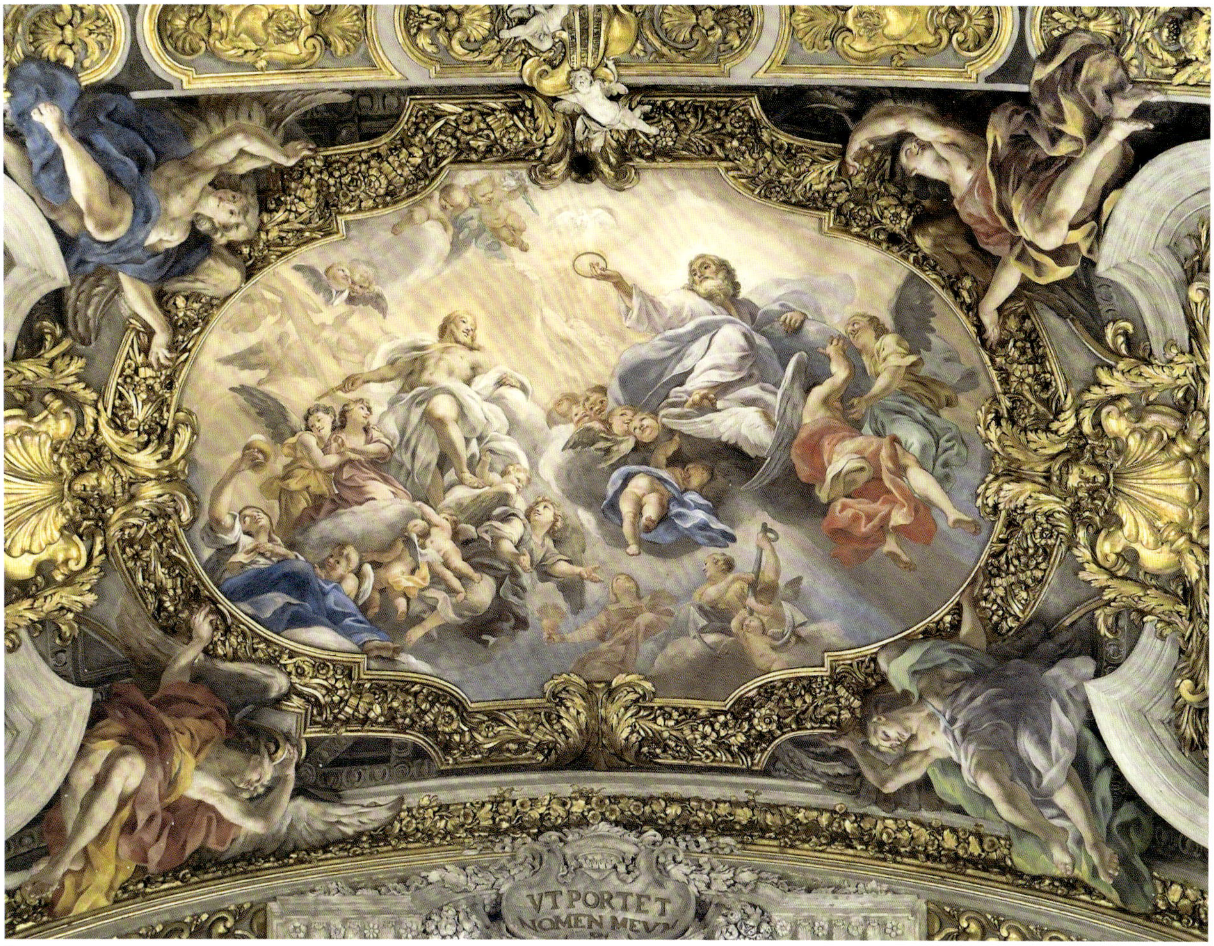

8

ment, furnishing physical evidence of Church history.[61] A century later, when Negroni agreed to renovate the Chapel of Francis Xavier, polychrome stone had become de rigueur in noble chapels.[62]

The Gesù lacked this ennobling treatment of marble revetment. Even the transept chapels dedicated, after 1622, to the Jesuits' principal saints, Ignatius of Loyola (left) and Francis Xavier (right), did not meet expectations for the visual rhetoric of holy spaces.[63] At the Gesù, the need to express devotion through material splendor might have been pressing as Jesuit churches in Palermo, Antwerp, and Naples outpaced the mother church.[64] In Naples, in the second quarter of the seventeenth century, the transept chapels dedicated to Francis Xavier in both the Gesù Vecchio and the Gesù Nuovo were ornamented with beautiful and expensive polychrome revetment.[65] This city also boasted the Treasury Chapel of San Gennaro, which contains its patron saint's blood relic and other relics in silver bust reliquaries. Helen Hills draws a symbiotic relationship between the Treasury Chapel's lavish silver and bronze objects, made through the physical process of transformation, and its key relic, San Gennaro's blood which transforms through liquefication to express divine presence and protection. This relationship infuses the silver bust reliquaries with "the promise of the glory of the saint's body transfigured for eternity, re-

FIG. 8. Giovanni Andrea Carlone, *The Trinity Welcoming Saint Francis Xavier into Heaven*, ca. 1672–1674. Chapel of Saint Francis Xavier, Il Gesù, Rome.

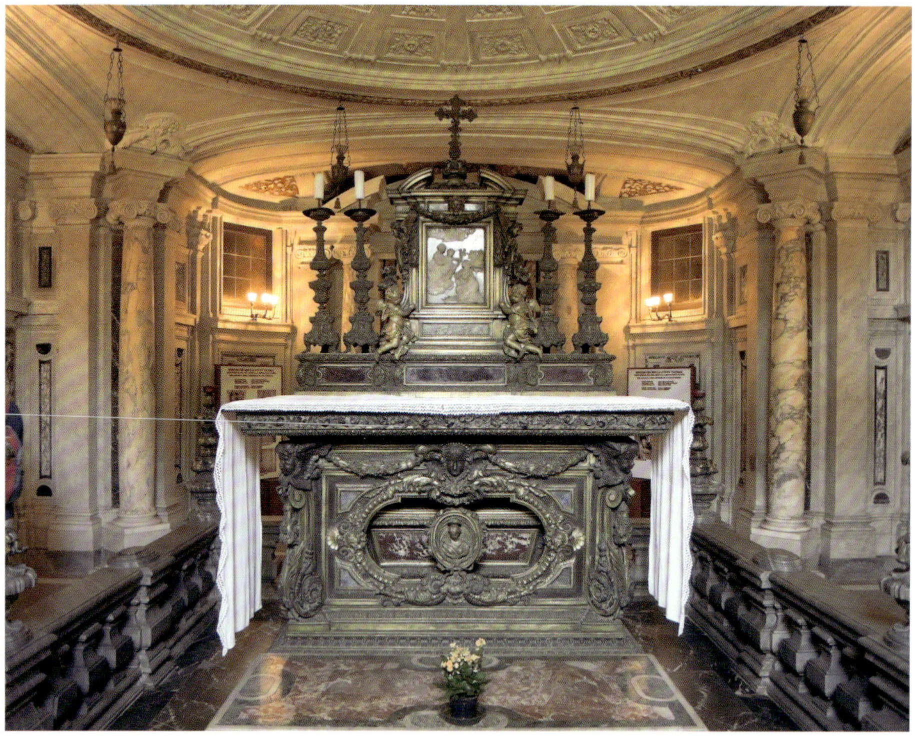

9

united with the soul, on earth and in heaven."[66] Similarly, the materials selected for the Chapel of Francis Xavier in the Gesù embody meanings specific to this saint.

Monsignor Negroni's patronage transformed the Chapel of Francis Xavier into a space that signified its special function as a reliquary chapel through its material splendor. Despite conflicting information about Negroni's willingness to be the chapel's patron, Oliva's letter of 1672 underscores the patron's fervent devotion to the relic, and his later insistence on controlling the relic's display confirms its vital role.[67] The material of hardstone—a visible sign of God—embeds the spiritual meaning of the relic in the space of the chapel.[68] The four columns and the wall revetment (FIG. 1) are *diaspro di Sicilia* (jasper). *Giallo antico* and *verde antico* are used for the pilasters behind the columns. The socles (FIG. 4) supporting the columns are made of, from bottom to top, *bianco e nero antico*, *portasanta*, *africano*, and again *bianco e nero antico*. The frieze of the aedicule is *verde antico*, and the frieze of the main entablature is alabaster.[69]

These hardstones conjure the heavenly Jerusalem, and the expensive jasper is a notable choice. Although we do not know with certainty who made the selection, Berrettini might have suggested it to the Jesuits or Negroni since he was an expert in hardstone.[70] Jasper is among the few stones mentioned in Revelation that could be obtained in monumental blocks to be cut into pieces to veneer columns and walls, which was impossible with gems such as sapphires, emeralds, and amethysts. Although the categorization of stones was nebulous, the value of semiprecious jasper derived in part from its association with these more valuable gems. Grand Duke Ferdinando de' Medici, whose workshops were famous for manufacturing objects of hardstones and gems,

FIG. 9. Pietro da Cortona, Reliquary altar of Saint Martina, ca. 1640–1650. Confessio Chapel, SS. Luca e Martina, Rome.

was obsessed with jasper. Emulating Philip II's "chapel of jasper" at the Escorial outside Madrid, Ferdinando I obtained large quantities of jasper from Tuscany, Corsica, and Sicily to use in his Cappella dei Principi, the Medici funerary chapel in Florence.[71] In the Chapel of Francis Xavier, the jasper unites the heavenly Jerusalem with the earthly container of the saint's body, blending spirit and matter as occurs during every Mass. It also has a specific connection to Xavier's biography, because, according to Albertus Magnus's *Book of Minerals*, it cures fevers.[72] Although there is no evidence that this specific meaning was intentional, viewers familiar with this well-known treatise might have made this association.

Through the animate nature of stones, the polychrome revetment associates the chapel's architecture with Xavier's incorrupt body. Since antiquity, stones were understood as being animate, like human beings, because both were divinely made. Lapidary materials were nature's flesh and blood. As such, ancient sculptors used stone to imitate the human body; the example par excellence is the use of purple-veined Phrygian marble to sculpt the battered body of the flayed Marsyas. In the early modern period, Pliny the Elder's popular *Natural History* continued to disseminate the concept of lapidary materials as imitating God's creation.[73] Drawing upon the tradition of stone as flesh and blood, Berrettini might have selected an abundance of stones with red hues (*diaspro di Sicilia*, *africano*, and *portasanta*) to evoke Xavier's corporeality which is *represented* in the altarpiece and *present* in the arm reliquary.

The profusion of Eucharistic imagery in the chapel—in one case overlaid on red-hued stone—supports this suggestion that the lapidary materials might have been chosen to conjure corporeality, both Xavier's and Christ's. The gilded reliefs of grapes and wheat on the red *portasanta* socles (FIG. 4), framing the altar, symbolize Christ's human sacrifice, which is reenacted in the Eucharistic sacrifice during every Mass at this altar. The baroque ciborium that holds the host continues the Passion imagery with the silver reliefs of Christ in the Garden at Gethsemane and angels holding symbols of the Passion.[74] Alighting on the balustrade, the bronze angels hold Christ's IHS monogram.[75] The references to Christ and his blood point to Xavier's devotion to the savior, his own incorruptibility, and the role of his blood in proving the miracle of his body. Xavier's blood made repeated appearances to attest to his body's defiance of deterioration, the first being the bloodstains on the white surplice that was placed on the saint's body to prepare it for burial.[76] Although Francis Xavier was not wearing the surplice at the time of his death, Maratti depicted the dying saint in this vestment.[77] In the space of the chapel, the altarpiece, the metalwork objects, the polychrome revetment, and the relic work together to produce the perception of Xavier's continuous miracle—his body's real presence—conjuring from the part in Rome the whole body in Goa.[78]

The Cortona-Berrettini enterprise followed an established practice of architects who used their expertise in stone to design polychrome architecture.[79] Other reliquary chapels by Cortona, with Berrettini as stonecutter, furnish evidence that this team selected polychrome stone for its potential meanings. In the 1640s and 1650s, Cortona designed and Berrettini (in part) executed the rich subterranean chapel of Santa Martina, in the church of Santi Luca e Martina.[80] The polychrome marble walls and columns enclose the elaborate gilt-bronze altar, raised on two steps of white-veined black marble and surrounded by the gray-streaked marble balustrade. Inside the altar table is the urn that contains the precious relic of Martina's partial skull (FIG. 9). Visually communicating Martina's sanctity, the materials stage the heavenly Jerusalem, from the hardstone walls to the gilt-bronze altar with its martyrdom imagery of cherubim, flower garlands, and palm fronds and the lapis lazuli, amethyst, and other stones. The deep red *portasanta* of the urn evokes the mortal remains contained within. Martina's relic assumes figural form in the altar's imagery: the urn has the *imago clipeata* of the saint, and the marble relief above the altar table represents the Virgin Mary and Christ receiving Martina into heaven, set against a lapis lazuli sky. The iconography and the materials evoke Martina's transformation from earthly mortal into heavenly saint. The Cortona-Berrettini enterprise repeated a similar, though less intricate, use of materials to encase another hidden martyr, whose body rests in the *portasanta* altar urn of the Chigi Chapel in Santa Maria della Pace (1656–1658).[81] Contemporaneously, Bernini used colored marble to represent the natural and divine realms, for instance, in the Cornaro Chapel of Santa Maria della Vittoria.[82] Building upon these precedents and experiences, Berrettini employed colored stone as a medium to visualize Xavier's incorruptibility in the Chapel of Francis Xavier.

The Frescoes

Soaring above the polychrome architecture of the Chapel of Francis Xavier, the five frescoes on the upper walls and vault (FIG. 6) reveal the most significant aspects of the iconography of the saint, especially in relation to his relic housed there. Here we aim to clarify the scenes depicted and offer a substantive analysis of them, as they have not been carefully or accurately identified in earlier scholarship and have never been evaluated appropriately.[83] These frescoes, although limited in number compared to other pictorial cycles of the saint, effectively illustrate the key aspects of Xavier's missionary work and miracles in Asia.[84] Based in the Portuguese city of Goa, the Jesuits' missionary base on the west coast of India, Xavier spent a great deal of time in southern India; his ministry is especially connected to the pearl fishery coast in Tamil Nadu and the coast of Travancore. The frescoes in Xavier's chapel primarily celebrate his missionary work in India, while recognizing his accomplishments in other parts of Asia, notably Indonesia and Japan. From the reliquary on the altar below, his right arm guides the viewer's attention to the painted decoration where it figures prominently. Thus, the scenes were selected to model the actions of the missionary saint, representing how Xavier's arm "performed" in life and how it continues to motivate the faithful.

From around 1672 to 1674, Giovanni Andrea Carlone (1639–1697) painted the five frescoes, two flanking the window and three in the vault. Carlone, an artist from Genoa, was likely selected by the patron Negroni due to their shared roots in that city.[85] Along with the representation of the saint's death in Maratti's altarpiece, these episodes of Xavier's missionary works are frequently included in the major (painted and sculpted) life cycles and printed *vite* of Xavier.[86] However, the selection of these specific scenes—and only these scenes—reveals that they were chosen for what they say about the saint as a model missionary and their relationship to the relic on the altar.

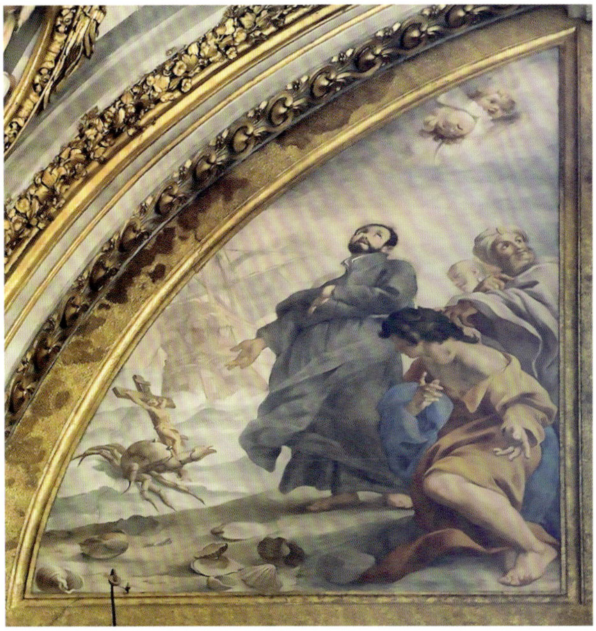

10

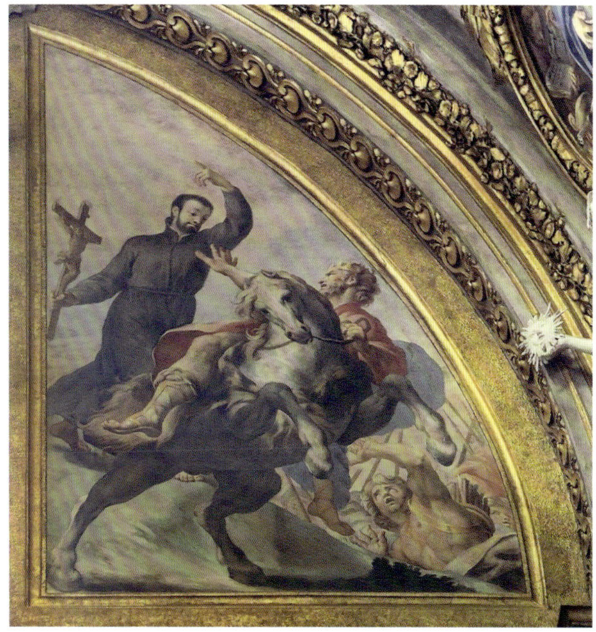

11

Flanking the window are two scenes depicting Xavier's miracles, the *Miracle of the Crab* (**FIG. 10**) and *Francis Xavier Driving Back the Badagas* (**FIG. 11**). Representing the power of the crucifix, they highlight his devotion to Jesus Christ. In the vault of the chapel, instead, are representations of Xavier engaged in the primary activities of his missionary work: *Francis Xavier Preaching to the Pearl Fishers* (**FIG. 12**) and *Francis Xavier Baptizing the Princess Neachile* (**FIG. 13**). These narratives flank the central scene of the *Trinity Welcoming Xavier into Heaven*, which links the frescoes to the works of art directly below. Francis Xavier is represented not in the Trinity fresco but in the stucco figure just below. As we have seen, this figure, like the *imago clipeata* on the altar frontal, embodying the saint's soul, connects Xavier's body—depicted in the altarpiece and encased in the gilded reliquary—to his reception into heaven.[87]

The *Miracle of the Crab* (**FIG. 10**) is one of the most commonly depicted scenes of Xavier's life, to the extent that the motif of the crab may be found in iconic representations of the saint, such as portraits.[88] In 1546, Xavier traveled through Indonesia; during his exploration of this territory, he sailed to two islands reportedly inhabited by headhunters called *alfuros*.[89] He was accompanied by Portuguese trader Joao Raposo and soldier Fausto Rodrigues. En route to the islands of Waranula and Seram, the boat encountered stormy seas. Xavier took hold of the crucifix, worn on a rope around his neck, and plunged it into the waters, asking God to calm them. His request was granted, but not before the boat's motion tore the crucifix from its rope and the saint lost hold of it. He thought it was lost forever, but when the group finally arrived on Seram, they discovered a crab walking along the beach toward them with the crucifix in his claw. Xavier, who as a missionary had never been without this potent symbol of his devotion to Christ, was grateful to have it back. During the process leading to Xavier's beatification, Rodrigues gave testimony of this great miracle.[90] Here Carlone focuses the composition on Francis Xavier, who gazes

FIG. 10. Giovanni Andrea Carlone, *Miracle of the Crab*, ca. 1672–1674. Chapel of Saint Francis Xavier, Il Gesù, Rome.

FIG. 11. Giovanni Andrea Carlone, *Francis Xavier Driving Back the Badagas*, ca. 1672–1674. Chapel of Saint Francis Xavier, Il Gesù, Rome.

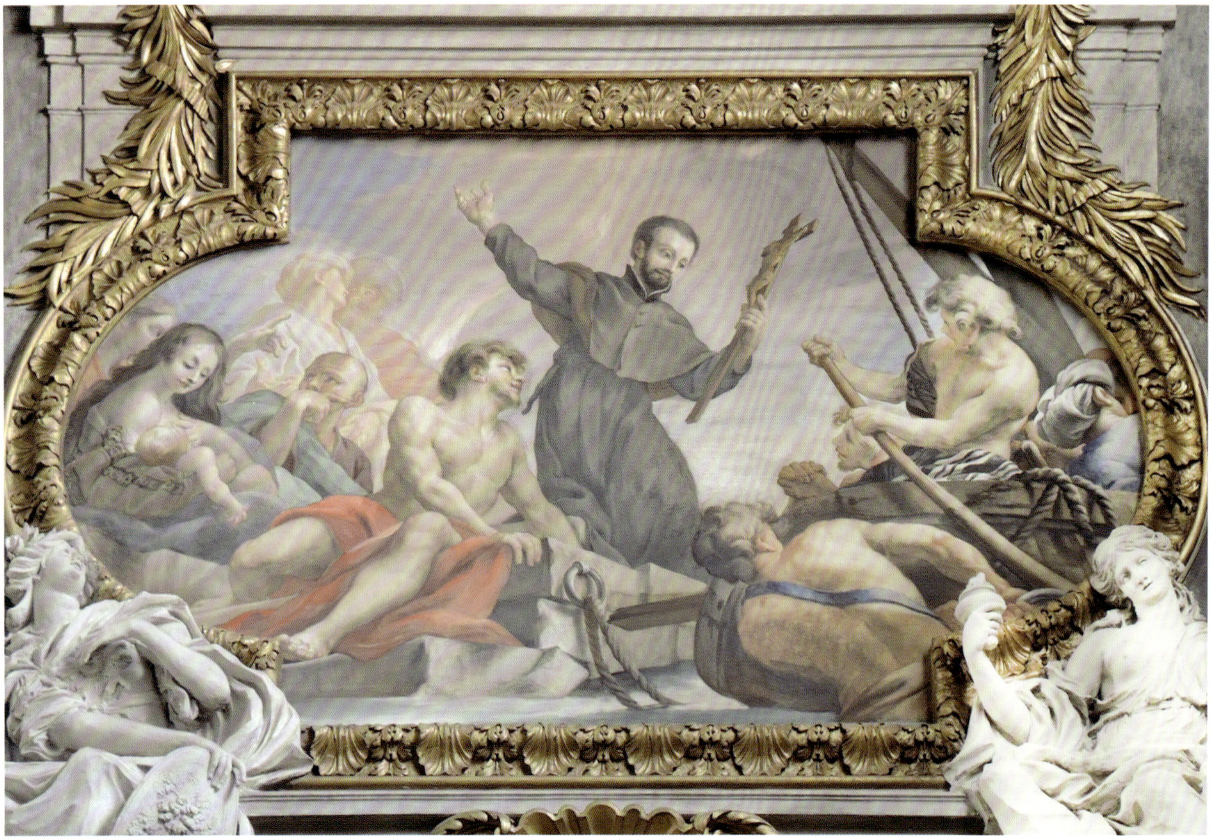

12

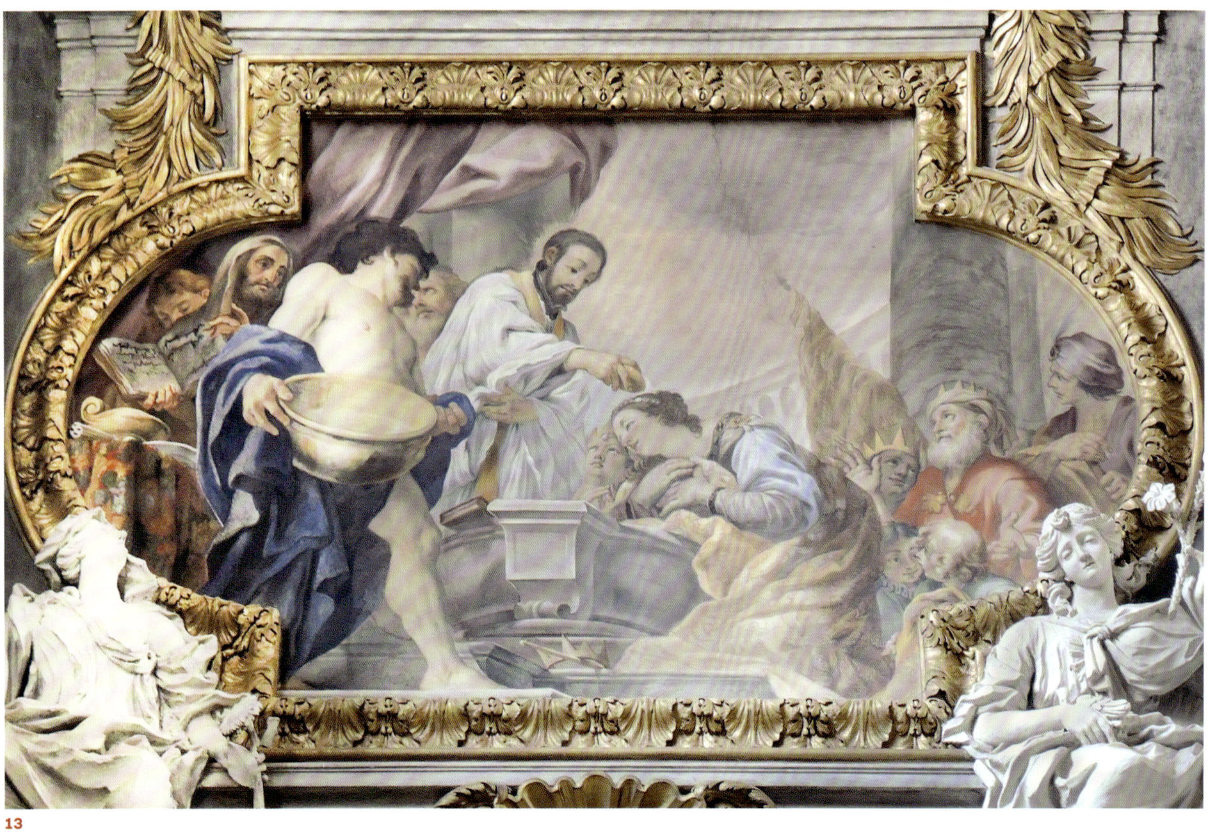

13

heavenward in gratitude for the crab's return of the crucifix, placed on the left in front of the ship. His companions and witnesses occupy the right edge of the painting, with the foreground figure (presumably the youthful Rodrigues) staring at the crab in disbelief.

The opposite fresco shows the Muslim challenge that Xavier faced in the Cape Comorin area (Travancore) of southern India.[91] In the year 52, Saint Thomas introduced Christianity into this area; during his first years in India centuries later, Xavier cultivated these Christians and converted many more.[92] The conflict between the Muslim Badagas and the Christians revolved around not only religion but also commercial interests, with both groups striving for control over fishing on this coast. The Badagas spent the summer of 1544 attacking the Christians, and Xavier devoted a great deal of time to protecting them. For months, soldiers had been unable to defeat the Badagas. Finally, Xavier strode into their midst, shouting at them and brandishing his crucifix, and repelled them. Here Carlone shows one Badaga already thrown to the ground and a second one attempting to hold off the calm yet strident Xavier, while being thrown from his rearing horse. The missionary earned the admiration and gratitude of not only the resident Christians but also a local king who gifted Xavier with a house and a church. Like the *Miracle of the Crab*, this scene is included in most major artistic cycles and printed *vite* of this period, representing a significant miracle, emphasizing the significance of Christ's guidance, and underscoring the ongoing fight against heresy.

The two side sections of the chapel's vault depict the most important undertakings of the missionary saint: preaching and baptizing (FIGS. 12–13). While representing these activities in a general manner, both use a specific episode of Xavier's interaction with the people of India to highlight his character as a missionary. As mentioned above, the Christians of the Pearl Fishery Coast were among those particularly cultivated by Xavier.[93] The left section of the vault illustrates Xavier preaching to the pearl fishers. He raises his crucifix as he gestures broadly while speaking to the fishermen, who are poised just on shore or still in their boats holding their oars. A woman holding a baby leans in from the left-hand edge of the painting, likely a reference to Xavier's resuscitation of the child who had drowned in a well, an event that took place at Cape Comorin.[94] Jacopo Curzietti identifies this scene as *Francesco Saverio accoglie a Macao la nave dispersa nella tempesta* (*Francis Xavier Welcomes to Macao the Ship Lost in the Storm*).[95] While Xaverian iconography includes numerous episodes involving ships—Xavier transformed sea water into fresh on one notable occasion, calmed storms with prayer, and steered ships safely away from pirates—the event in Macao is not especially well known or specifically represented in any other cycle. We argue, instead, that this fresco emphasizes the act of preaching. Aspects of the scene are similar to those in other representations, most notably an engraving from an illustrated *vita* of the saint (Rome, 1793) (FIG. 14), in which the caption identifies the subject as Xavier "Preaching to the Barbarians on the Fishery Coast."[96] This engraving similarly includes a mother and child at the edge of the scene and a group of figures listening to the preaching. In addition, Xavier's ministry to the pearl fishers was a particular focus of his time in India. They had become Christians in the late 1530s, prior to Xavier's arrival, but his discovery that they actually knew very little about Christianity prompted him to devote time to teaching them catechism and guiding them

FIG. 12. Giovanni Andrea Carlone, *Francis Xavier Preaching to the Pearl Fishers*, ca. 1672–1674. Chapel of Saint Francis Xavier, Il Gesù, Rome.

FIG. 13. Giovanni Andrea Carlone, *Francis Xavier Baptizing Princess Neachile*, ca. 1672–1674. Chapel of Saint Francis Xavier, Il Gesù, Rome.

in proper spiritual beliefs. This fresco highlights Xavier as preacher and illuminates the manner in which his arm gestures and blesses in that role and his particular devotion to the pearl fishers of southern India.

The right side of the vault features Xavier's arm in the act of baptism. Biographies of the saint describe the large numbers of baptisms he performed in Asia, and pictorial cycles represent both general scenes and baptisms of specific individuals.[97] This scene has traditionally been identified as the baptism of the princess Neachile, underscoring the Jesuit practice of converting the elites of society in order to encourage the rest of the population to follow suit. Here the three kings surround the princess at her baptism; her own crown has been removed and sits at her feet. Accounts of Xavier's life identify his meetings with, and conversions of, numerous kings, and artistic representations often depict their baptisms. One in particular was Dom Manuel Tabarija, king of Ternate, who may be one of the kings portrayed here; he was the son of Neachile.[98] Other illustrations of Xavier's missionary work are described more generally as preaching to or baptizing "heathens" or "Indians," although it should be noted that the term "Indies" is often used to characterize any number of places where Jesuit missionaries labored, including Naples.[99] While Xavier does not hold the crucifix in this scene of baptism, as he does in all of the other frescoes, his action does emphasize the use of his right arm—the relic possessed by the Jesuits and displayed in this chapel.

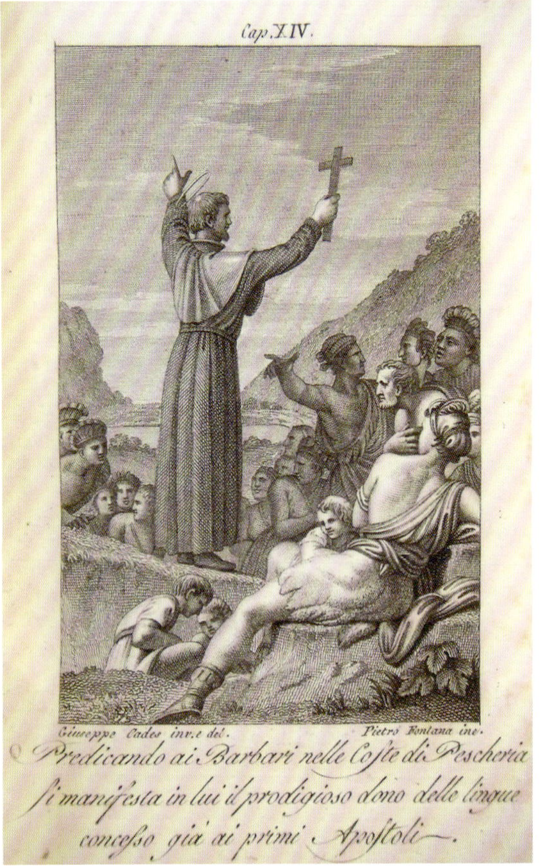

14

FIG. 14. *Preaching to the Pearl Fishers* (engraving), in Giuseppe Massei, *Compendio della Vita di S. Francesco Saverio della Compagnia di Gesù*, Roma 1793. Jesuitica Collection of John J. Burns Library, Boston College.

Together, the four episodes from the life of the missionary saint painted in this chapel showcase the saint actively using his arm and hand: blessing and gesturing while preaching, baptizing, holding the crucifix to work miracles, and reaching for that crucifix as it is returned to him after working another miracle. With the arm relic placed below the frescoes, they reinforce the actions that Francis Xavier performed in life, reminding the faithful of his missionary activities, miracles, power to heal, and incorrupt body. They also highlight the crucifix, held by Xavier in his missionary work, which reminds the viewer of Jesus Christ's significance to the Jesuits, who, from their very foundation, have regarded him as their companion. For Xavier, far from home, often alone or among unfamiliar persons and languages, Christ's companionship must have been especially important and comforting.

This chapel is home to the most significant part of the saint's body outside Asia, and although the narratives include limited scenes depicting his life and miracles, they were very carefully selected. The question of how the scenes were determined and why other events may have been omitted must be considered. As indicated earlier, other early modern *vite* and pictorial cycles typically include a dozen or more episodes, illustrating scenes of Xavier's life as well as his miraculous acts. Given what we know about the program for the entire chapel, we can envision how Negroni and the Jesuits thoughtfully considered how to effectively convey the salient points of the saint's life and miraculous acts and to designate which ones would have been most appropriate. There are two Roman works that would have been known to the Jesuits and should be considered as possible inspirations. The *Theatrum in Ecclesia* engraving, depicting the theater erected in St. Peter's for the 1622 canonization, features four small representations of Xavier's miracles in the upper right corner.[100] The engravings of Valérien Regnard document the (now lost) paintings celebrating Xavier's miracles, hung in the Gesù during the canonization festivities.[101] Both depict Xavier's principal miracles, with the four in the *Theatrum in Ecclesia* engraving—Xavier transforming salt water into fresh water, the resuscitation of a dead man, the raising of a boy who had drowned in a well, and the miracle of the crab—all repeated in Regnard's engravings.[102] Despite the prominence of the resuscitation scenes listed in the canonization bull and in these engravings connected to the canonization festivities, the frescoes in the Chapel of Francis Xavier do not include those miracles.[103] They focus instead on those missionary activities and miracles directed by the arm relic and emphasize the everyday actions of the missionary rather than the extraordinary ones. Like the other components of the chapel, the narratives work together to instruct and motivate the viewer, with the arm as a constant and consistent reminder of the incorruptible body as index of the saint.

Conclusion

The chapel persuasively verifies and celebrates the life, sanctity, and legacy of Francis Xavier for the Roman audience, a view that is essential to understanding how in the seventeenth century the Society of Jesus commemorated one of the first Jesuit saints in Rome. The focus on Xavier as missionary is constructed through the relic of his right arm with hand, extracted from his incorrupt corpse in Goa and brought to Rome to serve as the locus of his cult in the Society's principal church. The frescoes highlight Xavier's dedication to day-to-day missionary activities—baptizing the converted, preaching with crucifix in hand, and combatting heretics—as opposed to the miracles of healing and resurrection emphasized in other pictorial cycles of the period. The careful selection of stone and the vertical force that lifts the viewer's eyes from Xavier's earthly body to his welcome into heaven by the Trinity extend his story and its Christological meaning throughout the chapel. Following the founding principles of the Society of Jesus, Xavier emulated Christ in proselytizing and saving, and for his great devotion to this difficult and dangerous work, he was rewarded with incorruptibility. The coordinated design of the whole reliquary chapel motivates the Roman audience to reflect upon the crucial role of the Jesuit missions and its members as companions of Christ in the era of reform. As Vieira astutely observed in 1694, Xavier's arm relic—as index of his body—extends the spiritual value of his work in Asia back to Europe, allowing for his cult to be celebrated across the globe.[104]

Notes

1 — Levy 1999–2000, 381, 387: "dovesse sempre illustrare, qualificare, et arricchire, non l'altare solo, ma la cappella tutta." Trevisani (1980), first identified Negroni's patronage.
2 — Levy 1999–2000, 381–382.
3 — Levy (1999–2000) analyzed the chapel's patronage and architectural design within her study of the master plan to renovate the Gesù from 1672 to 1685.
4 — Schaar 1968; Trevisani 1980; Fischer Pace 1998; Levy 1999–2000; Leone 2013–2014.
5 — Curzietti 2011, 126–128. Scholars who mention but do not analyze the iconography include Pecchiai 1952, 275; Levy 1999–2000, 382–383; Dionisi 2004, 80; Levy 2018, 148.
6 — The primary bibliography on the chapel is Schaar 1968; Trevisani 1980; Fischer Pace 1998; Levy 1999–2000, 377–393; Leone 2013–2014, 452–457; Levy 2018, 148–151.
7 — The bibliography on chapels as integrated spatial environments is extensive, but especially salient here is Hahn 1997a. She demonstrates that medieval saints' shrines were carefully coordinated into a "visual rhetoric of sanctity that condenses holy past and sacred present within the particularities of a given space" (1997a, 1079). See also Palazzo 2010.
8 — For a comprehensive biography, see Schurhammer 1973–1982.
9 — Our approach is informed by Massimo Leone's concept (2014, esp. 54–55) of a relic as "an index of the body" and the "indexical relation between the sacred and a piece of its 'body.'"
10 — See n. 1 above.
11 — Gupta 2014, 27–77.
12 — Pinch 2011, 114. See also Brockey 2015, 47–48.
13 — For the state of the body from 1554 to 1624, see Gupta 2014, 27–77. On the Bom Jesus, see Osswald 2013.
14 — Schurhammer 1965; Osswald 2008.
15 — Gupta 2014; Brockey 2015, 54–60. For the elaborate marble base of the tomb, commissioned by Cosimo III de' Medici and sent from Florence in 1698, see Conforti 1991; Fleming 2020, forthcoming.
16 — Brockey 2015, 54–55, on Torsellino's biography (Rome, 1594) and that of Lucena (Lisbon, 1600).
17 — Pinch 2011; Brockey 2015, 55.
18 — The literature is extensive, but the fundamental study is Braun 1940. See also *Gesta*'s 1997 thematic issue (esp. Hahn 1997b); Hahn 2010a, 166–167; Hahn 2012, 134–141. For the quotation, see Cornelison 2004, 650.
19 — Maayan-Fanar 2006, 247–248.
20 — Hahn 2010a, 166.
21 — Hahn 2010b, 291.
22 — Hahn 2012, xiii.
23 — Maayan-Fanar 2006, 248. See also Hahn 1997b, 28.
24 — Gupta 2014, 66; the right arm was chosen because Xavier had used it for baptisms. The lower half (with hand) was shipped to Rome, whereas three pieces of the upper arm were later sent to Cochin, Malacca, and Macao. Brockey 2015, 41, 57.
25 — Gupta 2010, 86.
26 — Brockey 2015, 41–42.
27 — Vieira's sermon is quoted by Brockey 2015, 42.
28 — Geary (1978, 132–133) examines the notion that a saint could not be moved if he was unwilling. This justification is connected to many relic translations in the Middle Ages.
29 — Brockey 2015, 42.
30 — Angenendt 2010, 25–26. See also Palazzo 2010, 104–105.
31 — Bagnoli 2010, 141.
32 — Barry 2011, 602–604, on Bernini's contribution to this typology.
33 — Levy 1999–2000, 388.
34 — Levy 1999–2000, 385–386. The letter is preserved in the Jesuit Archives in Rome: Archivum Romanum Societatis Iesu (ARSI), Rome, 143, II, fol. 519 (modern pagination) and is published by Levy 1999–2000, 414, doc. 6.
35 — Levy 1999–2000, 386–387.
36 — Levy 1999–2000, 386, n. 17: "il disegno d'una medaglia, di Bronzo dorato, opera di Lucenti, e questa sostenuta da Angelo a volo, tutto egualmente di Bronzo dorato, e nella concavità di essa medaglia, restò racchiuso poi il Santo Braccio, frà due grandi Cristalli, da non potersi più aprire, così di conventione, havendo la santa Reliquia patito non poco, nel tempo della santa libertà, che godette, e così restò ristretto l'istesso santo Braccio, con l'accompagnamento suo pretioso, come appunto ora comparisce."
37 — Pecchiai (1952, 276, n. 1, 343–346) published the inventory.
38 — Pecchiai 1952, 344: "Questa cassa sigillata ed autentica sta incastrata dalla parte di dietro in una custodia d'argento dorato, che è divisa in due pezzi, uno ch'è tutto raggi, coperti con qualche gioia, l'altro è il piedestallo, dove a bassorilievo è scolpito un focone [braciere] con fuoco che arde."
39 — Levy 1999–2000, 387, fig. 14.
40 — Canepa 2007, 13–23.
41 — For representations of Xavier's flaming heart, see Vlam 1979, 48–49.
42 — On this dual function of reliquaries, see Bagnoli 2010, 138.
43 — Levy 2018, 150–151.
44 — Gupta 2014, 130.
45 — Levy (1999–2000) discusses the centrality of the relic to Negroni's chapel but does not argue that the whole chapel is a reliquary.
46 — For more on reliquary chapels that seamlessly integrate all elements of design, construction, and decoration, see Hahn 1997a. A key medieval example is the thirteenth-century Sainte-Chapelle in Paris (Cohen 2015). A notable early modern example is the "large-scale reliquary" for Saint Antoninus (d. 1459) in the renovated church of San Marco in sixteenth-century Florence (Cornelison 2012, 47–48).
47 — For more on the relics, miracles, and display of Saint Anthony, see McHam 1994, 7–16. The authors thank Sally Cornelison for suggesting this comparison.
48 — McHam 1994, 10.
49 — Gupta 2014; Brockey 2015.
50 — Ostrow 1996, 5–62. Its successor is the Pauline Chapel across the transept. Ostrow 1996, 118–183; Barry 2011, 603–604. As examples of exceptional chapels housing relics, tombs, and sacred images in this period, Cornelison (2012, 149) cites the St. Antoninus Chapel, San Marco, Florence; St. Anthony Chapel, Il Santo, Padua (1497–1594); Cappella Gregoriana, St. Peter's (1572–1584); and the Sistine Chapel. For more on relics in the early modern period, see Hahn 2017, 150–211.
51 — Scott 2003, 136, 374, n. 34.
52 — Scott 2003, 136.
53 — Hahn 2010b, 288–289, 311.
54 — Levy 1999–2000, 388–393; Leone 2013–2014, 452–457. See also Titi 1674–1763 [1987], 100; Trevisani 1980. The attribution to Cortona and Berrettini, however, continues to lack consensus. Cerutti Fusco and Villani 2002, 323–325; Merz 2008, 229. Canepa (2007, 18) found Negroni's account books that cite the architect Giacomo Costanzi, but his role and relationship to Berrettini have yet to be clarified.
55 — Levy (1999–2000, 391–393) analyzes the vertical architectural form but does not expand upon its iconographic

consequences. This discussion was developed by Leone 2013–2014, 454–455; and Levy 2018, 149.
56 — Schurhammer 1973–1982, 4, 640–643.
57 — Fischer Pace 1998, 220–228.
58 — Wittkower 1997, 262–263. The altar frontal was made by silversmith Giovanni Giardini (1646–1722), who also made the tabernacle. Canepa 2007, 18.
59 — On the substitution of the body in the chapel, see Leone 2013–2014, 455; Levy 2018, 149–150.
60 — Hahn 1997a, 1083–1084; Bagnoli 2010, 137–147.
61 — Ostrow (1990) was the first to make this point. See also Ostrow 2000, 241–243, and Fabio Barry's essay in this volume.
62 — Barry 2011, 552–652, with earlier bibliography.
63 — Levy 1993, 53–78; Levy 1999–2000, 375; Mormando 2018.
64 — For the churches in Palermo and Antwerp, respectively, see Hills 1999, 197–244; Knaap 2016.
65 — At the chapel in the Gesù Vecchio (1630–1654), Cosimo Fanzago was the sculptor. At the Gesù Nuovo, Giuliano Finelli, Donato Vannelli, and Antonio Solaro were responsible for the stone revetment (1642–1655). Pane 1984, 324, 331.
66 — Hills 2013, 57.
67 — Levy 1999–2000, 378–388, 412 (doc. 2).
68 — On the concept of materials producing (rather than representing) meaning in early modern chapels, see Nagel 2011, 261–285, on the high altar of Vicenza Cathedral (1534); Hills 2013 and Hills 2016, on the Treasury Chapel of San Gennaro, Naples.
69 — We thank Fabio Barry for help with identifying the stones.
70 — On Berrettini's role in the chapel, see Leone 2013–2014. On the purchase of the jasper, see Levy 1999–2000, 380–381.
71 — On the Cappella dei Principi and jasper, see Morrogh 2017, esp. 567–575.
72 — Albertus Magnus ed. 1967, II, ch. 8, 100.
73 — On the meaning of hardstone in antiquity and the early modern period, see Hills 1999, 35–40; Barry 2011, 54–61, 556–571; Barry 2016, 43.
74 — Pecchiai 1952, 276.
75 — Canepa 2007, 18.
76 — Gupta 2010, 85; Gupta 2014, 27–77; Brockey 2015, 52.
77 — Levy (2018, 149–150) is the first to interpret this important detail.
78 — On the relationship between the part and the whole body, see Brockey 2015, 62.
79 — Del Pesco 2016, who studies Giovanni Antonio Dosio (1533–1611) and Domenico Fontana (1543–1607).
80 — On the building history and architectural design (but without interpreting the materials and reliquary function), see Merz 2008, 61–65.
81 — Benedetti 2006, 113118; Leone 2013–2014, 449–450.
82 — Gallavotti Cavallero 2006; Barry 2009, 18; Barry 2016.
83 — For previous, cursory mentions of the frescoes and inconsistent identifications, see Pecchiai 1952, 275; Levy 1999–2000; Dionisi 2004, 80; Curzietti 2011, 126–128; Levy 2018, 148.
84 — Most other early modern artistic cycles or printed illustrations of Xavier contain at least a dozen images. Among the key works are Johann Bussemacher's "Wundervita" print (Cologne, ca. 1600) with fifteen vignettes around a portrait of Xavier; Andre Reinoso's cycle of twenty paintings in the sacristy of Sao Roque, Lisbon (1619); Valérien Regnard's set of twenty engravings documenting the paintings hung at the Gesù for his canonization celebration (Regnard ca. 1622); and the thirty-two relief panels on the silver casket of the saint's body in the Bom Jesus, Goa (1636–1637). Printed illustrated *vite* of the seventeenth and eighteenth centuries include up to forty-seven images; see Torres Olleta 2009.
85 — Trevisani 1980, 364; Curzietti 2011, 69–70, 124–128. For more on Carlone and his previous relationship with the Jesuits, see Rice 2018, 234–235.
86 — See n. 84 above. Curzietti (2011, 125–128) does briefly refer to Xavier's biographies.
87 — This representation parallels that of Saint Andrew in Sant'Andrea al Quirinale, Rome.
88 — One example is Marcos Orozco's engraving in Francisco Colin's *Labor evangelica, ministerios apostolicos de los obreros de la Compania de Jesus, fundacion y progressos de su provincia en las Islas Filipinas* (Madrid, 1663), in which the full-length figure of Xavier stands on an island, with the crab and his crucifix in the sea below him. The engraving is illustrated in Leone 2010, 413.
89 — Schurhammer 1973–1982, 3, 93–99.
90 — Schurhammer 1973–1982, 3, 98–99. Leone (2010, 409–410) also analyzes this episode.
91 — Schurhammer 1973–1982, 2, 439–456 (esp. 441–443).
92 — On Saint Thomas the Apostle in India and the Christian community established there, see Županov 2005, esp. 35–110; Županov 2018, 238–268.
93 — Schurhammer 1973–1982, 2, 311–321.
94 — For more on this miracle, see Schurhammer 1973–1982, 2, 345–346.
95 — Curzietti 2011, 127.
96 — Massei 1793, chap. XIV. For more on this *vita*, see Mormando and Thomas 2006, 81–104.
97 — Schurhammer (1973–1982, 2) recounts many baptisms performed by Xavier in India. Almost all pictorial cycles and *vite* noted earlier include at least one scene of baptism.
98 — See Schurhammer 1973–1982, 2, 250–254, for more on these persons.
99 — For a substantive examination of this issue, see Miller 2019. Prosperi 1982 has considered the multifaceted characterization of "the Indies."
100 - Anselmi 2005, 251–255, esp. fig. 295; Osswald 2002, 270–271; Casale 2011.
101 – *S. Francisci Xaverii Ind: Apli Societatis Iesu Quaeda Miracula* (Rome, after 1622) includes nineteen images, plus a title page. Elorza 1994. Regnard also produced a companion set of engravings depicting the miracles of St. Ignatius. Fleming 2012.
102 - Regnard's engravings are also believed to be the source for the silver relief panels on Xavier's casket in the Bom Jesus, Goa. Schurhammer 1965; Županov 2012; Fleming 2020, forthcoming.
103 - Of the four miracles represented in the *Theatrum in Ecclesia* engraving, only the miracle of the crab is incorporated into the chapel frescoes. However, Regnard's engravings include the subjects of all four frescoes and the *Death of Xavier* in the altarpiece.
104 - See n. 27 above.

A Chapel in Dialogue

THE CYBO CHAPEL IN SANTA MARIA DEL POPOLO

Fabrizio Federici

Although the Cybo Chapel in Santa Maria del Popolo (FIG. 1) is probably the most significant Roman monument entirely conceived and carried out during the pontificate of Innocent XI Odescalchi (1676–1689), the number of studies on it remains limited. Critics, among them notably Hellmut Hager, have examined the chapel primarily from an architectural perspective and for its significance in the career of its architect, Carlo Fontana;[1] less attention, however, has been given to the sumptuous decoration that characterizes the interior of the chapel.[2]

The purpose of this essay is twofold: on the one hand, it offers a precise reconstruction of the development of the project, based on various types of archival sources (payments, letters, and diary entries); on the other hand, it provides a detailed analysis of the chapel's pictorial imagery, tombs, and marble decorations in relation to the ambitions, taste, and strong personality of the patron, Cardinal Alderano Cybo (1613–1700)[3] (FIG. 2). Through this review and analysis of the history of the chapel's construction and decoration, it will be possible to point to a series of close connections between the Cybo Chapel and other significant spaces—based on emulation, allusion, and complementarity—which were purposefully created to celebrate the dual glory, civil and ecclesiastical, of the Cybo family. I will return to this "dialogue" between the chapel and other monuments later in this essay.

To reconstruct the history of the Cybo Chapel, we need to start from a few years before the actual beginning of the work. After the death of Pope Clement X Altieri (1670–1676), Cardinal Benedetto Odescalchi was elected pope on September 21, 1676, with the name of Innocent XI. At the time, Cardinal Alderano Cybo was one of the most prominent members of the College of Cardinals and had been one of the favored candidates when the conclave began. With Odescalchi's election, Cardinal Cybo lost any chance of earning a papal tomb in St. Peter's basilica; he therefore must have turned his thoughts to the family chapel in Santa Maria del Popolo as his final resting place and begun considering the possibility of renovating it. The new pope, out of gratitude for Cybo's mediation in his favor during the conclave and in the name of their long friendship, rewarded him with the post of secretary of state. This led to a marked increase in Cybo's income, encouraging him to intensify his activity as collector and patron of the arts and making his ambitious plans for the new chapel easier to attain.[4]

Soon, however, the relations between Pope Innocent XI and the cardinal soured, and Cybo's actual role as secretary of State became purely nominal.[5] The two figures were of profoundly contrasting character and taste, as evidenced by a comparison between the cardinal's ambitions for his chapel and the pope's virtual indifference toward the arts. While Cybo was having his funerary chapel built and decorated, Rome was permeated by a rigorous, "neo-Tridentine" cultural atmosphere imposed by the new pope. The cardinal employed the best artists active on the Roman scene to work on his magnificent monument at the same time that the Odescalchi pope was showing outright hostility toward artistic and sumptuary expenses.[6] Innocent's view was that gold was better spent on opposing the Ottoman empire, which was becoming increasingly a threat. The beginning of the work on the chapel neatly coincides, in fact, with the Turkish siege of Vienna (1683). The ideological climate of the Odescalchi pontificate is therefore the context in which the project

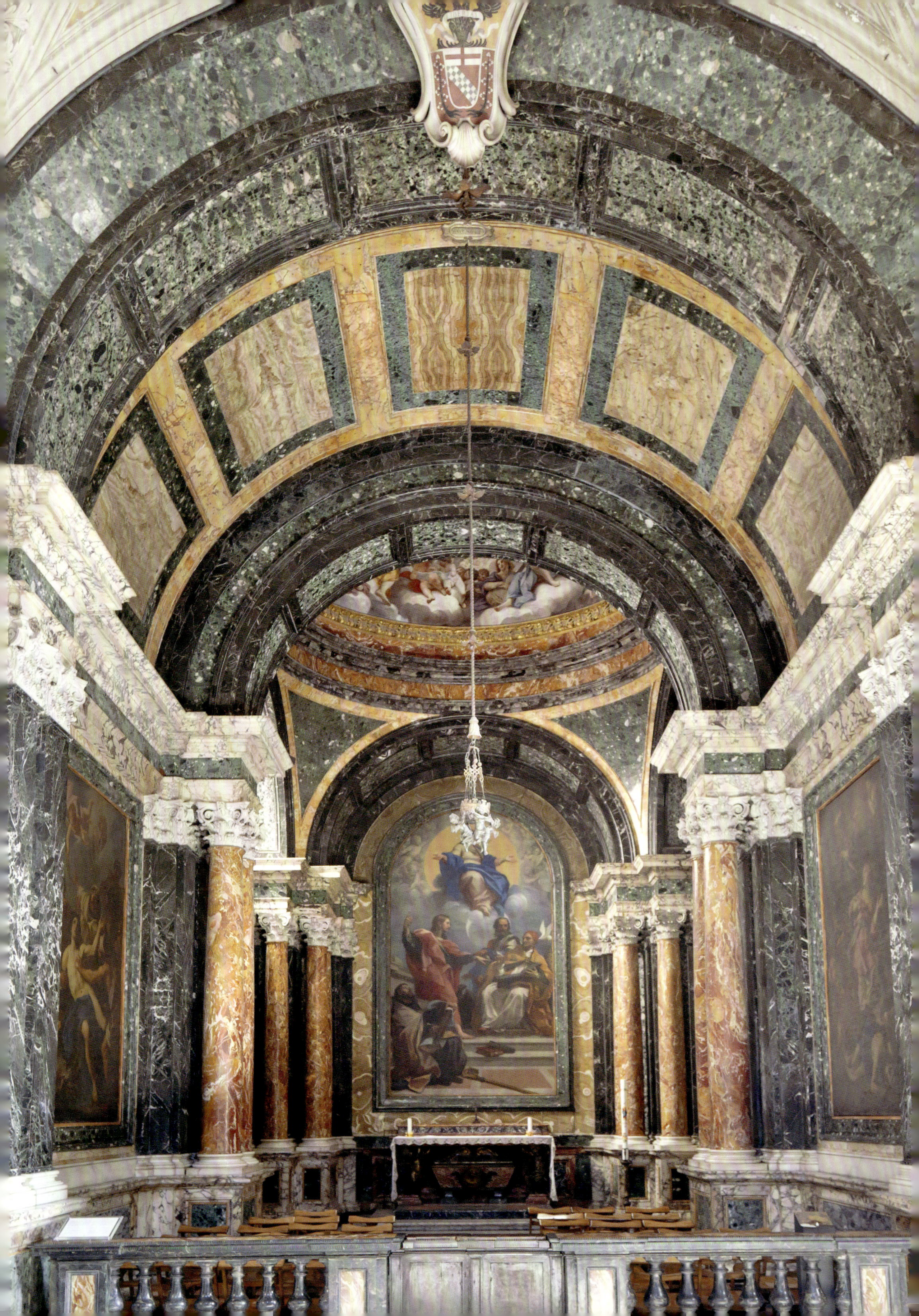

was conceived and launched—a context in which the Cybo Chapel must be seen as a form of radical dissension against the pope and his attitude toward the arts, a demonstration, in other words, of Cardinal Alderano's desire to participate in and extend the long tradition of patronage that had engendered the magnificent series of aristocratic chapels in the churches of Rome.

The chapel in Santa Maria del Popolo of which the Cybo had the *jus patronatus*—the second on the right from the entrance—was first built by Cardinal Lorenzo De Mari Cybo, nephew of Pope Innocent VIII (1484–1492), in the very early 1500s.[7] Its original decor must have been very similar to that of the other Renaissance chapels that open onto the side aisles of the basilica. It had a polygonal apse and was decorated with frescoes by Pinturicchio (who, with the help of collaborators, also frescoed other chapels in the church),[8] and hosted the funerary monument of Cardinal Lorenzo (FIG. 3), which, as correctly suggested by Francesco Caglioti, was sculpted in 1506–1507 by the Milanese Matteo Pellizzone, who was commissioned to carry out the work by the executors of the cardinal's will.[9] In the course of the sixteenth century, some funerary monuments to Genoese aristocrats were added to the chapel, that of Odoardo Cicada in 1545 and the marble and bronze tomb slab of his nephew, Cardinal Giovanni Battista Cicada, in 1570.[10] On July 12, 1605, the *jus patronatus* of the chapel passed from Ansaldo De Mari to the great-grandfather of Cardinal Alderano Cybo, Alberico I Cybo Malaspina, prince of Massa.[11]

To renovate the chapel, Cardinal Alderano turned first, in 1679, to the aging Gian Lorenzo Bernini, whom he had known since 1640, the time of Alderano's first stay in Rome.[12] Bernini's involvement is attested by an anonymous drawing in the Royal Collection at Windsor Castle, featuring a sketch of a tomb for a cardinal and the note: "Drawing made by cavalier Giovan Lorenzo Bernini, aged 81, for one of the tombs in the chapel that Cardinal Cybo was creating in Santa Maria del Popolo."[13] But on November 28, 1680, Bernini died, and the project came to nothing.[14]

At this point, Cardinal Alderano turned to Carlo Fontana, the best architect in Bernini's entourage.[15] A first project, filled with Berninian reminiscences, called for a chapel with a circular plan. Through a series of intermediate steps, however, Fontana veered toward a much more classical solution, one that excluded any curving walls and called for a Greek-cross plan and a dome, preceded by a rectangular vestibule and animated by no fewer than eight pairs of freestanding columns (FIG. 4). The inside was to be decorated by a luxurious lining of various polychrome marbles: black-veined marble (*portoro*), *verde antico*, *giallo antico*, *pavonazzetto*, white Carrara marble, and alabaster. The sixteen columns were to be of Sicilian jasper. These choices were clearly influenced by Cardinal Alderano, whose family ruled Carrara with its famous marble quarries[16] and who used polychrome marbles for all of the altars he commissioned, showing a particularly discerning judgment in this field.[17] And Fontana was ideally suited for implementing his patron's wishes. A few years earlier, the architect had richly decorated the interior of the Ginetti Chapel in Sant'Andrea della Valle with colored marbles—a project begun in 1671 but not consecrated until June 11, 1684, by Alderano Cybo himself.[18] In the Ginetti Chapel, the prominence of the marble revetment and sculptures over all other types of decorations astounded visitors[19] and no doubt influenced the decoration of the new Cybo Chapel.[20] At the same time, a collector of paintings like Alderano could

FIG. 1. Cybo Chapel, Santa Maria del Popolo, Rome.

not have a chapel without painted images, and thus a successful balance was achieved between marble decoration and painting. For the latter, the cardinal secured the services of the most famous painter of Rome, Carlo Maratti, to whom he entrusted the altarpiece, while two other notable artists, Luigi Garzi and Daniel Seiter, were assigned, respectively, the fresco on the vault of the dome and the paintings on the two lateral walls in the vestibule.

While the old Cybo Chapel was dedicated to Saint Lawrence, the new one was to be dedicated to the Immaculate Conception of the Virgin, to which Alderano, cardinal protector of the Franciscan Order, had a special devotion, as evidenced by the many images of the Virgin in his apartment and the paintings of the subject he commissioned.[21] In particular, in the same years in which the Cybo Chapel was being built, Alderano sent to Jesi an *Immaculata* attributed to Giacinto Brandi,[22] and for the altars in the transept of the church of San Francesco in Massa, he commissioned two paintings by Luigi Garzi, the *Disputation on the Immaculate Conception* and *The Holy Trinity and Saints*.[23]

It is difficult to fix an exact date for the actual beginning of the work on the new chapel. While the documents relating to the purchase of the materials and notices in contemporary sources would suggest 1682, a note in the *Chronicon* of the Augustinians of Santa Maria del Popolo reads as following: "1680. Cardinal Alderano Cybo presently began to decorate the chapel."[24] This, however, was probably a reference to the removal of some of the artworks from the chapel of Cardinal Lorenzo before its demolition—notably a portion of Pinturicchio's frescoes depicting the *Virgin and Child*, to which we will return below. The Cicada tombs were also removed and, after having been radically resized, were transferred to another chapel in Santa Maria del Popolo, the one dedicated to Santa Rita in the right transept of the church.[25] The funerary monument to Cardinal Lorenzo, without the *gisant* (now lost), was donated in 1685 by Alderano to the Franciscan tertiary minors of the convent of San Cosimato in Trastevere, to be used as an altar in their church.[26]

The chapel of Cardinal Lorenzo was therefore demolished between 1680 and 1681, and work on the new chapel must have begun immediately thereafter. For the materials and workforce, Cardinal Cybo proceeded in two ways. Like many Roman nobles and prelates of the time, he turned to the Reverenda Fabbrica di San Pietro (of whose congregation he had been nominated prefect in December 1679).[27] But he also independently acquired, in particular from Sicily and Carrara, some types of marble and had skilled stonemasons sent to Rome from his homeland.

The first deliveries of materials explicitly meant for the chapel arrived in the latter half of 1682.[28] On August 3, the stonemason Marcello Bigieri received from the Fabbrica five "pieces of travertine" which were to serve "for the work on the chapel of his high Eminence Signor Cardinale Cibo which he is having made in the church of Santa Maria del Popolo."[29] These were later followed by other deliveries of the same material.[30] It is clear that between 1681 and early 1682, the walls of the chapel had been finished, and workers had begun to line with travertine the lantern and the low tambour of the dome, as well as to decorate the exterior of the chapel's walls (whose aspect was later completely transformed by Giuseppe Valadier in the nineteenth century).

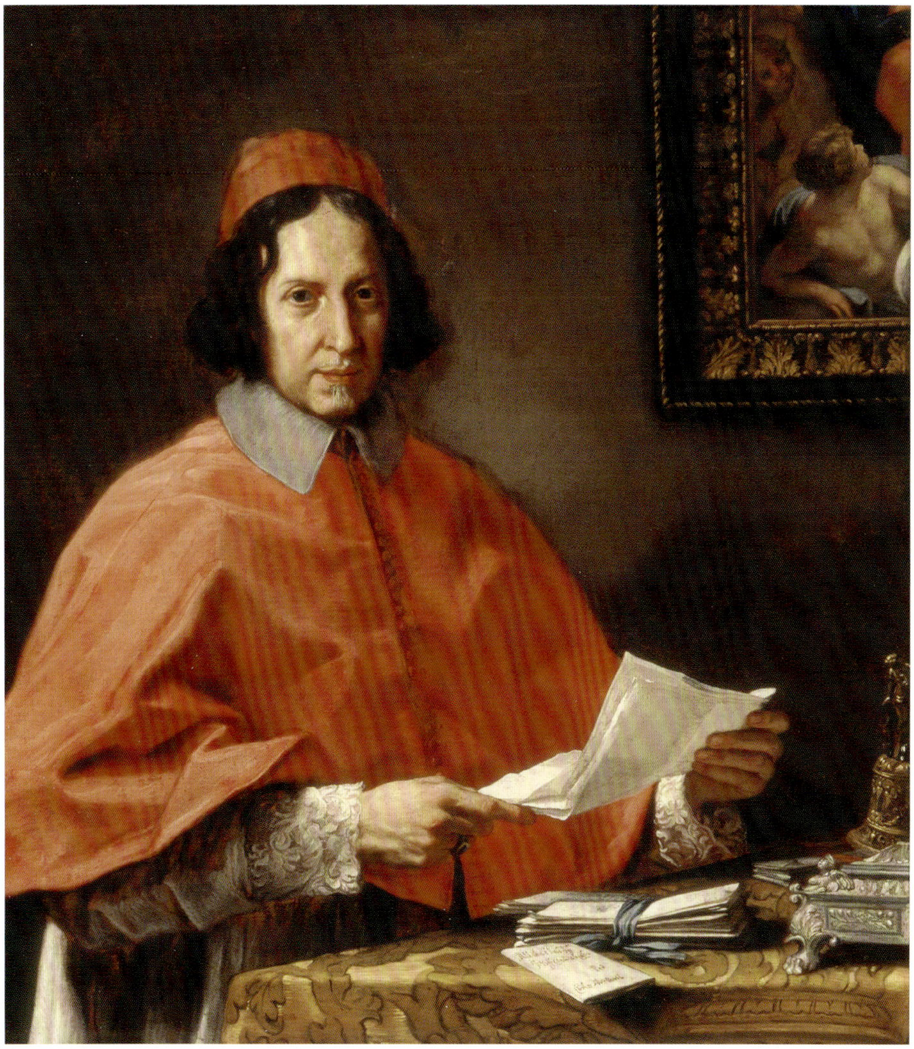

2

By the end of 1682, the space left by the demolition of the ancient chapel of Cardinal Lorenzo had been replaced by a new and much more monumental structure, which was already beginning to attract the attention of travelers and Romans. In the 1682 guide *Les merveilles de la ville de Rome*, we read that "Cardinal Cibo is having built a beautiful chapel," and Pietro Sebastiani, in his *Viaggio sagro, e curioso delle chiese più principali di Roma* (1683), writes that "cardinal Alderano Cybo, a family among the most powerful and ancient in Italy, has begun a famous chapel designed by Cavalier Fontana, with extremely rare and precious stones."[31]

The fact that in 1683 the chapel could already be termed "famous" gives us an idea of the expectations surrounding it, and in fact, the ambitious cardinal lost no occasion to publicize the grandiosity of his project and his intention of challenging the supremacy of the Chigi Chapel, the celebrated architectural masterpiece designed by Raphael that lies across the nave of the church, directly opposite the Cybo Chapel. That his ambitions were publicly known is evidenced by an *avviso* dated January 31, 1682, in which the anonymous writer

FIG. 2. Carlo Maratti, *Portrait of Cardinal Alderano Cybo*, ca. 1687. Musée des Beaux-Arts, Marseille.

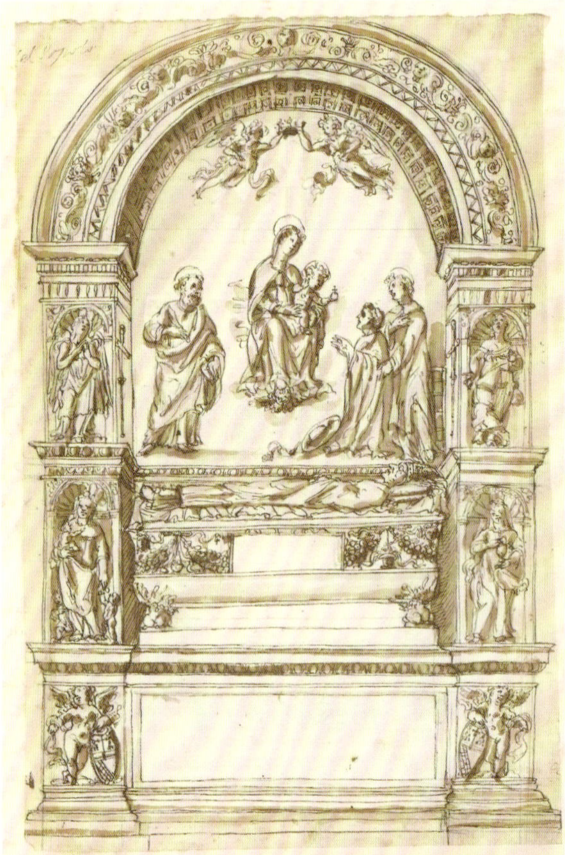

3

declared: "Cardinal Cybo has begun working on his chapel to be made in the church of Santa Maria del Popolo in front of that of Chigi, and he has decided to make all efforts so that it will not be inferior to it."[32]

This dialogue or, more accurately, competition with the Chigi Chapel was enacted through a series of allusions and formal imitations. They begin with the overall plan and design of the new chapel, which echoes Raphael's work not only with its "church within the church" structure, with a dome at the top, but also with the arrangement of the twin columns, which serve to evoke the cross-plan effect with chamfered corners of the Chigi Chapel. Then there is the altar, whose elegant form, without columns, with a simple ribbed frame for the altarpiece and an altar table, is clearly based on that in Raphael's chapel. Similarly, the gilt bronze putti supporting the altar table (a *unicum* in the works ordered by Cardinal Cybo) echo the bronze relief by Lorenzetto with *Christ and the Samaritan Woman* adapted by Bernini to serve as the altar frontal in the Chigi Chapel. Both chapels, too, are dedicated to the Virgin Mary—the Chigi to the Virgin of Loreto and the Cybo to the Immaculate Virgin. And from the dedications follows the affinity of the subjects of the two altarpieces, the *Birth of the Virgin* by Sebastiano del Piombo in the Chigi Chapel and the *Disputation on the Immaculate Conception* by Carlo Maratti in the Cybo. It is also possible that the technique of painting in oils directly on the walls used in the Cybo altarpiece and lateral paintings was inspired by that of Sebastiano, who had painted his altarpiece in oils on a wall lined with peperino.[33]

Through these references, Cardinal Cybo and Carlo Fontana clearly meant to harmonize the new chapel with the one opposite it; but by using marble decorations even more sumptuous than the ones in the Chigi Chapel and a solid perspectival structure created by the sequence of columns and pilasters, they intended to surpass the grandiosity and splendor of the celebrated model. The daring and determination with which Cybo launched himself into this *querelle entre les modernes* (quarrel among the moderns) earned him, in fact, the title "brave patron."[34]

Beginning in 1682–1683, work commenced on the polychrome marble revetment and on the twin sepulchers. As indicated by their funerary inscriptions, the tomb of Cardinal Lorenzo (FIG. 5), on the left wall, was finished in 1683 and that of Alderano (FIG. 6), on the right wall, one year later. Fontana's design combines austerity with sophistication, contrasting the black marble *specchiature* with the lighter stones—*bianco venato* and *giallo antico*—that frame them. Each tomb consists of a tall base with a sarcophagus above, surmounted by a cartouche in black marble and, at the top, a *giallo antico* oval bearing the bust of the praying cardinal in white marble. The only concessions to more decora-

FIG. 3. Anonymous draftsman, Sepulchral monument of Cardinal Lorenzo De Mari Cybo in its original arrangement, first half of the seventeenth century. Royal Library, Windsor Castle (RL 11744).

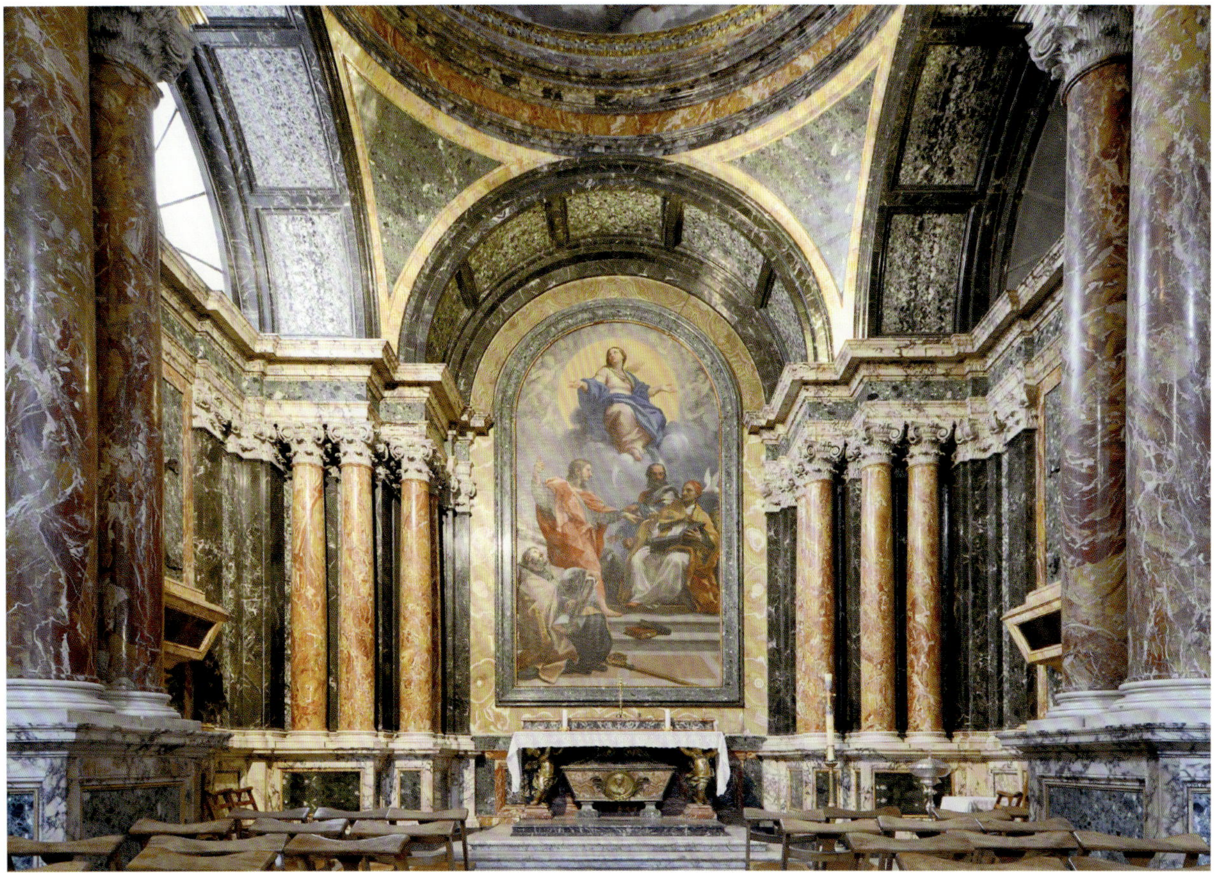

4

tive adornments are the fluttering ends of the cartouches and the acanthus-leaf flourishes at the upper center of the ovals.[35]

Both portraits of the cardinals had always been attributed, starting with Titi, to Francesco Cavallini from Carrara.[36] Later, however, a consensus developed about the attribution of Alderano's bust to the Florentine sculptor Anton Francesco Andreozzi, based on a document published by Lankheit.[37] It is likely that the attribution to Cavallini remains valid for the other bust, that of Lorenzo, the more so because the sculptor was a protégé of the cardinal, to whom he had been recommended by his brother Alberico II, duke of Massa, in 1677.[38]

When, at the end of 1686, Filippo Titi visited the "almost finished" chapel, he spoke of the two portraits as follows: "the portraits on the two tombs on the side walls under the dome … will be works worthy of the value of Francesco Cavallini."[39] His use of the future tense, "will be," suggests that the two busts had yet to be installed. Certainly, that of Alderano, if it was indeed Andreozzi who sculpted it, must have been realized, since the sculptor, as evident from Lankheit's document, was on the verge of leaving for Florence in June of that same year; the other bust was possibly still unfinished, since Cavallini was also working on the bronze altar. Cavallini's contributions to the altar cannot be definitively ascertained; while the general design of the altar and the alabaster urn beneath it should be attributed to Carlo Fontana, it is likely that Cavallini was responsible for designing the two putti supporting the altar table, as indi-

FIG. 4. Cybo Chapel (view toward the altar), Santa Maria del Popolo, Rome.

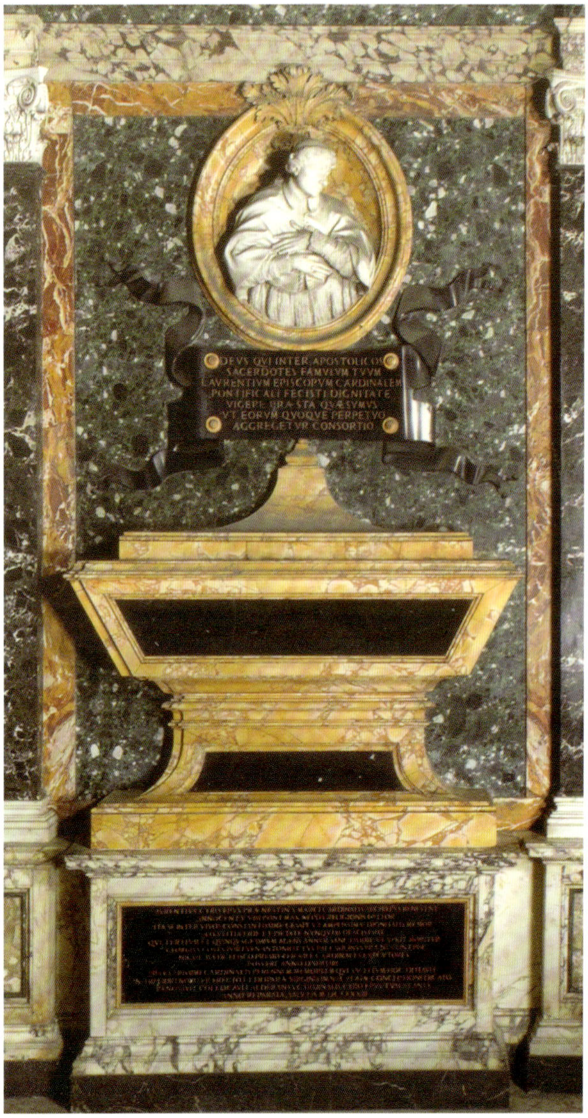

5

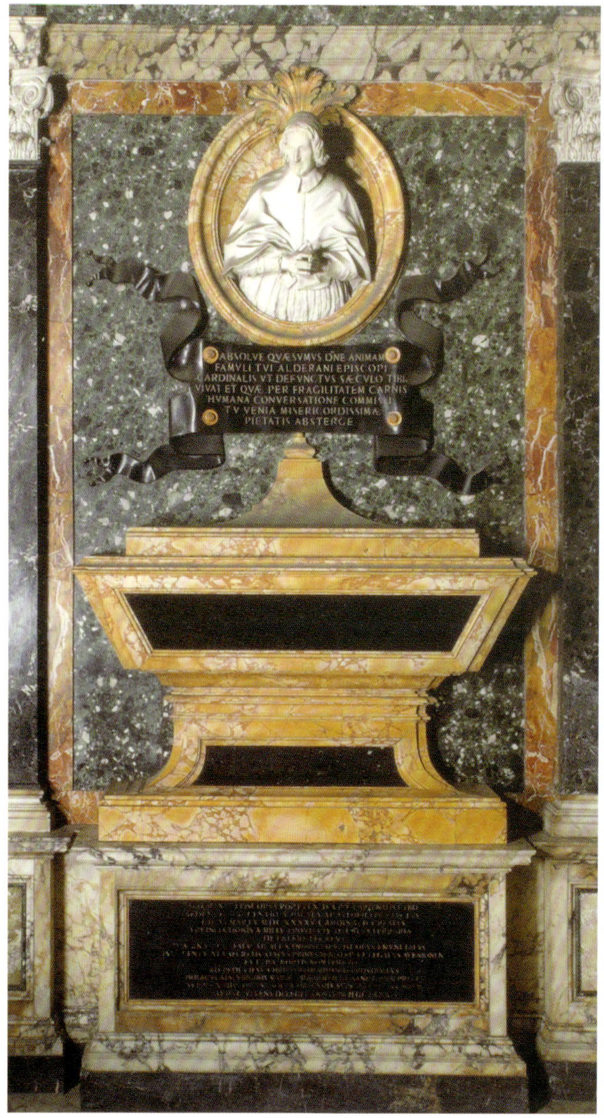

6

cated by Titi,[40] and for the medallion with the portrait of Saint Faustina Martyr that decorates the urn containing the remains of the saint.[41]

In the summer of 1683, work on the marble cladding of the walls was going apace, although no doubt Carlo Cartari was being too optimistic when he wrote that the chapel was close to "completion."[42] In this intense phase of the project, the cardinal decided to have some skilled stonemasons from Carrara brought to Rome. After discussing the matter with the sculptor Michele Antonio Grandi,[43] in September, Alderano wrote to his nephew Carlo Cybo Malaspina, prince of Carrara, asking for his help:

FIG. 5. Tomb of Cardinal Lorenzo De Mari Cybo, 1683. Cybo Chapel (left wall), Santa Maria del Popolo, Rome.

FIG. 6. Tomb of Cardinal Alderano Cybo, 1684. Cybo Chapel (right wall), Santa Maria del Popolo, Rome.

> To work in this chapel of mine in Santa Maria del Popolo, I would need the two young men Stefano Conti Cucurni and Agostino Molani, proposed and approved by Grandi; I would like Your Excellency to be so kind as to have them come here when it gets cooler, which will be toward late October, and to order Don Giovanni

> [Pizzuti][44] to give them the money they will need for the trip, which they will be able to do by sea.... You will learn from Grandi that the chapel is coming along very well and I wish it so, and it is my strong desire for the greater glory of our Lord and of the most Holy Virgin.[45]

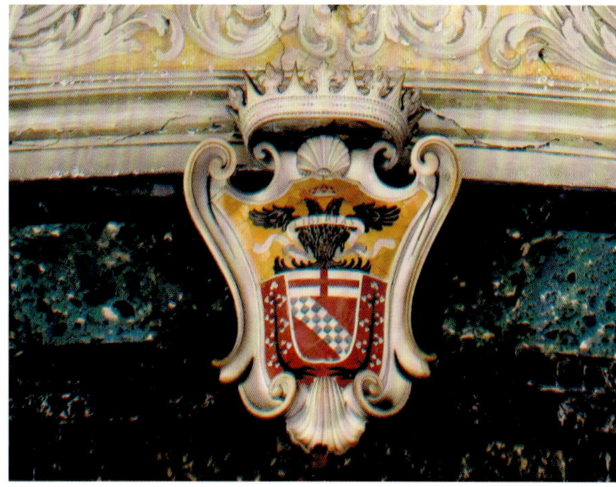

7

In the first few days of 1684, the jasper columns from Sicily arrived in Rome at the port of Ripa on the Tiber and were unloaded under the supervision of Giacomo Borzacchi. On January 4, Borzacchi received from the Fabbrica di San Pietro, on behalf of the cardinal, many tools needed for the unloading operations (see Appendix, doc. 1). These tools were returned to the Fabbrica on January 18. These two dates establish a time frame of about fourteen days for the unloading and transportation of the columns to the church. Not all of the sixteen columns, however, arrived on that occasion. Some did not arrive until a few months later, on July 22—by coincidence, the same day on which Bernini's equestrian statue of Louis XIV was being loaded on a ship for France.[46]

While work was being done to complete and install the columns, with their bases and capitals of white marble (on which little two-headed eagles were carved, alluding to the Cybo coat of arms), two workers, in the course of twelve days, from the end of February to the beginning of March 1684, undertook the preparation of the three large areas "where one has to paint," that is, the areas where the oil paintings were to be executed directly on the walls (see Appendix, doc. 2). This technique required a painstaking preparation of the surface: first linseed oil was passed between the bricks, and then the filler was prepared (a mixture of linseed oil, white lime, and travertine powder) and spread over the walls until a flat and compact surface was obtained for the painters to work on. Not all of this work was properly done, however, given that in the following years, the two paintings on the lateral walls rapidly deteriorated and had to be replaced, whereas in Maratti's altarpiece, the underlying bricks are visible on account of the "pozzolana mortar [having been] laid perhaps too thinly."[47]

As for the polychrome marble decorations, they proceeded swiftly, as attested by the delivery, in March 1684, of a "piece of *fiore di persico*" (see Appendix, doc. 2), and in August of the same year, the cardinal instructed his agent in Massa, Don Giovanni Pizzuti, to purchase the marbles necessary "to finish the chapel."[48] On January 6, 1684, Cartari again noted, this time correctly, that "the chapel ... is nearing perfection and they say that it is to have a place among the principal ones in Rome."[49]

In October 1684, one of the two stonemasons who had been called to Rome from Carrara following Grandi's indication returned home, suggesting that most of the work on the marble revetment was finished.[50] Satisfied with his work, the cardinal recommended him to his brother Duke Alberico:

> The stone-mason Agostino Molani returns after having satisfied with much punctuality and diligence and to my satisfaction the work he was given in this chapel of mine in the church of Santa Maria del Popolo; I wanted to bring the news to

FIG. 7. Ducal coat of arms of the Cybo Malaspina family, ca. 1684–1686. Cybo Chapel (entrance arch), Santa Maria del Popolo, Rome.

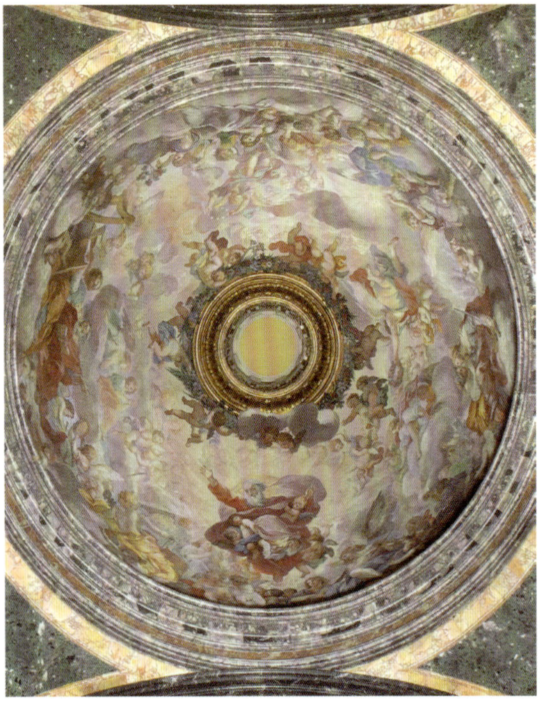

8

Your Excellency so that you would be so kind, as I pray you, to protect him in his need, for which thing I am so bold as to recommend him to Your Excellency as he deserves for the service rendered ... I pray [Your Excellency] to learn from the same the state of the chapel, which shall not displease you. I have decided to place in the arch of the entrance the coat of arms of Your Excellency and would like to know how it is to be done, whether with [the symbol of] Malaspina, or without it.[51]

The last sentence is of particular interest: the cardinal had decided to place in the entrance arch to the chapel not his coat of arms with the cardinal's hat, as would have been normal practice, but that of the Cybo Malaspina family with the ducal crown (FIG. 7).[52] The intention was clearly to emphasize his status as a member of one of the most aristocratic and ancient families of Italy, a family of "sovereign princes," which, unlike many other lineages, continued to exercise direct control over a portion, albeit a small one, of the Italian peninsula. Alderano followed up on his idea, placing the Cybo Malaspina coat of arms, with its blooming thorn, on the entrance arch, whereas his cardinal coat of arms was inlaid at the center of the pavement.[53] On the other hand, the Cybo family had placed many of its members at the top of the ecclesiastical hierarchy, and thus to give visual expression to their dual prestige, secular and religious, the ducal coat of arms was placed in direct relation to the coat of arms of Pope Innocent VIII (Cybo), which had been preserved in the keystone of the bay on which the chapel opens (or possibly placed there during the work on the new chapel).[54]

By the end of 1684, the appearance of the chapel must have been close to the present one. The two tombs had been finished (although, in all likelihood, still lacking their busts), and the marble cladding of the walls was also nearing its conclusion. All that remained to be carried out were the paintings, on which little, if anything, had been done—with the exception of preparatory studies—because the techniques chosen (fresco and oil painting on wall) required the paintings to be done on-site and only after the rest of the work was terminated or at least in a very advanced phase.

The cardinal entrusted the painting of the dome to Luigi Garzi, an artist whose services he used repeatedly in the 1680s.[55] Garzi painted the dome fresco in the course of 1684, alternating the work with that on two altarpieces commissioned by Cardinal Cybo for the church of San Francesco in Massa. On August 5, 1684, the cardinal wrote to his nephew Carlo that the second painting (for Massa), *The Holy Trinity and Saints*, "is coming along well, and we urge it [to be finished], indeed now, because the painter cannot apply himself to the dome we urge it for this reason."[56] Garzi, in other words, had been forced to temporarily suspend work on the fresco, possibly because of the arrival and installation of the second group of columns from Sicily (July 22) or because the excessive summer heat was not ideal for frescoing.

Garzi produced a highly attractive and decoratively effective fresco (FIG. 8), which echoes the work of Lanfranco and Pietro da Cortona, while ton-

FIG. 8. Luigi Garzi, Frescoes of the dome, 1684. Cybo Chapel, Santa Maria del Popolo, Rome.

FIG. 9. Cybo Chapel (view from the entrance), Santa Maria del Popolo, Rome.

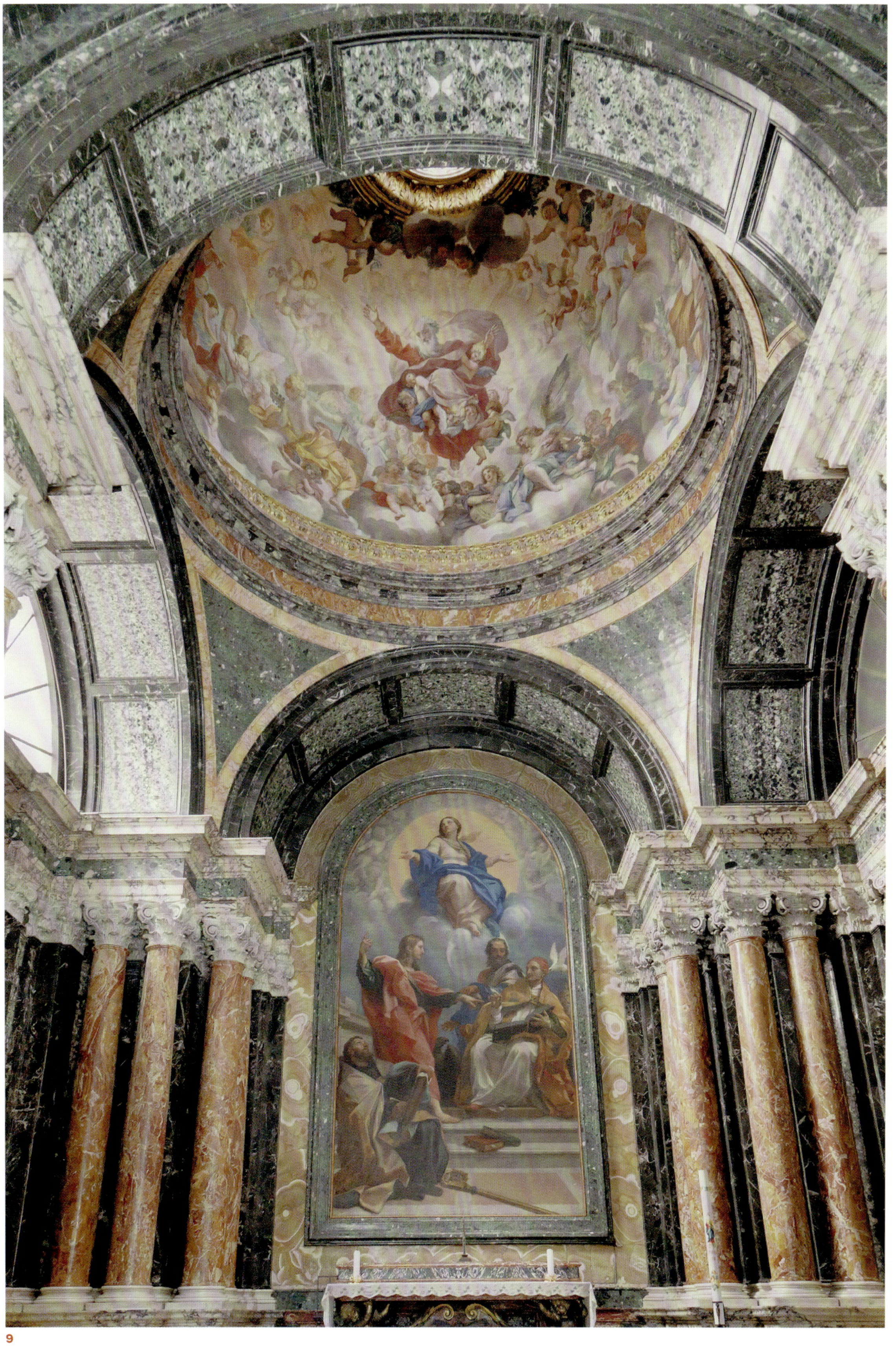

9

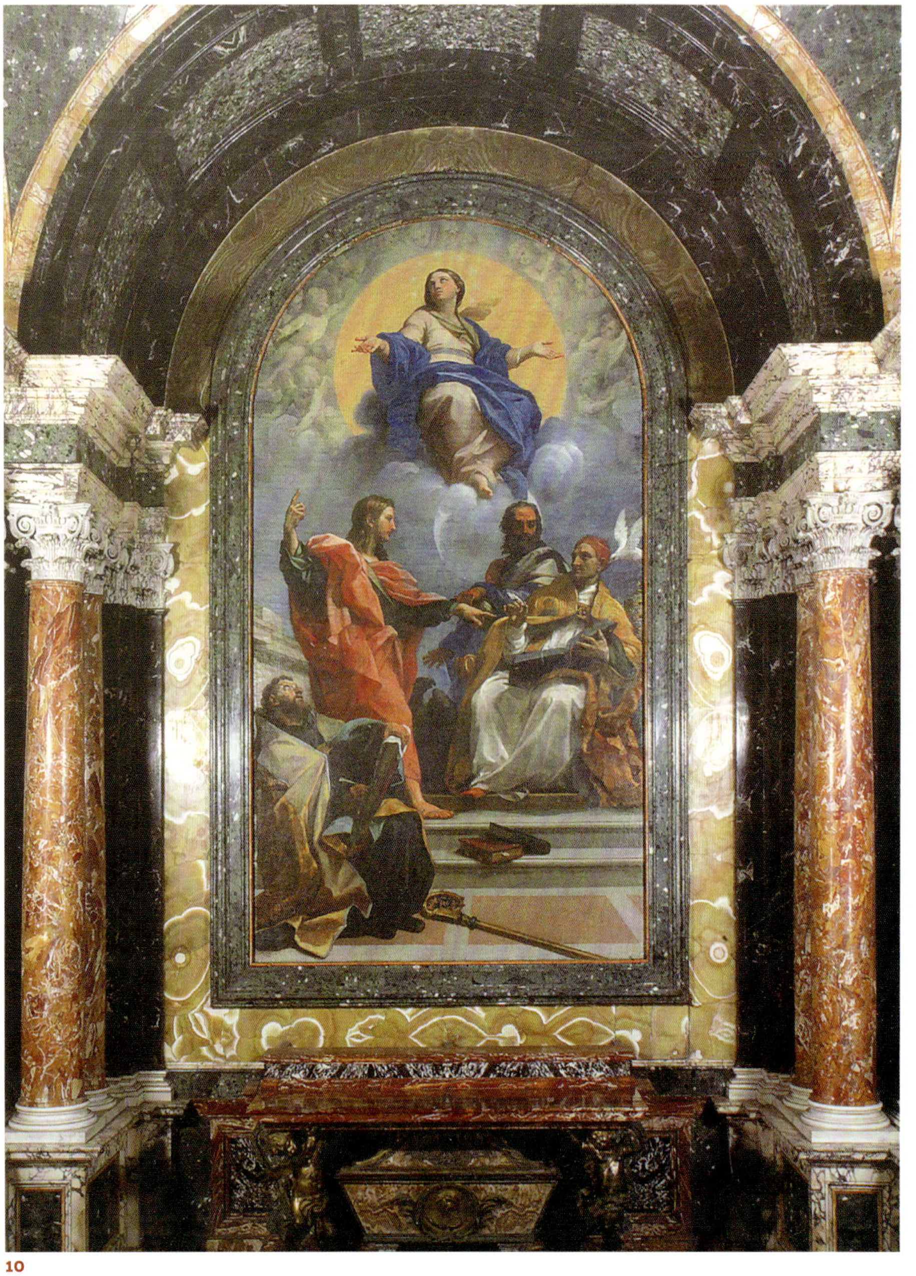

10

FIG. 10. Carlo Maratti, *Disputation on the Immaculate Conception*, 1684–1686. Cybo Chapel, Santa Maria del Popolo, Rome.

ing down their bravura in favor of a more graceful representation. The choice of depicting God the Father, surrounded by a crowd of angels, prophets, and Virtues arranged on paradisiacal clouds, may have been influenced, again, by the desire to echo the Chigi Chapel, on whose dome, in the lantern, there is a mosaic image of God the Father creating the world. However, a much more obvious reason could have been the desire to relate the dome fresco to the altarpiece by stressing the divine origin of the Virgin's privilege of immaculacy and purity, which is celebrated in Maratti's painting.[57] The image painted by Garzi, in other words, is not simply that of *God the Father in Glory*, as is often maintained; rather, it is God captured in the moment in which, with a solemn gesture, he grants Mary the privilege of the Immaculate Conception. The close connection between the figure of God the Father and that of the Virgin is ensured by the fact that the first is located just above the altarpiece on the same axis as the second, as is evident when one enters the chapel and proceeds toward the altar (FIG. 9).

Between the summer of 1684 and the summer of 1686, Carlo Maratti painted the altarpiece of the chapel, the oils-on-wall depicting the *Disputation on the Immaculate Conception* (FIG. 10).[58] Before the actual painting of the work, there was a phase of careful preparation, attested by a great number of sketches[59] and an oil-on-canvas study of the figure of the Virgin, now in the Bildergalerie of the Royal Palace of Sanssouci, in Potsdam.[60] The result is a masterpiece of crystalline composure, in which a number of saints gather to celebrate the Virgin: John the Evangelist (who had the vision of the Immaculate Virgin on Patmos), two Western Doctors of the Church, Gregory the Great and Augustine, and a Doctor of the Oriental Church, traditionally identified, following Bellori, as John Chrysostom[61] but who is more likely Athanasius of Alexandria, as maintained by some contemporary authors.[62]

From the very first glance, one is struck by the neo-Raphaelesque character of the altarpiece. The reference to Raffaello Sanzio is, of course, a constant in the work of Maratti, who had been hailed as a new Raphael and was a firm supporter of the supremacy of the master, affirming it through his painting as his mentor Giovan Pietro Bellori affirmed it in his writings.[63] In the case of the altarpiece in Santa Maria del Popolo, critics have seen in particular the influence of Raphael's fresco in the Vatican's Stanza della Segnatura, the *Disputation on the Holy Sacrament*, and his altarpiece known as the *Madonna of Foligno*.[64] In the case of the Cybo painting, however, we are dealing with something that goes much beyond mere influence, for the space in which Maratti sets his figures is exactly the same "open field with the beginning of a temple" where "the holiest senate of theologians and fathers" gathers—as Bellori described it—in Raphael's masterpiece in the Vatican.[65] The visual similarity is evident: we have the same pavement with ochre squares of terracotta tiles or bricks, contoured by white marble strips; the same two marble steps, leading in Raphael's *Disputation* to a marble platform on which are the altars and the chairs of the Doctors and in Maratti's painting to a more modest platform, possibly of wood, on which the chair of Saint Gregory is placed; and, in addition, the large plinth that is seen in the lower right corner of Raphael's fresco reappears in Maratti's work at the far left, behind Saint Augustine and Saint John.[66] These specific parallels are accompanied by a number of other citations that further reinforce the relationship between Maratti's altarpiece and Raphael's *Disputation*: Saint John the Evangelist's raised arm in Maratti's work evokes that of the character on the right of the altar in Raphael's fresco; the two books precariously positioned one on top of the other on the steps in the altarpiece recall the ones at the feet of the character in the fresco who is probably Origen. And the very pose of Maratti's Virgin and the solar disk against which she is placed echo the golden circle surrounding Christ in the Vatican fresco, even though in this case the crucial influence seems to have been Raphael's *Madonna of Foligno*.[67]

The *Disputation on the Immaculate Conception* in Santa Maria del Popolo was not the only work on this subject commissioned by Alderano in these years. As already mentioned, the cardinal had Luigi Garzi do another *Disputation* for the church of San Francesco in Massa. The use of this "militant" iconography is symptomatic of his profound devotion to the theme of the *sine macula* (without stain) conception of the Virgin and his desire for a rapid definition of the dogma. Unlike Garzi's *Disputation*, however, whose dynamism and dramatic quality make it fully "baroque",[68] Maratti's altarpiece is closely tied, as we have seen, to Raphael's classically restrained fresco, the theological disputation *par excellence*. Indeed, it can be described as a reenactment of the same. There may have been various reasons behind this choice, starting from the fact that in the same period (1684), probably through the influence of Cardinal Cybo, Maratti was nominated "custodian of the paintings" in the Vatican Stanze;[69] but a central role was certainly played by the cardinal, who wished to place on the same standing the belief in Mary's immaculacy and the fundamental dogmas of the Church celebrated in Raphael's fresco, thus formulating an exhortation, couched in a "Vatican" language for the reigning pope, to arrive quickly at the proclamation of the dogma of the Immaculate Conception.[70]

The two lateral paintings in the chapel (FIGS. 11–12) have a more complex history. The cardinal desired two martyrdom scenes to be represented, that of Saint Lawrence, to whom the original Cybo Chapel was dedicated, and that of Saint Catherine, for whom he had a special devotion. The story of how the works came to be commissioned from the Viennese painter Daniel Seiter, one of the most prominent artists of the time, is summarized by Pascoli as follows:

> The fame of his skill having circulated ... through all of Rome, there was not one connoisseur who did not go to see him, and no one went there more than Cardinal Cybo, who was decorating his chapel in Santa Maria del Popolo. He took him to see it and told him that he wanted him to paint the two laterals; and he gladly accepted the offer, and later began the work, and having finished the work [he] gained along with that of His Eminence the universal applause of all others.[71]

In reality, however, things were more complicated. Titi, a source contemporary to the building of the chapel and generally well informed, relates that at first, the cardinal had assigned to Seiter only one of the two laterals, commissioning the other from the Florentine painter Giovanni Maria Morandi. Titi offers this information in the 1686 edition of the *Studio di pittura*,[72] but in the appendix of his book, written toward the end of the year, which was dedicated to works under way at the time of printing, he rectifies it, mentioning only Seiter as the author of both the laterals.[73] The substitution must therefore have taken place in the course of 1686 and was probably a consequence of Morandi's prolonged absence from Rome.[74]

The two oils-on-wall by Seiter, hailed from the start as masterpieces (to the point of being, at times, preferred to Maratti's altarpiece),[75] brought extraordinary fame to the painter, earning him, in 1688, a commission of a number of works from the duke of Savoy for what is today the Royal Palace of Turin.[76] Unlike Maratti's altarpiece, however, Seiter's wall paintings rapidly deteriorated, forcing Cardinal Cybo to replace them in 1697 with paintings of the same subject on canvas, which Seiter himself executed in Turin and then shipped to Rome via Ferrara.[77] In these later versions of the two martyrdom scenes, Seiter repeats the arrangement of the oils-on-wall but makes the scenes more dramatic by resorting to emphatic gestures and intense chiaroscuro. Seiter's Venetian

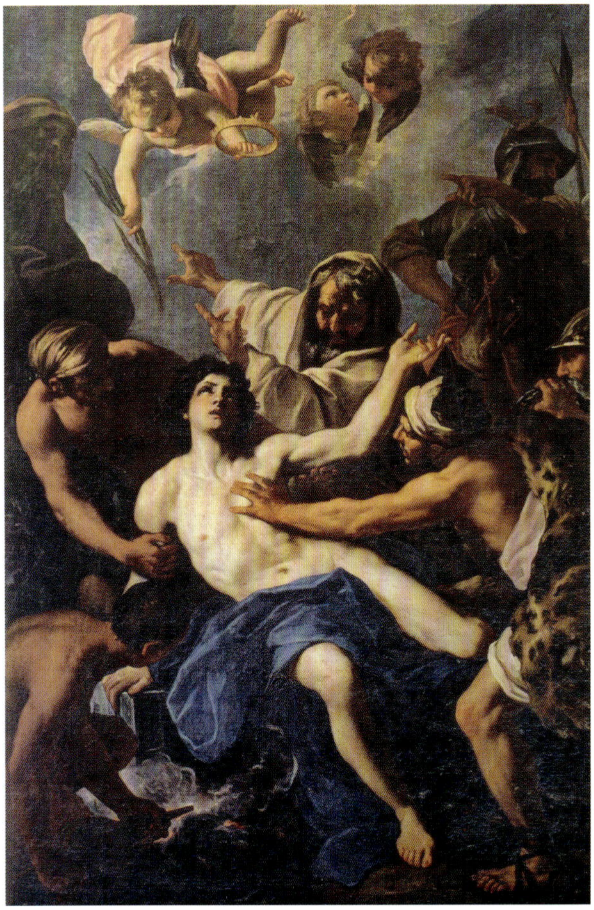

11

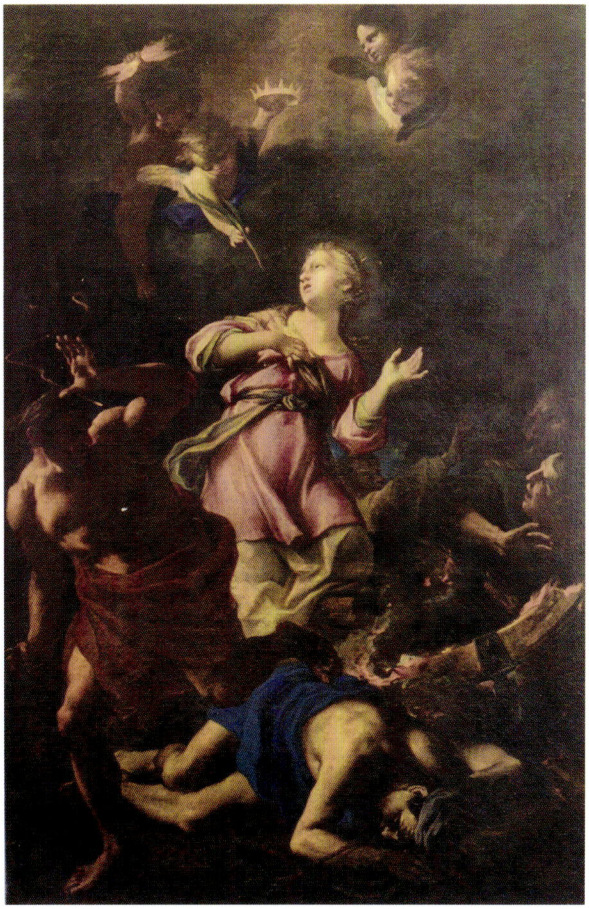

12

training is evident in the citations from such painters as Titian and Veronese, but in the *Martyrdom of Saint Lawrence* appear echoes of Poussin's *Saint Erasmus*. In the end, with their dramatic quality, Seiter's two later canvases function as an effective counterpoint to the crystalline purity of Maratti's *Disputation*.

In the autumn of 1686, the chapel was basically complete. In September of that year, Giovanni Prati printed his ode "on the unveiling" of the chapel,[78] and in the same month, Titi could write that the chapel was "almost finished."[79] Finally, in an entry in his diary dated October 19, 1686, Carlo Cartari informs us that "the chapel of Signor Cardinal Cybo in the church of Santa Maria del Popolo is finished, and will be unveiled very soon."[80] The consecration, however, was postponed for a few months, perhaps because the busts of the two cardinals were not yet put in place, as suggested by the fact, as noted above, that they were still absent when Titi visited the chapel for the second time.

Finally, in May 1687, all was ready for the consecration. Alderano, informing his brother Alberico of the imminent ceremony, manifested his profound satisfaction: "The chapel, made by me, and having the coat of arms of the House on the first arch is according to the judgment of the critics the most beautiful in Rome, with the exception of the two of Sixtus V and Paul V."[81] Although the judgment may have been exaggerated, the reference to the two papal chapels in Santa Maria Maggiore is of extreme interest, because the two monuments in many as-

FIG. 11. Daniel Seiter, *Martyrdom of Saint Lawrence*, 1697–1698. Cybo Chapel (left wall), Santa Maria del Popolo, Rome.

FIG. 12. Daniel Seiter, *Martyrdom of Saint Catherine*, 1697–1698. Cybo Chapel (right wall), Santa Maria del Popolo, Rome.

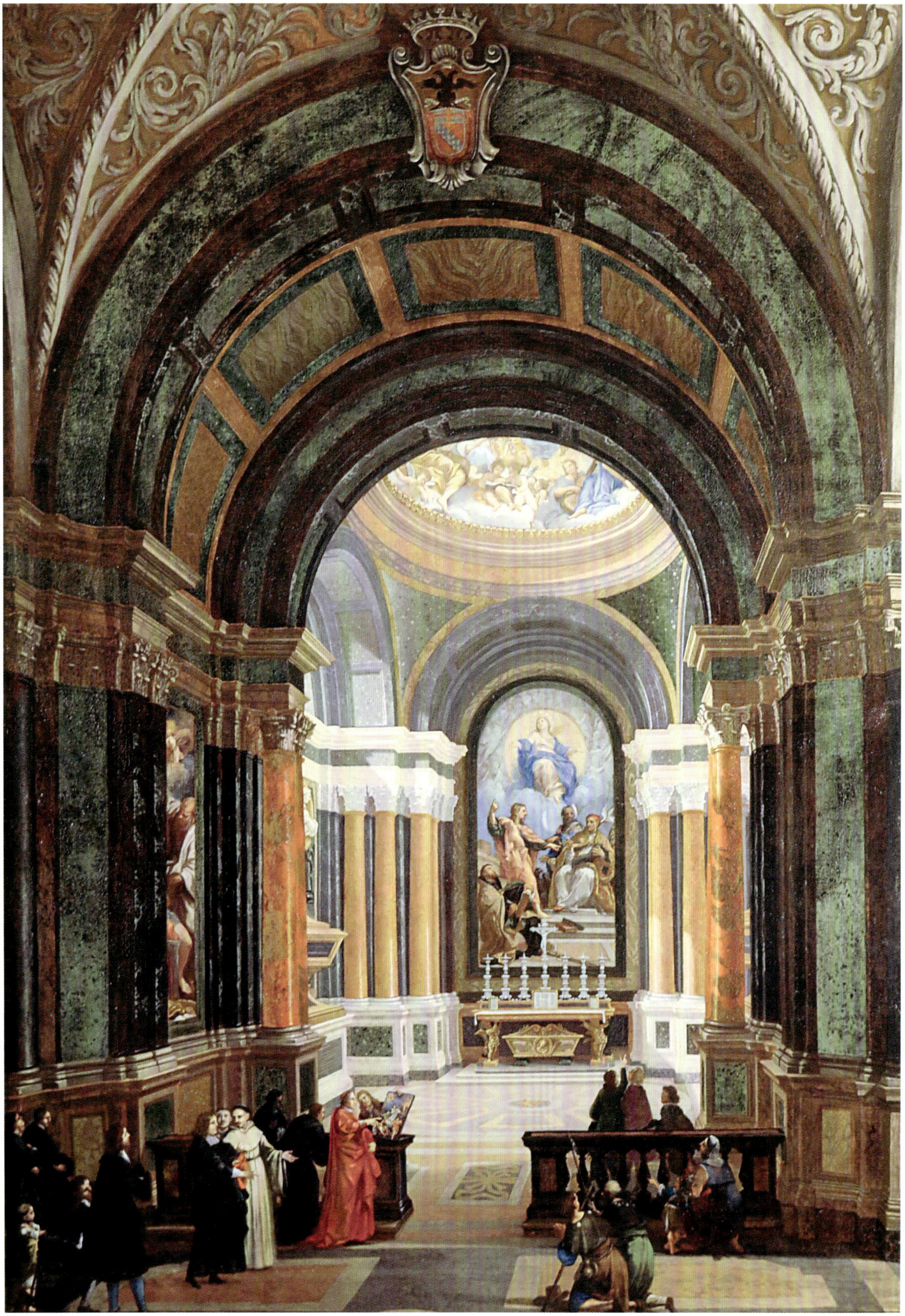

13

pects (the adoption of the central plan surmounted by a dome, the sumptuous lining with polychrome marbles, and the placing of twin funerary monuments on the lateral walls) must have been important models for the Cybo Chapel.[82]

On May 19, another of Alderano's brothers, Monsignor Odoardo Cybo, consecrated the chapel, greeted by "universal applause," as Duke Alberico II wrote to the cardinal, complimenting him on the event.[83] Since the aging duke could not visit the chapel in person, the cardinal commissioned an accurate depiction of the interior of the chapel, now in the Museo di Roma (FIG. 13), and to ensure maximum fidelity, he used the same artists who had done the original works, Maratti and Garzi, with the likely assistance of the painter of perspectives Pier Francesco Garoli.[84]

The entire project was thus carried out over a relatively short time span, ten years at most, unlike many other chapels, including the Chigi opposite it. This was certainly one of the reasons for the extraordinary architectural and artistic coherence that characterizes the interior of the chapel.[85] In the years immediately following its consecration, there were no major interventions, excluding the above-mentioned replacement of the two lateral paintings and, after the death of Cardinal Alderano (1700), the placing of a plaque with the date of his death at the bottom of his tomb slab. We have some precise information on the making of this lost inscription (which Forcella was still able to see and transcribe)[86] through a payment request by Carlo Fontana, from which we learn that the work had been entrusted to that same Marcello Bigieri (or Biggieri) who many years before had purchased the marbles from the Reverenda Fabbrica di San Pietro and had probably worked on the marble inlays. The same document also tells us about the restoration of the inscription on the tomb of Innocent VIII in St. Peter's, coincidentally associating the two foremost examples of art patronage by the Cybo family in Rome (see Appendix, doc. 3).

In the early nineteenth century, when Piazza del Popolo was completely renovated by Giuseppe Valadier, the external profile of the chapel was altered, as the structure was incorporated into the building annexed to the basilica that serves as one of the wings to the square. On that occasion, the right lunette in the chapel was closed, leaving the interior with very little natural light. On the other hand, Valadier showed his appreciation for the elegant profile of the chapel's dome by replicating it on a building on the left side of the Porta del Popolo. The two domes thus serve as a pendant pair, on a minor scale, to those of the two twin churches (Santa Maria dei Miracoli and Santa Maria in Montesanto) on the other side of the square.

To complete this historical "mosaic" of interventions, there is one additional and significant "tessera" that needs to be added. After having ordered the removal of Pinturicchio's *Madonna* (FIG. 14) during the demolition of the original chapel and having kept it with him for a few years, Cardinal Alderano decided in 1687 to send it to his family in Massa, where his brother Duke Alberico II had ordered the construction in the church of San Francesco of a burial chapel for the members of his family.[87] In October 1693, Pinturicchio's fresco was placed on the sumptuous polychrome marble altar of the chapel, designed by Domenico Martinelli (FIG. 15). For the occasion, Alberico's son Carlo II wrote to the cardinal, his uncle: "Yesterday, the image of Our Lady was raised, that Your Eminence sent to the Duke my father to be placed in the chapel of the House, having been removed from the ancient [chapel] of [Santa Maria] del Popolo."[88] Carlo's words

FIG. 13. Pier Francesco Garoli, Luigi Garzi, and Carlo Maratti, *View of the Cybo Chapel*, 1687. Museo di Roma, Rome.

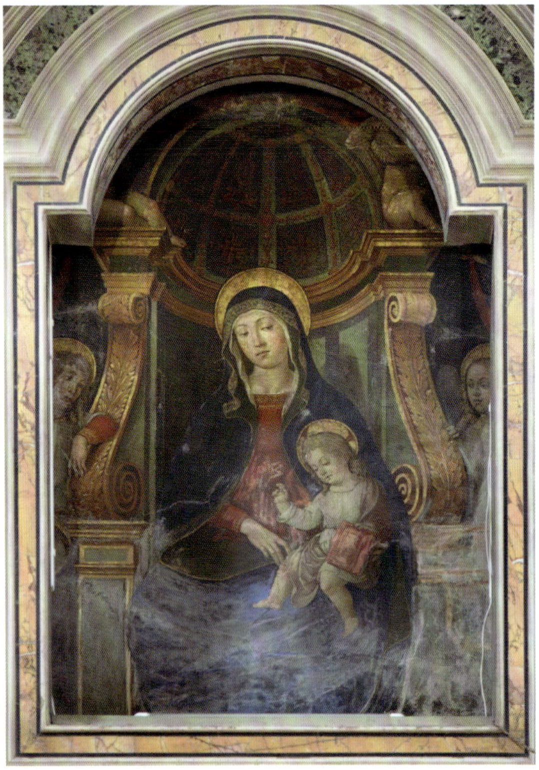

14

clearly evidence the role of Pinturicchio's fresco in establishing a bond between the two Cybo chapels, serving as a dynastic relic connecting the place in Massa dedicated to the celebration of the Cybo Malaspina as "sovereign princes" to the one celebrating the glory obtained by the family in Rome in service to the Church. To evidence the prestigious Roman provenance of the altarpiece, it was integrated with putti of white marble on alabaster clouds, sculpted by Andrea and Tommaso Lazzoni from Carrara; the lively cherubs do not simply support the sacred image but seem to be transporting it, as in the iconography of the translation of the Holy House to Loreto. Similarly, in the dome above, lined with the typically Roman *verde antico*, one can perhaps see an allusion to the chapel from which the fresco comes.

The relation between the two chapels, however, was not limited to their "complementarity" in celebrating the fame, civil and ecclesiastic, of the Cybo family; the Roman chapel also served clearly as an artistic and religious model for the one in Massa.[89] The colors of the Massa chapel, for one thing, echo those of the chapel in Santa Maria del Popolo. We find again columns of Sicilian jasper and use of alabaster and *verde antico* marble. In fact, much of the stone was sent as a present from Rome by Cardinal Alderano, and it is possible that some was left over from the decoration of the Cybo Chapel.[90] Furthermore, the Massa chapel is dedicated to the Nativity of the Virgin, "in imitation" of the cardinal who had dedicated his new chapel to the Immaculate Conception.[91] And this happened surprisingly without any actual images of the Nativity of Mary being placed in the chapel, which incidentally explains why Pinturicchio's *Madonna and Child* was for a long time mistaken for a *Saint Anne and the Young Mary*.[92]

In this essay, various "spaces" have been mentioned, mostly sacred, related in various ways to the Cybo Chapel. There are, of course, the chapels, starting with the Ginetti and concluding with the two papal chapels in Santa Maria Maggiore, that served as formal models for the Cybo, especially in terms of its plan and the marble lining of the walls. Other spaces, located in Rome (San Cosimato) and elsewhere (the ducal chapel in Massa) are related instead to the chapel in Santa Maria del Popolo on account of having inherited parts of the decorations of the old demolished chapel of Cardinal Lorenzo Cybo. Three spaces, however, have connections with the Cybo Chapel that are especially significant. The first is the Chigi Chapel in Santa Maria del Popolo, with which it has a relation of emulation and competition; then there is the Vatican Stanza della Segnatura, whose *Disputation* frescoed by Raphael served as model for Maratti's altarpiece, with strong theological implications; finally, there is the complex relationship with the chapel in Massa, which complemented the Cybo Chapel in celebrating the glory of the family and used it as a model, as suggested in particular by its being dedicated to the Nativity of the Virgin. These connections have different levels of legibility. While the reference to the Chigi Chapel would have been visually obvious to the public, the reference to the *Disputation* in the

FIG. 14. Bernardino di Betto, called Pinturicchio, *Madonna and Child* (from the Cybo Chapel in Rome), ca. 1503. Cappella Ducale (or Cappella del Santissimo Sacramento), Cathedral of SS. Pietro e Francesco, Massa.

FIG. 15. Cappella Ducale (or Cappella del Santissimo Sacramento), Cathedral of SS. Pietro e Francesco, Massa.

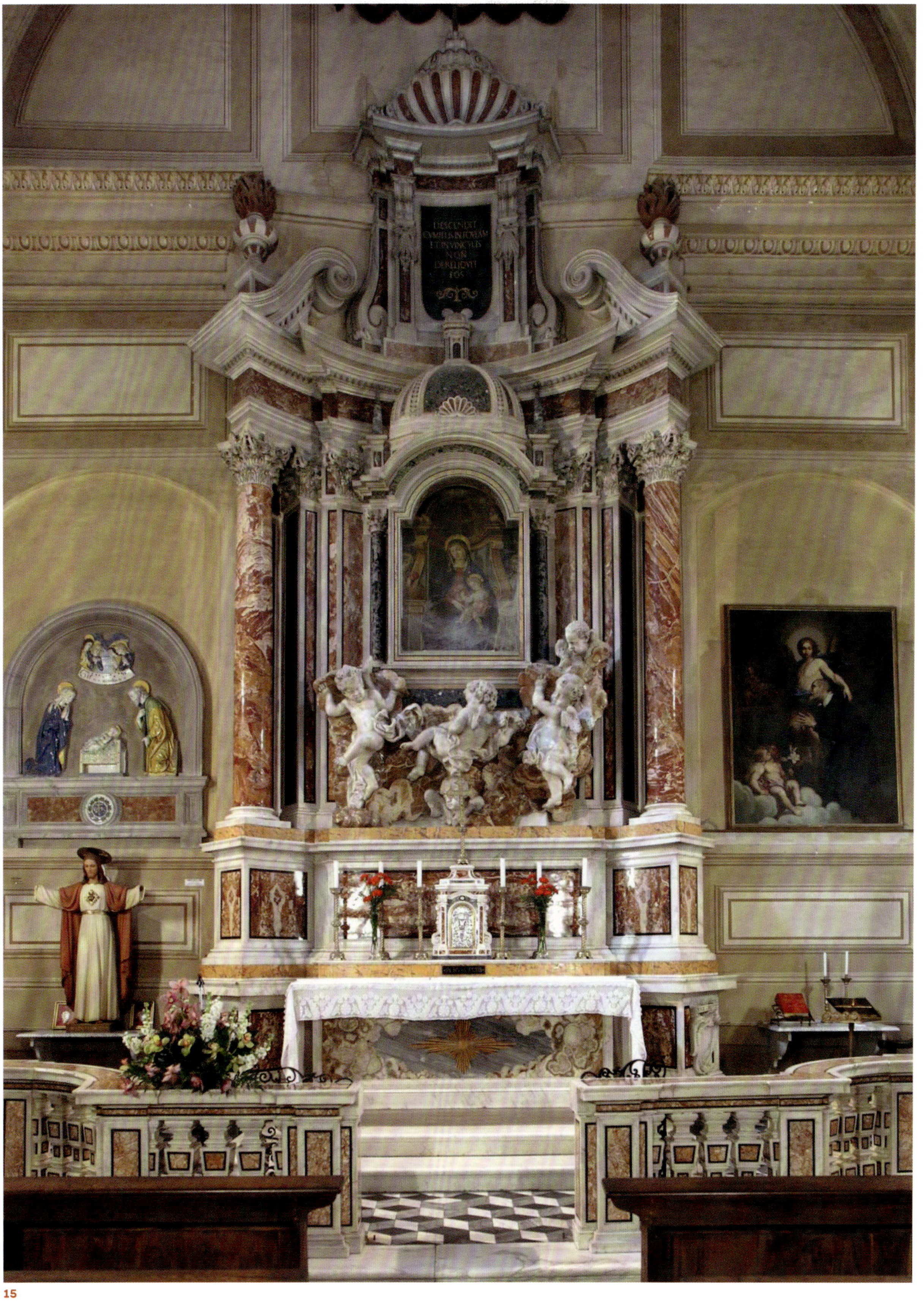

15

Vatican Palace is reserved for more educated viewers, capable of grasping the visual and doctrinal references of the scene (and among those who did get the message, many must have been struck by the boldness of the sacred representation orchestrated by Cardinal Alderano). Finally, the close correspondence with the Massa chapel could not be perceived in Rome, whereas in Massa, the connection with Rome was physically embodied by Pinturicchio's *Madonna* and underlined by the supporting angels beneath the fresco.[93]

Appendix

Doc. 1. Archivio Reverenda Fabbrica San Pietro (ARFSP), Arm. 26, rip. E, vol. 303, f. 34r:

> A dì 4 Gennaro 1684 si è consegniato per ordine delle Signor Cardinale Cibo a Jacomo Borzache le sottoscrite stiglie che devono servire per scarichare alcune peze di colone di marmo di Sicilia venute per servitio delle Signor Cardinale Cibo per la sua capella che fa alla chiesa della Madona del Popolo
> Due traglie di ferro con sue girele di metallo et ancho due altre traglie di fero con sue girelle di metallo che in tutte le sudette traglie sono n° 4
> et ancho due altre tragliette di fero con sue girele di metallo n° 2
> et ancho due canape grose buone lunghe palmi 75 l'uno n° 2
> et ancho una raganella buona n° 1
> et ancho due legni per la capa lunghe n° 2
> et ancho una pulea grosa con sua girella de metallo grosa n° 1
> Io Iacomo Borzatti [h]o ricuto tuta la sopradeta roba chonsegiata dall Signor Jacomo Blismeli fattore.
> A dì 18 gennaro 1684 il sudetto Jacomo Borzache [h]a riconsegniatto tutta la sudetta robba inmmisure [*sic*] e consegniata in mano delle Signor Giacomo Balsimelli fattore.
> A dì 27 dato allo sudeto una raspa da fare calcia n° 1.

Doc. 2. ARFSP, Arm. 26, rip. E, vol. 303, f. 35v:

> Aciò che ogniuno sapia tutto quello che [è] uscito dalla fabricha di San Pietro per servitio della capella che fa il Signor Cardinale Cibo all Chiesa della Madona delle Popolo qui sotto nottatto
> Adì 6 marzo 1684 nota di giornate che ha fatto Cosimo Rustichelli a dare l'olio di lino alli 3 quadri dove va dipinto e primo per olio di lino che si è auto dall Signor Girolamo Mugini in più volte prima per darlo tra li matoni in più volte e per impastare e fare lo stuco con la calce biancha e polvere di travertino e rimanegare detto stucho ricondotto in più volte
> olio di lino libbre 166 scudi 8.30
> Calcia biancha mesa in detto stucho pese tre n° 3 scudi 2.10
> Polvere di travertino scorzze n° 8 scudi [0.]80
> Giornate di due omini che [h]anno datto l'olio di lino alli muri e datto lo stucho in più volte che è stato Cosimo Rustichele e Giuseppe Coronette in tutto giornate
> n° 12 scudi 4.80
> [totale] scudi 16.00

viagi del caretiere a portare lo stucho all Chiesa delle Popolo e riportare li masteli alla Fabricha di San Pietro et ancho un viagio di un pezo di fiore di persicho preso alla fabricha di San Pietro che l'[h]a misurato il Signor Matia de Rose [Mattia de' Rossi] e notatto all libro dove si notta tuta la roba che della Fabricha esce sichè tutte li viagi delle caretiere sonno in tutte viagi n° 8 scudi 2.40

[totale] scudi 18.40

ARFSP, Arm. 27, rip. B, vol. 382, f. 21r:
A dì 14 marzo 1684 si è riauto dalla Signor Mugine olio di lino che [h]a servito per lo stucho della capella della Signor Cardinale Cibo alla Popolo in tre ricquadri grandi dato l'olio in prima alli detti 3 muri e fattollo stucho che in più volte detto oleo [fa] libbre 25 l. 61 l. 15 l. 23 che in tutto fa libbre 124.

Doc. 3. Archivio di Stato Massa (ASMs), *Arch. Ducale, Negozi dello Stato e della Casa*, vol. 127, conto di lavori svolti nella Cappella Cybo e al monumento sepolcrale di Innocenzo VIII in San Pietro, firmato da Carlo Fontana e indirizzato a monsignor Odoardo Cybo, patriarca di Costantinopoli:

A dì 10 febraro 1703. Misura, e stima delli lavori di scarpello, et altro fatti a tutta sua robba spesa, e fattura di mastro Marcello Biggieri capo mastro scarpellino, in haver fatto l'infrascritti lavori per servitio dell'Illustrissimo, e Reverendissimo Monsignore Cybbo Patriarca di Gierusalemme [*sic*] nella cappella posta nella chiesa della Madonna Santissima del Popolo in fare la nova iscrittione a piedi la sepoltura di detta cappella il tutto come qui sotto distintamente segue.
Per il commesso di gialdo [*sic*] antico del mastro di detta iscrittione, con sua fodera di peperino sotto commessa con dui cartocci d'acapo, e dui d'a piedi scartocciati di commesso simile contornati longhezza nel maggiore palmi 4½ altezza palmi 1/6, rotata, impomiciata, e lustra scudi 11.20

Per havere segnato, spartito, e intagliato n° 50 lettere dentro la sudetta iscritione alti l'uno palmi 1/6, e smaltate di negro scudi 2.60

[parziale] scudi 13.80

Per havere fatto la cassa attorno nel pavimento per incassare la suddetta iscritione, e incassata in conformità del suo contorno longhezza stes[s]a attorno palmi 14 altezza il levato palmi 1/4, e quadrato
Per havere pagato al muratore per farla mettere in opera speso de' propri

scudi [0].40

Per havere speso de' propri, in repulire, refondere le lettere, e resmaltarle in opera dell'iscritione della Santa Memoria di papa Innocenzo Ottavo nel suo deposito dentro la basilica di San Pietro scudi 8.50

[parziale] 9.50
13.80
[totale] 23.30

Fanno li sopradetti lavori e spese scudi ventitré baiocchi 30 moneta scudi 23.30.

Notes

1 — For an architectural analysis of the chapel, Hager 1974 is still fundamental; see also Hager 1976; Hager 1996; Hager 2009; Colonnese 2017.
2 — Bentivoglio and Valtieri 1976, 127–131; Carbonara Pompei 2009.
3 — For the biography and art patronage of the cardinal, see Stumpo 1981; Rudolph 1994; Federici 2003a.
4 — In addition to his salary as secretary of State (six thousand scudi per year), Cybo received the benefice (seven thousand scudi) of Avignon, where he served (*in absentia*) as papal legate since 1676, and the pension that he earned (more or less secretly) from the French monarchy (twelve thousand livres and, from 1683, eighteen thousand livres per year). See Michaud 1882, 479; Gérin 1894, II, 468–469, 567–568; Archivio di Stato di Roma (ASR), Archivio Cartari-Febei, b. 86, fols. 91r, 114r, 142v.
5 — Michaud 1882, 477–481; von Pastor 1943, 16; Neveu 1979.
6 — For a reevaluation of the approach of Innocent XI to the arts, see Bösel, Menniti Ippolito, and Spiriti 2014.
7 — A document of 1503 mentions the chapel as "noviter constructa" (Bentivoglio and Valtieri 1976, 127), and an inscription in praise of Cardinal Alderano Cybo, now in the sacristy of the church (Forcella 1869–1884, I, 1869, 392, n. 1498) refers to the construction of Cardinal Lorenzo's chapel with these words: "anno MDIII ... sacellum extruxit exornavit." A description of the previous chapel can be found in Alberici 1600, 18; Landucci 1646, 25–26, 165. The most detailed description is that by Benedetto Mellini, transcribed in Miarelli Mariani and Richiello 2009, II, 749–822. In the basilica is another chapel that belonged to the Cybo family (the Roman branch) and then passed to the Soderini; see Miarelli Mariani and Richiello 2009, I, 115–124.
8 — Gualdi 2009a; Gualdi 2009b.
9 — Caglioti 2002, 1019; Caglioti 2004, 353; Caglioti 2016, 142; Federici and Garms 2010, 95–97, cat. 30.
10 — Federici and Garms 2010, 97–98, cat. 31, 93–94, cat. 28.
11 — Bentivoglio and Valtieri 1976, 127.
12 — Federici 2003b.
13 — Brauer and Wittkower 1931, 171: "Disegno fatto dal cavalier Giovan Lorenzo Bernino di età d'anni 81 per uno delli depositi della cappella che doveva fare il cardinal Cibo al Popolo." See also Hager 1974, 47–48; and on the possible link between this drawing and the first project of the chapel by Fontana, see Federici 2003b.
14 — On the engagement of Bernini's disciple Antonio Valeri in the project, see Valeri 1958, 16–18; Pascoli 1730–1736 [1981], 235–236.
15 — Hager 1974; Hager 1976; Colonnese 2017.
16 — It seems, however, that among the marbles employed in the chapel, only the white comes from the Apuan Alps; the *portoro* comes from nearby Liguria (Portovenere), while the other stones come from other places (Sicily for the jasper) or from Rome itself (excavation marbles).
17 — Federici 2003a. The cladding of the altar wall with alabaster in the Cybo Chapel is notable. This stone adds further lightness to the luminous altarpiece painted by Maratti, which seems to float on clouds. The simple shape of the altar contributes to this effect of lightness. The altar design, inspired by that in the Chigi Chapel, inspired in turn the form of many altars built in and outside Rome in the first decades of the eighteenth century.
18 — ASR, Archivio Cartari-Febei, b. 90, fol. 200v. On the Ginetti Chapel, see Cavazzini 1999; Nater 2010.
19 — ASR, Archivio Cartari-Febei, b. 90, fols. 191r–v, diary of Carlo Cartari, June 16, 1684: "Osservai come cosa nuova, che la cuppola, e li pieducci erano tutti impellicciati, e incrostati di vaghi marmi coloriti; non già ornati di stucchi, oro e pitture, il che non si vede in alcuna altra cappella di Roma." ("I observed as a new thing that the cupola and the pendentives were entirely encrusted with beautiful colored marbles, not decorated with stuccos, gold, or paintings, something that one does not see in any other chapel in Rome.")
20 — The Ginetti Chapel also seems to have played the role of a "negative" model; that is to say that Cybo and Fontana wanted to avoid some faults that viewers had observed in the chapel in Sant'Andrea della Valle. See ASR, Archivio Cartari-Febei, b. 90, fols. 191r–v, diary of Carlo Cartari, June 16, 1684: "Osservai, che la faccia del cardinale non è troppo simile, e che è troppo grande il sito che si frapone tra il detto cardinale, e la cornice superiore del detto deposito. Osservai ancora, che l'inscrizzione è posta così in alto, che difficilmente può leggersi; onde per rimediare ... haverei stimato meglio, che la detta statua fosse stata collocata sopra un maestoso zoccolo, e che in questo si fusse incisa l'inscrizzione. Nel rimanente la cappella è nobile assai." ("I observed that the face of the cardinal does not resemble him, and that the space between the said cardinal and the upper cornice of the said tomb is too large. I also observed that the inscription is placed too high, making it difficult to read; thus to correct this ... I would have considered better, that the said statue should have been placed above an imposing socle, and in this would be incised the inscription. Otherwise, the chapel is very noble.")
21 — ASR, Notai Auditor Camerae, notary F. Franceschini, vol. 3231, fols. 617r–654r (inventory of cardinal's goods).
22 — Serafinelli 2015, II, 130.
23 — Federici 2018.
24 — Quoted in Bentivoglio and Valtieri 1976, 235: "1680. Cappella Cybo incominciata ad ornare, come al presente, dal cardinale Alderano Cybo."
25 — Federici and Garms 2010, 93–94, 97–98. For other marble fragments that may have come from the chapel, see Bentivoglio and Valtieri 1976, 76.
26 — Federici and Garms 2010, 95–97. In the new mounting of the monument in San Cosimato, the two side putti with coats of arms were inverted, as we can infer through a comparison of the tomb with the Windsor drawing that reproduces its original arrangement (fig. 3).
27 — Del Re 1952, 300.
28 — Already on September 23, 1679, the delivery of "un pezzetto di diaspro" for Cybo is recorded (Archivio Reverenda Fabbrica di San Pietro [hereafter ARFSP], Arm. 27, rip. B, vol. 377, fol. 5); this marks, according to Hager, the beginning of the fulfillment of Bernini's project, soon interrupted. We cannot exclude, however, the hypothesis that the delivery could be linked to other works commissioned by the cardinal where jasper is used, such as the main altar of the church of San Giovanni Battista in Jesi, finished and shipped in 1682 (see Federici 2006, 256–257).
29 — ARFSP, Arm. 27, rip. B, vol. 377, fols. 11v–12r.
30 — More travertine was given to Bigieri on August 6, 1682 (seven pieces),

August 19 (eight pieces), and November 26 (eleven pieces, including one "pezzo di feritora con occhi"); see ARFSP, Arm. 27, rip. B, vol. 377, fols. 11v–13v.

31 — Sources quoted in Westin and Westin 1975, 53: "Le cardinal Cybo y fait batir une belle chapelle," and "il cardinal Alderano Cybo, famiglia tra le più potenti, e antiche d'Italia, dà principio ad una famosa cappella architettata dal Cavalier Fontana di vaghissime, e pretiose pietre."

32 — Quoted in Rossi 1941, 438: "Ha messo mano nella sua cappella da farsi nella chiesa del Popolo a fronte di quella di Chigi il Cardinale Cybo, e pensa usare tutte le sue industrie, acciò non gli sia inferiore."

33 — We cannot exclude other reasons for this choice, such as a reference to Raphael's frescoes in the Vatican or the purpose of using a medium that is (theoretically, at least) more lasting than oils on canvas, thanks to its immobility.

34 — Rudolph 2000, 472. In prints, too, and especially in the collection *Disegni di vari altari e cappelle* by Giovanni Giacomo De Rossi (1713), we find the juxtaposition of and comparison between the two chapels of Santa Maria del Popolo; see Antinori 2017, 151.

35 — At first, Fontana had designed two monuments very different from the existing ones, with the full-length cardinals standing, flanked by allegorical figures and surmounted by circular windows; see Hager 1996, 246–249.

36 — Titi 1674–1763 [1987], 236.

37 — See Federici 2017, 218–219 (also for a bust of Cardinal Alderano linked to that in the chapel, formerly on the London art market).

38 — Archivio di Stato di Massa (hereafter ASMs), Archivio Cardinale Alderano Cybo, vol. XX, letter of Alderano to Alberico, May 22, 1677: "Francesco Cavallino da Carrara sarà da me assistito in tutte le sue occorrenze per servire a Vostra Eccellenza."

39 — Titi 1674–1763 [1987], 236.

40 — Titi 1674–1763 [1987], 236.

41 — The corpse of the martyr was donated to Cybo by Cardinal Gaspare Carpegna on October 15, 1686 (Bentivoglio and Valtieri 1976, 127); as Titi does not mention the urn, it probably had not yet been placed in the chapel at the end of 1686.

42 — ASR, Archivio Cardinale Alderano Cybo, b. 89, ff. 119v–120r, July 30, 1683.

43 — On the sculptor from Carrara Michele Antonio Grandi, who was famous especially for his astonishing marble musical instruments and who was probably employed in the realization of the marble decoration of the Cybo Chapel, see Federici 2003b; Bernardini 2005; Radicchi 2008.

44 — He was the agent of the cardinal in Massa.

45 — ASMs, Archivio Cardinale Alderano Cybo, vol. XXIII, letter of Alderano to Carlo, September 11, 1683: "Per lavorare in questa mia cappella del Popolo haverei bisogno delli due giovani Stefano Conti Cucurni, et Agostino Molani, proposti, et approvati dal Grandi; desidero che l'Eccellenza Vostra si compiaccia di disponerli a portarsi qua alla rinfrescata, che sarà verso il fine d'ottobre, e di ordinare a don Giovanni [Pizzuti] che gli somministri il denaro che gli bisognarà per il viaggio che potranno fare per mare.... Sentirà dal Grandi, che la cappella riesce molto bene et io lo desidero, e mi preme a maggior gloria di Dio e della Santissima Vergine."

46 — ASR, Archivio Cartari Febei, b. 90, f 277v: "Sabbato 22 di luglio [1684] viddi a Ripa Grande, che in quel giorno stesso si era dall'istesso luogo, dove furono alzate le colonne per la cappella del Signor Cardinale Cibo, calato il gran cassone, con dentro la statua a cavallo del Re di Francia, condottavi ... dalla scuola del cavalier Bernino." ("Saturday, July 22 [1684], I saw at Ripa Grande, that on that same day, from the same place that the columns for the chapel of the Signor Cardinal Cibo were unloaded [from a ship], was uploaded a large crate, inside of which [was] the equestrian statue of the King of France brought there ... by the workshop assistants of cavalier Bernino.)

47 — Giantomassi 2016, 280.

48 — ASMs, Archivio Cardinale Alderano Cybo, vol. XXIII, letter of Alderano to Carlo, August 12, 1684.

49 — ASR, Archivio Cartari Febei, b. 90, fols. 287r–v: "la cappella ... si va tuttavia riducendo a perfettione, dicendosi, che sia per haver luogo tra le principali di Roma."

50 — Still in 1686, however, purchases of marble from the Fabbrica di San Pietro are recorded: on February 14 of that year, two pieces of *paonazzo* marble were delivered to Marcello Bigieri, "scarpellino dell'Eminentissimo Signor Cardinale Cibo"; another piece of *paonazzo* and "una mezza colonna di bigio" were given to Bigieri, respectively, on May 28 and July 4. ARFSP, Arm. 27, rip. B, vol. 377, fols. 12r, 27v.

51 — ASMs, Archivio Cardinale Alderano Cybo, vol. XXIII, letter of Alderano to Alberico II, October 23, 1684: "Se ne ritorna costà Agostino Molani scarpellino dopo havere sodisfatto con molta puntualità, e diligenza, e con mia sodisfattione al lavoro che gl'è stato appoggiato in questa mia cappella della chiesa del Popolo; ho voluto portarne la notizia a Vostra Eccellenza afinché ella si compiaccia, come ne la prego, di protteggerlo nelle sue occorrenze per le quali prendo la confidenza di raccomandarlo all'Eccellenza Vostra com'egli merita per il buon servizio prestato.... prego [Vostra Eccellenza] sentire dallo stesso lo stato della cappella, che non le dispiacerà. Ho risoluto di mettere nell'arco dell'ingresso l'arma di Vostra Eccellenza et attendo sapere come la faccia se con la Malaspina, o senza."

52 — The double encomiastic purpose (individual and familiar) of the chapel's reconstruction is underlined by the cardinal at the end of the building works, in the letter to his brother Alberico of May 17, 1687: "La capella, fatta da me, e che ha l'arme della Casa nel primo arco." The emphasis on this point (see also the letter of the cardinal of January 7, 1690, in Federici 2002, 57: "io ho procurato di spender giustificatamente il mio denaro, di lasciare alla Casa questa cospicua memoria") seems to be motivated also by Cybo's wish to prevent potential criticisms of his choice to spend so much money on a Roman *fabbrica*, instead of using it for the construction of buildings and altars in Massa, as he had often done before. The emphasis on the familiar nature of the reconstruction of the chapel can also be discerned in the evident enlargement of the ducal coat of arms in the painting of the chapel's interior preserved at the Museo di Roma and ordered by the cardinal as a gift for his relatives in Massa.

53 — The balls of the Medici family, inserted in the Cybo family's coat of arms since 1487, were not depicted; see ASMs, Archivio Cardinale Alderano Cybo, vol. XXIII, letter of Alberico II to Alderano, November 12, 1684, and letter of Alderano to Alberico II, November 18, 1684. On the coat of arms on the

entrance arch of the chapel, see now Cantaro 2019, 229-232. In his own coat of arms, the cardinal never inserted either the Malaspina branch or the Medici balls; also for this reason, he is designated with the sole surname Cybo, while the sovereigns of Massa and Carrara bear the double surname Cybo Malaspina.

54 — On the coats of arms in Roman noble chapels, see Franceschini 2002. The painted decoration of the aisle's vault is contemporary to the building of the chapel (it is reproduced in the *veduta* of the Museo di Roma) and was probably executed by the same painter who decorated the location in San Cosimato in Trastevere, where Cardinal Lorenzo's monument, transformed into an altar, was placed.

55 — Federici 2013. On the fresco of the dome, see Sestieri 1972, 94; Federici 2018. On its restoration in 2000-2001, see Antellini Donelli 2009, 720-723.

56 — ASMs, Archivio Cardinale Alderano Cybo, vol. XXIII, letter of Alderano to Carlo, August 5, 1684: "riesce bene, e si sollecita, et hora, che il pittore non può applicare alla cupola si sollecita per questo."

57 — From this point of view, Garzi's God the Father is more similar to the one painted by Sebastiano del Piombo in his altarpiece of the *Nativity of the Virgin* than to the God of the lantern of the Chigi Chapel.

58 — Rudolph 1994, with previous bibliography; Rudolph 2000; Giantomassi 2016; Federici 2018. On the relationship between the artist and the cardinal, see Rudolph 1994; Federici 2008. The painting was restored at the beginning of the 1980s.

59 — For the preparatory drawings, see Prosperi Valenti Rodinò forthcoming, with previous bibliography.

60 — See Rudolph 1994; Federici 2008; Windt 2018. We cannot discard the hypothesis that the painting in Potsdam is actually a *ricordo* with variations and not a preparatory work. Cybo wanted a portion of the painting to be reproduced in his portrait by Carlo Maratti, now in Marseille (fig. 2).

61 — Bellori 1731, 186.

62 — See Federici 2018.

63 — On Maratti and Raphael, see Mena Marqués 1990; Ebert-Schifferer 2006.

64 — See especially Rudolph 1994, 23. In addition, the pose and the upward gaze of the Virgin (especially in the Potsdam version [see note 60]), can be seen as a tribute to one of the most famous depictions of Mary in Santa Maria del Popolo, Annibale Carracci's *Assumption of the Virgin* in the Cerasi Chapel.

65 — Quotations are taken from Bellori 1695, 26. On the *Disputa* by Raphael, see Reale 1998.

66 — On the various interpretations of the platform in Raphael's painting (as a reference to the construction of the new St. Peter's or as symbol of the victory over paganism, among others), see Reale 1998, 77. Its presence in Maratti's *Disputa* does not appear to carry a specific meaning but serves to reinforce the strong connection to Raphael's fresco.

67 — On Maratti's interest in this painting, see Rudolph 1994, 23. Even the choice of the oils-on-wall technique can be seen as a reference to the fresco technique employed by Raphael in the *Stanze*.

68 — For a comparison of the two *Disputations*, see Federici 2018.

69 — Federici 2018, 112-113.

70 — On Innocent's hesitancy to promote the Immaculate cult, see Vázquez Janeiro 1957; see also Anselmi 2008. Much later, and in a completely changed context, in the years immediately following the proclamation of the dogma of the Immaculate Conception (December 8, 1854), the painter Francesco Podesti, too, would have based his celebration of the Virgin, frescoed in the Sala dell'Immacolata in the Vatican Palaces, on Raphael's scene in the *Stanze*.

71 — Pascoli 1730-1736 [1992], 759: "Sparsasi ... per tutta Roma la fama della sua abilità non vi fu personaggio dilettante, che non l'andasse a trovare, e più d'ogni altro il cardinal Cybo, che ornar faceva la sua cappella alla Madonna del Popolo, v'andava. Condusselo a vederla, e gli disse, che voleva, che vi dipingesse i laterali; ed egli accettò volentieri il partito, e mise susseguentemente mano al lavoro, e compiutolo riportò con quello di Sua Eminenza l'applauso universale degli altri."

72 — Titi 1674-1763 [1987], 204.

73 — Titi 1674-1763 [1987], 236: "Oggi che mi è stato permesso di vederla [la cappella] quasi perfettionata, e trovo stabilite l'opere non in tutto nella conformità, che allora si era determinato; sono in obbligo in questa mia poca aggiunta discorrerne di nuovo."

74 — On this point and on the relationship between Cybo and Morandi, see Federici 2017. As the left side painting with *The Martyrdom of Saint Lawrence* was the first to be executed by Seiter, we can suppose that Cybo commissioned the right lateral panting from Morandi depicting *The Martyrdom of Saint Catherine*. Christoph Orth evocatively speculates that a drawing by Morandi representing the martyrdom of this saint could be a preparatory drawing for the never-realized Cybo painting; see Ketelsen and Orth 2015, 18-21).

75 — See the letter of the Piemontese ambassador De Gubernatis to the duke of Savoy, August 26, 1687: Seiter "è stato ultimamente impiegato dal Signor Cardinale Cibo per li quadri collaterali della cappella novamente fatta fabricare da Sua Eminenza nella chiesa della Madonna del Popolo, dove ha riuscito mirabilmente, a segno che messi in confronto coll'ancona dell'altare fatta da Carlo Maratta si reputano comunemente etiamdio per migliori." (Seiter "has recently been employed by the Signor Cardinal Cibo for the lateral paintings of the chapel newly built by His Eminence in the church of the Madonna del Popolo, where he has succeeded marvelously, evidenced by the fact that in comparison with the altarpiece made by Carlo Maratta, they [Seiter's paintings] are generally judged better.") Baudi Di Vesme 1963, III, 976.

76 — Cappelletti and Spione 2002.

77 — Pascoli 1730-1736 [1992], 759. For the appearance of the first versions, see Kunze 2000, 94, 98. On their removal, see Federici 2002, 60-61. On the execution in Turin of the second versions, see Mattiello 2016, 36.

78 — Prati 1686.

79 — Titi 1674-1763 [1987], 236.

80 — ASR, Archivio Cartari Febei, b. 94, fol. 203r.

81 — ASMs, Archivio Cardinale Alderano Cybo, vol. XXIV, letter of Alderano to Alberico II, May 17, 1687: "La capella, fatta da me, e che ha l'arme della Casa nel primo arco è riuscita a giuditio de' periti la più bella di Roma fuori delle due di Sisto Quinto, e di Paolo V."

82 — In another letter to his brother, sent on January 7, 1690, Alderano mentions again the chapel together with those in Santa Maria Maggiore; see Federici 2002, 57. On the two chapels of the Liberian Basilica, see Ostrow 1996.

83 — ASMs, Archivio Cardinale Alderano Cybo, vol. XXIV, note and letter of Alberico II to Cardinal Alderano, May 25, 1687, and letter of Alberico to Alderano, June 8, 1687. See also the appreciative words of Carlo Cartari, in ASR, Archivio Cartari Febei, b. 95, fol. 126r, May 25, 1687, where it is stated: "La spesa fatta dal Signor Cardinale dicono ascendere a ventiquattromila scudi." ("The expense made by the Signor Cardinal is said to amount to twenty-four thousand scudi.") In the following decades, this "universale applauso" diminished, together with the emergence of neoclassical aesthetic theory; and even if the Marquis de Sade in 1775 greatly praised the Cybo Chapel (Sade 1996, 56–57), a few years later, the severe Francesco Milizia wrote a stinging judgment: "Dal mezzo di questa chiesa, dove corrispondono le ricche cappelle di Cibo e di Chigi, si possono osservare i quattro stati più rimarchevoli dell'architettura romana dopo il ristabilimento delle belle arti: la sua alba e il suo rinascimento nel totale dell'edificio, il suo meriggio nella cappella Chigi diretta da Raffaello d'Urbino, e il suo occaso nella cappella Cibo architettata da un Fontana." ("From the center of this church, where the rich Cibo and Chigi chapels correspond, one can observe the four most remarkable states of Roman architecture after the reestablishment of the fine arts: its dawn and its renaissance in the entirety of the building, its noon in the Chigi chapel designed by Raphael of Urbino, and its sunset in the Cibo chapel built by Fontana.") Milizia 1787, 129–130. Nibby (1839, 457–458) quotes and disapproves of Milizia's words, underlining the architectural qualities of the Cybo Chapel.

84 — Federici 2002.

85 — A confirmation of this coherence, and of the cardinal's great care for it, is given by the fact that Cybo, when the side paintings had to be substituted, wanted the new versions to be painted by the same artist (Seiter) who had realized, ten years earlier, the original canvases (even if Seiter was then in Turin and far away from Rome).

86 — Forcella 1869–1884, I, 394, n. 1504. The inscription was placed at the entrance of the chapel, at the bottom of the still-extant tomb slab of the cardinal, decorated with *commesso* bones and cartouches.

87 — Staffetti 1900; Federici 2003a; Federici 2014. On the painting, see Gualdi 2009b, 270–271, where the author rejects the traditional attribution of the fresco and supposes that it should be assigned to a "collaborator of Pinturicchio under the influence of Antoniazzo Romano."

88 — ASMs, Archivio Cardinale Alderano Cybo, vol. XXVIII, draft of Carlo II, October 4, 1693: "Hieri si alzò l'imagine di Nostra Signora, che Vostra Eminenza inviò al Signor Duca mio padre per ponere nella cappella della Casa, già che fu levata dall'antica del Popolo."

89 — The close relationship between the two chapels, conceived and built in the same years (the project of the chapel in Massa is recorded already in 1675), is increased by the fact that the Roman chapel was meant to be the burial site not only of Alderano but also of the other cardinals of the family, those of the past (Lorenzo) and the future ones. From this point of view, the chapel was unsuccessful. Alderano's brother Odoardo, patriarch of Constantinople, moved from Rome to Massa at the end of his life and was buried there in 1705. His grandnephew Cardinal Camillo chose as his burial site the chapel he built in Santa Maria degli Angeli, where he was interred in 1743. On Camillo's decision not to be buried in the Cybo Chapel in Santa Maria del Popolo, see Bentivoglio and Valtieri 1976, 248; and on his chapel, see Brodini 2013.

90 — ASMs, Archivio Cardinale Alderano Cybo, vol. XXVIII, note of Carlo II, not dated [but from the end of 1692]: "manca il verde antico, ed un pezzo d'alabastro orientale, che forma nuvole, desidero sapere se a Vostra Eminenza può riuscire, di provedermene il compimento, supponendo io esserle facile di trovarlo negli avvanzi, che possono essere restati nella sua bellissima cappella già finita, di che la supplico farne fare ogni diligenza" ("lacking the *verde antico* and a piece of oriental alabaster, which forms the clouds, I want to know if Your Eminence can provide them, assuming that they would be easy to find among the leftover [materials] from your already finished beautiful chapel, for which I humbly ask that you do so with all care").

91 — ASMs, Archivio Cardinale Alderano Cybo, vol. XXIX, note of Carlo II, August 8, 1694: "Con tutta sollicitudine faccio terminare la capella della Casa in San Francesco, acciò sia all'ordine per la celebrazione della prima messa nel giorno della Beatissima Vergine di Settembre, che sarà il titolo della festa, e questo ad immitazione di Vostra Eminenza." ("With all solicitude I am completing the chapel of the [Cybo Malaspina] House in [the church of] San Francesco, so that it will be in order for the celebration of the first Mass on the feast of the Blessed Virgin in September, which will be dedicated to the feast [of the Nativity of the Virgin], and this in imitation of Your Eminence.")

92 — See Mussi (1935, 7), who writes of the "fresco representing the Virgin with the Heavenly Child and little joyful [*sic*] angels (not Saint Anne as erroneously believed)." The fresco is reproduced as a *Saint Anne* in Bonatti 1987, 173.

93 — A very small group of visitors, then, was able to appreciate the formal similarities between the two settings, because some of them had been in Rome and had seen the chapel in Santa Maria del Popolo or knew its aspect through the accurate *veduta* commissioned by Cardinal Alderano, which hung in one of the rooms of the Ducal Palace of Massa.

List of Abbreviations

AC — Archivio Caetani, Rome
ACCS — Archivio Storico della Congregazione per le Cause dei Santi, Vatican City
ACOR — Archivio della Congregazione dell'Oratorio, Rome
ARFSP — Archivio della Reverenda Fabbrica di San Pietro, Vatican City
ARSI — Archivum Romanum Societatis Jesu, Rome
ASC — Archivio Storico Capitolino, Rome
ASMs — Archivio di Stato di Massa
ASR — Archivio di Stato di Roma
ASUCBR — Archivio Storico Unicredit Banca di Roma, Vatican City
BAV — Biblioteca Apostolica Vaticana
BVR — Biblioteca Vallicelliana, Rome

Bibliography

Abromson 1976
Morton C. Abromson, *Painting in Rome during the Papacy of Clement VIII (1592–1605): A Documented Study*, PhD diss., Columbia University 1976.

Abromson 1981
Morton C. Abromson, *Painting in Rome during the Papacy of Clement VIII (1592–1605): A Documented Study*, New York and London 1981.

Accordi 1980
Bruno Accordi, "Michele Mercati (1541–1593) e la Metallotheca," *Geologica Romana*, 19, 1980, 1–50.

Acidini and Capretti 2009
Cristina Acidini and Elena Capretti eds., *Innocente e calunniato. Federico Zuccari (1539/40–1609) e le vendette d'artista*, exhib. catalogue (Firenze 2009–2010), Firenze 2009.

Acidini Luchinat 1991
Cristina Acidini Luchinat, "Tre madrigali e alcune osservazioni sulla Cappella Gaddi in Santa Maria Novella," *Studi di Storia dell'Arte*, 2, 1991, 295–320.

Acidini Luchinat 1998
Cristina Acidini Luchinat, *Taddeo e Federico Zuccari fratelli pittori*, I, Firenze 1998.

Affanni, Cogotti, and Vodret 1993
Anna Maria Affanni, Marina Cogotti, and Rossella Vodret, *Santa Susanna and San Bernardo alle Terme*, Roma 1993.

Agosti 2008
Barbara Agosti, *Paolo Giovio. Uno storico lombardo nella cultura artistica del Cinquecento*, Firenze 2008.

Agricola 1556
Georgius Agricola, *De Re Metallica Libri XII*, Basileae 1556.

da Alatri 1933
Ottavio da Alatri, "L'istituzione dell'incoronazione delle immagini mariane," *L'Italia francescana*, 8, 1933, 159–180.

Alberici 1600
Giacomo Alberici, *Compendio delle grandezze dell'illustre, et devotissima Chiesa di Santa Maria del Popolo di Roma*, Roma 1600.

Albertini 1510
Francesco Albertini, *Opusculum de mirabilibus novae et veteris urbis Romae*, Romae 1510.

Albertus Magnus ed. 1967
Albertus Magnus, *Book of Minerals*, trans. by Dorothy Wyckoff, Oxford 1967.

Aldrovandi and Mauro 1556
Ulisse Aldrovandi and Lucio Mauro, *Le antichità della città di Roma* [Ulisse Aldrovandi, *Delle statue antiche che per tutta Roma in diversi luoghi, e case si veggono*], Venetia 1556.

Alfarano 16th cent. [1914]
Tiberio Alfarano, *De Basilicae Vaticanae antiquissima et nova structura*, ed. by Michele Cerrati, Roma 1914.

Amadio 1986
Adele A. Amadio, *I mosaici di S. Costanza: disegni, incisioni e documenti dal XV al XIX secolo*, Roma 1986.

Amendola 2010
Adriano Amendola, *I Caetani di Sermoneta: storia artistica di un antico casato tra Roma e l'Europa*, Roma 2010.

Andaloro and Romano 2006–2017
Maria Andaloro and Serena Romano, *La pittura medievale a Roma, 312–1431. Corpus e Atlante*, 6 vols., Milano 2006–2017.

Angelelli 2010
Claudia Angelelli, *La basilica titolare di Santa Pudenziana. Nuove ricerche*, Città del Vaticano 2010.

Angenendt 2010
Arnold Angenendt, "Relics and their Veneration," in Bagnoli, Klein, Mann, and Robinson 2010, 19–28.

Annibali 2019, forthcoming
Luca Annibali, "Giovanni Battista Bianchi oltre il restauro di "anticaglie". Considerazioni sull'attività di uno scultore dimenticato," in *Circolazione, scambi e modelli: gli scultori a Roma nella seconda metà del Cinquecento*, conference proceedings (Rome 2019), ed. by Gregoire Extermann, Giovanna Ioele, and Livia Nocchi (forthcoming).

Anselmi 2005
Alessandra Anselmi, "Theaters for the Canonization of Saints," in *St. Peter's in the Vatican*, ed. by William Tronzo, Cambridge 2005, 244–269.

Anselmi 2008
L'Immacolata nei rapporti tra l'Italia e la Spagna, ed. by Alessandra Anselmi, Roma 2008.

Antellini Donelli 2009
Simona Antellini Donelli, "I restauri pittorici della Soprintendenza per i Beni Ambientali ed Architettonici di Roma (1993–2006)," in Miarelli Mariani and Richiello 2009, II, 705–727.

Antinori 2017
Aloisio Antinori, "La costruzione della carriera di Carlo Fontana: il ruolo delle stampe," in Bonaccorso and Moschini 2017, 148–154.

Antonucci 2018
Mario Antonucci, *La basilica di Santa Pudenziana*, Todi 2018.

Apollonj Ghetti 1965
Bruno M. Apollonj Ghetti, *Santa Susanna*, Roma 1965.

Apollonj Ghetti 1984
Bruno M. Apollonj Ghetti, "Le Confessioni semianulari nelle basiliche romane," in *Roma Sotterranea*, ed. by Roberto Luciani, Roma 1984, 203–213.

Aringhi 1788
Paolo Aringhi, *Memorie istoriche della vita del Padre Virgilio Spada Preposito della Congregazione dell'Oratorio di Roma e di poi Commendatore dell'Archiospitale di S. Spirito in Sassia*, Venezia 1788.

Armenini 1587
Giovanni Battista Armenini, *De' veri precetti della pittura, libri tre*, Ravenna 1587.

Arnolfini 1603
Paolino Arnolfini, *Narratione, et solenne essequie dell'Illustriss. et Reverendiss. Signor Cardinale Antonio Maria Salviati*, Roma 1603.

Augustine ed. 1853
Augustine of Hippo, *Expositions on the Book of Psalms*, trans. with notes and indices, V, Psalms CII–CXXV, Oxford 1853.

Augustine ed. 1948
Augustine of Hippo, *Basic Writings of St. Augustine*, trans. by Withney J. Oates, 2 vols., New York 1948.

Aurigemma 2004
Maria Giulia Aurigemma, "Committenze Caetani: dal Cinquecento al Seicento, dai feudi alla città," in *Bonifacio VIII, i Caetani e la storia del Lazio*, conference proceedings (Rome–Sermoneta 2000), ed. by Riccardo Cerocchi and Pier Giacomo Sottoriva, Roma 2004, 193–219.

Bacci 1625
Pietro Giacomo Bacci, *Vita di San Filippo Neri fiorentino fondatore della Congregazione dell'Oratorio*, Roma 1625.

Bacci ed. 1902
Pietro Giacomo Bacci, *The Life of St Philip Neri, Apostle of Rome and Founder of the Congregation of the Oratory*, 2 vols., ed. and trans. by Frederick Antrobus, London 1902.

Baglione 1642
Giovanni Baglione, *Le vite de' pittori scultori et architetti. Dal pontificato di Gregorio XIII del 1572. Insino a' tempi di papa Urbano VIII nel 1642*, Roma 1642.

Bagnoli 2010
Martina Bagnoli, "The Stuff of Heaven: Materials and Craftsmanship in Medieval Reliquaries," in Bagnoli, Klein, Mann, and Robinson 2010, 137–147.

Bagnoli, Klein, Mann, and Robinson 2010
Martina Bagnoli, Holger A. Klein, C. Griffith Mann and James Robinson eds., *Treasures of Heaven: Saints, Relics, and Devotion in Medieval Europe*, exhib. catalogue (Cleveland, Baltimore and London 2010–2011), New Haven 2010.

Bailey 2003
Stephen M. Bailey, "Taddeo Zuccaro's Early Ideas for the Altar Wall of the Frangipani Chapel," *Apollo*, 428, 2003, 8–13.

Balass 2001
Golda Balass, "Taddeo Zuccari's Decoration for the Frangipani Chapel in San Marcello al Corso," *Assaph* (Sect. B, Studies in Art History), 6, 2001, 177–204.

Baldini, Giusti, and Martelli 1979
Umberto Baldini, Anna Maria Giusti, and Annapaula Pampaloni Martelli eds., *La Cappella dei Principi e le pietre dure a Firenze*, Milano 1979.

Baldinucci 1681
Filippo Baldinucci, *Vocabolario toscano dell'arte del disegno*, Firenze 1681.

Balot 1998
Ryan K. Balot, "Pindar, Virgil, and the Proem to Georgic 3," *Phoenix*, 52, 1998, 12, 83–94.

Barchiesi 2017
Sofia Barchiesi, "La raccolta iconografica di san Filippo Neri dell'Archivio della Congregazione dell'Oratorio di Roma," in *Iconografia di un santo. Nuovi studi sull'immagine di san Filippo Neri*, ed. by Alberto Bianco, Roma 2017, 189–278.

Bargellini 1954
Piero Bargellini, *The Cloisters of Santa Maria Novella and the Spanish Chapel*, Florence 1954.

Barocchi 1960–1962
Paola Barocchi, *Trattati d'arte del Cinquecento tra manierismo e controriforma*, 3 vols., Bari 1960–1962.

Baronio 1586
Cesare Baronio, *Martyrologium Romanum*, Romae 1586.

Baronio 1588–1607
Cesare Baronio, *Annales ecclesiastici*, 12 vols., Antverpiae 1588–1607.

Baronio 1617
Cesare Baronio, *Annales ecclesiastici*, II, Antverpiae 1617.

Baronio 1656
Cesare Baronio, *Annali ecclesiastici*, trans. by Odorico Rinaldi, part I, Roma 1656.

Barral Altet and Bertelli 1988
Xavier Barral Altet and Carlo Bertelli, *Il mosaico*, Milano 1998.

Barroero 1984
Liliana Barroero, *Rione Monti I.III (Guide rionali di Roma)*, Roma 1984.

Barry 2009
Fabio Barry, "Sculpture in Painting/ Painting in Sculpture, c.1485–c.1660," in *Sculpture in Painting*, exhib. catalogue (Leeds 2009–2010), ed. by Penelope Curtis, Leeds 2009, 13–19.

Barry 2011
Fabio Barry, *Painting in Stone: The Symbolism of Colored Marbles in the Visual Arts and Literature from Antiquity until the Enlightenment*, PhD diss., Columbia University 2011.

Barry 2016
Fabio Barry, "Im/Material Bernini," in Levy and Mangone 2016, 39–67.

Barry 2017
Fabio Barry, "Painting in Stone: Early Modern Experiments in a Metamedium," *Art Bulletin*, 99, 2017, 3, 30–61.

Barry 2019, forthcoming
Fabio Barry, "'Perché vorrebbe uscire dall'ordinario': Architecture and the Paragone in Virgilio Spada's Chapel Designs for Sant'Andrea della Valle (1630–1634, 1662)," in *I colori del marmo*, study day (Pisa 2018), ed. by Cristiano Giometti and Cinzia M. Sicca, Pisa 2019 (forthcoming).

Barry and Gwynne, forthcoming
Fabio Barry and Paul Gwynne, *Ars Artem Invocat. Architecture and Poetry in Early Modern Rome* (forthcoming).

Bartola 2003
Alberto Bartola ed., *Il Regesto del Monastero dei SS. Andrea e Gregorio ad Clivum Scauri*, Roma 2003.

Bartoli 1963
Alfonso Bartoli, *Curia Senatus: lo scavo e il restauro*, Roma 1963.

Bartolocci 1675–1693
Giulio Bartolocci, *Bibliotheca Magna Rabbinica de scriptoribus & scriptis hebraicis*, 4 vols., Romae 1675–1693.

Bastogi 2002
Nadia Bastogi, *La pala di Santi di Tito nel Santuario di Santa Maria Soccorso*, Prato 2002.

Baudi di Vesme 1963
Alessandro Baudi di Vesme, *Schede Vesme: l'arte in Piemonte dal XVI al XVIII secolo*, 4 vols., Torino 1963.

Bauer 2013
Stefan Bauer, "La transizione storiografica tra Rinascimento e Controriforma: il caso di Onofrio Panvinio (1530–1568)," in *La transizione come problema storiografico: le fasi critiche dello sviluppo della modernità, 1494–1973*, ed. by Paolo Pombeni and Heinz-Gerhard Haupt, Bologna 2013, 129–149.

Bauer 2014
Stefan Bauer, "Onofrio Panvinio," in *Dizionario Biografico degli Italiani*, 81, Roma 2014, *ad vocem*.

Bauer 2019
Stefan Bauer, "History for Hire in Sixteenth-Century Italy: Onofrio Panvinio's Histories on Roman Families," *Erudition and the Republic of Letters*, 4, 2019, 397–438.

Beard 2003
Mary Beard, "Picturing the Roman triumph. Putting the Fasti Capitolini in their context," *Apollo*, 158, 2003, 497, 23–28.

Bedon 1983
Anna Bedon, "Uniatismo, apostolato e colonialismo religioso nell'età di Gregorio XIII, la chiesa di S. Atanasio di rito greco in Roma," *Antichità viva*, 22, 1983, 5–6, 49–57.

Bedon 1991
Anna Bedon, "La realizzazione del Campidoglio michelangiolesco all'epoca di Sisto V e la situazione urbana della zona capitolina," in *Il Campidoglio e Sisto V*, exhib. catalogue (Rome 1991), ed. by Luigi Spezzaferro and Maria Elisa Tittoni, Roma 1991, 76–84.

Bedon 2008
Anna Bedon, *Storia di un monumento civile nella Roma papale*, Milano 2008.

Beggiao 1978
Diego Beggiao, *La visita pastorale di Clemente VIII (1592–1600). Aspetti di riforma post-tridentina a Roma*, Roma 1978.

Bell 1985
Janice Bell, "The Life and Works of Matteo Zaccolini (1574–1630)," *Regnum Dei*, 41, 1985, 227–258.

Bellavia 2003
Silva Bellavia, "Il cardinale Girolamo Rusticucci e le sue committenze marchigiane," *Storia dell'arte*, 2003, 106, 25–43.

Bellini 1999
Federico Bellini, "La moderna Confessione di San Pietro; le proposte di Ferrabosco e Maderno," in *La Confessione nella basilica di San Pietro in Vaticano*, ed. by Alfredo Maria Pergolizzi, Cinisello Balsamo 1999, 43–55.

Bellini 2002
Federico Bellini, "La costruzione della Cappella Gregoriana in San Pietro, di Giacomo della Porta: cronologia, protagonisti e significato iconologico," in *Architettura: processualità e trasformazione*, conference proceedings (Rome 1999), published in *Quaderni dell'Istituto di Storia dell'Architettura*, 34–39, 2002, ed. by Maurizio Caperna and Gianfranco Spagnesi, Roma 2002, 333–346.

Bellini 2011
Federico Bellini, *La Basilica di San Pietro da Michelangelo a Della Porta*, 2 vols., Roma 2011.

Bellori 1672 [1976]
Giovan Pietro Bellori, *Le vite de' pittori, scultori e architetti moderni*, Roma 1672, ed. by Evelina Borea, Torino 1976.

Bellori 1672 [2005]
Giovan Pietro Bellori, *The Lives of the Modern Painters, Sculptors and Architects. A New Translation and Critical Edition*, trans. by Alice Sedgwick Wohl, notes by Hellmut Wohl, introduction by Tomaso Montanari, Cambridge 2005.

Bellori 1695
Giovan Pietro Bellori, *Descrizione delle immagini dipinte da Raffaelle d'Urbino nel Palazzo Vaticano, e nella Farnesina alla Lungara*, Roma 1695.

Bellori 1731
Giovan Pietro Bellori, "Vita di Carlo Maratti," in *Ritratti di alcuni celebri pittori del secolo XVII*, Roma 1731, 147–251.

Belting 2001
Hans Belting, *Bild-Anthropologie, Entwürfe für eine Bildwissenschaft*, München 2001.

Benati and DeGrazia 1999
Daniele Benati and Diane DeGrazia, eds., *The Drawings of Annibale Carracci. Catalog of an Exhibition Held at the National Gallery of Art*, exhib. catalogue (Washington DC 1999-2000), Washington DC 1999.

Benedetti 2006
Simona Benedetti, "Cappella Chigi in Santa Maria della Pace", in *Pietro da Cortona: piccole e grandi architetture*, ed. by Sandro Benedetti and Augusto Roca De Amicis, Roma 2006, 99–132.

Bentivoglio and Valtieri 1976
Enzo Bentivoglio and Simonetta Valtieri, *Santa Maria del Popolo*, Roma 1976.

Berger 2017
Susanna Berger, *The Art of Philosophy. Visual Thinking in Europe from the Late Renaissance to the Early Enlightenment*, Oxford and Princeton 2017.

Bernard ed. 1887
Bernard from Clairvaux, *Oeuvres completes de Saint Bernard*, III, Paris 1887.

Bernardini and Mignosi Tantillo 2001
Maria Grazia Bernardini and Almamaria Mignosi Tantillo eds., *Caravaggio, Carracci, Maderno. La Cappella Cerasi in Santa Maria del Popolo di Roma*, Cinisello Balsamo 2001.

Bernardini 2005
Maria Grazia Bernardini ed., *Un cembalo in marmo per Francesco II d'Este*, Modena 2005.

Bernardini and Fagiolo dell'Arco 1999
Maria Grazia Bernardini and Maurizio Fagiolo dell'Arco eds., *Gian Lorenzo Bernini. Regista del Barocco*, exhib. catalogue (Rome 1999), Milano 1999.

Bernia, Ambrosini, and Aldrovandi 1648
Marco Antonio Bernia, Bartolommeo Ambrosini, and Ulisse Aldrovandi, *Ulyssis Aldrovandi patricij Bononiensis musaeum metallicum in libros IIII distributum*, [Bononia] 1648.

Berthier 1910
Joachim Joseph Berthier, *L'Église de Sainte-Sabine a Rome*, Rome 1910.

Bevilacqua 2003
Mario Bevilacqua, "Residenze di ebrei conversi nella Roma del Seicento: Giovanni Antonio De Rossi e la costruzione di palazzo Boncompagni," in *Atlante tematico del Barocco in Italia. Il sistema delle residenze nobiliari. 2. Stato Pontificio e Granducato di Toscana*, ed. by Mario Bevilacqua, Marcello Fagiolo, and Maria Luisa Madonna, Roma 2003, 149–172.

Bianco 2009
Alberto Bianco, "Cesare Baronio e la conversione dei Corcos nei documenti d'archivio della Congregazione Oratoriana di Roma," in *Baronio e le sue fonti*, conference proceedings (Sora 2007), ed. by Luigi Gulia, Sora 2009, 154–165.

Biasiotti 1915
Giovanni Biasiotti, "La Basilica di S. Maria Maggiore di Roma prima delle innovazioni del secolo XVI," *Mélanges d'archéologie et d'histoire de l'École française de Rome*, 35, 1915, 15–40.

de Blaauw 1995
Sible L. de Blaauw, "Die Krypta in Stadtrömischen Kirchen: Abbild eines Pilzerfiels," in *Akten des XII. Internationalen Kongresses für christliche Archäologie*, conference proceedings (Bonn 1991), I, Münster 1995, 559–567.

Blunt 1982
Anthony Blunt, *Guide to Baroque Rome*, New York 1982.

Boden 2005
Anthony Boden, "The Life and Times of Thomas Tomkins and his Family," in *Thomas Tomkins: The Last Elizabethan*, ed. Anthony Boden, Aldershot 2005, 7–196.

Bösel, Menniti Ippolito, and Spiriti 2014
Richard Bösel, Antonio Menniti Ippolito, and Andrea Spiriti eds., *Innocenzo XI Odescalchi. Papa, politico, committente*, Roma 2014.

Bolzoni 2018
Marco Simone Bolzoni, "L'ultimo Salviati (1559–1563)," in *Autunno della Maniera*, ed. by Michela Corso and Alessia Ulisse, Milano 2018, 59–67.

Bombelli 1792
Pietro Bombelli, *Raccolta delle immagini della Beatissima Vergine Ornate della Corona d'Oro dal Reverendissimo Capitolo di San Pietro, con una breve ed esatta notizia di ciascuna imagine*, 4 vols., Roma 1792.

Bonaccorso and Moschini 2017
Giuseppe Bonaccorso and Francesco Moschini, eds., *Carlo Fontana 1638–1714 celebrato architetto*, conference proceedings (Rome 2014), Roma 2017.

Bonatti 1987
Franco Bonatti, *Massa Ducale*, Pisa 1987.

Bonaventure ed. 2008
Bonaventure from Bagnoregio, *Collations on the Seven Gifts of the Holy Spirit*, introd. and trans. by Zachary Hayes, notes by Robert J. Karris, New York 2008.

Bonci 2004
Paolo Bonci, *Madonne coronate in Italia e nel mondo, nel 3° Centenario dell'incoronazione di Maria SS. ma delle Grazie di San Giovanni Valdarno*, Fiesole 2004.

Bond 1916
Francis Bond, *The Chancel of English Churches: The Altar, Reredos, Lenten Veil, Communion Table, Altar Rails, Houseling Cloth, etc.*, Oxford 1916.

Borea 1986
Annibale Carracci e i suoi incisori, ed. by Evelina Borea, exhib. catalogue (Rome 1986), Roma 1986.

Borghini 1584
Raffaello Borghini, *Il Riposo*, Firenze 1584.

Borghini 1989
Gabriele Borghini ed., *Marmi antichi*, Roma 1989.

Borromeo 1577 [1962]
Carlo Borromeo, *Instructiones fabricae et supellectilis ecclesiasticae*, Mediolani 1577, in Barocchi 1960–1962, 3, 1962, 1–113.

Bosio 1650
Antonio Bosio, *Roma sotterranea*, with additions by Giovanni Severano, Roma 1650.

Bosman 2005
Lex Bosman, "Spolia and Coloured Marble in Sepulchral Monuments in Florence, Rome, and Bosco Marengo. Designs by Dosio and Vasari," *Mitteilungen des Kunsthistorischen Institutes in Florenz*, 49, 2005 (2006), 353–376.

van Boxel 2016
Piet van Boxel, *Jewish Books in Christian Hands. Theology, Exegesis and Conversion under Gregory XIII (1572–1585)*, Vatican City 2016.

Braconi 2015
Matteo Braconi, "Enrico Caetani e il restauro della basilica di S. Pudenziana a Roma: fatti e misfatti di un cantiere del tardo Cinquecento," *Rivista dell'Istituto Nazionale d'Archeologia e Storia dell'Arte*, 36, 2013(2015), 68, 61–99.

Braconi 2016
Matteo Braconi, *Il mosaico del catino absidale di Santa Pudenziana: la storia, i restauri, le interpretazioni*, Todi 2016.

Brauer and Wittkower 1931
Heinrich Brauer and Rudolf Wittkower, *Die Zeichnungen des Gianlorenzo Bernini*, Berlin 1931.

Braun 1924
Joseph Braun, *Der christliche Altar in seiner geschichtlichen Entwicklung*, 2 vols., München 1924.

Braun 1940
Joseph Braun, *Die Reliquiare des christlichen Kultes und ihre Entwicklung*, Freiburg 1940.

Brigidi 1885
Adamo Brigidi, "Cenno bibliografico intorno la vita e le opere di Lorenzo Frizolio da Sogliano, canonico della Cattedrale di Rimini," *Opuscoli religiosi, letterari e morali*, 18, 1885, 54, 347–357.

Brix 1995
Innocenzio Brix, "La Pentecoste filippina," *Memorie Oratoriane*, 17, 1995, 85–91.

Brockey 2015
Liam Matthew Brockey, "The Cruelest Honor: The Relics of Francis Xavier in Early-Modern Asia," *The Catholic Historical Review*, 101, 2015, 41–64.

Brodini 2013
Alessandro Brodini, "Il cardinale e il suo *thesaurus*: Camillo Cybo, Gaetano Fabrizi e la cappella delle reliquie nella basilica di Santa Maria degli Angeli in Roma," *Marburger Jahrbuch für Kunstwissenschaft*, 40, 2013, 149–189.

Brown 1981
Peter Brown, *The Cult of Saints. Its Rise and Function in Latin Christianity*, Chicago 1981.

Brunelli 2017
Giampiero Brunelli, "Rusticucci, Girolamo," in *Dizionario Biografico degli Italiani*, 89, Roma 2017, *ad vocem*.

Buchowiecki 1974
Walther Buchowiecki, *Handbuch der Kirchen Roms*, III, Wien 1974.

***Bullarium* 1868**
Bullarium Diplomatum et privilegiorum sanctorum romanum pontificum (ab. an. MDCXXIII ad an. MDCXXVIII), XIII, Augustae Taurinorum 1868.

Buttler 2011
Karen Buttler, "Rubens's First Painting for the High Altar of Santa Maria in Vallicella and His Unsuccessful Sales Strategy," in Feigenbaum and Ebert-Schifferer 2011, 17–38.

Caetani 1933
Gelasio Caetani, *Domus Caietana*, 2 vols., San Casciano Val di Pesa 1933.

Caffiero 2004
Marina Caffiero, *Battesimi forzati. Storie di ebrei, cristiani e convertiti nella Roma dei papi*, Roma 2004.

Caffiero 2016
Marina Caffiero, "Sainteté et conversions. Les procès de canonization comme source pour l'histoire des rapports entre juifs et chrétiens," in *Culture et Société au miroir des procès de canonization (XVIe–XXe siècle)*, ed. by Philippe Castagnetti and Christian Renoux, Saint-Étienne 2016, 167–80.

Caglioti 1997
Francesco Caglioti, "Sui primi temi romani d'Andrea Bregno: un progetto per il cardinale camerlengo Alvise Trevisan e un san Michele Arcangelo per il cardinale Juan de Carvajal," *Mitteilungen des Kunsthistorischen Institutes in Florenz*, 41, 1997(1998), 213–253.

Caglioti 2002
Francesco Caglioti, "La scultura del Quattrocento e dei primi decenni del Cinquecento," in *Storia della Calabria nel Rinascimento*, ed. by Simonetta Valtieri, Roma 2002, 977–1042.

Caglioti 2004
Francesco Caglioti, "Due 'Virtù' marmoree del primo Cinquecento napoletano emigrate a Lawrence, Kansas: i Carafa di Santa Severina e lo scultore Cesare Quaranta per San Domenico Maggiore," *Mitteilungen des Kunsthistorischen Institutes in Florenz*, 48, 2004(2005), 333–358.

Caglioti 2016
Francesco Caglioti, "La 'connoisseurship' della scultura rinascimentale: esperienze e considerazioni di un 'romanista' mancato," in *Il metodo del conoscitore. Approcci, limiti, prospettive*, conference proceedings (Rome 2015), ed. by Stefan Albl and Alina Aggujaro, Roma 2016, 125–152.

Caldwell 2011
Dorigen Caldwell, "A Neglected Papal Commission in Naples Cathedral: The Tomb of Cardinal Alfonso Carafa," *The Burlington Magazine*, 153, 2011, 1304, 712–717.

Caley and Richards 1956
Earle R. Caley and John C. Richards, *Theophrastus on Stones*, Columbus 1956.

Campana 1960
Augusto Campana, "Accursio, Mariangelo," in *Dizionario Biografico degli Italiani*, 1, Roma 1960, *ad vocem*.

Canepa 2007
Susanna Canepa, "Monsignor Giovanni Francesco Negrone: 'spirito e fuoco' per la Chiesa del Gesù in Roma," *La Casana*, 49, 2007, 361–370.

Canestrini and Desjardins 1875
Giuseppe Canestrini and Abel Desjardins eds., *Negotiacions diplomatiques de la France avec la Toscane. 5 Documents recueillis par Giuseppe Canestrini et publiés par Abel Desjardins*, Paris 1875.

Cantaro 2019
Maria Teresa Cantaro, *Gli stemmi di Santa Maria del Popolo: documenti di appartenenza*, Roma 2019

Cappelletti and Spione 2002
Francesca Cappelletti and Gelsomina Spione, *I fratelli Guidobono e Daniel Seiter. L'avvio della grande decorazione a Torino tra Seicento e Settecento*, Torino 2002.

Carbonara Pompei 2009
Sabina Carbonara Pompei, "L'apparato decorativo della Cappella Cybo," in Miarelli Mariani and Richiello 2009, II, 659–672.

Cardella 1793
Lorenzo Cardella, *Memorie storiche de' Cardinali della Santa Romana Chiesa*, V, Roma 1793.

Carinci 1870 [1893]
Giovanni Battista Carinci, *Lettere di Onorato Caetani, capitan generale delle fanterie pontificie nella Battaglia di Lepanto*, Roma 1870 (ed. 1893).

Casale 2011
Vittorio Casale, *L'Arte per le Canonizzazioni: l'attività artistica intorno alle canonizzazioni e alle beatificazioni del Seicento*, Torino 2011.

Castellani 1900
Giuseppe Castellani, "Medaglie Fanesi. I. Il Cardinale Rusticucci," *Rivista Italiana di Numismatica e Scienze Affini*, 13, 1900, 211–214.

***Catechismo* 1568**
Catechismo, cioe istruttione, secondo il decreto del Concilio di Trento, à parochi, publicato per comandamento del Santiss. S. N. Papa Pio V. & tradotto poi per ordine di S. Santità in lingua volgare, Venezia 1568.

Catitti 2013–2014
Silvia Catitti, "Balaustro e balaustrata tra metà Quattrocento e primo Cinquecento," *Quaderni dell'Istituto di Storia dell'Architettura*, 60–62, 2013–2014, 21–32.

Cavalieri 1584
Giovan Battista Cavalieri, *Descriptiones quaedam illius inhumanae et multiplicis persecutionis, quam in Anglia propter fidem sustinent catholice christiani*, Romae 1584.

Cavazzini 1999
Patrizia Cavazzini, "The Ginetti Chapel at S. Andrea della Valle," *The Burlington Magazine*, 141, 1999, 1156, 401–413.

Celio 1638
Gaspare Celio, *Memoria fatta dal Signor Gaspare Celio dell'habito di Christo delli nomi dell'artefici delle pitture che sono in alcune chiese, facciate e palazzi di Roma*, Napoli 1638.

Cerasoli 1894
Francesco Cerasoli, "Il monumento di Paolo IV nella chiesa della Minerva," *Studi e documenti di storia e diritto*, 15, 1894, 131–134.

Ceresa 1996
Massimo Ceresa, "Felini, Pietro Martire," in *Dizionario Biografico degli Italiani*, 46, Roma 1996, *ad vocem*.

Cerutti Fusco and Villani 2002
Annarosa Cerutti Fusco and Marcello Villani, *Pietro da Cortona Architetto*, Roma 2002.

Chacón 1576
Alonso Chacón, *Historia utriusque belli Dacici a Traiano Caesare gesti, ex simulachris quae in Columna eiusdem Romae visuntur collecta*, Romae 1576.

Chacón 1601
Alonso Chacón, *Vitae, et res gestae Pontificum Romanorum et S.R.E. Cardinalium*, Romae 1601.

Chacón 1630
Alonso Chacón, *Vitae et res gestae Pontificum Romanorum et S.R.E. Cardinalium*, II, Romae 1630.

Chase 2002
Steven Chase, *Angelic Spirituality: Medieval Perspectives on the Ways of Angels*, New York 2002.

Christian 2010
Kathleen Christian, *Empire Without End: Antiquities Collections in Renaissance Rome, c. 1350–1527*, New Haven and London 2010.

Ciappi 1591
Marco Antonio Ciappi, *Compendio delle heroiche et gloriose attioni et Santa Vita di Papa Gregorio XIII*, Roma 1591.

Ciappi 1596
Marco Antonio Ciappi, *Compendio delle heroiche et gloriose attioni, et Santa Vita Di Papa Gregorio XIII*, Roma 1596.

Cieri Via, Rowland, and Ruffini 2012
Claudia Cieri Via, Ingrid D. Rowland, and Marco Ruffini eds., *Unità e frammenti di modernità. Arte e scienza nella Roma di Gregorio XIII Boncompagni (1572–1585)*, conference proceedings (Rome 2004), Pisa 2012.

Cistellini 1989
Antonio Cistellini, *San Filippo Neri: l'Oratorio e la Congregazione Oratoriana. Storia e spiritualità*, 3 vols., Brescia 1989.

Cohen 2015
Meredith Cohen, *The Sainte-Chapelle and the Construction of Sacral Monarchy: Royal Architecture in Thirteenth-Century Paris*, Cambridge 2015.

Colantuono and Ostrow 2014
Anthony Colantuono and Steven F. Ostrow eds., *Critical Perspectives on Roman Baroque Sculpture*, University Park 2014.

Colonnese 2017
Fabio Colonnese, "'La Maestria di eccellenti artefici': note a margine di un rilievo della Cappella Cybo di Carlo Fontana," in Bonaccorso and Moschini 2017, 99–108.

Coltrinari 2016a
Francesca Coltrinari, *Artisti e committenti a Loreto (1538–1590): nuovi documenti*, Firenze 2016.

Coltrinari 2016b
Francesca Coltrinari, *Loreto cantiere artistico internazionale nell'età della Controriforma: i committenti, gli artisti, il contesto*, Firenze 2016.

Conforti 1991
Claudia Conforti, "Cosimo III de' Medici patrono d'arte a Goa: La tomba di S. Francesco Saverio di Giovan Battista Foggini," in *Lo Specchio del Principe. Mecenatismi paralleli: Medici e Moghul*, ed. by Dalu Jones, Roma 1991, 109–121.

Conforti 1993
Claudia Conforti, *Giorgio Vasari architetto*, Milano 1993.

Connor 1999
Carolyn L. Connor, "The Epigram in the Church of Hagios Polyeuktos in Constantinople and its Byzantine Response," *Byzantion*, 69, 1999, 2, 479–527.

Connors 1980
Joseph Connors, *Borromini and the Roman Oratory. Style and Society*, New York 1980.

Connors 1989
Joseph Connors, "Alliance and Enmity in Roman Baroque Urbanism," *Römisches Jahrbuch der Bibliotheca Hertziana*, 25, 1989, 207–294.

Cooper 1995
Alix Cooper, "The Museum and the Book: the Metallotheca and the History of an Encyclopaedic Natural History in Early Modern Italy," *Journal of the History of Collections*, 7, 1995, 1, 1–24.

Cordaro 1981
Michele Cordaro, "Circignani, Nicola," in *Dizionario Biografico degli Italiani*, 25, Roma 1981, *ad vocem.*

Cornelison 2004
Sally Cornelison, "Art Imitates Architecture: The Saint Philip Reliquary in Renaissance Florence," *Art Bulletin*, 86, 2004, 4, 642–658.

Cornelison 2012
Sally Cornelison, *Art and the Relic Cult of St. Antoninus in Renaissance Florence*, Farnham 2012.

Cornini 2012
Guido Cornini, "Pittura per l'eternità: lo studio del mosaico e la decorazione di San Pietro da Gregorio XIII a Pio VII," in *La basilica di San Pietro. Fortuna e immagine*, ed. by Giovanni Morello, Roma 2012, 371–443.

Corsi 1825
Faustino Corsi, *Catalogo ragionato d'una collezione di pietre di decorazione formata e posseduta in Roma*, Roma 1825.

***Le cose meravigliose della citta di Roma* 1544**
Le cose meravigliose della citta di Roma, Venezia 1544.

Cozzi Beccarini 1976
Antonietta Cozzi Beccarini, "La cappella Caetani nella Basilica di Santa Pudenziana," *Quaderni dell'Istituto di Storia dell'Architettura*, 22, 1976, 127–132, 143–158.

van Craneveldt and Svallemberg 1537
Frans van Craneveldt and Theodor Adam Svallemberg, *Procopii rhetoris et hystoriographi de Iustiniani Imp. aedificiis libri sex*, Parisiis 1537.

Cresti 1988
Carlo Cresti, "La Cappella dei Principi: un Pantheon foderato di pietre dure," in *Splendori di Pietre Dure. L'arte di corte nella Firenze dei Granduchi*, exhib. catalogue (Florence 1988–1989), ed. by Anna Maria Giusti, Firenze 1988, 62–73.

Cropper 2005
Elizabeth Cropper, *The Domenichino Affair. Novelty, Imitation, and Theft in Seventeenth-Century Rome*, New Haven and London 2005.

Cupperi, Ioele, and Extermann 2012
Walter Cupperi, Giovanna Ioele, and Grégoire Extermann eds., *Scultura a Roma nella seconda metà del Cinquecento*, San Casciano Val di Pesa 2012.

Curzietti 2011
Jacopo Curzietti, *Giovan Battista Gaulli: La decorazione della chiesa del SS. Nome di Gesù*, Roma 2011.

Dacos 1969
Nicole Dacos, *La découverte de la Domus Aurea et la formation des grotesques à la Renaissance*, London 1969.

Darsy 1961
Félix Darsy, *Santa Sabina*, Roma 1961.

Davies and Hemsoll 1983
Paul Davies and David Hemsoll, "Renaissance Balusters and the Antique," *Architectural History*, 26, 1983, 1–23, 117–122.

Davis 1962
Hugh H. Davis, "A Rosary Confraternity Charter of 1579 and the Cardinal of Santa Susanna," *The Catholic Historical Review*, 48, 1962, 321–342.

De Angelis d'Ossat 2011
Matilde De Angelis d'Ossat, "Le collezioni Barbo e Grimani di scultura antica," in *La storia del palazzo di Venezia. Dalle collezioni Barbo e Grimani a sede dell'ambasciata veneta e austriaca*, ed. by Maria Giulia Barberini, Matilde De Angelis d'Ossat, and Alessandra Schiavon, Roma 2011, 23–66.

Debenedetti 1991
Elisa Debenedetti, *La pittura del Settecento a Roma. 1. Da Clemente XI a Benedetto XIV*, Roma 1991.

De Caro 1973
Gaspare De Caro, "Caetani, Enrico," in *Dizionario Biografico degli Italiani*, 16, Roma 1973, *ad vocem.*

Degrassi 1943
A. Degrassi, "Le sistemazioni dei Fasti Capitolini," *Capitolium*, 12, 1943, 327–335.

Degrassi 1945–1946
A. Degrassi, "L'edificio dei Fasti Capitolini," *Atti della Pontificia Accademia di Archeologia. Rendiconti*, 21, 1945–1946, 57–104.

Degrassi 1962
A. Degrassi, "Le sistemazioni dei Fasti Capitolini e l'edificio dei Fasti Capitolini," in *Scritti vari di antichità*, I, Roma 1962, 229–281.

DeGrazia 1984
Diane DeGrazia, *Le stampe dei Carracci con i disegni, le incisioni, le copie e i dipinti connessi*, Bologna 1984.

Dejob 1881
Charles Dejob, *Marc Antoine Muret, un professeur français en Italie dans la seconde moitié du XVIe siècle*, Paris 1881.

Delbeke 2014
Maarten Delbeke, "'For We Are Made of Spectacle unto the World, and to Angels, and to Men': Alessandro Algardi's *Beheading of Saint Paul* and the Theatricality of Martyrdom," in Colantuono and Ostrow 2014, 141–164.

Del Bufalo 2000
Dario Del Bufalo, *Marmi antichi e pietre dure*, Lecce 2000.

Del Bufalo 2002
Dario Del Bufalo, "I luoghi dell'arte. I fasti della memoria," *Architectural Digest* (Italian edition), 250, 2002, March, 192–197.

De Lillo 2012
Alessandro De Lillo, "L'emblematica Gregoriana nelle Allusioni di Principio Fabrizi," in Cieri Via, Rowland, and Ruffini 2012, 131–150.

Delli Santi 2000
Maurizio Delli Santi, "Il reimpiego dei marmi antichi a Firenze nel XVI secolo: la Cappella Niccolini in Santa Croce," in Del Bufalo 2000, 91–102.

De Lotto 2009
Maria Teresa De Lotto, "Camillo Mariani," *Saggi e memorie di storia dell'arte*, 32, 2008 (2009), 21–223.

Del Pesco 2016
Daniela Del Pesco, "Giovan Antonio Dosio e Domenico Fontana in Napoli: decorazioni polimateriche e in marmo colorato," in Extermann and Varela Braga 2016, 261–272.

Del Re 1952
Niccolò Del Re, *La curia romana: lineamenti storico-giuridici*, Rome 1952.

Del Riccio ed. 1996
Agostino Del Riccio, *Istoria delle pietre*, ed. by Raniero Gnoli, Torino 1996.

De Maio 1978
Romeo De Maio, *Michelangelo e la Controriforma*, Roma and Bari 1978.

De Rossi 1713
Giovanni Giacomo De Rossi, *Disegni di vari altari e cappelle nelle chiese di Roma*, Roma 1713.

De Stefani 2011
Claudio De Stefani ed., *Paulus Silentiarius, Descriptio Sanctae Sophiae. Descriptio Ambonis*, New York 2011.

Di Castro 1994
Alberto Di Castro, *Marmorari e argentieri a Roma e nel Lazio tra Cinquecento e Seicento: i committenti, i documenti, le opere*, Roma 1994.

Dickerson III and Sigel 2016
Claude Douglas Dickerson III and Anthony Sigel, "Bernini/Not Bernini: Reflections on the Role of Technical Evidence in the Attribution of Bernini's Terracottas," in Levy and Mangone 2016, 187–217.

Dictionnaire de spiritualité 1937–1995
Dictionnaire de spiritualité, ascétique et mystique, Paris 1937–1995.

Diefenbach 2007
Steffen Diefenbach, *Römische Erinnerungsräume. Heiligen Memoria und kollektive Identitäten in Rom des 3. Bis 5. Jahrhunderts n. Chr.*, Berlin and New York 2007.

Diek 1997
Margarete Diek, *Die Spanische Kapelle in Florenz. Das trecenteske Bildprogramm des Kapitelsaals der Dominikaner von S. Maria Novella*, Frankfurt am Main 1997.

Di Federico 1983
Frank Di Federico, *The Mosaics of Saint Peter's: Decorating the New Basilica*, University Park 1983.

Di Giammaria 2012
Paola Di Giammaria, "L'attività di Giovanni Antonio Paracca, detto il Valsoldo, nella chiesa di Santa Susanna alle Terme e alcuni documenti inediti sul Valsoldo e sul Valsoldino," in Cupperi, Ioele, and Extermann 2012, 225–261.

Di Giammaria 2014
Paola Di Giammaria, "Novità biografiche e attributive su Giovanni Antonio Paracca il giovane detto il Valsoldino," *Storia dell'arte*, 45, 2014, 137–138, 75–92.

Dionisi 2004
Aurelio Dionisi, *Il Gesù di Roma: breve storia e illustrazione della chiesa-madre dei gesuiti*, Roma 2004.

Dombrowski 2014
Damian Dombrowski, "The Sculptural Altarpiece and its Vicissitudes in the Roman Church Interior: Renaissance through Baroque," in Colantuono and Ostrow 2014, 117–140.

Donati 2005
Angela Donati ed., "Dall'epistolario di Giovanni Cristofano Amaduzzi, Lettere a Girolamo Ferri (1759–1785), raccolte e trascritte da Giancarlo Donati, 2a parte (1770–1785)," in *Atti della Quarta giornata amaduzziana* (Savignano sul Rubicone 2004), Savignano sul Rubicone 2005, 137–263.

D'Onofrio 1989
Cesare D'Onofrio, *Visitiamo Roma nel Quattrocento. La città degli Umanisti*, Roma 1989.

Downey 1957
Glanville Downey, "Nikolaos Mesarites: Description of the Church of the Holy Apostles at Constantinople," *Transactions of the American Philosophical Society*, 47, 1957, 6, 855–924.

Duchesne 1892
Louis Duchesne ed., *Le Liber Pontificalis*, II, Paris 1892.

Duffy 2005
Eamon Duffy, *The Stripping of the Altars. Traditional Religion in England 1400–1580*, 2nd ed., New Haven and London 2005.

Durando 1612
Guglielmo Durando, *Rationale Divinorum Officiorum*, Lyon 1612.

Ebert-Schifferer 2006
Sybille Ebert-Schifferer, "Raffaello e le sue reincarnazioni," *Accademia Raffaello. Atti e studi*, I, 2006, 5–30.

Ebert-Schifferer and Ginzburg 2011
Sybille Ebert-Schifferer and Silvia Ginzburg eds., *Nuova luce su Annibale Carracci*, conference proceedings (Rome 2007), Roma 2011.

Egio 1547
Benedetto Egio, *Procopio Cesariense, de gli edifici di Giustiniano imperatore, di greco in volgare tradotti per Benedetto Egio da Spoleto*, Venetia 1547.

Eichberg 1994
Margherita Eichberg, "Un'architettura post-tridentina. La cappella Salviati in S. Gregorio al Celio," *Palladio*, 7, 1994, 13, 41–56.

Eichholz 1965
David E. Eichholz, *Theophrastus. De Lapidibus*, Oxford 1965.

Elorza 1994
Juan Iturriaga Elorza, "Hechos prodigiosos attribuidos a San Francisco Javier en unos grabados del siglo XVII," *Principe de Viana*, 55, 1994, 467–511.

Emerick 2005
Judson J. Emerick, "Altars Personified: The Cult of Saints and the Chapel System in Pope Paschal's S. Prassede (817–819)," in *Archaeology in Architecture. Studies in Honor of Cecil L. Striker*, ed. by Judson J. Emerick and Deborah M. Deliyannis, Mainz am Rhein 2005, 43–63.

Enggass and Enggass 1977
Catherine Enggass and Robert Enggass ed., *Nicola Pio, Le vite di pittori, scultori et architetti : [Cod. ms. Capponi 257]*, Roma 1977.

Eriksen 2001
Roy T. Eriksen, *The Building in the Text: Alberti to Shakespeare and Milton*, University Park 2001.

Eubel 1923
Konrad Eubel, Wilhem van Gulik, and Remigius Ritzler eds., *Hierarchia catholica medii aevi (…). Saeculum XVI ab anno 1503 complectens*, Monasteri 1923.

Eubel 1935
Konrad Eubel, Patrick Gauchat, Wilhem van Gulik, and Remigius Ritzler eds., *Hierarchia catholica medii aevi (…). A pontificatu Clementis papa VIII (1592) usque ad pontificatum Alexandri papae VII (1667)*, Monasteri 1935.

Extermann 2016
Grégoire Extermann, "Marmi romani in Piemonte. Pio V e il cantiere di Santa Croce a Bosco Marengo," in Extermann and Varela Braga 2016, 69–86.

Extermann and Varela Braga 2016
Grégoire Extermann and Ariane Varela Braga eds., *Splendor Marmoris. I colori del marmo, tra Roma e l'Europa, da Paolo III a Napoleone III*, conference proceedings (Rome 2012), Roma 2016.

Fabrizi 1588
Principio Fabrizi, *Delle allusioni, imprese, et emblemi del Signor Principio Fabricii*, Roma 1588.

Fagiolo 2006
Marcello Fagiolo, "Il gran teatro della Roma barocca," in *Roma barocca. Bernini, Borromini, Pietro da Cortona*, ed. by Marcello Fagiolo and Paolo Portoghesi, Roma 2006, 60–71.

Fagiolo and Fagiolo Dell'Arco 1967
Marcello Fagiolo and Maurizio Fagiolo dell'Arco, *Bernini. Una introduzione al gran teatro della Roma barocca*, Roma 1967.

Falcone 1998
Luigi Falcone ed., *Incunaboli e cinquecentine della biblioteca di Gregorio*

XIII Boncompagni. Dal Collegio Germanico alla Pontificia Università Lateranense, Città del Vaticano 1998.

Fanucci 1601
Camillo Fanucci, *Trattato di tutte l'opere pie di alma città di Roma*, Roma 1601.

Fara 2018a
Andrea Fara, *Vivere la città: domus e palazzi dei Frangipane nella Roma tra Quattrocento e Cinquecento*, in *Vivere la città. Roma nel Rinascimento*, ed. by Ivana Ait and Anna Esposito, Rome (in press).

Fara 2018b
Andrea Fara, "La famiglia Frangipane di Roma tra conservazione sociale e rinnovamento economico tra Quattro e Cinquecento: prime indagini," *Roma nel Rinascimento*, 2018, 363–390.

Farlati 1753
Daniele Farlati, *Illyrici Sacri. Tomus Secundus. Ecclesia Salonitana. A quarto saeculo aerae Christianae usque as excidium Salonae*, Venetiis 1753.

Federici 2002
Fabrizio Federici, "Tre pittori per un dipinto: l'*Interno della Cappella Cybo* del Museo di Roma," *Bollettino dei Musei Comunali di Roma*, 16, 2002, 49–66.

Federici 2003a
Fabrizio Federici, "La diffusione della 'prattica romana': il cardinale Alderano Cybo e le chiese di Massa (1640–1700)," *Atti e Memorie della Deputazione di Storia Patria per le antiche Provincie Modenesi*, s. XI, 2003, 25, 315–389.

Federici 2003b
Fabrizio Federici, "Un giovane prelato, Bernini e Borromini: il primo soggiorno romano di Alderano Cybo," *Ricerche di Storia dell'Arte*, 2003, 79, 93–107.

Federici 2006
Fabrizio Federici, "L''esilio' jesino del cardinale Alderano Cybo," in *Mistica e poesia. Il cardinale Pier Matteo Petrucci*, conference proceedings (Jesi 2001), ed. by Curzio Cavicchioli and Sabrina Stroppa, Genova and Milano 2006, 239–272.

Federici 2008
Fabrizio Federici, "Per Carlo Maratta ritrattista: un riesame del ritratto di Alderano Cybo," *Ricerche di Storia dell'Arte*, 2008, 96, 77–87.

Federici 2013
Fabrizio Federici, "Santi da chiesa e da camera: i dipinti di Luigi Garzi per il cardinale Alderano Cybo," *Predella. Journal of visual arts*, 8, 2013, 13–25.

Federici 2014
Fabrizio Federici, "'Ingressus ad requiem, regressus ad iudicium': il sepolcreto dei Cybo Malaspina nel duomo di Massa," in *Aspetti del tempo di Alberico II Cybo-Malaspina 1662–1690*, conference proceedings (Massa and Carrara 2013), ed. by Paolo Pelù and Olga Raffo, Modena 2014, 161–182.

Federici 2017
Fabrizio Federici, "Un'effigie in due tempi: il *Ritratto del cardinale Cybo* di Giovanni Maria Morandi nella Biblioteca Apostolica Vaticana e la sua versione preliminare," *Miscellanea Bibliothecae Apostolicae Vaticanae*, 23, 2017, 217–239.

Federici 2018
Fabrizio Federici, "Garzi e Maratta a confronto: due *Immacolate* per il cardinale Cybo," in *Luigi Garzi (1638–1721), pittore romano. Raccolta di studi*, ed. by Francesco Grisolia and Guendalina Serafinelli, Milano 2018, 107–118.

Federici and Garms 2010
Fabrizio Federici and Jörg Garms, "Tombs of Illustrious Italians at Rome. L'album di disegni RCIN 970334 della Royal Library di Windsor," *Bollettino d'Arte* (Volume speciale, 12), Firenze 2010.

Feigenbaum and Ebert-Schifferer 2011
Gail Feigenbaum and Sybille Ebert-Schifferer eds., *Sacred Possessions: Collecting Italian Religious Art, 1500–1900*, Los Angeles 2011.

Felini 1600
Pietro Martire Felini, *Trattato Nuovo delle cose maravigliose dell'Alma Città di Roma*, Rome 1600.

Felini 1610
Pietro Martire Felini, *Trattato Nuovo delle cose maravigliose dell'Alma Città di Roma*, Rome 1610.

Ferrari 1996
Oreste Ferrari, "Il secondo tempo della cappella Caetani," *Antologia di belle arte arti*, 20, 1996, 73–79.

Ferrari and Papaldo 1999
Oreste Ferrari and Serenita Papaldo, *Le sculture del Seicento a Roma*, Roma 1999.

Ferrary 1996
Jean Louis Ferrary, *Onofrio Panvinio et les antiquités romaines*, Roma 1996.

Fiorani 2007
Luigi Fiorani ed., *Palazzo Caetani: storia, arte e cultura*, Roma 2007.

Fiorani, Hunter, and Pugliatti 1983
Luigi Fiorani, John Hunter, and Teresa Pugliatti eds., *Girolamo Siciolante da Sermoneta (1521–1575). Storia e critica*, Roma 1983.

Fiore 2018
Camilla S. Fiore, "Gregorio XIII e i Greci di Sant'Atanasio a Roma tra fine Cinquecento e inizio Seicento," *Römisches Jahrbuch der Bibliotheca Hertziana*, 42 (2015–2016) 2018, 389–438.

Fischer Pace 1998
Ursula Verena Fischer Pace, "L'ultimo Pietro da Cortona nei suoi disegni," in *Pietro da Cortona*, conference proceedings (Rome and Florence 1997–1998), ed. by Christoph Luitpold Frommel and Sebastian Schütze, Milano 1998, 220–228.

Fleming 2012
Alison C. Fleming, "The 'Roles' of Illustrations of the Life of St. Ignatius of Loyola," in *Visibile Teologia: il libro sacro figurato in Italia tra Cinquecento e Seicento*, ed. by Erminia Ardissino and Elisabetta Selmi, Roma 2012, 115–125.

Fleming 2020, forthcoming
Alison C. Fleming, "Art and the Relics of St. Francis Xavier in Dialogue," in *The Interaction of Art and Relics in Late Medieval and Early Modern Art*, ed. by Livia Stoenescu, Turnhout 2020 (forthcoming).

Folli 1993
Irene Ventura Folli, "La Natura 'Scritta': La 'Libraria' di Ulisse Aldrovandi (1522–1605)," in *Bibliothecae selectae: da Cusano a Leopardi*, ed. by Eugenio Canone, Firenze 1993, 495–506.

Forcella 1869–1884
Vincenzo Forcella, *Iscrizioni delle chiese e d'altri edificii di Roma dal secolo XI fino ai giorni nostri*, 14 vols., Roma 1869–1884.

Fornasari 1996
Liletta Fornasari ed., *Pittura barocca in Valdichiana: Salvi Castellucci, allievo di Pietro da Cortona*, Città di Castello 1996.

Fortescue, O'Connell, and Reid 2009
Adrian Fortescue, J. B. O'Connell, and Alcuin Reid, *The Ceremonies of the Roman Rite Described*, 15th ed., London–New York 2009.

Fra Ilarino da Milano 1950
Fra Ilarino da Milano, "Incoronazione delle immagini di Maria santissima," in *Enciclopedia Cattolica*, VI, Città del Vaticano 1950, 1782–1783.

Fra Mariano 1518 [1931]
Fra Mariano da Firenze, *Itinerarium Urbis Romae*, Romae 1518, ed. by Enrico Bulletti, Roma 1931.

Franceschini 2002
Chiara Franceschini, "Ricerche sulle cappelle di famiglia a Roma in età moderna," in *Archivio Italiano per la Storia della Pietà*, 14, 2002, 345–413.

Franceschini 2017
Chiara Franceschini, *Storia del limbo*, Milano 2017.

Francino 1595
Girolamo Francino, *Le cose maravigliose dell'alma città di Roma*, Roma 1595.

Frangipane 1876
Camillo Trasmondo Frangipane, *Memorie sulla vita e i fatti del cardinale Alessandro Farnese per servire alla storia del XVI secolo*, Roma 1876.

Freiberg 1995
Jack Freiberg, *The Lateran in 1600: Christian Concord in Counter-Reformation Rome*, Cambridge and New York 1995.

Frizolio 1582
Lorenzo Frizolio, *Sacellum Gregorianum*, Romae 1582.

Frommel 2012
Cristoph Luitpold Frommel, "Pio V, la chiesa di Bosco Marengo e l'architettura della controriforma,"in *L'immagine del rigore. Committenza artistica di e per Pio V a Roma e in Lombardia*, ed. by Luisa Giordano and Giampaolo Angelini, Como 2012, 17–78.

Furlan and Tosini 2014
Caterina Furlan and Patrizia Tosini eds., *I cardinali della Serenissima: arte e committenza tra Venezia e Roma (1523–1605)*, Cinisello Balsamo 2014.

Furlotti 2016
Barbara Furlotti, "L'influence des mots, le pouvoir des images: acheter de l'art à distance en Italie aux XVIe et XVIIe siécles," *Seizième siècle*, 12, 2016, 125–143.

Galassi 2007
Cristina Galassi, *Nicolò Circignani, il Pomarancio: prattico e spedito pittore tra centro e periferia*, Città di Castello 2007.

Gallavotti Cavallero 2006
Daniela Gallavotti Cavallero, "I colori del barocco: l'arte dei marmi policromi," in *Roma barocca. Bernini, Borromini, Pietro da Cortona*, ed. by Marcello Fagiolo and Paolo Portoghesi, Milano 2006, 288–293.

Gallavotti Cavallero 2010
Daniela Gallavotti Cavallero, "L'iconografia di santa Prisca e l'immagine di Pietro dalla basilica Vaticana al titulus della santa sull'Aventino nei secoli XVI e XVII," in *L'Aventino dal Rinascimento a oggi: arte e architettura*, ed. by Mario Bevilacqua and Daniela Gallavotti Cavallero, Roma 2010, 56–71.

Gallonio 1591a
Antonio Gallonio, *Historia delle Sante Vergini Romane*, Roma 1591.

Gallonio 1591b
Antonio Gallonio, *Trattato de gli strumenti di martirio e delle varie maniere di martoriare usate da' gentili contro christiani*, Roma 1591.

Gallonio 1601
Antonio Gallonio, *Vita del B. P. Filippo Neri fiorentino*, Roma 1601.

Gallonio ed. 2005
Antonio Gallonio, *The Life of St. Philip Neri*, trans. by Jerome Bertram, Oxford 2005.

Gardi 1985
Andrea Gardi, *Il cardinale Enrico Caetani e la legazione di Bologna (1586–1587)*, Roma 1985.

Garnett and Rosser 2013
Jane Garnett and Gervase Rosser, *Spectacular Miracles: Transforming Images in Italy, from the Renaissance to the Present*, London 2013.

Geary 1978
Patrick J. Geary, *Furta Sacra: Thefts of Relics in the Central Middle Ages*, Princeton 1978.

Gere 1977
John Gere, "A new attribution to Correggio," *Master Drawings*, 15, 1977, 3, 256.

Gere and Pouncey 1983
John Gere and Philip Pouncey, *Italian Drawings in the Department of Prints and Drawings in the British Museum. Artists Working in Rome c. 1550 to c. 1640*, 2 vols., London 1983.

Gérin 1894
Charles Gérin, *Louis XIV et le Saint-Siège*, Paris 1894.

Ghisetti Giavarina 2009
Adriano Ghisetti Giavarina, "Tommaso Boscoli: note documentarie sull'attività di scultore, scalpellino e stuccatore," *Opus*, 9, 2008 (2009), 21–26.

Giantomassi 2016
Carlo Giantomassi, "Roma, Santa Maria del Popolo, Cappella Cybo, Carlo Maratti, Immacolata Concezione con i santi Giovanni Evangelista, Agostino, Gregorio e Giovanni Crisostomo: note di tecnica esecutiva," in *Maratti e la sua fortuna*, conference proceedings (Rome 2014), ed. by Sybille Ebert-Schifferer and Simonetta Prosperi Valenti Rodinò, Roma 2016, 277–284.

Gibelli 1888
Alberto Gibelli, *Memorie storiche ed artistiche dell'antichissima chiesa abbaziale dei santi Andrea e Gregorio al Clivio di Scauro sul Monte Celio*, Siena 1888.

Gigli 1996
Laura Gigli, *San Marcello al Corso*, Roma 1996.

Gilbert 1994
Peter L. Gilbert, *Person and Nature in the Theological Poems of St. Gregory of Nazianzus*, Washington DC 1994.

Gill 2014
Meredith J. Gill, *Angels and the Order of Heaven in Medieval and Renaissance Italy*, New York 2014.

Ginzburg 2011
Silvia Ginzburg, "Per la cronologia di Annibale Carracci (1602–1604)," in Ebert-Schifferer and Ginzburg 2011, 154–187.

Ginzburg Carignani 2000
Silvia Ginzburg Carignani, *Annibale Carracci a Roma: gli affreschi di Palazzo Farnese*, Roma 2000.

Giometti 2011
Cristiano Giometti, *Museo Nazionale del Palazzo di Venezia. Sculture in terracotta, Il Palazzo di Venezia e le sue collezioni di scultura*, IV, Roma 2011.

Giovenale 1929
Giovanni Battista Giovenale, *Il Battistero lateranense nelle recenti indagini della Pont. commissione di archeologia sacra*, Roma 1929.

Girot 2012
Jean-Eudes Girot, *Marc Antoine Muret: des isles fortunées au rivage romain*, Genève 2012.

Gloton 1998
Marie-Christine Gloton, "Giacinto Gimignani – Marseilles, 1668," in *Suite baroque: tableaux pour l'église des jésuites de Marseille, essais d'identification*, ed. by Marie-Paule Vial and Elisabeth Mognetti, Marseilles 1998, 30–41.

Gloton Rinville 1990
Marie-Christine Gloton Rinville, "Restaurations et nouvelles attributions: un tableau aixois rendu à l'école italienne," in *Seicento: la peinture italienne du XVIIe siècle et la France*, conference proceedings (Paris 1988), Paris 1990, 413–421.

Gnoli 1971
Raniero Gnoli, *Marmora romana*, Roma 1971.

Gnoli 1989
Raniero Gnoli, "Introduzione," in Borghini 1989, 13–17.

Gnoli and Sironi 1996
Raniero Gnoli and Attilia Sironi eds., *Agostino Del Riccio. Istoria delle pietre*, Torino 1996.

Gonzáles-Palacios 1988
Alvar Gonzáles-Palacios, "Itinerario da Roma a Firenze," in *Splendori di pietre dure. L'arte di corte nella Firenze dei Granduchi*, exhib. catalogue (Florence 1988–1989), ed. by Anna Maria Giusti, Firenze 1988, 43–52.

Gori 2007
Laura Gori, *I Caetani e le arti nella seconda metà del Cinquecento*, PhD diss., Università degli Studi Roma Tre 2007.

Gori 2011
Laura Gori, "Giovan Francesco Peranda, erudito e collezionista, dalla corte dei Gonzaga a quella dei Caetani," *Studi di Storia dell'arte*, 22, 2011, 97–106.

Gori 2012
Laura Gori, "La cappella Caetani in Santa Pudenziana: scultura e gusto antiquario in un cantiere di fine Cinquecento," in Cupperi, Ioele, and Extermann 2012, 263–298.

Gori 2014
Laura Gori, "Una famiglia filospagnola tra Cinquecento e Seicento: i Caetani di Sermoneta; dinamiche politiche e aspetti culturali," in *I rapporti tra Roma e Madrid nei secoli XVI e XVII*, conference proceedings (Rome 2011), ed. by Alessandra Anselmi, Roma 2014, 176–192.

Gori 2016
Laura Gori, "Due cantieri sul crinale tra Cinquecento e Seicento: la cappella Caetani e la cappella Rucellai," in Extermann and Varela Braga 2016, 119–135.

Grandolfo 2014
Alessandro Grandolfo, "Paracca, Giovanni Antonio di Pietro detto il Valsoldo," in *Dizionario Biografico degli Italiani*, 80, Roma 2014, *ad vocem*.

Gregorius Nazianzenus ed. 1504
Gregorii episcopi Nazanzeni Carmina ad bene, beateque uiuendum utilissima nuper e græco in latinum ad uerbum ferè traslata, Venetiis 1504.

Gregorius Nazianzenus ed. 1569
Divi Gregorii Nazianzeni, cognomento theologi opera omnia, ed. by Jacques de Billy, Parisiis 1569.

Gregorius Nazianzenus ed. 1583
D. Gregorii Nazianzeni, cognomento theologi opera omnia, ed. by Jacques de Billy, 2 vols., Parisiis 1583.

Griffith 2002
Terry Griffith, "'Εἴδωλον' as 'Idol' in Non-Jewish and Non-Christian Greek," *The Journal of Theological Studies*, 53, 2002, 1, 95–101.

Grisebach 1936
August Grisebach, *Römische Porträtbüsten der Gegenreformation*, Leipzig 1936.

Gualdi 2009a
Fausta Gualdi, "La decorazione pittorica della volta della cappella maggiore," in Miarelli Mariani and Richiello 2009, I, 411–426.

Gualdi 2009b
Fausta Gualdi, "Pintoricchio e collaboratori nelle cappelle della navata destra," in Miarelli Mariani and Richiello 2009, I, 257–294.

Guarraccino 2009
Monica Guarraccino, *Le pietre di Livorno: transito e lavorazione delle pietre dure per la Cappella dei principi di Firenze nel XVII secolo*, Livorno 2009.

Guerrieri Borsoi 1993
Maria Barbara Guerrieri Borsoi, "S. Maria dei Monti. Cappella Boncompagni (dell'Annunziata)," in Madonna 1993, 235–237.

Guerrieri Borsoi 1993
Maria Barbara Guerrieri Borsoi, "S. Susanna. Cappella Peretti (di S. Lorenzo)," in Madonna 1993, 279–283.

Guicciardi 1589
Orazio Guicciardi, *Sacello Gregoriano del Sig. Lorenzo Frizolio. Tradotto da M. Horatio Guicciardi Modonese, con una oda del medesimo sopra la Santa Casa di Loreto*, Bologna 1589.

Guidobaldi and Sabbi 2016
Federico Guidobaldi and Anna Sabbi, "Cripte semianulari e altri ambienti devozionali ipogei o semipogei delle chiese di Roma dall'età paleocristiana al medioevo: aspetti tipologici e cronologia," *Atti della pontificia academia romana di archeologia. Rendiconti*, ser. III, 88, 2016, 343–566.

Gupta 2010
Pamila Gupta, "Discourses of Incorruptibility: Of Blood, Smell, and Skin in Portuguese India," *Ler historia*, 28, 2010, 81–97.

Gupta 2014
Pamila Gupta, *The Relic State: St. Francis Xavier and the Politics of Ritual in Portuguese India*, Manchester 2014.

Hager 1974
Hellmut Hager, "La cappella del cardinale Alderano Cybo in Santa Maria del Popolo," *Commentari*, 25, 1974, 47–61.

Hager 1976
Hellmut Hager, "Un riesame di tre cappelle di Carlo Fontana a Roma," *Commentari*, 27, 1976, 252–289.

Hager 1996
Hellmut Hager, "Andrea Pozzo e Carlo Fontana, tangenze e affinità," in *Andrea Pozzo e il suo tempo*, conference proceedings (Trento 1992), ed. by Alberta Battisti, Milano 1996, 235–252.

Hager 2009
Hellmut Hager, "La Cappella Cybo," in Miarelli Mariani and Richiello 2009, II, 639–658.

Hahn 1997a
Cynthia Hahn, "Seeing and Believing: The Construction of Sanctity in Early-Medieval Saints' Shrines," *Speculum*, 72, 1997, 4, 1079–1106.

Hahn 1997b
Cynthia Hahn, "The Voices of the Saints: Speaking Reliquaries," *Gesta*, 36, 1997, 1, 20–31.

Hahn 2010a
Cynthia Hahn, "The Spectacle of the Charismatic Body: Patrons, Artists, and Body-Part Reliquaries," in Bagnoli, Klein, Mann, and Robertson 2010, 163–172.

Hahn 2010b
Cynthia Hahn, "What Do Reliquaries Do For Relics?," *Numen*, 57, 2010, 3–4, 284–316.

Hahn 2012
Cynthia Hahn, *Strange Beauty: Issues in the Making and Meaning of Reliquaries, 400–circa 1204*, University Park 2012.

Hahn 2017
Cynthia Hahn, *The Reliquary Effect: Enshrining the Sacred Object*, London 2017.

Haldrein 1538
Arnold Haldrein, *Procopii rhetoris et historici Caesariensis, de Iustiniani Augusti Caesaris aedificiis orationes sex*, Moguntiae 1538.

Hall 1979
Marcia B. Hall, *Renovation and Counter-Reformation. Vasari and Duke Cosimo in Sta Maria Novella and Sta Croce 1565–1577*, Oxford 1979.

Halleux 1974
Robert Halleux, *La problème des métaux dans la science antique*, Paris 1974, 97–128.

Harrison 2005
Stephen. J. Harrison, "Vergil and the Mausoleum Augusti: Georgics 3.12–18," *Acta Classica*, 48, 2005, 185–188.

Hecht 1997
Christian Hecht, *Katholische Bildertheologie im Zeitaltar von Gegenreformation und Barock. Studien zu Traktaten von Johannes Molanus, Gabriele Paleotti und anderen Autoren*, Berlin 1997.

Heimbürger Ravalli 1973
Minna Heimbürger Ravalli, *Alessandro Algardi scultore*, Roma 1973.

Heimbürger Ravalli 1977
Minna Heimbürger Ravalli, *Architettura e arti minori nel Barocco italiano: ricerche nell'Archivio Spada*, Firenze 1977.

Heisenberg 1908
August Heisenberg, *Grabeskirche und Apostelkirche, Zwei Basiliken Konstantins; Untersuchungen zur Kunst und Literatur des ausgehenden Altertums*, 2 vols., Leipzig 1908.

Hendler 2007
Sefy Hendler, "Les trois apparitions de saint Grégoire le Grand: le paragone peinture-sculpture au Seicento, d'une comparaison compétitive à une comparaison constructive," in *L'histoire de l'art et le comparatisme: les horizons du détour*, ed. by Marc Bayard, Paris 2007, 171–183.

Hess 1943
Jacob Hess, "Michelangelo and Cordier," *The Burlington Magazine*, 82, 1943, 480, 55–65.

Heydenreich 1977
Ludwig Heydenreich, "Baluster und Balustrade: eine 'invenzione' der toskanischen Frührenaissancearchitektur," in *Festschrift Wolfgang Braunfels*, ed. by Friedrich Piel and Jörg Träger, Tübingen 1977, 123–132.

Hibbard 1971
Howard Hibbard, *Carlo Maderno and Roman Architecture 1580–1630*, London 1971.

Hibbard 2001
Howard Hibbard, *Carlo Maderno*, Milano 2001.

Hills 1999
Helen Hills, *Marmi mischi siciliani: invenzione e identità*, Messina 1999.

Hills 2013
Helen Hills, "Through a Glass Darkly: Material Holiness and the Treasury Chapel of San Gennaro in Naples," in *New Approaches to Naples c. 1500–c. 1800: the Power of Place*, ed. by Melissa Calaresu and Helen Hills, Farnham 2013, 31–62.

Hills 2016
Helen Hills, *The Matter of Miracles: Neapolitan Baroque Architecture and Sanctity*, Manchester 2016.

Hubala 1965
Erich Hubala, "Roma sotterranea barocca," *Das Münster*, 18, 1965, 157–170.

Hülsen 1927 [2000]
Christian Hülsen, *Le chiese di Roma nel Medioevo*, Firenze 1927 (ed. Roma 2000).

Hunter 1983a
John Hunter, "Girolamo Siciolante da Sermoneta, committenti e committenza," in Hunter, Pugliatti, and Fiorani 1983, 9–76.

Hunter 1983b
John Hunter, *The Life and the Work of Girolamo Siciolante da Sermoneta*, PhD diss., University of Michigan 1983.

Hunter 1996
John Hunter, *Girolamo Siciolante, pittore da Sermoneta: (1521–1575)*, Roma 1996.

Hunter, Pugliatti, and Fiorani 1983
Girolamo Siciolante pittore da Sermoneta (1521–1575), ed. by John Hunter, Teresa Pugliatti, and Luigi Fiorani, Roma 1983.

Hurtubise 1985
Pierre Hurtubise, *Une famille-témoin: les Salviati*, Città del Vaticano 1985.

Ieni 1985
Giulio Ieni, "'Una superbissima sepoltura': il mausoleo di Pio V," in *Pio V e Santa Croce di Bosco: aspetti di una committenza papale*, exhib. catalogue (Bosco Marengo and Alessandria 1985), ed. by Carla Enrica Spantigati and Giulio Ieni, Alessandria 1985, 31–48.

Ieni 2002
Giulio Ieni, "La chiesa conventuale di Santa Croce e alcuni arredi fissi," in *Santa Croce di Bosco Marengo*, ed. by Fulvio Cervini and Carla Enrica Spantigati, Alessandria 2002, 52–65.

Incisa della Rocchetta 1961
Giovanni Incisa della Rocchetta, "Il conto della cena in occasione del battesimo dei quattro fratelli Corcos-Boncompagni," *L'Oratorio di S. Filippo Neri*, 18, 1961, 4–6.

Incisa della Rocchetta 1966
Giovanni Incisa della Rocchetta, "L'Armadio di Pietro Boncompagni," *L'Oratorio di S. Filippo Neri*, 23, 1966, 195–197.

Incisa della Rocchetta 1967
Giovanni Incisa della Rocchetta, "Un dialogo del P. Virgilio Spada sulla fabbrica dei Filippini," *Archivio della Società Romana di Storia Patria*, 90, 1967, 165–211.

Incisa della Rocchetta and Connors 1981
Giovanni Incisa della Rocchetta and Joseph Connors, "Documenti sul complesso borrominiano alla Vallicella (1617–1800)," *Archivio della Società Romana di Storia Patria*, 104, 1981, 159–326.

Incisa della Rocchetta and Vian 1957–1963
Giovanni Incisa della Rocchetta and Nello Vian, *Il primo processo per san Filippo Neri nel Codice Vaticano Latino 3798 e altri esemplari dell'Archivio dell'Oratorio di Roma*, 4 vols., Città del Vaticano 1957–1963.

Ioele 2012
Giovanna Ioele, "Profilo biografico del Cavaliere Giovan Battista Della Porta," in Cupperi, Ioele, and Extermann 2012, 151–201.

Ioele 2015
Giovanna Ioele, "Scultori fra le corti Farnese e Caetani," *Rivista dell'Istituto Nazionale d'Archeologia e Storia dell'arte*, 36, 2013 (2015), 68, 49–59.

Ioele 2016
Giovanna Ioele, *Prima di Bernini. Giovanni Battista Della Porta scultore (1542–1597)*, Roma 2016.

James and Webb 1991
Liz James and Ruth Webb, "To Understand Ultimate Things and Enter Secret Places: Ekphrasis and Art in Byzantium," *Art History*, 14, 1991, 1, 1–17.

Johnson 1995
Mark J. Johnson, "The Fifth-Century Oratory of the Holy Cross at the Lateran in Rome," *Architectura*, 25, 1995, 134–147.

Jones 2008
Pamela M. Jones, *Altarpieces and Their Viewers in the Churches of Rome from Caravaggio to Guido Reni*, Aldershot 2008.

Jungmann 1951
Joseph Jungmann, S. J., *The Mass of the Roman Rite: Its Origins and Development*, trans. Francis Brunner, 2 vols., New York 1951.

Kämpf 2015
Tobias Kämpf, *Archäologie offenbart. Cäciliens römisches Kultbild im Blick einer Epoche*, Leiden and Boston 2015.

Kelly 1987
Kristin A. Kelly, *Motifs in Opus Sectile and its Painted Imitation from the Tetrarchy to Justinian*, 2 vols., Ann Arbor 1987.

Ketelsen and Orth 2015
Thomas Ketelsen and Christoph Orth eds., *Giovanni Maria Morandi: ein Barockkünstler in Rom*, exhib. catalogue (Köln 2015), Köln 2015.

Kirsch 1918
Johann P. Kirsch, *Die römischen Titelkirchen im Altertum*, Paderborn 1918.

Knaap 2016
Anna C. Knaap, "Marvels and Marbles in the Antwerp Jesuit Church: Hendrick van Balen's Stone Paintings of the Life of the Virgin (1621)," in *Jesuit Image Theory*, ed. by Wietse de Boer, Karl A.E. Enenkel, and Walter S. Melion, Leiden 2016, 352-393.

Krautheimer 1942
Richard Krautheimer, "Introduction to an 'Iconography of Medieval Architecture'," *Journal of the Warburg and Courtauld Institutes*, 5, 1942, 1-33.

Krautheimer, Corbett, and Frankl 1937-1980
Richard Krautheimer, Spencer Corbett, and Wolfgang Frankl, *Corpus Basilicarum Christianarum Romae*, Ser. 2, vols. I-V, Città del Vaticano 1937-1980.

Kunze 2000
Matthias Kunze, *Daniel Seiter 1647-1705. Die Gemälde*, München and Berlin 2000.

Lamouche 2012
Emmanuel Lamouche, "Bastiano Torrigiani et les fondeurs de bronze de Sixte V: entre collaboration et création personelle," in Cupperi, Ioele, and Extermann 2012, 203-223.

Lamouche 2018
Emmanuel Lamouche, "La Cappella Gregoriana nella Basilica Vaticana: Il cantiere della decorazione attraverso i documenti della Tesoreria Segreta Pontificia (1578-1584)," in *Pratiche architettoniche a confronto nei cantieri italiani della seconda metà del Cinquecento*, conference proceedings (Mendrisio 2016), ed. by Maria Felicia Nicoletti and Paola Carla Verde, Milano 2018, 43-65.

Lanciani 1882
Rodolfo Lanciani, "Degli antichi edificii componenti la chiesa di SS. Cosma e Damiano," *Bullettino della Commissione Archeologica Comunale di Roma*, 10, 1882, 29-54.

Landucci 1646
Ambrogio Landucci, *Origine del tempio dedicato in Roma alla Vergine Madre di Dio Maria presso alla Porta Flaminia, detto hoggi del Popolo*, Roma 1646.

Lanciani 1902-1912
Rodolfo Lanciani, *Storia degli scavi di Roma*, 4 vols., Roma 1902-1912.

Lanciani 1989-2002
Rodolfo Lanciani, *Storia degli scavi di Roma*, 7 vols., Roma 1989-2002 (II ed.).

Leclercq 1914
Henri Leclercq, "Confessio," in *Dictionnaire d'archéologie chrétienne et de liturgie*, II.2, ed. by Fernand Cabrol and Henri Leclercq, Paris 1914, cols. 2503-2508.

Lenzo 2008
Fulvio Lenzo, "La cappella Spada in San Girolamo della Carità," *Römische Historische Mitteilungen*, 50, 2008, 383-428.

Leone 2010
Massimo Leone, *Saints and Signs: A Semiotic Reading of Conversion in Early Modern Catholicism*, Berlin 2010.

Leone 2014
Massimo Leone, "Wrapping Transcendence: The Semiotics of Reliquaries," *Signs and Society*, 2, 2014, 49-83.

Leone 2013-2014
Stephanie C. Leone, "Luca Berrettini (1609-1680): The Scalpellino-Merchant in Pietro da Cortona's Architectural Production and Baroque Rome," *Römisches Jahrbuch der Bibliotheca Hertziana*, 41, 2013-2014 (2017), 437-472.

Leuker 2009
Tobias Leuker, "Incisività sublime: l'arte epigrammatica di Aurelio Orsi nel giudizio di Giambattista Marino," in *The Neo-Latin Epigram: A Learned and Witty Genre*, ed. by Susanna de Beer, Karl A. E. Enenkel, and David Rijser, Leuven 2009, 233-254.

Leuker 2013
Tobias Leuker, "Per Lorenzo Frizolio - testo, datazione, e prima ricezione dell'ode *Ad Nubes* (con un elenco delle poesie dell'autore)," *Critica letteraria*, 41, 2013, 161, 697-724.

Levy 1993
Evonne Levy, *A Canonical Work of an Uncanonical Era: Re-Reading the Chapel of St. Ignatius in the Gesù of Rome (1695-1699)*, PhD diss., Princeton University 1993.

Levy 1999-2000
Evonne Levy, "The Institutional Memory of the Roman Gesù. Plans for Renovations in the 1670s by Carlo Fontana, Pietro da Cortona and Luca Berrettini," *Römisches Jahrbuch der Bibliotheca Hertziana*, 33, 1999-2000 (2003), 373-426.

Levy 2018
Evonne Levy, "The Honor of the Altar, the Fate of the Cults: Jesuit Saints in Roman Churches (1670-1713)," in *The Holy Name: Art of the Gesù, Bernini and his Age*, ed. by Linda Wolk-Simon, Philadelphia 2018, 145-183.

Levy and Mangone 2016
Evonne Levy and Carolina Mangone eds., *Material Bernini*, London and New York, 2016.

Llewellyn 1977
Nigel Llewellyn, "Two notes on Diego da Sangredo," *Journal of the Warburg and Courtauld Institutes*, 40, 1977, 292-300.

Lo Bianco 1995
Anna Lo Bianco, "Pietro da Cortona e gli Oratoriani," in *La regola e la fama*, 1995, 174-193.

Loffredo 2011
Fernando Loffredo, "Pedro de Toledo, lo stemma di Castelcapuano e Francesco da Sangallo a Napoli," in *Castelcapuano da reggia a tribunale: architettura e arte nei luoghi della giustizia*, ed. by Fabio Mangone, Napoli 2011, 42-69.

Loisel 2014
Catherine Loisel, "Attributions traditionelles et identifications certaines: dessins de N. Circignani, V. Strada, P. F. Mola, A. Gherardi et G. D. Piastrini pour des travaux romains," *Paragone*, 65, 2014, 775, 52-64.

Loisel 2015
Catherine Loisel, "Chantiers de la Contr-Réforme: 1580-1600," in *La fabrique de saintes images: Rome-Paris 1580-1660*, exhib. catalogue (Paris 2015), ed. by Louis Frank and Philippe Malgouyres, Paris 2015, 78-89.

Loisel Legrand 1999
Catherine Loisel Legrand, "Saint Gregory Praying for Souls in Purgatory," in Benati and DeGrazia 1999, 79, 251–252.

Lombardi 1993
Sergio Lombardi, "Fuccheri, Stefano," in Madonna 1993, 558.

Lotz 1955
Wolfgang Lotz, "Die ovalen Kirchenräume des Cinquecento," *Römisches Jahrbuch für Kunstgeschichte*, 7, 1955, 7–99.

Lotz 1977
Wolfgang Lotz, "Notes on the Centralized Church of the Renaissance," in Wolfgang Lotz, *Studies in Italian Renaissance Architecture*, Cambridge 1977, 66–73.

Lucidi 1796
Emmanuele Lucidi, *Memorie storiche dell'antichissimo municipio, ora terra, dell'Ariccia e delle sue colonie Genzano, e Nemi*, Roma 1796.

Luschi 1998
Licia Luschi, "Gli antichi edifici della basilica dei SS. Cosma e Damiano: osservazioni su disegni ligoriani," in *XLIII Corso di cultura sull'arte ravennate e bizantina*, ed. by Raffaella Farioli Campanati, Ravenna 1998, 429–452.

Maayan-Fanar 2006
Emma Maayan-Fanar, "The Fragmentary Body: The Place of Human Limbs in Byzantine Illuminated Initials," *Byzantion*, 76, 2006, 241–263.

Macioce 1984
Stefania Macioce, "San Marcello al Corso, Cappella Frangipani," in *Oltre Raffaello. Aspetti della cultura figurativa del Cinquecento romano*, exhib. catalogue (Rome 1984), ed. by Luciana Cassanelli and Sergio Rossi, Roma 1984, 112–118.

Macioce 1990
Stefania Macioce, *Undique Splendent. Aspetti della pittura sacra nella Roma di Clemente VIII Aldobrandini (1592–1605)*, Roma 1990.

Mackie 1997
Gillian Mackie, "The Santa Croce Drawings: A Re-examination," *RACAR*, 24, 1997, 1, 1–13.

Macrides and Magdalino 1988
Ruth Macrides and Paul Magdalino, "The Architecture of Ekphrasis: Construction and Context of Paul the Silentiary's Poem on Hagia Sophia," *Byzantine and Modern Greek Studies*, 12, 1988, 47–82.

Madonna 1993
Maria Luisa Madonna ed., *Roma di Sisto V. Le arti e la cultura*, Roma 1993.

Maffei 1742
Giovanni Pietro Maffei, *Degli annali di Gregorio XIII., Pontefice Massimo*, 2 vols., Rome 1742.

Mâle 1951
Emile Mâle, *L'art religieux de la fin du 16. siècle, du 17. siècle, et du 18. siècle. Études sur l'iconographie après le Concile de Trent: Italie, France, Espagne, Flandres*, Paris 1951.

Malvasia 1678 [1841]
Carlo Cesare Malvasia, *Felsina Pittrice: vite de' Pittori Bolognesi del Conte Carlo Cesare Malvasia con aggiunte, correzioni e note inedite del medesimo Autore di Giampietro Zanotti e di altri scrittori viventi del Conte Carlo Cesare Malvasia*, 2 vols., Bologna 1678, ed. Bologna 1841.

Malvasia 1980
Carlo Cesare Malvasia, *The Life of Guido Reni*, trans. and with an introduction by Catherine Enggass and Robert Enggass, University Park and London 1980.

Mancini ca. 1620 [1956–1957]
Giulio Mancini, *Considerazioni sulla pittura* [ca. 1620], ed. by Adriana Marucchi and Luigi Salerno, Roma 1956–1957.

Mancini 1966–1967
Adele Mancini, "La chiesa medioevale di S. Adriano nel Foro Romano," *Atti della Pontificia Accademia Romana di Archeologia*, 39, 1966–1967, 191–245.

Mangia Renda 1993
Paola Mangia Renda, "S. Girolamo degli Schiavoni," in Madonna 1993, 145–149.

Mansour 2013
Opher Mansour, "The Visitation of Clement VIII and the Visual Arts," in *The Sensuous in the Counter-Reformation Church*, ed. by Marcia B. Hall and Tracy E. Cooper, New York 2013, 136–160.

Marchetti 2004
Elisabetta Marchetti, "Nuove ricerche sull'Arciconfraternita di San Girolamo della Carità," *Quaderni di Scienza della Conservazione*, 4, 2004, 239–258.

Marcucci 1991
Laura Marcucci, *Francesco da Volterra: un protagonista dell'architettura post-tridentina*, Roma 1991.

Marcucci 1999
Laura Marcucci, "Il Vignola, Francesco da Volterra e la committenza Caetani nella seconda metà del Cinquecento," in *Sermoneta e i Caetani*, conference proceedings (Rome and Sermoneta 1993), ed. by Luigi Fiorani, Roma 1999, 501–532.

Marliano 1549
Bartolomeo Marliano, *Consulum, dictatorum censorumque Romanorum series una cum ipsorum triumphis, quae marmoribus scalpta [sic] in foro reperta est, atque in Capitolium translata*, Romae 1549.

Martellacci 1995
Rosamaria Martellacci, "Cappelle gentilizie fiorentine in epoca di controriforma," in *Architettura di altari e spazio ecclesiale. Episodi a Firenze, Prato e Ferrara nell'eta della Controriforma*, ed. by Carlo Cresti, Firenze 1995, 75–113.

Martin 1581 [1969]
Gregory Martin, *Roma Sancta*, ed. by George Bruner Parks, Rome 1969.

Martin 1998
Thomas Martin, *Alessandro Vittoria and the Portrait Bust in Renaissance Venice: Remodelling Antiquity*, Oxford 1998.

Martinelli 1644
Fioravante Martinelli, *Roma ricercata nel suo sito, e nella scuola di tutti gli Antiquarij*, Roma 1644.

Martinelli 1653
Fioravante Martinelli, *Roma ex ethnica sacra sanctorum Petri, et Pauli praedicatione profuso sanguine*, Roma 1653.

Masetti Zannini 1973
Gian Ludovico Masetti Zannini, "Il processo e l'assoluzione di Alessandro Algardi per un incendio alla Lungara," *Commentari*, 24, 1973, 235–240.

Massei 1793
Giuseppe Massei, *Compendio della Vita di S. Francesco Saverio della Compagnia di Gesù*, Roma 1793.

Matile 1997
Michael Matile, *"Quadri laterali" im sakralen Kontext. Studien und Materialien zur Historienmalerei in venezianischen Kirchen und Kapellen des Cinquecento*, München 1997.

Mattiello 2016
Simone Mattiello, "Daniel Seiter per Vittorio Amedeo II nel Palazzo Ducale," *Palazzo Reale a Torino: allestire gli appartamenti dei sovrani (1658–1789)*, ed. by Giuseppe Dardanello, Torino 2016, 29–37.

Mauro and Aldrovandi 1556
Lucio Mauro and Ulisse Aldrovandi, *Le antichità della città di Roma* (Ulisse

Aldrovandi, *Delle statue antiche che per tutta Roma in diversi luoghi, e case si veggono*), Venezia 1556.

McHam 1994
Sarah Blake McHam, *The Chapel of St. Anthony at the Santo and the Development of Venetian Renaissance Sculpture*, New York 1994.

McPhee 2002
Sarah McPhee, *Bernini and the Bell Towers. Architecture and Politics at the Vatican*, New Haven and London 2002.

McTavish 2008
David McTavish, "A Drawing in Rennes for the Vault of the Caetani Chapel in Santa Pudenziana in Rome," *Bulletin de l'Association des Historiens de l'Art Italien*, 13, 2007 (2008), 5–11.

Meban 2008
David Meban, "Temple Building, Primus Language, and the Proem to Virgil's Third Georgic," *Classical Philology*, 103, 2008, 2, 150–174.

Medici 1701
Paolo Sebastiano Medici, *Catalogo de neofiti illustri usciti per la misericordia di Dio dall'Ebraismo e poi rendutisi gloriosi nel Cristianesimo*, Firenze 1701.

Meiss 1951
Millard Meiss, *Painting in Florence and Siena after the Black Death*, Princeton 1951.

Mena Marqués 1990
Manuela B. Mena Marqués, "Carlo Maratti e Raffaello," in *Raffaello e l'Europa*, conference proceedings (Rome 1990), ed. by Marcello Fagiolo and Maria Luisa Madonna, Roma 1990, 541–563.

Mercati 1717
Michele Mercati, *Metallotheca*, Roma 1717.

Mercati 1944
Angelo Mercati, "La nomina di Carlo Maratta a soprintendente di tutte le pitture del Palazzo Vaticano," in *Il Giudizio Universale di Michelangelo*, ed. by Deoclecio Redig de Campos and Biagio Biagetti, Roma 1944, 181–184.

Merz 2008
Jorg M. Merz, *Pietro da Cortona and Roman Baroque Architecture,* New Haven 2008.

Miarelli Mariani and Richiello 2009
Ilaria Miarelli Mariani and Maria Richiello eds., *Santa Maria del Popolo. Storia e restauri*, 2 vols., Roma 2009.

Michaud 1882
Eugène Michaud, *Louis XIV et Innocent XI*, Paris 1882.

Milizia 1787
Francesco Milizia, *Roma delle belle arti del disegno*, Bassano 1787.

Miller 2019
Rachel Miller, "Converting 'the Indies' of Naples in Luca Giordano's 'Saint Francis Xavier Baptizing Indians' Altarpiece," *Journal of Jesuit Studies*, 2019, 6, 249–269.

***Missale Romanum* 1661**
Missale Romanum: Ex Decreto Sacrosancti Concilii Tridentini Restitutum, Pii V. Pont. Max. Iussu Editum, Et Clementis VIII. Primum, Nunc Denuo Urbani Papae Octavi Auctoritate Recognitum. In quo Missae propriae de Sanctis ad longum positae sunt ad maiorem celebrantium commoditatem, Monachii 1661.

Mittarelli and Costadoni 1764
Johannes Benedictus Mittarelli and Anselmo Costadoni, *Annales Camaldulenses Ordinis Sancti Benedicti: Quibus plura interferuntur tum ceteras Italico-monasticas res, tum historiam Ecclesiasticam remque Diplomaticam illustrantia*, vol. 8: *Complectens res gestas ab anno Christi MDXV ad annum MDCCLXIV*, Venetiis 1764.

Möller 2013
Gina Möller, *Die Cappella Caetani an San Pudentiana*, Magisterarbeit, Rheinische Friedrich-Wilhelms-Universität 2013.

Möller 2018
Gina Möller, *Romische Papstkapellen des Cinquecento: Buntmarmor, Materialästhetik und Kunstpatronage in post-tridentinischer Zeit*, Petersberg 2018.

Montagu 1970
Jennifer Montagu, "Antonio and Gioseppe Giorgetti: Sculptors to Cardinal Francesco Barberini," *Art Bulletin*, 52, 1970, 278–298.

Montagu 1977
Jennifer Montagu, "Alessandro Algardi and the Statue of St. Philip Neri," *Jahrbuch der Hamburger Kunstsammlungen*, 22, 1977, 75–100.

Montagu 1985
Jennifer Montagu, *Alessandro Algardi*, 2 vols., New Haven and London 1985.

Montagu 1990
Jennifer Montagu, "Alessandro Algardi (Bologna, 1598 – Roma, 1654). Estasi di san Filippo Neri, 1635–1636," in Romano 1990, 171–177.

Montagu 1992
Jennifer Montagu, "Alessandro Algardi (Bologna, 1598 – Roma, 1654). Estasi di san Filippo Neri, 1635–1636," in *Per la storia della scultura. Materiali inediti e poco noti*, ed. by Massimo Ferretti, Torino 1992, 92–99.

Montagu 2009
Jennifer Montagu, "Scultori di ritratti del primo barocco romano," in *I marmi vivi. Bernini e la nascita del Barocco romano*, exhib. catalogue (Florence 2009), ed. by Andrea Bacchi, Tomaso Montanari, Beatrice Paolozzi Strozzi, and Dimitrios Zikos, Firenze 2009, 181–205.

Montini 1953
Renzo U. Montini, *Iconografia mariana di Roma*, Roma 1953.

Montini 1960
Renzo U. Montini, *Santa Pudenziana*, Roma 1960.

Mormando 2011
Franco Mormando, *Bernini. His Life and His Rome*, Chicago 2011.

Mormando 2018
Franco Mormando, "Gian Paolo Oliva: The Forgotten Celebrity of Baroque Rome," in *The Holy Name: Art of the Gesù. Bernini and his Age*, ed. by Linda Wolk-Simon, Philadelphia 2018, 185–224.

Mormando and Thomas 2006
Franco Mormando and Jill G. Thomas eds., *Francis Xavier and the Jesuit Missions in the Far East*, Chestnut Hill 2006.

Moroni 1840–1879
Gaetano Moroni, *Dizionario di erudizione storico-ecclesiastica*, 103 vols., Venezia 1840–1861.

Morrogh 1985
Andrew Morrogh, "Vasari and Coloured Stones," in *Giorgio Vasari: tra decorazione ambientale e storiografia artistica*, conference proceedings (Arezzo 1981), ed. by Gian Carlo Garfagnini, Firenze 1985, 309–320.

Morrogh 2017
Andrew Morrogh, "The Cappella dei Principi under Ferdinand I de Medici," in *San Lorenzo*, ed. by Robert Gaston and Louis A. Waldman, Florence 2017, 567–610.

Muffel 1452 [1999]
Nikolaus Muffel, *Descrizione della città di Roma nel 1452*, ed by Gerhard Wiedmann, Bologna 1999.

Mulhern 2003
P. F. Mulhern, "Holy Spirit, Gifts of," in *The New Catholic Encylcopedia*, 2nd ed., VII, Washington DC 2003, 47–49.

Muñoz 1919
Antonio Muñoz, *La Basilica di Santa Sabina in Roma*, Milano 1919.

Muñoz 1938
Antonio Muñoz, *Il Restauro della Basilica di Santa Sabina*, Roma 1938.

Mussi 1935
Luigi Mussi, *Il Cardinale Alderano dei Principi Cibo Malaspina dai documenti del R. Archivio di Stato di Massa*, Massa 1935.

Musso 1590
Cornelio Musso, *Prediche sopra il Simbolo degli Apostoli, le due dilettioni di Dio, e del prossimo, il sacro decalogo, & la passione di nostro Signor Giesu Christo*, Venezia 1590.

Mussolin 2009
Mauro Mussolin ed., *Michelangelo architetto a Roma*, exhib. catalogue (Rome 2010), Cinisello Balsamo 2009.

Nagel 2011
Alexander Nagel, *The Controversy of Renaissance Art*, Chicago and London 2011.

Napoleone 1989
Caterina Napoleone, "Il collezionismo dei marmi e pietre colorate dal secolo XVI al secolo XIX," in Borghini 1989, 99–115.

Nater 2010
Carol Nater, "Streit um den Platz in der Ewigkeit: die Ginetti-Kapelle in S. Andrea della Valle im Spannungsfeld konkurrierender römischer Aufsteigerfamilien im Seicento", in *Vom Nachleben der Kardinäle: römische Kardinalsgrabmäler der Frühen Neuzeit*, ed. by Arne Karsten Philipp Zitzlsperger, Berlin 2010, 197–219.

Neppi 1975
Lionello Neppi, *Palazzo Spada*, Roma 1975.

Neveu 1979
Bruno Neveu, "Episcopus et princeps Urbis: Innocent XI reformateur de Rome d'après des documents inédits (1676–1689)," in *Römische Kurie. Kirchliche Finanzen. Vatikanisches Archiv. Studien zu Ehren von Hermann Hoberg*, ed. by Erwin Gatz, Rom 1979, II, 597–633.

Newlands 2013
Carole E. Newlands, "Architectural Ecphrasis in Roman Poetry," in *Generic Interfaces in Latin Literature. Encounters, Interactions and Transformations*, ed. by Theodore D. Papanghelis, Stephen J. Harrison, and Stavros Frangoulidis, Berlin and Boston 2013, 55–78.

Nibby 1839
Antonio Nibby, *Roma nell'anno MDCCCXXXVIII*, Roma 1839.

Notter and Daguerre de Hureaux 2002
Annick Notter and Alain Daguerre de Hureaux eds., *Lubin Baugin*, exhib. catalogue (Orleans and Toulouse 2002), Paris 2002.

Orbaan 1919
Johannes Albertus Franciscus Orbaan, "Der Abbruch Alt-Sankt-Peters 1605–1615," *Jahrbuch der Preuszischen Kunstsammlungen*, 39, 1919, 21–117.

Orsolini 1701
Ignazio Orsolini, *Riflessioni spirituali, e morali sopra la vita di S. Filippo Neri, Fondatore della Congregazione dell'Oratorio nella città di Roma*, Roma 1701.

Oryshkevich 2003
Irina T. Oryshkevich, *The History of the Roman Catacombs from the Age of Constantine to the Renaissance*, PhD diss., Columbia University 2003.

Osswald 2002
Maria Cristina Osswald, "The Iconography and Cult of Francis Xavier, 1552–1640," *Archivum Historicum Societatis Iesu*, 71, 2002, 142, 259–277.

Osswald 2008
Maria Cristina Osswald, "Aspectos de Devoción e Iconografía del Túmulo de San Francisco Javier en Goa," in *Misión y Aventura: San Francisco Javier, sol en Oriente*, ed. by Ignacio Arellano and Delio Mendonça, Madrid 2008, 223–251.

Osswald 2013
Maria Cristina Osswald, *Written in Stone: Jesuit buildings in Goa and their artistic and architectural features*, Goa 2013.

Ostrow 1990
Steven F. Ostrow, "Marble Revetment in Late Sixteenth-Century Roman Chapels," in *IL60. Essays in Honor of Irving Lavin on his Sixtieth Birthday*, ed. by Marilyn Aronberg Lavin, New York 1990, 253–266.

Ostrow 1996
Steven F. Ostrow, *Art and Spirituality in Counter-Reformation Rome. The Sistine and Pauline Chapels in S. Maria Maggiore*, Cambridge and New York 1996.

Ostrow 2000
Steven F. Ostrow, "La decorazione architettonica," in *La Basilica di San Pietro in Vaticano*, ed. by Antonio Pinelli, II, Modena 2000, 241–251.

Ostrow 2009
Steven F. Ostrow, "The 'Confessio' in Post-Tridentine Rome," in *Arte e committenza nel Lazio nell'età di Cesare Baronio*, conference proceedings (Frosinone and Sora 2007), ed. by Patrizia Tosini, Roma 2009, 19–32.

Ostrow 2015
Steven F. Ostrow, "The Ludovisi Saint Peter: a New Work by Bastiano Torrigiani in the Minneapolis Museum of Art," in *The Eternal Baroque. Studies in Honour of Jennifer Montagu*, ed. by Carolyn H. Miner, Milano 2015, 409–426.

Ostrow 2016
Steven F. Ostrow, "Giovanni Angelo Frumenti and His Tomb in S. Maria Maggiore: a Proposed New Work by Gian Lorenzo Bernini," *The Burlington Magazine*, 158, 2016, 1360, 518–528.

Ottley and Tomkins 1818
William Young Ottley and Peltro William Tomkins, *Engravings of the Marquis of Stafford's Collection of Pictures in London*, II, London 1818.

Palazzo 2010
Eric Palazzo, "Relics, Liturgical Space, and the Theology of the Church," in Bagnoli, Klein, Mann, and Robinson 2010, 99–109.

Paleotti 1582 [2012]
Gabriele Paleotti, *Discorso sopra le immagini sacre et profane*, Bologna 1582, Engl. ed. *Discourse on Sacred and Profane Images*, introduction by Paolo Prodi, trans. by William McCuaig, Los Angeles 2012.

Palla 1989–1998
Roberto Palla, "Alle fonti della prima edizione Billiana dei carmi di Gregorio Nazianzeno," in *Polyanthema: studi di letteratura cristiana antica offerti a Salvatore Costanza*, ed. by Gianvia Resta, Messina 1989–1998, 3, 83–114.

Palla 2002
Roberto Palla, "Tra filologia e motivi confessionali: edizioni e traduzioni latine di Gregorio Nazianzeno dal 1569 al 1583," in *I padri sotto il torchio: le edizioni dell'antichità cristiana nei secoli XV–XVI*, ed. by Mariarosa Cortesi, Firenze 2002, 167–188.

Palla, Moroni, Crimi, and Dessì 2010
Roberto Palla, Maria Grazia Moroni, Carmelo Crimi, and Antonino Dessì eds., *Gregorio di Nazianzo in Occidente. 1: Edizioni e traduzioni latine a stampa 1500–1549*, Pisa 2010.

Palladio 1554
Andrea Palladio, *Descritione de le chiese, stationi, indulgenze e reliquie dei corpi santi che sono in la città di Roma*, Roma 1554.

Palmerio and Villetti 1989
Giancarlo Palmerio and Gabriella Villetti, *Storia edilizia di S. Maria sopra Minerva in Roma, 1275–1870*, Roma 1989.

Pampalone 2000
Antonella Pampalone, "La Pentecoste di san Filippo Neri. Iconografia e iconologia," in *San Filippo Neri nella realtà romana del XVI secolo,* conference proceedings (Rome 1995), ed. by Maria Teresa Bonadonna Russo and Niccolò del Re, Roma 2000, 145–188.

Pampalone 2017
Antonella Pampalone, "La vita di san Filippo Neri nei cicli figurativi," in *Iconografia di un Santo. Nuovi studi sull'immagine di san Filippo Neri*, ed. by Alberto Bianco, Roma 2017, 9–188.

Panciroli 1600
Ottavio Panciroli, *I tesori nascosti nell'alma città di Roma*, Roma 1600.

Panciroli 1625
Ottavio Panciroli, *Tesori nascosti nell'alma città di Roma*, Roma 1625.

Pane 1984
Roberto Pane ed., *Seicento Napoletano. Arte costume e ambiente*, Milano 1984.

Panvinio 1557
Onofrio Panvinio, *Fasti et Triumphi Rom. A Romulo Rege usque ad Carolum V*, Venetiis 1557.

Panvinio 1558
Onofrio Panvinio, *Fastorum libri V a Romulo rege usque ad Imp. Caes. Carolum V*, Venetiis 1558.

Panvinio 1570
Onofrio Panvinio, *Le sette chiese principali di Roma*, Roma 1570.

Papalexandrou 2001
Amy Papalexandrou, "Text in Context: Eloquent Monuments and the Byzantine Beholder," *Word & Image*, 17, 2001, 3, 259–283.

Parente 1990
Fausto Parente, "De Monte, Andrea," in *Dizionario Biografico degli Italiani*, 38, Roma 1990, *ad vocem*.

Parlato 2009
Enrico Parlato, "Enrico Caetani a S. Pudenziana: antichità, magnificenza decorativa e prestigio del casato nella Roma di fine Cinquecento," in *Arte e committenza nel Lazio nell'età di Cesare Baronio*, conference proceedings (Frosinone and Sora 2007) ed. by Patrizia Tosini, Roma 2009, 143–164.

Parlato 2014
Enrico Parlato, "Esequie e sepolture romane dei cardinali veneziani," in Furlan and Tosini 2014, 329–365.

Pascoli 1730–1736 [1981]
Lione Pascoli, *Vite de' Pittori, Scultori ed Architetti Moderni*, 2 vols., Roma 1730–1736, ed. by Isa Belli Barsali, Treviso 1981.

Pascoli 1730–1736 [1992]
Lione Pascoli, *Vite de' Pittori, Scultori ed Architetti Moderni*, 2 vols., Roma 1730–1736, ed. by Francesco F. Mancini, Perugia 1992.

Passeri 17th cent. [1934]
Giovanni Battista Passeri, *Vite de' pittori, scultori ed architetti che hanno lavorato in Roma, morti dal 1641 fino al 1673*, ed. by Jacob Hess (*Die Künstlerbiographien von Giovanni Battista Passeri nach den Handschriften des Autors herausgegeben und mit Anmerkungen versehen von Jacob Hess*), Leipzig and Wien 1934.

Passeri 1934 [1995]
Giovanni Battista Passeri, *Die Künstlerbiographien von Giovanni Battista Passeri*, ed. by Jacob Hess, Leipzig 1934 (ed. Worms am Rhein 1995).

Pastor von 1943
Ludwig von Pastor, *Storia dei papi dalla fine del Medioevo*, XIV.2, Roma 1943.

Pastor von 1951
Ludwig von Pastor, *The History of the Popes from the Close of the Middle Ages*, XVII, ed. by Ralph Francis Kerr, London 1951.

Paul 2015
Benjamin Paul, "Bad Colours for the Pope: Tintoretto, Giovanni Grimani and the Decoration of the Cappella Gregoriana in New St Peter's," in *Artistic Practices and Cultural Transfer in Early Modern Italy: Essays in Honour of Deborah Howard*, ed. by Nebahat Avcıoğlu and Alllison Sherman, Farnham 2015, 29–43.

Pecchiai 1952
Pio Pecchiai, *Il Gesù di Roma,* Roma 1952.

Pecchiai and Montini 1958
Pio Pecchiai and Renzo U. Montini, *San Giacomo in Augusta*, Roma 1958.

Pedrocchi 1993
Anna Maria Pedrocchi, *San Gregorio al Celio. Storia di un'abbazia*, Roma 1993.

Peranda 1601
Giovan Francesco Peranda, *Lettere del Sig. Gio. Francesco Peranda*, Venezia 1601.

Petraroia 1993
Pietro Petraroia, "Bastiano Torrigiani detto il Bologna," in Madonna 1993, 565.

Piazza 1675
Carlo Bartolomeo Piazza, *Santuario overo Menologio romano perpetuo per la visita delle chiese, feste, indulgenze, stazioni, reliquie de santi, e cose sacre memorabilia di Roma*, Roma 1675.

Piazza 1679
Carlo Bartolomeo Piazza, *Opere Pie di Roma descritte secondo lo stato presente dall'Abbate Carlo Bartolomeo Piazza*, Roma 1679.

Piazza 1690
Carlo Bartolomeo Piazza, *Emerologio sagro di Roma cristiana e gentile*, I, Roma 1690.

Piazza 1702
Carlo Bartolomeo Piazza, *Eorterologio overo le sacre stazioni romane, e feste mobili*, Roma 1702.

Piazza 1703
La Gerarchia Cardinalizia a Clemente XI Pontefice Massimo, Roma 1703.

Picone 1995
Leo Picone, "I busti dei Frangipane in San Marcello al Corso," *Lazio ieri e oggi*, 31, 1995, 41–43.

Picozzi 2007
Maria Grazia Picozzi, "Le collezioni di antichità: le raccolte Caetani sino al XVIII secolo," in *Palazzo Caetani: storia, arte e cultura*, ed. by L. Fiorani, Roma 2007, 267–282.

Pierguidi 2017
Stefano Pierguidi, *Pittura di marmo: storia e fortuna delle pale d'altare a rilievo nella Roma di Bernini*, Firenze 2017.

Pinch 2011
William Pinch, "The Corpse and Cult of Francis Xavier, 1552–1623," in *Engaging South Asian Religions: Boundaries, Appropriations, and Resistances*, ed. by Mathew N. Schmalz and Peter Gottschalk, Albany 2011, 113–132.

Pisanelli 1575
Baldassarre Pisanelli, *Sopra il dragone di fuoco apparso in Roma alli 29 di gennaro 1575 ad un'hora di notte*, Bologna 1575.

Pittiglio 2012
Gianni Pittiglio, "La traslazione di S. Gregorio di Nazianzo tra urbanistica

e opere di misericordia," in Cieri Via, Rowland, and Ruffini 2012, 89–110.

Pollak 1928–1931
Oskar Pollak, *Die Kunsttätigkeit unter Urban VIII*, 2 vols., Wien 1928–1931.

Polzer 1995
Joseph Polzer, "Andrea di Bonaiuto's Via Veritas and Dominican Thought in Late Medieval Italy," *Art Bulletin*, 77, 1995, 262–289.

Poma 1993
Luigi Poma, "Apocrifi tassiani," in *Le tradizioni del testo. Studi di letteratura italiana offerti a Domenico De Robertis*, ed. by Franco Gavazzeni e Guglielmo Gorni, Milano and Napoli 1993, 201–208.

Pometti 1901
Francesco Pometti, "Il ruolo dei Lettori del MDLXVIIII-MDLXX ed altre notizie sull'università di Roma," in *Scritti vari di filologia dedicata a Ernesto Monaci*, Roma 1901, 67–93.

Ponnelle and Bordet 1986
Louis Ponnelle and Luigi Bordet, *San Filippo Neri e la società romana del suo tempo (1515–1595)*, Firenze 1986.

Portoghesi 1953
Paolo Portoghesi, "La cappella Spada in S. Gerolamo della Carità," *Quaderni dell'Istituto di storia dell'architettura*, 4, 1953, 7–13.

Posner 1971
Donald Posner, *Annibale Carracci. A Study in the Reform of Italian Painting around 1590*, 2 vols., London and New York 1971.

Possanzini 1985
Laura Possanzini, "Croce, Baldassarre," in *Dizionario Biografico degli Italiani*, 31, Roma 1985, *ad vocem*.

Posterla 1707
Francesco Posterla, *Roma sacra e moderna*, Roma 1707.

Prati 1686
Giovanni Prati, *Nel discoprirsi la sontuosa capella fatta dalla splendidissima pietà dell'Eminentissimo Signor Cardinale Alderano Cybo [...]*, Roma 1686.

Preimesberger 1993
Rudolf Preimesberger, "Alessandro Algardis Statue des heiligen Philippus Neri: zum Thema Wort und Bild im römischen Barock," *Kunsthistorisches Jahrbuch Graz*, 25, 1993, 153–162.

Pressouyre 1984
Sylvia Pressouyre, *Nicolas Cordier: recherches sur la sculpture à Rome autour de 1600* (Collection de l'Ecole Française de Rome, 73), Rome 1984.

Prete 2001–2002
Cecilia Prete, "Il cardinale Rusticucci e le arti: episodi di committenza tra Roma e le Marche alla fine del Cinquecento," *Notizie da Palazzo Albani*, 30–31, 2001–2002, 153–165.

Priedl 2001
Elisabeth Priedl, "La pittura architettonica: da portatore di immagine a portatore di significato. Baldassare Croce nella Chiesa di Santa Susanna," in *Viterbo, Palazzo dei Priori: La Sala Regia. La storia, il restauro*, ed. by Massimo G. Bonelli and Laura P. Bonelli, Viterbo 2001, 109–123.

Priedl 2004
Elisabeth Priedl, *Santa Susanna. Die beiden Susannen des Kardinals Girolamo Rusticucci. Zum didaktischen Bildprogramm von Santa Susanna in Rom*, Wien 2004.

Priedl 2014
Elisabeth Priedl, "The Making of Santa Susanna. Medium, Diskurs, und Ritual der posttridentinischen Erzeugung von Evidenz," in *Autopsia: Blut- und Augenzeugen. Extreme Bilder des christlichen Martyriums*, ed. by Carolin Behrmann and Eisabeth Priedl, München 2014, 145–166.

Prosperi 1982
Adriano Prosperi, "'Oltras Indias': Missionari della controriforma tra contadini e selvaggi," in *Scienze, credenze occulte, livelli di cultura*, conference proceedings (Florence 1980), Firenze 1982.

Prosperi Valenti Rodinò, forthcoming
Simonetta Prosperi Valenti Rodinò, *Carlo Maratti: i disegni*, Roma (forthcoming).

Przyborowski 1982
Claudia Przyborowski, *Die Ausstattung der Fürstenkapelle an der Basilica von San Lorenzo in Florenz: Versuch einer Rekonstruktion*, PhD diss., 2 vols., Technische Universität Berlin 1982.

Pucci 1621
Benedetto Pucci, *Genealogia degl'illustrissimi Signori Frangipani romani*, Venezia 1621.

Pugliatti 1983
Teresa Pugliatti, "Girolamo Siciolante da Sermoneta considerazioni e proposte per una ricostruzione del percorso stilistico," in Fiorani, Hunter, and Pugliatti 1983, 77–108.

Pupillo 1998
Marco Pupillo, "Fuccari, Stefano," in *Dizionario Biografico degli Italiani*, 50, Roma 1998, *ad vocem*.

Radicchi 2008
Patrizia Radicchi, "Gli strumenti musicali in marmo di Michele Antonio Grandi, 'intagliator de' violini, gravicembali ed altri musicali stromenti'," *Accademia dei Rinnovati, Massa. Atti e Memorie*, 2003–2007 (2008), 97–134.

Raspe 2000
Martin Raspe, "Das Schaubild als monumentale Form. Zur 'Medialisierung' der Architektur bei Bramante, Domenichino, Cortona, Borromini und anderen," *Kritische Berichte*, 28, 2000, 3, 5–20.

Raspe 2014
Martin Raspe, "Cesare Domenichi, Die Cappella Gregoriana in Neu-St. Peter, Rom: Aufriss und Querschnitt," in *Architektur- und Ornamentgraphik der Frühen Neuzeit: Migrationsprozesse in Europa / Gravures d'architecture et d'ornement au début de l'époque moderne: processus de migration en Europe*, eds. Sabine Frommel and Eckhard Leuschner, exhib. catalogue (Gotha 2014), Roma 2014, 40–41 (Kat. Nr. 15).

Reale 1998
Giovanni Reale, *Raffaello, la 'Disputa': una interpretazione filosofica e teologica dell'affresco con la prima presentazione analitica dei singoli personaggi e dei particolari simbolici e allegorici emblematici*, Milano 1998.

Redle 1967
M. J. Redle, "Beatific Vision," in *New Catholic Encyclopedia*, II, New York 1967, 186–193.

Regnard ca. 1622
Valérien Regnard, *S. Francisci Xaverii Indiarum Apostoli Societatis Iesu quaedam Miracula*, Romae ca. 1622.

***La regola e la fama* 1995**
La regola e la fama. San Filippo Neri e l'arte, exhib. catalogue (Rome 1995), Milano 1995.

Restaino and Zampino 2012
Concetta Restaino and Giuseppe Zampino eds., *Tesori del regno: l'ornamentazione delle cripte delle cattedrali di Salerno e Amalfi nel XVII secolo*, Pozzuoli 2012.

Ribadeneyra 1604
Pedro Ribadeneyra, *Flos Sanctorum, cioè Vite de Santi*, Venezia 1604.

Riccoboni 1942
Alberto Riccoboni, *Roma nell'arte: la scultura nell'evo moderno da Quattrocento ad oggi*, Roma 1942.

Rice 1997
Louise Rice, *The Altars and Altarpieces of New St. Peter's: Outfitting the Basilica, 1621–1666*, Cambridge and New York 1997.

Rice 2018
Louise Rice, "Joshua and the Jesuits: The Battle for the Apse of the Gesù," in *The Holy Name: Art of the Gesù, Bernini and his Age*, ed. by Linda Wolk-Simon, Philadelphia 2018, 225–251.

Rickert 1998
Franz Rickert, "Zum Inkrustationsschmuck von S. Sabina in Rom," in *Chartulae: Festschrift für Wolfgang Speyer*, ed. by Ernst Dassmann, Münster 1998, 263–270.

Riebesell 1991
Christina Riebesell, "Giovanni Battista Di Bianchi," in *Dizionario Biografico degli Italiani*, 39, Roma 1991, *ad vocem.*

Righini 2012
Davide Righini, *Gli Spada in Romagna e a Bologna. Architettura, arte e collezionismo nei secoli XVI e XVII*, Faenza 2012.

Riikonen 1982
Hannu Riikonen, "*Ad Nubes*--The Horatian Ode of Torquato Tasso," *Turun Yliopiston Julkaisuja–Annales Universitatis Turkuensis*, 1982, 156, 9–39.

Ripa 1593
Cesare Ripa, *Iconologia overo descrittione dell'Imagini universali cavate dall'Antichità ed da altri luoghi*, Roma 1593.

Robertson 1992
Clare Robertson, *Il Gran Cardinale: Alessandro Farnese, Patron of the Arts*, New Haven and London 1992.

Romano 1990
Giovanni Romano ed., *Da Biduino ad Algardi: pittura e scultura a confronto. Antichi Maestri Pittori*, exhib. catalogue (Turin 1990), Torino 1990.

Romano 1991
Marco Romano, "Materiale di spoglio nel battistero di San Giovanni in Laterano: un riesame e nuove considerazioni," *Bollettino d'Arte*, 76, 1991, 70, 31–70.

Romano 1996
Marco Romano, "L'Oratorio della S. Croce al Laterano. Preliminari di un'indagine archeologica-topografica," *Zeitschrift für Kunstgeschichte*, 59, 1996, 341–349.

Romano 1976
Serena Romano, "Due affreschi nel Cappellone degli Spagnoli: problemi iconologici," *Storia dell'arte*, 1976, 26–28, 181–213.

Romano 2017
Serena Romano, *Apogeo e fine del Medioevo, 1288–1431*, in Andaloro and Romano 2006–2017, VI, 2017.

Rossi 1941
Ermete Rossi, "Roma ignorata", *Roma*, XIX, 1941, 10, 438–439.

Rudolph 1994
Stella Rudolph, "Premessa ad un'indagine sul mecenatismo del cardinale Alderano Cybo devoto dell'Immacolata nonché parziale a Guercino e a Maratti," *Bollettino dei musei comunali di Roma*, 8, 1994, 5–31.

Rudolph 2000
Stella Rudolph, "Carlo Maratti", in *L'Idea del Bello. Viaggio per Roma nel Seicento con Giovan Pietro Bellori*, exhib. catalogue (Rome 2000), ed. by Evelina Borea and Carlo Gasparri, with Luciano Arcangeli, Roma 2000, 456–479.

Rudolph 2011
Conrad Rudolph, "Inventing the Exegetical Stained-Glass Window: Suger, Hugh, and a New Elite Art," *Art Bulletin*, 93, 2011, 399–422.

Ruffini 2005
Marco Ruffini, *Le imprese del drago. Politica, emblematica e scienze naturali alla corte di Gregorio XIII Boncompagni (1572–1585)*, Roma 2005.

Ruffini 2009
Marco Ruffini, "A Dragon for the Pope: Politics and Emblematics at the Court of Gregory XIII," *Memoirs of the American Academy in Rome*, 54, 2009, 83–105.

Rupert of Deutz ed. 1854
Rupert of Deutz, "De operibus Spiritus Sancti," in *Patrologiae Cursus Completus... Series Latina*, ed. by Jacques-Paul Migne, CLXVII, Paris 1854, cols. 1528–1571.

de Sade ed. 1996
Donatien-Alphonse-François Marquis de Sade, *Viaggio in Italia*, ed. Torino 1996.

Santi 1588
Fra Santi, *Stationi delle chiese di Roma per tutta la Quaresima con una breve narratione della fondatione, & Consecratione di dette Chiese*, Roma 1588.

Satkowski 1993
Leon Satkowski, *Giorgio Vasari: Architect and Courtier*, Princeton 1993.

Schaar 1968
Eckhard Schaar, "Carlo Marattis 'Tod von Heiligen Franz Xaver' im Gesù," in *Munuscula Discipulorum: kunsthistorische Studien; Hans Kauffmann zum 70. Geburtstag 1966*, ed. by Tilman Buddensieg and Matthias Winner, Berlin 1968, 247–264.

Schraven 2014
Minou Schraven, *Festive Funerals in Early Modern Italy. The Art and Culture of Conspicuous Commemoration*, Farnham 2014.

Schurhammer 1965
Georg Schurhammer, "Der Silberschrein des Hl. Franz Xaver in Goa. Ein Meisterwerk Christlich-Indischer Kunst," *Varia*, 1, 1965, 561–567.

Schurhammer 1973–1982
Georg Schurhammer, *Francis Xavier. His Life, His Times*, trans. by M. Joseph Costelloe, 4 vols., Rome 1973–1982.

Scorza Barcellona 2000
Francesco Scorza Barcellona, "Pio I", in *Enciclopedia dei Papi*, Roma 2000, I, 220–222.

Scott 2003
John Beldon Scott, *Architecture for the Shroud: Relic and Ritual in Turin*, Chicago 2003.

Sénécal 1995
Robert Sénécal, "The Caetani Chapel in S. Pudenziana, Rome: Late Sixteenth-Century Chapel Decoration," *Apollo*, 142, 1995, 401, 37–42.

Sénécal 2000
Robert Sénécal, "Carlo Borromeo's Instructiones Fabricae et Supellectilis Ecclesiasticae and Its Origins in the Rome of His Time," *Papers of the British School at Rome*, 68, 2000, 241–267.

Serafinelli 2011
Guendalina Serafinelli, "Guido Reni, Clemente Boncompagni Corcos e lo Stendardo doppio di San Francesco: rinvenimenti d'archivio," *Rivista d'Arte*, 1, 2011, 175–203.

Serafinelli 2015
Guendalina Serafinelli, *Giacinto Brandi (1621–1691). Catalogo ragionato delle opere*, Torino 2015.

Serafinelli 2020, forthcoming
Guendalina Serafinelli, "Diventare bolognese: l'ebreo converso Ippolito Boncompagni e i suoi legami con Guido Reni, Guido Signorini e Domenichino," *Römisches Jahrbuch der Bibliotheca Hertziana*, 43, 2017–2018 (forthcoming).

Sestieri 1972
Giancarlo Sestieri, "Per la conoscenza di Luigi Garzi," *Commentari*, 23, 1972, 89–111.

Sicca 1996
Cinzia M. Sicca, "Le Pompe Della Fede," *FMR*, 15, 1996, 118, 110–126.

Sickel 2011
Lothar Sickel, "Virgilio Spada im Streit mit Gian Lorenzo Bernini: eine merkwürdige Episode in der unbekannten Geschichte des Palazzo Cybo," in *Ordnung und Wandel in der römischen Architektur der Frühen Neuzeit*, ed. by Hermann Schlimme and Lothar Sickel, Rom 2011, 215–234.

Sickel 2014
Lothar Sickel, "Guglielmo Della Porta's last Will and the Sale of his Passion of Christ to Diomede Leoni," *Journal of the Warburg and Courtauld Institutes*, 77, 2014, 229–239.

Sigonio 1550
Carlo Sigonio, *Regum, Consolum, Dictatorum, ac Censorum Romanorum Fasti*, Mutina 1550.

Sigonio 1556
Carlo Sigonio, *Fasti Consulares*, Venetiis 1556.

Sinding-Larsen 1965
Staales Sinding-Larsen, "Some Functional and Iconographical Aspects of the Centralized Church in the Italian Renaissance," *Acta ad archeologiam et artium historiam pertinentia*, 2, 1965, 203–252.

Smith O'Neil 1985
Maryvelma Smith O'Neil, "The Patronage of Cardinal Cesare Baronio at San Gregorio Magno: Renovation and Innovation," in *Baronio e l'arte*, conference proceedings (Sora 1984), ed. by Agostino Borromeo and Romeo De Maio, Sora 1985, 145–171.

Spagnolo 2013
Maddalena Spagnolo, "Giovio's Puns and Vasari's Curly Tuft," in *Renaissance Studies in Honor of Joseph Connors* (Villa i Tatti Series, 29), ed. by Maecht Israëls and Louis A. Waldman, Florence 2013, II, 519–524.

Spalding 1982
Jack Spalding, *Santi di Tito*, New York and London 1982.

Spear 1969a
Richard E. Spear, "Algardi's Saint Proculus," *The Burlington Magazine*, 111, 1969, 793, 220–223.

Spear 1969b
Richard E. Spear, "The Cappella Della Strada Cupa: A Forgotten Domenichino Chapel," *The Burlington Magazine*, 111, 1969, 790, 12–23.

Spear 1982
Richard E. Spear, *Domenichino*, New Haven and London 1982.

Staffetti 1900
Luigi Staffetti, *Spigolature di storia artistica massese: un affresco di Bernardino Pinturicchio nel Duomo di Massa*, La Spezia 1900 (offprint of *Giornale storico e letterario della Liguria*, 1.1900).

Steinberg 1959
Leo Steinberg, "Observations in the Cerasi Chapel," *Art Bulletin*, 41, 1959, 183–190.

Steinemann 1995
Holger Steinemann, *Baldassare Croce, ein Maler der katholischen Reform*, Magisterarbeit Thesis, University of Stuttgart 1995.

Stern 1958
Henri Stern, "Les mosaïques de l'église de Sainte-Constance à Rome," *Dumbarton Oaks Papers*, 12, 1958, 159–218.

Strinati 1984
Claudio Strinati, "San Marcello al Corso, Cappella Frangipani," in *Oltre Raffaello. Aspetti della cultura figurativa del Cinquecento romano*, exhib. catalogue (Rome 1984), ed. by Luciana Cassanelli and Sergio Rossi, Roma 1984, 118–124.

Strinati 1992
Claudio Strinati, "La scultura a Roma nel Cinquecento," in *L'arte a Roma nel secolo XVI*, 2, ed. by Daniela Gallavotti Cavallero, Francesco d'Amico, and Claudio Strinati, Roma 1992, 301–342.

Strinati 2001
Claudio Strinati, "L'Assunzione della Vergine di Annibale Carracci," in Bernardini and Mignosi Tantillo 2001, 77–85.

Stroud 2012
James W. Stroud, *Thomas Aquinas' Exposition of the Gifts of the Holy Spirit: Developments in His Thought and Rival Interpretations*, PhD diss., The Catholic University of America 2012.

Stumpo 1981
Enrico Stumpo, "Cibo, Alderano", in *Dizionario Biografico degli Italiani*, 25, Roma 1981, *ad vocem*.

Suggit 1985
John Neville Suggit, "1 John 5: 21: Τεκνία, φυλάξατε ἑαυτὰ ἀπὸ τῶν εἰδώλων," *The Journal of Theological Studies* 36, 1985, 2, 386–390.

Summers 2006
Kirk M. Summers, *The Iuvenilia of Marc-Antoine Muret*, Columbus 2006.

Sutherland Harris and Schaar 1967
Ann Sutherland Harris and Eckhard Schaar eds., *Die Handzeichnungen von Andrea Sacchi und Carlo Maratta* (*Katalog des Kunstmuseums Düsseldorf*, 3/1), Düsseldorf 1967.

Tafuri 1976
Manfredo Tafuri, "Capriani, Francesco," in *Dizionario Biografico degli Italiani*, 19, Roma 1976, *ad vocem*.

Tancredi 1998
Romolo Tancredi, "La costruzione della chiesa di S. Atanasio dei Greci a Roma (1578–1583)," *Palladio*, 21, 1998, 13–34.

Tancredi 2000
Romolo Tancredi, "Giacomo della Porta e Martino Longhi il Vecchio nella chiesa di S. Atanasio dei Greci a Roma," *Opus*, 6, 2000, 139–172.

Taylor 1950
Lily Ross Taylor, "Degrassi's Edition of the Consular and Triumphal Fasti," in *Classical Philology*, 45, 1950, 84–95.

Tellini Santoni and Manodori 1995
Barbara Tellini Santoni and Alberto Manodori eds., *Messer Filippo Neri Santo. L'apostolo di Roma*, exhib. catalogue (Rome 1995), Roma 1995.

Testa 2015
Simone Testa, "Peranda, Giovan Francesco," in *Dizionario Biografico degli Italiani*, 82, Roma 2015, *ad vocem*.

Thomas Aquinas ed. 2006
Thomas Aquinas, *Summa Theologiae*, 24, *The Gifts of the Spirit*, ed. and trans. by Edward D. O' Connor, Cambridge 2006.

Thumser 1991
Matthias Thumser, "Die Frangipane: Abriss der Geschichte einer Adelsfamilie im hochmittelaterlichen Rom," *Quellen und Forschungen aus italienischen Archiven und Bibliotheken*, 71, 1991, 106–162.

Titi 1674–1763 [1987]
Filippo Titi, *Studio di pittura, scoltura, et architettura nelle chiese di Roma*, 2 vols., ed. by Bruno Contardi and Serena Romano, Firenze 1987.

Titi 1763
Filippo Titi, *Descrizione delle Pitture, Sculture e Architetture esposte in Roma*, Roma 1763.

Toesca 1965
Ilaria Toesca, "Due opere del Siciolante," *Paragone*, 16, 1965, 187, 57–5x.

Torricelli, Tugnoli Pattaro and Scappini 1993
Maria Pia Torricelli, Sandra Tugnoli Pattaro, and Cristiana Scappini, *Lo Studio Aldrovandi in Palazzo pubblico. 1617–1742*, Bologna 1993.

Torres Olleta 2009
Maria Gabriela Torres Olleta, *Redes iconograficas: San Francisco Javier en la cultura visual del Barroco*, Madrid 2009.

Tosini 2003
Patrizia Tosini, "Giovan Battista Ricci and Cristoforo Greppi at the Castellani Chapel in S. Francesco a Ripa, Rome," *The Burlington Magazine*, 145, 2003, 1202, 366–370.

Tosini 2008
Patrizia Tosini, *Girolamo Muziano, 1532–1592. Dalla Maniera alla Natura*, Roma 2008.

Tosini 2010
Patrizia Tosini, "Il Duomo di Orvieto nella seconda metà del Cinquecento: un modello per la pittura della Controriforma," in *Storia di Orvieto. Quattrocento e Cinquecento*, 3.2, ed. by Carla Benocci, Giuseppe Della Fina, and Corrado Fratini, Pisa 2010, 469–488.

Tosini 2012
Patrizia Tosini, "Girolamo Muziano e Gregorio XIII: Un rapporto privilegiato," in Cieri Via, Rowland, and Ruffini 2012, 277–297.

Totti 1638
Pompilio Totti, *Ritratto di Roma Moderna*, Roma 1638.

Trevisani 1980
Filippo Trevisani, "Giovanni Battista Negroni committente dell'altare di S. Francesco Saverio al Gesù di Roma," *Storia dell'arte*, 38–40, 1980, 361–369.

Trivellone 2007
Alessia Trivellone, "Il cosiddetto oratorio mariano della chiesa di S. Pudenziana e i suoi affreschi: nuove considerazioni," in *Roma e la Riforma gregoriana*, conference proceedings (Lausanne 2004), ed. by Serena Romano and Julie Enckell Julliard, Roma 2007, 305–330.

Tromp 1959
Sebastian Tromp, "De Primis Secretariis S. Congregationis Concilii," *Gregorianum*, 40, 1959, 3, 523–531.

Tuena 1988
Filippo Tuena, "Appunti per la storia del commesso romano," *Antologia di Belle Arti*, 12, 1988, 54–69.

Tuena 1989a
Filippo Tuena, "Un bando del 1572 per la regolamentazione degli scavi in Roma," *Xenia*, 17, 1989, 91–94.

Tuena 1989b
Filippo Tuena, "I marmi commessi del tardo Rinascimento romano," in Borghini 1989, 81–97.

Turner 1583
Robert Turner, *Panegyrici sermones duo, de D. Gregorio Nazianzeno translato unus, alter de triumpho, quo post conditam ecclesiam Leodiam celeberrimo Illustrissimus Bavariae Dux Ernestus fuit Episcopus Leodius inauguratus*, Ingolstadt 1583.

Turriziani 2011
Simona Turriziani, "Le immagini mariane nell'arte musiva della Basilica," in *San Pietro in Vaticano, i mosaici e lo spazio*, ed. by Christof Thoenes and Vittorio Lanzani, Milano 2011, 206–233.

Ugonio 1588
Pompeo Ugonio, *Historia delle Stationi di Roma che si celebrano la Quadragesima*, Roma 1588.

Ugonio 1603
P. Ugonio, *In funere amplissimi cardinalis Antonii Mariae Salviati oratio ad sacrum Senatum, habita in Romae in Templo S. Iacobii in Augusta...*, Romae 1603.

Ugurgieri Azzolini 1649
Isidoro Ugurgieri Azzolini, *Le pompe sanesi, o' vero Relazione delli huomini e donne illustri di Siena e del suo Stato*, 2 vols., Pistoia 1649.

Urban 1961–1962
Günter Urban, "Die Kirchenbaukunst des Quattrocento in Rom," *Römisches Jahrbuch für Kunstgeschichte*, 9–10, 1961–1962, 9–10, 74–287.

Uttaro and Gigli 2003
Eliana Uttaro and Laura Gigli, *Palazzo Boncompagni Corcos a Monte Giordano: programmi e immagini*, Roma 2003.

Vai and Cavazza 2006
Gian Battista Vai and William Cavazza, "Ulisse Aldrovandi and the Origin of Geology and Science," *Geological Society of America*, special paper, 411, 2006, 43–63.

Valentino 1583
Ascanio Valentino, *Sacelli Gregoriani descriptio*, Florentiae 1583.

Valentino 1584
Ascanio Valentino, *Sacellum Gregorianum ex ipso opere, ut extat, descriptum*, Ingolstadii 1584.

Valeri 1958
Ugo Valeri, *L'ultimo allievo del Bernini: Antonio Valeri*, Roma 1958.

Vanmaele 1965
Basile Vanmaele, *L'église pudentienne de Rome (Santa Pudenziana): contribution à l'histoire de ce monument insigne de la Rome chrétienne ancienne du IIe au XXe siècle (Bibliotheca Analectorum Praemonstratensia, 6)*, Averbode 1965.

Vasari 1550–1568 [1966–1997]
Giorgio Vasari, Le vite dei più eccellenti pittori, scultori ed architettori, Firenze 1550–1568, ed. by Paola Barocchi and Rosanna Bettarini, 11 vols., Firenze 1966–1997.

Vasari 1568 [1906]
Giorgio Vasari, *Le vite dei più eccellenti pittori, scultori ed architettori*, Firenze 1568, ed. and annotated by Gaetano Milanesi, VII, Firenze 1906.

Vázquez Janeiro 1957
Isaac Vázquez Janeiro, *Las negociaciones inmaculistas en la Curia Romana durante el Reinado de Carlos II de España (1665–1700)*, Madrid 1957.

Verde 2009
Paola Carla Verde, "Domenico Fontana, regio ingegnere nel Regio di Napoli (1592–1607)," in *Studi sui Fontana; una dinastia di architetti a Roma tra Manierismo e Barocco*, ed. by Marcello Fagiolo and Giuseppe Bonaccorso, Roma 2009, 81–96.

Visceglia 2001
Maria Antonietta Visceglia, "'Non si ha da equiparare l'utile quando vi fosse l'honore': scelte economiche e reputazione; intorno alla vendita dello stato feudale dei Caetani (1627)," in *La nobiltà romana in età moderna: profili istituzionali e pratiche sociali*, ed. by Maria Antonietta Visceglia, Roma 2001, 203–223.

Vlam 1979
Grace A.H. Vlam, "The Portrait of S. Francis Xavier in Kobe," *Zeitschrift für Kunstgeschichte*, 42, 1979, 1, 48-60.

***Vocabolario degli Accademici della Crusca* 1612**
Vocabolario degli Accademici della Crusca, Venezia 1612.

***Vocabolario degli Accademici della Crusca* 1691**
Vocabolario degli Accademici della Crusca, 3rd ed., Firenze 1691.

Voelker 1977 [2008]
Evelyn Carole Voelker, *Charles Borromeo's Instructiones fabricae et supellectilis ecclesiasticae*, 1577, Book I and II, a translation with commentary and analysis, PhD diss., Syracuse University 1977, now available the complete translation and commentary on line on: http://evelynvoelker.com

Webb 1999a
Ruth Webb, "The Aesthetics of Sacred Space: Narrative, Metaphor and Motion in Ekphraseis of Church Buildings," *Dumbarton Oaks Papers*, 53, 1999, 59-74 (Webb 1999a).

Webb 1999b
Ruth Webb, "Ekphrasis Ancient and Modern: the Invention of the Genre," *Word & Image*, 15, 1999, 1, 7-18 (Webb 1999b).

Weißenberger 2007
Johanna Weißenberger, *Römische Mariengnadenbilder 1473-1590. Neue Altäre für alte Bilder: zur Vorgeschichte der barocken Inszenierungen*, PhD diss., Heidelberg Universität 2007.

Westin and Westin 1975
Jean K. Westin and Robert H. Westin eds., *Carlo Maratti and his Contemporaries. Figurative Drawings from the Roman Baroque*, exhib. catalogue (University Park 1975), University Park 1975.

Whitby 2006
Mary Whitby, "The St. Polyeuktos Epigram (Ap 1.10): A Literary Perspective," in *Greek Literature in Late Antiquity: Dynamism, Didacticism, Classicism*, ed. by Scott Fitzgerald Johnson, Aldershot 2006, 159-187.

Wiedmann 2004
Gerhard Wiedmann, "Il cardinale Anton Maria Salviati e il pittore Giovan Battista Ricci in S. Giacomo in Augusta a Roma," in *Per la storia dell'arte in Italia e in Europa. Studi in onore di Luisa Mortari*, ed. by Mimma Pasculli Ferrara, Roma 2004, 228-233.

Wilkinson 1970
Lancelot Patrick Wilkinson, "Pindar and the Proem to the Third Georgic," in *Forschungen zur römischen Literatur: Festschrift zum 60. Geburtstag von Karl Büchner*, ed. by Walter Wimmel, Wiesbaden 1970, 286-290.

Windt 2018
Franziska Windt, "Die Unbefleckte Empfängnis trifft auf erotische Hingabe - Die "Maria Immaculata" von Carlo Maratti in König Friedrichs II. Bildergalerie von Sanssouci," in *Texte des RECS* #17, https://recs.hypotheses.org/2287/(08.02.2018).

Wittkower 1981
Rudolf Wittkower, *Gian Lorenzo Bernini. The Sculptor of the Roman Baroque*, 3rd ed., Oxford 1981.

Wittkower 1990
Rudolf Wittkower, *Bernini. Lo scultore del Barocco romano*, Milano 1990.

Wittkower 1997
Rudolf Wittkower, *Bernini: The Sculptor of the Roman Baroque*, London 1997.

Wuescher-Becchi 1900
E. Wuescher-Becchi, "Sulla ricostruzione di tre dipinti descritti da Giovanni Diacono ed esistenti al suo tempo (Sec. IX) nel convento di S. Andrea ad Clivum Scauri," *Nuovo Bullettino di Archeologia Cristiana*, 6, 1900, 235-251.

Zander 2016
Pietro Zander, *La Madonna 'del Soccorso' nella Basilica Vaticana*, Città del Vaticano 2016.

Zander 2020, forthcoming
Pietro Zander, *La Madonna 'del Soccorso' nella cappella Gregoriana in San Pietro. Storia e restauro*, in *Gregorio XIII Boncompagni. Arte dei moderni e immagini venerabili nei cantieri della nuova* Ecclesia, conference proceedings (Rome 2018), ed. by Valentina Balzarotti and Bianca Hermanin (forthcoming).

Zazzera d'Aragonia 1617
Francesco Zazzera d'Aragonia, *Della famiglia Frangipani*, Napoli 1617.

Zollikofer 2016
Kaspar Zollikofer, *Die Cappella Gregoriana. Der erste Innenraum von Neu-Sankt-Peter in Rom und seine Genese*, Basel 2016.

Zuccari 1984
Alessandro Zuccari, *Arte e committenza nella Roma di Caravaggio*, Torino 1984.

Zuccari 1985
Alessandro Zuccari, "Restauro e filologia baroniani," in *Baronio e l'arte*, conference proceedings (Sora 1984), ed. by Agostino Borromeo and Romeo De Maio, Sora 1985, 489-510.

Zuccari 2001
Alessandro Zuccari, "Benedetto Giustiniani e i pittori di S. Prisca," in *Caravaggio e i Giustiniani: Toccar con mano una collezione del Seicento*, exhib. catalogue (Rome 2001), ed. by Silvia Danesi Squarzina, Milano 2001, 81-86.

Zuccari 2004
Alessandro Zuccari, "'Rhetorica christiana' e pittura: il cardinal Rusticucci e gli interventi di Cesare Nebbia, Tommaso Laureti e Baldassarre Croce nel presbiterio di S. Susanna," *Storia dell'arte*, 2004, 107, 37-80.

Zuccari 2012
Alessandro Zuccari, "Baronio e l'iconografia del martirio," in *Cesare Baronio tra santità e scrittura storica*, conference proceedings (Rome 2007), ed. by Giuseppe Antonio Guazzelli, Raimondo Michetti, and Francesco Scorza Barcellona, Roma 2012, 445-501.

Županov 2005
Ines Županov, *Missionary Tropics: The Catholic Frontier in India (16th and 17th centuries)*, Ann Arbor 2005.

Županov 2012
Ines Županov, "Passage to India: Jesuit Spiritual Economy between Martyrdom and Profit in the Seventeenth Century," *Journal of Early Modern History*, 16, 2012, 121-159.

Županov 2018
Ines Županov, "South Asia" in *A Companion to Early Modern Catholic Global Missions*, ed. by Ronnie Po-Chia Hsia, Leiden 2018, 238-268.

Contributors

Fabio Barry received his PhD from Columbia University in 2007. He formerly taught at the University of St. Andrews and is now Assistant Professor in the Department of Art and Art History at Stanford University. His research often concentrates on art in Rome, particularly baroque architecture, but he has also published extensively on medieval and antique art, especially sculpture. He is the author of *Painting in Stone: Architecture and the Poetics of Marble from Antiquity until the Enlightenment* (forthcoming in 2020 with Yale University Press) and coeditor of *The Serpent and the Stylus: Essays on G. B. Piranesi* (University of Michigan Press, 2006) and *The Rome of Piranesi in the Great "Vedute"* (Artemide, 2006). His articles and essays have appeared in numerous journals and edited volumes.

Fabrizio Federici studied Art History at the University of Pisa and at the Scuola Normale Superiore. From 2008 to 2012 he was the team leader of the project "Osservatorio Mostre e Musei" of the Scuola Normale, and from 2016 to 2019 he was a postdoctoral fellow at the Bibliotheca Hertziana in Rome. His interests include art patronage and collecting in the seventeenth century, the history of antiquarianism, and the reception of medieval art in the early modern age. He is the author, with Jörg Garms, of the book *Tombs of Illustrious Italians at Rome. L'album di disegni RCIN 970334 della Royal Library di Windsor* (Olschki, 2010).

Alison C. Fleming is Professor of Art History at Winston-Salem State University. Her research investigates art produced in the service of religion in the early modern world, especially the visual and material culture created by and associated with the Society of Jesus. She is associate editor of *The Cambridge Encyclopedia of the Jesuits* (Cambridge University Press, 2017), guest editor of a thematic issue on Jesuit visual culture in the *Journal of Jesuit Studies* (2019), and the author of a number of journal articles and essays in collected volumes on Benedictine and Jesuit art.

Chiara Franceschini received her PhD in 2008 from the Scuola Normale Superiore. After working at the Warburg Institute and teaching at University College London, she joined the Ludwig Maximilian University in Munich as Professor for Early Modern Art History in 2016. She is the author of *Storia del limbo* (Feltrinelli, 2017) as well as of several articles and essays on early modern art and religion, the political use of antiquities, and family chapels in Rome; she coedited *Classifying Content: Photographic Collections and Theories of Thematic Ordering* (Special Issue of *Visual Resources*, 2014). Currently, she directs the ERC-funded project "SACRIMA: The Normativity of Sacred Images in Early Modern Europe" on interrelations between art, religion, and cultural geography in Renaissance and Counter-Reformation Europe.

Stephanie C. Leone, Professor of Art History at Boston College, is a specialist in Italian Renaissance and baroque art and architecture, especially in Rome. Her research focuses on patronage, the papal court, secular architecture, architectural production, the building industry, art collecting, and material culture. She is the author of *The Palazzo Pamphilj in Piazza Navona: Constructing Identity in Early Modern Rome* (Harvey Miller, 2008) and the editor of and contributor to *The Pamphilj and the Arts: Patronage and Consumption in Baroque Rome* (McMullen Museum of Art, 2011). She is currently writing a book titled *Innocent X Pamphilj: Building Baroque Rome.*

Steven F. Ostrow received his PhD from Princeton University in 1987. After teaching at Vassar College and the University of California, Riverside, he moved in 2006 to the University of Minnesota, where he served as chair of the Art History Department until 2015. A specialist in early modern Italian (especially Roman) visual culture, he is the author of *Art and Spirituality in Counter-Reformation Rome: The Sistine and Pauline Chapels in S. Maria Maggiore* (Cambridge, 1996) and coeditor of and contributor to *Dosso's Fate* (Getty Research Institute, 1998), *Bernini's Biographies: Critical Essays* (Penn State, 2006), and *Critical Perspectives on Roman Baroque Sculpture* (Penn State, 2014). His articles and essays have appeared in numerous journals and edited volumes.

Enrico Parlato received a degree at Sapienza University (Rome, 1980), and an MPhil at Columbia University (1985). A Professor at the Università della Tuscia (Viterbo), he has published widely on painting and sculpture in fifteenth-century Rome, with particular attention to Filarete and Filippino Lippi, and liturgical and ceremonial aspects of artistic creation. He has also worked on the relations between Rome and Venice in the sixteenth century, with studies on Sebastiano del Piombo, book illustrations, and printed images. Recently, he was the curator of an exhibition on Filippo Lippi's *Madonna di Tarquinia* (Roma, Palazzo Barberini, 2017).

Louise Rice received her PhD from Columbia University in 1992 and taught for a decade at Duke University before joining the faculty of New York University in 2002. She is the author of *The Altars and Altarpieces of New St Peter's: Outfitting the Basilica 1621–1666* (Cambridge, 1997) and of numerous articles and essays on the art and architecture of baroque Rome, as well as the coauthor, with Joseph Connors, of *Specchio di Roma barocca. Una guida inedita del XVII secolo*. Rice's current research is directed at prints; she is writing a typological and cultural history of the thesis print in seventeenth-century Rome.

Guendalina Serafinelli is a specialist in early modern art history. After receiving her PhD from Sapienza University of Rome, she was a postdoctoral research associate at CASVA (National Gallery of Art, Washington D.C.) and a postdoctoral fellow at the Bibliotheca Hertziana, Max-Planck-Institut für Kunstgeschichte, Rome, where she now serves as scientific collaborator of the photo archive. She currently teaches at the Rome campus of the University of St. Thomas. She is the author of *Giacinto Brandi (1621–1691). Catalogo ragionato delle opere* (Umberto Allemandi, 2015) and coeditor of and contributor to *Luigi Garzi (1638–1721). Pittore romano* (Officina Libraria, 2018).

Patrizia Tosini received her PhD from Sapienza University of Rome in 1999. She is Assistant Professor in Art History at Roma Tre University. She is the author of many publications about the arts in Rome during the Counter-Reformation age, including the monographs *Girolamo Muziano. Dalla Maniera alla Natura (1532–1592)* (Ugo Bozzi, 2008) and *Immagini ritrovate. Decorazione a Villa Peretti Montalto tra Cinque e Seicento* (De Luca Editori, 2015). She also coedited the volumes *Arte e committenza nel Lazio nell'età di Cesare Baronio* (Gangemi Editore, 2009); *I Cardinali della Serenissima. Arte e committenza tra Venezia e Roma (1523–1605)* (Silvana Editoriale, 2014); *After 1564. Michelangelo's Legacy in Late Cinquecento Rome* (De Luca Editori, 2016); *Intrecci Virtuosi. Letterati, artisti e accademie tra Cinque e Seicento* (De Luca Editori, 2017); *L'Ospedale del SS. Salvatore tra Medioevo ed età moderna* (Silvana Editoriale, 2017).

Index of Names

Page numbers in italics refer to illustrations

Index of Places

Page numbers in italics refer to illustrations

Photo Credits

Photo at p. 8: Ministero dell'Interno, Dipartimento per le Libertà civili e l'Immigrazione, Direzione Centrale per l'Amministrazione del Fondo Edifici di Culto (FEC) / Photo Mauro Coen.

Photo at p. 15: The Trustees of the British Museum.

Photo at pp. 16–17: New York, The Metropolitan Museum of Art.

TOSINI
1: Ministero dell'Interno, Dipartimento per le Libertà civili e l'Immigrazione, Direzione Centrale per l'Amministrazione del Fondo Edifici di Culto (FEC) / Photo Mauro Coen; 2–7; 9–13: Bibliotheca Hertziana, Max-Planck-Institut für Kunstgeschichte, Rom / Ministero dell'Interno, Dipartimento per le Libertà civili e l'Immigrazione, Direzione Centrale per l'Amministrazione del Fondo Edifici di Culto (FEC); 8: Roma, Sovrintendenza Capitolina ai Beni Culturali.

BARRY
1: Archivio fotografico della Reverenda Fabbrica di San Pietro; 2: Universität Erfurt, Forschungsbibliothek Gotha; 3–4, and cover: Wormsley Library; 5, 9–11: Public domain; 6–8: Author.

PARLATO
1–5, 9–10, 13: Ministero dell'Interno, Dipartimento per le Libertà civili e l'Immigrazione, Direzione Centrale per l'Amministrazione del Fondo Edifici di Culto (FEC) / Photo Mauro Coen; 8: Rennes, Musée des Beaux-Arts; 12: Ministero dell'Interno, Dipartimento per le Libertà civili e l'Immigrazione, Direzione Centrale per l'Amministrazione del Fondo Edifici di Culto (FEC) / Photo Giulio Archinà; 6–7, 11, 14–15: Author.

OSTROW
1, 3–8, 10–12: Author; 2: after Apollonj Ghetti 1965, fig. 15.

FRANCESCHINI
1–8, 10–12, 14–16, 21: Ministero dell'Interno, Dipartimento per le Libertà civili e l'Immigrazione, Direzione Centrale per l'Amministrazione del Fondo Edifici di Culto (FEC) / Photo Mauro Coen; 9: after Krautheimer, Corbett, and Frankl 1937, I, n. 8; 13, 19: The Trustees of the British Museum; 17: Bridgewater Gallery, London; 18: Devonshire Collection, Chatsworth / reproduced by permission of Chatsworth Settlement Trust / Bridgeman Images; 20: The Royal Collection Trust, Her Majesty Queen Elizabeth II 2019.

SERAFINELLI
3–5, 8: Author; 7: Archivio della Congregazione dell'Oratorio, Rome; 1–2, 6, 9–11: Ministero dell'Interno, Dipartimento per le Libertà civili e l'Immigrazione, Direzione Centrale per l'Amministrazione del Fondo Edifici di Culto (FEC).

RICE
1–3, 15: Author; 4: after Heimbürger Ravalli 1977, fig. 88; 5: London, British Library; 6: Public domain; 7, 12: The Trustees of the British Museum; 8: Sotheby's; 9: County Durham, Bowes Museum; 10: Paris, Bibliothèque nationale de France; 11: New York, The Metropolitan Museum of Art; 13: Amsterdam, Rijksmuseum; 16: Postcard.

FLEMING-LEONE
1, 5: Photo Mauro Coen; 2, 6, 8–11: Alison Fleming; 3–4: Bibliotheca Hertziana – Max-Planck-Institut für Kunstgeschichte, Rom; 7: after Levy 1999–2000, 387, fig. 14; 12: Alison Fleming (reproduced with permission of John J. Burns Library, Boston College).

FEDERICI
1, 9: Bibliotheca Hertziana – Max-Planck-Institut für Kunstgeschichte, Rom / Ministero dell'Interno, Dipartimento per le Libertà civili e l'Immigrazione, Direzione Centrale per l'Amministrazione del Fondo Edifici di Culto (FEC); 2: Marseille, Musée des Beaux-Arts; 3: The Royal Collection Trust, Her Majesty Queen Elizabeth II 2009; 4–8, 10–12, 14–15: Author; 13: Roma, Sovrintendenza Capitolina ai Beni Culturali, Museo di Roma.

FSC
www.fsc.org
MIX
Paper from
responsible sources
FSC® C018150

ex Officina Libraria Jellinek et Gallerani

Printed in Italy